Lecture Notes in Computer Science 5737

Commenced Publication in 1973
Founding and Former Series Editors:
Gerhard Goos, Juris Hartmanis, and Jan van Leeuwen

Editorial Board

David Hutchison
Lancaster University, UK

Takeo Kanade
Carnegie Mellon University, Pittsburgh, PA, USA

Josef Kittler
University of Surrey, Guildford, UK

Jon M. Kleinberg
Cornell University, Ithaca, NY, USA

Alfred Kobsa
University of California, Irvine, CA, USA

Friedemann Mattern
ETH Zurich, Switzerland

John C. Mitchell
Stanford University, CA, USA

Moni Naor
Weizmann Institute of Science, Rehovot, Israel

Oscar Nierstrasz
University of Bern, Switzerland

C. Pandu Rangan
Indian Institute of Technology, Madras, India

Bernhard Steffen
University of Dortmund, Germany

Madhu Sudan
Microsoft Research, Cambridge, MA, USA

Demetri Terzopoulos
University of California, Los Angeles, CA, USA

Doug Tygar
University of California, Berkeley, CA, USA

Gerhard Weikum
Max-Planck Institute of Computer Science, Saarbruecken, Germany

Yong Dou   Ralf Gruber   Josef M. Joller (Eds.)

Advanced
Parallel Processing
Technologies

8th International Symposium, APPT 2009
Rapperswil, Switzerland, August 24-25, 2009
Proceedings

 Springer

Volume Editors

Yong Dou
National University of Defense Technology
Department of Computer Science
Changsha 410073, P.R.China
E-mail: yongdou@nudt.edu.cn

Ralf Gruber
Ecole Polytechnique Fédérale de Lausanne (EPFL)
Dépt. Physique
1015 Lausanne, Switzerland
E-mail: Ralf.Gruber@epfl.ch

Josef M. Joller
HSR - Hochschule für Technik Rapperswil
Oberseestr. 10
8640 Rapperswil, Switzerland
E-mail: jjoller@hsr.ch

Library of Congress Control Number: 2009931946

CR Subject Classification (1998): B.2.1, B.4.3, B.5.1, B.6.1, C.1.2, C.1.4, D.1.3, F.1.2, G.1

LNCS Sublibrary: SL 1 – Theoretical Computer Science and General Issues

ISSN   0302-9743
ISBN-10   3-642-03643-0 Springer Berlin Heidelberg New York
ISBN-13   978-3-642-03643-9 Springer Berlin Heidelberg New York

This work is subject to copyright. All rights are reserved, whether the whole or part of the material is concerned, specifically the rights of translation, reprinting, re-use of illustrations, recitation, broadcasting, reproduction on microfilms or in any other way, and storage in data banks. Duplication of this publication or parts thereof is permitted only under the provisions of the German Copyright Law of September 9, 1965, in its current version, and permission for use must always be obtained from Springer. Violations are liable to prosecution under the German Copyright Law.

springer.com

© Springer-Verlag Berlin Heidelberg 2009
Printed in Germany

Typesetting: Camera-ready by author, data conversion by Scientific Publishing Services, Chennai, India
Printed on acid-free paper   SPIN: 12736133   06/3180   5 4 3 2 1 0

Preface

This volume contains the papers presented at the 8th International Conference on Advanced Parallel Processing Technologies, APPT 2009. This series of conferences originated from collaborations between researchers from China and Germany and has evolved into an international conference for reporting advances in parallel processing technologies. APPT 2009 addressed the entire gamut of related topics, ranging from the architectural aspects of parallel computer hardware and system software to the applied technologies for novel applications.

For this conference, we received over 76 full submissions from researchers all over the world. All the papers were peer reviewed in depth and qualitatively graded on their relevance, originality, significance, presentation, and the overall appropriateness for their acceptance. Any concerns raised were discussed by the Program Committee. The Organizing Committee did an excellent job in selecting 36 papers for presentation. In short, the papers included here represent the forefront of research from China, Switzerland, Germany, and other countries.

APPT 2009 was made possible by the collective efforts of many people and organizations. We would like to express our special thanks to the Architecture Professional Committee of China Computer Federation, HSR University of Applied Sciences in Rapperswil, Switzerland, National Laboratory for Parallel and Distributed Processing, China, and the Computer Science and Technology School of Harbin Institute of Technology, China. Without the extensive support from many communities for both the technical program and the local arrangements, we would not have been able to hold the conference in time. Our thanks also go to Springer for its assistance in putting the proceedings together.

We would like to take this opportunity to thank all the authors, many of whom traveled great distances to participate in this conference and make their valuable contributions. We would also like to express our gratitude to the Program Committee members for reviewing the large number of papers submitted. Last but not least, our thanks also go to the local Organizing Committee for the great job in making the local arrangements and organizing an attractive social program.

August 2009

Yong Dou
Ralf Gruber
Josef Joller

Organization

General Co-chairs

Hermann Mettler   HSR University of Applied Sciences of Eastern
Switzerland
Xingming Zhou   Chinese Academy of Sciences, China

Program Co-chairs

Yong Dou   NUDT, China
Ralf Gruber   EPFL, Switzerland
Josef Joller   HSR University of Applied Sciences of Eastern
Switzerland

Technical Program Committee

Hamid R. Arabnia   The University of Georgia, USA
Peter Arbenz   ETHZ, Switzerland
Arndt Bode   TU Munich, Germany
Tianzhou Chen   Zhejiang University, China
Wenzhi Chen   Zhejiang University, China
Frederic Desprez   Ecole Normale Superieure, France
Beniamino Di Martino   Seconda Universita' di Napoli, Italy
Ramon Doallo   University of A Coruña, Spain
Xiaoshe Dong   Jiaotong University, China
Aristides Efthymiou   University of Edinburgh, UK
Xiaoya Fan   Northwestern Polytechnical University, China
Len Freeman   University of Manchester, UK
Walter Gander   ETHZ, Switzerland
Georgi Gaydadjiev   TU Delft, The Netherlands
Minyi Guo   University of Aizu, Japan
Lifeng He   Aichi Prefectural University, Japan
Xiangdong Hu   Jiangnan Computing Institute, China
Zhenzhou Ji   Harbin Institute of Technology, China
Gerhard R. Jouber   Technical University of Clausthal, Germany
Pierre Kuonen   University of Applied Sciences of Western Switzerland
Arjen Lenstra   Laboratory for Cryptologic Algorithms EPFL,
Switzerland
Yijun Liu   Guangdong University of Technology, China
Chaoguang Men   Harbin Engineering University, China
Tsuyoshi Nakamura   Nagoya Institute of Technology, Japan

Thomas Rauber	University of Bayreuth, Germany
Wolfgang Rosenstiel	University of Tübingen, Germany
Marie-Christine Sawley	ETHZ, group CERN, Switzerland
Ruth Shaw	University of New Brunswick, Canada
Ruedi Stoop	UZH, ETHZ, Switzerland
Ruppa K. Thulasiram	University of Manitoba, Canada
Dongsheng Wang	Tsinghua University, China
Ji Wang	National Laboratory of Parallel and Distributed Processing, China
Xingwei Wang	North-East University, China
Chenggang Wu	Institute of Computing Technology, China
Minyou Wu	Shanghai Jiao Tong University, China
Zhibo Wu	Harbin Institute of Technology, China
Jie Xu	University of Leeds, UK
Jingling Xue	The University of New South Wales, Australia
Ramin Yahyapour	University of Dortmund, Germany
Laurence T. Yang	St. Francis Xavier University, Canada
Pen-Chung Yew	University of Minnesota, USA
Zhiwen Yu	Kyoto University, Japan
Binyu Zang	Fudan University, China
Zhao Zhang	Iowa State University, USA
Eckart Zitzler	ETH, Switzerland

Organization and Publicity Chair

Tina Sasse	Abricot GmbH, Switzerland

Table of Contents

I Architecture

II   Graphical Processing Unit

III   Grid

IV   Grid Scheduling

V   Mobile Applications

VI   Parallel Applications

VII   Parallel Libraries

VIII   Performance

A Fast Scheme to Investigate Thermal-Aware Scheduling Policy for Multicore Processors

Liqiang He and Cha Narisu

College of Computer Science, Inner Mongolia University
Hohhot, Inner Mongolia 010021 P.R. China
{liqiang,csnars}@imu.edu.cn

Abstract. With more cores integrated into one single chip, the overall power consumption from the multiple concurrent running programs increases dramatically in a CMP processor which causes the thermal problem becomes more and more severer than the traditional superscalar processor. To leverage the thermal problem of a multicore processor, two kinds of orthogonal technique can be exploited. One is the commonly used Dynamic Thermal Management technique. The other is the thermal aware thread scheduling policy. For the latter one, some general ideas have been proposed by academic and industry researchers. The difficult to investigate the effectiveness of a thread scheduling policy is the huge search space coming from the different possible mapping combinations for a given multi-program workload. In this paper, we extend a simple thermal model originally used in a single core processor to a multicore environment and propose a fast scheme to search or compare the thermal effectiveness of different scheduling policies using the new model. The experiment results show that the proposed scheme can predict the thermal characteristics of the different scheduling policies with a reasonable accuracy and help researchers to fast investigate the performances of the policies without detailed time consuming simulations.

1 Introduction

Chip Multicore Processor (CMP) has become the mainstream in nowadays microprocessor industry. Dual core and Quad core processor from Intel and AMD have been widely used by general users. The product to integrate more cores into one silicon chip can also be seen in not far away future. CMP processor improves the overall performance through exploiting both instruction-level parallelism and thread-level parallelism from the concurrent running multiple threads in it.

With more cores integrated into one single chip, the overall power consumption from the multiple running programs increases dramatically in a CMP processor which causes the thermal problem becomes more and more severe than that of the traditional superscalar processor. High power density in a processor unit can potentially cause a high temperature at the unit, named Hot-spot phenomenal. A temperature surpassing the chip thermal threshold can greatly reduce the reliability of the processor, even broken it at an extreme circumstance.

Y. Dou, R. Gruber, and J. Joller (Eds.): APPT 2009, LNCS 5737, pp. 1–10, 2009.
© Springer-Verlag Berlin Heidelberg 2009

To leverage the thermal problem of a multicore processor, two kinds of orthogonal technique can be exploited. One is the commonly used Dynamic Thermal Management techniques, such as DVFS (Dynamic Voltage and Frequency Scaling) and Clock Gating. The other is the thermal aware thread scheduling policy. For the latter one, some general ideas have been proposed by academic and industry researchers, for example moving the hottest thread to the coldest core [1,2] or core hopping based on some neighborhood thermal information [5]. One big difficult to investigate or evaluate the effectiveness of a thread scheduling policy is the huge searching space coming from the different possible mapping combinations for a given multiple program workload. Most previous researches [1,2,3] justify their works through comparing their proposed thermal aware scheduling policy with the base one that does not consider the thermal information at all, and seldom works [4] have been done to compare the effectiveness of different thermal aware policies. To our best knowledge, there is no work to investigate the best thermal case for a given multi-program workload with different scheduling policies.

To search a thread scheduling solution with a lowest temperature for a given multi-program workload, it needs to explore a huge searching space of different mapping combinations. Using traditional cycle-by-cycle simulating scheme, it will be very time consuming or even impossible when the number of cores is greater than eight, In this paper, we extend a simple thermal model with polynomial complexity originally used in a single core processor to a multicore environment and propose a fast scheme to search or compare the thermal effectiveness of different mappings for a multi-program workload using the new model. Comparing with the simulating scheme, our scheme is two orders faster. Also, experiment results show that the proposed scheme can predict the thermal characteristics of the different mappings with a reasonable accuracy and help researchers to fast investigate the performance of different scheduling policies.

The rest of this paper is organized as follows. Section 2 presents our extended thermal model for a multicore processor. Section 3 and 4 give the experimental methodology and results. Section 5 discusses the related works, and Section 6 concludes this paper.

2 Thermal Model for a Multicore Processor

In this section, first, we introduce a simple thermal model used by single core processor. Then we extend the model to our multicore environment and propose a fast scheme to help exploring the searching space or comparing the thermal effectiveness of different thermal aware scheduling policies.

2.1 Thermal Model for Single Core Processor

Han et al [6] proposes a simple thermal model used for temperature aware floorplanning in traditional superscalar processor. The basic idea of temperature or thermal aware floorplanning is to adjust the placement of the units of a processor according to their power densities and areas in order to obtain a lower average/peak temperature in the final chip. Temperature aware floorplanning is a multi-objective optimization problem and the thermal model is the basis of it. There are many proposals for floorplanning in academic and industry literature, but discussion of them is out of the scope of this paper. In this paper, we only care of the thermal model used by them.

In Han's model, each unit i ($i = 1, \cdots, n$) is a block with a fixed area A_i and the height and width are h_i and w_i. The power consumption of unit i is P_i. To estimate the maximum temperature of a floorplanning, the model needs to calculate the potential temperatures for all the units. The particular temperature of a unit depends not only on its own power dissipation but also on the temperatures of the adjacent blocks. Because the power density d_i of an **isolate** block is linear to its temperature, the model uses the power density as an estimation of the temperature. So the heat diffusion between two adjacent blocks with *shared_length* longer common edge can be expressed as follow:

$$H(d1, d2) = (d1 - d2) * shared\_length \tag{1}$$

For each block, its total heat diffusion from all the neighbor blocks d_i is :

$$H(d) = \sum H(d, d_i) \tag{2}$$

To estimate the maximum temperature of a chip, the model picks the top m ($1 \leq m \leq n$) possibly hot blocks and calculates the final thermal diffusion D by summing all the heat diffusions H_i. D is used as the approximation of the maximum temperature of the chip.

In Han's experiment, the selection of 2 possibly-hot blocks produces the best temperature estimation result for the Alpha processor.

2.2 Extended Model for Multicore Processor

To evaluate the effectiveness of different thermal aware scheduling policies, we need compare the average/peak temperatures of them. Two types of policies exist for multicore processor in literature. One is for the case that the number of threads being scheduled is greater than the number of cores. At this case, the scheduling policy selects a thread from the waiting queue and puts the thread to an available core according to a pre-defined policy, for example to the coldest core or to the core with most cooler neighbors [2, 5]. For this case, the most effort is spent to select the thread, not to determine where to put the thread. Another type of policy, more accurate speaking, mapping policy, focuses on how to select the target core such as to obtain a lower average/peak run-time temperature. The first one does not relay much on the thermal model or it assumes a simple basic model, and the final temperature is worse than the second one which considers more about the thermal relationship of the mapped threads.

Figure 1 shows a simple experiment result which maps one eight-thread workload on a sixteen cores processor using hundred of different mappings. The difference of average temperatures of the mappings is close to 1 °C, whereas the difference of peak temperatures can be up to 5 °C in Figure 1. The blue lines

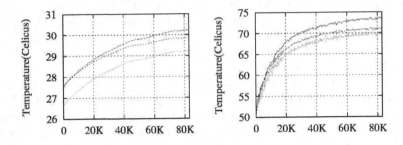

Fig. 1. The average (left) and peak (right) temperature of different mapping schemes for a eight program workload, the blue lines are the temperatures of mapping scheme in Fig.2

art		twolf	mesa
fma3d			
			applu
perl.	face.		crafty

Fig. 2. Mapping scheme for the eight program workload in Fig.1 corresponding to the blue temperature line

show the result of one particular mapping shown in Figure 2. In this paper, we focus on the effectiveness of second type of policies, and try to come up with a fast scheme to investigate or evaluate different mapping schemes using our extended thermal model in this section.

In a multicore processor, an unit becomes the hottest block so as to have a highest temperature over the chip either Figure 1 when it is the hottest block in a core and all the neighbor blocks are in the same core and all the units in other cores have lower temperatures than it, or Figure 2 when it is surrounded by hot units that some of them belong to the same core and some others belong to the adjacent cores, and the temperature is boosted by the heat spreading from the surrounded blocks. In case Figure 1, the peak temperature of the chip does not depend on the mapping scheme. It only depends on the workload itself. But in case Figure 2, the peak temperature does depend on the mappings. Different mappings can put different surrounded blocks for the unit such as getting a different temperature of it. A good mapping scheme can put relative cooler blocks around a potential hot unit such as to obtain less heat diffusion from the neighbors. Combining both above two cases, we give our extended model to estimate the maximum temperature of a chip multicore processor with n cores as follows:

$$D_{cmp} = MAX(D_i, A) \quad i = 1, 2, 3, \cdots, n \tag{3}$$

Where

$$D_i = \sum_{j=1,\cdots,m} H(d_j) \qquad (4)$$

In formula (4), D_j is the j th block among the m possibly hot blocks in core i and does not adjacent to the blocks in other cores; If block d_j is an internal block, $H(d_j)$ is computed using formula (2). But if block d_j sits at the edge of the chip it can dissipate heat to the ambient and thus decrease the temperature of the core. At this case, due to the ability of heat dissipation of ambient is more than the intra-blocks in the same core, we need use formula (5) to calculate $H(d_j)$.

  $H(d1, d2) = (d1 - d2) * shared\_length$ where d2 is internal neighbor block;
  $H(d1,A)=\alpha *(- d1) * length$ where A is ambient and α is a parameter;

$$H(d_j) = \sum H(d_j, d_m) + H(d_j, A) \qquad (5)$$

In addition,if core i does not have a program running, then D_i equals to zero. So D_i measures the maximum temperature of the running core i.
  In formula (3),

$$A = \sum_{i=1,\cdots,n} A_i \qquad (6)$$

Where

$$A_i = \sum H'(d_k) \qquad (7)$$

and d_k is the k th block at the edge of core i. Where $H'(d) = \sum H'(d, d_l)$ and d_l is the l th block around block d which is either in the same core as d or in the neighbor cores. $H'(d_1, d_2)$ is similar as $H(d_1, d_2)$ in section 2.1 and presented as follows. Where $shared\_length'$ is the length of the shared edge between block d_l in core i and block d_2 in core j.

$$H'(d_1, d_2) = (d_1 - d_2) * shared\_length' \qquad (8)$$

Here, if d_l is in a neighbor core which does not have a program running, then $H'(d, d_l)$ equals to zero. So a measures the heat spreading effect of the blocks at the edges of all the running cores.
  The basic idea of this model is to consider all the potential hot blocks inside the cores and the heat spreading effect between the running cores and peak the maximum value D_{cmp} as the estimation of the peak temperature of the chip.

2.3   Scheme to Fast Searching Space Exploring

Using the thermal model of last section, we can simply investigate or compare the effectiveness of different mapping policies through computing and comparing the estimated temperature values D_{cmp} shown in the following algorithm.

```
lowest_temp = MAX_TEMP;
For each Mᵢ in possible mappings
   d = D_cmp(Mᵢ);
   if (lowest_temp < d)
      { lowest_temp = d; lowest_mapping = i; }
end.
```

The complexity to compute one D_{cmp} is $O(n*(j+k))$ where n is the number of cores, j is the selected hottest block inside a core, and k is the number of blocks at the edge of a core. So the overall complexity to investigate the effectiveness of different m mappings is $O(n*m)$.

Discussion: When the number of mappings being compared is not much, the algorithm in the algorithm works well. But if we want to find a best mapping with lowest peak temperature, we need to compute and compare all the possible D_{cmp}. It is very time consuming or even impossible if a processor has more then sixteen cores and the workload includes more then eight threads. This is a common limitation for all the technologies that wants to find an optimal solution among a huge search space. A more smart mechanism, such as heuristics based scheme, is needed to help to reduce the space so as to get a sub-optimal result. This is part of our future work.

In addition, although the target in this paper is not the fist type of scheduling policy discussed in last section the above algorithm can also be used to compare the different thermal performances after the particular policy has made the mapping decision.

3   Methodology

To validate our multicore thermal model, we compare the results from our model and a trace-driven thermal simulator ATMI [7]. We construct three workloads, one is eight threads, one is twelve threads, and the other is sixteen threads, as shown in Table 1. We then randomly generate different mappings for them. The power densities are from an in-house cycle-by-cycle multicore simulator. We get 70K sample points during the program running, and use the average value as the input power densities of our model and ATMI simulator. The sample interval is 1ns. The architecture of the simulated multicore chip is a sixteen cores homogeneous CMP processor organized as a 4X4 grid where each core has an Alpha EV6 [8] like organization.

4   Experiment Result

Figure 3,4 and 5 show our estimated peak temperatures and the temperatures obtained from ATMI for three workloads.

Table 1. Workloads in our experiment

NO.	Workload
1	art-applu-crafty-facerec-fma3d-mesa-perlbmk-twolf
2	art-applu-crafty-facerec-fma3d-mesa-perlbmk-twolf-galgel-vortex-swim-mcf
3	art-applu-crafty-facerec-fma3d-mesa-perlbmk-twolf-galgel-vortex-swim-mcf -eon-wupwise-gzip-gap

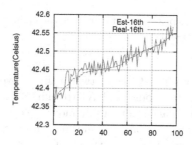

Fig. 3. Estimated and real peak temperatures for the sixteen-thread workload with different mapping schemes (x-axis)

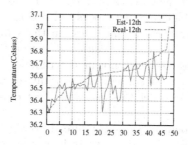

Fig. 4. Estimated and real peak temperatures for the twelve-thread workload with different mapping schemes (x-axis)

For sixteen-thread workload (Figure 3), the estimated temperatures are very close to the values from the accurate thermal simulator. The maximum difference for a specific mapping between the two schemes is less than 0.05 $°C$. In term of simulating speed, the time to simulate a 70K power densities and get the thermal values for a sixteen cores processor needs about 3 days in an Intel Core Due processor with 2.8GHz clock frequency if we set the maximum number (18) of sensors for each core. If we use the average power densities for 70K sample points as the inputs of ATMI and calculate the steady-state temperature, it takes about 3 to 5 minutes. But in our model, it talks less than 1 second to calculate the value. The speedup is 200 to 300 times faster.

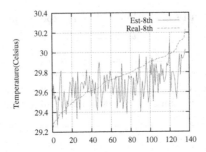

Fig. 5. Estimated and real peak temperatures for the eight-thread workload with different mapping schemes (x-axis)

Figure 4 shows the temperatures of twelve-thread workload. The difference between the values of our model and ATMI simulator can be up to 0.3 °C, but we can tolerate the inaccuracy in our model because it can still show the trend and give the correct comparison information between different mappings at most cases. One source of the inaccuracy of our model comes from the not-running holes in the processor which affects the heat diffusion values calculated by formula (6). Another reason is due to the heat dissipation effects from the blocks at the edge of the chip. Different mappings have different number of threads running in the edge cores, and different threads in the edge cores have different potential hot blocks. Some blocks can become the hottest spot due to the heat spreading from the internal blocks in the same core, but also it can reduce temperature due to the edge position close to ambient. The combination effects from internal blocks and ambient determines the final temperature of the edge block, and some inaccuracies are introduced. In our experiment, α in formula (5) is set to 5 in order to enlarge the heat dissipation effect from the ambient.

In Figure 5, the temperatures of eight-thread workload are given. Due to half of the cores have no thread running, more inaccuracies are introduced in our model. Although the trend is similar as the one from the ATMI simulator, the maximum temperature difference is close to 0.6 °C. The reasons are same as in twelve-thread case which calls for a more accurate model for the few thread running cases in a multicore processor and is part of our future work.

5   Related Works

There are many thermal-aware thread scheduling policies proposed in academic and industry literature. [1] proposes a policy which considers the power load balance and uses energy as a represent of thermal for embedded system, but unfortunately power or energy do not always reflect the temperature in a real system. [2] gives two simple policies, one is sending workload to the coldest core, another is similar but gives priority to the core with more "idle" neighbors so as to dissipate more heat to the idle ones. In [3], Choi considers the heat balance for

SMT processor in system software level. The basic idea is to assign hot task and cold task to each core in order to create opportunities for leverage temporal heat slack. [4] compares some temperature-aware scheduling policies in a same infrastructure. The targets of the policies can be lowest average temperature, highest peak temperature in order to extract maximum performance, or minimum safe temperature to avoid performance degradation. In [5], different parameters, the intra hot spots, the idle neighbors, the busy neighbors, and the edge blocks, are considered together in order to get a final lowest average temperature. Our work is similar as [5], but we use different thermal model and our target is to find a lowest temperature mapping scheme among a huge possible mapping search space.

In addition, Chen [9] uses fuzzy logic to calculate the suitability between programs and cores for heterogeneous multicore system in order to save energy consuming. Zhou [10] et al use the similar principles as [5] to adjust the task allocation in a 3D processor.

6   Conclusion

Multiple thermal-ware scheduling policies have been proposed for chip multicore processor. Most of the works compare or validate their policies with the baseline policy which does not consider temperature when scheduling at all. For a multicore processor, a huge number of possible mapping schemes exist for a given multi-program workload. Different mapping schemes reflect different scheduling decisions at a given running interval. In our motivation experiment, there can be as high as 5 °C temperature difference for a eight-thread workload with more than hundred of random generate mappings. So how to evaluate the effectiveness of different thermal aware scheduling policies in an efficient way becomes important for a multicore processor. This paper presents a simple multicore thermal model which combines multiple parameters into together and calculates a value as an estimation of the real temperature for a specific mapping scheme. Our model can be used to compare the effectiveness of different thermal aware scheduling policies, and also can be used to find the lowest peak temperature among a huge number of possible mapping decisions. We validate our model against an accurate analytic thermal model ATMI using a sixteen cores processor. The experiment results show that our model can match the temperatures from ATMI at most cases, and some inaccuracy will be fixed in our future work. In term of speedup, our model is two orders faster than ATMI simulator which shows that our method is a fast scheme to investigate the thermal-aware scheduling policy for multicore processor.

Acknowledgement

This work is supported by Inner Mongolia Natural Science Foundation Project No. 20080404ms0901, and the Ph.D Research Startup Foundation of Inner Mongolia University No. 208041.

References

1. Bautista, D., Sahuquillo, J., Hassan, H., Petit, S., Duato, J.: A Simple Power-Aware Scheduling for Multicore Systems when Running Real-Time Applications. In: 22rd IEEE International Symposium on Parallel and Distributed Processing, pp. 1–7. IEEE Press, Los Alamitos (2008)
2. Coskun, A.K., Rosing, T.S., Whisnant, K.: Temperature Aware Task Scheduling in MPSoCs. In: Design Automation and Test in Europe (DATE), pp. 1659–1664 (2007)
3. Choi, J., Cher, C., Franke, H.: Thermal-aware Task Scheduling at the System Software Level. In: IEEE International Symposium on Low Power Electronics and Design, pp. 213–218 (2007)
4. Kursun, E., Cher, C.-Y., Buyuktosunoglu, A., Bose, P.: Investigating the Effects of Task Scheduling on Thermal Behaviour. In: 3rd Workshop on Temperature-Aware Computer System, conjunction with ISCA-33 (2006)
5. Stavrou, K., Trancoso, P.: Thermal-aware scheduling for future chip multiprocessors. J. EURASIP Embedded Syst. (2007)
6. Han, Y., Koren, I., Moritz, C.A.: Temperature Aware Floorpalnning. In: 2nd Workshop on Temperature-Aware Computer System, conjunction with ISCA-32 (2005)
7. Michaud, P., Sazeides, Y., Seznec, A., Constantinou, T., Fetis, D.: An Analytical Model of Temperature in Microprocessors. Research report RR-5744, INRIA (November 2005)
8. McLellan, E.J., Webb, D.A.: The Alpha 21264 Microprocessor Architecture. In: Proc. of the International Conference on Computer Design (1998)
9. Chen, J., John, L.K.: Energy-Aware Application Scheduling on a Heterogeneous Multi-core System. In: IEEE International Symposium on Workload Characterization (2008)
10. Zhou, X., Xu, Y., Du, Y., Zhang, Y., Yang, J.: Thermal Management for 3D Processors via Task Scheduling. In: 37th International Conference on Parallel Processing, pp. 115–122 (2008)

Dealing with Traffic-Area Trade-Off in Direct Coherence Protocols for Many-Core CMPs

Alberto Ros, Manuel E. Acacio, and José M. García

Departamento de Ingeniería y Tecnología de Computadores
Universidad de Murcia, 30100 Murcia, Spain
{a.ros,meacacio,jmgarcia}@ditec.um.es

Abstract. In many-core CMP architectures, the cache coherence protocol is a key component since it can add requirements of area and power consumption to the final design and, therefore, it could restrict severely its scalability. Area constraints limit the use of precise sharing codes to small- or medium-scale CMPs. Power constraints make impractical to use broadcast-based protocols for large-scale CMPs.

Token-CMP and DiCo-CMP are cache coherence protocols that have been recently proposed to avoid the indirection problem of traditional directory-based protocols. However, Token-CMP is based on broadcasting requests to all tiles, while DiCo-CMP adds a precise sharing code to each cache entry. In this work, we address the traffic-area trade-off for these indirection-aware protocols. In particular, we propose and evaluate several implementations of DiCo-CMP which differ in the amount of coherence information that they must store. Our evaluation results show that our proposals entail a good traffic-area trade-off by halving the traffic requirements compared to Token-CMP and considerably reducing the area storage required by DiCo-CMP.

1 Introduction

Current chip multiprocessors (CMPs) have a relatively small number of cores, which are typically connected through a shared medium, i.e., a bus or a crossbar (e.g., the dual-core IBM Power6 [1] and the eight-core Sun T2 [2]). However, CMP architectures that integrate tens of processor cores (usually known as many-core CMPs) are expected for the near future [3], making undesirable elements that could compromise the scalability of these designs. For example, the area required by a shared network becomes impractical as the number of cores grows [4]. Therefore, tiled CMPs designed as arrays of replicated tiles connected over a point-to-point network are a scalable alternative to current small-scale CMP designs and they will help in keeping complexity manageable.

In these architectures, each tile contains at least one level of private caches which are kept coherent by using a cache coherence protocol. The cache coherence protocol is a key component since it adds requirements of area and power consumption, which can condition systems scalability. Although a great deal of attention was devoted to scalable cache coherence protocols in the last decades

Y. Dou, R. Gruber, and J. Joller (Eds.): APPT 2009, LNCS 5737, pp. 11–27, 2009.
© Springer-Verlag Berlin Heidelberg 2009

in the context of shared-memory multiprocessors, the technological parameters and constrains entailed by many-core CMPs demand new solutions to the cache coherency problem [5]. One of these constrains is the use of unordered networks, that prevent from using the popular snooping-based cache coherence protocol.

Two traditional cache coherence protocols aimed to be used with unordered networks are *Hammer* [6], implemented in the AMD Opteron^{TM}, and *Directory* [7]. *Hammer* avoids keeping coherence information at the cost of broadcasting requests to all cores. Although it is very efficient in terms of area requirements, it generates a prohibitive amount of network traffic, which translates into excessive power consumption. On the other hand, *Directory* reduces network traffic compared to *Hammer* by storing in a directory structure precise information about the private caches holding memory blocks. Unfortunately, this storage could become prohibitive for many-core CMPs [3]. Since neither the network traffic generated by *Hammer* nor the extra area required by *Directory* scale with the number of cores, a great deal of attention was paid in the past to address this traffic-area trade-off [8,9,10].

On the other hand, these traditional cache coherence protocols introduce the well-known indirection problem. In both protocols, the ordering point for the requests to the same memory block is the *home* tile. Therefore, all cache misses must reach this ordering point before performing coherence actions, a fact that introduces extra latency in the critical path of cache misses. Recently, Token-CMP [11] and DiCo-CMP [12] protocols have been proposed to deal with the indirection problem. These indirection-aware protocols avoid the access to the home tile through alternative serialization mechanisms. Token-CMP only cares about requests ordering in case of race conditions. In those cases, a persistent requests mechanism is responsible for ordering the different requests. In DiCo-CMP the ordering point is the tile that provides the block in a cache miss and indirection is avoided by directly sending the requests to that tile. These indirection-aware protocols reduce the latency of cache misses compared to *Hammer* and *Directory*, which translates into performance improvements. Although Token-CMP entails low memory overhead, it is based on broadcasting requests to all tiles, which is clearly non-scalable. Otherwise, DiCo-CMP sends requests to just one tile, but it adds a bit-vector field that keeps track of sharers to each cache entry, which does not scale with the number of cores.

The aim of this work is to address the traffic-area trade-off of indirection-aware protocols for many-core tiled CMPs. Although this trade-off has been widely studied for traditional protocols, in this work we consider protocols that try to avoid indirection. Particularly, we perform this study by relaxing the accuracy of the sharing codes used in DiCo-CMP. The other important contribution of this work is the evaluation of the state of the art in cache coherence protocols for future many-core CMPs in a common framework.

We have implemented and evaluated several cache coherence protocols based on the direct coherence concept which differ in the amount of coherence information that they store. Particularly, *DiCo-LP-1*, which only stores the identity of one sharer along with the data block, and *DiCo-NoSC*, which does not store any coherence information along with the data caches, are the best alternatives. *DiCo-LP-1* presents a good traffic-area trade-off by requiring slightly more area than *Token-CMP* (1% for 32 cores, and same complexity order $-O(log_2 n)-$) and slightly increasing network traffic compared to *DiCo-CMP* (11% on average for 32 cores). *DiCo-NoSC* does not need to modify the structure of caches to add any extra field and, therefore, introduces less area requirements than *Token-CMP* (4% for 32 cores). However, it increases network traffic by 35% compared to *DiCo-CMP*, but still halving the traffic when compared to *Token-CMP*.

The rest of the paper is organized as follows. Section 2 discusses the cache coherence protocols that could be be used in many-core CMPs. DiCo-CMP and the implementations evaluated in this work are described in Section 3. Section 4 focus on the evaluation methodology. Section 5 shows performance results. In Section 6 we present the related work. Finally, Section 7 concludes the paper.

2   Background on Cache Coherence Protocols

This section describes the cache coherence protocols proposed in the literature aimed to be used in systems with unordered networks. We describe their implementation for a tiled CMP, in which each tile includes private L1 caches (both instruction and data caches) and a slice of the L2 cache. The L2 cache is physically distributed and logically shared among the different processing cores (L2 NUCA architecture [13]). Each memory block is assigned to a particular cache bank (or tile) which is called its *home* bank (or *home* tile). We focus on the cache coherence protocol employed for avoiding inconsistencies between data stored in the L1 caches. We also assume that caches use MOESI states, and that L1 and L2 caches are non-inclusive. We classify these cache coherence protocols into *traditional* protocols, in which cache misses suffer from indirection, and *indirection-aware* protocols, which try to avoid the indirection problem.

2.1   Traditional Protocols

In traditional protocols, the requests issued by several cores to the same block are serialized through the home tile, which enforces cache coherence. Therefore, all requests must be sent to the home tile before coherence actions can be performed. Then, the request is forwarded to the corresponding tiles according to the coherence information (or it is broadcast if the protocol does not maintain any coherence information). All processors that receive the forwarded request answer to the requesting core by sending either an acknowledgment (invalidating the block in case of write misses) or the requested data block. The requesting core can access the block when it receives all the acknowledgment and data messages. The access to the home tile introduces indirection, which causes that cache misses take three hops in the critical path.

Examples of these traditional protocols are *Hammer* and *Directory*. As commented in the introduction, *Hammer* has the drawback of generating a considerable amount of network traffic. On the other hand, directory protocols that use a precise sharing code to keep track of cached blocks introduce an area overhead that does not scale with the number of cores.

Hammer-CMP. *Hammer* is the cache coherence protocol used by AMD in their Opteron systems. Like snooping-based protocols, *Hammer* does not store any coherence information about the blocks held in private caches and it relies on broadcasting requests to solve cache misses. The advantage with respect to snooping-based protocols is that *Hammer* targets systems that use a point-to-point interconnection. However, the ordering point in this protocol is the home tile, a fact that introduces indirection for every cache miss. In this work we evaluate an implementation of the AMD's Hammer protocol for tiled CMPs, that we call *Hammer-CMP*. As an optimization for tiled CMPs, our implementation adds a small structure to each home tile which stores the tag of the blocks that are held in the private L1 caches. This optimization avoids off-chip accesses when the block can be obtained on-chip, and uses a small structure whose size does not increase with the number of cores.

Directory-CMP. The *directory*-based protocol that we have implemented is similar to the intra-chip coherence protocol used in Piranha [14]. This protocol avoids broadcasting requests by storing in the home tile precise information about the state of each block in the private caches. This information consists in a full-map (or bit-vector) sharing code employed for keeping track of the sharers, and a pointer identifying the owner tile, i.e., the tile that provides the data block. The bit-vector field allows the protocol to send invalidation messages just to the caches currently sharing the block. The owner field is used in a MOESI protocol to avoid forwarding requests to all sharers on read misses. In this way, requests are only forwarded to the tile that provides the block. This precise directory information allows the protocol to reduce considerably network traffic compared to *Hammer-CMP*.

2.2   Indirection-Aware Protocols

Recently, new cache coherence protocols have been proposed to avoid the indirection problem of traditional protocols. *Token-CMP* avoids indirection by broadcasting requests to all tiles and maintains coherence through a token counting mechanism. Although the area required to store the tokens of each block is reasonable, network requirements are prohibitive for may-core CMPs. On the other hand, *DiCo-CMP* keeps traffic low by sending requests to only one tile. However, coherence information used by its previous implementations [12] include bit-vector sharing codes, which are not scalable in terms of area requirements.

Token-CMP. Token coherence is a framework for designing coherence protocols whose main asset is that it decouples the correctness substrate from the performance policies. Token coherence protocols avoid both the need of a totally ordered network and the introduction of indirection. They keep cache coherence by assigning T tokens to every memory block, where one of the T is the owner token. Then, a processor can read a block only if it holds at least one token for that block. On the other hand, a processor can write a block only if it holds all tokens for that block. Token coherence avoids starvation by issuing a

Table 1. Summary of cache coherence protocols

	Traditional	Indirection-aware
Traffic-intensive	Hammer-CMP	Token-CMP
Area-demanding	Directory-CMP	DiCo-CMP

persistent request when a processor detects potential starvation. In this paper, we evaluate Token-CMP [11], which is a performance policy aimed to achieve low-latency cache-to-cache transfer misses. Token-CMP uses a distributed arbitration scheme for persistent requests, which are issued after a single retry to optimize the access to contended blocks.

DiCo-CMP. Direct coherence protocols where proposed both to avoid the indirection problem of traditional directory-based protocols and to reduce the traffic requirements of token coherence protocols. In direct coherence, the ordering point for the requests to a particular memory block is the current owner tile of the requested block. In this way, the tile that must provide the block in case of a cache miss is the one that keeps coherence for that block. Indirection is avoided by directly sending requests to the corresponding owner tile instead to the home one. In this paper we evaluate DiCo-CMP [12], an implementation of direct coherence for CMPs. Particularly, we implement the *base* policy presented that work because it is the policy that incurs in less area and traffic requirements and it obtains similar execution times than Token-CMP.

2.3   Summary

Table 1 summarizes the described protocols. Hammer-CMP and Token-CMP are based on broadcasting requests on every cache miss. Although the storage required to keep coherence in these protocols is small, they generate a prohibitive amount of network traffic. On the other hand, Directory-CMP and DiCo-CMP achieve more efficient utilization of the interconnection network at the cost of increasing storage requirements compared to Hammer-CMP and Token-CMP.

3   Traffic-Area Trade-Off in Direct Coherence Protocols

3.1   DiCo-CMP Basis and Storage Requirements

As previously discussed, traditional protocols introduce indirection in the critical path of cache misses. Figure 1(a) (left) gives an example of a cache miss suffering from indirection in Directory-CMP. When a cache miss takes place it is necessary to access the home tile to obtain the directory information and order the requests before performing coherence actions (*1 Get*). In case of a cache-to-cache transfer, the request is subsequently sent to the owner tile (*2 Fwd*) where the block is provided (*3 Data*). As it can be observed, the miss is solved in three hops. Moreover, other requests for the same block cannot be processed

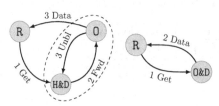
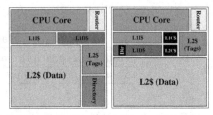

(a) Cache-to-cache transfer in Directory-CMP (left) and DiCo-CMP (right). (R=Requester; H=Home; D=Directory; O=Owner).

(b) Organization of a tile in Directory-CMP (left) and DiCo-CMP (right). Black boxes are the elements added by DiCo-CMP.

Fig. 1. Behavior and tile design of Directory-CMP and DiCo-CMP

by the directory until it receives the unblock message (*3 Unbl*). As shown in Figure 1(a) (right), DiCo-CMP sends directly the request to the owner tile (*1 Get*). In this way, data is provided by it (*2 Data*), thus requiring only two hops to solve the miss. This is achieved by assigning the task of keeping cache coherence and ensuring ordered accesses to the owner tile. Therefore, DiCo-CMP extends the tags' part of the L1 data caches with a bit-vector field (L2 caches already include this field in Directory-CMP) to allow the protocol to keep track of sharers of a block along with its owner copy. In contrast, DiCo-CMP does not need the directory structure in the home tile that traditional directory protocols require. Additionally, by keeping together the owner block and the directory information, control messages between them are not necessary, thus saving some network traffic.

On the other hand, the drawback of DiCo-CMP is that the owner tile can change on write misses and, therefore, finding it could be difficult in some cases. Hence, DiCo-CMP needs two extra hardware structures that are used to record the identity of the owner cache of every memory block: the *L1 coherence cache* and the *L2 coherence cache*, as shown in Figure 1(b).

- *L1 coherence cache* (L1C$): The information stored in this structure is used by the requesting core to directly send local requests to the owner tile. Therefore, this structure is located close to each processor's core. Although DiCo-CMP can update this information in several ways, we consider in this work the *base* policy presented in [12], in which this information is updated by using the coherence messages sent by the protocol, i.e., invalidation and data messages.
- *L2 coherence cache* (L2C$): Since the owner tile can change on write misses, this structure is responsible for tracking the owner cache for each block allocated in any L1 cache. The L2C$ replaces the directory structure required by Directory-CMP and it is accessed each time a request fails to locate the owner tile. Therefore, this information is updated through control messages whenever the owner tile changes.

3.2   DiCo-CMP Cache Coherence Protocol

When a processor issues a request that misses in its private L1 cache, the request is directly sent to the owner tile in order to avoid indirection. The identity of the potential owner tile is obtained from the L1C$, which is accessed at the time that the cache miss in detected. If there is a hit in the L1C$, the request is sent to the owner tile. Otherwise, the request is sent to the home tile, where the L2C$ will be accessed to get the identity of the current owner tile.

If the request is received by a tile that is not the current owner of the block, it is simply re-sent to the home tile, where the L2C$ is accessed. Then, in case of a hit in the L2C$, the request is sent to the current owner tile. In absence of race conditions the request will reach the owner tile. If there is a miss in the L2C$ the request is solved by providing the block from main memory, where, in this case, a valid copy of the block resides. In this case, a new entry pointing to the current L1 owner tile has to be allocated in the L2C$.

If the request reaches the owner tile, the miss can be immediately solved. If the owner is the home tile all requests (reads and writes) are solved by deallocating the block from the home tile and allocating it in the L1 cache of the requester. Again, the identity of the new owner tile is stored in the L2C$.

When the owner is the L1 cache, read misses are completed by sending a copy of the block to the requester and adding it to the sharing code field. Write misses are solved by sending invalidation messages to all the tiles sharing the block and by sending the data block to the requester. Acknowledgement messages are collected at the requesting cache as in all protocols evaluated in this work.

Finally, since the L2C$ must store up-to-date information regarding the owner tile, every time that the owner tile changes, a control message is sent to the L2C$ indicating the identity of the new owner. These messages must be processed by the L2C$ in the very same order in which they were generated. Otherwise, the L2C$ could fail to store the identity of the current owner. The order is guaranteed by sending an acknowledgement from the L2C$ to the new owner. Until this message is not received by the new owner, it cannot give the ownership to another tile. Note that these two control messages are not in the critical path of the current miss.

3.3   Reducing Storage Requirements for DiCo-CMP

DiCo-CMP needs two structures that keep the identity of the tile where the owner copy of the block resides. These two structures does not compromise scalability because they have a small number of entries and each one stores a tag and a pointer to the owner tile ($log_2 n$ bits, where n is the number of cores). The L2C$ is necessary to solve cache misses in DiCo-CMP, since ensures that the tile that keeps coherence for each block can always be found. On the other hand, the L1C$ is necessary to avoid indirection in cache misses and, therefore, it is essential to obtain good performance.

Apart from these structures, DiCo-CMP also adds a full-map sharing code to each cache entry. Since the memory overhead of this field can become prohibitive for many-core CMPs, we study some alternatives that differ in the amount of coherence information stored. These alternatives have at least area requirements of order $O(log_2n)$, due to the L1C\$ and the L2C\$. The particular compressed sharing code employed only impacts on the number of invalidations sent for write misses, because in DiCo-CMP cache misses are solved from the owner tile and, therefore, read misses are never broadcast. Next, we comment on the alternatives evaluated in this work.

DiCo-CV-K is a DiCo-CMP protocol that reduces the size of the sharing code field by using a *coarse vector* [10]. In a coarse vector, each bit represents a group of K tiles, instead of just one. A bit is set when at least one of the tiles in the group holds the block in its private cache. Therefore, if one of the tiles in the group holds the block, all tiles belonging to that group will receive an invalidation message. Particularly, we study two configurations using a coarse vector sharing code with values for K of 2 and 4. Although this sharing code reduces the memory required by the protocol, its size still increases linearly with the number of cores.

DiCo-LP-P employs a *limited pointers* sharing code [9]. In this scheme, each entry has a limited number of P pointers for the first P sharers of the block. Actually, since DiCo-CMP always stores the information about the owner tile in the L2C\$, the first pointer is employed to store the identity of the second sharer of the block. When the sharing degree of a block is greater than $P + 1$, write misses are solved by broadcasting invalidations to all tiles. However, this kind of misses is not very frequent since the sharing degree of applications is usually low [7]. The overhead of this sharing code is $O(P \times log_2n)$. In particular, evaluate this protocol with a value for P of 1.

Finally, *DiCo-NoSC* (no sharing code) does not maintain any coherence information along with the owner block. In this way, this protocol does not need to modify the structure of data caches to add any field. This lack of information implies broadcasting invalidation messages to all tiles upon write misses, although this is only necessary for blocks in shared state because the owner tile is always known in DiCo-CMP. This scheme incurs in more network traffic compared to *DiCo-CV-K* or *DiCo-LP-P*. However, it incurs in less traffic than *Hammer-CMP* and *Token-CMP*. *Hammer-CMP* requires broadcasting requests on every cache miss, and what is more expensive in a network with multicast support, every tile that receives the request answers with a independent control message. On the other hand, although *Token-CMP* avoids unnecessary acknowledgements, it also relies on broadcasting requests for all cache misses.

4   Simulation Environment

We perform the evaluation using the full-system simulator Virtutech Simics [15] extended with Multifacet GEMS 1.3 [16], that provides a detailed memory system timing model. Since the network modeled by GEMS 1.3 is not very precise, we have extended it with SICOSYS [17], a detailed interconnection network simulator. We simulate CMP systems with 16 and 32 tiles to show that our proposals

Table 2. System parameters

GEMS Parameters		SICOSYS Parameters	
Processor frequency	4 GHz	Network frequency	2 GHz
Cache hierarchy	Non-inclusive	Topology	4x4 & 8x4 Mesh
Cache block size	64 bytes	Switching technique	Wormhole, Multicast
Split L1 I & D caches	128KB, 4 ways, 4 hit cycles	Routing technique	Deterministic X-Y
Shared unified	1MB/tile, 4 ways,	Data message size	4 flits
L2 cache	7 hit cycles	Control message size	1 flit
L1C$ & L2C$	512 sets, 4 ways, 2 hit cycles	Routing time	2 cycles
Directory cache	512 sets, 4 ways, 2 hit cycles	Link latency (one hop)	2 cycles
Memory access time	200 cycles	Link bandwidth	1 flit/cycle

scale with the number of cores. Table 2 shows the values of the main parameters used for the evaluation, where cache latencies have been calculated using the CACTI 5.3 tool [18] for 45nm technology. We also have used CACTI to measure the area of the different structures needed in each one of the evaluated protocols. In this study, we assume that the length of the physical address is 44 bits, like in the SUN UltraSPARC-III architecture [19].

The ten applications used in our simulations cover a variety of computation and communication patterns. *Barnes* (8192 bodies, 4 time steps), *FFT* (256K points), *Ocean* (258x258 ocean), *Radix* (1M keys, 1024 radix), *Ray-trace* (teapot), *Volrend* (head) and *Water-Nsq* (512 molecules, 4 time steps) are scientific applications from the SPLASH-2 benchmark suite [20]. *Unstructured* (Mesh.2K, 5 time steps) is a computational fluid dynamics application. *MPGdec* (525_tens_040.m2v) and *MPGenc* (output of *MPGdec*), are multimedia applications from the APLBench suite [21]. We account for the variability in multithreaded workloads by doing multiple simulation runs for each benchmark in each configuration and injecting random perturbations in memory systems timing for each run.

5   Evaluation Results

5.1   Impact on Area Overhead

First, we compare the memory overhead introduced by coherence information for all the protocols considered in this work. Although some protocols can entail extra overhead as a consequence of the additional mechanisms that they demand (e.g., timeouts for reissuing requests in *Token-CMP*), we only consider the amount of memory required to keep coherence information. Figure 2 shows the storage overhead introduced by these protocols in terms of both number of bits and estimated area, varying the number of cores from 2 to 1024.

Although the original *Hammer* protocol does not require coherence information, our optimized version for CMPs adds a new structure to the home tile. This structure is a 512-set 4-way cache that contains a copy of the tags for blocks stored in the private L1 caches but not in the shared L2 cache. However, this structure introduces a slight overhead which however keeps constant when the number of cores increases.

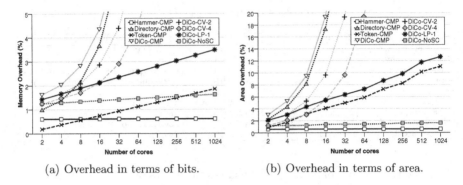

(a) Overhead in terms of bits.   (b) Overhead in terms of area.

Fig. 2. Overhead introduced by the coherence protocols evaluated in this work

Directory-CMP stores the directory information either in the L2 tags, when the L2 cache holds a copy of the block, or in a distributed directory cache, when the block is stored in any of the L1 caches but not in the L2 cache. Since the information is stored by using a bit-vector, the number of required bits is n and, consequently, the width of each entry grows linearly with the number of cores.

Token-CMP keeps the token count for any block stored both in the L1 and L2 caches, which requires $log_2(n+1)$ bits (the owner-token bit and non-owner token count). These additional bits are stored in the tags' part of both cache levels. Therefore, *Token-CMP* has an acceptable scalability in terms of area.

DiCo-CMP stores directory information for owner blocks stored in any L1 or L2 cache. Therefore, a full-map sharing code is added to each cache line. More-over, it uses two structures that store the identity of the owner tile, the L1C$ and the L2C$. Each entry in these structures contains a tag and an owner field, which requires $log_2 n$ bits. Hence, this is the protocol with more area requirements.

In this work, we propose to reduce this overhead by introducing compressed sharing codes in DiCo-CMP. *DiCo-CV-2* and *DiCo-CV-4* save storage compared to *DiCo-CMP* but they are still non-scalable. In contrast, *DiCo-LP-1*, which only adds a pointer for the second sharer of the block (the first one is given by the L2C$) has better scalability $-O(log_2 n)-$. Finally, *DiCo-NoSC*, which does not require to modify data caches to add coherence information, is the implementa-tion of DiCo with less overhead (although it still has order $O(log_2 n)$ due to the presence of the L1 and L2 coherence caches), at the cost of increasing network traffic. Finally, we can see that a small overhead in the number of required bits results in a major overhead when the area of the structures is considered.

5.2   Impact on Network Traffic

Figure 3 compares the network traffic generated by the protocols discussed pre-viously for the 16-core and the 32-core configurations. Each bar plots the number of bytes transmitted through the interconnection network normalized with re-spect to *Hammer-CMP*.

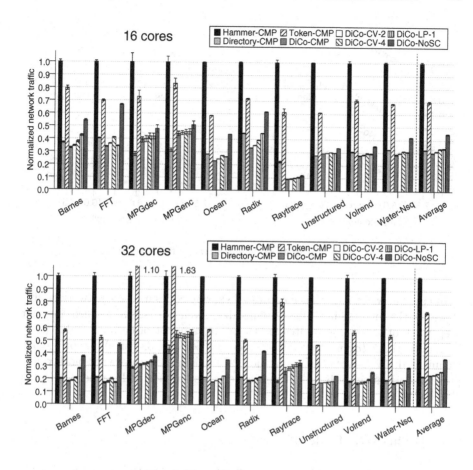

Fig. 3. Normalized network traffic

As expected, *Hammer-CMP* introduces more network traffic than the other protocols due to the lack of coherence information, which implies broadcasting requests to all cores and receiving the corresponding acknowledgements. *Directory-CMP* reduces considerably traffic by adding a bit-vector that filters unnecessary invalidations. *Token-CMP* generates more network traffic than *Directory-CMP*, because it relies on broadcast, and less than *Hammer-CMP*, because it does not need to receive acknowledgements from tiles without tokens (i.e., the tiles that do not share the block). However, for some applications, like *MPGdec* and *MPGenc*, *Token-CMP* generate more traffic than *Hammer-CMP* for the 32-core configuration. This increase is due to two main factors. First, in Hammer-CMP, read misses that found the data block in the L2 cache do not broadcast requests whereas Token-CMP always needs to broadcast read requests. Second, the high contention found in these applications increases the amount of reissued persistent requests in *Token-CMP*. Finally, we can also observe that *DiCo-CMP* has similar traffic requirements than *Directory-CMP*.

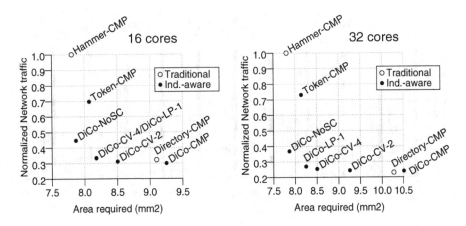

Fig. 4. Traffic-area trade-off

In general, we can see that compressed sharing codes increase network traffic. However, the increase in traffic is admissible. Even *DiCo-NoSC*, which does not keep track of sharers, generates an acceptable amount of network traffic (36% less traffic than *Token-CMP* for 16 cores and 50% for 32 cores). As previously commented, *DiCo-NoSC* stores in the L2C$ a pointer to the owner block which prevent read misses of broadcasting requests, as happens in Hammer-CMP and Token-CMP.

5.3   Traffic-Area Trade-Off

Figure 4 shows the traffic-area trade-off for all the protocols evaluated in this work. The figure also differentiates between traditional and indirection-aware protocols. We can see that, in general, the base protocols aimed to be used with tiled CMPs do not have a good traffic-area trade-off: both *Hammer-CMP* and *Token-CMP* are constrained by traffic while both *Directory-CMP* and *DiCo-CMP* are constrained by area.

However, the use of different compressed sharing codes for DiCo-CMP can lead to a good compromise between network traffic and area requirements. The *DiCo-CV* approaches have low traffic overhead but the area requirements considerably increase with the number of cores. Both *DiCo-LP-1* and *DiCo-NoSC* are very close to an ideal protocol with the best of the base protocols. The difference is that *DiCo-LP-1* is more efficient in terms of generated traffic while *DiCo-NoSC* is more efficient in terms of area requirements. Particularly, *DiCo-LP-1* requires slightly more area than *Token-CMP* (1% for 32 cores, and same complexity order $-O(log_2 n)-$) and slightly increases network traffic compared to *DiCo-CMP* (11% on average for 32 cores). On the other hand, *DiCo-NoSC* does not need to modify the structure of caches to add any extra field and, therefore, introduces less area requirements than *Token-CMP* (4% for 32 cores), but with the same complexity

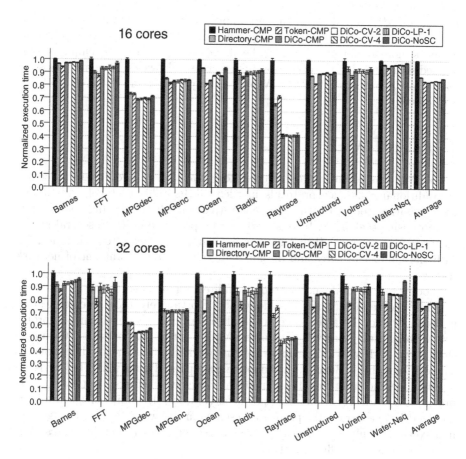

Fig. 5. Normalized execution times

order $-O(log_2 n)-$. However, it increases network traffic by 35% compared to *DiCo-CMP*, but still halving the traffic when compared to *Token-CMP*.

5.4   Impact on Execution Time

Figure 5 plots the average execution times for the applications evaluated in this work normalized with respect to *Hammer-CMP*. Compared to *Hammer-CMP*, *Directory-CMP* improves performance for all applications as a consequence of an important reduction in terms of network traffic. Moreover, on each miss *Hammer-CMP* must wait for all the acknowledgement messages before the requested block can be accessed. On the contrary, in *Directory-CMP* only write misses must wait for acknowledgements.

On the other hand, indirection-aware protocols reduce average execution time when compared to traditional protocols. Particularly, *Token-CMP* obtains average improvements of 16% compared to *Hammer-CMP* and 4% compared to

Directory-CMP for 16 cores. Similar improvements are obtained with *DiCo-CMP*. For 32 cores, the average improvements of indirection-aware protocols becomes more significant. On the other hand, when *DiCo-CMP* employs compressed sharing codes, the execution time increases. However, it remains close to *DiCo-CMP*, except for *DiCo-NoSC* mainly when a 32-core CMP is considered.

6   Related Work

DiCo-CMP was recently proposed by Ros *et al.* [12] to avoid the indirection of traditional coherence protocols in tiled CMPs. This protocol adds a bit-vector sharing code to each cache entry (particularly, in the tags part), thus compromising scalability. In this work, we propose and evaluate several implementations of DiCo-CMP that use compressed sharing codes to scale gracefully with the number of cores and do not require a prohibitive amount of network traffic.

Snoopy protocols do not introduce indirection because they are based on a totally-ordered interconnection network. Unfortunately, these interconnection networks are not scalable. Some proposals have focused on using snoopy protocols with arbitrary network topologies. Martin. *et al.* [22] present a technique that allows SMPs to utilize unordered networks (with some modifications to support snooping). Bandwidth Adaptive Snooping Hybrid (BASH) [23] is an hybrid coherence protocol that dynamically decides whether to act like snoopy protocols (broadcast) or directory protocols (unicast) depending on the available bandwidth. In contrast, the protocol presented in this work does not changes dynamically, but only broadcast requests for a small number of cache misses, thus obtaining network traffic reductions.

Cheng *et al.* [24] adapt already existing coherence protocols for reducing energy consumption and execution time in CMPs with heterogeneous networks. In particular, they assume a heterogeneous network comprised of several sets of wires, each one with different latency, bandwidth, and energy characteristics, and propose to send each coherence message through a particular set of wires depending on its latency and bandwidth requirements. Our proposals are orthogonal to this work and the ideas presented in [24] could also be applied to direct coherence protocols.

Martin *et al.* propose to use destination-set prediction to reduce the bandwidth required by a snoopy protocol [25]. Differently from our proposals, this approach is based on a totally-ordered interconnect, which is not suitable for large-scale tiled CMPs. Regarding indirection avoidance, Cheng *et al.* propose to convert 3-hop read misses into 2-hop read misses for memory blocks that exhibit the producer-consumer sharing pattern [26] by using extra hardware to detect when a block is being accessed according to this pattern. In contrast, direct coherence obtains 2-hops misses for read, write and upgrade misses without taking into account sharing patterns.

7   Conclusions

Tiled CMP architectures have recently emerged as a scalable alternative to current small-scale CMP designs, and will be probably the architecture of choice for future many-core CMPs. On the other hand, although a great deal of attention was devoted to scalable cache coherence protocols in the last decades in the context of shared-memory multiprocessors, the technological parameters and power constrains entailed by CMPs demand new solutions to the cache coherence problem. New cache coherence protocols, like *Token-CMP* and *DiCo-CMP*, have been recently proposed to cope with the indirection problem of traditional protocols. However, neither *Token-CMP* nor *DiCo-CMP* scale efficiently with the number of cores.

This work addresses the traffic-area trade-off of indirection-aware cache coherence protocols through several implementations of direct coherence for CMPs. We evaluate several cache coherence protocols that differ in the amount of coherence information that they store. Particularly, *DiCo-LP-1*, which only stores the identity of one sharer along with the data block, and *DiCo-NoSC*, which does not store any coherence information in the data caches, are the alternatives that achieve a best compromise between traffic and area. Note that both approaches include the coherence caches required by direct coherence protocols. *DiCo-LP-1* presents a good trade-off by requiring slightly more area than *Token-CMP* (1% for 32 cores and same order $-O(log_2 n)-$) and slightly increasing network traffic compared to *DiCo-CMP* (11% for 32 cores). *DiCo-NoSC* does not need to modify the structure of caches and, therefore, has less area requirements than *Token-CMP* (4% for 32 cores), but with the same complexity order $-O(log_2 n)-$. However, it increases network traffic by 35% compared to *DiCo-CMP*, but still halving the traffic when compared to *Token-CMP*. Finally, *DiCo-LP-1* improves execution time compared to *DiCo-NoSC* due to reductions in network traffic. Finally, we believe that both alternatives can be considered for many-core tiled CMPs depending on the particular system constraints.

References

1. Le, H.Q., et al.: IBM POWER6 microarchitecture. IBM Journal of Research and Development 51(6), 639–662 (2007)
2. Shah, M., et al.: UltraSPARC T2: A highly-threaded, power-efficient, SPARC SOC. In: IEEE Asian Solid-State Circuits Conference, November 2007, pp. 22–25 (2007)
3. Azimi, M., et al.: Integration challenges and tradeoffs for tera-scale architectures. Intel. Technology Journal 11(3), 173–184 (2007)
4. Kumar, R., Zyuban, V., Tullsen, D.M.: Interconnections in multi-core architectures: Understanding mechanisms, overheads and scaling. In: 32nd Int'l. Symp. on Computer Architecture (ISCA), June 2005, pp. 408–419 (2005)
5. Bosschere, K.D., et al.: High-performance embedded architecture and compilation roadmap. Transactions on HiPEAC I, 5–29 (January 2007)
6. Owner, J.M., Hummel, M.D., Meyer, D.R., Keller, J.B.: System and method of maintaining coherency in a distributed communication system. U.S. Patent 7069361 (June 2006)

7. Culler, D.E., Singh, J.P., Gupta, A.: Parallel Computer Architecture: A Hardware/Software Approach. Morgan Kaufmann Publishers, Inc., San Francisco (1999)
8. Agarwal, A., Simoni, R., Hennessy, J.L., Horowitz, M.: An evaluation of directory schemes for cache coherence. In: 15th Int'l. Symp. on Computer Architecture (ISCA), May 1988, pp. 280–289 (1988)
9. Chaiken, D., Kubiatowicz, J., Agarwal, A.: LimitLESS directories: A scalable cache coherence scheme. In: 4th Int. Conf. on Architectural Support for Programming Language and Operating Systems (ASPLOS), April 1991, pp. 224–234 (1991)
10. Gupta, A., Weber, W.D., Mowry, T.C.: Reducing memory traffic requirements for scalable directory-based cache coherence schemes. In: Int'l. Conference on Parallel Processing (ICPP), August 1990, pp. 312–321 (1990)
11. Marty, M.R., Bingham, J., Hill, M.D., Hu, A., Martin, M.M., Wood, D.A.: Improving multiple-cmp systems using token coherence. In: 11th Int'l. Symp. on High-Performance Computer Architecture (HPCA), February 2005, pp. 328–339 (2005)
12. Ros, A., Acacio, M.E., García, J.M.: DiCo-CMP: Efficient cache coherency in tiled cmp architectures. In: 22nd Int'l. Parallel and Distributed Processing Symp. (IPDPS) (April 2008)
13. Kim, C., Burger, D., Keckler, S.W.: An adaptive, non-uniform cache structure for wire-delay dominated on-chip caches. In: 10th Int. Conf. on Architectural Support for Programming Language and Operating Systems (ASPLOS), October 2002, pp. 211–222 (2002)
14. Barroso, L.A., et al.: Piranha: A scalable architecture based on single-chip multiprocessing. In: 27th Int'l. Symp. on Computer Architecture (ISCA), June 2000, pp. 12–14 (2000)
15. Magnusson, P.S., et al.: Simics: A full system simulation platform. IEEE Computer 35(2), 50–58 (2002)
16. Martin, M.M., et al.: Multifacet's general execution-driven multiprocessor simulator (GEMS) toolset. Computer Architecture News 33(4), 92–99 (2005)
17. Puente, V., Gregorio, J.A., Beivide, R.: SICOSYS: An integrated framework for studying interconnection network in multiprocessor systems. In: 10th Euromicro Workshop on Parallel, Distributed and Network-based Processing, January 2002, pp. 15–22 (2002)
18. Thoziyoor, S., Muralimanohar, N., Ahn, J.H., Jouppi, N.P.: Cacti 5.1. Technical Report HPL-2008-20, HP Labs (April 2008)
19. Horel, T., Lauterbach, G.: UltraSPARC-III: Designing third-generation 64-bit performance. IEEE Micro. 19(3), 73–85 (1999)
20. Woo, S.C., Ohara, M., Torrie, E., Singh, J.P., Gupta, A.: The SPLASH-2 programs: Characterization and methodological considerations. In: 22nd Int'l. Symp. on Computer Architecture (ISCA), June 1995, pp. 24–36 (1995)
21. Li, M.L., Sasanka, R., Adve, S.V., Chen, Y.K., Debes, E.: The ALPBench benchmark suite for complex multimedia applications. In: Int'l. Symp. on Workload Characterization, October 2005, pp. 34–45 (2005)
22. Martin, M.M., et al.: Timestamp snooping: An approach for extending SMPs. In: 9th Int. Conf. on Architectural Support for Programming Language and Operating Systems (ASPLOS), November 2000, pp. 25–36 (2000)
23. Martin, M.M., Sorin, D.J., Hill, M.D., Wood, D.A.: Bandwidth adaptive snooping. In: 8th Int'l. Symp. on High-Performance Computer Architecture (HPCA), January 2002, pp. 251–262 (2002)

24. Cheng, L., Muralimanohar, N., Ramani, K., Balasubramonian, R., Carter, J.B.: Interconnect-aware coherence protocols for chip multiprocessors. In: 33rd Int'l. Symp. on Computer Architecture (ISCA), June 2006, pp. 339–351 (2006)
25. Martin, M.M., Harper, P.J., Sorin, D.J., Hill, M.D., Wood, D.A.: Using destination-set prediction to improve the latency/bandwidth tradeoff in shared-memory multiprocessors. In: 30th Int'l. Symp. on Computer Architecture (ISCA), June 2003, pp. 206–217 (2003)
26. Cheng, L., Carter, J.B., Dai, D.: An adaptive cache coherence protocol optimized for producer-consumer sharing. In: 13th Int'l. Symp. on High-Performance Computer Architecture (HPCA), February 2007, pp. 328–339 (2007)

An Efficient Lightweight Shared Cache Design for Chip Multiprocessors*

Jinglei Wang, Dongsheng Wang, Yibo Xue, and Haixia Wang

Tsinghua National Laboratory for Information Science and Technology
Department of Computer Science and Technology, Tsinghua University,
Beijing 100084, China
wjinglei00@mails.tsinghua.edu.cn, {wds,yiboxue}@tsinghua.edu.cn

Abstract. The large working sets of commercial and scientific work-loads favor a shared L2 cache design that maximizes the aggregate cache capacity and minimizes off-chip memory requests in Chip Multiprocessors (CMP). The exponential increase in the number of cores results in the commensurate increase in the memory cost of directory, restricting its scalability severely. To resolve this hurdle, a novel *Lightweight Shared Cache* design is proposed in this paper, which applies two small fast caches to store and manage the data and directory vectors for the blocks recently cached by L1 caches in each tile of CMP. The proposed cache scheme removes the directory vectors from L2 cache, thus decreases on-chip directory memory overhead and improves the scalability. Moreover, the proposed cache scheme brings significant reductions in terms of the L1 cache miss latencies, which lead to the improvement of program performance by 6% on average, and up to 16% at best, with 0.18% storage overhead.

Keywords: Chip Multiprocessors (CMP), Directory-based Cache Coherence Protocol, Lightweight Shared Cache.

1 Introduction

The large working sets of commercial and scientific workloads favor a shared L2 cache design that maximizes the aggregate cache capacity and minimizes off-chip memory requests in Chip Multiprocessors (CMP). Current CMP systems, such as Piranha [18], Sun Niagara [19], XLR [20] and Power 5 [21], employ shared L2 caches to maximize the on-chip cache capacity. Physical and manufacturing considerations suggest that future CMP integrating hundreds of cores on chip will be probably designed as tiles connected over a switched direct network [1, 2, 3, 4]. In most current proposals, each tile contains a processor core, a private L1 cache, a bank of shared cache (commonly, the L2 cache) and a router. Private caches are kept coherent by using directory-based cache coherence protocol [5].

* This work has been supported by NSFC grants No. 60833004, No. 60773146 and No. 60673145.

Y. Dou, R. Gruber, and J. Joller (Eds.): APPT 2009, LNCS 5737, pp. 28–40, 2009.
© Springer-Verlag Berlin Heidelberg 2009

In tiled CMP, the directory structure is distributed within each L2 cache bank, usually included in the L2 tags' portion. In this way, each tile keeps the directory vectors of blocks mapped to its L2 cache bank. L1 cache misses are sent to the corresponding home node, which looks up the directory vector and performs the actions needed to ensure coherence. The directory access latency is equal to the L2 cache bank access time.

The exponential increase in the number of cores results in the commensurate increase in the memory cost of directory vectors, restricting its scalability severely. For example, considering cache line size is 64Bytes and full-map bit-vector is adopted, the memory cost of directory vectors will be 100% of L2 cache when the number of cores increases to 512 [14]. Since CMP designs are constrained by area, the directory should occupy a small fraction of the total chip area.

In fact, only a small fraction of data blocks are caching in L1 caches at a particular time (temporal locality). In L2 cache, when a data block is cached to L1 caches, its directory vector is used to track the locations of L1 caches. In the worst cases, the number of directory vectors used in L2 cache is equal to the number of data blocks of L1 caches able to contain at any time when CMP is running. Since the capacity of L1 caches is far smaller than that of L2 cache, most of directory vectors are unused and wasted.

In this paper, we firstly analyze the occupation of directory vectors in shared L2 cache of CMP. Experiment results show that the average number of blocks cached to L1 caches does not exceed 41% of the capacity of L1 caches due to redundant copies existing in L1 caches. In the worst cases, up to 96.8% of the directory vectors are vacant.

Motivated by the observation and analysis, we propose a *Lightweight Shared Cache* design that applies a *Shared Data Cache (SDC)* and a *Victim Directory Cache (VDC)* to store and manage data and directory vectors for the blocks recently cached by L1 caches in each tile of CMP. The *SDC* stores data and directory vectors for the local blocks cached by L1 caches. The *VDC* stores only directory vectors for those blocks evicted from the *SDC*. In this way, directory vectors are removed from L2 cache.

The proposed lightweight shared cache design shows the following benefits: (1) Decreases on-chip directory memory overhead and improves the scalability of CMP by removing directory vectors from L2 cache. (2) Reduces L1 cache miss latencies by accelerating the access to shared data blocks. (3) Obtains less number of off-chip memory requests by increasing the capacity of on-chip cache.

Since shared data access and directory maintenance are correlated with network communication, the proposed scheme embeds *SDC* and *VDC* into the network interface of each router to decrease L1 cache miss latency further.

Full-system simulations of 16-core CMP show that the lightweight shared cache scheme provides the robust performance: it decreases L1 miss latency by 20% on average and reduces off-chip memory requests by 13% on average. Consequently, this leads to 6% improvement in execution time on average, and up to 16% at best, with 0.18% storage overhead.

The rest of the paper is organized as follows: Section 2 presents a review of the related work. Section 3 analyzes the occupation of directory vectors in L2 cache. Section 4 describes the lightweight shared cache design and the cache coherence protocol required by it. Section 5 evaluates the performance of the lightweight shared cache. And finally, section 6 concludes the paper and points out some future work.

2   Related Work

Most of previous work about directory structure of cache coherence protocol focused on the private L2 cache design in CC-NUMA multiprocessors. In CC-NUMA, directory is stored in main memory, and implies memory overhead and long L2 miss latencies.

Directory caches have been originally proposed in [6] for cutting down directory memory overhead, which can also be used for reducing the latency of L2 misses by obtaining directory information from a much faster structure than main memory. Fox example, in [7, 8] the integration of directory caches inside the coherence controllers was proposed to minimize directory access time. In [9], the remote memory access latency is reduced by placing caches in the crossbar switches of the interconnection network to capture and store shared data as they flow from the memory module to the requesting processor. In [10], a 3-level directory organization was proposed, including a directory cache on chip and a compressed directory structure in main memory.

The lightweight directory architecture proposed in [12] adds directory information to the L2 caches, thus removing the directory structure from main memory. However, this structure increases the number of cache misses as a result of the premature invalidations that arise when a particular memory block is replaced from the L2 cache of the corresponding home node. To minimize such premature invalidations, a new L2 cache design [13] was proposed which splits the cache structure into two different parts: one for storing data and directory information for the blocks requested by the local processor, and another one for storing only directory information for blocks accessed by remote processors.

This paper studies the directory structure of shared L2 cache design in CMP. In CMP, directory is stored in L2 cache, and implies the similar problem as CC-NUMA: memory overhead and long miss latencies. But the directory capacity and the directory access latency have significantly difference between CMP and CC-NUMA. The directory capacity of CMP is much smaller than that of CC-NUMA, but it will consume the constrained on-chip resource. The directory access latency of CMP is much lower than that of CC-NUMA, but the directory accesses are more frequent than that in CC-NUMA due to different L2 cache design. Thus, the directory access latency can also lead to long miss latency in CMP.

In this paper, we propose a lightweight shared cache design to decrease memory overhead of on-chip directory and reduce the L1 miss latencies in CMP.

3   Characterizing CMP Directory

In CMP, only a small fraction of data blocks in shared L2 cache are cached in the L1 caches at a particular time. We analyzes the average and maximum number of data blocks cached to L1 caches in L2 cache, through running multithreads and single-thread programs in 16-core CMP simulator. Section 5 describes the simulation environment and workloads in detail.

Table 1. Number of Data Blocks Cached by L1 Caches in L2 Cache

| Benchmarks | CMP: 16 cores, L1 Cache:32KB, L2 Cache Bank: 1MB, Cache Line: 64B | | | |
| | *Average number of data blocks* | | *Maximum number of data blocks* | |
	% of L1 capacity	*% of L2 capacity*	*% of L1 capacity*	*% of L2 capacity*
fft	29.3%	0.9%	92.0%	2.9%
lu	41.0%	1.3%	99.6%	3.2%
radix	40.0%	1.3%	98.2%	3.1%
radiosity	23.2%	0.7%	45.9%	1.4%
raytrace	29.9%	0.9%	52.3%	1.6%
ocean	30.5%	1.0%	60.5%	1.9%
art	15.4%	0.5%	31.4%	1.0%
apsi	25.0%	0.8%	47.3%	1.5%

Table 1 gives the number of data blocks cached by L1 caches in L2 cache. In L2 cache, the average number of data blocks cached by L1 caches accounts for 15.4-41.0% of the capacity of L1 caches, and accounts for 0.5-1.3% of the capacity of L2 cache. The maximum number of data blocks cached by L1 caches in L2 cache is 31.4-99.6% of the capacity of L1 caches, and is 1.0-3.2% of the capacity of L2 cache.

From table 1, we observe that:

(1) In the worst cases, up to 96.8% directory vectors in L2 cache are unused and wasted.

(2) The number of data blocks recently cached by L1 caches does not exceed 41% of the capacity of L1 caches on average.

Motivated by the observation, we propose a lightweight shared cache to store the data blocks recently cached by L1 caches and ensure their coherence. The directory vectors removed from L2 cache to save on-chip resources are justly used to compensate for the cost of the proposed lightweight shared cache.

4   The Lightweight Shared Cache Design

In this section, we present the structure of the lightweight shared cache, as well as the coherence protocol required by it.

4.1   Structure of the Lightweight Shared Cache

The lightweight shared cache proposed in this paper stores data and directory vectors for the blocks recently cached by L1 caches to reduce on-chip directory overhead and decrease L1 cache miss latencies.

To reduce on-chip directory overhead, directory vectors in L2 cache are removed due to its low utilization rate. The lightweight shared cache should contain enough directory vectors to satisfy the demand of L1 cache misses. Previous experiment and analysis show that the maximum number of data blocks recently cached by L1 caches in L2 cache is close to the capacity of L1 caches in the worst cases. So the number of directory vectors stored in the proposed lightweight shared cache should be larger than the maximum number of data blocks recently cached by L1 caches.

To decrease L1 cache miss latencies, the lightweight shared cache should contain data blocks recently cached by L1 caches. From previous experiment, the number of data blocks recently cached by L1 caches in L2 cache does not exceed 41% of the capacity of L1 caches on average. According to temporal locality, we place these data blocks in the proposed lightweight shared cache in the home node. Most of L1 miss requests sent to this home node will be satisfied in the lightweight shared cache and need not travel to L2 cache bank to access data blocks. The lightweight shared cache should have desirable space to contain blocks recently cached by L1 caches.

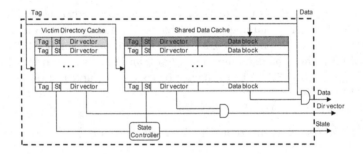

Fig. 1. The lightweight shared cache

The proposed lightweight shared cache consists of two structures as shown in figure 1:

(1) The *Shared Data Cache (SDC)* that maintains both local data blocks and corresponding directory vectors recently cached by L1 caches. In SDC, a cache line contains tag, coherence state, directory vector and data block. Because the goal of SDC is to reduce L1 cache miss latencies, the SDC should be able to contain the blocks recently cached by L1 caches, larger SDC will waste on-chip resource. According to previous analysis, when the size of SDC is equal to that of L1 cache, most of L1 misses could be satisfied in the SDC.

(2) The *Victim Directory Cache (VDC)* that stores only directory vectors for the local blocks recently cached by L1 caches and not present in SDC. As the name implies, VDC works as a victim directory cache of SDC. Because the limited capacity, the SDC increases the number of L1 cache misses as a result of the premature invalidations that arise when a particular data block is replaced from the SDC. To minimize the number of premature invalidations, when a data block is replaced from SDC, the evicted directory vector is stored in the VDC. The aim of VDC is to increase the capacity of directory vectors in the proposed lightweight shared cache. In VDC, a cache line contains tag, coherence state and directory vector, but not containing data block.

Since the lightweight shared cache is small and its function is correlated with network communication, it is embedded into the network interface of router to reduce the access latency of data blocks and directory vectors further. The modified router is shown in Figure 2.

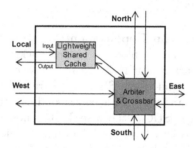

Fig. 2. Modified Router Structure

Differently from conventional router, the modified router adds a lightweight shared cache module into the network interface. The lightweight shared cache module intercepts and captures local/remote L1 cache requests sent to the local L2 cache bank at local input/output port respectively. The lightweight shared cache's requests and responses sent to local L1 cache and L2 cache bank are transmitted through local output port. The lightweight shared cache's requests and responses sent to remote L1 caches are injected into network through the local input port.

4.2   Cache Coherence Protocol for Lightweight Shared Cache

The proposed lightweight shared cache design requires a cache coherence protocol similar to MSI [14] with some minor modifications. These modifications are performed to ensure that the lightweight shared cache can intercept and capture the messages transmitted between L1 caches and local L2 cache bank to handle all operations related to coherence maintenance. Although implementing a full-map MSI protocol, the proposed cache scheme has no special limits to directory-based coherence protocol.

Read and Write Requests: Each L1 read or write miss request is sent to L2 cache bank in home node.

(1) At home node, the lightweight shared cache intercepts and captures local/remote L1 miss request at local input/output port, then snoops SDC and VDC.

(2) In case of a SDC hit, the SDC is responsible for providing the data and sending the reply to the requestor. After updating directory vector, the reply is directly sent to local L1 cache, or is injected into network to transmit to the remote L1 cache through local input port.

(3) In case of a VDC hit, VDC requests data from local L2 cache bank. After receiving the requested data from local L2 cache bank, the directory vector is updated and the reply is forwarded to requestor like (2).

(4) If the requested address is not present in SDC and VDC, SDC requests data from local L2 cache bank through local output port. After receiving the requested data from local L2 cache bank through local input port, SDC stores this data and updates directory vector, and then sends reply to requestor.

Lightweight Shared Cache Replacement: When a cache line is replaced from the SDC, the evicted data block is written back to local L2 cache bank, while the evicted directory vector is stored in the VDC. When a cache line is replaced from the VDC, and if the SDC has a free line, VDC will store the directory vector in SDC, and then reads corresponding data block from local L2 cache bank and stores it in SDC. Otherwise, VDC sends invalidations to shared L1 caches. After having collected all invalidation acknowledges, the cache line is removed from VDC. If VDC has received write back message, it forwards this message to local L2 cache bank to store the data block.

L2 Requests from Lightweight Shared Cache: When local L2 cache bank receives read request from SDC or VDC, L2 cache bank returns data block to the requestor. If the request is from SDC, the requested data block is removed from L2 cache bank. The data blocks stored in SDC need not hold in L2 cache bank. Thus, the capacity of on-chip cache increases.

5   Evaluation Results and Analysis

The lightweight shared cache improves the performance of CMP by reducing L1 cache miss latencies and decreasing the number of off-chip memory requests.

In this section, we evaluate the performance of the proposed lightweight shared cache in terms of total execution time as well as we analyze the impact on L1 cache miss latencies, the number off-chip memory requests and the number of L1 cache misses. We compare the proposed lightweight shared cache design with the conventional shared L2 cache design. The CMP structure adopting the lightweight shared cache is shown in Figure 3. Differently from a conventional CMP, the directory is removed from L2 cache and a lightweight shared cache is added to router in the CMP.

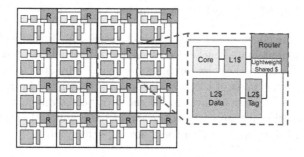

Fig. 3. CMP Architecture with the lightweight shared cache

5.1   Simulation Environment

This paper uses GEMS simulator [11] to evaluate the performance of the lightweight shared cache. Table 2 shows the detailed system parameters. The benchmarks are selected from SPLASH-2 [16] and SPEC2000 [17]. Table 3 shows the benchmarks used in this evaluation. In this evaluation, the size of SDC is equal to the size of L1 cache, and the number of entries of VDC is equal to that of L1 cache. The impact on the performance of CMP when different size of SDC and VDC are adopted will be evaluated in future work.

Table 2. System parameters

Processors: 16 cores, Cache line size: 64B
L1 I/D Cache: 32KB -2way, 1 cycle
L2 Cache: 6 cycles, 1MB-16way/bank, (Total 16MB)
Lightweight Shared Cache: 16-way, 1 cycle, SDC: 32KB, VDC: 512 Entries
L1/L2/SDC/VDC Replacement Policy: Psuedo-LRU
Network: 4 x 4 Mesh; One-hop latency: 3 cycles
External memory latency: 256 cycles

Table 3. Benchmarks parameters

Benchmarks	Parameters
fft	256K complex doubles
lu	1024 x 1024 matrix
radiosity	room environment
radix	1M keys, 1024 radix
raytrace	car environment
ocean	258 x 258 grid
art	lgred input
apsi	lgred input

5.2   Impact on L1 Cache Miss Latencies

Figure 4 shows the normalized L1 cache miss latencies. As it can be observed, the proposed lightweight shared cache decreases the L1 cache miss latencies by from 15% to 25%. The L1 cache miss latencies are reduced by 20% on average. One of the reasons is that most of L1 cache misses can be satisfied in the lightweight shared cache, and need not travel to L2 cache to access directory vectors and data blocks. Another reason is the reduction of the number of off-chip memory requests which will be discussed in the following subsection.

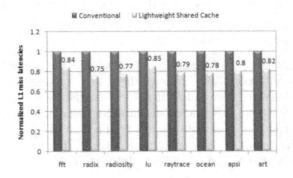

Fig. 4. Reduced L1 cache miss latencies

5.3   Impact on Off-Chip Memory Requests

Figure 5 shows the normalized number of off-chip memory requests. The proposed lightweight shared cache decreases the number of off-chip memory requests by from 2% to 24%. The number of off-chip memory requests is reduced by 13% on average. The reason is that the lightweight shared cache increases the capacity of on-chip cache through moving blocks recently accessed by L1 caches to the SDC. Reduced off-chip memory requests can significantly decrease the latency of off-chip memory access, which result in the reduction of L1 miss latency. As can be seen in Figure 4 and Figure 5, less number of off-chip memory requests will lead to lower L1 miss latency relatively.

5.4   Impact on L1 Cache Miss Ratio

Figure 6 shows that the proposed lightweight shared cache increases the L1 miss ratio of each workload by 1-33% except lu. For lu workload, the L1 miss ratio does not increase, but decrease by 12%. The reason is that we selected a "-c" parameter in lu's command line, which means that non-locally allocated blocks will be copied to local memory before they are needed. Well spatial locality makes lu obtain lower L1 miss ratio than conventional CMP. In addition, the L1 miss

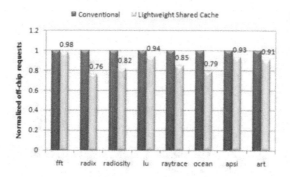

Fig. 5. Reduced off-chip memory requests

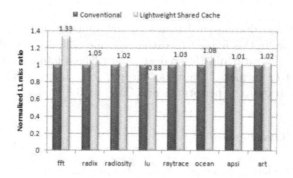

Fig. 6. Normalized L1 miss ratio

ratio of fft increases by 33%, which is far higher than that of other workloads. This is due to its lower spatial locality. The L1 cache miss ratio increases by 5% on average. The increase of L1 cache miss ratio is caused by the limited capacity of the lightweight shared cache.

5.5 Impact on Execution Time

For benchmarks running on CMP, their execution time is decided by the latency of memory system which further depends on the L1 miss latency and the L1 miss ratio. For example, we assume the L1 miss ratio is Rm, the L1 miss latency is Lm, and the L1 hit latency is 1. So the average latency of memory system (L) will be described as follow:

$$L = 1 - Rm + Rm * Lm \qquad (1)$$

Figure 7 shows that the lightweight shared cache reduces the execution time of each benchmark by 3-16%. As discussed above, although the L1 miss ratio

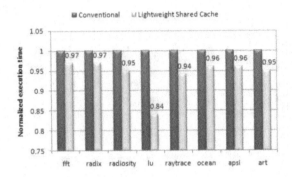

Fig. 7. Improvement of the total performance

increases, the larger decrease of L1 miss latencies finally lead to the reductions of execution time. In this figure, the execution time of lu is reduced by 16% due to its lower L1 miss ratio and 15% reduction of L1 miss latency. This is because that lu has better memory locality as the previous analysis. The lightweight shared cache improves the performance of CMP by 6% on average.

5.6   Storage Overhead

The lightweight shared cache will consume some on-chip resource, while the memory space of directory in L2 cache is saved. Compared to conventional shared L2 cache design, the lightweight shared cache design increases on-chip storage by only 0.18%. The detailed storage overhead can be seen in Table 4. As the number of cores increases, the saved directory storage from L2 cache will increase significantly, while the storage overhead of the proposed scheme will increase far slower. So, the proposed lightweight shared cache design can provide much better scalability than the conventional shared L2 cache design.

Table 4. Storage Overhead Comparison (in Each Tile of CMP)

	Conventional scheme	Proposed cache scheme
L1 cache	32KB	32KB
L2 cache	1MB	1MB
L2 directory	32KB	0
Lightweight shared cache	0	SDC data blocks: 32KB SDC directory: 1KB VDC directory: 1KB
Total	1088KB	1090KB
Normalization	1	1.0018

6 Conclusions and Future Work

This paper proposes an efficient *Lightweight Shared Cache* design that applies *Share Data Cache (SDC)* and *Victim Directory Cache (VDC)* to store and manage data and directory vectors for the blocks recently cached by L1 caches in CMP. In this way, directory vectors are removed from L2 cache, thus decreasing the on-chip directory overhead and improving the scalability of CMP. The proposed lightweight shared cache also reduces the L1 cache miss latencies and increases the capacity of on-chip cache, which translates into reductions in applications' execution time. This paper evaluates the performance of the proposed lightweight shared cache. Simulation results show that the proposed cache scheme provides the robust performance: it decreases L1 miss latency by 20% on average and reduces off-chip memory requests by 13% on average. Consequently, this leads to 6% improvement in execution time on average, with 0.18% storage overhead. When the data blocks of applications are locally allocated, the lightweight shared cache can improve their performance significantly by up to 16%.

For future work, we plan to evaluate the performance of the lightweight shared cache when the different size of SDC and VDC are adopted. We will also evaluate the performance of the lightweight shared cache when the number of cores increases. Another area of interest is to study the method to improve data blocks' locality. Finally, in order to reduce even more directory memory overhead, we would like to evaluate the effect of limited pointers or compressed sharing codes in the lightweight shared cache design.

References

1. Taylor, M.B., Kim, J., Miller, J., et al.: The raw microprocessor: A computational fabric for software circuits and general purpose programs. IEEE Micro. 22(2), 25–35 (2002)
2. Zhang, M., Asanovic, K.: Victim replication: Maximizing capacity while hiding wire delay in tiled chip multiprocessors. In: 32nd Int'l. Symp. on Computer Architecture (ISCA 2005), June 2005, pp. 336–345 (2005)
3. Azimi, M., Cherukuri, N., Jayasimha, D.N., Kumar, A., Kundu, P., Park, S., Schoinas, I., Vaidya, A.S.: Integration challenges and tradeoffs for tera-scale architectures. Intel. Technology Journal 11(3), 173–184 (2007)
4. Vangal, S., Howard, J., Ruhl, G., et al.: An 80-tile 1.28tflops network-on-chip in 65nm cmos. In: IEEE Int'l. Solid-State Circuits Conference (ISSCC) (February 2007)
5. Chaiken, D., Fields, C., Kurihara, K., Agarwal, A.: Directory-based cache coherence in large-scale multiprocessors. Computer 23(6), 49–58 (1990)
6. Gupta, A., Weber, W., Mowry, T.: Reducing Memory Traffic Requirements for Scalable Directory-Based Cache Coherence Schemes. In: Int'l. Conference on Parallel Processing (ICPP 1990), August 1990, pp. 312–321 (1990)
7. Nanda, A., Nguyen, A., Michael, M., Joseph, D.: High-Throughput Coherence Controllers. In: 6th Int'l. Symposium on High-Performance Computer Architecture (HPCA-6), January 2000, pp. 145–155 (2000)

8. Michael, M., Nanda, A.: Design and Performance of Directory Caches for Scalable Shared Memory Multiprocessors. In: Fifth International Conference on High Performance Computer Architecture, HPCA-5 (1999)

9. Iyer, R., Bhuyan, L.: Switch Cache: A Framework for Improving the Remote Memory Access Latency of CC-NUMA Multiprocessors. In: 5th Int'l. Symposium on High-Performance Computer Architecture (HPCA-5), January 1999, pp. 152–160 (1999)

10. Acacio, M.E., Gonzalez, J., Garcia, J.M., Duato, J.: An architecture for highperformance scalable shared- memory multiprocessors exploiting on-chip integration. IEEE Transactions on Parallel and Distributed Systems 15(8), 755–768 (2004)

11. Martin, M.M., Sorin, D.J., Beckmann, B.M., Marty, M.R., Xu, M., Alameldeen, A.R., Moore, K.E., Hill, M.D., Wood, D.A.: Multifacet's general execution-driven multiprocessor simulator (GEMS) toolset. Computer Architecture News 33(4), 92–99 (2005)

12. Ros, A., Acacio, M.E., Garca, J.M.: A Novel Lightweight Directory Archi-tecture for Scalable Shared-Memory Multiprocessors. In: Cunha, J.C., Medeiros, P.D. (eds.) Euro-Par 2005. LNCS, vol. 3648, pp. 582–591. Springer, Heidelberg (2005)

13. Ros, A., Acacio, M.E., Garca, J.M.: An efficient cache design for scalable glueless shared-memory multiprocessors. In: Proceedings of the 3rd conference on Computing frontiers, pp. 321–330 (2006)

14. Culler, D.E., Singh, J.P., Gupta, A.: Parallel Computer Architecture: A Hardware/Software Approach, 2nd edn. Harcourt Asia Pte Ltd. (2002)

15. Woodacre, M., Robb, D., Roe, D., Feind, K.: The SGI AltixTM 3000 global shared-memory architecture.Technical Whitepaper, Silicon Graphics, Inc. (2003)

16. Woo, S.C., Ohara, M., Torrie, E., Singh, J.P., Gupta, A.: The SPLASH-2 programs: Characterization and methodological considerations. In: 22nd Int'l. Symp. on Computer Architecture (ISCA 1995), June 1995, pp. 24–36 (1995)

17. SPEC2000, http://www.spec.org

18. Barroso, L., et al.: Piranha: a scalable architecture based on single-chip multiprocessing. In: ISCA-27, Vancouver, BC, Canada (May 2000)

19. Krewell, K.: Sun's Niagara pours on the cores. Microprocessor Report 18(9), 11–13 (2004)

20. Raza Microelectronics, Inc. XLR processor product overview (May 2005)

21. Sinharoy, B., Kalla, R., Tendler, J., Eickemeyer, R., Joyner, J.: Power5 System Microarchitecture. IBM Journal of Research and Development 49(4) (2005)

A Novel Cache Organization for Tiled Chip Multiprocessor*

Xi Zhang, Dongsheng Wang, Yibo Xue, Haixia Wang, and Jinglei Wang

Tsinghua National Laboratory for Information Science and Technology,
Department of Computer Science & Technology,
Tsinghua University, Beijing 100084, China
{zhang-xi06,wjinglei00}@mails.tsinghua.edu.cn
{wds,yiboxue,hx-wang}@tsinghua.edu.cn

Abstract. Increased device density and working set size are driving a rise in cache capacity, which comes at the cost of high access latency. Based on the characteristic of shared data, which is accessed frequently and consumes a little capacity, a novel two-level directory organization is proposed to minimize the cache access time in this paper. In this scheme, a small Fast Directory is used to offer fast hits for a great fraction of memory accesses. Detailed simulation results show that on a 16-core tiled chip multiprocessor, this approach reduces average access latency by 17.9% compared to the general cache organization, and improves the overall performance by 13.3% on average.

Keywords: Chip Multiprocessor(CMP), Tiled Architecture, Multi-level Directory, Cache Organization.

1 Introduction

Chip multiprocessor (CMP) is proposed to maintain the expected performance advances within the power and design complexity constraints. Future CMP will integrate more cores on a chip to increase the performance, meanwhile will increase the on-chip cache size to reduce access latency. The increasing number of cores and growing cache capacity will challenge the design of on-chip cache hierarchy which is now working well on 2 or 4-core CMP.

When CMP is scaled to tens or even hundreds of cores, the organization of on-chip cache and the design of cache coherence will become one of the key challenges. There have been dance-hall CMP architectures with processing cores on one side and shared L2 cache on the other side, which are connected by bus or network [25]. But dance-hall architecture is not well scalable because minimum L2 hit latency increases with the number of cores. Hence, to design CMP with more cores, tiled architecture which has better scalability and can reduce the design efforts is considered to be more appropriate. Directory-based cache

---

* This work is supported by the Natural Science Foundation of China under Grant No. 60673145, No. 60773146 and No. 60833004.

Y. Dou, R. Gruber, and J. Joller (Eds.): APPT 2009, LNCS 5737, pp. 41–53, 2009.
© Springer-Verlag Berlin Heidelberg 2009

coherence protocols have been widely used in large-scale multichip multiprocessor [1,2], which have been proved to be scalable, will be adopted by future CMP together with tiled architecture [24].

Advancements in semiconductor technology enable designers to exploit more transistors to improve performance. To minimize average access latency, increasing on-chip cache sizes to reduce the number of off-chip memory access is an effective solution. At the same time, growing application working sets can benefit from enlarging on-chip cache capacity as more cache lines can be kept on-chip. Manufacturers also ship CMP with large on-chip cache size (e.g., Intel Dual-Core Xeon 7100 [3] with 16MB cache, and Dual-Core Intel Itanium 2 with 24MB [4]). However, large cache size result in the increasing of hit latency-e.g. 4cycles in Intel Pentium III and 14cycles in Dual-Core Itanium 2, which penalty the performance. Nikos Hardavellas et al [5] investigate performance of database workloads on modern CMP. When the capacity of L2 cache is enlarged from 1MB to 26MB, the performance increases at first but begins to decrease quickly, even before the cache captures the entire working sets. The phenomenon indicates that merely increasing on-chip cache capacity is no longer enough to attain maximum performance, because bottleneck will be shifted from off-chip memory access to on-chip L2-hits. The on-chip cache hit latency mainly depends on the organization of last-level cache (LLC). Access latency of LLC generally consists of two parts: the network latency depending on the distance between requesting core and data, and the cache-bank access latency. There has been a flurry of researches on cache line replication or migration to place data close to requesting core, which can reduce network latency [6,7,8,9,10], but not suitable to cache-bank access latency. Our research is focusing on how to reduce the LLC cache-bank access latency.

Previous works [8,20,21,23] observe the characteristic of shared data: a small set of shared data which consumes small capacity in LLC serves a substantial fraction of total memory accesses. Moreover, shared data has good temporal locality. This observation indicates the bottleneck of existing cache organization: most of the memory accesses involve only a small fraction of total cache lines in LLC, but the access of such a small fraction of cache lines has to suffer from high latency incurred by large LLC.

Motivated by the observation, we propose a novel two-level directory organization to reduce LLC access latency while avoid issuing more off-chip memory accesses. The first-level directory is a small cache named FAST Directory, which is placed in each tile to offer fast hit for frequently accessed lines. The Second-level directory is the large L2 cache slice to reduce the number of off-chip memory accesses. We evaluate the two-level directory organization on a range of scientific workloads and show that 13.3% speedup in execution time in 16-core CMP, and up to 38.1% at best.

The rest of this paper is organized as follows. Section 2 presents background and related work. Section 3 describes our two-level organization in detail. In section 4 we evaluate the design with cycle-accurate full-system simulation, and finally we conclude in section 5.

2   Background and Related Work

Tiled architecture is considered to be main architecture of large-scale CMP for its good scalability and simple design [27]. A typical tiled CMP comprises of multiple tiles which are replicated to fill the die area. Each tile includes a processor core, network router, private L1 data and instruction caches and an L2 cache slice. The L2 cache slice can be either private to its local core or can be one slice of a monolithic shared L2. We base our design on shared L2 scheme due to its simplicity in maintaining cache coherence and less storage overhead [10]. Though shared L2 scheme can lead to long wire delays on chip, there have been a flurry of previous works on how to manage it [6,7,8,9,10]. These proposed techniques are aiming at reducing network latency by decreasing the distance between the requesting node and data. The motivation of our proposed approach is to reduce the high L2 cache bank access latency which constitutes the overall L2 cache access latency together with the network latency. Hence, these techniques and our work aim at different parts of L2 cache access latency, and can be combined.

Liu et al. [22] and Guz et al. [23] added a central cache which holds shared data to a DNUCA-based CMP. The central cache is surrounded by processing cores, which can reduce access latency to shared data. The central cache is relatively small to speed up accessing to shared cache lines, which is similar to our work. But their architecture is asymmetric which fits for 4 or 8-core, and don't scale well to large-scale CMP. Moreover, several cores access the same shared cache may incur heavy contention and form a hot spot on chip. In our design, the same cache is in banks and distributed across chip, avoiding heavy contention and hot spot.

There is a lot of previous research on SMP-based multi-level directory architecture, which is used to solve the scalability of directory memory overhead [12,13,14]. Michael et al. [11] implemented directory cache on directory controller chip. Gonzalez et al. [13] and Acacio et al. [14] moved off-chip main memory directory to SMP processor chip. In their approach based on SMP, off-chip directory access latency can be reduced, but it doesn't reduce the on-chip cache hit latency. Brown et al [15] suggested a directory cache on CMP chip, which caches the frequent accessed directory entries to reduce off-chip memory access times, and improve average access latency. But there is still a directory in off-chip memory, which leads to large memory overhead. Unlike these multi-level directory designs, our proposal focus on reducing on-chip cache hit latency incurred by large L2 cache capacity. Hence the added Fast Directory, which holds frequent accessed L2 cache lines, lies between L1 and L2 cache on CMP chip. To reduce memory overhead, there is no directory in off-chip memory.

3   Two-Level Directory Cache Organization

3.1   Overview

The characteristic of shared data indicates that a small number of shared cache lines which reside only a small fraction of total LLC lines are accounting for a significant fraction of total memory accesses, which suggests that a relatively small cache is sufficient for serving the majority of memory accesses [23]. Thus, the basic idea of two-level directory organization given in this paper is to place frequently accessed cache lines in a relatively small cache to provide fast access while preserve the L2 cache slice to keep on-chip capacity. As a result, reduction in access latency for these frequently accessed lines leads to reduction in average access latency.

The basic idea is implemented based on a shared L2 tiled CMP scheme. Compared to this scheme, a small cache named Fast Directory is placed in each tile. The small cache holds the recently accessed cache lines and can provide low hit latency. According to temporal locality of shared data [20], there is a great possibility that the recently accessed cache lines will be accessed by other processors in a short while. Thus, subsequent accesses to this cache line will be served by Fast Directory. If there is a conflict, less frequently accessed lines will be replaced first, as same as a general cache replacement strategy. Therefore, the more frequently cache line is accessed, the longer it will reside in Fast Directory. As a result, more reduction in average access latency can be expected.

Besides Fast Directory, the large L2 cache slice is used to store more data and directory information on chip. If the L2 cache slice is removed or the size is decreased, more replacements and off-chip memory accesses will lead to performance degradation.

Throughout this paper, a standard directory-based MSI protocol [16] is assumed, but our approach can be applied to any directory protocol. The organization and mechanism of two-level directory will be described in detail as below.

3.2   Structure

The two-level directory structure for the case of 16-core CMP is shown in Fig.1. A shared L2 tiled scheme is taken as baseline. A Fast Directory is added between router and L2 cache slice in each tile. The Fast Directory is an inclusive cache,

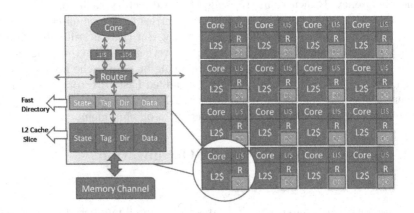

Fig. 1. Two-level Directory organization

that is, cache lines in Fast Directory are a subset of L2 cache slice. Each cache line contains three fields aside from Data: the Tag used to identify the block, the State which is one of the 3 states used by the MSI protocol, and the Dir used to specify which nodes' L1 cache are actively sharing the data.

In such organization, one most important problem is to decide which directory maintains coherence, and how to ensure the coming request see the latest coherence information. Fast Directory, which is accessed more frequently, is used to keep the latest State, Data and Dir information. If a cache line resides both in Fast Directory and L2 cache, coherence of this line is maintained by Fast Directory. Otherwise, the cache line will be fetched from L2 cache slice and saved in Fast Directory. When Fast Directory cache line is replaced, the latest State and Dir field value of that line will be written back to L2 cache slice.

3.3 Two-Level Cache Coherence

Two-level directory cache coherence is implemented based on a generic directory-based MSI protocol. States in Fast Directory and L2 cache have the same meaning. M (Modified) state means the cache line was modified, and the latest data is in L1 cache of some node, which is specified by Dir field of this line. S (Shared) state means the cache line has a clean copy, but other nodes' L1 cache may also have copies. I (Invalid) state means the cache line has been invalidated. The NP (Not Present) state means the cache line is not in the cache, so it is not a real state saved in cache line.

The state transitions diagram for Fast Directory is shown in Fig.2. Since a great deal of memory accesses which are acknowledged by L2 cache slice in baseline are now processed by Fast Directory, the state transitions of Fast Directory are much similar to that of a general L2 cache. So we emphasize the difference with broken lines in Fig.2. Actions triggered during state transition from I to M(S) are the same as those triggered when state transition takes place from NP to M(S) (not shown in Fig.2 for simplicity).

The events triggering Fast Directory state transition have two sources: local router and L2 cache slice. Compared to baseline protocol, several types of messages are added for communication between two level directories. The added types of messages are summarized in Table 1.

The state transitions of L2 cache slice in two-level directory are shown in Fig.3. Messages triggering L2 cache transitions are GETLINE and PUTLINE from Fast Directory. Upon receiving the PUTLINE, State and Dir field in L2 cache line are updated if a match is found. When cache line in L2 cache slice is replaced, the INVLINE, which comprises of State and Dir of the cache line, will be sent to Fast Directory.

3.4 Memory Access Walkthrough

To tie the state transitions in Fig.2 and Fig.3 together, three typical walkthrough cases are presented. Each step is described in detail below. Fig.4, Fig.5 and Fig.6 describe the operations of Fast Directory miss, Fast Directory Replacement, and L2 cache replacement respectively.

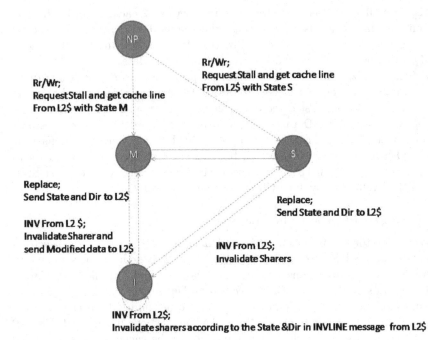

Fig. 2. Fast Directory state transitions

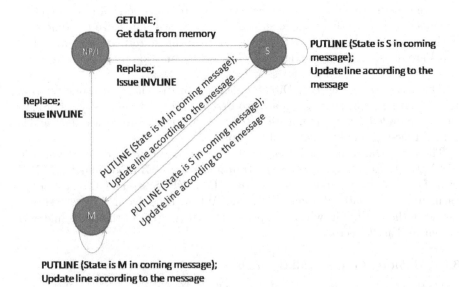

Fig. 3. L2 cache state transitions

Fast Directory issues **GETLINE** message to local L2 cache slice;
Upon L2 is receiving the **GETLINE** message,
   If the requested cache line cached in L2 *then*
      L2 cache returns the requested cache line to Fast Directory.
   Else L2 cache
      Fetch data from off-chip memory;
      Allocate a new line to keep data;
      Set the new line to **state S**;
      Send the new line to Fast Directory.
Fast Directory reissues the stalled memory requests;
Subsequent operations perform as Fast Directory hit.

Fig. 4. Pseudo code of operations of Fast Directory miss

Fast Directory issues **PUTLINE** message to local L2 cache slice;
Upon receiving the **PUTLINE** message, L2 cache,
   Update the corresponding cache line;
   Send a **PUTLINE_ACK** to Fast Directory.
Upon receiving the **PUTLINE_ACK**, Fast Directory,
   Set the replaced line to **state I**.

Fig. 5. Pseudo code of operations of Fast Directory replacement

L2 cache sends an **INVLINE** message to Fast Directory;
Upon Fast Directory receiving the **INVLINE** message,
   If there is a hit in the Fast Directory *then*
      Fast Directory issues invalidations to all sharers according to
     the Dir vector in Fast Directory;
   Else Fast Directory
      Send invalidations to sharers according to Dir vector in the
      INVLINE message;
      If receives all invalidation **ACKs** *then*
         If the line exists *then*
            Set the cache line to **state I**.
      Else if receives the latest data from an exclusive node *then*
         Send data to L2 cache;
         If the line exists *then*
            Set the cache line to **state I**.
     Send **INVLINE_ACK** to L2 cache.
Upon receiving **INVLINE_ACK** message, L2 cache,
   Set the replaced cache line to **state I**;
   If the latest data arrives *then*
      Write it back to memory.

Fig. 6. Pseudo code of operations of Fast Directory replacement

Table 1. Messages between Fast Directory and L2 cache

Message	Description
GETLINE	Message from Fast Directory to L2 cache to fetch cache line.
RETLINE	Message from L2 cache to Fast Directory to acknowledge the GETLINE request.
	The message includes all four fields of the corresponding cache line in L2 cache.
PUTLINE	Message from Fast Directory to L2 cache to update the corresponding cache line in L2 cache.
	The message includes a Tag, State, Dir field of the requested line.
PUTLINE_ACK	Message from L2 cache to Fast Directory to acknowledge PUT-LINE.
INVLINE	Message from L2 cache to Fast Directory to invalidate the corresponding line in Fast Directory.
	The message includes Tag, State, Dir field of the requested line.
INVLINE_ACK	Message from Fast Directory to L2 cache to acknowledge INVLINE.

4   Evaluation

4.1   Experiment Setup

By using full-system simulation based on Simics [17] and the GEMS toolset [18], we evaluate our two-level directory scheme against baseline.

The parameters of configurations are given in Table 2. Fast Directory is implemented with two alternative sizes: 32KB and 64KB. All designs use write-back, write-allocate caches. The L2 cache is inclusive with the L1 caches as well as the Fast Directory. The network-on-chip is modeled in detail, including all messages required to maintain coherence. We study our design using six scientific workloads from SPLASH-2 [19] as shown in Table 3.

4.2   Memory Access Latency

Fig.7 presents normalized reduction of access latency. For all the 6 workloads, 17.9% savings in average access latency can be gained relative to baseline with 32KB Fast Directory configuration. With 64KB configuration, the savings are 19.1%, a little more than that of 32KB configuration. However, the results are based on the assumption that 32KB and 64KB Fast Directory have the same hit latency. But in reality, larger cache may result in more cycles to access, which may penalty the performance.

4.3   Hit Ratio of Fast Directory

The hit ratios of Fast Directory are shown in Table 4. Hit ratios in 64KB configuration are a little higher than that in 32KB configuration. Except radix with

Table 2. Processor and cache/memory/network parameters

Component	Parameter
CMP Size	16-core
Processing Core	Sparc V9 ISA/in-order/ 1.4GHz
Cache Line Size	64B
L1 I-Cache Size/ Associativity	32KB /2-way
L1 I-Cache Size/ Associativity	32KB /2-way
L1 Load-to-Use Latency	2-cycle
L1 Replacement Policy	Psuedo-LRU
Fast Directory (per tile)	32KB/16-way and 64KB/16-way
Fast Directory Load-to-Use Latency	2-cycle
Network Configuration	4x4 Mesh
One-hop Latency	3-cycle
External Memory Latency	300-cycle

Table 3. Workloads description

Workload	Problem Set
FFT	256K points
LU	1024*1024 matrix, 16x16 blocks
RADIX	1048576 keys, radix=1024
RAYTRACE	Teapot.env
OCEAN	258 x 258 ocean
WATER	512 molecules

Table 4. Hit ratios of Fast Directory in different configurations

	fft	lu	ocean	radix	raytrace	water
32KB Fast Directory	97.19%	98.18%	97.87%	86.84%	99.47%	98.28%
64KB Fast Directory	97.43%	98.57%	98.50%	89.92%	99.58%	98.70%

3.28% increase, the average increase in hit ratios of other 5 workloads is only 0.36%, which indicates that 32KB Fast Directory is sufficient to hold frequently accessed cache lines.

4.4 Execution Time

Fig.8 shows speedups in execution time of 6 workloads relative to baseline. Results of 32KB Fast Directory configuration show that the average speedup

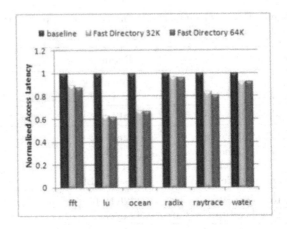

Fig. 7. Normalized reduction in access latency

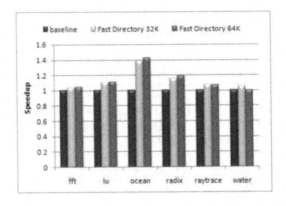

Fig. 8. Speedup in execution time

is 13.3%, and the best case is 38.1% in ocean. For 64KB Fast Directory, the average speedup is 13.7%, nearly the same as that of 32KB configuration. Considering only a half of storage overhead against 64KB configuration, 32KB configuration is a more appropriate choice for leveraging performance and overhead. For workload water, the execution time of the 64KB configuration is a little more than that of 32KB though the reduction in access latency is more than that of 32KB configuration. Considering some indeterminism in multithreaded application execution, such a little difference is in a reasonable scope.

4.5   Overhead

Area overhead is introduced in implementing the Fast Directory. Storage space (in bits) is used for estimating the area overhead. The added storage space is dominantly decided by the capacity of the Fast Directory. In our configuration, the capacity of Fast Directory is in two configurations: 32KB and 64KB, which increase on-chip storage space by 3% and 6% respectively. Area overhead of 32KB configuration is comparable to that of Cooperative Caching [11]. We do not model the area of point-to-point network connecting Fast Directory and L2 cache slice as it requires consideration of many physical constraints, which is not our focus. We believe it is comparable to the existing and future network-on-chip.

4.6   Impact of Associativity

In order to find the optimal configuration for our scheme, we performed different configurations of Fast Directory. With the 32KB size of Fast Directory, we evaluate 3 configurations of associativity for the lu workload: 8-way, 16-way and 32-way, and hit ratios are shown in Table 5. Results show that hit ratio is increasing with more ways of associatively. It can be explained that more ways of associativity results in higher utilization ratio of Fast Directory capacity. Moreover, increasing associativity from 8-way to 16-way improves hit ratio more, while increasing from 16-way to 32-way changes it much less. Since more ways of associativity leads to more area overhead and power consumption, 16-way configuration is a compromise between performance and overhead.

Table 5. Hit ratios of 32KB Fast Directory with different ways of associativity for workload lu

Associativity	Fast Directory Hit Ratio
8-way	97.26%
16-way	98.18%
32-way	98.34%

5   Conclusions and Future Work

The trend of increasing on-chip cache sizes comes at the cost of high on-chip hit latency, which challenges cache organization design. There is a lot of previous work on decreasing the latency of on-chip communication, while this paper focuses on how to reduce access latency of cache slice. By utilizing characteristic of shared data, a two-level directory organization is proposed, which offers fast access for a great fraction of memory accesses. Evaluated on a 16-core CMP, our proposal reduces average access latency by 17.9%, and improves the overall performance by 13.3% on average.

Organization and mechanics of Fast Directory can be optimized further. In addition, LLC bank access latency is only part of the overall access latency, while wire delays and limited off-chip bandwidth are also challenging the memory hierarchy design of CMP. Techniques to manage wire delays and off-chip bandwidth can be explored to combine with our work.

References

1. Briggs, F., et al.: Intel 870: A Building Block for Cost-Effective Scalable Servers. IEEE Micro., 36–47 (March-April 2002)
2. Chaiken, D., Fields, C., Kurihara, K., Agarwal, A.: Directory-based cache coherence in large-scale multiprocessors. IEEE Computer, 49–58 (June 1990)
3. Rusu, S., et al.: A Dual-Core Multi-Threaded Xeon Processor with 16MB L3 Cache. In: IEEE International Solid-State Circuits Conference Digest of Technical Papers (February 2006)
4. Wuu, J., Weiss, D., Morganti, C., Dreesen, M.: The Asynchronous 24MB On-Chip Level-3 Cache for a Dual-Core Itanium-Family Processor. In: IEEE International Solid-State Circuits Conference Digest of Technical Papers (February 2005)
5. Hardavellas, N., Pandis, I., Johnson, R., Mancheril, N., Ailamaki, A., Falsafi, B.: Database servers on chip multiprocessors: limitations and opportunities. In: CIDR (2007)
6. Zhang, M., Asanovic, K.: Victim Replication: Maximizing Capacity while Hiding Wire Delay in Tiled Chip Multiprocessors. In: Proc. of the 32nd International Symposium on Computer Architecture, June 2005, pp. 336–345 (2005)
7. Zhang, M., Asanovic, K.: Victim Migration: Dynamically Adapting between Private and Shared CMP Caches. MIT Technical Report MIT-CSAIL-TR-2005-064,MIT-LCS-TR-1006 (October 2005)
8. Beckmann, B.M., et al.: ASR: Adaptive Selective Replication for CMP Caches. In: Proc. of the 39th Annual IEEE/ACM International Symposium on Microarchitecture, December 2006, pp. 443–454 (2006)
9. Chang, J., et al.: Cooperative Caching for Chip Multiprocessors. In: Proc. of the 33rd Annual International Symposium on Computer Architecture, ISCA 2006, May 2006, pp. 264–276. IEEE, Los Alamitos (2006)
10. Eisley, N., Peh, L.-S., Shang, L.: Leveraging On-Chip Networks for Cache Migration in Chip Multiprocessors. In: Proceedings of 17th International Conference on Parallel Architectures and Compilation Techniques (PACT), Toronto, Canada (October 2008)
11. Michael, M.M., Nanda, A.K.: Design and Performance of Directory Caches for Scalable Shared Memory Multiprocessors. In: 5th Int'l. Symposium on High Performance Computer Architecture (January 1999)
12. Acacio, M.E., Gonzalez, J., Garcia, J.M., Duato, J.: A Two-Level Directory Architecture for Highly Scalable cc-NUMA Multiprocessors. IEEE Transactions on Parallel and Distributed Systems 16(1), 67–79 (2005)
13. Ros, A., Acacio, M.E., García, J.M.: A Novel Lightweight Directory Architecture for Scalable Shared-Memory Multiprocessors. In: Cunha, J.C., Medeiros, P.D. (eds.) Euro-Par 2005. LNCS, vol. 3648, pp. 582–591. Springer, Heidelberg (2005)
14. Acacio, M.E., Gonzalez, J., Garcia, J.M., Duato, J.: An Architecture for High-Performance Scalable Shared-Memory Multiprocessors Exploiting On-Chip Integration. IEEE Transactions on Parallel and Distributed Systems 15(8), 755–768 (2004)
15. Brown, J., Kumar, R., Tullsen, D.: Proximity-Aware Directory-based Coherence for Multi-core Processor Architectures. In: Proceedings of SPAA-19. ACM, New York (June 2007)
16. Lenoski, D., Laudon, J., Gharachorloo, K., Weber, W., Gupta, A., Henessy, J., Horowitz, M., Lam, M.: The stanford DASH multiprocessor. IEEE Computer (1992)

17. Virtutech AB. Simics Full System Simulator, http://www.simics.com/
18. Wisconsin Multifacet GEMS Simulator, http://www.cs.wisc.edu/gems/
19. Woo, S.C., Ohara, M., Torrie, E., Singh, J.P., Gupta, A.: The SPLASH-2 Programs: Characterization and Methodological Considerations. In: Proceedings of the 22nd Annual International Symposium on Computer Architecture, June 1995, pp. 24–37 (1995)
20. Wang, H., Wang, D., Li, P.: Exploit Temporal Locality of Shared Data in SRC enabled CMP. In: Li, K., Jesshope, C., Jin, H., Gaudiot, J.-L. (eds.) NPC 2007. LNCS, vol. 4672, pp. 384–393. Springer, Heidelberg (2007)
21. Beckmann, B.M., Wood, D.A.: Managing wire delay in large chip multiprocessor caches. Micro. 37 (December 2004)
22. Liu, C., Sivasubramaniam, A., Kandemir, M., Irwin, M.J.: Enhancing L2 organization for CMPs with a center cell. In: IPDPS 2006 (April 2006)
23. Guz, Z., Keidar, I., Kolodny, A., Weiser, U.C.: Utilizing shared data in chip multiprocessors with the Nahalal architecture. In: Proceedings of the 20th Annual ACM Symposium on Parallelism in Algorithms and Architectures (SPAA 2008), New York, NY, USA, pp. 1–10 (2008)
24. Azimi, M., Cherukuri, N., Jayasimha, D.N., Kumar, A., Kundu, P., Park, S., Schoinas, I., Vaidya, A.S.: Integration challenges and trade-offs for tera-scale architectures. Intel. Technology Journal (August 2007)
25. Haff, G.: Niagara2: More Heft in the Weft. Sun Analyst Research Reports (August 2007)

A Performance Model for Run-Time Reconfigurable Hardware Accelerator*

Gang Wang, Du Chen, Jian Chen, Jianliang Ma, and Tianzhou Chen

ZJU-INTEL Technology Center
College of Computer Science, Zhejiang University
Hangzhou, Zhejiang, P.R. China
{gangwang,xiaoyin,jianjian,majl,tzchen}@zju.edu.cn

Abstract. The reconfigurable devices such as CPLD and FPGA become more popular for its great potential on accelerating applications. They are widely used as an application-specified hardware accelerator. Many run-time reconfigurable platforms are introduced such as the Intel® QuickAssist Technology. However, it's time consuming to design a hardware accelerator while the performance is hard to determine because of the extra overheads it involved. In order to estimate the efficiency of the accelerator, a theoretical analysis of such platforms was done in our paper. Three factors which impact the performance of the accelerator were concluded as well: speed up ratio, reconfiguration overhead and communication overhead. Furthermore, a performance model was established and an experiment on bzip2 was done to verify the model. The results showed that the model's estimation is very close to the real world and the average error on the efficiency's threshold is less than 5%.

1 Introduction

Today reconfigurable devices have been widely used because of their flexibility and high performance [1] . The RTR logic is a popular design alternative in SoC system [2][4], which achieves great speedup over a general processor by implementing applications on reconfigurable devices, making them application-specified hardware accelerator. Intel® QuickAssist Technology [19][20][21] brings such a reconfigurable hardware accelerator (RHA) based platform. The programming model is similar to a function call with registered procedure: if the programmer wants to use a pre-designed accelerator, she or he has to register the accelerator in the system. As soon as the accelerator finishes configuration, it can be called to execute.

Much research has been done in the fields of RTR platform. That research can be classified into two categories: platforms hardware and RTR based applications. The former concentrates on the platform hardware design such as the reconfigurable devices properties, the power consuming, hardware interface and etc. The latter focuses

---

* Supported by the National Natural Science Foundation of China under Grant No. 60673149 and the National High-Tech Research, Development Plan of China under Grant Nos.863-2007AA01Z105 and the Research Foundation of Education Bureau of Zhejiang Province under Grant No. Y200803333.

Y. Dou, R. Gruber, and J. Joller (Eds.): APPT 2009, LNCS 5737, pp. 54–66, 2009.
© Springer-Verlag Berlin Heidelberg 2009

on the accelerator design and the usage model of the platform. With the sophistical design, the accelerator can achieve great speedup over general CPU. However, the RHA is not suitable for every situation. In some applications, the overhead involved by the accelerator may eclipse the performance improvement or even make the platform slower. Estimating the accelerators performance will help to using the reconfigurable hardware efficiently.

In this paper, we give a theoretical analysis of the factors of the reconfigurable platform. A performance model is established according to our work. The model estimates the accelerators performance and help to find the efficiency threshold. Experimental results based on bzip2 are presented in order to evaluate our model.

In next section, there is the related work. The key features of the RTR platform are discussed in section 3 and section 4 analyzes the performance influencing factors and introduces the performance model. To evaluate our model, experimental results is shown in section 5. The conclusion is described in section 6, and finally, the references are listed.

2 Related Work

Due to its potential to greatly accelerate a wide variety of applications, RTR platforms have been explored much in recently years. [1] gave a survey on reconfigurable computing, mainly on the hardware and software architecture. On-chip, reconfigurable coprocessor such as Garp [5] and off-chip reconfigurable accelerator such as Intel® QuickAssist Technology introduce the reconfigurable accelerator based platform to us. Not only the hardware but also the software for RTR platform is researched. HybridOS [6] is an operation system designed for the reconfigurable accelerator based platform. Applications on RTR platforms are researched as well such as the digital signal processing [7], scientific computing like grid [8], logic comparison [9], network intrusion detection [10] and etc. At the same time, the overhead caused by the reconfigurable logic also attracts much attention. Techniques such as configuration context prefetching [11][12], configuration cache [13][14], partial reconfiguration [15][18] and configuration scheduling [17][16] are focusing on reducing the reconfiguration overhead of the reconfigurable logic. [2] introduced a hybrid reconfigurable computer and gives the statistic results on the performance and overhead.

Previous works on RTR platform are mostly on the individual aspect such as specific application's performance enhancement, physical hardware design and overhead reduction. Our work focuses on an overview of the reconfigurable accelerator in the platform and gives a performance model to measure the accelerators efficiency. The next section will describe the key features of the RTR platform and give a theoretical analysis.

3 Key Features of RTR Platform

Like co-processor architecture, the general RTR platform's architecture is showed in Figure 1 . The general processor and the RHA are connected by the hardware interface including the FSB, PCI-E and other attaching technologies. In most cases, a local memory is attached with it.

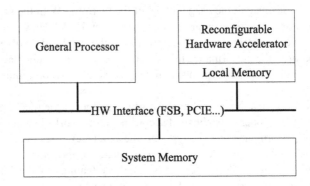

Fig. 1. Architecture of RTR platform

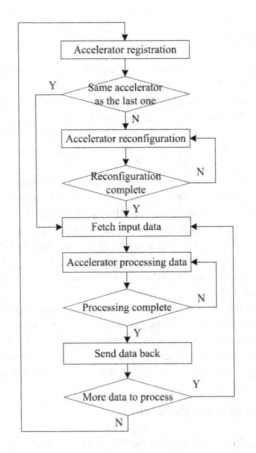

Fig. 2. Work flow of the RHA of the platform

The work flow is described in Figure 2 . First the accelerator is registered to the platform and then the platform check whether the accelerator is the same type as last one. If it matches, the reconfiguration procedure can be omitted. Otherwise it needs to be reconfigured. Once the reconfiguration is complete, the data processing begins. The input data is fetched though the hardware interfaces by DMA or other technique. They are sent back to the platform as soon as they are processed.

From the work flow, we find that the performance enhancement is achieved during the data processing stage. The reconfiguration stage is the extra stage compared to the normal platforms, which takes extra time to execute. In addition, the data fetching and sending stages increase the overhead of the platform. In conclusion, the key feature of the run-time reconfigurable platform including the speed up ratio of the data processing stage, the reconfiguration overhead and the communication overhead caused by the data transferring. In next section, we will analyze each of the key features and give an overall performance model based on them.

4   Factors Affecting the Performance and Modeling

4.1   Hardware Speedup Ratio

Amdahl's law shows the relation between the speedup part and the whole system. According to the Amdahls law, the better performance improvement comes from greater fraction of the accelerating part. Another important factor of performance is the frequency of the accelerator. High frequency is desired, however, the design of the RHA is restricted by the reconfigurable device's limited resource. For that reason, the clock frequency of general-purpose processors is about 20 times of typical FPGA implementations [3]. Our work focuses on the RHA's speedup ratio rather than the platforms. What we want is to give a performance model that can help the compiler or the programmer to decide whether the situation is suitable for using the RHA.

In order to compare the RHA with the software, we define the operation time as Equation (1) where SUR = speed up ratio of the RHA

Time_{CPU} = execution time of the general CPU
Time_{acc} = execution time of the RHA
Cycle_{CPU} = Total cycle of the CPU runs
Freq_{CPU} = Frequency of the general purpose processor
CPI = Average number of clock cycles per instruction
Time_{saved} = The operation time saved by using the RHA

$$Time_{saved} = Time_{CPU} - TIME_{acc}$$
$$= Time_{CPU} * (1 - \frac{1}{SUR})$$
$$= \frac{Cycle_{CPU}}{Freq_{CPU}} * (1 - \frac{1}{SUR}) \qquad (1)$$

4.2   Communication Overhead

The communication overhead of the RTR platform comes from the data transfer, including the control process. The control process contains the data channel establishing, protocol acting and etc. The data transfer refers to the time of moving the data between the accelerator and the platform, which mainly depends on the interconnection. The control process takes a constant time as long as the protocol is designed. We combine it with the data transfer and discuss them together.

As the difference types of the interconnection, the data transfer rate ranges from 133MB/s to 8.6GB/s, which is showed in Table 1 . Theoretically, the faster data transfer ratio is, the less communication overhead it brings. The Intel® QuickAssist Technology introduced several attaching technologies including the PCI-Express and FSB with a software level called AAL [20][21](abstract accelerator level). It provides a uniform set of platform services for using the reconfigurable hardware accelerators. The FSB based platform is tightly coupled while the PCI-Express based one is loosely coupled [20][21]. Because of the different interconnection; the communication overhead will be different.

In order to evaluation the communication overhead, we also use a Equation to describe the model. Since the data transfer is related with the number that the accelerator is called, we define the overhead as Equation (2) , where NoT_{acc} = the number of times that the accelerator is called

$Data_{size}$ = the size of data that transfer between the accelerator and the platform for each call

$Trans_{ratio}$ = the specific attach technology's data transfer ratio

$$Overhead_{comm} = NoT_{acc} * (Ctrl + Trans)$$
$$= NoT_{acc} * (Ctrl + \frac{Data_{size}}{Trans_{ratio}}) \quad (2)$$

Table 1. Data transfer ratio of Attaching technologies

Attaching technology	Data transfer ratio
PCI	133MB/s
AGP-1X	266MB/s
AGP-2X	533MB/s
AGP-4X	1.0GB/s
AGP-8X	2.1GB/s
PCI Express 1X	500MB/s
PCI Express 2X	1GB/s
PCI Express 4X	2GB/s
PCI Express 8X	4GB/s
PCI Express 16X	8GB/s
Intel FSB 400MHz	3.6GB/s
Intel FSB 533MHz	4.2GB/s
Intel FSB 800MHz	7.2GB/s
Intel FSB 1066MHz	8.6GB/s

4.3   Reconfiguration Overhead

Besides the communication, the reconfiguration overhead is another dominative factor that has to be taken into consideration. Like the communication overhead, it is a negative affecter.

Today the most popular reconfigurable device is CPLD or FPGA. But even the most advanced device such as the Xilinx Vertex5 [23], the reconfiguration process takes several milliseconds. According to the user guide of the Xilinx FPGA, the configuration has 8 modes [24]. The differences between them are bandwidth, clock, interface and storages. No matter what mode is, the reconfiguration is made up with three basic steps: setup, bitstream loading and finishing. The reconfiguration overhead can be defined as Equation (3)

$$Overhead_{reconfig} = Overhead_{setup}$$
$$+ Overhead_{bitstream\_load} \quad (3)$$
$$+ Overhead_{finish}$$

Among these parts, the bitstream loading takes much more time than the other steps. For convenience, we omit the time taken by the setup and finishing steps. Then we get

$$Overhead_{reconfig} \approx Overhead_{bitstream\_load} \quad (4)$$

The bitstream loading can be calculated by three parameters: the bit file size, the data width of configuration and the configuration clock frequency. The bit file size depends only on the FPGA type [24]. We list some of Virtex-5 bitstream length in Table 2. Since the bitstream length is a fixed value, we modify Equation (4) into Equation (5), which is our final reconfiguration overhead model.

$$Overhead_{reconfig} = \frac{Bitfile_{size}}{Bus_{width} * Freq_{reconfig}} \quad (5)$$

There are much research on reducing the overhead of reconfiguration such as configuration context prefetching [11][12], configuration cache [13][14], partial reconfiguration [15][18] , configuration scheduling [17][16] , configuration overlapping and etc. The model we presented here is one of the cases, which do not include any overhead reducing technique. Specific model can substitute here when specific overhead reducing technique is put to use.

Table 2. Virtex-5 Bitstream Length

Device	Total Number of Configuration Bits
XC5VLX30	8,374,016
XC5VLX110	29,124,608
XC5VLX30T	9,371,136
XC5VLX110T	31,118,848
XC5VFX30T	13,517,056
XC5VFX100T	39,389,696
XC5VFX200T	70,856,704

4.4   Performance Modeling

Whether a program is suitable for the RHA depends on the three factors we discussed: the speed up ratio of the accelerator, the communication overhead and the reconfiguration overhead. Some statistic work is done in [2] but without a theoretical model. In order to establish the performance model, We define EFF_{acc} as the accelerators efficiency. It is the performance's measurement showed in Equation (6),

$$EFF_{acc} = \frac{Time_{saved}}{Overhead_{comm} + Overhead_{reconfig}} \tag{6}$$

$$EFF_{acc} = \frac{\frac{Cycle_{cpu}}{Freq_{cpu}} * (1 - \frac{1}{SUR})}{NoT_{acc} * (Ctrl_{overhead} + \frac{Data_{size}}{Trans_{ratio}}) + \frac{Bitfile_{size}}{Bus_{width} * Freq_{reconfig}}} \tag{7}$$

$$EFF_{acc} = \frac{\frac{NoT_{acc} * CyclePerCall}{Freq_{cpu}} * (1 - \frac{1}{SUR})}{NoT_{acc} * (Ctrl_{overhead} + \frac{Data_{size}}{Trans_{ratio}}) + \frac{Bitfile_{size}}{Bus_{width} * Freq_{reconfig}}} \tag{8}$$

Bigger EFF_{acc} shows greater performance improvement. The efficiencys threshold is when the EFFacc equals 1. We define that point as EFF point. EFF_{acc} is greater than 1 means the accelerator can improve the performance of the system. We put the previous equations into the definition yields the Equation (7) . $Cycle_{cpu}$ is NoT_{acc} multiplied by CPU cycles per call of the accelerator, where the NoT_{acc} is the accelerator called times. Then we get Equation (8). In the next section, an experiment based on bzip2 is presented to evaluate the performance model and shows how it works to guide the usage of the accelerator.

5   Performance Model Evaluation

5.1   Experiment Platform

Our experiment is made on a RTR platform with a Xilinx Vertex5 FPGA (xc5vlx110t) installed. The interconnection between the RHA and general PC is through PCI-Express. The accelerator is a hardware version of MoveToFront (MTF) function of bzip2, which is made by hand translation without much optimize. It is an encoding of data designed to improve the performance of entropy encoding techiques of compression. It takes advantage of local correlation of frequencies to reduce the entropy of message. Burrows-Wheeler transform producing a sequence that exhibits local frequency correlation in bzip2 and after that, MTF handle the sequence. More detailed information can be find in [25]. The reason we choose the MTF function is by our profiling results, which is showed in table 3 . The average value tells that the MTF function takes much time (38.48%) in the software version of bzip2.

From the Figure 3 we can see that the MTF unit is a module designed, sequential working unit. The MTF unit is constructed in three layers. The upper layer is the interconnection. In our implementation, the data transfer is by DMA through the PCIE

Table 3. Profiling results of CPU2006 bzip2

Module Name	Input.com	Input.pro	Chicken.jpg	Input.source	Text.html	Liberty.jpg	Avg.
mainGtU	35.12%	28.18%	2.29%	52.72%	24.44%	1.38%	24.02%
MTF	17.53%	38.36%	76.94%	8.07%	11.11%	78.84%	38.48%
mainSort	3.78%	11.62%	9.69%	14.26%	18.89%	7.61%	10.98%
sendMTF	2.60%	8.41%	5.84%	5.91%	12.22%	6.09%	6.85%
mainQSort	1.45%	5.55%	0.60%	9.34%	11.11%	0.83%	4.81%
copy_input	0.96%	3.17%	1.51%	3.97%	5.56%	0.97%	2.69%
mainSimple	0.41%	2.25%	0.84%	3.96%	2.22%	0.69%	1.73%
others	38.15%	2.46%	2.29%	1.77%	14.45%	3.59%	10.45%

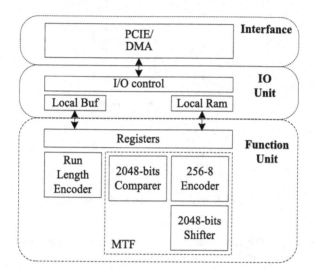

Fig. 3. Architecture of the MTF unit

Table 4. Device utilization summary of MTF unit

Logic Utilization	Used	Utilization
Slice Registers	8537	12%
Slice LUTs	31859	46%
Fully used Bit Slices	4398	12%
Bonded IOBs	16	2%
RAM/FIFO	56	37%
BUFG/BUFGCTRLs	7	21%
PLL ADVs	1	16%

channel. The middle layer is called IO unit, it is the local storage with the controller. IO units task is arranging the local storage for both the accelerator and the PCIE channel. The bottom is the core layer of the MTF unit. The MTF work is done here.

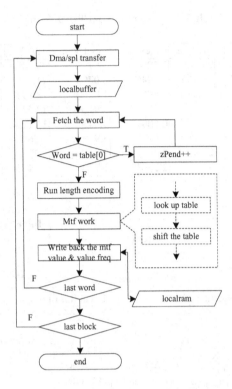

Fig. 4. Work flow of the MTF unit

Table 5. Input file size, MTF called times and speedup ratio. The number following the name means the times it was enlarged according to the original file.

File name	File size (MB)	MTF called times	Speedup ratio
chicken.jpg	0.62	1	4.52
chicken2.jpg	1.24	2	4.02
chicken4.jpg	2.48	3	4.05
chicken8.jpg	4.96	6	4.06
chicken16.jpg	9.92	12	4.01
chicken32.jpg	19.84	24	4.03
chicken64.jpg	39.68	47	4.04
chicken128.jpg	79.36	93	4.05
chicken256.jpg	158.72	186	3.91
chicken512.jpg	317.44	371	3.88

Our hardware MTF's work flow is similar to the software version as shown in Figure 4. The slight difference is the additional hardware controlling demand. When using the accelerator, the programmer should register the RHA and prepare the input data, when everything is ready, call the pre-defined system call to start the RHA. The platform first configures the FPGA board. The data is read into the RHA by DMA when configuration is completed. After that, the platform will halt until the RHA finishes the job and write the results back. The speedup achieved is mainly on the parallel hardware look up table compared with the software loops. The hardware resource the RHA used is showed in Table 5 , which is generated from the ISE9.2.02i. Both the MTF RHA and the PCIE interface runs at 125 MHz and the data width is 64 bits.

5.2   Experiment Result and Analysis

According to the performance model, the reconfiguration overhead can be estimated while other parameter depends on the input file. The bit file of xc5vlx110t is about 3800KB [24] including the PCIE interface IP and the MTF RHA. The maximum configuration frequency is about 60MHz with the x32 bits data width. The reconfiguration overhead is about 16 ms. In order to evaluate the parameter that depends on the input source we choose a standard input of SPEC CPU 2006: chicken.jpg. To make the results more obvious, we extend the input file several times to increase the times the accelerator is called. As Table 5 shows, the chicken.jpg is extended at most 512 times, whose size is 317.44 MB. The MTF times increases with the enlargement of the input file. We compare the RHA with a software version of MTF on a general PC with Intel® Celeron® CPU 2.40GHz and 1G RAM. The speedup ratio collected from our experiment shows it is not related with the file enlargement. The reason is the enlargement does not change the property of the original input file. Figure 5-8 shows the results that we get from the chicken.jpg. The x-axis indicates the MTF routine called times that each input file gets.

In Figure 5, the execution time of hardware MTF is compared with the software implementation and the average speed up ratio is about 4. With the MTF times increasing, the time that the RHA saved is increasing according to the speed up ratio.

Figure 6 shows the comparison of time saved by the RHA and the overhead it brings. From it we can find that between the 93 and 186 MTF times (represents the

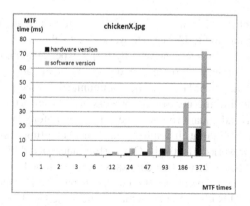

Fig. 5. Comparison of MTF execution time between hardware version and software version on the series of chickenX.jpg

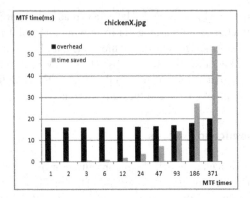

Fig. 6. Comparison of time saved by the RHA and the overhead it brings on series of chickenX.jpg

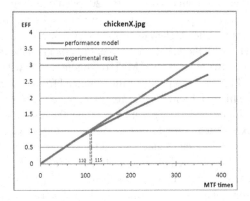

Fig. 7. EFF value generated by the real data and calculated by the performance model on the series of chickenX.jpg

chicken128.jpg and chicken256.jpg), the saved time becomes greater than the overhead. It means from that point, the RHA begin to work effectively.

Figure 7 gives the EFF value generated by bzip2 experiment and calculated by the performance model. For the performance model, the speed up ratio is 4, the CPU cycles is about 465925183.92 per MTF call. The communication time per MTF call equals about 376.5 us including the controlling process and the data transfer process. The reconfiguration overhead equals 16 ms as we calculated before. What needs to be emphasized here is the EFF point. It implies that if the MTF times are greater than that value, the accelerator works effectively. Our performance model gives the point where MTF times equals 110 while the real data shows the point at 115. The error between them is about 4.37%. The gap grows with the increasing of MTF times. That is because the performance model is ideal. Some factors are neglected such as parts of the reconfiguration steps and hardware error checking. More MTF times brings more inaccuracy. However, the performance model gives important EFF point and is precise enough for trend analysis.

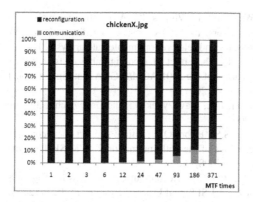

Fig. 8. Overhead partition figure represents the relation between the reconfiguration and the communication on the series of chickenX.jpg

The Figure 8 indicates the composition of the overhead and shows the relation between the reconfiguration and the communication overhead. It can be seen that though the communication overhead is increased by the growth of the MTF times; the reconfiguration overhead still occupies a great part. Even the MTF times is 371, the reconfiguration overhead takes more than 80%. It shows the bottleneck of the platform is the reconfiguration process if no special technique is used to reduce it.

6   Conclusion

In this paper, we analyzed the performance factors of the RTR platform. The object of our analysis is to identify the RHAs factors that contribute to the performance improvement and bring the overhead. A performance model on those platforms is established according to three major factors: speed up ratio, communication overhead and reconfigurable overhead. We also evaluate the performance model by introducing an experiment based on bzip2. The MTF routine is translated into hardware and implemented on the FPGA as the RHA. The results show that our performance model gives a very close estimate of the real world and the average error of the efficient point is under 5%. We believe our performance model not only gives a guidance of when to use the accelerator on RTR platforms but also gives the accelerator designer view of the RHA in the system. In conclusion, our performance model is a theoretical estimation of RTR platform, which shows the efficient point and the trend of the RHA in the platform.

References

1. Compton, K., Hauck, S.: Reconfigurable computing: a survey of systems and software. ACM Comput. Surv., P171–P210 (2002)
2. Fidanci, O.D., Poznanovic, D., Gaj, K., El-Ghazawi, T., Alexandridis, N.: Performance and Overhead in a Hybrid Reconfigurable Computer. In: IPDPS 2003: Proceedings of the 17th International Symposium on Parallel and Distributed Processing. IEEE, Los Alamitos (2003)

3. Guo, Z., Najjar, W., Vahid, F., Vissers, K.: A quantitative analysis of the speedup factors of FPGAs over processors. In: FPGA 2004: Proceedings of the 2004 ACM/SIGDA 12th international symposium on Field programmable gate arrays (2004)

4. Carrillo, J.E., Chow, P.: The effect of reconfigurable units in superscalar processors. In: FPGA 2001: Proceedings of the 2001 ACM/SIGDA ninth international symposium on Field programmable gate arrays (2001)

5. Callahan, T.J., Hauser, J.R., Wawrzynek, J.: The Garp Architecture and C Compiler. Computer, P62–P69 (2000)

6. Kelm, J.H., Lumetta, S.S.: HybridOS: runtime support for reconfigurable accelerators. In: FPGA 2008: Proceedings of the 16th international ACM/SIGDA symposium on Field programmable gate arrays (2008)

7. Shoa, A., Shirani, S.: Run-Time Reconfigurable Systems for Digital Signal Processing Applications: A Survey. J. VLSI Signal Process. Syst., P213–P235 (2005)

8. Dydel, S., Benedyczak, K., Bala, P.: Enabling Reconfigurable Hardware Accelerators for the Grid. In: PARELEC 2006: Proceedings of the international symposium on Parallel Computing in Electrical Engineering. IEEE, Los Alamitos (2006)

9. Platzner, M.: Reconfigurable Accelerators for Combinatorial Problems. Computer, P58–P60 (2000)

10. Mitra, A., Najjar, W., Bhuyan, L.: Compiling PCRE to FPGA for accelerating. In: SNORT IDS ANCS 2007: Proceedings of the 3rd ACM/IEEE Symposium on Architecture for networking and communications systems (2007)

11. Li, Z., Hauck, S.: Configuration prefetching techniques for partial reconfigurable coprocessor with relocation and defragmentatio. In: FPGA 2002: Proceedings of the 2002 ACM/SIGDA tenth international symposium on Field-programmable gate arrays (2002)

12. Resano, J., Mozos, D., Catthoor, F.: A Hybrid Prefetch Scheduling Heuristic to Minimize at Run-Time the Reconfiguration Overhead of Dynamically Reconfigurable Hardware. In: DATE 2005: Proceedings of the conference on Design, Automation and Test in Europe (2005)

13. Li, Z., Compton, K., Hauck, S.: Configuration Caching Management Techniques for Reconfigurable Computing. In: FCCM 2000: Proceedings of the 2000 IEEE Symposium on Field-Programmable Custom Computing Machines (2000)

14. Sudhir, S., Nath, S., Goldstein, S.C.: Configuration Caching and Swapping. In: Brebner, G., Woods, R. (eds.) FPL 2001. LNCS, vol. 2147, p. 192. Springer, Heidelberg (2001)

15. Robertson, I., Irvine, J.: A design flow for partially reconfigurable hardware. Trans. on Embedded Computing Sys., P257–P283 (2004)

16. Mtibaa, A., Ouni, B., Abid, M.: An efficient list scheduling algorithm for time placement problem. Comput. Electr. Eng., P285–P298 (2007)

17. Resano, J., Mozos, D.: Specific scheduling support to minimize the reconfiguration overhead of dynamically reconfigurable hardware. In: DAC 2004: Proceedings of the 41st annual conference on Design automation. IEEE, Los Alamitos (2004)

18. McDonald, E.J.: Runtime FPGA Partial Reconfiguration. In: IEEE Aerospace Conference (2008)

19. Intel Corp., http://www.intel.com/

20. Intel Corp. Intel QuickAssist Technology White Paper (2007)

21. http://www.intel.com/technology/platforms/quickassist/

22. Xilinx Solutions Guide for PCI Express

23. Xilinx Virtex-5 FPGA User Guide

24. Xilinx Virtex-5 FPGA Configuration User Guide

25. bzip2 source code, http://www.bzip.org/

SPMTM: A Novel ScratchPad Memory Based Hybrid Nested Transactional Memory Framework

Degui Feng, Guanjun Jiang, Tiefei Zhang, Wei Hu, Tianzhou Chen, and Mingteng Cao

College of Computer Science, Zhejiang University, Hangzhou, Zhejiang, 310027, China
{loosen,libbug,tfzhang,ehu,tzchen}@zju.edu.cn,cmt75827@gmail.com

Abstract. Chip multiprocessor (CMP) has been the mainstream of processor design with the progress in semiconductor technology. It provides higher concurrency for the threads compared with the traditional single-core processor. Lock-based synchronization of multi-threads has been proved as an inefficient approach with high overhead. The previous works show that TM is an efficient solution to solve the synchronization of multi-threads. This paper presents SPMTM, a novel on-chip memory based nested TM framework. The on-chip memory used in this framework is not cache but scratchpad memory (SPM), which is software-controlled SRAM on chip. TM information will be stored in SPM to enhance the access speed and reduce the power consumption in SPMTM. Experimental results show that SPMTM can obtain average 16.3% performance improvement of the benchmarks compared with lock-based synchronization and with the increase in the number of processor core, the performance improvement is more significant.

Keywords: Chip multiprocessor, synchronization, transactional memory, scratchpad memory.

1 Introduction

More than one processor is integrated into a single chip as chip multiprocessor (CMP) to solve the problem of performance improvement, power consumption and design cost in sing-core processor [1]. CMP provides higher concurrency probability to explore thread level parallelism (TLP) for applications. Traditional lock-based synchronization is used to manage the shared objects in programming for CMP. Though these lock-based synchronization methods can provide ready-made solutions, the locks are the source of contention perhaps becuase they will block the potential parallel threads which are non-interference between each other [2].

Transactional memory (TM) is proposed to improve the performance of multi-threads programming [3,4]. There are three types of TM in the literature: hardware transactional memory (HTM) [5,6,7,8,9,10,23], software transactional memory (STM) [4,11,12,13,14] and hybrid transactional memory (HybridTM)

Y. Dou, R. Gruber, and J. Joller (Eds.): APPT 2009, LNCS 5737, pp. 67–81, 2009.
© Springer-Verlag Berlin Heidelberg 2009

[15,16,17,18,19,24] according to the dependence on hardware, software or a hybrid of hardware and software during the design and implementation. These studies have proved that TM can avoid deadlock and reduce the overhead in management of shared resources, so TM is efficient in multi-thread programming.

This paper proposes SPMTM, a novel on-chip memory based hybrid nested transactional memory framework. Scratchpad memory (SPM), which is a special type of on-chip memory, is used in this framework. SPM is software-controlled on-chip SRAM and used in embedded system traditionally [20]. Compared with cache, SPM has faster access time, lower power consumption and simpler structure [21,22]. SPMTM introduces SPM into CMP architecture as the architectural support for TM framework. The hybrid nested transactional memory framework is designed based on SPM. SPMTM tries to take advantages of SPM to provide better performance and lower power consumption. SPMTM will have less execution time and power consumption. It will have lower complexity compared with the existing methods.

The rest of this paper is organized as follows. Section 2 describes the related work. Section 3 describes the SPMTM hardware. Section 4 presents the open nested transactions in SPMTM. Section 5 provides the experimental results. And at last, Section 6 offers conclusions and future work.

2   Related Work

Herlihy and Moss proposed architectural supported transactional memory from the transaction concept of database [7]. The transactions of transactional memory are code segments with atomicity, consistency and isolation to provide synchronization mechanism for multi-threads [5]. TM can support concurrency of multiple transactions if there are no conflicts and has higher performance than lock-based synchronization. More and more designs and implementations were proposed concerning transactional memory after Herlihy and Moss.

HTM is architectural supported transactional memory. Special hardware designs are provided for transaction operations in typical HTM. Most HTM will add new special buffers and new cache tags for transactions. The buffers are used to store the intermediate results of the shared data. And the write/read operations of the shared data in transactions are marked by the new cache tags. Transactional memory coherence and consistency (TCC) [23] is typical HTM. TCC added a write buffer and read tag of cache for a single processor core. Additionally "commit control" component was also added to control the commit of the transactions, detects the conflicts and insure the coherence of the shared data. [5,6,7,8,9,10] were similar to it with their special features for TM. [24] and [25] extended the instruction set architecture (ISA) to support transactions. [26] proposed a different HTM, in which the main modification is the additional hardware primitives. STM is TM implemented in software [5] and it provides shared data management as transactions through software programming. Typical STM focuses on the following concerns: programming interfaces, running environments and TM grain etc. [4] presented a basic model of software transactional memory. Locks were still important in this STM, they were used to protect the shared data. It would not make the transactions in waiting state, which was different from the locks in traditional lock-based synchronization methods. STM is non-blocking for the conflict detection and arbitration of the transactions. [11,12,13,14] were also typical software transactions.

HTM can provide strong atomicity and be faster than the other TM methods through the architectural support. But the additional hardware has higher cost and limited resources. STM will have no cost in hardware and can be implemented on existing hardware. But the efficiency of STM is lower for its complexity. The comparison research in [24] shows that STM may slow down each thread by 40% or more. HybridTM is the combination of HTM and STM. HybridTM tries to combine the advantages of HTM and STM to solve the synchronization problem of CMP. Architectural support will be added and at the same time the corresponding features of STM will also be defined according to the architectural support. The existing HybridTM [15,16,17,18,19,24] are different in design and implementation according to their different combination of hardware and software. The main disadvantage of HybridTM is that the architectural support is still limited and lacks of flexibility from the perspective of the programmers.

SPMTM proposed in this paper introduces scratchpad memory as the architectural support for transactions. SPM is on-chip SRAM with the same level with cache in the memory hierarchy. But SPM has different hardware structure from cache. SPM does not need the tag arrays and comparators, which are necessary for caches. SPM has 34% smaller die and 40% lower energy consumption comparison with cache of the same capacity [22]. SPM is used in embedded system including embedded multi-core processor based embedded system traditionally. Though SPM is on-chip, it is software-controlled memory and different from the hardware-controlled caches. The allocation of the SPM will be controlled by the compiler or the programmers. The studies on SPM focus on the allocation of the hotspot of the programs to SPM [26,27,28] and SPM has been proved that it can be expected to continue to gain improved performance. SPMTM explores the utilization of SPM in CMP architecture to support transactions and designs the corresponding software transaction mechanism according to the features of SPM.

3   SPMTM Hardware

3.1   Architecture

Traditionally cache is the main type of on-chip memory, which is managed by hardware and invisible to software. SPMTM introduces another type of on-chip memory (SPM) to provide more flexibility for software. The processor architecture adopted in SPMTM is shown in Fig. 1. Each processor core has two types of on-chip memory: private data cache and scratchpad memory. The private data cache is used for non-transaction data. SPM is integrated onto the chip for transactions. The data in cache and the data in SPM will be not overlapped for the isolation of transactions.

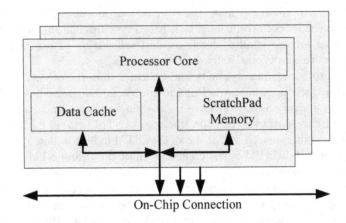

Fig. 1. Processor architecture of SPMTM

The address space of SPM is a part of the whole address space of the system. All the SPM space of the processor cores will be mapped to the entire unified memory space. The local SPM space of a processor core is called local SPM (LS) and the SPM space of other processor cores is called remote SPM (RS). A processor core can access its local SPM space or remote SPM space. Each SPM will be divided into different blocks for management. These blocks will be same to the page size of main memory. The blocks of SPM are called SPM pages (SP) in this paper. When the transactions are executing, the transaction data will be transferred to the SPM pages.

When the transactions access SPM, they can access LS or RS. But during the access, the data in RS will not be fetched to the LS. The fetch operations need more time for transmission. In fact, the data in RS means that they are transaction data and may be used by another transaction. Thus there are shared data conflicts perhaps. Though there are some delays in remote access, the data in RS can not be fetched to arbitrarily to reduce such delays. At the same time, the access speed of SPM is very fast and then the delays are not prominent. Thus the data access can be divided into LS access (LSA) and RS access (RSA) in SPMTM.

3.2   Transactions on SPM

When the transactions are executing, the data of these transactions will be fetched and stored in SPM. The size of SPM is limited. SPM should be well organized to support the execution of transactions in SPM. The organization of SPM is shown in Fig. 2 (a). The basic space in SPM for transactions is divided into different transaction blocks. The data used during the transactions will be stored in these transaction blocks. And it is convenient to protect the transaction data.

Transaction information blocks (TIB), which is a data structure for transactions in SPM, are stored in SPM. The structure of TIB is shown in Fig. 2 (b).

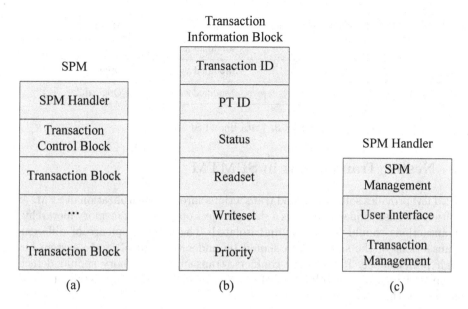

Fig. 2. The structure of SPM data. (a) The organization of SPM; (b) the structure of transaction information block; (c) SPM handler structure.

TIB records the control information of transactions including transaction ID, transaction status, readset and writeset etc. Transaction ID is used to identify the different transactions. The status of the transactions will be recorded in transaction status. Readset and writeset are used to record the read/write operations of the transactions respectively. Priority is also stored in TIB. A special field of TIB named PT ID is the father transaction ID of the transaction. The definition of father transaction is described in subsection 4.3.

There is also one special component titled SPM handler (SPMH) designed in SPMTM for management as shown in Fig. 2 (c). SPMH is used to manage the SPM and the transactions in SPM, it has three parts including SPM management, user interface, and transaction management. SPM management is used to manage memory space of SPM including the memory allocation, memory deallocation and the protection of SPM space. User interface will provide the operation interface on transactions and SPM space to the users. Transaction management will be implemented via TIB. SPMH can add, modify and delete the TIBs of the transactions to manage the transactions.

The data in SPM can be locked if the data are shared. Each data line of SPM has two tag bits for read/write lock as shown in Fig. 3. The owner ID is the tag to denote the owner transaction of the data line. It means that the data line is first used by this transaction and the original value is fetched to LS of this transaction. Read tag and write tag are set to denote the read/write operations of the special data line. The modified data and original data are both recorded. Original data is recorded to restore the data when the owner transaction of the data is aborted.

Owner ID	Read Tag	Write Tag	Data Line	Data Line
T_1	0	0	Modified X	Original X
T_1	1	0	Modified Y	Original Y
T_2	0	1	Modified Z	Original Z

Fig. 3. Data line of SPM

4   Nested Transactions in SPMTM

SPMTM provides software nested transactions through the utilization of SPM. A software transactional memory is a shared object operating on memory hierarchy. Transactions should be atomic and isolated. The access sequence of different transactions of the shared data should be under the control of the system for high performance. If there are conflicts, transactional memory should detect them and provide the solutions. SPMTM will be described in detail of these aspects in this section.

4.1   Basic Transaction Model

Each transaction is an instruction sequence including the access of local memory and shared memory [4]. The lifecycle of a transaction has four stages: initialization, execution, committing and committed in SPMTM as shown in Fig. 4 (a). During the execution stage, there will be conflicts perhaps. The conflicts will emerge under the following circumstances:

- During the procedure of the read operation of transaction T1, T1 finds that the target object is under the write operation of some other transaction;
- During the procedure of the write operation of transaction T1, T1 finds that the target object is under the write or read operation of some other transaction.

The solution of conflicts in SPMTM will be described in subsection 4.2.

Each transaction in SPMTM has five states during its execution including active, suspended, aborted, committing and committed as shown in Fig. 4 (b).

- Active: transactions are executing on the rails;
- Suspended: when the conflicts are from the read conflicts, the transactions will not be aborted directed. These transactions will be suspended. The cost of transaction resume is lower than that of restart.
- Aborted: the transactions are judged to be aborted by the conflict policy.
- Committing: The operations of transactions are all completed and waiting for final commit.
- Committed: The commits of transactions are completed.

SPMTM provides the transaction interfaces of the different state transitions through the library. The main interfaces are listed in the following:

- TMBegin (): it defines the beginning of the transactions.

- Suspend (): it will suspend some transactions when there are conflicts.

- Resume (): it will resume the execution of the suspended transactions.

- Abort (): it will abort the transactions, which are judged to be aborted by the conflict policy.

- getStatus(): the state of the transactions can be obtained through this interface.

- Commit (): It will complete the commit operation of the transactions.

(a)   (b)

Fig. 4. The lifecycle of transactions in SPMTM; (b) the states and states transitions of transactions in SPMTM

4.2 Conflict Arbitration Policy

As mentioned in subsection 4.1, data operations of the transactions will have conflicts during the execution of them. When the conflict occurs, there are two transactions impacted by the conflict at least. Which one of the transactions in conflict should be aborted or delayed plays an important role in transaction performance. Different Conflict arbitration policies have different operations on the conflicted transactions. The transactions in conflicts will not have the same priorities in different conflict arbitration policies. Conflict arbitration policy is also defined in SPMTM to detect conflicts and provide the corresponding solutions.

The conflict arbitration policy in SPMTM is priority-based policy. The quantity of write/read operations completed is important in software supported transactional memory. When a conflict occurs, aborting a transaction with many write/read operations completed will have more penalty than aborting a transaction in initialization stage. Thus it is more efficient to abort the transaction with less write/read operations.

Each transaction in SPMTM has a priority (TPri) with the initial value zero in its initialization stage. After each write/read operation, TPri will be increased

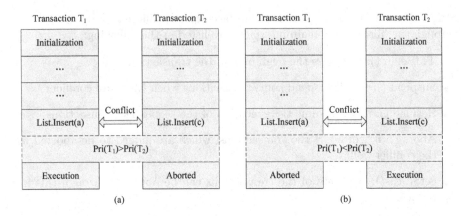

Fig. 5. Conflict arbitration in SPMTM. The operations are insertions of a list: (a) if priority of transaction T1 (Pri (T1)) > priority of transaction T2 ((Pri(T2)), T2 is aborted; (b) if Pri(T1) < Pri(T2), T1 is aborted.

by one. When the conflict occurs, the TPri of the conflicted transactions will be compared. The transaction with higher TPri will continue and the transaction with lower TPri will be suspended or aborted. Fig. 5 shows the detail of the execution of two conflicted transactions in SPMTM.

When the conflicts are read conflicts, the transactions with lower priorities will not be aborted at once. These transactions are suspended first. These suspended transactions are called TSu and the transactions which continue to execute are called TCo. TSu must wait in suspended state for the availability of the shared data after the release from TCo. When the shared data is available, TSus are resumed to execute. If TCos are aborted, the corresponding TSus will also be aborted. If transactions are aborted, their Pri values will not be cleared. The Pri will be inherited when the aborted transactions are restarted. Thus the transactions will not be in starvation.

4.3 Nested Transactions

Nested transactions will improve the performance of the transactional memory. When there are no conflicts in semantics, two or more transactions can be nested during the execution. SPMTM supports open nesting for transactional memory. SPMH can keep tracks on the data modification through readset, writeset and the original data records. The old data of the transactions can be obtained through SPMH. If the conflicts occur, SPMH can restore the old data to eliminate the operations of the aborted transactions.

The outer transaction of the nested transactions is called the parent transaction (PT); and the inner transaction of the nested transactions is called the leaf transaction (LT). All the outer transactions of a transaction can be a set called the ancestor transaction set (ATS). During the execution of a transaction, the operations of committed transactions will be combined into its PT. The operations of each LT will be combined into its PT. At last, all the operations will be

...

Transaction T_1

    T_1_Begin

    ...

    Transaction T_2

        T_2_Begin

     ...

        T_2_Committed

        T_2_End

  ...

  T_1_Committed

  T_1_End

...

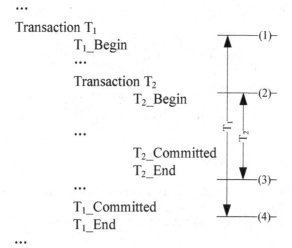

Fig. 6. An example of nested transactions in SPMTM

combined into the most outer transaction. The modification from the operations of each committed LT will be kept even if its PT is aborted. Fig. 6 shows an example of the nested transactions.

There are two nested transactions (T1 and T2) in Fig. 6. T1 is the outer transaction (PT) of T2 (T2 is the leaf transaction). There are four time points in these nested transactions. Time point (3) is the committed time of T2. SPMH will combine the committed data to T1. And then SPMH will delete the TIB of T2 from SPM. All the modification to the original data by T2 will not be found through TIB. And all the modifications can not be restored.

5   Experiments

5.1   Experiment Setup

Simics [29] is adopted as the simulation platform for the experiments in this paper. The configuration of the CMP system is shown in Table 1. The simulated processors have two cores, four cores and eight cores respectively. All the process cores in the same processor are all same to each other. The processor cores are connected by the on-chip bus. The access time of SPM, cache and off-chip memory is set to two cycles, two cycles and two hundred cycles respectively.

The List and HashMap in Java class library are selected as the benchmarks in these experiments. All the operations are created with random. During the experiments each time unit of these experiments is twenty seconds. The baseline of the experiments is the basic traditional lock-based method. The List and hashMap are tested on the simulated processors with different cores.

Table 1. The configuration of the processors with multi-cores

Core Numbers	2	4	8
Frequency	2.9GHz	2.9GHz	2.9GHz
L1 Cache	32KB	64KB	64KB
L2 Cache	2MB	4MB	4MB
SPM	256K	256K	256K
Main Memory	2GB	2GB	2GB

5.2   Experimental Results

The experiments have two different types: one tests the number of committed transactions of List and HashMap and the other tests the execution time of SPMTM compared with the traditional lock-based synchronization method for multi-threads.

The numbers of committed transactions in List and HashMap are shown in Fig. 7 and Fig. 8 respectively. When the number of processor cores is increased, more transactions in system will be created accordingly. The committed transactions are also increased during the execution. When the threads are more created for higher currency, more transactions will also be created. When the number of threads and cores is increased, it means that the concurrency is increased. Thus there are more concurrent transactions. Though there is still possibility of conflicts in these transactions, more transactions are committed successfully. The experimental results show that SPMTM is efficient for the high concurrency of CMP. And as the increase of the core number, SPMTM will have better performance.

Transactional memory is waiting-free compared with traditional lock-based synchronization. The performance of SPMTM and lock-based synchronization (as "Locks" shown in Fig. 9 and Fig. 10) is compared with each other of List

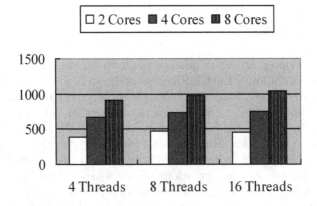

Fig. 7. Number of committed transactions in List

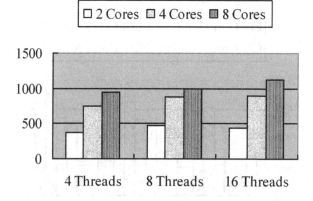

Fig. 8. Number of committed transactions in HashMap

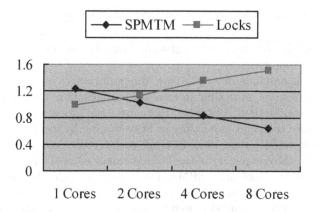

Fig. 9. List: Performance comparison of SPMTM and lock-based synchronization

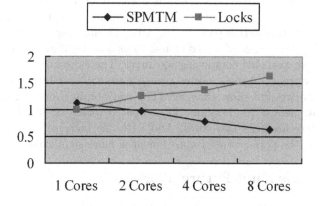

Fig. 10. HashMap: Performance comparison of SPMTM and lock-based synchronization

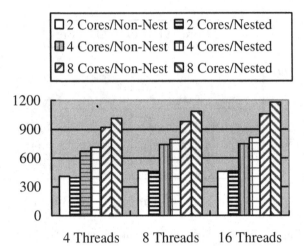

Fig. 11. The performance comparison of nested and non-nested transactions

and HashMap. The experimental results are shown in Fig. 9 and Fig. 10 for List and HashMap respectively.

When there is only one processor core, the performance of locks is better for SPMTM will consume more time in creation, initialization, abortion and other operations on transactions. But when there are more processor cores than one, the threads have to spend more time in busy-waiting by locks. Thus SPMTM has better performance than locks in CMP architecture. When there are more processor cores, the complexity of the locks is enhanced, and the time consumed in waiting is more. Contrarily SPMTM can provide high concurrency of the transactions with the increase of processor cores.

SPMTM has also supported nested transactions. The performance of nested transactions and non-nested transactions is compared as shown in Fig. 11. As shown in Fig. 11, when the number of processor cores is small (two cores), the performance of non-nested transactions is better than nested transactions. The reason is that when there are only limited processor cores, the nested transactions will have more abortion penalty. But when the number of processor cores is increased, the performance of nested transactions is better than non-nested transactions for more available computing resources. The experimental results when there are many processor cores, nested transactions will have better performance.

Experimental results show that SPMTM can obtain average 16.3% performance improvement of the benchmarks compared with lock-based synchronization when there are only two cores. And with the increase in the number of processor core, the performance improvement is more significant.

6   Conclusions and Future Work

Chip multiprocessor (CMP) can provide higher concurrency for the integrated more processor cores on chip. Though the traditional lock-based synchronization can be used in such architecture for thread level parallelism, this mechanism may block the threads without contentions. The overhead is the main problem of performance improvement. Transactional memory is proposed to solve this problem. The existing research shows that TM is efficient for synchronization in CMP processors. In this paper, a new type of on-chip memory, titled scratchpad memory (SPM), is introduced as the architectural support of transactional memory. SPM is software-controlled on-chip memory and its address space is a part of the whole address space of the system. And then the hybrid nested transactional memory framework titled SPMTM is designed based on SPM. SPMTM can take advantages of SPM to provide better performance and lower power consumption as shown by the experimental results.

SPM is on-chip memory with more flexibility. SPMTM is an exploration of transactional memory on such type of on-chip memory. The following areas will have important impacts on the performance of transactional memory including the distribution of processor cores, different organization of SPM and the address organization of SPM space etc. SPMTM will be improved in these areas in the future.

Acknowledgments. This work is supported by National Nature Science Foundation of China (No. 60673149), the National High-Tech Research and Development Program of China (863) (No. 2007AA01Z105) and the Research Foundation of Education Bureau of Zhejiang Province (No. Y200803333).

References

1. Nayfeh, B.A., Olukotun, K.: A single-chip multiprocessor. IEEE Computer 30(9), 79–85 (1997)
2. Herlihy, M., Luchangco, V., Moir, M., Scherer, W.N.: Software transactional memory for dynamic-sized data structures. In: The twenty-second annual symposium on Principles of distributed computing (PODC 2003), pp. 92–101. ACM Press, New York (2003)
3. Larus, J.R., Rajwar, R.: Transactional Memory. Morgan and Claypool (2007)
4. Shavit, N., Touitou, D.: Software transactional memory. Distributing Computing 10, 99–116 (1997)
5. Blundell, C., Devietti, J., Lewis, E.C., Martin, M.K.: Making the fast case common and the uncommon case simple in unbounded transactional memory. In: The 34th Annual International Symposium on Computer Architecture (ISCA 2007), San Diego, California, USA, pp. 24–34 (2007)
6. Bobba, J., Moore, K.E., Volos, H., Yen, L.: Performance pathologies in hardware transactional memory. In: The 34th Annual International Symposium on Computer Architecture (ISCA 2007), San Diego, California, USA, pp. 81–91 (2007)
7. Herlihy, M., Moss, J.: Transactional memory: Architectural support for lock-free data structures. In: The Twentieth Annual International Symposium on Computer Architecture (ISCA 1993), San Diego, California, United States, pp. 289–300 (1993)
8. Sanchez, D., Yen, L., Hill, M.D., Sankaralinga, K.: Implementing Signatures for Transactional Memory. In: The 40th Annual IEEE/ACM International Symposium on Microarchitecture, pp. 123–133. IEEE Computer Society, Los Alamitos (2007)

9. Agrawal, K., Leiserson, C.E., Sukha, J.: Memory models for open-nested transactions. In: The 2006 workshop on Memory system performance and correctness, San Jose, California, pp. 70–81. ACM Press, New York (2006)

10. Saha, B., Adl-Tabatabai, A.R., Jacobson, Q.: Architectural Support for Software Transactional Memory. In: The 39th Annual IEEE/ACM International Symposium on Microarchitecture, pp. 185–196. IEEE Computer Society, Los Alamitos (2006)

11. Abadi, M., Birrell, A., Harris, T., Isard, M.: Semantics of transactional memory and automatic mutual exclusion. In: The 35th annual ACM SIGPLAN-SIGACT symposium on Principles of programming languages, San Francisco, California, USA, pp. 63–74. ACM Press, New York (2008)

12. Scherer, W.N., Scott, M.L.: Advanced contention management for dynamic software transactional memory. In: The twenty-fourth annual ACM symposium on Principles of distributed computing, Las Vegas, NV, USA, pp. 240–248 (2005)

13. Riegel, T., Fetzer, C., Felber, P.: Time-based transactional memory with scalable time bases. In: The nineteenth annual ACM symposium on Parallel algorithms and architectures, San Diego, California, USA, pp. 221–228 (2007)

14. Felber, P., Fetzer, C., Riegel, T.: Dynamic performance tuning of word-based software transactional memory. In: The 13th ACM SIGPLAN Symposium on Principles and practice of parallel programming, Salt Lake City, UT, USA, pp. 237–246 (2008)

15. Shriraman, A., Spear, M.F., Hossain, H.: An integrated hardware-software approach to flexible transactional memory. In: The 34th annual international symposium on Computer architecture (ISCA 2007), San Diego, California, USA, pp. 104–115 (2007)

16. Chung, J.W., Minh, C.C., McDonald, A., et al.: Tradeoffs in transactional memory virtualization. In: Thirteenth International Conference on Architectural Support for Programming Languages and Operating Systems (ASPLOS 2006), San Jose, California, USA, pp. 371–381 (2006)

17. Kumar, S., Chu, M., Hughes, C.J., et al.: Hybrid transactional memory. In: The eleventh ACM SIGPLAN symposium on Principles and practice of parallel programming (PPoPP 2006), New York, USA, pp. 209–220 (2006)

18. Moravan, M.J., Bobba, J., Moore, K.E., et al.: Supporting nested transactional memory in logTM. In: Thirteenth International Conference on Architectural Support for Programming Languages and Operating Systems (ASPLOS 2006), San Jose, California, USA, pp. 359–370 (2006)

19. Ananian, C.S., Asanovic, C., Kuszmaul, B.C., Leiserson, C.E., Lie, S.: Unbounded Transactional Memory. In: The 11th International Symposium on High-Performance Computer Architecture (HPCA-11 2005), pp. 316–327 (2005)

20. Avissar, O., et al.: An optimal memory allocation scheme for scratch-pad-based embedded systems. ACM Trans. on Embedded Computing Sys. 1(1), 6–26 (2002)

21. Delaluz, V., et al.: Energy-Oriented Compiler Optimizations for Partitioned Memory Architectures. In: International Conference on Compilers, Architecture, and Synthesis for Embedded Systems, pp. 138–147. ACM Press, New York (2000)

22. Banakar, R., et al.: Scratchpad memory: A design alternative for cache on-chip memory in embedded systems. In: 10th International Symposium on Hardware/Software Codesign (CODES), pp. 73–78. ACM Press, New York (2002)

23. Hammond, L., Wong, V., Chen, M., Carlstrom, B.D., et al.: Transactional Memory Coherence and Consistency. In: The 31st annual international symposium on Computer architecture, pp. 102–113 (2005)

24. Minh, C.C., Trautmann, M., Chung, J.W., McDonald, A., et al.: An effective hybrid transactional memory system with strong isolation guarantees. In: The 34th annual international symposium on Computer architecture, San Diego, California, USA, pp. 69–80 (2007)
25. McDonald, A., Chung, J.W., Carlstrom, B.D., Minh, C.C.: Architectural Semantics for Practical Transactional Memory
26. Panda, P.R., et al.: On-chip vs. off-chip memory: The data partitioning problem in embedded processor-based systems. ACM Trans. Des. Autom. Electron. Syst., 5(3), 682–704 (2000)
27. Paulin, P.G., et al.: Embedded software in realtime signal processing systems: Application and architecture trends. Proceedings of IEEE 85(3), 419–435 (1997)
28. Zhang, C., et al.: On combining iteration space tiling with data space tiling for scratchpad memory systems. In: The 2005 conference on Asia South Pacific design automation, pp. 973–976. ACM Press, New York (2005)
29. Virtutech Simics, http://www.virtutech.com/products

Implementation of Rotation Invariant Multi-View Face Detection on FPGA

Jinbo Xu, Yong Dou, Yuxing Tang, and Xiaodong Wang

National Laboratory for Parallel and Distributed Processing
National University of Defense Technology
Changsha, P.R. China, 410073
{xujinbo,yongdou,tyx,xdwang}@nudt.edu.cn

Abstract. This paper aims at detecting faces with all -/+90-degree rotation-out-of-plane and 360-degree rotation-in-plane pose changes fast and accurately under embedded hardware environment. We present a fine-classified method and a hardware architecture for rotation invariant multi-view face detection. A tree-structured detector hierarchy is designed to organize multiple detector nodes identifying pose ranges of faces. We propose a boosting algorithm for training the detector nodes. The strong classifier in each detector node is composed of multiple novelly-designed two-stage weak classifiers. Each detector node deals with the multi-dimensional binary classification problems by means of a shared output space of multi-components vector. The characteristics of the proposed method is analyzed for fully exploiting the spatial and temporal parallelism. We present the design of the hardware architecture in detail. Experiments on FPGA show that high accuracy and amazing speed are achieved compared with previous related works. The execution time speedups are significant when our FPGA design is compared with software solution on PC.

Keywords: Face Detection, Rotation Invariant, Multi-View, Hardware Architecture, FPGA.

1   Introduction

Great advances have been achieved on face detection research [14] (for example [6][8][10]). The breakthrough happened in 2001 when Viola and Jones [10] developed their Boosted Cascade Framework whose remarkable performance owes to the fast speed of Haar-like feature calculation based on the integral image, the high accuracy of boosted strong classifiers, and the asymmetric decision making of the cascade structure.

Although many early researches have good performance for detection of frontal faces, Rotation Invariant Multi-View Face Detection (RIMVFD), which is used to detect faces with both ±90-degree rotation-out-of-plane (ROP) and 360-degree rotation-in-plane (RIP) pose changes, remains a challenging problem due to the much more complicated variation within the multi-view face class.

Y. Dou, R. Gruber, and J. Joller (Eds.): APPT 2009, LNCS 5737, pp. 82–94, 2009.
© Springer-Verlag Berlin Heidelberg 2009

In the past few years, many derivatives of Viola's work have been proposed for rotation invariant frontal face detection and multi-view face detection (MVFD), which can be categorized into four aspects: the detector structure (for example [12][3]), designing of strong classifiers (for example [7][3]), training of weak classifiers (for example [12][4]), and selecting of features (for example [1]). Most of these works focus on increasing the detection accuracy. However, these methods are only evaluated with software solution, which can hardly achieve real-time MVFD for some time-constraint applications.

To meet the needs of various applications, using dedicated hardware to accelerate RIMVFD is an effective solution. In the literature, there are hardware implementations of frontal face detection based on Neural Networks(for example [9]) and AdaBoost(for example [13]). However, few researches focus on hardware implementation of RIMVFD.

In this paper, a fine-classified method and an FPGA-based hardware architecture for RIMVFD are presented. Firstly, a tree-structured detector hierarchy is designed to organize detector nodes for RIP and ROP pose changes. To train branching nodes of the detector tree, a fine-classified boosting algorithm with a novel two-stage weak classifier design is proposed. Then, the temporal and spatial parallelism of the proposed method is fully exploited. Next, the hardware architecture for RIMVFD is designed and implemented on FPGA. The main contributions of this paper are: (1) RIMVFD with all 90-degree ROP and 360-degree RIP pose changes is achieved using tree-structured detector hierarchy and fine-classified Vector Boosting; (2) The execution time of the classification procedure is significantly reduced by fully exploiting the parallelism.

2   Design of Our RIMVFD Method

2.1   Framework of AdaBoost-Based Face Detection

Face detection based on AdaBoost algorithm has been accepted by the computer vision community as the state-of-the-art in terms of speed and accuracy. The basic idea of AdaBoost is that a combination of single rules or "weak classifiers" gives a "strong classifier". Viola and Jones proposed the use of Haar-like features which can be computed efficiently with integral image [11]. In Viola's cascade framework, a group of features composes a classification stage based on AdaBoost. The outcome of a stage determines whether the examined image region contains a face or not. When the base size is processed for all regions, the features are enlarged in subsequent scales, and evaluated for each scale to

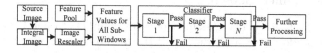

Fig. 1. Framework of AdaBoost-based face detection

be able to detect faces of larger sizes. Additional algorithm details can be found in [11]. The algorithm outline is shown in Figure 1.

The difference between our RIMVFD method and the framework in Figure 1 is mainly reflected in the classifier part. The integral image computation and image rescaler are the same. In this paper, we will focus on the classifying strategy for RIMVFD.

2.2   Tree-Structured Detector Hierarchy

For RIMVFD, pose changes should be identified in addition to face/non-face classification. There have been some related works, such as [12][3]. Huang claimed his tree structure [3] can balance the face/non-face distinguishing and pose identification tasks, so as to enhance the detector in both accuracy and speed. Limited by the parallel processing ability in general-purpose processor, Huang's tree structure only divides all faces into 5 categories according to ROP to control the computational cost.

As illustrated in Figure 2, we design a fine-grained tree structure with more detector nodes so as to achieve more accuracy and speed with the aid of hardware acceleration. The tree structure covers all ±90-degree ROP and 360-degree RIP pose changes and the detection granularities in ROP and RIP are 20 degrees and 30 degrees respectively. The coarse-to-fine strategy is adopted to divide the entire face space into smaller and smaller subspaces. Which branches a sample should be sent to is determined by computing a determinative vector $\mathbf{G}(\mathbf{x}) = [\mathbf{g_1}(\mathbf{x}), ..., \mathbf{g_n}(\mathbf{x})]$ for each node except the leaves, where n is the number of branches of a node. The sample is processed from the root node down to the leaf nodes. After the sample is processed by some selected leaf nodes, the RIP and ROP ranges where the sample belongs are determined.

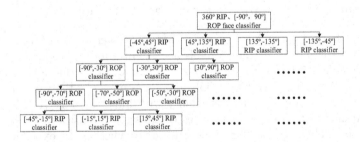

Fig. 2. Illustration of the proposed fine-grained tree structure

2.3   Fine-Classified Boosting

This section proposes a fine-classified boosting method to get $\mathbf{G}(\mathbf{x})$ fast and accurately. The designing and training of the method are detailed.

Many derivations from the basic AdaBoost method have been proposed for MVFD (for example [7][3]). Huang proposed Vector Boosting [3] in which both its weak learner and final output are vectors rather than scalars. Vector Boosting deals with the decomposed binary classification problems in a unified framework by means of a shared output space of multi-components vector. Each binary problem has its own "interested" direction in this output space, denoted as its projection vector. For each binary problem, a confidence value is calculated using an extended version of the Real AdaBoost. Then the strong classifier with Boolean outputs is got with a threshold vector $\mathbf{B}$. Classification criterion only uses single threshold for each dimension and only considers the discrimination in the current dimension of multiple classes. The disadvantage is that some classes may be unnecessarily considered as candidate classes to which a sample may belong. If $\mathbf{G(x)}$ is (1, 0, 1, 0) when the classification criterion uses single threshold, it may be refined to (1, 0, 0, 0) when the criterion is improved.

Therefore, we propose a fine-classified boosting method. It is configured to handle a complicated problem in a k-dimensional output space, which can be decomposed into n binary ones. Figure 3 gives the generalized description of the proposed method. We define the training set of m samples as $S = (\mathbf{x_1}, \mathbf{v_1}, \mathbf{y_1}), ..., (\mathbf{x_m}, \mathbf{v_m}, \mathbf{y_m})$, where $\mathbf{x_i}$ belongs to an instance space χ, $\mathbf{v_i}$ belongs to a finite k-dimensional projection vector set Ω and the label $y_i = \pm 1$.

The primary idea is that each weak classifier has two stages. The first stage $\mathbf{h'_t} : \chi \rightarrow \mathbb{R}^k$ based on piecewise function is trained to assign each sample a real-value confidence vector $x_i | i = 1, ..., k$ for k dimensions based on a sample's Haar-like feature. Each element in the vector indicates the probability whether the sample belongs to the corresponding class. Then the second stage $\mathbf{h''_t} : \mathbb{R}^k \rightarrow \{-1 | +1\}^k$ based on hyper-rectangles is trained to output a Boolean value for each dimension to further determine whether a sample belongs to the i-th class based on the confidence vector. $\mathbf{h'_t} : \chi \rightarrow \mathbb{R}^k$ and $\mathbf{h''_t} : \mathbb{R}^k \rightarrow \{-1 | +1\}^k$ are merged to form the final weak classifier $\mathbf{h^*_t} : \chi \rightarrow \{-1 | +1\}^k$, which estimates whether a sample belongs to the i-th class or not, $i = 1, ..., k$.

For a classification problem that has been decomposed into n binary ones, given:

(1) Projection vector set $\Omega = \{\omega_1, ..., \omega_n\}$, $\omega_i \in \mathbb{R}^k$

(2) Sample set $S = \{(\mathbf{x_1}, \mathbf{v_1}, y_1), ..., (\mathbf{x_m}, \mathbf{v_m}, y_m)\}$, where $\mathbf{x} \in \chi$, $\mathbf{v} \in \Omega$ and its label $y = \pm 1$

●   Initialize the sample distribution $D_1(i) = 1/m$ for all $i = 1, ..., m$.

●   For $t = 1, ..., T$

     ✧   Under current distribution, train a weak classifier: $\mathbf{h^*_t}(\mathbf{x}) : \chi \rightarrow \{-1|+1\}^k$.(weak learner)

     ✧   Calculate the weighted error ε_t of $\mathbf{h^*_t}$: $\varepsilon_t = \sum_{i=1}^{m} D_t(i) I(y_i \neq \mathbf{v_i} \bullet \mathbf{h^*_t}(\mathbf{x_i}))$.

     ✧   Compute the coefficient α_t: $\alpha_t = \frac{1}{2} \log\left(\frac{1-\varepsilon_t}{\varepsilon_t}\right)$.

     ✧   Update the sample distribution: $D_{t+1}(i) = \frac{D_t(i) \exp(-\alpha_t y_i (\mathbf{v_i} \bullet \mathbf{h^*_t}(\mathbf{x_i})))}{Z^*_t}$, where Z^*_t is the

     normalization factor so as to keep D_{t+1} as a probability distribution.

●   Stop if $\varepsilon_t = 0$ or $\varepsilon_t \geq 1/2$ and set $T = t-1$.

●   The final output space is: $\mathbf{H(x)} = \sum_{t=1}^{T} \alpha_t \mathbf{h^*_t(x)}$.

●   The confidence space is: $\mathbf{F(x)} = \mathbf{AH(x)}$, where the transformation matrix $\mathbf{A} = \{\omega_1, ..., \omega_n\}^T$.

●   The final strong classifier is: $\mathbf{G(x)} = sgn(\mathbf{F(x)})$.

Fig. 3. A generalized description of the fine-classified boosting method

The weak learner is called repeatedly under the updated distribution to form a highly accurate classifier. The margin of a sample $\mathbf{x_i}$ with its label y and projection vector $\mathbf{v_i}$ is defined as $y_i(\mathbf{v}_i \bullet \mathbf{h}_t^*(\mathbf{x}_i))$. Thus, the orthogonal component of a weak classifier's output makes no contribution to the updating of the sample's weight. The final output is the linear combination of all trained weak classifiers. A $n \times k$ matrix A made up of all n projection vectors in set Ω is used to transform the k-dimensional output space into n-dimensional confidence space. Each dimension of the confidence space corresponds to a certain binary problem. Finally, the output of the strong classifier is the sign of $\mathbf{F}(\mathbf{x})$.

The first stage is based on piecewise function [12], which is more efficient than threshold-type function and can be efficiently implemented with Look Up Table (LUT). The objective of the training procedure is to minimize the normalization factor of current round if adopting greedy strategy. A piecewise function is configured by two parts: the division of feature space and the constant for each division (i.e. bin). For the training of classifier in the i-th dimension, assuming the feature value of each training sample f_{Haar} has been normalized, the feature space is divided evenly into p sub-ranges: $bin_j = [(j-1)/p, j/p], 1 \le j \le p$. A partition on the range corresponds to a partition on χ. Thus, $\mathbf{h}_t'$ can be defined as: $f_{Haar}(\mathbf{x}) \in bin_j \Rightarrow h_t'(\mathbf{x}) = c_j$, where c_j can be easily trained with a proper optimization algorithm such as Newton-Step method. Finally, $\mathbf{h}_t'$ can be expressed as :

$$\mathbf{h}_t'(\mathbf{x}) = \sum_{j=1}^{p} \mathbf{c}_j^* B_p^j(f_{Haar}(\mathbf{x})) \tag{1}$$

where $B_p^j(u) = \begin{cases} 1 & u \in [(j-1)/p, j/p) \\ 0 & u \notin [(j-1)/p, j/p) \end{cases}, j = 1, ..., p, \mathbf{c}_j^* = \{c_{j(i)}|i = 1, ..., k\}$
and $\mathbf{h}_t' = \{h_{t(i)}'|i = 1, ..., k\}$.

The second stage will learn the distribution of the confidence vectors for all samples, and generate a precise criterion to discriminate different classes. In this paper, the second stage is based on hyper-rectangles. It has been proved that decision functions based on hyper-rectangles instead of a single threshold give better results [2] and can be easily implemented in parallel. We define the generalized hyper-rectangle as a set H of $2k$ thresholds and a class y_H, with $y_H \in \{-1, +1\} : H = \{\theta_1^l, \theta_1^u, \theta_2^l, \theta_2^u, ..., \theta_k^l, \theta_k^u, y_H\}$, where θ_i^l and θ_i^u are the lower and upper limits of a given interval in the i-th dimension. The decision function is

$$\begin{cases} h_H(\mathbf{x}) = y_H \Leftrightarrow \prod_{i=1}^{k} ((x_i > \theta_i^l) \text{and} (x_i < \theta_i^u)), \\ h_H(\mathbf{x}) = -y_H, \text{otherwise}. \end{cases} \tag{2}$$

The core of the training procedure is the hyper-rectangle set S_H determination from a set of samples S. We use the training method proposed in [5]. The basic idea is to build around each sample $\mathbf{x}_i, \mathbf{y}_i \in S$ a hyper-rectangle $H(\mathbf{x}_i)$ containing no sample of opposite classes, where $\mathbf{x}_i$ is the confidence vectors of all samples in this section and $y_i = \pm 1$.

3   Proposed Hardware Architecture for RIMVFD

3.1   The Global Structure

We exploit the temporal and spatial parallelism of the proposed RIMVFD method first. The phase of acquiring frames, computing integral frames and classifying faces within frames can form a pipeline. The image rescaler and the classification procedure can work in parallel. In our work, we rescale the image instead of the features, which means each iteration of rescaling has a corresponding rescaled integral image. In the classification procedure, different levels in the detector tree work on different sub-windows in a pipelined fashion, and different detector nodes in the same level work in parallel (see Figure 2).

According to the parallel characteristics of the system, the global architecture for RIMVFD is designed as illustrated in Figure 4. The key parts of the system are the Integral Image Computer, the Face Detector Module and Image Rescaler. The results of Integral Image Computer are required by Face Detector Module and Image Rescaler. The rescaled integral image data generated by Image Rescaler are required by Face Detector Module, too. In each detector node, a Feature Calculator and a Face Classifier are included. The intermediate results of these processing modules are stored in the Main Memory via the multi-port Memory Interface for later use. For the computation of integral image and the rescaling of image, they have been researched in many related works (e. g. [13][15]). Therefore, we will not discuss them in this paper and focus on the design of Face Detector Module.

The number of detector nodes as shown in Figure 2 can be reduced about 75% without significantly affecting the speed. The reason is that the detector branches for [-45°, 45°], [45°, 135°], [135°, -135°] and [-135°, -45°] RIP ranges can reuse the same structure. The only differences among them are the data acquisition addresses during the feature calculation procedure. Therefore, only the [-45°, 45°] RIP classifier and its child nodes are configured into the system at first, together with the root node (i.e. 360° RIP, [-90°, 90°] ROP face classifier). If a sub-window is rejected by the root node, it is considered as non-face; otherwise, it flows into the [-45°, 45°] RIP classifier. The locations of sub-windows rejected by the [-45°, 45°] RIP classifier are buffered and reprocessed by the same detector tree, except that the data acquisition scheme in the feature calculation part is

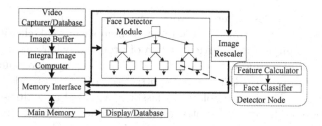

Fig. 4. Global architecture of the RIMVFD system

updated to rotate the feature values for 90 degrees, 180 degrees and 270 degrees successively. Only sub-windows rejected by the previous 90-degree RIP classifier are sent into the successive one. Since most multi-view faces concentrate in [-45°, 45°] RIP range in real world, the number of sub-windows that are rejected by the [-45°, 45°] RIP classifier will be tiny. Therefore, although the number of detector nodes as shown in Figure 2 is reduced from 161 to 41, the detection speed is hardly affected and the detection accuracy remains unchanged.

3.2   Design and Implementation of the Detector Hierarchy

Different nodes in the detector tree have similar structure with different classification parameters. The inputs of each node are some feature values of sub-windows, and an Enable Signal indicating whether the node needs to be activated. The output is a Boolean value indicating whether a sub-window belongs to the current face class. All direct child nodes of a parent node use the same feature set calculated by the Feature Calculator. If the node is not a leaf, the output will be sent into all its child nodes in the next level as their Enable Signals; otherwise, the output is the final result for a sub-window. In each node, cascaded structure [10] is also adopted to organize strong classifiers, where simple classifiers at early stages can filter out most negative sub-windows efficiently. The output of the previous cascade stage is connected with the Enable Signals of its successive stage. Different stages work on the sub-windows in a pipelined fashion. In Figure 5, we pick up several detector nodes from two adjacent levels to illustrate the structure and their communications.

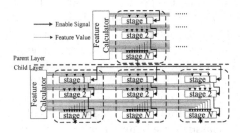

Fig. 5. Structure of detector nodes and their communications

In the detector nodes, different strong classifiers have similar structure with different classification parameters and different number of weak classifiers. Each strong decision function is a particular sum of products, where each product is made of a constant α_t and the value -1 or +1 depending on the output of h_t^*. In our design, the results of additions and subtractions of α_t are encoded into LUT units beforehand. The outputs of weak classifiers are used as addresses of LUT units. The more additions and subtractions are encoded in a LUT unit, the less online addition operations are required in the hierarchy of adders. The structure of the strong classifier with 16-bit LUT unit is presented in Figure 6(a).

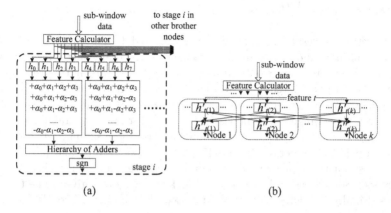

(a)   (b)

Fig. 6. Structure of the strong classifier and the weak decision function. (a)strong classifier; (b)weak decision function.

Next, we will introduce the hardware structure of the two-stage weak classifiers. The first stage $\mathbf{h}_t^{'} : \chi \to \mathbb{R}^k$ has the form as shown in Equation (1), and $\mathbf{c}_j^*$ is trained off-line. The second stage : $\mathbf{h}_t^{''} : \mathbb{R}^k \to \{-1| + 1\}^k$ has the form of Equation (2) for each dimension of the k classes. For the t-th weak classifier, the feature value is sent into all dimensions of $\mathbf{h}_t^{'}$ first, where each dimension corresponds to each direct child node of a parent node. All k outputs of $\mathbf{h}_t^{'}$ are sent into each dimension of $\mathbf{h}_t^{''}$ for further hyper-rectangle-based decision. Figure 6(b) shows the dataflow.

Different $\mathbf{h}_t^{'}$ have similar structure. The piecewise decision function can be easily implemented on hardware by using LUT units, as shown in Figure 7(a). Each element in a LUT corresponds to the constant value for a feature bin. The input is the normalized feature value, which is used as the address for LUT. If the feature value is located at the j-th bin of all p bins, c_j in the LUT will be selected as output. Different $\mathbf{h}_t^{''}$ have similar structure, too. The hyper-rectangle-based decision function can be easily implemented on hardware only by using some comparison units and logical operation units, as illustrated in Figure 7(b).

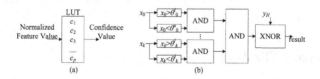

Fig. 7. Structure of the two-stage weak classifier. (a) the first stage; (b) the second stage.

4   Experimental Results

In this section, several experiments are performed to evaluate the proposed RIMVFD method and hardware architecture. More than 85,000 face samples are collected by cropping from various sources, which are normalized to the standard 24×24 pixel patch and cover all ±90-degree ROP and ±45-degree RIP pose changes. We partition the sample space into smaller and smaller subspaces of narrower view ranges. The nodes in the detector tree are trained by using the training method introduced in Section 2.3 upon these samples. As described in Section 3.1, the detection in the [45°, 135°], [135°, -135°] and [-135°, -45°] RIP ranges can be implemented by simply rotating the trained classifiers for 90 degrees, 180 degrees and 270 degrees clockwise. Figure 8 gives some training samples. Finally the detector tree is composed of 41 nodes in 5 levels.

Fig. 8. Some training samples

A prototype of the proposed design has been implemented in an FPGA testbed for evaluation, which includes a large capacity FPGA chip and a SDRAM module, connecting to the host processor through USB interface. Our target device is Altera Stratix II EP2S130F1020C5, containing 106,032 ALUTs and 6,747,840 bits of on-chip memory. The SDRAM module with capacity of 1G Bytes is deployed as off-chip memory. The host processor functions as the Video Capture Device and Display/Store Device as shown in Figure 4. The FPGA implementation is coded with Verilog HDL, simulated with Mentor Graphics ModelSim, and synthesized with Quartus II.

To give an overall evaluation, we test our system on the CMU profile set, which consists of 208 images with 441 faces. Since the CMU profile set can not evaluate the rotation invariant characteristics well, we also collect a database of 360-degree rotation invariant test images from various sources, containing 213 images with 682 rotation invariant multi-view faces. The CMU+MIT frontal face test set containing 130 images with 507 main frontal faces is also used to evaluate the frontal face detection performance. Some detection results generated by the proposed system are shown in Figure 9.

4.1   Resource Utilization

We synthesize the design using Quartus II. The size of the sub-window for classification, x_0-by-y_0, is 24×24. The scanning steps in the x- and y-direction S_x and S_y are set to be 1 pixel, and the scaling factor r is 1.25. The number of detector nodes is 41, which are organized as described in Section 3.1. The number of cascade stages in each detector node, and the number of weak classifiers in

Fig. 9. Some detection results of the proposed system

Table 1. Resource utilization for different parts of the system

Modules	Area (ALUTs)	On-Chip Memory(bits)
Video Capturer/Database Interface	238	67239
Results Display/Database Interface	322	8325
Main Memory Controller	819	19200
Integral Image Computer	657	48921
Face Detector Tree	102512	69038
Image Rescaler	579	32973
Total	105127	245696

each cascade stage are determined by selecting operating points within a receiver operator characteristic (ROC) curve. Finally, 3820 weak classifiers are included in the detector tree. Based on the synthesis results, the clock speed of the entire design reaches 98MHz. Table 1 gives the resource utilization for different parts of the system. We can see that the Face Detector Tree occupies most of the ALUT resources. The reason is that the number of weak classifiers in it is pretty large.

4.2 Speed Comparison with Software Solution and Related Works

We compare the processing speed of the hardware implementation with that of the software solution on PC with a Pentium IV 2.8GHz CPU and 1GB memory bank. The software solution is implemented based on OpenCV. The program code is written in Visual C++ language under WindowsXP OS. Table 2 gives the comparison of execution latency for detecting rotation invariant multi-view faces in one image frame using these two solutions and the off-chip memory bandwidth requirements. Test images with different sizes are used. We can see that although the system clock speed is only 98MHz, which is much slower than that of PC (i.e. Pentium IV 2.8GHz), the processing speed of the hardware solution is still faster than that of the software solution. The detection speed

Table 2. Performance comparison between the hardware and software solution and the off-chip memory bandwidth requirements

Image Size	Execution Latency(ms)		Speed Up	Bandwidth (MB/s)
	Hardware	Software		
160×120	1.58	23.2	14.68	99.8
192×144	2.06	33.6	16.31	110.7
320×240	5.36	93.9	17.52	158.7
384×288	7.27	135.4	18.62	168.5
480×320	9.71	188.2	19.38	175.4
640×480	18.42	376.6	20.45	185.1
768×576	26.08	542.5	20.8	188.3
800×600	28.22	588.7	20.86	188.9

is also much faster than other related works tested on PC or FPGA [12][3][15]. The reason is that our design uses tree-structured detector hierarchy, and the temporal/spatial parallelism is fully exploited to construct highly parallel and pipelined hardware architecture. The off-chip memory bandwidth requirements for different image sizes are also described in Table 2. The available off-chip memory bandwidth in our prototype system is about 200MB/s, which can meet the requirements.

4.3   Accuracy Comparison with Related Works

Frontal face detection test on CMU+MIT frontal face. As frontal faces are very useful in face-related applications, we first evaluate the proposed method on the CMU+MIT frontal face test set, and compare the results with those of Rowley's ANN method [6], Viola's cascade detector [10] and Wu's parallel cascade method [12]. Figure 10(a) gives the detection results and the corresponding ROC curves. We can see that our proposal has a much higher detection rate.

MVFD test on CMU profile set. We compare the proposed method with Schneiderman's Bayesian decision rule method [8], Wu's parallel cascade method [12] and Huang's WFS tree method [3] for MVFD. All tests are based on the CMU profile set. Figure 10(b) gives the detection results and the corresponding ROC curves.

RIMVFD test on our own database. For the rotation invariant MVFD, since there is no available standard test set, we use our own collected database containing 213 images with 682 rotation invariant multi-view faces. Wu's parallel cascade method [12] and Huang's WFS tree method [3] did some experiments on RIMVFD, but they didn't give the ROC curves. In our experiment, the ROC curve of our proposal on our own test set is given in Figure 10(c).

The main reason why our proposal achieves a better performance is that the outputs of the first stage in weak classifiers are further classified by the second stage. Consequently, faces belonging to each class can be well separated

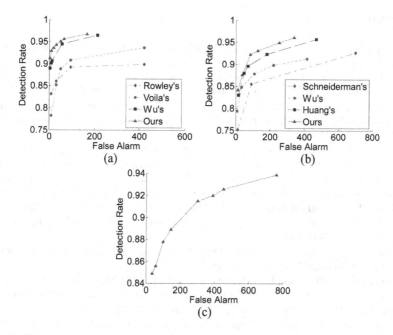

Fig. 10. ROC curves on (a)CMU+MIT frontal face set; (b)CMU profile set; (c)our own test set

from other classes. Since the Haar-like feature values of face samples are mainly reflected by the color differences of different organs in the face and not the absolute color values, the face objects can be distinguished from other objects with similar color such as shirts on people, and face colors of various races (white, black,) will not influence the detection accuracy too much.

5   Conclusions

We presented a fine-classified method and an FPGA-based hardware architecture for detecting rotation invariant multi-view faces with all -/+90-degree ROP and 360-degree RIP pose changes. A tree-structured detector hierarchy was designed to organize multiple detector nodes. We proposed a fine-classified boosting algorithm to train each detector node, where each weak classifier has a novel two-stage structure. The proposed method achieves higher accuracy than related works. Due to the highly parallel and pipelined design of the hardware architecture for RIMVFD and the reusability of detector nodes, amazing speed were realized compared with previous related works.

Acknowledgments. This work is supported in part by the National Science Foundation of China through grants 60633050 and 60833004.

References

1. Baluja, S., Sahami, M., Rowley, H.A.: Efficient Face Orientation Discrimination. In: IEEE International Conference on Image Processing (ICIP), pp. 589–592 (2004)
2. DeMacq, I., Simar, L.: Hyper-Rectangular Space Partitioning Trees, a Few Insight. Technical report, Universite Catholique de Louvain, Belgium (2002)
3. Huang, C., Li, Y., Ai, H.Z., Lao, S.H.: Vector Boosting for Rotation Invariant Multi-View Face Detection. In: IEEE International Conference on Computer Vision (ICCV), pp. 446–453 (2005)
4. Mita, T., Kaneko, T., Hori, O.: Joint Haar-Like Features for Face Detection. In: IEEE International Conference on Computer Vision (ICCV), pp. 1619–1626 (2005)
5. Mitéran, J., Matas, J., Bourennane, E., Paindavoine, M., Dubois, J.: Automatic Hardware Implementation Tool for a Discrete Adaboost-Based Decision Algorithm. EURASIP Journal on Applied Signal Processing 2005(1), 1035–1046 (2005)
6. Rowley, H.A.: Neural Network-Based Human Face Detection. PhD thesis, Carnegie Mellon University (1999)
7. Schapire, R.E., Singer, Y.: Improved Boosting Using Confidence-Rated Predictions. Machine Learning 37(3), 297–336 (1999)
8. Schneiderman, H., Kanade, T.: A Statistical Method for 3D Object Detection Applied to Faces and Cars. In: IEEE Computer Society Conference on Computer Vision and Pattern Recognition (CVPR), pp. 746–751 (2000)
9. Theocharides, T., Link, G., Vijaykrishnan, N., Irwin, M., Wolf, W.: Embedded Hardware Face Detection. In: IEEE International Conference on VLSI Design (ICVLSI), pp. 133–138 (2004)
10. Viola, P., Jones, M.: Rapid Object Detection Using a Boosted Cascade of Simple Features. In: IEEE Computer Society Conference on Computer Vision and Pattern Recognition (CVPR), pp. 511–518 (2001)
11. Viola, P., Jones, M.: Robust Real-Time Face Detection. International Journal of Computer Vision 57(2), 137–154 (2004)
12. Wu, B., Huang, C., Ai, H.Z., Lao, S.H.: Fast Rotation Invariant Multi-View Face Detection Based on Real Adaboost. In: IEEE International Conference on Automatic Face and Gesture Recognition (FGR), pp. 79–84 (2004)
13. Yang, M., Wu, Y., Crenshaw, J., Augustine, B., Mareachen, R.: Face Detection for Automatic Exposure Control in Handheld Camera. In: IEEE International Conference on Computer Vision Systems, pp. 17–24 (2006)
14. Yang, M.H., Kriegman, D.J., Ahuja, N.: Detecting Faces in Images: A Survey. IEEE Transactions on Pattern Analysis and Machine Intelligence (PAMI) 24(1), 34–58 (2002)
15. Yu, W., Xiong, B., Chareonsak, C.: FPGA Implementation of Adaboost Algorithm for Detection of Face Biometrics. In: IEEE International Workshop on Biomedical Circuits and Systems, pp. 17–20 (2004)

The Design and Evaluation of a Selective Way Based Trace Cache*

Deze Zeng[1,2], Minyi Guo[1,3], Song Guo[1], Mianxiong Dong[1], and Hai Jin[2]

[1] School of Computer Science and Engineering, The University of Aizu,
Aizu-Wakamatsu, Fukushima, 965-8580, Japan
{m5112104,sguo,d8101104}@u-aizu.ac.jp
[2] School of Computer Science and Technology, Huazhong University of Science and
Technology, Wuhan, 430074, China
hjin@hust.edu.cn
[3] Department of Computer Science and Engineering, Shanghai Jiao Tong University
Shanghai, 200030, China
guo-my@cs.sjtu.edu.cn

Abstract. Energy efficient and performance efficient instruction fetch unit is a critical issue in modern processor design. Trace cache which stores dynamic basic-block stream can significantly improve performance efficiency. Conventional trace cache (CTC) usually adopts set associative structure which requires probing all the data ways in parallel such that only the output of the matched way is used, but the energy for accessing the other ways is wasted. In this paper, we propose a selective way based trace cache (SWTC), which probes only the selected way(s) instead of probing all the data ways. In SWTC, traces are divided into several types and stored into cache by type. Then the trace cache is partially activated and accessed. Based on these design principles, a SWTC model is proposed and evaluated in this paper. Simulation results show that compared to CTC, SWTC can reduce energy consumption on the fetch unit by 20.1% on average, while providing almost the same performance in terms of number of instructions per cycle.

Keywords: computer architecture; instruction fetch unit design; energy efficient; trace cache; selective way.

1 Introduction

The development of superscalar processors has placed great demand on the instruction fetch mechanism. The instruction fetch unit is desired to fetch instructions as many as possible, by fully utilizing the datapath resources to achieve

* This work is supported by the National 973 Basic Research Program of China under grant No.2007CB310900, National High-Tech Research and Development Plan of China (863 Plan) under Grant Nos. 2008AA01Z106 and 2006AA01Z202, the National Natural Science Foundation of China under Grant Nos. 60811130528, 60725208 and 60533040, Shanghai Pujiang Plan No. 07pj14049 and Research Fellowships of the Japan Society for the Promotion of Science for Young Scientists Program.

Y. Dou, R. Gruber, and J. Joller (Eds.): APPT 2009, LNCS 5737, pp. 95–109, 2009.
© Springer-Verlag Berlin Heidelberg 2009

a higher instruction level parallelism (ILP). Higher instruction fetch rate can potentially increase the performance of the processor [1]. On the other side, energy efficiency has become an important issue in modern processor design. The instruction fetch unit consumes a considerable proportion of the total power consumption in a processor [2][3]. The design of fetch unit for future superscalar processors should achieve a high instruction fetch rate in an energy efficient way.

The capacity of conventional fetch units is limited as it can only fetch at most one block from instruction cache per cycle. In order to improve the instruction fetch rate, many novel fetch mechanisms have been proposed, such as Braid [1], branch address cache (BAC) [4], collapsing buffer (CB) [5] and trace cache (TC) [6]. Among them, trace cache has received much attention from both academia [7][8][9][10] and industry [11]. Trace cache was first proposed by Rotenberg et al. in [6], known as conventional trace cache (CTC). It has been proved that trace cache can improve performance and save energy over the instruction cache [8]. Recent research shows that the energy efficiency of CTC can be improved further.

There are at least two drawbacks resulting in energy inefficiency of CTC. One is its low utilization of cache space. Some literatures [15][16] improve the cache space utilization of trace cache by optimizing fill-in policy of CTC. Another is the simultaneous access to both trace cache and instruction cache in every fetch cycle. Previous work, such as sequential trace cache (STC), selective trace cache (SLTC) [17] and dynamic direction prediction based trace cache (DPTC) [18], all try to avoid the simultaneous access to reduce energy consumption.

Cache usually adopts a set associative structure because it can lower miss rate as well as minimize access time. However it has to probe all the data ways in parallel using tag lookup and only data from only the matched way is used. The energy spent for accessing other unmatched ways can be viewed as a waste of energy. It has been proved that the wasted energy can be reduced by predicting the way to be possibly matched and then only accessing the predicted way [12][13][14]. This mechanism is known as the selective way access.

In this paper, the selective way access technique is applied to trace cache and a selective way based trace cache (SWTC) for reducing energy consumption of trace cache is proposed. A natural characteristic of trace cache is exploited to realize selective access. The basic idea is that the partial access can make trace cache more energy efficient. We notice that trace cache itself is endowed with the capacity of way selection. One trace is specified by its start address and the branch outcomes in the trace. So, according to their branch outcomes in the trace, traces can be divided into several types. Trace cache is also divided into a set of ways and traces are allocated into different ways by type. Then, the multiple-branch prediction [22] is used as the prediction of the matched way. Only the possibly matched way is selected by this prediction and activated. Therefore, the energy for activating other invalid ways can be saved.

Based on this principle, a SWTC architecture model is introduced in this paper. In the model, trace cache is evenly divided into 6 ways and each way can accept one or two types of trace. In each fetch cycle, two ways are selected, activated and accessed using a three-branch prediction while the other four ways remain in a quiescent state. Experimental results show that compared to CTC, SWTC can reduce energy consumption on the fetch unit by 20.1% on average while achieving 1.2% close to the performance of CTC.

The remaining part of this paper is structured as follows. Section 2 introduces selective ways cache techniques and summarizes the related work which made efforts on reducing power dissipation of trace cache. Section 3 presents the design principles and a architecture model of SWTC. Simulation model and experimental results are presented in Section 4. Section 5 concludes our findings and points out several future research problems.

2   Related Work

As reducing energy consumption, especially cache energy consumption, is one of the most important issues in modern processor design, some work have pioneered in proposing efficient solutions. One trend is to partition cache into smaller ways and to access one way selectively. On the other hand, since trace cache is an effective way to achieve high performance, some work have also been done to reduce energy consumption on trace cache.

2.1   Selective Way Cache

Selective cache ways [12] can achieve good performance by partitioning the set associative caches into subarrays such that some ways of the cache can be disabled during the periods when full cache functionality is not needed. The cache is partitioned and tailored to the requirements of different applications based on a performance on-demand approach that can achieve energy saving. Another way is to predict the cache way that will be accessed on each cache access. Inoue et al. [13] evaluated one such scheme that predicts the most-recently used way to be accessed to reduce energy consumption in set associative caches. Powel et al. [14] further refined the way prediction scheme by selective direct-mapping. In order to increase the prediction accuracy, a selective direct-mapping scheme was exploited. Nonconflicting blocks are placed in a direct-mapping way while conflicting blocks still use the set associative mapping. Therefore, it can be determined whether the direct-mapping way or the set-associative mapping way should be used by predicting whether a block is conflicting or nonconflicting. However, all these way prediction schemes have a drawback that if a misprediction occurs, the rest of the ways need to be accessed in the following cycle, which results in performance degradation. SWTC, different from previous work, as a selective way cache, can guarantee that the access missed in the selected way will not hit in the unselected way either. This can be viewed as an immediate trace cache miss and the instruction fetch will proceed normally from instruction cache instead of probing other unselected ways in the next cycle.

2.2   Energy Efficient Trace Cache

There has been a lot of research work on reducing energy consumption of trace cache. Some work mainly exploits the "hot/cold trace" principle to optimize trace cache building. Hot traces are executed many times and contribute to the majority of committed instructions. Cold traces are rarely executed but may be written into trace cache many times. Using trace filtering methodology to prevent cold traces from entering trace cache can significantly improve its space utilization of trace cache, improve performance and reduce the energy consumption at the same time. Kosyakovsky et al. [15] propose a profile-based trace cache management. They use profiling to identify the "hot traces" and supply the hardware with hints to store hot traces. Michael Behar at al. [16] propose a trace cache sampling filter which selects traces to be stored in trace cache on a periodic basis. It selects traces into trace cache randomly, without any prior knowledge of trace behavior. Since most traces are cold traces, by preventing them from being written into trace cache, this mechanism can reduce much power consumption.

There are also some work exploiting the way to try to avoid simultaneous access to both trace cache and instruction cache at each fetch stage. Hu et al. propose two fetch models: Selective trace cache (SLTC) [17] and dynamic direction prediction based trace cache (DPTC) [18]. SLTC uses profile information to get the locality of traces, and then use a modified ISA, compiler optimization and hardware support to control trace cache lookup. DPTC is a pure hardware theme to implement selective access to trace cache and instruction cache. It augments the branch targe buffer entry with two additional saturating counters to predict next fetch direction either to instruction cache or to trace cache.

In [19], Dynamic Voltage and Frequency Scaling (DVFS) technique is applied to trace cache, in which the first basic block is not voltage-scaled while all other blocks are voltage-scaled down so as to reduce energy consumption.

Our current work is also a pure hardware scheme, but it takes a completely different approach from all previous work on reducing energy consumption of trace cache. It can be incorporated into existing work to achieve even higher energy efficiency.

3   Selective Way Based Trace Cache

In this section, some fundamentals of trace cache and principle of SWTC will be discussed first. A selective way based trace cache micro-architecture will then be proposed based on the principle.

3.1   Fundamentals of Trace Cache

Trace cache captures dynamic sequential blocks in dynamic program order, called trace, instead of static program order generated by compiler in each cache line. Each trace is specified by its start address and branch outcomes. A trace can be formally denoted by a tuple, $T = \{A, C\}$, where A is the start address and C is the branch outcomes.

The microarchitecture of the CTC fetch unit is shown in Fig. 1. Trace cache mainly consists of instruction trace, line-fill buffer logic and control information.

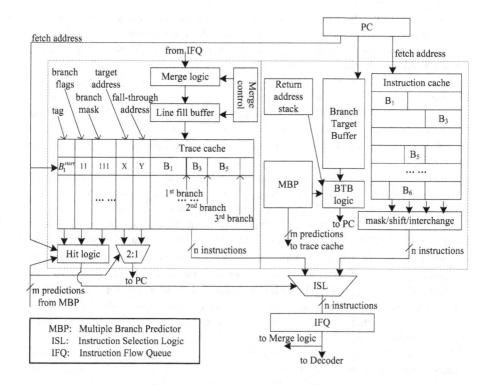

Fig. 1. Microarchitecture of the CTC fetch unit

Control information has two functions. One is to specify the instruction trace by its tag, branch flags and branch mask. Tag identifies the start address of the trace. Branch flags are the branch outcomes within the trace and the branch mask indicates the number of branches in the trace. The other function of control information is to produce the next fetch address after the current trace. The last bit of the branch mask indicates whether the trace ends with a branch or not. If it ends with a branch and the last branch in the trace is predicted as taken, target address will be selected as the next fetch address. Otherwise, fall-through address will be selected.

In CTC, trace cache is accessed simultaneously when instruction cache is accessed. If the fetch address matches the tag and the results from the multiple branch predictor (MBP) match the branch flags, trace cache hits and instruction selection logic (ISL) will feed the corresponding trace into instruction fetch queue (IFQ). The data from instruction cache are bypassed.

3.2 Principle of SWTC

Power dissipation in CMOS circuits mainly consists of two parts, static power dissipation due to leakage current and dynamic power dissipation due to logic switching current, the charging and discharging of the load capacitance. Let P_{static} and $P_{dynamic}$ be the static power dissipation and the dynamic power dissipation of trace cache, respectively. In N way set associative cache, the N ways are accessed simultaneously, resulting in the power dissipation being equals to N * $P_{dynamic}$. In a selective way cache, if only one selected way is activated while all other ways stay in a quiescent state, the power dissipated can reduce to: 1 * $P_{dynamic} + (N\text{-}1) * P_{static}$ In the above power expressions, the power dissipation consists of several component, such as tag array power dissipation, data array power dissipation, etc. These components are not detailed, but sufficient for our discussion.

In trace cache, each trace consists of several basic blocks. The number of basic blocks is limited by the capacity of cache line and the number of branch prediction that can be made in each cycle. Each trace should at least have two basic blocks and can accommodate up to N basic blocks, there are at least 1 branch and up to $N\text{-}1$ branches in one trace. Let i be the number of branch in a trace $(1 \leq i \leq N\text{-}1)$, the total number of possible branch outcomes is equal to $\sum_{i=1}^{N-1} 2^i = 2^N - 2$. Since each trace is denoted by $T = \{A, C\}$, traces can be classified into 2^N-2 types by branch outcomes C. If traces are stored in different ways by type, branch prediction can be viewed as trace type prediction to select the possible matched way. Then, instead of probing all the data ways in CTC, only the selected way is accessed for saving energy.

It is ideal that only one way is selected to access if every trace has the same number of basic blocks. But in general, traces can consist of various number of basic blocks, so for each multiple-branch prediction, more than one way may be valid. For example, in a trace cache where each trace can accommodate up to 4 basic blocks, suppose the multiple-branch prediction is "1001". Traces with branch outcomes "1", "10" and "100" are all possibly valid. If each trace can accommodate up to N basic blocks, $N\text{-}1$ types should be selected to access simultaneously in SWTC. Suppose both CTC and SWTC have the same trace cache size, if trace cache in SWTC is divided into 2^N-2 ways equally and each way accept one type of trace . A more general case, in which each way can accept more than one type of trace, will be discussed in the next section. Here we only consider a one-to-one rule. Regarding the power expression shown above, the relationship between the trace cache power dissipation in each access of SWTC and CTC can be obtained as the following formula:

$$\frac{P_{SWTC}}{P_{CTC}} = \frac{(2^N - 2 - (N-1)) * P_{static} + (N-1) * P_{dynamic}}{(2^N - 2) * P_{dynamic}}$$

Since dynamic power dissipation contributes to most of the total power dissipation as shown in the above formula, we can conclude that SWTC has a great power efficiency advantage over CTC. However, this can not guarantee that SWTC has also a energy advantage to CTC because energy is approximately the product of power and time. If performance of SWTC is much lower than CTC, it is possible that SWTC may finally consume more energy than CTC. On the other hand, performance efficiency is also an important issue in modern processor design. So we cannot evaluate efficiency of SWTC only in terms of energy consumption of each trace cache access without the consideration of performance.

When it comes to the performance evaluation of systems with trace cache, the first thing to be concerned is how many instructions can be fetched from trace cache since more instructions from trace cache are fetched, more benefits from trace cache are obtained. In general, the bigger the trace cache is, the more instructions from the trace cache can be fetched. However, for trace cache with the same capacity, the utilization of the physical capacity should also be taken into account. In CTC, a trace can be filled into any way of trace cache according to the mapping rule and replacement policy. While in SWTC, a trace can only be filled into one way determined by its type. It can be concluded that SWTC has lower space utilization than CTC. In other words, CTC may be more performance efficient than SWTC.

However, the above conclusion is not always true. Recall that while filling a trace into trace cache, some other trace in the trace cache may be evicted. It is possible that the trace is evicted out before it will be used again. This is known as the cache pollution problem. In CTC, trace in any set has the same possibility to be evicted out since new trace can be inserted into any cache set. However in SWTC, the new trace can only be filled into the way specified by its branch outcomes and therefore only trace within the same way can be evicted out. This property makes less chances of performance degradation due to the cache pollution problem compared to CTC.

By the discussion above, we predict that SWTC may suffer some performance degradation compared to CTC, but it should have a great energy efficiency advantage over CTC.

3.3 Microarchitecture of a SWTC Model

Based on the design principle discussed, a microarchitecture model of SWTC is proposed. The microarchitecture of SWTC is shown in Fig. 2. Comparing Fig. 2 with Fig. 1 roughly, we can observe that only little modifications over CTC are required. It implies that the hardware cost is similar to the original system.

Since it is difficult to make a precise prediction for over three branches due to the technical limitations [20], a three-branch predictor is adopted in our SWTC model. So one trace can accommodate 2 or 3 blocks and the number of branch outcomes in each trace is 1 or 2, respectively. By the branch outcomes, traces can be classified into six types, represented as TC00, TC01, TC10, TC11, TC0 and TC1. The notations are in binary form and each bit represents one branch outcome. The relationship between each multiple-branch prediction and the possibly matched traces is shown in Table 1. For each branch prediction, there are two types of possibly matched trace. By the principle discussed in previous section, trace cache is divided into six ways and one way accepts one type of trace. As shown in Fig. 2, each way corresponds to one trace type, such as Way00 to TC00, Way01 to TC01, Way1 to TC1 and so on. At each fetch stage, two types

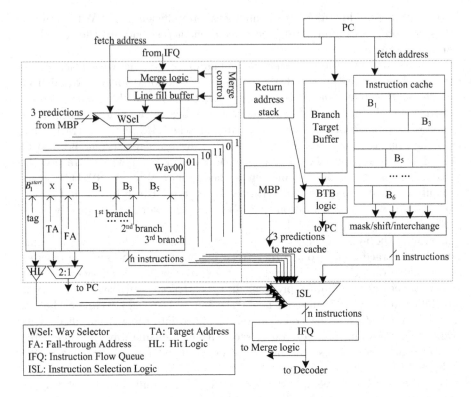

Fig. 2. Microarchitecture of six-way SWTC fetch unit

Table 1. Relationship between multiple-branch prediction and matched trace

	Prediction00	Prediction01	Prediction10	Prediction11
TC00	√			
TC01		√		
TC10			√	
TC11				√
TC0	√	√		
TC1			√	√

of trace may be valid for each multiple-branch prediction as shown in Table 1 and two corresponding ways should be activated.

Now we consider a more general case that each way can accept multiple types of traces such that the number of trace cache ways can be reduced to four. For example, Way00 can accpet not only TC00 but also TC0. In summary, each way accepts two types of traces, the relationship between cache way and trace type is as following: Way00{TC00, TC0}, Way01{TC01, TC0}, Way10{TC10,

Start Address	Trace	Target Address	Fall-through Address	Branch Flags	Branch Mask

Fig. 3. Structure of line-fill buffer

TC1}, Way11{TC11, TC1}. Now two ways should be probed simultaneously during each access. For example, upon obtaining the branch prediction result "01", both Way01 and Way00 should be probed because there may exist TC0 locating in either Way00 or Way01. Since other two ways stay in a quiescent state, approximately 50% dynamic energy consumption can be saved compared to CTC.

To select the possibly matched way or to allocate traces into the right way, a Way Selector (WSel) is needed, as shown in Fig. 2. It plays the key role in SWTC. First of all, it can be viewed as located between line-fill buffer and trace cache. To access trace cache selectively by branch prediction, it is the first requirement that all the traces are stored in different ways according to their type determined by the branch outcomes. As a result, WSel is to select one way of trace cache and put the trace from line-fill buffer to the selected way. The structure of line-fill buffer is the same as in CTC, as shown in Fig. 3. But the fill-in process is different from CTC in that the trace should be filled into the specified way with the help of WSel. While filling in a trace, Branch Flags and Branch Mask are first used by WSel to select the right way. Start Address is then used to find an entry from the selected way(s) according to the mapping rule and replacement policy. Finally the trace as well as its corresponding control information is inserted into the entry.

After allocating traces into different ways, how to extract the wanted trace at fetch stage should be considered. Now, WSel can be viewed as located between PC and trace cache. Since traces have been classified and stored into different ways according to their branch outcomes. Before access to trace cache, multiple-branch prediction from MBP is used by WSel to select and activate the possible matched ways. And at the same time, fetch address is sent to the selected ways. As presented before, two ways may be valid for each three-branch prediction. So at each fetch stage, WSel activates two ways and send fetch address the two ways to see whether there is an entry whose tag matches fetch address while leaving the other four ways stay in quiescent state. If one entry matches in the selected ways, there is trace cache hit.

If there is a trace cache hit, instructions should be fetched from the matched entry. This requires that which way hits should be known accurately. Since there are six ways in SWTC, there are six datapaths from trace cache to instruction fetch queue (IFQ). Each way has its own hit logic (HL). If there is a hit in one way, its HL will signal instruction selection logic (ISL) to select instructions from the datapath of that way correspondingly. The entire trace of instructions is then fed into IFQ and the instruction cache will be bypassed. If none of the ways hits, fetching just proceeds normally from the instruction cache.

4 Experiment and Analysis

4.1 Experimental Methodology

All the experiments were performed on a modified SimpleScalar Toolset [21]. A cycle-accurate execution-driven out-of-order simulator executing the Alpha ISA was extended to a conventional trace cache (CTC) following Fig. 1. Based on CTC, the trace cache as well as the fetch unit were redefined to simulate SWTC. The SWTC has a four-way trace cache, in which each way accept two types of trace. Each trace is defined to accommodate two or three basic blocks, up to 16 instructions. Besides, a three-branch predictor MGAg [22] capable of generating three branch predictions is also implemented to support trace cache.

We configured a highly parallelizing execution core with 128 instruction queue entries, 128 physical registers and 128 load/store queue entries. It can fetch, execute and commit as many as 16 instructions per cycle. The configuration of our simulator model is summarized in Table 2. All the experiments in our work are based on the configuration.

To evaluate energy consumption, we also augmented Wattch [23] infrastructure by including the ability to calculate the energy consumption of trace cache,

Table 2. Basic simulator model

Processor Core		Memory Hierachy	
Instruction queue	128 entries	L1 instruction cache	32KB, 4-way, LRU,
Physical register	128 entries		1-cycle latency
Load/store queue	128 entris	Trace cache	32KB, 4-way, LRU, 1-cycle
Fetch width	16 instructions		latency
Execute width	16 instructions	L1 data cache	64KB,2-way, LRU,
Commit width	16 instructions		write-back,
ALU unit	16 IntAddALU, 4 IntMult/Div		1-cycle latency
	16FPAddALU, 4 FPMulti/Div	Unified L2 cache	512KB, 4-way LRU,
	4 memory ports		write-back, 6-
Branch Predictor			cycle latency
BTB	2K-entry, 2-way	Main memory	First chunk: 128-cycle latency
RAS	32 entry	TLB	ITLB:4-way 128-entry,
Branch predictor	MGAg, 16-bit branch history		DTLB: 4-way 128-entry,
	register, 4K-entry		30-cycle miss penalty

which consists of dynamic energy consumption and static energy consumption. In our experiments, we consider that the trace cache (or one way of the cache) not in use consumes 10% of energy when in use. This setting also applies to all other ports or units, i.e., instruction cache. Fetch unit energy is defined as the sum energy consumption of instruction cache, trace cache and branch predictor (including two-level branch predictor, return address stack and branch target buffer).

All the experiments were carried out with the programs from SPEC CPU-2000INT benchmark suite and all the programs were run into competition with the MinneSPEC reduced input sets [24].

4.2   Experimental Results

The main purpose of this work is to reduce the overall energy consumption of trace cache so as to reduce energy consumption of fetch unit. Fig. 4 shows the trace cache energy consumption of one instruction for the benchmarks. The energy consumption consists of two parts, dynamic energy consumption and static energy consumption. The lower part of each bar shows the dynamic energy consumption of trace cache for each program while the higher part shows the static energy consumption. In Fig. 4, we observe that SWTC saves 46.1% dynamic energy of CTC on average, which is consistent with the analysis in section 3. But this can not demonstrate the energy efficiency of SWTC since energy consumption consists of dynamic and static energy consumption. However, keeping some ways of trace cache quiescent will increase the static energy component that can not be ignored. Furthermore, static energy consumption is linearly with the execution time. Taking both static and dynamic energy into consideration, the energy reduction of SWTC is still significant. For example, SWTC can save up to 45.2% on the dynamic energy and 36.0% on the overall energy for gcc compared to CTC. For the overall trace cache energy consumption over all benchmark programs, SWTC can save 39.2% energy consumption of CTC.

When it comes to the overall fetch unit energy consumption, both instruction cache and branch predictor are also taken into account with trace cache. Fig. 5 shows our experimental results of average fetch unit energy consumption of one instruction for each benchmark program. Thanks to the energy reduction in the trace cache of SWTC, SWTC also shows energy efficiency advantage over CTC on the whole fetch unit. SWTC has an average energy reduction of 20.1% compared to CTC. From Fig. 5, we ,can conclude that we have achieved our first goal, to reduce the overall energy consumption of fetch unit.

However, we can not analyze energy consumption without consideration of performance. First of all, a good architecture should reduce energy consumption while maintaining the performance. On the other hand, recall that energy consumption is approximately linear with the execution time that the performance also has some influence on the energy consumption. Fig. 6 depicts performance of SWTC and CTC for each benchmark in terms of number of Instruction Per Cycle (IPC). From Fig. 6, we can see that SWTC has almost the same IPC with CTC for all benchmark programs. The simulation result shows that SWTC can

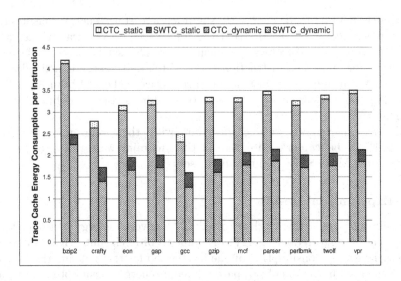

Fig. 4. Average Trace Cache Energy Consumption comparison between CTC and SWTC

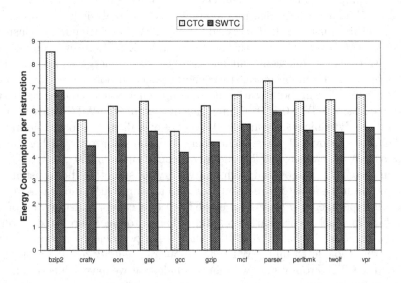

Fig. 5. Average Fetch Unit Energy Consumption comparison between CTC and SWTC

achieve 1.2% close to the performance of CTC. The result is consistent with our analysis in Section 3.2 that SWTC may suffer little performance degradation compared to CTC. Now, we can conclude that SWTC is a good solution to design both performance efficient and energy efficient processor with trace cache.

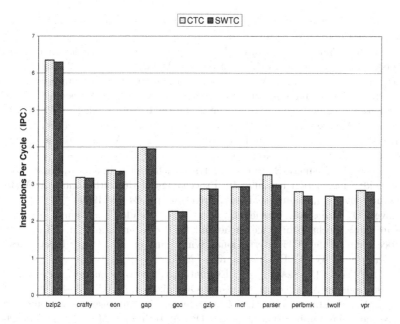

Fig. 6. Performance comparison between CTC and SWTC, measured in Instruction Per Cycle(IPC)

5   Conclusion

In this paper, we have discussed a selective way based trace cache (SWTC) principle, in which traces are divided into several types according to their branch outcomes. Traces are stored into different ways by type. In the fetch cycle, multiple-branch prediction is used as trace type prediction to select the possible matched ways. Only selected ways are activated while leaving other unselected ways in a quiescent state to achieve energy saving. Based on the SWTC principle, a microarchitectural model is also proposed and evaluated in this paper. Simulation results show that compared to CTC, SWTC can reduce energy consumption on the fetch unit by 20.1% on average, while providing almost the same performance in terms of number of instructions per cycle. The measurement testifies the soundness of SWTC principle and implies that SWTC is an efficient solution to design performance and energy efficient processor with trace cache. Beyond the model proposed in this paper, the principle of SWTC can be applied to other architectures with trace cache and can be also integrated with the other energy efficient optimization technique to trace cache to reduce energy consumption further.

References

1. Tseng, F., Patt, Y.N.: Achieving Out-of-Order Performance with Almost In-Order Complexity. In: ISCA 2008: Proceedings of the 35th International Symposium on Computer Architecture, pp. 3–12. IEEE Computer Society, Los Alamitos (2008)

2. Wilcox, K., Manne, S.: Alpha processors: A history of power issues and a look to the future Cool-Chips. Tutorial (1999)
3. Manne, S., Klauser, A., Grunwald, D.: Pipeline gating: speculation control for energy reduction. ACM SIGARCH Comput. Archit. News 26, 132–141 (1998)
4. Yeh, T., Marr, D.T., Patt, Y.N.: Increasing the instruction fetch rate via multiple branch prediction and a branch address cache. In: ICS 1993: Proceedings of the 7th international conference on Supercomputing, pp. 67–76. ACM, New York (1993)
5. Conte, T., Menezes, K., Mills, P., Patel, B.: Optimization of instruction fetch mechanisms for high issue rates. In: Proceedings of the 22nd Annual International Symposium on Computer Architecture, pp. 333–344 (1995)
6. Rotenberg, E., Bennett, S., Smith, J.: Trace cache: a low latency approach to high bandwidth instruction fetching. In: Proceedings of the 29th annual ACM/IEEE international symposium on Microarchitecture, pp. 24–35 (1996)
7. Chaver, D., Rojas, M., Pinuel, L., Prieto, M., Tirado, F., Huang, M.: Energy-aware fetch mechanism: trace cache and BTB customization. In: ISLPED 2005. Proceedings of the 2005 International Symposium on Low Power Electronics and Design, pp. 42–47. IEEE, Los Alamitos (2005)
8. Co, M., Weikle, D., Skadron, K.: Evaluating trace cache energy efficiency. ACM Transactions on Architecture and Code Optimization (TACO) 3, 450–476 (2006)
9. Hu, J., Vijaykrishnan, N., Irwin, M., Kandemir, M.: Optimising power efficiency in trace cache fetch unit. Computers and Digital Techniques, IET 1, 334–348 (2007)
10. Kim, C., Hwang, I., Chae, C., Choi, D., Jung, T., Chung, S.: Energy-Effective Instruction Fetch Unit for Embedded Processors. In: 5th IEEE Consumer Communications and Networking Conference, 2008. CCNC 2008, pp. 734–735 (2008)
11. Hinton, G., Sager, D., Upton, M., Boggs, D., Carmean, D., Kyker, A., Roussel, P.: The microarchitecture of the Pentium 4 processor. Intel Technology Journal 5, 1–13 (2001)
12. Albonesi, D.: Selective cache ways: On-demand cache resource allocation. In: Proceedings. 32nd Annual International Symposium on Microarchitecture, 1999. MICRO-32, pp. 248–259 (1999)
13. Inoue, K., Ishihara, T., Murakami, K.: Way-predicting set-ssociative cache for high performance and low energy consumption. In: Proceedings of the 1999 international symposium on Low power electronics and design, pp. 273–275. ACM, New York (1999)
14. Powell, M., Agarwal, A., Vijaykumar, T., Falsafi, B., Roy, K.: Reducing set-associative cache energy via way-prediction and selective direct-mapping. In: Proceedings of the 34th annual ACM/IEEE international symposium on Microarchitecture, pp. 54–65 (2001)
15. Kosyakovsky, O., Mendelson, A., Kolodny, A.: The Use of Profile-based Trace Classification for Improving the Power and Performance of Trace Cache Systems. In: 4th Workshop on Feedback-Directed and Dynamic Optimization (2001)
16. Behar, M., Mendelson, A., Kolodny, A.: Trace cache sampling filter. ACM Trans. Comput. Syst. 25, 3 (2007)
17. Hu, J., Irwin, M., Vijaykrishnan, N., Kandemir, M.: Selective Trace Cache: A Low Power and High Performance Fetch Mechanism. Pennsylvania State University, Dept. of Computer Science and Engineering, College of Engineering (2002)
18. Hu, J., Vijaykrishnan, N., Irwin, M., Kandemir, M.: Using dynamic branch behavior for power-efficient instruction fetch. In: IEEE Computer Society Annual Symposium on VLSI, 2003. Proceedings, pp. 127–132 (2003)

19. Jang, H.B., Choi, L., Chung, S.W.: A Trace Cache with DVFS Techniques for a Low Power Microprocessor. In: ICCIT 2008: Proceedings of the 2008 Third International Conference on Convergence and Hybrid Information Technology, pp. 587–592. IEEE Computer Society, Los Alamitos (2008)
20. Hennessy, J., Patterson, D., Goldberg, D., Asanovic, K.: Computer Architecture: A Quantitative Approach, 4th edn., p. 129. Morgan Kaufmann, San Francisco (2003)
21. Burger, D., Austin, T.: The SimpleScalar Tool Set, Version 2.0
22. Yeh, T., Patt, Y.: Alternative implementations of two-level adaptive branch prediction. In: International Symposium on Computer Architecture, pp. 451–461 (1998)
23. Brooks, D., Tiwari, V., Martonosi, M.: Wattch: a framework for architectural-level power analysis and optimizations. In: Proceedings of the 27th annual international symposium on Computer architecture, pp. 83–94 (2000)
24. KleinOsowski, A., Lilja, D.: MinneSPEC: A New SPEC Benchmark Workload for Simulation-Based Computer Architecture Research. Computer Architecture Letters 1, 10–13 (2002)

A Fine-Grained Pipelined Implementation for Large-Scale Matrix Inversion on FPGA

Jie Zhou[1], Yong Dou[1], Jianxun Zhao[2], Fei Xia[1], Yuanwu Lei[1],
and Yuxing Tang[1]

[1] National Laboratory for Parallel & Distributed Processing, NUDT, Changsha,
P.R. China, 410073
{zhoujie,yongdou,xcyphoenix,yuanwulei,tangyuxing}@nudt.edu.cn
[2] Academy of Armored Forces Engineering, Beijing, China, 100072
ajianbear@163.com

Abstract. Large-scale matrix inversion play an important role in many
applications. However to the best of our knowledge, there is no
FPGA-based implementation. In this paper, we explore the possibility of
accelerating large-scale matrix inversion on FPGA. To exploit the computational potential of FPGA, we introduce a fine-grained parallel algorithm for matrix inversion. A scalable linear array processing elements
(PEs), which is the core component of the FPGA accelerator, is proposed to implement this algorithm. A total of 12 PEs can be integrated
into an Altera StratixII EP2S130F1020C5 FPGA on our self-designed
board. Experimental results show that a factor of 2.6 speedup and the
maximum power-performance of 41 can be achieved compare to Pentium
Dual CPU with double SSE threads.

1 Introduction

Large-scale matrix inversion is widely used in many fields, such as signal processing [8][17], large image processing [9], computational fluid dynamics [2] and
computational structure dynamics [15]. But it is a tremendous time-consuming
algorithm with the computation complexity of $O(n^3)$. To accelerate it, the traditional methods tie to parallel programming executing on parallel computers
[1][4][16][19][11]. In contrast, the FPGA-based design for large-scale matrix inversion has not been previously reported.

Recently, many works [18][7][14][5][6][3] have been spent on studying how to
implement small-scale (4×4 etc) or mid-scale (64×64 etc) matrix inversion on
FPGA. Small-scale matrix inversion is usually used in the real-time systems. To
satisfy the computation speed, two-dimension systolic structure array including
$O(n^2)$ processing elements is generally adopted [18][7][14]. It can achieve high
parallelzation and performance, but consumes a mass of hardware resources. For
the limitation of chip area and power dissipation, it is hard to map a mid-scale
matrix inversion into a full pipeline of two-dimension systolic structure array
currently [12]. To implement mid-scale matrix inversion, researchers have proposed various mapping and folding approaches to fold the two-dimension systolic

Y. Dou, R. Gruber, and J. Joller (Eds.): APPT 2009, LNCS 5737, pp. 110–122, 2009.
© Springer-Verlag Berlin Heidelberg 2009

structure into one-dimension [5][6][3]. [5] maps the traditional triangular array architectures employing $O(n^2)$ processing elements onto a scalable linear array architecture with $O(n)$ processing elements. And the mapping and folding methods introduced in [6][3] are similar to [5]. However, the number of the processing elements is increasing with the matrix size.

In this paper, we explore the possibility of accelerating large-scale matrix inversion on FPGA. For this purpose, there exists two main challenges: limited external DRAM bandwidth and on-chip memory resource. On the one hand, a mass of on-chip storage is needed for large-scale matrix inversion to reduce the external DRAM access. And on the other hand, the limited on-chip storage cannot hold all $O(n^2)$ matrices, especially for large ones, resulting in long-latency data load from external DRAM. For limited external DRAM bandwidth, this paper proposes a fine-grained parallel algorithm which introduces none extra external DRAM access with varying the number of PEs. And we design the accelerator system as Ping-Pong DRAM structure to double the DRAM access bandwidth. For the bottleneck of on-chip memory, we present dynamic access mechanism to reuse the FPGA memory blocks, which can save one half of on-chip storage. Furthermore, we propose a hardware design on FPGA for large-scale matrix inversion fine-grained pipeline implementation with Givens Rotation, which is based on a scalable linear array of processing elements. Our hardware design for fine-grained design has implemented into an Altera StratixII EP2S130F1020C5 FPGA on our self-designed development board with two 1 GB SDRAMs running at 100 MHz. A total of 12 PEs can be integrated into this FPGA, on which the run time of matrix inversion for size of 4096×4096 is 106.404s, outperforming the performance of 2.0GHz Pentium Dual CPU with double SSE threads by the factor of 2.6. Moreover, our design can achieve 41 times of the power-performance efficiency compare with the Pentium Dual CPU. Note that one PE in this paper includes one FGR-PE and one InvMul-PE, which are used to operate the QR decomposition and up-triangular matrix inversion and matrix multiplication respectively.

The remainder of this paper is organized as follows. Section 2 gives some brief background and related work. Section 3 describes the fine-grained parallel algorithm and performance model. Section 4 presents the fine-grained pipeline FPGA implementation for matrix inversion. Section 5 provides the experimental results and section 6 concludes this paper.

2   Fine-Grained Parallel Algorithm and Performance Model

In this section, we present a fine-grained parallel algorithm by analyzing the data dependency of QRD-based matrix inversion and a model to project performance.

2.1   Fast Givens Rotation

Many fields, such as signal processing [10][13], image processing [9], need QR-based matrix inversion which are a class of algorithms with good numerical

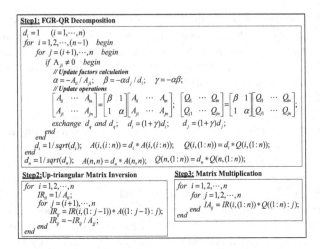

Fig. 1. Matrix inversion with fast Givens Rotation

stability. And Givens Rotation is most stable algorithm of QR decomposition and more suitable for fine-grained implementation on FPGA [20]. So we choose the matrix inversion with fast Givens Rotation (FGR) as our implementation algorithm. Figure 1 shows the algorithm of matrix inversion with fast Givens Rotation, which is composed of QR decomposition, up-triangular matrix inversion and matrix multiplication. The first step produces the up-triangular matrix A (covering the raw matrix) and the transpose of orthogonal matrix Q. The second step execute the calculation of up-triangular matrix inversion and matrix multiplication is operated in the third step.

2.2 Data Dependency of QRD-Based Matrix Inversion

Figure 2 illustrates the data dependency of fast Givens Rotation shown the first step of Figure 1. Here, $up(i,j)$ of the left part denotes the jth inner loop of the ith outer loop and $op(i,k)$ of the right part denotes one update operation. The inner loops of one outer loop must be calculated in sequence and the calculation of the ith outer loop depends the i-1's results. But further analysis reveals that the ith outer loop can be started as soon as the needed update result is produced by the $(i$-$1)th$ outer loop, as shown in the right part of Figure 2. That is to say, we can extract pipeline parallelism between the successive outer loops for fast Givens Rotation.

We suppose that matrix IR is the inversion of up-triangular matrix R. Figure 3 shows the data dependency for calculating one element of IR. The calculation of IR_{ij} needs the jth column of R and the produced elements of ith row of IR. Furthermore, the elements of IR should be stored in external memory for large number of data. To avoid storing of IR by combining up-triangular inversion and matrix multiplication, we develop another version of up-triangular inversion as the third step shown in Figure 1. For differentiating, we call it as

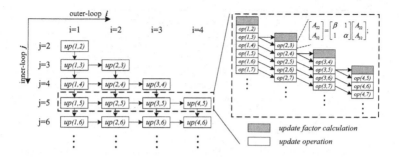

Fig. 2. Data dependency of fast Givens Rotation

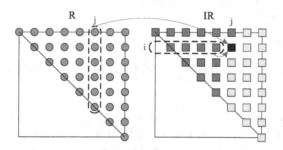

Fig. 3. Data dependency of up-triangular matrix inversion

row-oriented up-triangular matrix inversion for it produces the elements of IR row by row.

2.3   Fine-Grained Parallel Algorithm

As implied by Figure 2, the outer loops can be executed by fine-grained pipeline in parallel. For load balance, we adopt the "one-row-cyclic" task partitioning in this paper, where each PE holds one outer loop cyclically in turn. Let n and p be the size of raw matrix A and the total number of PEs respectively, assuming that p is less than n. By four-phase organization, Figure 4 describes the fine-grained parallel fast Givens Rotation algorithm in a Single Program Multiple Data (SPMD) style with message passing primitives. And the primary message primitives are defined as:

$Load(pid,X)$: PE(pid) loads array X from external DRAM;
$\overline{Store(pid,X)}$: PE(pid)stores array X to external DRAM;
$\overline{Store\_QR(pid,X,Y)}$: PE($pid$)stores array X and Y to external DRAM;
$\overline{Send(pid,X)}$: send array X to PE(pid);
$\overline{Rcv(pid,X)}$: receive array X from PE(pid);

The fist part of Figure 4 shows variable, parameter definitions and symbol illuminations. At the initial phase, each FGR-PE assigns its PE identifier, pid, to the row index indicating the initial row assignment. Here, each FGR-PE updates

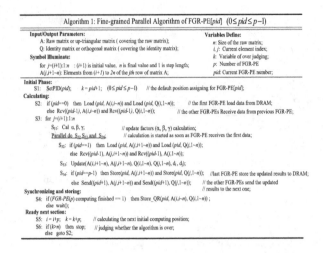

Fig. 4. The fine-grained parallel algorithm for FGR-PE[pid]

the assigned row with all rows behind it in sequence and finally produces one row of matrix R and Q. The first FGR-PE loads data from external DRAM and the others receive data from their previous ones as shown in S32. And as shown in S34, the last FGR-PE stores the updated results to external DRAM, the others send their updated results to the next ones. Each updated result of FGR-PE[pid] is sent to the next one as soon as it is produced. And each FGR-PE is driven when receiving the first effective data. Therefore, S32, S33 and S34 can be executed in parallel. When one row of matrix R and Q are produced, the FGR-PE enters the synchronizing and storing phase. When the last FGR-PE completes all update operations, indicating all FGR-PEs complete the update task assigned, the final results of matrix R and Q are stored to external DRAM. In ready next section phase, each FGR-PE adds p to its row index and judges whether it accomplishes all tasks assigned.

To avoid storing inversion of up-triangular matrix to external DRAM, we intercross the calculation of up-triangular matrix inversion and matrix multiplication. Similar to fast Givens Rotation, Figure 5 lays out the description of fine-grained parallel up-triangular matrix inversion and matrix multiplication algorithm in a SPMD style. Each InvMul-PE produces one row of inversion of up-triangular matrix and one row of inversion of the raw matrix. What's more, its execution procedure resembles to FGR-PE. But each InvMul-PE sends data, received from the previous InvMul-PE, to the next one directly except the last InvMul-PE.

2.4 Performance Model

In this sub-section, we analyze the scalability of proposed parallel algorithm detailedly. And in our performance model, a single linear array is considered.

Algorithm 2: Fine-grained Parallel Up-Triangular Matrix Inversion and Matrix
Multiplication Algorithm of InvMul-PE[*pid*] (1≤ *pid* ≤ *p*)

Input Parameters:	**Variables Define:**
R: Upper triangular matrix; Q: Orthonormal matrix;	*n*: Size of the raw matrix;
Output Parameters:	*i,j*: Current element index;
IA: Inversion of the raw matrix;	*p*: Number of InvMul-PE
Symbol Illuminate:	*k*: Variable of over judging;
for *j*=1:1:*n* : 1 is initial value, *n* is final value and 1 is step length;	*pid*: Current PE number;
R((1:*j*-1),*j*) : Elements from *1* to (*j-1*) of the *j*th column of matrix R;	IR: Inverse matrix of R;
Q(*,*j*): The *j*th column of matrix Q;	

Initial Phase:
S1: SetPID(*pid*); *k* = *pid*+1;   (1≤ *pid* ≤ *p*);   // the default position assigning for InvMul-PE[*pid*];
Inversion Calculating:
S2: if (*pid* == 1)   then Load (*pid*, R(*i,i*));   // the first InvMul-PE load data from DRAM;
      else Receive (*pid*-1, R(*i,i*));   // the other InvMul-PEs Receive data from the previous one;
S3: Cal IR(*i,i*);
S4: for *j*=(*i*+1):1:*n*
      Parallel do S₄₁, S₄₂ and S₄₃;   // calculation is started as soon as InvMul-PE receives the first data;
      S₄₁: if (*pid*==1)   then Load (*pid*, R((1:*j*-1),*j*));
            else Receive (*pid*-1, R((1:*j*-1),*j*));
      S₄₂: Cal IR(*i,j*);
      S₄₃: if (*pid* != *p*) then Send (*pid*+1, R((1:*j*-1),*j*));   // send R((1:*j*-1),j) to the next InvMul-PE as soon as
                                                                                            // receiving from the the previous one, except the last one;
Matrix Multiplication:
S5: for *j*=1:1:*n*
      Parallel do S₅₁, S₅₂ and S₅₃;   // calculation is started as soon as InvMul-PE receives the first data;
      S₅₁: if (*pid*==1)   then Load (*pid*, Q(*,*j*));
            else Receive (*pid*-1, Q(*,*j*));
      S₅₂: Cal IA(*i,j*);
      S₅₃: if (*pid* != *p*) then Send (*pid*+1, Q(*,*j*));   // send the *j*th row of Q to the next InvMul-PE as soon as
                                                                                            // receiving from the previous one, except the last one;
Synchronizing and storing:
S6: if (InvMul-*PE*(*p*) computing finished == 1) then Store (*pid*, IA(*i*,*));   // store the *i*th row of IA to DRAM ;
      else wait;
Ready next section:
S7: *i* = *i*+*p*;   *k* = *k*+*p*;   // calculating the next initial computing position;
S8: if (*k*>*n*) then stop; else goto S2;   // judging whether the algorithm is over;

Fig. 5. The fine-grained parallel algorithm for InvMul-PE[pid]

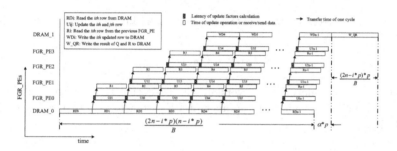

Fig. 6. Time estimation for fine-grained pipeline of fast Givens Rotation

To analyze the scalability of the proposed fine-grained fast Givens Rotation parallel algorithm, we built an analytical performance model for one sweep execution as shown in Figure 6. And here, we call one outer loop execution of all FGR-PEs as one sweep. The overhead of data communication among FGR-PEs is almost fully overlapped with pipelined computation. And efficiency of the pipeline is mainly limited by the external DRAM access bandwidth. To present the parallel algorithm's performance and scalability, we assume the following notations: (1) n - size of the matrix; (2) p - the number of FGR-PE, here $n >> p$; (3) α - pipeline depth of update operation, and $n >> \alpha$; (4) B - external DRAM access bandwidth; (5) F - execution frequency. Then the execution time of one sweep mainly consists of external DRAM read, pipeline flushing of update operation and external DRAM writing of Q and R results. For the ith sweep, the corresponding overheads are $(2n - i*p)(n - i*p)/B$, $\alpha*p/F$ and $(2n - i*p)*p/B$ respectively. That is to say, the execution time of the ith sweep of matrix R and Q is:

$$T_i = \frac{(2n^2 + 2np) - (np - p^2)i + p^2i^2}{B} + \frac{\alpha p}{F} \tag{1}$$

Here $0 \leq i \leq s$ and $s = \lfloor n/p \rfloor$.

Then the total execution time is:

$$T_{FGR} = T_0 + T_1 + \cdots + T_s = \frac{5n^3}{6pB} + \frac{5n^2}{B} - \frac{5np}{6B} + \frac{\alpha n}{F} \tag{2}$$

Since $n >> p$ and $n >> \alpha$, the total execution time can be approximately considered as:

$$T_{FGR} = \frac{5n^3}{6pB} \tag{3}$$

Similar to fast Givens Rotation parallel algorithm, the execution time of up-triangular matrix inversion and matrix multiplication is:

$$T_{InvMul} = \frac{2n^3}{3pB} \tag{4}$$

Then the total execution time of the parallel algorithm of matrix inversion is:

$$T = T_{FGR} + T_{InvMul} = \frac{3n^3}{2pB} \tag{5}$$

So, for the large-scale matrix inversion, the execution time of our parallel algorithm is increasing with the number of PEs, showing good parallelism and scalability.

3   Hardware Implementation on FPGA

Based on the proposed fine-grained parallel algorithm, we present a scalable linear array structure for large-scale matrix inversion and its FPGA implementation in this section.

3.1   Hardware Structure

As shown in Figure 7, the structure for large-scale matrix inversion is mainly composed of an FPGA chip, two SDRAM modules and one I/O channel to the host PC. The FPGA chip integrates a linear array of PEs, SDRAM Controller, Phase Controller and on-chip memories, including Rams and FIFOs. We set two SDRAM modules in order to double the SDRAM access bandwidth and form full pipeline structure. The I/O channel is responsible for transferring the initial data, final results and the commands between the accelerator and the host.

The on-chip memories, Rams, are used to store the middle or final results of one row of matrix R and Q during the QR decomposition phase. And they are used to store one row of inversion of up-triangular matrix or raw matrix

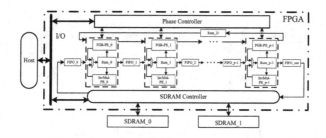

Fig. 7. Structure for fine-grained pipeline implementation

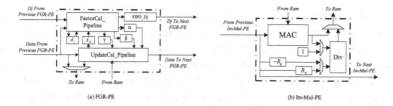

(a) FGR-PE   (b) InvMul-PE

Fig. 8. The structure of FGR-PE and InvMul-PE

during up-triangular matrix inversion and matrix multiplication phase. So the capability of RAM block is increasing with the matrix size. The two phases are not executed at the same time. Therefore, Rams and FIFOs, connecting the PEs and SDRAM controller, can be reused and nearly one half of on-chip RAM blocks will be saved.

The computational core of the FPGA matrix inversion accelerator is a cluster of FGR-PEs and InvMul-PEs, as shown in Figure 8. FGR-PEs produce matrix R and Q and InvMul-PEs execute the computation of the inversion of up-triangular matrix and matrix multiplication. FGR-PE is composed of FactorCal_Pipeline module, FIFO_Dj, UpdateCal_Pipeline module, a selector and some registers. FactorCal_Pipeline module performs the update factors (α, β and γ) calculation and updates the parameters $d_i(1 \leq i \leq n)$ receiving from the previous FGR-PE. FIFO_Dj is used to cache parameters d_j ($i < j \leq n$), which will send the next FGR-PE for further updating. The updated data executing by UpdateCal_Pipeline module include two parts, one loaded from Ram and the other received from the previous FGR-PE. And the corresponding results are stored back into Ram and sent to the next FGR-PE separately. When all update tasks is completed, the final results, one row of matrix R and Q, stay in Ram. InvMul-PE, which is simpler compared to FGR-PE, is mainly composed of Multiply-Add Cumulation (MAC), division module, a selector and some registers. MAC module executes the Multiply-Add-Cumulation operations during the up-triangular inversion and matrix multiplication. And the division module performs the division operations during up-triangular inversion. Finally, one row of the raw matrix inversion is stored in Ram.

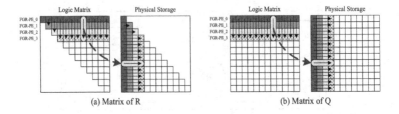

(a) Matrix of R   (b) Matrix of Q

Fig. 9. Storage methods of R and Q

3.2 Storage Method of Matrix R and Q

In QR decomposition phase, each FGR-PE produces one row of matrix R and Q^T (transposition matrix of Q). But matrix R and Q^T need to be accessed by column during up-triangular matrix inversion and matrix multiplication phase. If we store the results of R and Q^T in sequence of row, n times of row-store operations are needed. However, $(n^2 - p^2)/2p$ times of column-load operation are needed during up-triangular matrix inversion and matrix multiplication phase. And the bandwidth of column access is about $1/8$ of that of row access [21]. So we store the results of R and Q^T in sequence of column. To store the columns efficiently, we pack the produced elements of the same column by FGR-PEs into one packet and store the results packet by packet, as shown in Figure 9. Suppose that the number of FGR-PE is p and the extra cyclic of once storage is λ, then the element number of each packet is p and $(\lambda + p)/(\lambda + 1)$ times of storage efficiency can be achieved. So the efficiency of column storage is increase with the number of FGR-PE.

4 Experimental Results

We implement the fine-grained pipeline accelerator for matrix inversion on our self-designed development board, which is composed of an FPGA chip of Altera Stratix EP2S130F1020C5, two 1GB SDRAMs of Micron MT16LSDT12864A and an USB 2.0 interface to the Host. All modules including FGR-PE, InvMul-PE, Phase Controller, SDRAM Controller and USB 2.0 interface are coded in Verilog and synthesized with Altera QuartusII 6.0. And the power dissipations are estimated by PowerPlay Power Analyzer. In addition, we measure the software execution time on the platforms of 2.80GHz Intel Celeron CPU and 2.0GHz Intel(R) Pentium Dual CPU E2180 with.

4.1 FPGA Resources Usage

The scalable array FPGA accelerator is implemented by parameterized design methodology, which makes them execute the problems of different size, and the maximum size is 4096 × 4096. Then a tool is designed to automatically generate Verilog codes that describe the connection between the Verilog modules. So we

Table 1. Single precision floating-point operations circuit statistics

	Adder	Multiplier	Divider	SquareRoot
Pipeline depth	8	3)	13	25
ALUTs)	554	107	1791	1152
Registers	365	91	921	1056
DSP Blocks	0	8	0	0
Frequency(MHz)	227.32	164.17	150.35	255.95

Table 2. Synthesis results for different modules

	SDRAM Controller	USB 2.0 Controller	FGR-PE	InvMul-PE
ALUTs)	458	952	4888	3130
Registers	363	612	3278	1848
Memory Bits	13824	2048	2647	801
M4Ks	0	0	2	0
DSP Blocks	0	0	24	8
Fmax(MHz)	213.86	206.36	130.07	130.67
Power Dissipation (mW)	54.98	49.75	530.79	529.11

can specify the number of PEs to generate different length of linear arrays. In addition, the two SDRAMs operate in Ping-Pong model so that the current step's output data will be input data for the next step, speeding up the pipeline of PEs.

The synthesis results of single precision floating-point operation, which are resource-consuming, are shown in Table 1. The floating-point divider may occupy more areas than the other operations and also be the critical path of the hardware design. Table 2 details the synthesis results for different modules implemented on FPGA. The frequency of SDRAM controller and USB2.0 interface modules is higher than 200MHz, while the power dissipations are about 50 mW.

Figure 10 illustrates the resources utilization ratio, power dissipation and frequency of the hardware design with varying number of PEs. To operate large-scale matrix inversion, the local storages are implemented using M4Ks and M-RAMs blocks. And to utilize the RAM blocks efficiently, we firstly try to use the M4Ks blocks and then M-RAMs blocks. As shown in Figure 10, a total of 12 PEs can be integrated into one EP2S130F1020C5 FPGA chip due to the limitation of ALUTs, M4Ks and M-RAMs resources. But for larger matrix inversion implementation, such as $8k \times 8k$, the M4Ks and M-RAMs blocks will be the limited resources. In addition, the utilization of other resources are increasing linearly with the number of PEs. The right part of Figure 10 shows that the power dissipation also increases linearly as the number of PEs increases. And the power dissipation of the 12-PE accelerator is 4031mW . However, as the number of PEs increases from 1 to 12, the degradation in achievable maximum frequency is less 13%. The achievable maximum frequency is 103Mhz for the hardware design of 12 PEs, which can still correctly operate at 100MHz on our development board.

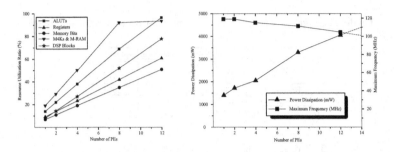

Fig. 10. Resource utilization ratio, power dissipation and frequency with varying number of PEs

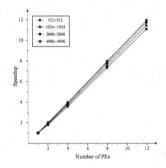

Fig. 11. Speedup with varying the number of PEs

4.2 Performance

Figure 11 shows the speedup of the scalable linear array FPGA accelerator for matrix inversion comparing to one PE. More detailedly, our FPGA accelerator can achieve nearly linear speedup, but introduces none external DRAM access bandwidth with the number of PEs. Furthermore, the speedup of 4096×4096 matrix is larger than that of 512×512 matrix. Because the external DRAM bandwidth is increasing with the size of matrix and the larger matrix can use the external DRAM bandwidth and calculation pipelines more efficiently.

Table 3 shows the execution time on 2.80GHz Intel Celeron CPU, 2.0GHz Intel(R) Pentium Dual CPU E2180 and our FPGA accelerator running at 100MHz

Table 3. Performance and speedup on different platforms

		512×512		1024×1024		2048×2048		4096×4096	
		Time(s)	Sp	Time(s)	Sp	Time(s)	Sp	Time(s)	Sp
Celeron	C++	3.907	1.000	30.844	1.000	242.734	1.000	1862.539	1.000
	SSE(1)	1.407	2.777	10.797	2.857	81.282	2.986	616.813	3.020
Pentium	C++	3.187	1.226	25.781	1.196	203.953	1.190	1703.635	1.093
	SSE(1)	0.578	6.760	4.687	6.581	39.422	6.157	306.797	6.071
	SSE(2)	0.531	7.358	4.031	7.652	34.891	6.957	265.245	7.022
FPGA accelerator		0.236	16.555	1.758	17.545	13.551	17.931	106.404	17.504

platforms. The 2.80 Intel Celeron CPU has the features of 1GB Memory, 12kB L1 cache and 256kB L2 cache. And the Intel(R) Pentium Dual CPU E2180 has the features of 1GB Memory, 32kB*2 L1 cache and 1MB L2 cache. For general-purpose CPUs, the C++ code is written in VC++ 6.0 environment and compiled into release version. And SSE(1) and SSE(2) in Table 3 denote single- and double-thread with SSE separately. For the hardware platform, the FPGA accelerator is consisted of 12 PEs. Taking C++ code on Celeron CPU as the base, our FPGA accelerator can achieve more than 17 times speedup on average. And compare to Pentium Dual CPU with double SSE threads, our FPGA accelerator also can achieve the factor of 2.6 times speedup. Moreover, the power dissipation of 12-PE accelerator is 4.031W. That is say, the FPGA accelerator can reach the maximum power-performance of 41 than the Pentium Dual CPU with the power dissipation of 65W.

5   Conclusion

This paper presents an FPGA implementation for large-scale matrix inversion. And to the best of our knowledge, this is the first reported FPGA-based implementation. To exploit the computational potential of FPGA, we propose a fine-grained parallel algorithm. And a scalable linear array of PEs is introduced to implement the proposed parallel algorithm on our self-designed board. What's more, one half of on-chip memory resource can be save due to the reusing of RAM blocks. The experimental results show that linear array accelerator can achieve nearly linear speedup with the number of PEs. And compare to Pentium Dual CPU with double SSE threads, our FPGA accelerator can achieve a factor of 2.6 times speedup and the maximum power-performance of 41.

Acknowledgments

This work is supported in part by the National Science Foundation of China through grants 60633050 and 60833004.

References

1. Bailey, D.H., Ferguson, H.R.: A strassen-newton algorithm for high-speed parallelizable matrix inversion. In: Proceedings of Supercomputing 1988, pp. 419–424. IEEE, Los Alamitos (November 1988)
2. Batchelor, G.: Introduction to Fluid Dynamics, 2nd edn. Cambridge University Press, Cambridge (2000)
3. Bigdeli, A., Biglari-Abhari, M., Salcic, Z., Lai, Y.T.: A new pipelined systolic array-based architecture for matrix inversion in fpgas with kalman filter case study. EURASIP Journal on Applied Signal Processing archive 2006(1), 75 (2006)
4. Caron, E., Utard, G.: Parallel out-of-core matrix inversion. In: Proceedings of International Parallel and Distributed Processing Symposium (IPDPS 2002), pp. 71–76 (2002)

5. Echman, F., Owall, V.: A scalable pipelined complex valued matrix inversion architecture. In: IEEE International Symposium on Circuits and Systems, vol. 5, pp. 4489–4492 (2005)
6. Edman, F., Owall, V.: Implementation of a scalable matrix inversion architecture for triangular matrices. In: 14th IEEE Proceedings on Personal, Indoor and Mobile Radio Communications, vol. 3, pp. 2558–2562 (2003)
7. El-Amawy, A.: A systolic architecture for fast dense matrix inversion. IEEE Transactions on Computers 38(3), 449–455 (1989)
8. Farina, A., Timmoneri, L.: Parallel algorithms and processing architectures for space-time adaptive processing. In: Proceedings of CIE International Conference of Radar, pp. 770–774 (1996)
9. Fischer, B., Modersitzki, J.: Fast inversion of matrices arising in image processing. Computer Science 22(1), 1–11 (1999)
10. LaRoche, I., Roy, S.: A efficient regular matrix inversion circuit architecture for mimo processing. In: Proceedings of IEEE International Symposium on Circuits and Systems, May 2006, pp. 4819–4822 (2006)
11. Lau, K., Kumar, M., Venkatesh, S.: Parallel matrix inversion techniques. In: Proceedings of the 16th Annual Symposium on Foundations of Computer Science, October 1975, pp. 11–12 (1975)
12. Lightbody, G., Walke, R., Woods, R., McCanny, J.: Linear qr architecture for a single chip adaptive beamformer. Journal of VLSI Signal Processing Systems archive 24(1), 67–81 (2000)
13. Lim, C.H., Mulgrew, B.: Prediction of inverse covariance matrix (picm) sequences for stap. IEEE Signal Processing Letters 13(4), 236–239 (2006)
14. Milovanovic, E., Milovanovic, I., Stojcev, M., Jovanovic, G.: Fault-tolerant matrix inversion on processor array. Electronics Letters 28(13), 1206–1208 (1992)
15. Ojalvo, I.: Proper use of lanczos vectors for large eigenvalue problems. Computers & Structures 20(1-3), 115–120 (1985)
16. Quintana, E.S., Quintana, G., Sun, X., van de Geijn, R.: Efficient matrix inversion via gauss-jordan elimination and its parallelization. Technical Report TR-98-19, Dept. of Computer Sciences, The University of Texas at Austin (1998)
17. Rabideau, D., Kogon, S.: A signal processing architecture for space-based gmti radar. In: The Record of the 1999 IEEE Radar Conference, pp. 96–101 (1999)
18. Singh, C.K., Prasad, S.H., Balsara, P.T.: Vlsi architecture for matrix inversion using modified gram-schmidt based qr decomposition. In: 20th International Conference on VLSI Design, pp. 836–841 (2007)
19. Xiaodong, W., Roychowdhury, V.: Minimizing communication overhead for matrix inversion algorithms on hypercubes. In: Proceedings of the 9th International Parallel Processing Symposium, April 1995, pp. 446–450 (1995)
20. Yong, D., Jie, Z., Xiaoyang, C., Yuanwu, L., Jinbo, X.: Fpga accelerating three qr decomposition algorithms in the unified pipelined framework. In: FPL 2009 (2009)
21. Yong, D., Jie, Z., Yuanwu, L., Xingming, Z.: Fpga sar processor with window memory accesses. In: IEEE International Conf. on Application-specific Systems, Architectures and Processors, pp. 95–100 (2007)

L1 Collective Cache: Managing Shared Data for Chip Multiprocessors

Guanjun Jiang, Degui Fen, Liangliang Tong, Lingxiang Xiang, Chao Wang,
and Tianzhou Chen

College of Computer Science, Zhejiang University, China
Department of Computer Science, Hongkong University, China
{libbug,loosenvon,lxxiang,cw,tzchen}@zju.edu.cn,
lltong@cs.hku.hk

Abstract. In recent years, with the possible end of further improvements in single processor, more and more researchers shift to the idea of Chip Multiprocessors (CMPs). The burgeoning of multi-thread programs brings on dramatically increased inter-core communication. Unfortunately, traditional architectures fail to meet the challenge, as they conduct such a kind of communication on the last level of on-chip cache or even on the memory.This paper proposes a novel approach, called Collective Cache, to differentiate the access to shared/private data and handle data communication on the first level cache. In the proposed cache architecture, the share data found in the last level cache are moved into the Collective Cache, a L1 cache structure shared by all cores. We show that the mechanism this paper proposed can immensely enhance inter-processors communication, increase the usage efficiency of L1 cache and simplify data consistency protocol. Extensive analysis of this approach with Simics shows that it can reduce the L1 cache miss rate by 3.36%.

Keywords: CMP, cache design, L1 cache.

1   Introduction

The Chip-Multiprocessors technology, which allows more than one executing processor to be integrated in a single chip, has substituted traditional single processor as future architectures for high-performance computing. As Chip-Multiprocessors emerge in mainstream systems, they must provide better performance for general workloads, especially for those that require intense data communication between different on-chip processors, like the multi-thread programs. It imposes challenges on the design of CMPs, in particular on the corresponding on-chip storage system, for it acts as the key that defines the system performance.

Computer systems normally adopt a 2- or 3-level hierarchy for cache architecture. As for how to design each cache level, however, different researchers propose various approaches. Such as for the L2 caches, Some CMP systems, for example the IBM Power5 [2] and Sun Niagara [3], employ shared L2 caches to

Y. Dou, R. Gruber, and J. Joller (Eds.): APPT 2009, LNCS 5737, pp. 123–133, 2009.
© Springer-Verlag Berlin Heidelberg 2009

maximize available on-chip capacity to each processor by preventing data replications, whereas [4] [5] provide an alternative way of private L2 caches, as it suits with the characteristics of current NUCA and leads to average reductions in access latency to on-chip cache. In private L2 caches structure data can be replicated to make it close to the requesting processor, yet it also sacrifices effective capacity and incurs more miss compared with shared L2 cache structure.

Recent cache architecture designs mainly focus on the L2 cache, as researchers regard L2 cache as the key role of defining the performance of on-chip storage system for Chip Multiprocessors. Most of these researches seek to gain a balance between access latency and capacity efficiency, by techniques like replicating data blocks and thus migrating them among different on-chip processors, etc. For example, Cooperative Caching [6] employs data replications and migration mechanism for a normal private L2 cache infrastructure, whereas [7] dynamically allocates the ownership of each L2 cache blocks to requesting processors, and proposes to keep hot blocks that responsible for inter-processor misses in a specially designed Processor Owned Private (POP) caches. These schemes perform relatively better than simply designed shared cache structure or private cache structure. But mechanisms like data replications and migration, however, inevitably decrease cache capacity efficiency, and to some extent complicate the cache coherency protocols. As the data communication among cores rise dramatically, particularly for execution of multi-thread programs, they also see limitations on providing a high-efficiency data sharing and exchanging scheme.

Interestingly, although most of the researchers perceive L1 caches as the most important role to determine system performance, they scarcely pay any attention to improve L1 cache for Chip Multiprocessors, but simply use the private L1 cache architecture which is designed for traditional single processor. This paper realizes the critical position of L1 caches and proposes collective cache for it accordingly.

The highlight of our mechanism is to propose to add a collective cache to traditional L1 cache architecture and differentiate on-chip processor access to two kinds of data: Shared Data and Private Data. It is the former data that are responsible for data communication and exchange among on-chip processors. Generally speaking, collective cache can be seemed as a special L1 cache that is shared by every on-chip processors, which can fetch data from L2 cache in the same way as other private L1 caches do. The only difference between them is that shared data are fetched into collective cache, while private data into private cache. Our design requires few changes to lower storage level such as on-chip L2 cache or off-chip memory.

We make the following contributions in this paper:

1. We present the importance of L1 cache architecture to performance enhancement of CMPs, for it is the first level of storage system that processors can access.

2. We propose to add collective cache to differentiate processor access to shared and private data. The mechanism of storing shared data in collective cache and private data in private L1 caches brings the level of data commu-

nication from L2 cache or memory to L1 cache, thus immensely enhance the corresponding efficiency. By prohibiting replications it also helps to increase cache capacity efficiency and simplify coherency protocol.

3. In order to guarantee the implementation of collective cache, we furthermore suggest a 4T mechanism to facilitate design: parallel hunting, single writing, early evicting and late invalidating.

4. We extensively evaluate the above approaches in Simcs and GEMS, which shows an average 3.36% L1 cache misses reduction for Splash2 benchmark.

The reminder of this paper is organized as follows. After characterizing CMP data access distributions in section 2, Section 3 detail the design and implementation of collective cache, while section 4 presents simulation results. The related works are discussed in section 5, and section 6 summarizes the entire work.

2   Characterizing CMP Data Access

Before demonstrating the merits of our mechanism, we firstly analyze the characteristics of processors' requests for cache data.

Unlike single processor, there may be more than one on-chip processor in CMPs to request concurrently for the same data block. Such a distinguishing feature brings on many challenges in design CMPs architecture. The possible performance enhancement thus depends on cache blocks' sharing types.

According to the request characteristics, on-chip data can be classified into two distinct types: shared data and private data. The former kind of data is accessed by more than one on-chip processors while the latter by a single processor, so private data are irresponsible for data communication. This paper concentrates on the management of shared data, for it not only defines communication workload but also is the reason for data replications and consistency protocols. Beckmann et al. [8] makes an in-depth exploration into such a kind of sharing type. They show that although many requests are to the shared data, single requestor blocks consume the majority of the cache capacity. Furthermore, shared blocks exhibit strong locality, especially for shared read-only blocks, as averagely 10% shared blocks account for 70% of request to all the shared data.

Our study simulated a four-processor CMP executing Splash2 benchmark under the red-hat 7.3 operating system, and Table 1 lists the result of simulation, which accords with that of [8].

Table 1. L2 cache request capacity characteristics

Benchmark	Single requests		Shared requests	
	% of all requests	% of capacity	% of all requests	% of capacity
FFT	20	70	80	30
Cholesky	99	99	1	1
Lu non	19	93	81	7
Water	94	98	6	2

Instead of L1 Cache, we analyze the profile of L2 cache requests, the reason for which will be explained in the following section.

On how to handle these shared data, previous researches focus on data replications and migration in a private L1 cache and shared/private L2 cache structure. The impact of replications falls into two aspects: Firstly, although replicating blocks can reduce the cache access latency, it also decreases the effective L2 cache size [8], because multiple replications for a single blocks must be present in the private L2 cache or L1 cache; secondly, the existence of transverse replications in the same cache level complicates cache coherency protocol. The use of these complex protocols, for example the snoop protocol, produces more coherency misses for caches. Due to the afore-mentioned matters, we thus propose the collective cache to manage shared data in CMPs.

3   Collective Cache

In this section we explore into the details of design and optimization of collective cache for L1 caches. The content includes the overall framework of our mechanism and how will the processors operate after collective cache is added.

3.1   Frameworks

After adding collective cache, the new CMPs architecture looks like that in Figure 1.

As depicted in Figure 1, each on-chip processor owns an independent private L1 cache, whereas the collective cache is shared by all of them. The low-lever L2 caches could be design as private or shared, as both of them will be supported by the collective cache.

The basic aim of this architecture is to differentiate processors access to shared data and private data. It works based on the following concepts:

1. Shared data were all stored in collective cache. Every processor requests data by fetching data from L1 caches. In the following part we will show how to collect the shared data to collective cache.

2. Private data were all stored on the private cache of requesting processor. Private data will only be used by the requesting processor, so it is beneficial to only fetch it into the corresponding private cache.

In the last section we analyze the requesting characteristics for L2 cache data blocks in CMPs. General speaking, L1 cache data come from L2 caches. If the data blocks in L2 caches are marked as shared or private, and fetched to L1 collective cache and L1 private cache separately based on the marks, we could probably implement the proposed mechanism.

Figure 2 show the cooperation between L1 caches and L2 caches. The upper level of figure is L1 cache including both private L1 cache and collective cache, the strip of green and blue is L2 cache. Whether a cache block is shared or not is up to the requesting status: If there are more one processors that are requesting for this datum block, then it is marked as shared, otherwise it is private data.

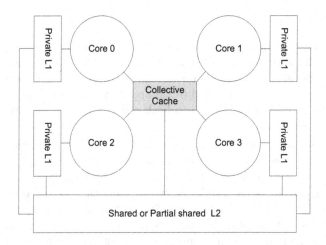

Fig. 1. The proposed cache architecture for a 4-core CMP

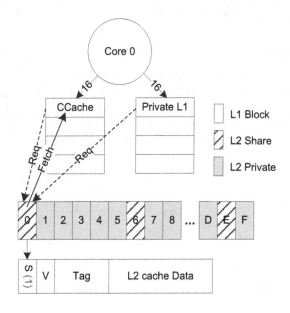

Fig. 2. Example of how processors request data

When the data request for L1 cache turn out to be a miss, the L1 cache controller will put a miss signal on the bus in order to fetch data from L2 cache. The L2 cache controller will look itself for possible address matches. If found, based on the status of this datum block, the controller will return the data to L1 collective cache if it is shared, or private L1 cache if it is private.

3.2   Operations

Here we demonstrate how the cache operate after collective cache is added by a solid example, as depicted in Figure 2, which is the case happens in miss. For simplifications we assume that the number of sets for L1 cache is 4, L2 cache 16, L1 and L2 cache are all direct-mapped. When Core 0 releases a data requesting instruction of address 16 to both collective cache and private cache, three possibilities may arise:

1. One hit and one miss. This is the most favorite case, when the cache just needs to return the requesting processor with the relating datum.

2. Two misses. The request meets with misses both in collective cache and corresponding private cache. The L1 cache controller then must redirect the miss address 16 to L2 cache. For the L2 cache is direct-mapped, cache controller will look for set 0 for matching tag. In this circumstance it is found shared. So the L2 cache disables the request from L1 private cache and responds the L1 collective cache with the requesting datum.

3. Two hits. This possibility must be strictly prohibited from happening, the reason for which we will explain immediately in the following part.

3.3   Methodology

In order to furthermore realize the functions collective cache, we proposed the 4T mechanisms as ways of implementations methodology. They are: Parallel HunTing, Exclusive WriTing, Early EvicTing, and Replacing InvalidaTing, namely "4T". Parallel Hunting. L1 caches locate in the critical path of system execution, whose access time can influence the performance immensely, so we introduce

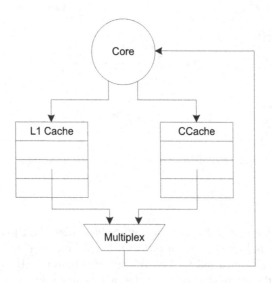

Fig. 3. Parallel hunting

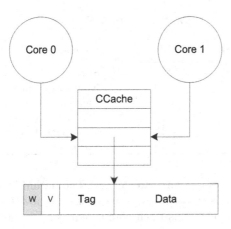

Fig. 4. Exclusive writing

parallelism into the L1 collective cache. As depicted in Figure 3, when the processor plans to request for a datum, it will release the corresponding instruction to both private cache and collective cache. This will help to maintain the L1 cache access time at its minimum.

Exclusive Writing. The circumstance of writing to one datum block concurrently by different processors must be prevented, for it will lead to writing collapse that result in fault actions.

As depicted in Figure 4, we propose to add a writing bit (W) to each block in collective cache. When a processor starts writing to a block, the writing bit will be accordingly set to 1. This bit will not be set to 0 again until the writing action is finished.

Early Evicting. The mechanism prepares for the circumstance when request hits both in collective cache and private cache, and it demands the precondition that the cache write policy is write through. When there are two hits on L1 cache level, early evicting tells the cache controller to evict or invalidate the datum block in private cache while preserve the one in collective cache. In the following part we will describe the other ways to manage this circumstance. Replacing Invalidating. The sharing status of a block in L2 cache will not be removed until the eviction of its corresponding peer datum block in L1 cache or the eviction of itself.

Care must be taken that our mechanism is proposed aiming at the L1 data cache. The instruction cache is not included, for there is no writing for instruction cache. Now we make more in-depth explorations into the reason and settlements of two hits.

Firstly core 0 starts fetching data. If there are misses both in collective cache and private cache, controller will request the L2 cache for the datum, which is found private. It is then returned to the private L1 cache of core 0 to facilitate the future usage. If before this datum's eviction from the private cache, core 1 also requests for it. For core 1 has no right to access the private cache of processor

Table 2. Critical N values

Parameter for L1 private cache	Value	Parameter for L2 cache	Value
Size	32KB	Size	1024KB
Number of lines	1024	Number of lines	32768
Line size	32B	Line size	32B
Associativity	2	Associativity	4
Replacement policy	LRU	Replacement policy	LRU
Write policy	Write through	Write policy	Write back

0, this request still ends up with two misses. The datum in the second time is fetch to L1 cache, but is stored in collective cache, for now it is requested by two processors. If shortly after this fetch core 0 requests for this datum again, the circumstance of two hits happens.

Previously we said that if the cache write policy is writing through, we could employ early evicting to avoid possible data inconsistency. For writing back, the corresponding mechanism must be changed. After the miss of L1 cache hunting, the cache controller must monitor the status of relating datum block. If this block changed from single to shared, controller must issue a write back signal to the up-level private L1 cache that owns the block to write the data back to L2 cache, or to transmit the corresponding datum block to collective cache.

Further optimizations can be applied to our design, like to a more practical protocol for two hits, or enhance the communication between collective cache and private caches. We leave them for future works.

3.4   Evaluation

By using full-system simulation based on Simics [9] and GEMS toolset [10], we implement our mechanism in order to evaluate its performance.

3.5   Platform Setup

Here a 4-core CMP is used as the baseline. For each core, we assume an in-order execution model and set the write policy of L1 cache to writing through. The parameter of collective cache is the same as the private. The only difference is collective cache's size, which is 4KB. For Simics is a full-system simulator we execute the programs in redhat 7.3 operating system with kernel of Linux-2.4.18. We use Stanford Splash2 as the benchmark.

3.6   Experiment Result

Figure 5 depicts the L1 cache miss rate achieved by traditional MESI protocol and our proposed mechanism. The result shows that our proposed mechanism reduces the L1 cache miss rate by 3.36% on average and achieves suitable enhancement in the system performance, compared with traditional MESI protocol based CMPs architecture.

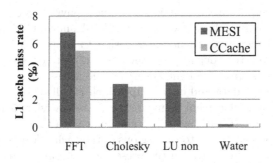

Fig. 5. L1 cache miss rates for MESI and CCache

3.7 Mechanism Analysis

This part analyzes the merits of our mechanism.

1. Data Communication. We put all the shared data in the L1 collective and thus all the data sharing is conducted on the L1 cache level, which can enhance the communication efficiency.

2. Capacity Efficiency. Employing our mechanism data replications for shared data can be prevented, so it will boost the capacity efficiency of L1 cache.

3. Protocol simplification. Remove of transverse data replications will inevitably simplify the cache coherency protocol, such as snoop protocol and directory-based protocol.

4 Related Works

4.1 Chip Multiprocessors

The concept of Chip Multiprocessors (CMPS) is firstly proposed in 1997 [11]. In order to examine possible design space for CMPs, [12] analyzes several design energy/performance trade-offs for parallel applications when varying core complexity, L2 cache size and the number of cores, and arrives at the following conclusions that on-chip cache is very important to the system performance. As there exist two distinct ways to implement on-chip cache, [13] compares the memory system for CMPs which draws the conclusion that both hardware-managed coherent caches and software-managed streaming memory are practical and useful for on-chip memory system design. That which method outperforms depends on the environment. Owing to the critical role of cache, in the following section we will briefly discuss its current researches.

4.2 CMPs On-Chip Storage System

Nowadays researches on CMPs on-chip storage system mainly concentrate on L2 cache architecture. As increases in on-chip communication delays make the hit time of large on-chip caches a function of a line's physical location within the cache, [14] first proposes physical designs for Non-Uniform Cache Architectures (NUCAs), and furthermore extend their design to support data migration on the same cache level. In order to place the vast majority of frequently-accessed data in the fast sub-arrays and thus decrease the access time, [15] suggests to separate the access of data and of tags up, which is called Non-Uniform access with replacement and placement using Distance associativity cache (NuRAPID cache). Some researches, such as [16], point out that although NUCA reduces latency by allowing fast access to the regions of the cache close to the processor, it may turn out to be ineffective in the presence of sharing because each sharer pull the block toward it, leaving eventually the block in the middle, far away from all the sharers. Because neither pure shared not pure private cache accommodate the objects, [17] extends the NuRAPID mechanism and proposes to adopt a hybrid design of private, per-processor tag arrays and a shared data array. As an alternative, [18] proposes Shared Processor-Based Split L2 to capture the benefits of shared/private organizations.

Although many researches have been conducted in CMPs L2 cache design, the investigations on L1 cache are relatively insufficient. Among them [19] just briefly mentions L1 prefetching mechanism as a possibility to hide average hit latencies, and [16] talks something about stride-based prefetching between L1 and L2 caches to improve performance. Many of L2 cache researches propose data replications and migration in L2 cache to reduce access time, but to some extent they reduce capacity efficiency and complicate cache coherency protocol, which our proposed mechanism can handle better.

5   Conclusions

As the trend of multi-thread programming steps further, it imposes more and more challenges on on-chip communication efficiency for CMPs. Although many researches have been conducted to balance the on-chip access latency and capacity efficiency, their mechanisms, such as data replications and migration, result in either capacity inefficiency or longer access time. The existence of complex cache coherency protocols also leads to decline of communication efficiency, sometimes even gives rise to coherency storm.

In this paper, we propose to construct the collective cache framework and differentiate access to on-chip shared/private data. Our mechanism puts mass of data sharing in L1 cache level to accelerate data communication, at the same time it prevents possible data replications on the same cache level thus increases capacity efficiency and simplifies coherency protocols. The result is a more efficient cache hierarchy that suits small CMPs system.

References

1. Monchiero, M., Canal, R., Gonzalez, A.: Design space exploration for multicore architectures: A power/performance/thermal view. In: IEEE conference on supercomputing (June 2006)

2. Sinharoy, B., Kalla, R., Tendler, J., Eickemeyer, R., Joyner, J.: Power5 System Microarchitecture. IBM Journal of Research and Development 49(4) (2005)
3. Kongetira, P.: A 32-way Multithreaded SPARC? Processor. In: Proceedings of the 16th HotChips Symposium (August 2004)
4. Krewell, K.: UltraSPARC IV Mirrors Predecessor. In: Microprocessor. Report, November 2003, pp. 1–3 (2003)
5. McNairy, C., Bhatia, R.: Montecito: A Dual-Core Dual-Thread Itanium Processor. IEEE Micro. 25(2), 10–20 (2005)
6. Chang, J., Sohi, G.S.: Cooperative cache for chip multiprocessors. In: ISCA (2006)
7. Srikantaiah, S., Irwin, M.K.M.J.: Adaptive set pinning: Managing shared caches in Chip Multiprocessors. In: ASPLOS 2008 (2008)
8. Beckmann, B.M., Marty, M.R., Wood, D.A.: ASR: Adaptive selective replication for CMP caches. In: MICRO (2006)
9. Peter, S.: Magnusson: Simics: a full system simulator. IEEE Computer Society, Los Alamitos (2002)
10. Martin, M.M.K.: Multifacet's general execution-driven multiprocessor simulator (GEMS) toolset. In: Computer Architecture News (September 2005)
11. Hammond, L., Nayfeh, B.A., Olukotun, K.: A single-chip multiprocessor. IEEE Computer Society, Los Alamitos (1997)
12. Monchiero, M., Canal, R., Gonzalez, A.: Design space exploration for multicore architectures: A power/performance/thermal view. In: IEEE conference on super-computing (June 2006)
13. Leverich, J., Arakida, H., Solomatnikov, A.: Comparing memory systems for chip multiprocessors. In: ISCA (2007)
14. Kim, C., Burger, D., Keckler, S.W.: An adaptive, non-uniform cache structure for wire-delay dominated on-chip caches. In: ASPLOS (2002)
15. Cgushti, Z., Powell, M.D., Vijaykumar, T.N.: Distance associativity for high-performance energy-efficient non-uniform cache architectures. In: MICRO (2003)
16. Beckmann, B.M., Wood, D.A.: Managing Wire Delay in Large Chip-Multiprocessor Caches. In: Proc. 37th Int'l. Symp. Microarchitecture (MICRO-37) (December)
17. Chishti, Z., Powell, M.D., Vijaykumar, T.N.: Optimizing Replication, Communication, and Capacity Allocation in CMPs. In: Proc. 32nd Ann. Int'l. Symp. Computer Architecture (ISCA 2005) (June 2005)
18. Liu, C., Sivasubramaniam, A., Kandemir, M.: Organizing the last line of Defense before hitting the memory wall for CMPs. In: 10th HPCA (2004)
19. Huh, J., Kim, C.: A NUCA substrate for flexible CMP cache sharing. IEEE transactions on parallel and distributed systems (2007)

Efficient Multiplication of Polynomials on Graphics Hardware

Pavel Emeliyanenko

Max-Planck-Institut für Informatik, Saarbrücken, Germany
asm@mpi-inf.mpg.de

Abstract. We present the algorithm to multiply univariate polynomials with integer coefficients efficiently using the Number Theoretic transform (NTT) on Graphics Processing Units (GPU). The same approach can be used to multiply large integers encoded as polynomials. Our algorithm exploits fused multiply-add capabilities of the graphics hardware. NTT multiplications are executed in parallel for a set of distinct primes followed by reconstruction using the Chinese Remainder theorem (CRT) on the GPU. Our benchmarking experiences show the NTT multiplication performance up to 77 GMul/s[1]. We compared our approach with CPU-based implementations of polynomial and large integer multiplication provided by NTL and GMP[2] libraries.

Keywords: large integer arithmetic, parallel computations, graphics hardware, GPU, CUDA.

1   Introduction

Large integer and polynomial arithmetic constitutes the core of many scientific computations. For instance, algorithms in algebraic geometry involve a substantial amount of symbolic computations performed over integer polynomials in one or more variables (e.g., polynomial subresultants and derived quantities [5]). The performance of public key cryptosystems also relies on the efficiency of large integer arithmetic.

Schönhage and Strassen [21] have shown that the Number Theoretic transform (NTT), as generalization of discrete Fourier transform to finite fields, is asymptotically the fastest known way to multiply two large integers. Moreover, the inherent parallel structure of the NTT and the absence of round-off errors, as opposed to floating-point Fourier transforms, makes it very tempting candidate for realization on parallel architectures. Unfortunately, the graphics hardware, driven by the needs of the game industry, was originally designed for efficient low-precision floating-point arithmetic.

---

[1] GMul/s stands for "10^9 modular multiplications per second", not to confuse with GFlop/s, see Section 6 for explanations.

[2] NTL: http://www.shoup.net/ntl, GMP: http://gmplib.org

Y. Dou, R. Gruber, and J. Joller (Eds.): APPT 2009, LNCS 5737, pp. 134–149, 2009.
© Springer-Verlag Berlin Heidelberg 2009

Although floating-point Fourier transforms are also applicable to integer convolutions[3], the number of bits to be stored in a floating-point number to guarantee the provably correct rounding is substantially limited (see [20] for precise estimates). As a result, single-precision floating-point is practically not applicable for error-free integer convolutions, while the double-precision arithmetic is still relatively slow on modern GPUs. The NVIDIA's CUDA API [2] makes it possible to utilize graphics processors for integer computations.

Main contribution. we present the algorithm to compute integer polynomial products using the NTT on graphics processors. We use efficient 24-bit modular multiplication which reflects the native multiplication capabilities of the GPU. Our algorithm operates on partially reduced 24-bit residues represented by 32-bit integers, deferring the final reduction as long as possible. This enables us to avoid a great deal of expensive operations. Optimized FFT-kernels utilize fused multiply-add capabilities of the graphics hardware. The reconstruction of convolution digits is performed on the GPU using the Chinese Remainder theorem (CRT) allowing us to multiply polynomials with moderate coefficient bit-length entirely on the GPU.

The remaining part of the paper is structured as follows. In Section 2 we survey existing algorithms for modular techniques and large integer multiplication on parallel architectures. Section 3 gives an overview of 3D graphics hardware and CUDA programming model. Some background theory underlying the Number Theoretic transforms and the CRT reconstruction is presented in Section 4. In Section 5 we discuss the algorithm and its mapping to the GPU in detail. Then, in Section 6 we compare our algorithm with existing CPU-based implementations and draw conclusions in Section 7.

2 Related Work

Over the past years there was a lot of research carried out to implement efficient FFT algorithms on graphics processors ([10], [1], [17]). Unfortunately, all of them operate in a single-precision floating-point arithmetic and, hence, are not suitable for integer convolutions. There were attempts to emulate extended precision using a pair or a quad of low-precision floating-point numbers ([12], [11]). However, this leads to rather complicated arithmetic operations thereby annihilating all the advantages of the floating-point and, moreover, it doubles the memory bandwidth between the host and the graphics card which is a major performance killer for GPU algorithms.

There are two recent papers employing modular techniques on the GPU ([18], [24]). Despite the fact that they are concentrated on the acceleration of modular exponentiation, it is interesting within our context how they deal with the modular reduction after multiplication.

The authors of [18] used a traditional shader approach to program the GPU. As a result, they could only handle integers that fit the floating-point mantissa

---

[3] By convolution we mean here the integer polynomial product (acyclic convolution) which is a cyclic convolution of zero-padded sequences, see Section 4.

(24 bits). They suggested to use composite moduli consisting of 2 primes whose product fits in 24 bits. Hence, unfolding the CRT over these two primes, the modular multiplication can proceed without intermediate values that exceed 24 bits. We find that this method involves too many arithmetic operations and does not take any advantage of the floating-point nature of the arithmetic.

The second paper [24] used CUDA framework and all computations were carried out in integer arithmetic. The authors reported that, while the graphics hardware supports fast 24-bit integer multiplication, CUDA does *not* expose an intrinsic to obtain the most-significant 16 bits of the product. Therefore, they were constrained to use full 32-bit moduli and slow 32-bit multiplication. Luckily, we have been able to deal with this limitation (see Section 5.3). Unfortunately, their paper does not explain in a concrete way how the 32-bit modular reduction is realized.

An interesting approach to large integer multiplication on parallel architectures appears in [8]. It uses multi-dimensional Fermat Number transform (FNT)[4]. Although, the FNT has clear advantages credited to Schönhage and Strassen, we believe that the modular approach with CRT is more suitable for GPU implementation because of its relative simplicity (as opposed to multi-dimensional transform) and flexibility since it allows us to convolve variable length sequences using the same transform length. On the contrary, dimensionality of the FNT depends on the length of input sequences. Moreover, according to [8], 1024-point FNT requires 2^{13} processors arranged in a 4-dimensional hypercube to work cooperatively. This number exceeds by far the maximal number of threads allowed per one GPU's thread block while threads of different blocks cannot communicate with each other directly (see Section 3).

3   Overview of the GPU Architecture and CUDA Framework

In this overview we only consider the GPUs with NVIDIA Tesla architecture [16]. However, the new standard for heterogeneous programming OpenCL [19] will provide a unified API (which is very similar to that of CUDA) and will be supported by many other vendors. The NVIDIA Tesla architecture unifies vertex and fragment processors in streaming multiprocessors (SMs) that can execute any shader programs as well as general-purpose parallel programs. For instance, GeForce GTX 280 GPU contains 30 SMs.

The GPU executes instructions in a SIMT – *single-instruction, multiple-thread* – fashion. In other words, the SM's instruction issue unit (MT issue, see Figure 1) applies a single instruction to a group of 32 threads called *warps*. As a result, threads of a single warp are always executed synchronously. When the threads follow different execution paths (diverge on a branch instruction), the warp has to serially execute all taken branch paths. The full efficiency is attained when

---

[4] A well-known restriction of using Fermat ring to compute convolutions relates to the fact that the maximal transform length is proportional to the modulus bit-length. Multi-dimensional techniques are supposed to overcome this difficulty.

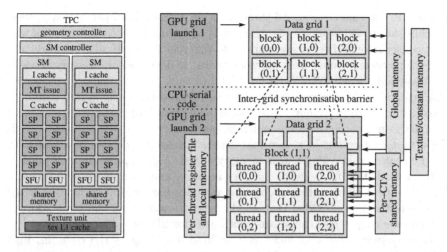

Fig. 1. Texture/processor cluster (TPC) comprising two SMs (left); CUDA execution model, thread and memory hierarchy (right)

a branch condition is *warp-aligned*. Different warps are independent from each other and can execute disjoint paths without penalties.

Each SM contains two special function units (SFU) and eight streaming processors cores (SP), see Figure 1. The SM processes simple arithmetic instructions in *four* clock cycles for the entire warp. These instructions also include single-precision floating-point multiply/multiply-add and 24-bit integer multiply/multiply-add. Integer division and modulo are particularly costly and should be avoided, we use floating-point arithmetic instead.

CUDA is a heterogeneous *serial-parallel* programming model, i.e., a parallel GPU code is interleaved with a serial code executed on the host (see Figure 1). On the top level, threads are grouped into *cooperative thread arrays* (CTAs) or *thread blocks*. Each block consists of up to 512 concurrent threads which execute the same CUDA code, can share the results of computations and synchronize their execution with barriers. In its turn, blocks are organized in a *grid* of thread blocks which is launched on a single CUDA program. Threads of different blocks cannot communicate with each other explicitly but can share the results by means of global memory[5]. *Inter-grid synchronization* can be achieved by serialized grid launches. The CTA model implements a coarse-grained parallelism as opposed to fine-grained parallelism achieved by warps.

Memory system of the GPU is organized as follows: each thread has its own *register file*. The SM has a fixed number of registers split evenly between threads of a block, by exceeding this amount registers get spilled into slow *local memory*

---

[5] Block independence naturally comes from the scalability requirements allowing a binary program to run unchanged on any number of SMs. However, it imposes additional difficulties in algorithms' realization. In this respect, we find the Intel's Larrabee architecture more advantageous, see Section 7.

residing in external DRAM. All threads within a single block can access the fast on-chip *shared memory* (see Figure 1). It is organized in 16 *banks* in such a way that consecutive addresses are mapped to different banks. If all 16 threads of a half-warp access memory from different banks, no delays occur. Memory accesses with a stride s where $GCD(s, 16) \neq 1$ lead to *bank conflicts* and are serialized[6]. The remaining three memory spaces – read-write *global memory* and read-only *constant* and *texture memory* – are visible to all threads of the entire grid. Global memory is not cached and has much higher latency than shared memory, it is important to access it in a way that separate memory accesses of a half-warp can be coalesced in a single wide memory access. A good programming practise is to preload data from global memory at once, and then use shared memory for subsequent computations. Constant memory has on-chip cache, amortized access to it is fast provided that all threads of a warp read the same address. Texture memory is also cached and optimized for 2D spatial locality.

High memory access latencies can be hidden as long as the code has high arithmetic intensity and the SM has enough warps to switch between in order to interleave memory access with ALU operations.

4   Mathematical Preliminaries

In this section we overview some basic facts from the number theory underlying fast multiplication algorithms in finite fields and recall the *Chinese remainder theorem* (CRT) to recover multidigit result after modular multiplication.

4.1   Number Theoretic Transforms and Fast Convolutions

The forward and backward Number Theoretic transforms are defined respectively as follows:

$$X_k \equiv_m \sum_{j=0}^{N-1} x_j \alpha^{jk} \quad \text{and} \quad x_j \equiv_m N^{-1} \sum_{k=0}^{N-1} X_k \alpha^{-jk},$$

where $j, k = 0, \ldots, N-1$, all arithmetic is performed over Z/mZ and α is an N-th primitive root of unity (an element of order N). The necessary and sufficient conditions for existence of such transforms are [7]:

- $N \mid GCD\{(p_i - 1), i = 1, \ldots, l\}$, where $m = \prod_{i=1}^{l} p_i^{r_i}$;
- $GCD(N, m) = 1$ (existence of modular inverse);
- $\alpha^s \neq 1 \pmod{m} : \forall s = [1, 2, \ldots, N-1]$.

A *cyclic convolution* of two length-n sequences $a = [a_0 \ldots a_{n-1}]$ and $b = [b_0 \ldots b_{n-1}]$ is a length-n sequence $h = a * b$ with $h_j = \sum_{i=0}^{n-1} a_i b_{(j-i) \bmod n}$. Once the conditions above are satisfied, the transform possesses the so-called

---

[6] Bank conflicts only occur within a half-warp – a group of 16 threads.

cyclic convolution property (CCP) allowing for fast convolutions in Z/mZ. The CCP states that if

$$X_k \equiv_m \sum_{j=0}^{N-1} x_j \alpha^{jk} \quad \text{and} \quad Y_k \equiv_m \sum_{j=0}^{N-1} y_j \alpha^{jk}, \text{ then for } h = x * y,$$

$$h_j \equiv_m N^{-1} \sum_{k=0}^{N-1} H_k \alpha^{-jk} \quad \text{where} \quad H_k \equiv_m X_k \cdot Y_k.$$

Accordingly, the usual polynomial product of a and b, defined as $r_j = \sum_{i=0}^{n-1} a_i b_{j-i}$, is a cyclic convolution of zero-padded sequences, i.e., $[a_{n/2} \dots a_{n-1}] = 0$ and $[b_{n/2} \dots b_{n-1}] = 0$. To multiply two K-bit integers using this technique, they are first partitioned into $N/2$ chunks of $P = 2K/N$ bits each, where N is the size of the transform. Then, the resulting sequences a and b are zero-padded and convolved, i.e., $r \equiv_m a * b$. The modulus m is chosen to be large enough so that the "convolution digits" are recovered exactly (see estimates in Section 5.1). Finally, one obtains the resulting product by evaluating: $z = \sum_{i=0}^{N-1} r_i \cdot 2^{Pi}$.

In our approach we use 24-bit prime moduli of the form $m = 2^n \cdot k + 1$ (for transforms of length 2^n). The reasons for that are: first, the number of 24-bit primes of this form is considerably large, which is suitable for the CRT reconstruction. Second, the modular reduction with 24-bit primes can be performed efficiently in floating-point arithmetic.

4.2   Chinese Remainder Theorem

Let $(m_1, m_2, \dots, m_k)$ be pairwise coprime moduli and $M = \prod_{i=1}^{k} m_i$ (M is called dynamic range). Then, for the set of residues $(x_1, x_2, \dots, x_k)$ with $0 \leq x_i < m_i$ ($1 \leq i \leq k$) there exists a unique X ($0 \leq X < M$), such that: $x_i = X \bmod m_i$.

A classical approach for incremental Chinese remaindering is the one of Szabo and Tanaka [23] based on Mixed Radix System (MRS). Here X is defined by the associated mixed-radix digits $(\alpha_1, \alpha_2, \dots, \alpha_k)$ in the following way:

$$X = \alpha_1 M_1 + \alpha_2 M_2 + \dots + \alpha_k M_k$$

where $M_1 = 1$, $M_j = m_1 m_2 \dots m_{j-1}$ ($2 \leq j \leq k$). We omit precise formulae for α_i for brevity. There exist efficient MRS conversion algorithms based on look-up tables (see [14], [3]), however the size of the tables they require is proportional to the modulus bit-length which draw them impractical for the GPUs[7]. We have decided in favour a simple algorithm from [25] which rearranges Szabo and Tanaka formulae in a more structured way, thereby exposing some parallelism. The α_i are computed as below ($1 \leq i \leq k$):

$$\alpha_1 = x_1, \quad \alpha_2 = (x_2 - \alpha_1) c_2 \bmod m_2$$

---

[7] Using large look-up tables residing in external DRAM turn to be inefficient on the GPU due to the high memory latencies and the lack of *gather* operation.

$$\alpha_3 = ((x_3 - \alpha_1)c_3 - (\alpha_2 M_2 c_3 \bmod m_3)) \bmod m_3$$
$$\alpha_i = ((x_i - \alpha_1)c_i - (\alpha_2 M_2 c_i \bmod m_i) - \ldots$$
$$- (\alpha_{i-1} M_{i-1} c_i \bmod m_i)) \bmod m_i$$

where $c_i = (m_1 m_2 \ldots m_{i-1})^{-1} \bmod m_i$. Here c_i and $M_j c_i \bmod m_i$ can be pre-computed in advance.

5   Mapping Multiplication Algorithm to Graphics Processor

In this section we consider the multiplication algorithm step-by-step. First, we present our approach at a high-level to give the reader an intuitive feeling about the algorithm. Then, we describe how the FFT algorithm is mapped to the graphics hardware to achieve even work distribution between threads. The next sections cover the efficient modular reduction and optimizations aimed to utilize fused multiply-add capabilities of the GPU and reduce the amount of reductions using redundant residue representation. At the end, we discuss how the CRT reconstruction is realized on the graphics processor.

5.1   Algorithm Overview

The multiplication on the GPU proceeds as follows: we are given a set of N integer polynomials of degree at most 2^{n-1}, where 2^n is the size of the transform[8]. Polynomials of higher degree can be processed by encoding them in fixed degree polynomials using the binary segmentation [9]. Large integers are handled by partitioning them into respective number of pieces.

Each piece (or polynomial coefficient) is reduced modulo a set of distinct 24-bit primes, the number of primes K is chosen such that the resulting products can be recovered exactly[9]. The GPU executes $N \times K$ NTT modular multiplications in parallel. Once all products are ready, another kernel groups every K modular products and recovers multiprecision digits using the CRT (see Section 5.5). K is chosen to be small enough (typically $K < 10$), so that the CRT reconstruction can proceed entirely on the GPU. However, this is not a restriction – the GPU can run modular convolutions for large values of K and recover multiprecision digits only partially, leaving the final reconstruction for the CPU.

The number of primes required to recover the product of two large integers is estimated as follows: each "digit" after 2^n-point convolution is bounded by $2^{2M} \cdot 2^{n-1}$, where M is a bit-length of an input sequence digit. Hence, a "convolution digit" has at most $2M + n - 1$ bits. For the CRT reconstruction with c primes, it holds that: $2M + n - 1 = 23 \cdot c$ or $M_c = (23 \cdot c - n + 1)/2$, here we assumed that each prime is 23-bits long on the average. Thus, c convolutions with different moduli

---

[8] Recall that, the input sequences must be initially zero-padded, hence these numbers.
[9] For small values of K, the initial modular reduction can be done directly on the graphics processor.

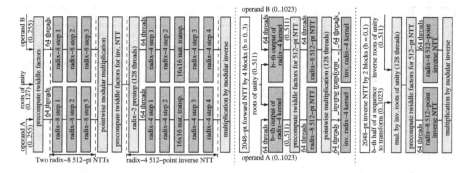

Fig. 2. Schematic view of 512-point (left) and 2048-point (right) NTT multiplication on the GPU

are enough to multiply numbers of $2^{n-1}M_c$ bit-length. For example, with $c = 4$, 2048-point transform can be used to multiply integers having at most $1024 \cdot 41$ bits each (1312 32-bit machine words).

5.2   The FFT Algorithm

Parallel FFT algorithms are commonly based on the Stockham out-of-place FFT. We use Bailey's variation of this algorithm [4]. This is a self-sorting algorithm, such that an expensive index permutation phase (as opposed to the classical Cooley-Tukey FFT [6]) can be skipped. Moreover, all data fetches and stores are performed solely with unit strides, hence, no bank conflicts occur. Roots of unity are still accessed with power-of-two strides but this can be alleviated by storing the roots in contiguous arrays for each FFT step. In contrast to floating-point transforms, the roots of unity in Z/mZ cannot be computed on-the-fly, but must be precomputed in advance and loaded to the GPU. We have implemented Bailey's FFT for transform sizes 512, 1024 and 2048.

Figure 2 depicts the mapping of 512- and 2048-point NTTs to the graphics hardware, 1024-point transform is realized by analogy. The core of the algorithm constitute radix-2, -4 and -8 kernels (or "butterfly" operations). The radix-n FFT-kernel is defined as: $[y_0, \ldots, y_{n-1}] = F_n diag(1, \alpha^k, \ldots, \alpha^{(n-1)k})[x_0, \ldots, x_{n-1}]$, where α^k is a twiddle factor and F_n is an $n \times n$ Fourier matrix, i.e., $F_n = [w_n^{j \cdot k}]_{j,k=0,\ldots,n-1}$ (w_n is an n-th root of unity). In the following subsections we consider optimized FFT-kernels in detail.

The 512-point NTT multiplication is done by a single block of 128 threads, after each radix-4/-8 step the data is reordered in shared memory. The forward 2048-point transform is run by 4 blocks collectively, they first evaluate a radix-4 kernel for both multiplicands. Then, the outputs are split evenly between the blocks, each single block processes its parts, multiplies them elementwise and runs the first radix-4 step of the inverse transform. By multiplying the operands early in the forward kernel, we effectively reduce the memory bandwidth because only one (resulting) sequence is written out to global memory. The inverse

---

Algorithm 1. 24-bit modular multiplication: computes $a \cdot b \bmod m$

1:	**procedure** MUL_MOD(a, b, m, invm)	▷ $invm = 2^{16}/m$ (in floating-point)
2:	hi = _umul24hi(a, b)	▷ compute upper 32 bits of the product
3:	prodf = _fmul_rn(hi, invm)	▷ multiplication in floating-point
4:	l = _float2uint_rz(prodf)	▷ integer truncation: $l = \lfloor hi \cdot 2^{16}/m \rfloor$
5:	**return** (_umul24(a, b) − _umul24(l, m))	▷ in $[-m + \varepsilon; m + \varepsilon]$ with $0 \le \varepsilon < m$
6:	**end procedure**	

2048-point NTT is run by 2 blocks, each block transforms its 1024-element part separately.

5.3   Multiplication and Modular Reduction

The reason for choosing 24-bit primes was that the graphics hardware does not support a full 32-bit integer multiplication natively. It provides only 24-bit multiplication realized in mul24.lo/hi instructions[10]. mul24.lo computes multiplies 24 least significant bits (LSB) of the operands and returns 32 LSB of 48-bit product, it is available via _umul24 intrinsic. mul24.hi returns 32 most significant bits of the product respectively. Strangely enough, it is not accessible from a high-level CUDA code. Fortunately, we have been able to rebuild the *nvopencc* (which is based on *open64*) from sources to insert the "missing intrinsic", in what follows we will refer to it as _umul24hi[11].

Having all prerequisites at hand, we now discuss how the modular arithmetic is realized on the GPU. We consider only modular multiplication in detail (see Algorithm 1) as the remaining operations (addition and subtraction) are rather trivial. Algorithm 1 splits the product in two parts, i.e., $a \cdot b = 2^{16} hi + lo$ (32 and 16 bits), and the following holds ($0 \le r < m$):

$$2^{16} hi + lo = (m \cdot l + r) + lo \equiv_m r + lo = 2^{16} hi + lo - m \cdot l = a \cdot b - l \cdot m$$

Observe that, $l = \lfloor 2^{16} hi/m \rfloor$ is at most 24-bits long, thus it is exactly representable with 24-bit mantissa. Let $\gamma = a \cdot b - l \cdot m = lo + r$, hence $\gamma \in [0; m + \varepsilon]$ ($0 \le \varepsilon < m$)[12]. As a result, γ fits into 32 bits and is computed as a difference of 32 LSB of both products using _umul24 intrinsic. The final reduction needs two additional steps to map the range $[-m + \varepsilon; m + \varepsilon]$ to $[0; m - 1]$. Owing to the redundant representation of residues, these steps can be deferred until the next modular multiplication takes place. We discuss this and other optimizations in the following section.

---

[10] The 32-bit integer multiplication gets demoted to a more primitive operations and is 4 times slower than its 24-bit counterpart.

[11] The compiler built for Linux platform with a set of new intrinsics is available at http://www.mpi-inf.mpg.de/~emeliyan/cuda-compiler

[12] According to our tests, $\gamma \in [-m+\varepsilon; m+\varepsilon]$ due to the loss of accuracy when converting hi to floating-point but this is not critical for us.

Algorithm 2. Realization of radix-2 kernel (FMA_BFY2) and modular reduction of 32-bit operand (REDUCE_MOD)

1: **procedure** FMA_BFY2(x_0, x_1, w, m, invm)   ▷ $invm = 2^{16}/m$ (in floating-point)
2:     hi = _umul24hi(x_1, w)   ▷ compute upper 32 bits of the product
3:     prodf = hi * invm + 2.0f   ▷ floating-point multiply-add
4:     l = _float2uint_rz(prodf)   ▷ integer truncation: $l = \lfloor hi \cdot 2^{16}/m \rfloor + 2$
5:     y_0 = x_0 + _umul24(x_1, w) − _umul24(l, m)   ▷ a pair of 24-bit multiply-adds
6:     **return** [y_0, sad(x_0, y_0, x_0)]   ▷ $y_1 = |x_0 − y_0| + x_0 = 2x_0 − y_0$
7: **end procedure**
8: **procedure** REDUCE_MOD(a, m, invm)   ▷ $invm = 1/m$ (in floating-point)
9:     ai = a + _umul24(100, m)   ▷ make sure a is positive
10:    af = _fmul_rn(_uint2float_rn(ai), invm)   ▷ multiply in floating-point
11:    l = _float2uint_rz(af)   ▷ integer truncation: $l = \lfloor a/m \rfloor + 100$
12:    r = ai − _umul24(l, m)   ▷ $r \in [−m + \varepsilon; \varepsilon]$ with $0 \le \varepsilon < m$
13:    **if** r < 0 **then** r = r + m   ▷ adjust the result in case of negative sign
14:    **return** r
15: **end procedure**

5.4 FMA-Optimized FFT Kernels and Exploiting Redundancy in Residue Representation

The graphics hardware has fused multiply-add (FMA) capabilities. Namely, it supports floating-point FMA as well as 24-bit integer FMA instructions. To achieve the full efficiency, it is therefore important to respect these hardware features. In our implementation we use both of them. Our radix-4 and -8 FFT kernels are based on the FMA-optimized factorization of a matrix product given in [15]. In its core it has a primitive radix-2 "butterfly" defined as ($[y_0, y_1] = \mathsf{fma\_bfy2}([x_0, x_1], w)$): $y_0 \leftarrow x_0 + x_1 \cdot w$ and $y_1 \leftarrow 2 \cdot x_0 − y_0$. Its realization is given by procedure FMA_BFY2 of Algorithm 2. Remark that, y_1 cannot be computed with 24-bit FMA because x_0 can exceed 24 bits (when redundant representation is used). Remarkably, the GPU has a native $\mathsf{sad}(x, y, z)$ instruction which computes $|x − y| + z$. Thus, if we ensure that $x_0 − y_0 > 0$, we can use sad to compute y_1. We guarantee this by adding 2 to *prodf* in line 3 of the algorithm. Indeed, $x_0 − y_0 = l \cdot m − x_1 \cdot w = \gamma$, and, according to the estimates above, $\gamma \in [−m + \varepsilon; m + \varepsilon]$. Altogether, the fma_bfy2 is compiled in *6 flops* on the GPU[13].

Remark that, y_0 and y_1 in general are not valid residues, while _umul24 can only handle 24-bit operands. To this end, the argument x_1 of the next fma_bfy2 must be reduced prior to multiplication, this is achieved by procedure REDUCE_MOD of Algorithm 2. By adding $100 \cdot m$ to a we ensure that $l = \lfloor a/m \rfloor + 100$ is positive and, hence, _umul24(l, m) delivers the correct result[14]. We will refer to

---

[13] Generated low-level GPU assembly code can be inspected using the *decuda* tool: http://www.cs.rug.nl/~wladimir/decuda

[14] It can be estimated that a never deviates from 0 by more than $100 \cdot m$, thus, $a + 100 \cdot m$ is guaranteed to be positive and fits within 32 bits.

reduce_mod(x_1) followed by fma_bfy2($[x_0, x_1, w]$) as fma_red_bfy2. FMA-optimized radix-4 kernel is defined below ($[y_0, \ldots, y_3] = $ fma_bfy4($[x_0, \ldots x_3], u$)):

$$[d_0, d_1] = \text{fma\_red\_bfy2}([x_0, x_2], u^2) \quad [d_2, d_3] = \text{fma\_red\_bfy2}([x_1, x_3], u^2)$$
$$[y_0, y_2] = \text{fma\_red\_bfy2}([d_0, d_2], u) \quad [y_1, y_3] = \text{fma\_red\_bfy2}([d_1, d_3], u \cdot w_4),$$

here $u = \alpha^k$ denotes a twiddle factor and w_4 is 4-th root of unity. Radix-8 kernel is realized by analogy. Note that, the first step of the FFT algorithm does not need any twiddle factors and FFT-kernels are simplified. Moreover, the input sequences are initially zero-padded, hence the first stage of the forward transform can be simplified even further.

The redundancy in residue representation is exploited as follows: *modular reductions after addition/subtraction as well as correction steps after multiplication are performed on demand only*. In other words, they are deferred until either the next multiplication takes place or until the very last stage of the NTT algorithm.

5.5   CRT Reconstruction on the GPU

Owing to the fact that each "convolution digit" is recovered independently, it is advantageous to run the CRT reconstruction directly on the GPU provided that the number of moduli k is small (typically $k \leq 10$). We compute the MRS digits α_i defined in Section 4.2 in a straightforward way. Threads are split logically into groups of $P = (k-2)/2$ threads each. We require P to be a *power-of-two*, so that the groups of P threads are always warp-aligned and access to shared memory proceeds without synchronization. We have chosen the block size of 64 threads[15].

We assume that the moduli are sorted, i.e., $m_1 < m_2 < \ldots < m_k$. Thus, for respective residues $x_1, x_2, \ldots, x_k$, it holds that $x_i < m_j$ for $1 \leq i < j \leq k$. This enables us to save on reductions when the quantities of the form $(x_j - x_i) \bmod m_j$ are computed. Each thread computes two values of x_i in one step (we refer to them by $\delta = \{1, 2\}$). Let $j = 1 \ldots k/2$, the algorithm takes $k - 1$ steps:

step 1: for threads $i = 1 \ldots P$: $x_{2i+\delta} \leftarrow (x_{2i+\delta} - x_1)c_{2i+\delta} \bmod m_{2i+\delta}$. For the 1st thread additionally: $x_2 \leftarrow (x_2 - x_1)c_2 \bmod m_2$;
step (2j): for threads $i = j \ldots P$: $x_{2i+\delta} \leftarrow (x_{2i+\delta} - x_{2j}M_{2j}c_{2i+\delta}) \bmod m_{2i+\delta}$;
step (2j + 1): for threads $i = j - 1 \ldots P$: $x_{2i+\delta} \leftarrow (x_{2i+\delta} - x_{2j-1}M_{2j-1}c_{2j+\delta}) \bmod m_{2j+\delta}$, a thread $i = j - 1$ computes only x_{2i+2}.

The number of threads involved decrements every 2 steps, this way we achieve sufficiently even work distribution. We use precomputed values for c_i and $s_i^l = M_l c_i \bmod m_i$ defined in Section 4.2. Once MRS digits are computed, the resulting "convolution digit" is recovered as: $X = \alpha_1 M_1 + \alpha_2 M_2 + \ldots + \alpha_k M_k$. We extract some parallelism by evaluating this expression in a "tree-like" fashion. To realize multiprecision additions required here, we use addition-with-carry intrinsics provided by our *nvopencc* compiler.

---

[15] As we only need P threads to work cooperatively, a small block size is reasonable since the GPU has more freedom in scheduling light-weight blocks to hide memory access latencies.

6   Experimental Results and Comparison

We have tested our algorithm on the *GeForce GTX 280* graphics processor and compared it with GMP 4.2.1 (http://gmplib.org) for large-integer multiplication and with NTL 5.5 (http://www.shoup.net/ntl) for polynomial multiplication. As a target CPU we have used *Quad-Core Intel Xeon E5420* clocked at 2.5Ghz with 12MB L2 cache and 8Gb RAM. Both libraries were built under native 64-bit Linux platform (Debian Etch), such that they were able to benefit from AMD64 instruction set.

For benchmarks we have implemented two versions of the CRT reconstruction: a completely inlined one using 4 moduli where each digit is processed separately by a single thread, and the 6-moduli CRT which realizes the algorithm from Section 5.5. The *initial modular reduction* of input digits was performed directly on the GPU prior to modular multiplications because the digits' bit-length is small. The bit-length of numbers to be multiplied depending on the CRT size and the transform length was estimated using the formula from Section 5.1. We use these estimates to compare our multiplication with that of provided by GMP and NTL. For instance, 1024-point NTT with 6-moduli CRT is enough to multiply 512·64-bit numbers exactly. Hence, GMP was used to multiply numbers of 512·64 bit-length, while NTL – to multiply 512-degree polynomials with 64-bit coefficients.

Remark that, our algorithm does not perform the digit adjustment after multiplying two integers encoded as polynomials. In other words, we do not compute the sum of "convolution digits", i.e., $z = \sum_{i=0}^{N-1} r_i \cdot 2^{Pi}$ (see Section 4.1). Nevertheless, we suppose this would not make our comparison with GMP unfair

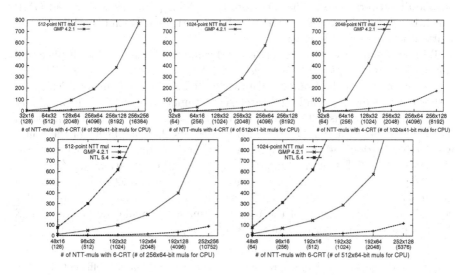

Fig. 3. Time comparison of batched large integer/polynomial multiplication with GMP/NTL implementations. **Top row:** 512-(left), 1024-(middle) and 2048-point(right) NTTs with 4-moduli CRT. **Bottom row:** 512-(left) and 1024-point(right) NTTs with **6-moduli** CRT. All times are in milliseconds.

Table 1. Performance of the 512-point and 2048-point convolutions in "GMul/s": 10^9 modular multiplications per second

# of 512-point NTTs	32x16	64x32	128x64	256x64	256x128	256x256
time (ms)	0.26	0.98	4.04	7.78	15.22	29.13
GMul/s	68	72	73	75	77	77
# of 2048-point NTTs	32x8	64x16	128x32	256x32	256x64	256x128
time (ms)	0.74	2.49	9.83	19.34	38.39	76.55
GMul/s	58	67	72	73	73	74

because this step is rather cheap as it only involves additions[16]. Moreover, the digit adjustment is not required in case of polynomial multiplication.

Figure 3 shows the time comparisons for batched multiplications. The labels along x-axes have the following meaning: for instance, on the top-left plot 32x16(128) denotes that the CPU performs 128 multiplications of 256×41-bit numbers while the GPU runs 16 512-point convolutions for each of 32 moduli (total of 512 convolutions) since a group of every 4 moduli contributes to a single multiplication. The GPU timing includes the time taken for memory transfer to the GPU and back to the host for a more objective comparison. We use *page-locked* memory to achieve higher bandwidth. From Figure 3 one can see that the GPU is superior for batched multiplications with moderate bit-lengths. Moreover, the gap increases for larger transforms. Increasing the number of CRT moduli is also advantageous for our algorithm, although it is yet unclear whether increasing the transform length or increasing the number of moduli is overall more efficient. Note that, NTL performs worse than GMP which is expectable because GMP uses hand-optimized assembly while NTL is written in a high-level language.

Table 1 summarizes the "effective" performance of the NTT multiplication, computed as: $GMul/s = 10^{-9} \cdot batch \cdot (3 \cdot 2.5N \log_2 N + 2N)/t$, here $2.5N \log_2 N$ is the complexity of the Cooley-Tukey style NTT (N is the transform length), t is the elapsed time in seconds and *batch* is the number of parallel multiplications. Each multiplication uses 2 forward and 1 backward transform, hence, the factor 3 in front of the formula. The term $2N$ represents the complexity of the point-wise multiplication and the multiplication by modular inverse. Remark that, the Cooley-Tukey NTT bound counts the number of multiplications in Z/mZ. To evaluate the "real" performance in *flops* recall that fma_bfy2 realizing modular multiplication executes in 6 flops (see Section 5.4). Hence, 77 GMul/s is roughly equivalent to 462 GFlop/s of the real performance[17], while the GeForce GTX 280 has peak parallel performance of 933 GFlop/s.

---

[16] Carry propagation after mutliprecision addition can be realized efficiently, for instance, using Hillis-and-Steele-style reductions [13].

[17] It worth mentioning that the Cooley-Tukey bound tends to overestimate the number of multiplications, nevertheless it is a commonly used tool to evaluate the FFT/NTT performance.

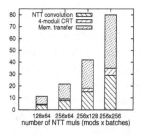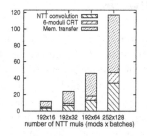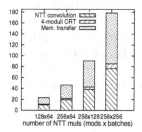

Fig. 4. Time breakdown (in milliseconds) for 512-(left), 1024-(middle) and 2048-point(right) transforms. Abbreviations along x-axis are the same as in Figure 3.

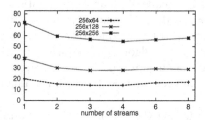

Fig. 5. The number of parallel streams influencing the overall time (in milliseconds) for 512-point NTTs including the memory transfer

Figure 4 depicts the time distribution over algorithm stages. Observe that, the CRT reconstruction is rather cheap while the time needed for memory transfer comprises the major part. This is known to be the main bottleneck for GPU algorithms. Fortunately, CUDA allows us to split a single kernel launch into several *streams* which execute asynchronously such that the memory transfer of one stream can overlap with a kernel execution of another stream[18]. Figure 5 evaluates the performance of 512-point NTTs with several streams. The figure shows that the optimal number of streams is 4.

To sum-up, our algorithm outperforms GMP and NTL for batched multiplications with moderate bit-length. We agree that this is not an objective picture because, for instance, GMP is particularly fast when the numbers of million bits are multiplied. We were not able to benchmark our algorithm on such instances due to the lack of implementation of larger transform lengths which is an object of ongoing research. Still, we believe that the this gives a good estimate of what the GPUs are practically capable of, because this area of GPU application is yet not well-explored.

---

[18] At the time of writing the new CUDA 2.2 has been released. It supports allocation of *pinned memory* mapped to the device's address space (cudaHostAllocMapped). Due to the time limitations we have not been able to test its performance.

7 Summary and Outlook

We have presented the algorithm to multiply polynomials on the GPU using the NTT modular convolution with the CRT reconstruction. Our approach shows a good performance for batched multiplication of polynomials with moderate coefficient bit-length. Clearly, the approach presented here is only the first step in realization of a robust large integer and polynomial arithmetic on the GPU.

Note that, this application domain is pretty novel for the graphics hardware and we see many promising perspectives for future work. First, we would like to increase the NTT transform length and make it adaptable to the bit-lengths of numbers to be multiplied. Second, we would like to realize multiprecision addition on the GPU using parallel reductions in order to be able to reconstruct multiprecision numbers by means of binary segmentation. It is also worthwhile to try out the technique called *GPU virtualization* given in [10] to handle inputs that do not fit in a single grid launch due to the hardware limitations. Finally, we would like to realize other algorithms requiring multiprecision arithmetic on the GPU using the modular approach, for example, evaluation of matrix determinants with large integer coefficients which is a fundamental operation in many scientific fields.

We also find very promising the oncoming Intel's Larrabee architecture [22] and would like to test our algorithm with it. It has a number of salient features lacked on the current GPUs. First, Larrabee's 16-wide Vector Processing Unit (VPU – somewhat similar to SM) supports double-precision arithmetic at full speed[19], which allows us to increase the moduli bit-length (up to 54 bits) or employ floating-point transforms for integer convolutions. Second, Larrabee has a coherent L2 cache, such that the data is transparently shared between all processor cores (in contrast, GPU thread blocks can share data only through a high-latency GDDR memory). This considerably simplifies the realization of large FFT transforms which are realized by a hierarchy of grid launches on the GPU. Moreover, Larrabee supports scatter/gather operations, i.e., VPU lanes can access data at non-contiguous addresses while uncoalesced global memory access by a half-warp is considerably slow and should be avoided.

Acknowledgements. We would like to thank Michael Kerber for reviewing the paper and for useful and pragmatic suggestions.

References

1. CUDA CUFFT library. NVIDIA Corp. (2007)
2. NVIDIA CUDA: Compute Unified Device Architecture. NVIDIA Corp. (2007)
3. Akkal, M., Siy, P.: A new Mixed Radix Conversion algorithm MRC-II. J. Syst. Archit. 53, 577–586 (2007)
4. Bailey, D.H.: A High-Performance FFT Algorithm for Vector Supercomputers. International Journal of Supercomputer Applications 2, 82–87 (1988)

---

[19] The GPU has only one double-precision FPU per SM, therefore the double-precision arithmetic is 8 times slower than the single-precision.

5. Basu, S., Pollack, R., Roy, M.-F.: Algorithms in Real Algebraic Geometry (Algorithms and Computation in Mathematics). Springer, New York (2006)
6. Cooley, J.W., Tukey, J.W.: An Algorithm for the Machine Calculation of Complex Fourier Series. Mathematics of Computation 19, 297–301 (1965)
7. Elliott, D.F., Rao, K.R.: Fast Transforms: Algorithms, Analyses, Applications. Academic Press, Inc., Orlando (1983)
8. Fagin, B.S.: Large integer multiplication on hypercubes. J. Parallel Distrib. Comput. 14, 426–430 (1992)
9. von zur Gathen, J., Gerhard, J.: Modern Computer Algebra. Cambridge University Press, Cambridge (1999)
10. Govindaraju, N.K., Lloyd, B., Dotsenko, Y., Smith, B., Manferdelli, J.: High performance discrete Fourier transforms on graphics processors. In: SC 2008, pp. 1–12. IEEE Press, Los Alamitos (2008)
11. Graça, G.D., Defour, D.: Implementation of float-float operators on graphics hardware. CoRR **abs/cs/0603115** (2006)
12. Hida, Y., Li, X.S., Bailey, D.H.: Algorithms for Quad-Double Precision Floating Point Arithmetic. In: Proceedings of the 15th Symposium on Computer Arithmetic, pp. 155–162. IEEE Computer Society Press, Los Alamitos (2001)
13. Hillis, W.D., Steele Jr., G.L.: Data parallel algorithms. ACM Commun. 29, 1170–1183 (1986)
14. Huang, C.H.: A Fully Parallel Mixed-Radix Conversion Algorithm for Residue Number Applications. IEEE Trans. Computers 32, 398–402 (1983)
15. Karner, H., Auer, M., Ueberhuber, C.W.: Accelerating FFTW by Multiply-Add Optimization. Tech. rep., Institute for Applied and Numerical Mathematics, Vienna University of Technology, TR1999-13 (1999)
16. Lindholm, E., Nickolls, J., Oberman, S., Montrym, J.: NVIDIA Tesla: A Unified Graphics and Computing Architecture. IEEE Micro. 28, 39–55 (2008)
17. Moreland, K., Angel, E.: The FFT on a GPU. In: HWWS 2003. Eurographics Association, pp. 112–119. ACM Press, New York (2003)
18. Moss, A., Page, D., Smart, N.: Toward Acceleration of RSA Using 3D Graphics Hardware. In: Galbraith, S.D. (ed.) Cryptography and Coding 2007. LNCS, vol. 4887, pp. 364–383. Springer, Heidelberg (2007)
19. Munshi, A.: OpenCL: Parallel Computing on the GPU and CPU. SIGGRAPH 2008 (2008) (presentation)
20. Percival, C.: Rapid multiplication modulo the sum and difference of highly composite numbers. Mathematics of Computation 72, 241, 387–395 (2003)
21. Schönhage, A., Strassen, V.: Schnelle Multiplikation grosser Zahlen. Computing 7, 281–292 (1971)
22. Seiler, L., Carmean, D., Sprangle, E., Forsyth, T., Abrash, M., Dubey, P., Junkins, S., Lake, A., Sugerman, J., Cavin, R., Espasa, R., Grochowski, E., Juan, T., Hanrahan, P.: Larrabee: a many-core x86 architecture for visual computing. ACM Trans. Graph. 27, 1–15 (2008)
23. Szabo, N., Tanaka, R.: Residue arithmetic and its applications to computer technology. SIAM 11, 103–104 (1969)
24. Szerwinski, R., Güneysu, T.: Exploiting the Power of GPUs for Asymmetric Cryptography. In: Oswald, E., Rohatgi, P. (eds.) CHES 2008. LNCS, vol. 5154, pp. 79–99. Springer, Heidelberg (2008)
25. Yassine, M.: Matrix Mixed-Radix Conversion For RNS Arithmetic Architectures (1991)

Performance Optimization Strategies of High Performance Computing on GPU*

Anguo Ma, Jing Cai, Yu Cheng, Xiaoqiang Ni,
Yuxing Tang, and Zuocheng Xing

National Laboratory for Parallel and Distributed Processing, School of Computer,
National University of Defense Technology,
ChangSha, China
{anguo.ma,jing.cai,y.cheng,xq.ni,tyx,zcxing}@nudt.edu.cn
http://www.nudt.edu.cn

Abstract. Recently GPU is widely utilized in scientific computing and engineering applications, owing primarily to the evolution of GPU architecture. Firstly, we analyze some key performance characters of GPU in detail, and the relationships among GPU architecture, programming model and memory hierarchy. Secondly, we present three performance optimization strategies: Prefetching, Streamlizing, and Task Division. Adequate experiments have been done to abstract the relationships among different factors and efficiency. Finally, we map the HPL benchmark to testify our strategies and achieve certain speedup.

Keywords: GPGPU, Optimization Strategy, Stream Computing, Task Division, HPL Benchmark.

1 Introduction

Driven by new demands of emerging applications, computing architectures keep on improving with the support of CMOS technology scaling. Whereas today how to harness the theoretic peak performance of the powerful multi-core processors is the key to high performance computing. Exposing and utilizing parallelism in different levels rely on the efforts of architecture designer and programmer. Although great efforts has been made to modeling underline hardware architecture into special software platform, the gap between the ability of parallel hardware and the ability of software to use the parallisim continues expanding.

Besides the huge effort to create a brand-new architecture with high-efficient parallel programming models, there are two directions to save both commercial vendors and academic researchers from the dilemma: to make the general processor more powerful or to make the custom processor more general, both with advanced developing environment. Many commercial vendors and academic

---

* This work is supported by National High Technology Development 863 Program of China under Grant No.2009AA01Z102 and National Natural Science Foundation of China under Grant No.60873016.

Y. Dou, R. Gruber, and J. Joller (Eds.): APPT 2009, LNCS 5737, pp. 150–164, 2009.
© Springer-Verlag Berlin Heidelberg 2009

Table 1. Environment Configuration

Environment	Platform1	Platform2
CPU	Intel Core2 E7200	Intel Core i7
GPU	NVIDIA GeForce 9800GTX	NVIDIA GTX280
Motherboard	GIGABYTE EDP43-DS3L	GIGABYTE EX58-UD4

researchers have made great efforts. New arechitecture with own programming model has been proposed, such as Imagine, Cell, RAW, Many-core plan, Fusion plan and so on. Meanwhile, new multi-core programming platforms have been stimulated to grow rapidly to face the era of parallel computing on multi-core computing hardware, such as Ct [1], SWARM [2], and RapidMind [3].

In the way of making custom processor more general, GPU is one of the most successful candidates. GPU architecture has achieved revolutionary progress to support scientific computing and engineering applications, along with new programming platforms which is convenient for mapping these applications onto it. As the explosion of GPGPU applications shows, GPU can be widely used in the general-purpose and scientific computing field, besides the traditional graphics processing.

Because many scientific computing applications are full of dense linear algebra [4], hence the performance of Linpack is the most important criterion to evaluate the capability of supercomputers. HPL (High Performance Linpack), an advanced implementation of Linpack, solves the dense linear algebra in double precision (64-bits) arithmetic on distributed-memory computers. Matrix multiplication and LU factorization are the key parts of HPL. HPL also provides a testing and timing program to quantify the accuracy of the obtained solution as well as the time it took to compute it [5].

In this paper, based on three optimizing methods: prefetching, streamlizing, and task division, we speedup Matrix multiplication on different GPU hardware platforms. The core of optimization is to improve the ratio of computing operations to memory accesses, and hide the transfer latency in different memory levels. Ths task division can utilize the computing power of CPU and GPU at the same time. We summarized the relationship between advisable division factor and a large variety of factors including the capability of GPU and CPU in the heterogeneous system and transfer bandwidth. Moreover, we tried to hide the transfer latency in system level by packing subsets of transfer operations and computing operations into multiple streams. In final experiment, the HPL benchmark was optimized on our heterogeneous hardware platforms. Specifications of two platforms used in our experiments are listed in Table. 1.

2 Background and Overview

2.1 GPGPU Trend

The emergence of development platforms and SDKs - CUDA from NVIDIA and Brook+ from AMD - has attracted the attention of researchers and programmers devoted to scientific computing and parallel programming, and also guided them to find that GPUs could be reharnessed for tasks other than graphics easily [6]. And the trend mapping general-purpose applications onto GPU is called GPGPU (General Purpose Computing on GPU). Masses of successful implementations have proved that GPU can be used widely and efficiently in fields of Computational Biology [7][8], Physically Based Simulation[9][10][11], Computational Biophysics[12][13][14], Signal and Image Processing[15][16] and so on.

2.2   GPU Architecture and Programming Model

Over the past few decades, GPU architecture has developed dramatically and changed rapidly. Targeting load balance and high hardware utilization, GPU has evolved from fixed-function architecture to general parallel programmable architecture, which merged special-purpose shaders - Programmable Vertex Processor and Programmable Fragment Processor - into the unified shader. Early in 2005, AMD implemented the first unified shader architecture in Xenos GPU, and later in 2006 announced the AMD Stream Processor with CTM (Close To Metal) runtime, addressing the needs of high-performance computing. Meanwhile, NVIDIA introduced CUDA (Compute Unified Device Architecture) in November 2006. The main strategy of them is to utilize the powerful computing resources efficiently by scheduling masses of threads dynamically.

In contrast to CPU, GPU addresses throughput related issues other than latency, and GPU architecture is designed for data parallel applications with high arithmetic density. As to NVIDIA, GTX280 is composed of 10 Thread Processing Clusters (TPC), each of them consisting of 3 Streaming Multiprocessor (SM), which is made up of 8 Streaming Processor (SP), a 64 bit fused multiply-add

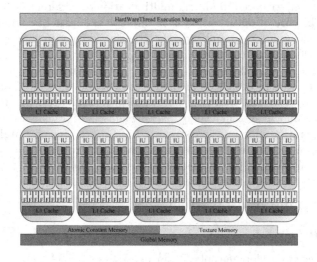

Fig. 1. GTX280 Architecture

unit and a Special Function Unit (SFU) sharing a front-end, similar to a 8-wide SIMD CPU.

With respect to different types of data structure in diverse applications, it implements a complex memory hierarchy and related texture and render output pipelines to reuse data on chip including temporal computing result adequately and to hide the data transfer delay. GTX280 employs 1GB off-chip global memory which is shared by all the threads on GPU to link GPU and CPU by PCIe interface. Computing kernels run on GPU can access the global memory directly, or access read-only texture memory and constant memory via texture cache and constant cache. Each SM has 16KB on-chip shared memory and 16KB 32-bit registers. Shared memory is organized into 16 banks and partitioned among thread blocks dynamically, while registers are partitioned among active thread blocks on SM dynamically and assigned to a given thread statically. Without bank conflict, access to shared memory is as fast as that of register file, while access to global memory may take multiple hundreds of cycles. Data will be spilled out to private local memory located in global memory when registers assigned are not enough in a thread.

Only one program can be performed on single GPU device, and the program launched to device by CPU(host) is called kernel, which is executed in manner of SPMD(Single Program Multiple data), running thousands of threads in parallel on different data sets. The thread grid is divided into many thread blocks with the same dimension and mapped onto SMs after the kernel is launched. The maximum number of active blocks per SM is 8, and at most 1024 threads can be executed on single SM concurrently. The practical numbers are limited by resource demands of single thread. Every 32 threads in one block are grouped as a warp and performed in SIMD manner by 8 SPs. The SM in device of Compute Capability 1.3 can have as many as 32 active warps, which are switched periodically to hide the latency of stalled threads. Threads in the same block can cooperate via shared memory using synchronization instruction, yet communication among threads from different blocks isn't supported at present.

2.3   GPGPU in High Performance Computing

Though the development platforms and SDKs(software development kits) have been introduced to facilitate utilizing powerful hardware efficiently, it is still not easy for programmers used to traditional programming, owing to insufficient details exposed to programmer and intrinsic limitations inherited from graphics. Many efforts have been made to enhance the performance of linear algebra algorithms like matrix multiplication on GPU from aspects of parallel programming, compiling optimization and heterogeneous computing and so on.

Volkov et al. [17] concluded the characters of modern GPU in a special view and useful experiences being of benefit to code optimization. Their work presented the size and latency of cache and TLB in GPU memory system. Considering the parallel computing of CPU and GPU in heterogeneous system, their matrix-matrix multiply routine ran up to 60% faster than CUBLAS1.1 and achieved 80-90% of the peak GEMM rate.

Massimiliano Fatica [18] analyzed the bandwidth between host (CPU) and device (GPU), then concluded the division factor used in dividing tasks to perform simultaneously on both CPU and GPU.

Castillo et al. [19] ported libFlame, developed from PLAPACK application programming interface(API), to a multi-GPU system using a wrapper for the CUBLAS, and achieved an ideal speedup.

Quintana-Orti et al. [20] testified FLAME methodology by adapting FLAME to a complex heterogeneous system including multiple types of accelerator, CPU, GPU and CELL B.E.

3   GPU Features

The performance of an application depends on many factors including the capabilities of different system computing resources and transfer bandwidth between host (CPU) and devices (other computing resources). Kernel running on GPU can access global memory directly, but it may take several hundreds of cycles greater than that of on-chip memory, hence how to utilize limited registers and shared memory have a great effect on algorithms. In this section we analyze the transfer bandwidth between CPU and GPU, and the layout of passed parameters of kernel and located shared memory space.

3.1   Transfer Bandwidth between CPU and GPU

Although GPU is more and more powerful, how to feed them with data in time is a great problem for programmers. CUDA2.2beta released recently introduces a new runtime feature called zero-copy, which can hide data transfer latency automatically. According to the programming guide released by NVIDIA officially, transfer with Pinned memory is faster than that of Pageable memory, because it can eliminate an extra copy existing right before DMA transfer between CPU and GPU[18]. Unfortunately, this transfer speedup comes at the cost of CPU performance, because Pinned memory is page-locked and can't be used until it is released.

We tested different transfer modes with different data sizes on different platforms, and motherboards in both of them are compatible with PCIe2.0 x16 standard, the ideal bandwidth of which can approach 8.0GB/s.

As presented in Fig. 2, bandwidth of Pinned memory is much higher than that of Pageable memory apparently. Bandwidth of Pinned memory increases with data amount, then reaches and maintains 4.6GB/s steadily. As for Pageable memory, the steady bandwidth only can approach 1.7 GB/s when transfer data from host to device, in the opposite direction, the steady bandwidth is 1.55 GB/s.

Testing on platform 2, we got a better result. As presented in Fig. 3, the steady H2D bandwidth of Pinned memory can reach 5.7 GB/s, and that of opposite direction is 5.4 GB/s. The bandwidths of Pageable memory in both directions tend toward the same 2.3 GB/s.

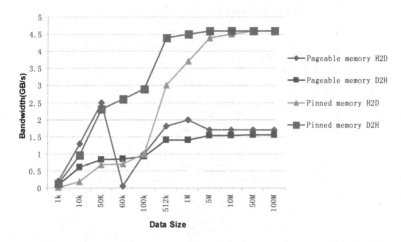

Fig. 2. Transfer Bandwidth between CPU and GPU on Platform1 (H2D: host to device D2H: device to host)

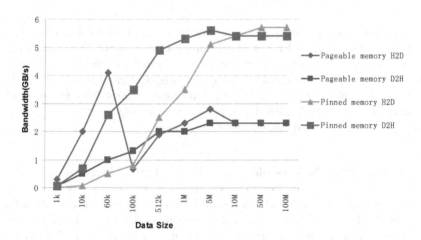

Fig. 3. Transfer Bandwidth between CPU and GPU on Platform2

3.2 Layout of Shared Memory

Threads in a block can cooperate using a synchronize operation, and communicate with each other via shared memory. Moreover, shared memory also can be used to reuse data on-chip among threads and mitigate pressure of limited register file. As demonstrated above, access to shared memory is as fast as register access in absent of bank conflicts. When a kernel is launched from host to device, the execution configuration parameters and kernel parameters are passed to device and kept in shared memory. Using several benchmarks with different configuration and shared memory usage, as presented in Table. 2, we can find

Table 2. Layout of Shared Memory

Random data
Extern __shared__ memory   *(Start from the first address divide 16B exactly)*
Random data
__shared__ memory
Parameter n   Parameter n-1   . . .   Parameter 0
Zero(4B)
Dg.y(2B)   Dg.x(2B)   Db.z(2B)   Db.y(2B)   Db.x(2b)   *(Start from address 0)*

that execution configuration parameters are kept from address 0 in order (Db and Dg are Dim3 type, and Db is dimension of a block, while Dg is dimension of a grid), after 4B unknown space storing zero, kernel parameters are kept in sequence. Then there is a memory space allocated statically according to the code, while the memory space allocated dynamically starts from the first address dividing 16B exactly after the last data in static space. And the data in between static space and dynamic space are random.

3.3   Optimization Methodology and Performance Analysis

The basic principle of optimization is to make the most of computing units in the whole system effectively during the entire execution period. So we emphasize the load balance in three levels. Firstly, we optimized the scalable algorithms by improving the ratio of computing operations to memory accesses, and made great efforts to increase data reusage to avoid high latency of off-chip memory access. By comparison, we abstracted an appropriate prefetching stride factor to guide scheduling instructions manually in instruction level, based on the assemble code generated by decuda[20]. Furthermore, in order to overlap kernel execution with transfers between CPU and GPU, we wrapped related transfer and computing operations into several streams, and analyzed the relationship between the amount of streams and performance. Based on the above works, we tried to figure out the most appropriate factor when we divide the whole application into several tasks running on different processors in the system concurrently.

According to the Amdahl's Law, optimizing the part of application with high computing ratio is the most effective method to improve the overall performance. As to the HPL benchmark, it is matrix multiplication. So we focus on the matrix multiplication algorithm, and the corresponding optimization strategies are described in following sections.

3.4 Prefetching

Compiler always works in a relatively conservative way. Hence there still is a vast space for programmer to schedule instructions or assemble operations. Placing irrelevant instructions between instructions with data dependence could hide the instruction stalls, however inadequate scheduling may lower the performance. Prefetching is a popular scheduling strategy aiming at hiding the latency of memory access. Global memory access in GPU takes several hundreds of cycles and hurt much performance. We use prefetching strategy in our matrix multiplication algorithm, and bring some global memory access operations forward and place them between instructions in data hazard. How many memory access operations should be brought forward depends on the ratio of memory access latency and computing overhead. Furthermore, because of active thread warps being scheduled periodically, there is a complex relationship between the period and scheduling. So we move different amount of irrelevant memory access operations up in main loop.

When the dimensions of both matrices are 2048*2048, our matrix multiplication application scheduled two memory access operations runs up to 8.5% faster than algorithm without prefetching. However, when four or eight memory access operations are moved up, it only reaches 38% of original performance.

3.5 Stream Computing

Many types of operations in CUDA runtime are asynchronous, such as cudaMemcpyAsync, kernel launch operation, cudaEventRecord and so on, control is returned to host after they are launched. Hence we can utilize the parallelism in system level and stream level. A subset of transfer operations and kernels can be wrapped into a stream, and operations from different streams without resource conflict can be performed in parallel. Although there are some restrictions, especially for stream 0, it is still worth streamlizing the application to overlap operations from different streams.

As illustrated by Fig. 4, the traditional way of GPU computing can be described as: transfer data and code into device, kernel execution on device, and then transfer results to host from device. Due to the data parallelism in application and the SPMD manner of GPU computing, an application can be divided into several streams, which are performed in parallel partially as illustrated in Fig. 5.

Apparently, streamlizing application will increase the amount of operations, incurring more launch overhead. Furthermore, limited by global memory, the transfer of divided data input possibly can't make use of the peak bandwidth between CPU and GPU. In addition, the streamlizing strategy targets hiding the transfer latency from computing, hence little speedup could be gained when

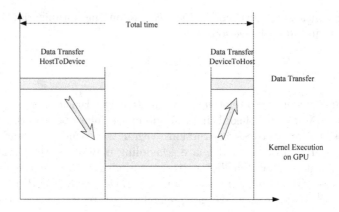

Fig. 4. Traditional Way of GPU Computing

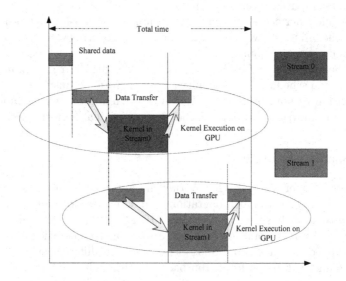

Fig. 5. Stream Computing in GPU

the ratio of transfer time to computing time is very small or very large, and even performance is likely to be worse.

In Fig. 6, compared to unstreamlized routine, 4% speedup is achieved averagely with nstreams being 3. When nstreams is 6, streamlized routine runs up to 5% faster than the original routine, except for some special situation as described above.

As Fig. 7 presented, when the matrix dimension exceeds 4096, a steady 2.3% speedup can be achieved with nstreams being 4. And when the matrix dimension is under 4096, streamlized applications behave not well, even worse.

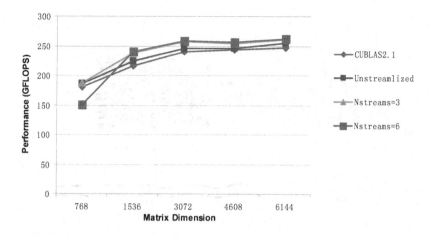

Fig. 6. Performance comparison on platform1. *Nstreams is the number of streams.*

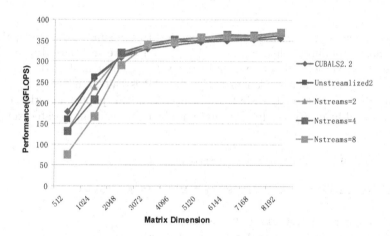

Fig. 7. Performance comparison on platform2

3.6   Task Division for CPU and GPU

After kernel is launched, control is returned to host, consequently host can process in parallel with GPU. So we divide the application into two work sets, and make them run in different hardware concurrently as illustrated in Fig. 8. The division factor relies on the capabilities of device and host, and the transfer bandwidth between them.

As for matrix multiplicaiton A*B=C, matrix A is divided into two submatrices A_{host} and A_{device} by division factor, so the equation A*B=C is divided into A_{host}*B=C_{host} and A_{device}*B=C_{device}. Because the launch overhead can be ignored, it can be assumed that the ideal factor should be G_{device} / (G_{host}

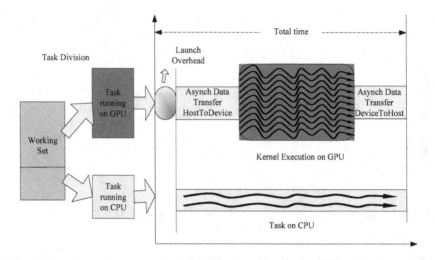

Fig. 8. Task Division

$+ G_{device}$), that is the ratio of device capability to the sum of device capability and host capability. Then matrices A_{device} and B are transferred to device asychronously, kernel is launched, and matrix C_{device} is transferred from device to host asychronously. Concurrently, $A_{host}*$B is calculated on host using MKL10.1.0.018 (mentioned as MKL later throughout this paper), and the result C_{host} is stored in host directly. The division algorithm is demonstrated simply as follows.

Pseudo Code of parallel computing in system level

```
For(;division factor < 1;division factor += stride)
{
    Async transfer matrix B to device
    Async transfer matrix A partially to device
    Kernel lanuch
    Async transfer matrix C partially to device
    Cblas_sgemm // task running on host
    cudaThreadSynchronize()
    //blocking until task on device complete
}
```

As presented in Fig. 9, the performance of device improves while the size of matrix increases. As a whole, the speedup is rough equal to G_{host} / G_{device}. For example, when the matrix dimension is 4096, G_{host} is 35GFLOPS and G_{device} is 301GFLOPS. And the system achieves the peak performance of 341GFLOPS with the factor being 0.875 which approaches 0.89, the theoretical result of G_{device} / ($G_{host} + G_{device}$). And the practical speedup is 13%, which is close to 12%, the result of G_{host} / G_{device}.

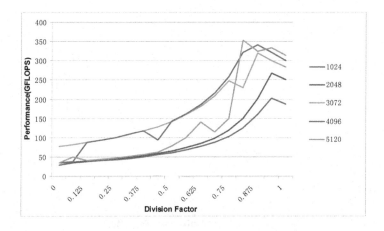

Fig. 9. Task Division on Platform 2

3.7 Streamlizing the Divided Task on Device

Based on the above attempts, three task division routines, CUBLAS2.2 with MKL, optimized algorithm with MKL, and streamlized algorithm with MKL, are tested on platform2 and compared with each other.

In Fig. 10, owing primarily to the extra launch overhead and transfer bandwidth, the advantage of streamlization reveals until the matrix dimension is big enough to approach the peak transfer bandwidth. With appropriate division factor, streamlized routine with 6 streams can run up to 436GFLOPS, about 2% faster than optimized routine, and 18% faster than the vendor's implementation optimized by task division strategy. Compared with the traditional way of GPU computing, the streamlized routine using task division strategy runs up to 23.5% faster than the vendor's implementation.

4 Accelerating HPL Benchmark in Heterogeneous System

4.1 Key Parameters

There are two controllable parameters playing important roles in tuning the practical implementation of HPL benchmark targeting at the peak performance. N is the matrix dimension, and NB is the block sizes one wants to run, which can be used to control the width of matrix A and the hieght of B. Therefore we analyze effects of N and NB on the performance of benchmark firstly.

Using CUBLAS2.1 and Pageable memory, we test HPL benchmark on Platform2. As presented by Fig. 11, both N and NB have a positive effect on the performance for the most part. Furthermore, as NB increases, the effect of NB on performance becomes weaker and weaker.

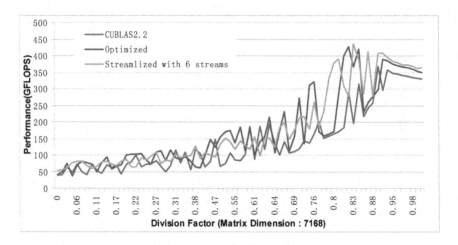

Fig. 10. Performance comparison of three routines using MKL

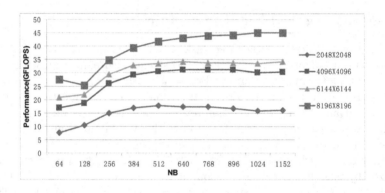

Fig. 11. N and NB's effects on performance

4.2   Acceleration Results

HPL benchmark is divided into different working sets running on host and device in parallel, using CUBLAS2.1 and MKL respectively. Before utilizing the capability of the whole system, the performances of HPL on device and host are tested apart and compared in Fig. 12.

Apparently, as N increases linearly, the performance of HPL implemented using CUBLAS improves remarkably on the whole and becomes sustained at last, while the performance of HPL running on host using MKL improves slowly in waves. Because of the transfer overhead, the application using MKL behaves better than the application implemented with CUBLAS. When the transfer overhead is hidden by the advantage brought by GPU's computing capability, the situation reversed.

The theoretical Double Precision performance of host and device on Platform 2 are 40GFLOPS and 78GFLOPS respectively. According to the division

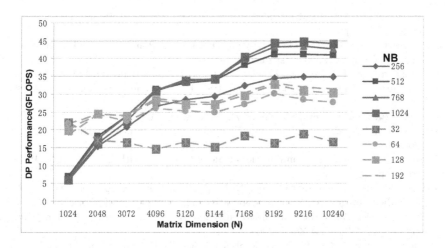

Fig. 12. HPL performance using CUBLAS and MKL. Real line is on behalf of CUBLAS2.1, Broken line is on behalf of MKL

Table 3. DP performance of HPL (N=12288)

Division factor(ratio)	0.64	0.65	0.66	0.67	0.68	0.69
DP Performance(GFLOPS)	61.28	61.64	62.62	62.07	61.55	60.94

equation $G_{device}\ /\ (G_{host}\ +\ G_{device})$, the best division factor should be 0.66, which is confirmed by our later experiment results in Table. 3. Moreover, the parallel implementation delivers 62.62GFLOPS, 53% of the 118GFLOPS system peak performance. Given more memory on device, we will take advantage of under-utilized hardware further.

5   Conclusions and Future Work

Although we have achieved considerable speedup for matrix multiplication algorithm and HPL benchmark by means of three basic optimization strategies, there still is a wide optimization space with limited transfer bandwidth. Addressing the load balance issue, effective instruction scheduling and application streamlizing would introduce much more improvements. Furthermore, we will explore the optimization space of sparse linear algebra, tune the optimization factors and improve our experimental theory.

References

1. Ghuloum, A., Sprangle, E., Fang, J., Wu, G., Zhou, X.: Ct: A Flexible Parallel Programming Model for Tera-scale Architectures. Technical report, Intel Research (2007)

2. Gutowitz. H.: A tutorial introduction to Swarm. Technical report, The Santa Fe Institute (1993)
3. Monteyne, M.: RapidMind: Multi-Core Develpment Platform, RapidMind Official Page (2007), http://www.rapidmind.net/
4. Dongarra, J.J., Luszczek, P., Petitet, A.: The LINPACK Benchmark: Past, Present, and Future. Concurrency and Computation: Practice and Experience 15, 803–820 (2003)
5. http://www.netlib.org/benchmark/hpl/index.html
6. Halfhill, T.R.: Parallel Processing With CUDA. Microprocessor Report (January 2008)
7. Stone, J.: Accelerating Computational Biology by 100x with CUDA. In: NVISION (2008) (presentation)
8. Hartley, T.D.R., Catalyurek, U., Ruiz, A., Igual, F., Mayo, R., Ujaldon, M.: Biomedical image analysis on a cooperative cluster of gpus and multicores. In: ICS 2008: Proceedings of the 22nd annual international conference on Supercomputing, pp. 15–25. ACM, New York (2008)
9. Bond, A.: Havok FX: GPU-accelerated physics for PC games. In: Proceedings of Game Developers Conference 2006 (2006)
10. Hagen, T.R., Lle, K.-A., Natvig, J.R.: Solving the Euler equations on graphics processing units. In: Alexandrov, V.N., van Albada, G.D., Sloot, P.M.A., Dongarra, J. (eds.) ICCS 2006. LNCS, vol. 3994, pp. 220–227. Springer, Heidelberg (2006)
11. Zeller, C.: Cloth simulation on the GPU. In: ACM SIGGRAPH 2005 Conference Abstracts and Applications (2005)
12. Elsen, E., Houston, M., Vishal, V., Darve, E., Hanrahan, P., Pande, V.S.: N-Body simulation on GPUs. In: Proc. 2006 ACM/IEEE Conf. on Supercomputing, p. 188 (2006)
13. Phillips, J.C., Braun, R., Wang, W., Gumbart, J., Tajkhorshid, E., Villa, E., Chipot, C., Skeel, R.D., Kale, L., Schulten, K.: Scalable molecular dynamics with NAMD. J. Comp. Chem. 26, 1781–1802 (2005)
14. Stone, J.E., Phillips, J.C., Freddolino, P.L., Hardy, D.J., Trabuco, L.G., Schulten, K.: Accelerating molecular modeling applications with graphics processors. J. Comp. Chem. 28, 2618–2640 (2007)
15. Stone, S.S., Haldar, J.P., Tsao, S.C., Hwu, W.W., Liang, Z., Sutton, B.P.: Accelerating advanced MRI reconstructions on GPUs. In: ACM Computing Frontier Conference (2008)
16. openVIDIA, http://openvidia.sourceforge.net/
17. Volkov, V., Demmel, J.W.: Benchmarking GPUs to tune dense linear algebra. In: SC 2008: Proceedings of the 2008 ACM/IEEE conference on Super-computing, pp. 1–11. IEEE Press, Los Alamitos (2008)
18. Fatica, M.: Accelerating Linpack with CUDA on heterogenous clusters. In: GPGPU 2009. ACM, New york (2009)
19. Castillo, M., Chan, E., Igual, F.D., Mayo, R., Quintanaorti, E.S., Quintana-orti, G., Van De Geijn, R., Van Zee, F.G.: Making Programming Synonymous with Programming for Linear Algebra Libraries, FLAME Working Note #31. The University of Texas at Austin, Department of Computer Sciences. Technical Report TR-08-20 (April 17, 2008)
20. Quintana-Orti, G., Igual, F.D., Quintana-Orti, E.S., van de Geijn, R.: Solving Dense Linear Systems on Platforms with Multiple Hardware Accelerators. In: PPoPP, pp. 121–129 (2009)
21. decuda, http://www.cs.rug.nl/~wladimir/decuda/

A Practical Approach of Curved Ray Prestack Kirchhoff Time Migration on GPGPU*

Xiaohua Shi, Chuang Li, Xu Wang, and Kang Li

School of Computer Science,
Beihang University, Beijing 100083, China
xhshi@buaa.edu.cn, whlichuang@126.com,
{xu.wang,kang.li}@sei.buaa.edu.cn

Abstract. We introduced four prototypes of General Purpose GPU solutions by Compute Unified Device Architecture (CUDA) on NVidia GeForce 8800GT and Tesla C870 for a practical Curved Ray Prestack Kirchhoff Time Migration program, which is one of the most widely adopted imaging methods in the seismic data processing industry. We presented how to re-design and re-implement the original CPU code to efficient GPU code step by step. We demonstrated optimization methods, such as how to reduce the overhead of memory transportation on PCI-E bus, how to significantly increase the kernel thread numbers on GPU cores, how to buffer the inputs and outputs of CUDA kernel modules, and how to utilize the memory streams to overlap GPU kernel execution time, etc., to improve the runtime performance on GPUs. We analyzed the floating point errors between CPUs and GPUs. We presented the images generated by CPU and GPU programs for the same real-world seismic data inputs. Our final approach of Prototype-IV on NVidia GeForce 8800GT is 16.3 times faster than its CPU version on Intel's P4 3.0G.

Keywords: General Purpose GPU, Prestack Kirchhoff Time Migration, CUDA.

1 Introduction

The main goal of earth exploration is to provide the oil and gas industry with knowledge of the earth's subsurface structure to detect where oil can be found and recovered. To do so, large-scale seismic surveys of the earth are performed, and the data recorded undergoes complex iterative processing to extract a geological model of the earth. The data are then interpreted by experts to help decide where to build oil recovery infrastructure[1].

In practice, seismic data processing is divided into two steps. The first step applies signal processing algorithms to normalize the signal over the entire survey

---

* This work was supported by grants from the National High Technology Research and Development Program of China (863 Program) No.2007AA01A127 and the Specialized Research Fund for the Doctoral Program of Higher Education (New Faculty) 2007006028.

Y. Dou, R. Gruber, and J. Joller (Eds.): APPT 2009, LNCS 5737, pp. 165–176, 2009.
© Springer-Verlag Berlin Heidelberg 2009

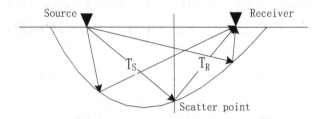

Fig. 1. Relationship between source, receiver, scatter point and their corresponding migration curve in PKTM. T_S is the sending time from the source to the scatter point. T_R is the reflecting time from the scatter point to the receiver.

and to increase the signal-to-noise ratio. Hundreds of mathematical algorithms are available during this step, from which geophysical specialist will select the particular candidates for seismic data by experience. The second step, which is the most time-consuming one, is designed to correct for the effects of changing subsurface media velocity on the wave propagation through the earth. Prestack Kirchhoff Time Migration (PKTM) algorithm used in the second step is one of the most widely adopted imaging methods in the seismic data processing industry.

Fig. 1 shows the relationship between the source, receiver and scatter point as well as their corresponding migration curves used in PKTM algorithm. It assumes that the energy of a sampled point on an input trace is the superposition of the reflections from all the underground scatter points that have the same travel time. The purpose of the migration processing is to spread the points on an input trace to all possible scatter points in the 3D space. Each input trace is independent of the others when it is migrated, and this makes this problem suitable for parallelization on the cluster. After all input traces are migrated, the migrated samples are accumulated to get the migrated image. The algorithm is heavily time-consuming because of the huge number of iterations at runtime.

A PKTM program, especially Curved Ray PKTM (CR-PKTM) program [2], usually runs days or weeks to process a typical seismic job on clusters with hundreds of machines. Fig. 2 illustrates a typical approach of CR-PKTM on cluster [3]. Process 1–N on different nodes will get the same amount of trace data as inputs. And the calculation work on each node is almost the same. Clearly, one of the efficient ways to improve the overall performance of CR-PKTM is to improve the average calculating performance for each node in the cluster.

In a matter of just a few years, the programmable graphics processor unit has evolved into an absolute computing workhorse. With multiple cores driven by very high memory bandwidth, today's GPUs offer incredible resources for both graphics and non-graphics processing [4]. The GPUs could achieve up to hundreds or even thousands of GFLOPS, comparing to the general CPUs that only have dozens of GFLOPS so far.

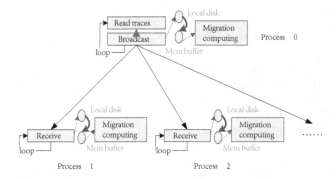

Fig. 2. A parallelized CR-PKTM program on cluster

The main reason behind such an evolution is that the GPU is specialized for compute-intensive, highly parallel computation - exactly what graphics rendering is about - and therefore is designed such that more transistors are devoted to data processing rather than data caching and flow control. When GPUs are used as general platforms to exploit data-level-parallelism (DLP) for non-graphic applications, they are known as General Purpose GPUs (GPGPUs).

As a leading role in the seismic data processing industry, Compagnie Generale de Geophysique (CGG) has evaluated the GPGPU and Compute Unified Device Architecture (CUDA) as accelerating platforms in its migrating software [1]. For the DLP programming models on GPU, there are a lot of research works. I. Buck et al. presented the Brook system for GPGPU [5]. Brook extends C to include simple data-parallel constructs, enabling the use of the GPU as a streaming coprocessor. D.Tarditi et al. presented Accelerator, a system that uses data parallelism to program GPUs for general-purpose uses instead [6]. Peakstream Corp. developed a DLP programming platform for GPGPU [7]. The Peakstream platform was a new software development platform that offered an easy-to-use stream programming model for multi-core processors and accelerators such as GPUs.

In this paper, we demonstrate how to utilize CUDA [4], GeForce 8800GT and Tesla C870 GPUs of NVidia, to exploit the data-level-parallelism for a practical CR-PKTM program.

2 Implement Curved Ray Prestack Kirchhoff Time Migration on GPGPU

Fig. 3 presents the simplified pseudo code of a practical CR-PKTM program. There are four-layer loops in the program. The outer two layers survey the incoming floating points that represent different coordinates on the earth surface, choose the appropriate candidates and pass them to the inner two loops to be migrated on a particular cluster node.

```
for(loopcount1){
  for(loopcount2){ ...
    while(condition1){ ...
      if(condition2){ ...
        for(loopcount3){... ...}
      }else if(condition3){ ...
        for(loopcount4){... ...}
      }else{
        for(loopcount5){... ...}
      }
      ... ...
    }//while
  }//for loopcount2
}//for loopcount1
```

Fig. 3. Simplified pseudo code of a practical CR-PKTM program

Comparing with the Kirchhoff migration CPU code of PeakStream [7], the practical CR-PKTM program has more branches, one more layer loop and more complicated floating point calculations. As we known, the branches will hurt the efficiency of the SIMD instructions of GPGPU at runtime.

2.1   Prototype I

There are four-layer loops in the practical CR-PKTM program in Fig. 3. The outer two-layer loops select appropriate coordinates to be migrated in the inner two-layer loops. Rewriting the inner two-layer loops from CPU code to CUDA code is an easy way to utilize the GPGPU. Fig. 4 illustrates how Prototype-I works. For every selected coordinate, we send the input data from CPU memory to the GPU memory, start CUDA kernels on the GPU [4], calculate the migration results, and then send the result back to CPU memory.

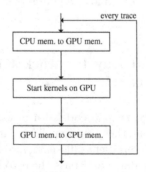

Fig. 4. Flowchart of Prototype-I

However, there are serious bandwidth issues in Prototype-I. Because the input data for every trace, including the original collected data, the pre-processed data and the result array, are as large as more than 100M bytes, the average transporting overhead between CPU memory and GPU memory could be 150–160ms (for about 300M bidirectional data), with an ideal transporting rate about 5GB/s and practical transporting rate about 2GB/s. Although the GPU could finalize every thread in 5ms, the total cost of calculation and data transportation is much higher than the original CPU code, which could be less than 15ms on Intel's P4 3.0G.

2.2   Prototype II

With a deeper study on the CR-PKTM program in Fig.3, we found the input data for every trace include a large data array with more than 100M bytes, which record the migration result and are partly used in the next traces. We could keep these arrays in the GPU memory until them out of usage. For the 512M GPU memory, we could keep up to 300 traces of data in the GPU memory.

Fig.5 presents the flowcharts of Prototype-II. Comparing to Prototype-I, Prototype-II pre-sends the large data arrays to GPU memory before the loop, and only transports about 1M bytes between CPU memory and GPU memory for every trace. The transportation overhead between the two memories is less than 1ms per trace. Because the CUDA code of the inner two-layer loops could be finalized in 5ms, the GPU code on NVidia GeForce8800GT could be more than 4 times faster than the CPU code on Intel's P4 3.0G.

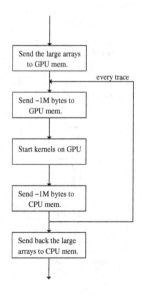

Fig. 5. Flowchart of Prototype-II

Although Prototype-II dramatically decreased the transportation overhead between CPU and GPU memories, the straightly translated CUDA code from CPU code did not take advantage of the powerful SIMD cores of GPU well. For every incoming trace, there are at most 256 coordinates will be selected to the inner loops, that means at most 256 threads on the GPU will be triggered. For the NVidia GeForce8800GT GPU, there are 14 multiprocessors and every multiprocessor has 8 stream processors. Every stream processor will run less than 3 threads on average. That means most stream processors will be idle during the calculation.

Furthermore, there are a lot of branch instructions in the inner loops. These branches will seriously hurt the runtime efficiency of the SIMD cores also.

2.3   Prototype III

Fig. 6 demonstrates the flowcharts of Prototype-III. The original CR-PKTM program has been separated in 5 steps, *Step0–Step4*. *Step0* runs on CPU, initializes the input data and send them to the GPU memory.

Step1–Step4 run on GPU as CUDA kernels. *Step1* starts one thread for every incoming coordinate. It will survey every coordinate, select the appropriate candidates, do some pre-migration calculations and send the results to *Step2*.

Step2 starts one thread for every appropriate coordinate, deals with the same calculation work as the 3rd layer loop (the while loop) in Fig. 3. There is an *if-elseif-else* conditional statement in the 3rd layer loop. The *for* loop with *loop-count3* will be rewritten to the CUDA code in *Step3*, and the *for* loop with

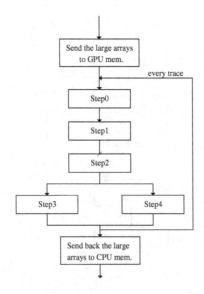

Fig. 6. Flowchart of Prototype-III

loopcount4 will be rewritten to the CUDA code in *Step4* also. The *for* loop with *loopcount5* is never executed in practical, so we just ignore it.

Step2 makes the decision which Step, *Step3* or *Step4* will be executed next.

Step3 and *Step4* are well designed CUDA kernels for NVidia's SIMD cores. According to the iteration times of the more inner loops, *Step3* will trigger at least 3000 threads, and *Step4* will trigger at least 1000 threads, respectively.

Prototype-III redesigned the original CPU code to fit the GPU and CUDA features better, and improved the runtime efficiency more than 7.2 times comparing with the CPU code on Intel's P4 3.0G.

2.4 Prototype IV

Using CUDA Profiler to analyze the runtime performance of Prototype-III, we can find *Step2* dominated the executing time, like Fig. 7. *Step2* starts one thread for every appropriate coordinate, deals with the same calculation work as the 3rd layer loop (the *while* loop) in Fig. 3. There are at most 256 threads will be triggered in *Step2* for every input trace. However, for GPUs like 8800GT or Tesla C870 with more than 100 cores, the thread number is too small to utilize the cores well. These threads will spend more time in waiting I/O instead of kernel code.

One efficient way to improve the runtime performance of *Step2* is to increase the thread number of it. Because *Step2* uses the output of *Step1* as input, we applied input and output buffers for both steps. The buffers save multiple input and output trace data. With the input and output buffers, *Step1* and *Step2* could start *N**256 threads before *Step3* and *Step4*, respectively, in which *N* is the buffered trace number. Fig. 8 presents the flowchart of Prototype-IV.

Fig. 9 demonstrates how many traces should be buffered to get the best runtime performance in *Step1* and *Step2*. For the 8800GT and Tesla C870 GPUs we used, the best trace number is 20. That means there are at most 20*256, about 5120 threads, will be trigger in *Step1* and *Step2*.

Fig. 10 shows the profiling data of Prototype-IV. The memcopy function instead of any Steps dominates the execution time now. The memcopy functions before *Step3* and *Step4* send a large array namely *WAVE*, from CPU to GPU.

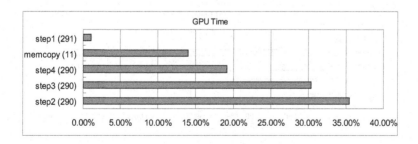

Fig. 7. CUDA profiling data of Prototype-III

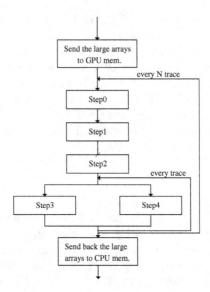

Fig. 8. Flowchart of Prototype-IV

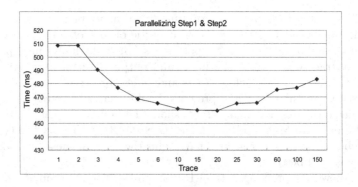

Fig. 9. Parallelizing *Step1* and *Step2* by buffering their inputs and outputs for multiple traces

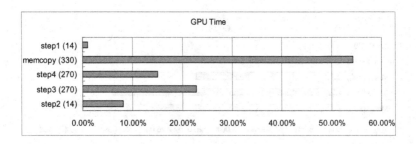

Fig. 10. CUDA profiling data of Prototype-IV

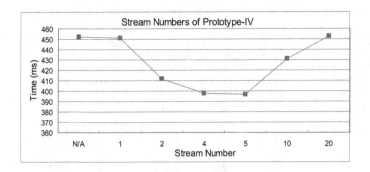

Fig. 11. Streaming Prototype-IV from 0 to 20

We can use the CUDA streams to overlap the I/O time by kernel execution time. Fig. 11 shows how many streams should be applied to get the best runtime performance. The best stream number should be 5 under this scenario.

The Prototype-IV with streams support is more than 16.3 times faster than its CPU version on Intel's P4 3.0G.

3   Floating Point Errors

The Curved Ray PKTM accumulates the floating point errors. Fig. 12 demonstrates a piece of CR-PKTM code at the image generating phase. The image buffer WOT will be accumulated times and times, before the final image been generated. It is easy to know, the floating point errors will be accumulated times and times too, if they do exist.

Both 8800GT and Tesla C870 have IEEE-compliant additions and multiplications. However, the two operations are often combined into a single multiply-add

```
for(...)
{
   int ITM1 = KTM1>>12;

   WOT(IT,KF,MC,N4,NOFF)= WOT(IT,KF,MC,N4,NOFF)
                          -TA1*( WAVE(ITM1-KP1,1,1,NTNEW,NBAND)
                          -WAVE(ITM1,1,1,NTNEW,NBAND)
                          -WAVE(ITM1,1,1,NTNEW,NBAND)
                          +WAVE(ITM1+KP1,1,1,NTNEW,NBAND));

   KTM1=KTM1 + KDELT;
   TA1=TA1 + ADELT;
}
```

Fig. 12. Sample CR-PKTM code at image generating phase

Table 1. Relative floating point errors between CPU and GPU results

Relative Error %	1 Trace	10 Traces	50 Traces	100 Traces	300 Traces
0	26974088	26960697	26787671	26584427	26041297
⩽ 0.0001	124528	104584	225252	358052	734273
⩽0.001	5340	34188	78441	135211	268185
⩽0.01	0	3460	8164	16866	31859
⩽0.1	1	377	873	1869	3787
⩽1	1	83	490	1230	5129
⩽10	14	310	2000	4180	13981
⩽100	43	286	1022	1989	4920
> 100	17	47	119	208	601
Errors/Total %	0.479	0.529	1.167	1.917	3.921

instruction fmad, which truncates the intermediate result of the multiplication and has a maximum error more than 0.5 ulp (unit in the last place). For other operations, like divisions, sqrtf, etc., the maximum ulp errors could up to 3–4. CPU operations have the similar ulp problems also. That means, the two different types of processors may get different calculation results for the same code fragment, cf. Fig. 12.

For instance, the integer number KTM1 in Fig. 12 is rounded from floating points. It will be right shifted 12 bits, to get an index number of array *WAVE*. If CPU and GPU get different *KTM1* numbers before, like 13000704 and 13000703, they will get different shifted indexes like 3174 and 3173. The two different indexes of WAVE will cause totally different calculation results of *WOT*.

Table 1 shows the relative errors of final images between CPU and GPU code. The outputs of CPU code, which are assumed to be more accurate, are selected as baseline. The relative error rates have been accumulated trace by trace, from 0.479% to 3.921% after 300 traces.

4   Performance Evaluation

We implemented the practical CR-PKTM program on NVidia 8800GT and Tesla C870 GPUs, which have 512M and 1G GPU memory, respectively, and both have PCIE-16X and CUDA2.0 support. The GPUs could achieve up to 336GFLOPs and 350GFLOPs in terms of single-precision floating point calculation, respectively. The host machine of 8800GT has an Intel's P4 3.0G CPU and 2G DDR400 memory. The Tesla's has an AMD Athlon64 3000+ CPU and 2G DDR400 memory. The operation systems are Linux 2.4.21. The GCC version is 3.2.3.

For 30000 traces of input data, Prototype-III and Prototype-II on 8800GT are 7.2 times and 4 times faster than the CPU code on Intel's P4 3.0G, respectively, like Fig. 13. Prototype-IV on 8800GT and Prototype-IV on Tesla C870 are 16.3 and 11.6 times faster than the CPU code, respectively. It is interesting that 8800GT is faster than Tesla C870, although it is not a strictly "apple-to-apple" comparison because they have different types of host machines.

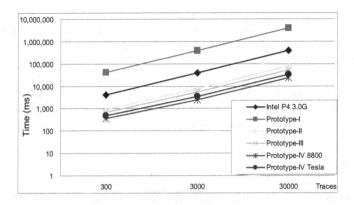

Fig. 13. Performance of CPU code, Prototype I, Prototype-II, Prototype-III and Prototype-IV

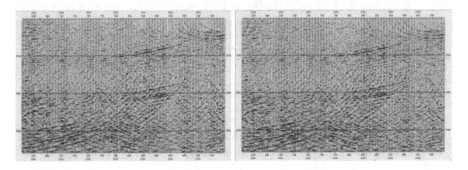

Fig. 14. Final images on CPU and GPU. The Left image was generate by CPU code, the right image was generated by GPU code.

Prototype-I on 8800GT is much slower, almost 10 times, than the CPU code on P4, because of the significantly heavy transportation overhead between CPU and GPU memories, as what we have aforementioned in Section 2.1.

Fig. 14 shows the final images generated by the CPU and GPU CR-PKTM programs for the same input traces. Although Section 3 describes that the floating point errors could be a serious issue when implementing CR-PKTM on GPUs, the final images do not have distinct difference and are all acceptable by geophysicists.

5 Conclusion

For seismic data processing, GPGPU is an appropriate accelerating platform. Many seismic data processing applications, like CR-PKTM, accept the single-precision results of floating point calculation. As we known so far, comparing with the double precision, the single precision is the strength of GPU in terms of performance and power consumption.

However, it is not a "free lunch" to port the original CPU code to GPGPU code. It is not easy to transform the sequential CPU code, C or Fortran programs, to data-parallelized GPU code with hundreds and thousands threads and more suitable to the SIMD cores.

In this paper, we introduced a serial of GPGPU prototypes for a practical CR-PKTM program, and presented the not-easy code migration work. We hope this work could be helpful for the future GPGPU applications, especially the seismic data procession applications, and the GPGPU programmers.

References

1. Deschizeaux, B., Blanc, J.Y.: Imaging Earth's Subsurface Using CUDA, http://developer.download.nvidia.com/books/gpu_gems_3/samples/gems3_ch38.pdf
2. Taner, M.T., Koehler, F.: Velocity spectra-digital computer derivation and application of velocity functions. Geophysics 34, 859–881 (1969)
3. Zhao, C.H., Shi, X.H., Yan, H.H., Wang, L.: Exploiting coarse-grained data parallelism in seismic processing. In: Proceedings of the 2008 Workshop on Architectures and Languages for Throughput Applications: Held in conjunction with the 35th International Symposium on Computer Architecture, Beijing, China (2008)
4. NVidia, NVidia CUDA Computer Unified Device Architecture Programming Guide, Version 2.0 (2008)
5. Buck, I., Foley, T., Horn, D., Sugerman, J., Fatahalian, K., Houston, M., Hanrahan, P.: Brook for GPUs: Stream Computing on Graphics Hardware, ACM 0730-0301/04/0800-0777, pp. 777–786. ACM Press, New York (2004)
6. Tarditi, D., Puri, S., Oglesby, J.: Accelerator: Using Data Parallelism to Program GPUs for General-Purpose Uses. In: Proceedings of ASPLOS 2006, pp. 325–335 (2006)
7. Papakipos, M.: The PeakStream Platform: High-Productivity Software development for Nulti-Core Processors, Writepaper, PeakStream Corp. (2007)

GCSim: A GPU-Based Trace-Driven Simulator for Multi-level Cache

Han Wan, Xiaopeng Gao, Xiang Long, and Zhiqiang Wang

State Key Laboratory of Virtual Reality Technology and System,
School of Computer Science and Engineering, Beihang University
Xueyuan Rd.37, 100191, Beijing, China
{wanhan,gxp,long,wangzhiqiang}@les.buaa.edu.cn

Abstract. We describe the design of parallel trace-driven cache simulation for the purposes of evaluating different cache structures. As the research goes deeper, traditional simulation methods, which can only execute simulation operations in sequence, are no longer practical due to their long simulation cycles. An obvious way to achieve fast parallel simulation is to simulate the independent sets of a cache concurrently on different compute resources. We considered the use of generic GPU to accelerate cache simulation which exploits set-partitioning as the main source of parallelism. But we show this technique is not efficient in the case that just simulating one cache configuration, since a high correlation of the activity between different sets. Trace-sort and multi-configuration simulation in one single pass techniques are developed, taking advantage of the full programmability offered by the Compute Unified Device Architecture (CUDA) on the GPU. Our experimental results demonstrate that the cache simulator based on GPU-CPU platform gains 2.44x performance improvement compared to traditional sequential algorithm.

Keywords: parallel algorithms; caches; trace-driven simulation; GPGPU; CUDA.

1 Introduction

Caches are small high-speed buffer memories that shorten the performance gap between the CPU and memory in the computer systems. Consequently, as part of the design of a new system, many different cache architectures are evaluated and compared. Such analysis is generally performed by trace-driven Cache simulator [1]. Compared to execution-driven cache simulator [2] and model analysis [3], trace-driven simulator has the advantage of yielding better accuracy and being of more flexibility.

As the cache architecture grows in complexity, trace-driven simulation demand lots of storage for reference and computer time to produce statistically reliable results. It becomes worthwhile to consider parallel methods for cache simulation. An algorithm for parallel simulation is the subject of this paper.

Several researchers have contributed techniques for reducing the simulation time. For example, one single pass simulation [4] is able to compute statistics for

Y. Dou, R. Gruber, and J. Joller (Eds.): APPT 2009, LNCS 5737, pp. 177–190, 2009.
© Springer-Verlag Berlin Heidelberg 2009

different sizes of cache within a single pass. But it is confined to certain range of parameters and may create large overhead as flexibility increases. Trace reduction technique [5] can greatly reduce trace length but cannot guarantee the accuracy of performance metrics. There are also parallel simulation method such as time-parallel simulation [6] and SIMD massive parallel simulation [7]. Compared to the time-parallel simulation, the method proposed in this paper exploits both set-parallelism and search-parallelism in the trace-driven cache simulation. Our method can simulate the behavior of the cache accurately without extra processing for simulation result correction. Furthermore, our algorithm is of more flexibility as it is not limited to LRU simulation or other acceleration condition.

In this paper, we introduce a general parallel method to accelerate the simulation of multi-level cache, which utilizes the computation ability of GPU. Extension of our proposed method can be applied to GPU based multi-core cache simulator.

For implementation, we map our parallel trace-driven simulation algorithm to the SIMD computation model in GPU. A trace-driven simulator for two-level cache is constructed based on the GeForce 8800GTX with Compute Unified Device Architecture (CUDA). With different parallel granularities, we implemented several parallel algorithms for our experiment. The most efficient algorithm shows 2.44x speedup compared to traditional CPU-based serial algorithm.

The paper is organized as follows: section 2 describes concepts of Graphics Processing Unit and parallel processing model. Section 3 presents our CUDA based parallel algorithm as well as related techniques. Section 4 gives the implementation of simulation algorithms. Section 5 elaborates the results of experiments. Finally, Section 6 summarizes the results.

2   Preliminaries

2.1   Traditional Trace-Driven Cache Simulator

Sequential simulation algorithm in traditional trace-driven cache simulator can be described as fellows:

For each memory reference address, the cache simulator computes its set number and tag information according to cache parameters such as the block size and associativity. Then simulator checks corresponding set to find out whether there is a cache line has the same tag as current memory reference. And finally set status and metrics will be updated accordingly.

2.2   General-Purpose Computation on GPUs

In the last decade, GPU performance has been increasing so fast that even out paces the speed of integrated circuit predicted by Moore's Law. This rapid increase in GPU performance takes advantage of the highly parallel nature of visual computing. State of the art graphic architectures provide tremendous memory bandwidth and computational power. Besides performance improvement of the hardware, the programmability also has been significantly increased. These improvements make GPU a compelling platform for general-purpose computing as well as visual computing.

Advanced GPU architecture offers significant level of parallelism with relatively low cost. The operations executed in GPU are similar to the well known vector processing model, which is also known from Flynn's taxonomy as Sing Instruction Multiple Data or SIMD. Therefore it can be predicted that many applications use to be hosted on vector supercomputers in the past can be deployed on GPU platform. With the ever increasing programmability, specific powerful programming tools (e.g. CUDA [8] and CTM [9]) can be used for implementation of algorithms. For example, GPU has been utilized as a math co-processor in special games and physics simulations in [10]; [11] introduces a GPU based implementation of Reyes-style adaptive surface subdivision; [12] presents fast algorithms for scan and segmented scan on GPUs; [13] develops a programming framework on the graphics architectures and applies it to a variety of problems (e.g. matrix multiplication); [14] introduces a framework for the implementation of linear algebra operators on GPUs; And in [15], Fast Fourier Transform is implemented on NVIDIA graphics architecture.

Among the various applications of GPU programming, the major challenge is how to map the algorithm to units of graphics architecture. As shown in the GPGPU technique, applications need be partitioned into independent parallel sections. And each section needs to be implemented as a kernel executes on a processing unit. While input and output of a kernel are stored in the memory of GPU.

2.3   Parallel Processing Model

It has been observed that the simulation process of each memory reference shows a weakly partial order. Whether current reference is a cache hit is dependent on cache status, which is modified by the memory references that have been simulated. This observation implies that memory references belonging to the same cache set should be simulated jointly while simulation of different sets need to be carried separately.

During cache simulation, the following operations are performed on an address:

☐ Fetch address from the trace;

☐ Break address into tag, block number, block offset;

☐ Calculate set number;

☐ Search blocks in corresponding set;

☐ Update the set status and metrics.

Among all five steps, step 4 and step 5 are the two most time-consuming steps, which can be performed independently on different sets. This observation leads to exploit of set-parallelism (i.e. trace-driven cache simulation can be performed in parallel on a set base). Parallel simulation algorithm first classifies trace by set numbers, and then implements simulation kernel. In addition to set-parallelism, searching in the step 4 can also work in parallel.

In a coarse granularity, multi-configuration can be parallelized using the computational resource on GPU. Once trace file is read into memory, the simulator can generate metrics for cache with different parameters within a single pass. Together with set-parallelism and search-parallelism in the process of cache simulation are explored, the cache simulator acceleration utilizing GPU is feasible.

3   Parallel Simulation Scheme on CUDA

3.1   CUDA

Modern NVIDIA GPUs, such as GeForce 8800 GTX are fully programmable manycore chips built around an array of parallel processors as shown in Fig. 1. The GPU consists of an array of SM multiprocessors, each can support up to 1024 concurrent threads. A single SM contains 8 scalar SP processors, each with 1024 32-bit registers, for total of 64KB on-chip memory that has very low access latency and high bandwidth. A read-only constant/texture cache is shared by all the processors and serves the purpose of speeding up reads from the constant/texture memory. The local and global memory spaces are implemented as read-write regions of device memory and are not cached. All thread management including creation, scheduling, and synchronization is performed entirely in hardware by the SM.

CUDA provides the means for developers to execute parallel programs on the GPU. It issues and manages computations on GPU as a data-parallel computing

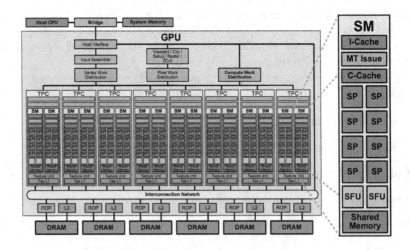

Fig. 1. Block Diagram of a G80 GPU

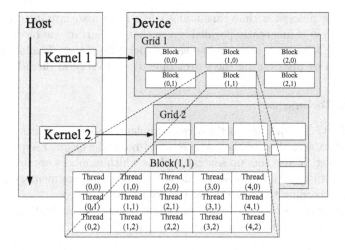

Fig. 2. CUDA Programming Model

device without the need of mapping computation to a graphics API. When programming CUDA, programmers take GPU as a processing device capable of executing a large number of threads in parallel. In the CUDA programming model, an application is organized into a sequential host program that may execute parallel program, referred to as kernels, on a parallel device as shown in Fig. 2.

Host can request services of the device via specific programming interfaces. Each kernel is executed as a batch of threads which are organized as a grid of thread blocks. A thread block is a cluster of threads that communicate with each other efficiently via fast shared memory and synchronize their execution for memory access competition. Synchronization points are specified in the kernel. Once such a point exists, threads in a block will be suspended until they all reach the synchronization point. There is a limitation on the maximum number of threads that a block can host. However, blocks of same dimensionality and size that execute the same kernel can be clustered into a grid of blocks. Therefore the total number of threads that can be launched in a single kernel invocation is much larger than single block limitation. But threads in different thread blocks from the same grid cannot communicate and synchronize with each other.

3.2 Parallel Simulation Algorithm Based on CUDA

As analyzed in section 2.3, we can utilize the GPU parallel architecture to optimize the following computations:

☐ The simulation processes on different cache sets are independent. And the computations on different thread blocks are also independent. Therefore the parallel simulation on different cache set can be implemented by distributing the simulation process of each cache set to a separate thread block in GPU.

☐ Searching process is time-consuming when large associativity presents. As this process is inherently parallel, given that threads in one block can communicate with each other in the same block, the search-parallelism can be exploited by distributing the search operations to several threads.

3.3   Key Techniques

Bucket Sort. The original sort process is implemented on the CPU. It classifies the trace data according to the cache set, and holds the original sequence of the same cache set. It also sets up several buckets which numbers are in accordance to the set numbers. And ultimately, the sort process matches memory references to buckets according to the sequence in cache sets.

Since the sort process needs lots of time in the whole simulation, we finally sorted trace on the GPU using radix sorting algorithm.

Ping-pong Buffer. In general, as cache lines are stored in static arrays in memory, they need to be reordered after searching process is over. Ping-pong buffer is therefore adopted to parallelize the reordering process.

☐ The information about one cache set is stored in two buffers: Buf0 and Buf1. Assume initial input is Buf0;

☐ After each searching process, all information stored in Buf0 is copied to Buf1 according to the replacement policy and updating policy, then set the input as Buf1 and output as Buf0;

☐ After each memory reference is simulated, exchange the position of input and output buffer until the whole trace file is simulated. And the input buffer at the time is the final status.

Memory Model on the GPU. Different memories on GPU vary greatly in terms of bandwidth, which has a significant impact on the performance of the simulator. The memory model adopted here is:

☐ Since the trace data is large, it can be only stored in the global memory;

☐ The information about the cache set, such as the cache lines, tag, status and metrics, which needs high memory access speed, is stored in the shared memory.

Stream Management. In order to improve performance, we use two streams to parallelize cache simulation process and bucket sort process. As trace data can be divided into multiple segments, one stream prepares the bucket sort for next phase, while the other stream executes the simulation process on the sorted stream. Parallelizing the two streams, we can achieve approximate 2x speedup compared to one stream implementation.

There are specific limitations about the feature of supporting overlapped memory copy concurrently with kernel execution using new stream management interface. Overlapping is only allowed on the 1.1 architectures (g84/g86/g92), and it will revert to serial operation on the 1.0 architectures (g80).

4   The General Algorithm

When programming on the CUDA, users need to allocate device memory first, then transfer data from host to device, and finally get results back from device when computation is finished.

4.1   Parallel Simulation Algorithms for a Single-Level Cache Simulation

The five parallel algorithms for single-level cache simulator are described as follows:

Parallel Simulation Algorithm 1. *Example of a references process Program about one cache set on a thread block*

```
program references process (reference)
   begin
     repeat
       If(the memory reference is mapped to this cache set)
        simulation the reference process;
       Else
        Discard it;
     until reference = NULL
end.
```

In this algorithm, Trace data is not sorted, but simply stored in an array. The simulation is parallelized at both set-parallelism level and search-parallelism level. One thread block is dedicated to the simulation of one cache set, and each thread in the block is in charge of searching in one cache line. For every memory reference, each thread block needs to compute whether this data belongs to the cache set it is simulating, and simulates the cache function in case the memory reference does. Since there are multiple threads executing the search process and they work independently, synchronization is needed to find out if the memory reference is hit, and then to update status and metrics.

Parallel Simulation Algorithm 2. Perform bucket sort on trace data. One thread block is dedicated to the simulation of one cache set. And each thread in the block is in charge of searching in one cache line.

Parallel Simulation Algorithm 3. Perform bucket sort on trace data. One thread block is dedicated to the simulation of one cache set. Only one thread in each thread block is in charge of searching.

The difference between algorithm 2 and 3 is the searching process. While algorithm 2 does searching in parallel, algorithm 3 does it in sequential. This improvement to algorithm 3 is based on the consideration that the thread synchronization consumes lots of computation cycles.

Parallel Simulation Algorithm 4. Similar to algorithm 2, but it using the ping-pong buffer to accelerate the update process.

Parallel Simulation Algorithm 5. The simulation of multi-configuration is implemented in a single pass. Since the sort process takes lots of cycles, sorted trace data are used to simulate caches with different degrees of associativity. In this algorithm, each thread block is dedicated to the simulation of one cache set, while each thread within this thread block is dedicated to the simulation under different degrees of associativity.

4.2   Algorithm for Multi-level Cache Simulator

Single-Configuration. *Example of a Multi-level Cache Simulator Program*

```
program CacheSimulation (Output){
  initializeCache();
  While (reference needs to be simulated)
  {
    Compute the access type and address of the reference;
    If (access type == data access)
    {
        Find in the L1 cache data;
        If (hit)
            Update the cache set;
        Else (miss)
        {
            Replace and update;
            Find in the next level cache, if hit, data copy to L1 cache,
            else find in the next level till the memory;
        }
    }
    Else (access type == instruction read)
    {
        Find in the L1 instruction cache;
        If (hit)
            Update the cache set;
        Else (miss)
```

```
    {
            Replace and update;
            Find in the next level cache, if hit, data copy to L1 cache,
            else find in the next level till the memory;
    }
  }
}
Write the dirty cache block to the memory;
Output the statistic;}
```

Multi-configuration parallel simulation in a single pass. When parallel simulating the multi-configuration in a single pass, we use several threads to parallel simulate traces belong to different cache set. One thread block simulates one cache set, and each thread in this thread block takes charge of one configuration simulation.

5   Performance

We use DineroIV sequential uniprocessor cache simulator for our evaluation. The experiments were conducted on a test bed equipped with an Intel core 2 E6550 and GeForce 8800 GTX graphics card.

Our experiments consist of the simulation on various input traces which are obtained from the NMSU Trace Base facility. The traces are collections of memory references from programs in the SPEC 92 benchmark suite.

5.1   Time Measurement

The CPU simulation time does not include the time that read trace file from disk to memory. While the GPU simulation time includes the bucket sort time, the time of data transfer from CPU to GPU, GPU simulation time, and the time of results feed back from GPU to CPU.

5.2   Single Configuration Simulation for Single Level Cache

We simulate one trace file of 10MBytes to get the GPU simulation time distribution as shown in TABLE II. The cache is 64 sets, 4-way set associative, with 16B line size, using LRU and write back policy.

It can be observed from the results Fig. 3: bucket sort process occupies a great amount of time in simulation; Data download time is bounded to the memory bandwidth between CPU and GPU; and data upload is very fast and not significant compared to the others.

The rest experiments and analysis adopt alvinn.din as an example.

Process	Average Time (ms)	Percentage
Bucket sort	40.09	36.609%
Data download	7.05	6.438%
Kernel executing	62.35	56.935%
Data upload	0.02	0.018%

Fig. 3. GPU Simulation Time Distributions

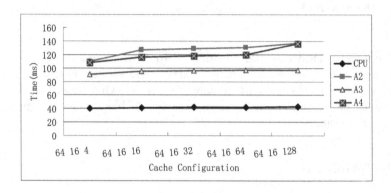

Fig. 4. Simulation Time Curve with Increasing Set Number

Increasing the Associativity. As shown in Fig. 4, A2-A4 represent parallel algorithm 2-4 respectively. And we choose LRU as replacement policy, write-back as updating policy in this experiment. X-axis represents cache configuration in following format: number of sets (64), block size (16) and associativity (4—16—64—128).

We found that the time using by A1 is several dozen times longer than others so we do not show it in this figure. The reason behind this is that the unsorted trace data is large and stored in the global memory. Thus A1 experiences long memory access latency.

As the degree of associativity increase:

☐ Serial simulation time increased slowly. It benefits from the principle of locality. Hit rate is high since the memory reference is located centralized in an address range. When associativity is increased, hit rate would not increase dramatically, and thus the simulation time is not improved significantly.

☐ A2 and A4 simulation time increased. Since the thread number is increased when associativity is increased in A1, this results in much more time spending on synchronization.

☐ A1's simulation time increased evidently. Since each thread block needs to access all memory references, synchronization time is increased.

☐ A3 simulation time increased slowly. As each thread block has only one
thread, the sequential searching time is increased as the associativity increase. When hit rate increased, searching time increment is negligible.

Increasing Set Number. Fig. 5 shows simulation time curves with increasing
set number when the cache block size and associativity are fixed.

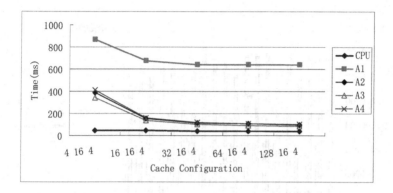

Fig. 5. Simulation Time Curve with Increasing Set Number

As set number increase:

☐ Sequential simulation time reduces slowly. Hit rate increases as the set number increased. Since the degree of associativity is 4, the replacement and
update execution on CPU is fast.

☐ A1, A2, A3 and A4 simulation time first reduces fast and then slows down.
Hit rates are low when there are few sets. And hit rate increases as set
number increases.

Single Configuration Simulation Summary. Results have shown that A1-
A4 algorithms cannot speed up the simulation of single cache configuration:

☐ Too much time is spent on bucket sort process;

☐ Fetching data from the global memory of GPU suffers from long latency and
the computation density on the GPU is small.

☐ The computation capability of CPU is much larger than that of the single
processor in the GPU.

☐ A high correlation of the activity between different sets.

Using Radix Sort Algorithm to Speedup Sort Process. Since the sort process occupies a great amount of time in simulation, we adopted radix sorting algorithm to speed up the sort process.

The sort process classifies the trace data according to the cache set number, and holds the original sequence. We implemented a radix sorting algorithm on the GPU to accelerate this process. The key which is processed by sorting algorithm is the set number of the trace address.

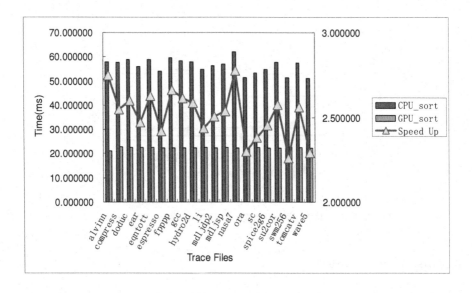

Fig. 6. Speedup of Radix Sorting Algorithm

As shown in Fig. 6, we use 10 bits as the key's length to implement the sort algorithm, which means the number of keys is 2^{10}. We can sort 1024 sets' references. The minimum and average speedup of radix sorting algorithm is 2.26 and 2.52.

5.3 Multi-configuration Simulation in Single Pass for Single-Level Cache

Fig. 7 shows the speedup of GPU multi-configuration simulation for single level cache in single pass. The cache is 128 sets, with 32B line size, and the degree of associativity is varied from 1 to 32. The average speedup is 2.76.

5.4 Multi-configuration Simulation in Single Pass for Two-Level Cache

Fig. 8 shows the speedup of GPU multi-configuration simulation for two-level cache in single pass. The first level cache is 32 sets, with 32B line size, and the

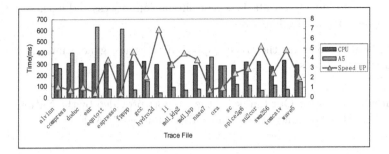

Fig. 7. Simulation Time of Multi-configuration in Single Pass for Single Level Cache

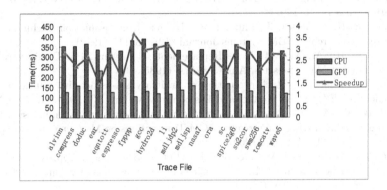

Fig. 8. Simulation Time of Multi-configuration in Single Pass for Two Level Cache

degree of associativity is varied from 1 to 32. The second level cache is 4096 sets, with 32B line size. The average speedup is 2.44.

6 Conclusion and Future Work

In this paper, we suggest that the trace-driven cache simulator can be accelerated on the GPU. Our experiments show that this method is low-cost and easy to use. Performance is analyzed according to the GPU architecture and CUDA programming environment.

The functionality and performance of our GPU based simulator could be easily improved by incorporating the following changes:

☐ Improve our method to make use of hardware and the extensive features of SDK;

☐ When simulate cache coherency in multi-core system, it needs to execute cache simulation of different cores on different thread blocks and use global memory to simulate the coherency;

☐ Use two streams to parallelize cache simulation process and bucket sort process on 1.1 graphics hardware;

☐ Use Pin to generate the trace, pipelined the trace generation process and simulation process.

Acknowledgments. Our thanks to the support provided by the National High Technology Research and Development Program (2007AA01Z183).

References

1. Uhlig., R.A., Mudge, T.N.: Trace-driven Memory Simulation: A survey. ACM Computing surveys 29 (1997)
2. Mattson, R.L., Gecsei, J., Slutz, D.R., Traiger, I.L.: Evaluation Techniques for Storage Hierarchies. IBM Systems Journal 9(2), 78–117 (1970)
3. Puzak, T.R.: Analysis of Cache Replacement Algorithms. Ph. D. Dissertation, University of Massachusetts, Amherst, MA (1985)
4. Wu, Y., Muntz, R.: Stack evaluation of arbitrary set-associative multiprocessor caches. IEEE Tram on Parallel and Distribured Systems 6(9), 930–942 (1995)
5. Milenkovi'c, A., Milenkovi'c, M.: An efficient single-pass trace compression technique utilizing instruction streams. ACM Transactions on Modeling and Computer Simulation 17(1), Article 2 (2007)
6. Ingalls, R.G., Rossetti, M.D., Smith, J.S., Peters, B.A. (eds.): Approximate Time-parallel Cache simulation. In: Proceedings of the 2004 Winter Simulation Conference, vol. 1, pp. 337–346 (2004)
7. Kiesling, T., Pohl, S.: Time-Parallel Simulation with Approximative State Matching, pads. In: 18th Workshop on Parallel and Distributed Simulation, pp. 195–202 (2004)
8. NVIDIA CUDA Programming Guide, http://developer.nvidia.com/cuda
9. ATI CTM Guide, http://ati.de/companyinfo/researcher/documents.html
10. Zamith, M.P.M., Clua, E.W.G., Conci, A., Montenegro, A., Leal-Toledo, R.C.P., Pagliosa, P.A., Valente, L., Feijo, B.: A game loop architecture for the GPU used as a math coprocessor in real-time applications. In: Computers in Entertainment (CIE), pp. 1–19 (2008)
11. Patney, A., Owens, J.D.: Real-time Reyes-style adaptive surface subdivision. In: ACM SIGGRAPH Asia 2008 papers, pp. 1–8 (2008)
12. Dotsenko, Y., Govindaraju, N.K., Sloan, P.-P., Boyd, C., Manferdelli, J.: Fast scan algorithms on graphics processors. In: Proceedings of the 22nd annual international conference on Supercomputing, pp. 205–213 (2008)
13. Thompson, C.J., Hahn, S., Oskin, M.: Using Modern Graphics Architectures for General-Purpose Computing: A Framework and Analysis. In: Proceedings of International Symposium on Microarchitecture, Istanbul, pp. 306–317 (2002)
14. Krüger, J., Westermann, R.: Linear algebra operators for GPU implementation of numerical algorithms. In: ACM SIGGRAPH 2005 Courses, p. 234 (2005)
15. Romero, S., Trenas, M.A., Gutierrez, E., Zapata, E.L.: Locality-improved FFT implementation on a graphics processor. In: Proceedings of the 7th WSEAS International Conference on Signal Processing, Computational Geometry Artificial Vision, pp. 58–63 (2007)

A Hybrid Parallel Signature Matching Model for Network Security Applications Using SIMD GPU

Chengkun Wu*, Jianping Yin, Zhiping Cai, En Zhu, and Jieren Chen

School of Computer Science,
National University of Defense Technology,
410073, Changsha, Hunan Province, China
{chengkun_wu,jpyin,enzhu,zpcai,jrchen}@nudt.edu.cn

Abstract. High performance signature matching against a large dictionary is of great importance in network security applications. The many-core SIMD GPU is a competitive choice for signature matching. In this paper, a hybrid parallel signature matching model (HPSMM) using SIMD GPU is proposed, which uses pattern set partition and input text partition together. Then the problem of load balancing for multiprocessors in the GPU is discussed carefully, and a balanced pattern set partition method (BPSPM) employed in HPSMM is introduced. Experiments demonstrate that using pattern set partition and input text partition together can help achieve a better performance, and the proposed BPSPM-Length works well in load balancing.

Keywords: signature matching, parallel model, network security, GPU.

1 Introduction

Signature matching against a large dictionary or a set of many patterns is of great importance in network security applications.Typical applications include digital forensics tools, intrusion detection/prevention systems, antivirus software, etc. Signature matching usually becomes the performance bottleneck in those applications. Take the famous open source network intrusion detection system Snort for example, signature matching can consume up to 70% of the execution time [1].

A conventional way to improve the performance of signature matching is to use hardware technologies like ASIC [2], FPGA [3,4,5] and TCAMs [6,7]. Those solutions can achieve a throughput up to tens of gigabits per second, compared to several hundreds of kilobits per second of software solutions on general purpose CPUs. However, the hardware solutions are usually very weak in adaptability and scalability, and they are very expensive, thus confine their applications.

---

* This work is supported by the National Natural Science Foundation of China (NO.60603015, NO.60603062), Science Foundation of Hunan Province (06JJ3035).

Y. Dou, R. Gruber, and J. Joller (Eds.): APPT 2009, LNCS 5737, pp. 191–204, 2009.
© Springer-Verlag Berlin Heidelberg 2009

The rapid development of multi-core technologies makes it possible to develop flexible and cheaper high-performance solutions. Solutions based on current multi-core CPUs can achieve a throughput about hundreds of megabits per second. Yet it's still not fast enough. Application Specific Instruction Processor (ASIP) is another choice, for example, the multi-core network processors (NP) can combine the flexibility of commodity processors with the high performance of ASICs. The throughput of NP-based solutions can be up to several gigabits per second [8,9], which is not that far from the fastest solutions using hardware technologies. NPs are optimized for network packet processing, and often appear as part of network devices, which can be suitable for network applications but not applications like antivirus software and host forensics tools.

Many-core and SIMD Graphic Processing Unit (GPU) becomes another potential alternative. The mainstream GPUs like Nvidia G80 [10] comprise many general purpose stream processors, and support thousands of concurrent threads executed in the SIMD fashion. SIMD GPU has demonstrated its power in computationally intensive applications. Many attempts have been made to use SIMD GPUs for security purpose applications like digital forensics tools, intrusion detection or prevention systems, and anti-virus software.

In this paper, we proposed a hybrid parallel signature matching model using SIMD GPU, called HPSMM. In HPSMM, we used pattern set partition and input text partition together, and we introduced a balanced pattern set partition method (BPSPM) to balance the workload of different multiprocessors inside the GPU. Then we presented experiments about pattern set partition and input text partition, at last we evaluated the efficiency of BPSPM.

The paper is organized as follows: in Section 2, we give an overview of a typical SIMD GPU at first, then we perform a survey of most recent related work. In Section 3, we propose a hybrid parallel signature matching model using SIMD GPU. Then in Section 4, we describe the BPSPM algorithms in detail. In Section 5, we present our experiments and evaluate the correctness of our model and the efficiency of BPSPM. Finally, in Section 6, we draw some conclusions and outline some ideas for future work.

2   Related Work

2.1   Overview of a Typical SIMD GPU

Nvidia G80 [10] series GPUs are typical SIMD GPUs. The G80 series and later are designed to be highly parallel,massive-threading, and many-core processors. They're optimized for compute-intensive applications that execute the same program on many data elements in parallel, namely, the SIMD fashion. A G80 GPU consists of sixteen multiprocessors. Each multiprocessor is composed of eight Stream Processors (SPs), two special function units, on-chip shared memory, and a shared Instruction Unit. A sketch map is depicted in Fig.1 [11].

Each multiprocessor executes one or more thread blocks, and each block has the same number of threads. The number of threads in a block can be up to 768 for devices with Compute Capability 1.0 [11], limited by the number of on-chip

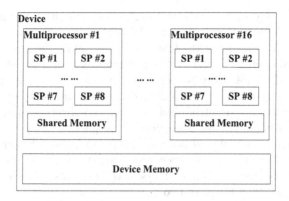

Fig. 1. The G80 GPU Architecture

registers. The maximum number of blocks supported is 65535. Threads within a block can communicate with each other through the shared memory, they can also synchronize by a barrier synchronization intrinsic. But threads in different blocks cannot synchronize with each other.

The G80 GPU is programmed through the Compute Unified Device Architecture (CUDA) [11], which is a parallel programming model for using the GPU as a general purpose SIMD processor. CUDA consists of a set of extension to the C language, a supporting library that provides control to the GPU from the host, and some built-in functions and data types. With the help of CUDA, we can write a program for a thread, specify the parameters that determine the number of threads, and then CUDA will organize all the threads to execute the instructions of the program in SIMD fashion. Moreover, CUDA can support multiple GPUs at the same time, which can provide more computation power.

2.2 A Brief Survey of Signature Matching Using SIMD GPU

L. Marziale, et al. illustrated that binary string searches can be substantially sped up by utilizing a SIMD GPU (Nvidia 8800GTX) [12]. In their work, the 8800GTX GPU executes a kernel that creates 65,536 threads; each thread is responsible for a portion of the incoming data; a simple sequential string search is used to avoid thread divergence. Experiments against multi-threaded and multi-core CPUs are carried out to prove that GPU can provide higher performance at a lower cost than adding additional cores or CPUs. The search algorithm employed in their GPU implementation is the naive brute-force method whereas a more efficient algorithm, the Boyer-Moore algorithm is used in CPU implementations, thus the GPU implementation can be further optimized and improved to obtain even higher performance.

G. Vasiliadis, et al. presented a Snort based prototype system Gnort assisted by GPU and explored how SIMD GPUs like Nvidia G80 can be used to speed up the processing throughput of NIDS by offloading the signature matching operations to the GPU [13]. The multi-pattern matching Aho-Corasick algorithm [14] was used. In the preprocessing phase, the deterministic finite automaton (DFA) of the state machine is stored as a two-dimensional array, each element in the array is made up of four bytes: the first two bytes contain the next state to move and the last two contain the ID of the matching pattern if the state is final or zero otherwise; the DFA array is then copied to the texture memory to utilize the texture memory cache. In the search phase, two different approaches splitting the computation were introduced: one packet per multiprocessor, in which each thread in a block process a portion of the packet; one packet per stream processor, in which each thread process a different packet. Experiment results showed that the performance of two counterparts were almost the same. Gnort could achieve a throughput of 2.3 Gbit/s in the best case, which outperformed conventional Snort by a factor of two.

N. Goyal, et al. analyzed the basic memory, control flow, and concurrency properties of signature matching for network processing in detail [15]. Different platforms for signature matching such as ASICs, FPGAs, network processors, general purpose processors, and SIMD architectures were compared. They also identified the feasibility of using SIMD architecture for signature matching applications. Results showed that SIMD GPUs can provide significantly higher performance at a cost similar to general purpose processors. Two methods for signature matching were examined: deterministic finite automata (DFAs) based and extended finite automata (XFAs) [16] based. The DFA based method is simple and uniform in per byte processing, which map it naturally to the SIMD architecture. The XFA method has been proved to be a high performance solution at much lower memory cost on general purpose microprocessors [16], but it's more complex and less uniform, and requires auxiliary storage and extra operations which will cause threads divergence. A SIMD design that supports both methods was outlined and an implementation with a speed up of 6X to 9X was achieved using Nvidia G80 GPU compared to normal schemes using Pentium 4 CPU. It was also concluded that a number of other applications like virus scanning could benefit from SIMD architectures.

3   A Hybrid Parallel Signature Matching Model Using SIMD GPU

In this section, an analysis of the parallelism inside signature matching against a large pattern set in network security applications is performed at first, then a hybrid parallel processing model using an SIMD GPU as a signature matching co-processor to a multi-core CPU is proposed.

3.1   Data Parallelism Analysis

In this paper, we mainly focus on data parallelism as we are using the SIMD GPU, which is weak in the sophisticated and complex control brought by instruction parallelism. There are two kinds of data in the signature matching procedure of security applications: the input text and the signature set with a large number of patterns.

The input text can be split into chunks and different chunks can be processed by different processors in parallel, some previous works like [13] make use of this method. If the chunks are equal, then the working load of all the different processors will be the same. The method can reduce the processing time of each input text to a degree.

The signature set can be partitioned into several smaller subsets then each multiprocessor is responsible for matching the input text against one or several smaller signature subsets. The partition can be done once when the system is initialized, no overhead will be introduced at runtime. Our experiments in Section 5 proved that pattern set partition can help increase the throughput of each multiprocessor.

Some parallelism exists outside the GPU too. An important point in our paper is that the SIMD GPU is used as the co-processor for CPU, which means the concurrency between CPU and GPU should also be taken into consideration. The CUDA enables the CPU continue to execute instructions while the GPU are running a kernel (the program that runs on GPU) by using the asynchronous function calls. At the same time, CUDA supports multiple GPUs around one CPU, thus the concurrency between the GPUs will be taken account of.

3.2   The Hybrid Parallel Signature Matching Model

Our HPSMM (hybrid parallel signature matching model) is depicted in Fig.2. In this model, the SIMD GPU is used as a co-processor of a multi-core CPU. Inside the GPU, pattern set partition for multiprocessors and input text partition for stream processors within a multiprocessor are introduced to gain maximum parallelism.

On the CPU side, input texts are buffered in order to transfer the data from the CPU to the GPU in batches, which can reduce the overhead associated with the memory copy from CPU to GPU. The number of buffers will be twice as many as the number of GPUs, that is, dual buffers for each GPU, thus the CPU can continue collecting input texts while the data in the fully filled buffer is being transferred to the GPU. Besides, once a new kernel (the program that runs on GPU) is launched, the CPU can perform other operations like post processing for results generated by preceding GPU kernel launch or preprocessing for the next kernel launch.

On the GPU side, the pattern set is partitioned into several subsets, and the number of the subsets is no less than the number of multiprocessors on the GPU. Each subset is processed by one multiprocessor, and one multiprocessor might possess multiple subsets. The partition is done on the host, and copied to the GPU in the form of the data structures required by specific pattern matching algorithms and stored in the cached texture memory. Input text partition is introduced inside each multiprocessor to decrease the processing time of each multiprocessor, stream processors (SP) will operate on equally split chunks, each chunk will be assigned to a unique SP, as depicted in Fig.3. The results are all written to the result buffer residing on the global memory. When the pattern matching on the GPU is finished, the content of the result buffer is copied to the host for post-processing in a single operation.

The HPSMM model can be easily extended to the multi-GPUs scheme, and the scheme of four GPUs is shown in Fig.4, which can be implemented easily with the help of CUDA. A dispatcher is added, which is essential for load balancing among different GPUs. Each GPU is allocated a dual buffer. The results generated by each GPU will be integrated on the CPU, the post processing and final result generation will be done on the CPU too. The operation of transferring data between the CPU and GPUs will be organized in streams in case of the memory bandwidth problem.

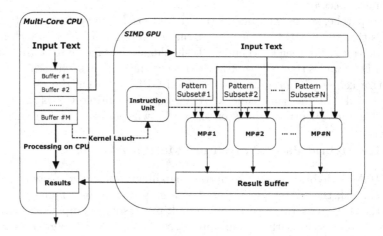

Fig. 2. The hybrid parallel signature matching model - HPSMM

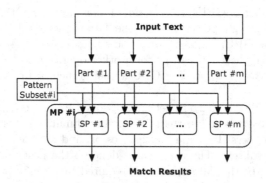

Fig. 3. Input text partition inside each multiprocessor

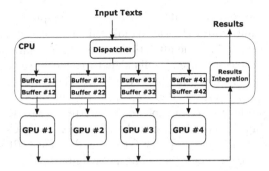

Fig. 4. Multi-GPU scheme for HPSMM

3.3   Analysis of HPSMM

Three types of parallelism are considered in HPSMM: parallelism inside the SIMD GPU, parallelism between CPU and GPU, parallelism among multi-GPUs.

Inside the GPU, pattern set partition and input text partition is carefully examined at the level of data parallelism. Theoretically, input text partition can reduce the processing time by a factor of the number of processors. However, the experiments in Section 5 demonstrate that the processing time decreases when the number of processors increases, which turned out to be a smoothly lower down curve rather than a straight line. This phenomenon is caused by the memory access operations. The input text is stored in the GPU's cached texture memory, but the cache size is quite small, up to 16 KB [11]. Input text partition will cause more cache misses, thus affects the performance. On the contrary, smaller pattern set will have better locality, which can increase the chance of cache hits.

In HPSMM, pattern set partitioning and input text partitioning are combined in the following way: for different multiprocessors, each input text is sent to every multiprocessor, each pattern subset obtained from the pattern set partitioning is sent to one single multiprocessor, so different multiprocessors operate on the same input text but on different pattern subset; for different stream processors inside a multiprocessor, they operate on the same pattern subset allocated to the multiprocessor, but different stream processors will handle different parts of the input text assigned to the multiprocessor. In other words, pattern set partitioning is introduced at the multiprocessors' level while input text partitioning is introduced between different stream processors. By doing this, SPs inside a multiprocessor operate on different text chunks in parallel, and different MPs process the same input text but on different pattern set, thus we maximize the parallelism inside the GPU.

We are emphasizing the use of multi-core CPU for two reasons: the first is that in security applications there are some preprocessing need to be done before the signature matching begins, such as capturing packets, decoding and so on. Instead of waiting for the matching results, we want the CPU to do the preprocessing for the coming input while the preceding input are being processed by the GPU, the multi-core CPU can handle this well; the second is that some more processing need to be done after the matching procedure on GPU, for example, some Snort rules require specific signatures to appear at certain offset, and checking this is not a job that suits the SIMD GPU well.

When using multiple GPUs, there are also two methods to distribute the workloads: the input flow segmentation and the pattern set partition. The former one will split the input flows and assign them to different GPUs. The latter one will broadcast the input data to every GPU but different GPUs will work one different pattern subsets. Load balancing is an important issue that must be covered in both methods, and that's not an easy question, because in security applications there are many extra requirements, this part will not be discussed in this paper. Another possible problem is that different GPUs may perform memory copy operations between the host and GPU through PCI-E16 bus at the same time, solutions to this problem will be discussed in future work rather than in this paper.

4   Load Balancing Inside the GPU

In this section, we will discuss the problem of load balancing inside the GPU, which includes load balancing for input text partition and load balancing for pattern set partition.

4.1   Load Balancing When Using Input Text Partition

As described in Section 3, the input text partition will be split into chunks that are equal in length, and that's a pretty good load balancing strategy. There's no need to employ other sophisticated strategy, the reasons run as follows:

(1) More complex load balancing strategies require more control, in which the SIMD GPU is weak.

(2) In most commonly used multi-pattern matching algorithm, the length of the input text will affect the performance most rather than the content of the input text, thus partition the text by equal length is well enough.

4.2   BPSPM: The Balanced Pattern Set Partition Method

The balanced pattern set partition method (BPSPM) is proposed to balance the workload of different multiprocessors when performing pattern set partition. The idea is to make each subset as similar as possible. If two pattern subsets have the approximate number of patterns and the structure of the patterns are close to each other, then we consider the two subsets to be similar.

BPSPM uses the round-robin dispatch, which will make the number of patterns in pattern subsets approximately the same, the difference between any subset will be at most one pattern.

To make the structures of patterns in different subsets similar, BPSPM sorts the patterns. Two typical methods for sorting strings are the length-first sorting and the lexically sorting. Both are considered for BPSPM, called *BPSPM-Length* and *BPSPM-Lexical,* respectively. Our experiments in Section 5 shows the *BPSPM-Length* algorithm outperforms its counterpart on Snort signature set.

The *BPSPM-Length* algorithm can be finished in $O(rlogr)$ time (r is the number of patterns), and will be executed only once at the initial phase of the calling application. The *BPSPM-Lexical* algorithm is obtained by replacing the **Length-First-Sort** function in *BPSPM-Length* with a lexically string sorting function.

The *BPSPM-Length* algorithm is listed as follows:

Algorithm 1. BPSPM-Length: The Length First Balanced Pattern Set Partition Method

---

Input:
  The pattern set $P = \{p^1, p^2, \ldots, p^r\}$;
  The number of output subsets m
Output:
  A set of pattern subset $\{P_1, P_2, \ldots, P_m\}$,
  where $P_i \subset P$, and $\bigcup\limits_{i=1}^{m} P_i = P, \forall i, j, P_i \cap P_j = \emptyset$

Boolean Function Pattern-Compare(pattern p^i , pattern p^j)
Begin
    if $|p^i| = |p^j|$ and $p^i < p^j$ return TRUE;
    if $|p^i| < |p^j|$ then return TRUE;
    return FALSE;
End
Procedure Length-First-Sort(Pattern-Set P)
Begin
    Sort the elements in P such that
        for any i, j, **Pattern-Compare**(p^i, p^j) = TURE;
End
Begin
    (1) **Length-First-Sort(P)**;
    (2) for $i:=1$ to m do $P^i = \oslash$
    (3) for $j:=1$ to $\frac{r}{m}$ do
        for $i:=1$ to m do $P_i = P_i \cup \{p^{m \times (j-1)+i}\}$;
End

---

5   Experiments and Results

In this section, we present our experiments about pattern set partition and input text partition.

We use a SIMD GPU GTX 9800+, whose architecture is similar to the G80 series. The input texts are constructed randomly on the ASCII alphabet, and the size is 128MB. The Snort signature set and the ClamAV signature set are chosen because of their different pattern length distribution characteristics: the signature set of Snort has shorter average length and the most frequent patterns are the 5 bytes patterns; the signature set of ClamAV has longer average length and the most frequent patterns are the 38 bytes patterns.

5.1 Experiments on Pattern Set Partition and Input Text Partition

We measured the average throughput of the multiprocessors using the pattern partition based method *BPSPM-Length*. The experiments were carried out using the Aho-Corasick algorithm [14] both on Snort and ClamAV signature sets. The number of subsets is equal to the exponent of 2, ranging from 4 to 2048; the throughput of a single multiprocessor is obtained for each division. We can see that the throughput will increase with the number of subsets until the number is greater than 2048, as is depicted in Fig.5. The result demonstrates that pattern partition introduced in our model can help improve the throughput.

We also measured the maximum execution time of all the stream processors inside a multiprocessor using both the pattern partition based and text partition based methods. The experiments were carried out using the Aho-Corasick algorithm [14] both on Snort and ClamAV signature sets.

The pattern partition method is the same as the antecedent experiment of throughput variation. When using the text partition method, the input text T is split into equal chunks TC_i, and $|TC_i| = \frac{|T|}{m} + p_{maxl}, 1 \le i \le m$, where $|T|$ is the length of the input text, $|TC_i|$ is the length of chunk i, m is the number of chunks per text, and p_{maxl} is the max pattern length. The number of chunks per text is equal to the exponent of 2, ranging from 4 to 2048; the maximum execution time of the stream processors inside a multiprocessor is obtained for each division.

On the Snort signature set, the maximum execution time decreases if the number of pattern subsets increases when the patterns are partitioned, as is shown in Fig.6(a); the maximum execution time also decreases if the number of

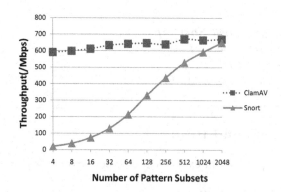

Fig. 5. The throughput variation using pattern set partition

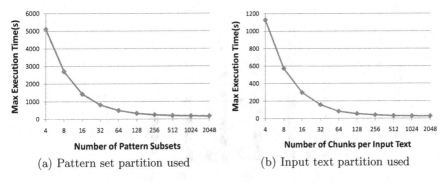

(a) Pattern set partition used   (b) Input text partition used

Fig. 6. The max execution time variation on Snort signature set

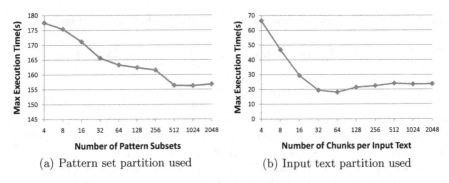

(a) Pattern set partition used   (b) Input text partition used

Fig. 7. The max execution time variation on ClamAV signature set

chunks increases when the input texts are split, as is presented in Fig.6(b). But the former max execution time is 5 times larger than the latter one.

On the ClamAV signature set, similar results can be obtained, which is depicted in Fig.7(a) and Fig.7(b), and the maximum execution time of the former one is 3~5 times larger than the latter one.

This proves that both pattern set partition and input text partition can help reduce the processing time of stream processors. But text partition based method has smaller maximum execution time than pattern set partition based methods. That is why input text partition is introduced inside the multiprocessor between different stream processors, while the pattern set partition is introduced between multiprocessors. And the correctness and feasibility of the idea adopted in HPSMM that considers combining pattern set partition and input text partition is verified.

5.2   Effects of Load Balancing

As discussed in Section 4, input text partition works well at load balancing, so we only present experiments of the load balancing effect of BPSPMs. The time Coefficient Variant (C.V) is introduced as a measurement of load balancing

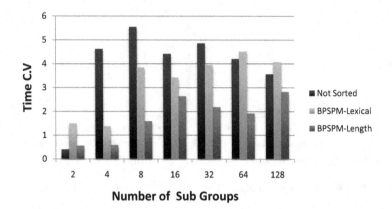

Fig. 8. Time C.V variation with the number of pattern subsets on Snort signature set

effect. For an array of data $d = \{d_1, d_2, \ldots, d_n\}$, C.V of d is defined as:

$$C.V(d) = \frac{\sum_{i=1}^{n} (d_i - \overline{d})^2}{n * \overline{d}} . \tag{1}$$

From the above equation, greater C.V value means a more dispersive distribution of data which represents poor effect of load balancing, and zero means a uniform distribution which represents perfect effect of load balancing.

We performed signature matching on pattern subsets generated from Snort signature set, and then we calculated the C.V of the signature matching time on different pattern subsets. The same procedure was executed three times using the *BPSPM-Lexical*, *BPSPM-Length* and the not sorted pattern set partition method respectively. The results are depicted in Fig.8. We can see that *BPSPM-Length* outperforms the other two, which demonstrates the power of our method.

5.3   Comparison with Hardware Based Methods

Our method is quite different from the hardware based methods in many ways, such as performance, cost, scalability, and adaptability. A comparison is listed in Table.1.

A GPU that supports CUDA costs no more than several hundred dollars, which is approximate to the price of a general purpose CPU, while dedicated hardware cost much more; the GPU based signature matching applications can

Table 1. Comparison between GPU based and hardware based methods

Parameters	GPU based method	Hardware based method
Performance	medium	high
Cost	low	high
Scalability	high	low

be run on any host with a GPU that supports CUDA, rather than a small number of devices, while hardware based methods is usually designed to run on certain hardware such as FPGA,TCAM,etc; the performance of GPU based methods is much higher than that of CPU based methods, but it is still not that high as hardware based methods.

However, there are some applications like network situation awareness and network attack prediction, which require a massive number of high performance network sensors, hardware based methods are too expensive and not scalable enough, but GPU based methods can be quite suitable.

6 Conclusions

In this paper, the SIMD GPU is introduced to speed up the signature matching in network security applications. A thorough analysis of the data parallelism when using the SIMD GPU to speed up signature matching is made at first. Then an HPSMM using SIMD GPU is presented, which combines the pattern set partition and input text partition to gain more parallelism. The load balancing problem of HPSMM is discussed carefully, and a load balance method based on pattern set partition BPSPM is proposed. Experiment results on a SIMD GPU GTX 9800+ demonstrate the feasibility and rationality of the HPSMM model, and the load balancing effect of *BPSPM-Length* is proved to be good.

There are four points that differentiate our work from previous ones:

(1) A hybrid architecture that combines pattern set partition and input texts partition to maximize parallelism inside the GPU.

(2) An effective load balancing method is proposed for the multiprocessors inside the GPU.

(3) Multi-core CPUs are used, which help increase the concurrency between the host and the GPU device.

(4) Multi-GPUs scheme is outlined, which introduce more processing power.

Further study will focus on the workload balancing when multi-GPUs are employed.

References

1. Antonatos, S., Anagnostakis, K.G., Markatos, E.P.: Generating realistic workloads for network intrusion detection systems. In: ACM SIGSOFT Software Engineering Notes, vol. 29, pp. 207–215 (2004)
2. Tuck, N., Sherwood, T., Calder, B., Varghese, G.: Deterministic memory-efficient string matching algorithms for intrusion detection. In: Proc. of INFOCOM, vol. 4, pp. 2628–2639 (2004)
3. Clark, C.R., Schimmel, D.E.: Scalable Pattern Matching for High Speed Networks. In: Proceedings of the 12th Annual IEEE Symposium on Field-Programmable Custom Computing Machines, pp. 249–257. IEEE Computer Society, Washington (2004)

4. Tan, L., Sherwood, T.: A High Throughput String Matching Architecture for Intrusion Detection and Prevention. In: Proceedings of the 32nd annual international symposium on Computer Architecture, vol. 4, pp. 112–122 (2005)
5. Dharmapurikar, S., Lockwood, J.W.: Fast and scalable pattern matching for network intrusion detection systems. IEEE Journal on Selected Areas in Communications 24, 1781–1791 (2006)
6. Yu, F., Katz, R.H., Lakshman, T.V.: Gigabit rate packet pattern-matching using TCAM. In: Proceedings of the 12th IEEE International Conference on Network Protocols, 2004, pp. 174–183 (2004)
7. Alicherry, M., Muthuprasanna, M., Kumar, V.: High speed pattern matching for network IDS/IPS, pp. 187–196. IEEE Computer Society, Los Alamitos (2006)
8. Lei, S., Yue, Z., Jianming, Y., Bo, X., Bin, L., Jun, L.: On the Extreme Parallelism Inside Next-Generation Network Processors. In: Proceedings of INFOCOM, pp. 1379–1387 (2007)
9. Ni, J., Lin, C., Chen, Z., Ungsunan, P.: A Fast Multi-pattern Matching Algorithm for Deep Packet Inspection on a Network Processor. In: International Conference on Parallel Processing (2007)
10. Nvidia G80 Specs, http://www.nvidian.com/page/8800_features.html
11. Nvidia CUDA Programming Guide 2.1.,
    http://developer.download.nvidia.com/compute/cuda/2_1/NVIDIA_CUDA_
    Programming_Guide_2.1.pdf
12. Marziale, L., Richard, G.G., Roussev, V.: Massive threading: Using GPUs to increase the performance of digital forensics tools. Digital Investigation 4, 73–81 (2007)
13. Vasiliadis, G., Antonatos, S., Polychronakis, M., Markatos, E.P., Ioannidis, S.: Gnort: High performance network intrusion detection using graphics processors. In: Lippmann, R., Kirda, E., Trachtenberg, A. (eds.) RAID 2008. LNCS, vol. 5230, pp. 116–134. Springer, Heidelberg (2008)
14. Aho, A.V., Corasick, M.J.: Efficient String Matching: An Aid to Bibliographic Search. Communications of the ACM 18, 333–340 (1975)
15. Goyal, N., Ormont, J., Smith, R., Sankaralingam, K., Estan, C.: Signature Matching in Network Processing using SIMD/GPU Architectures. UW CS technical report 1628 (January 2008)
16. Smith, R., Estan, C., Jha, S., Kong, S.: Deflating the big bang: fast and scalable deep packet inspection with extended finite automata. In: Proceedings of the ACM SIGCOMM 2008 conference on Data communication, pp. 207–218. ACM, New York (2008)

HPVZ: A High Performance Virtual Computing Environment for Super Computers

Kai Lu, Wanqing Chi, Yongpeng Liu, and Hongwei Tang*

School of Computer Science in National University of Defense Technology,
Changsha, 410073, P.R. China
kai_lu@263.net,
chiwq@yahoo.com,
liupy@nudt.edu.cn,
hwtang@nudt.edu.cn

Abstract. Because of the features of isolation, security and consolidation, virtual machine technology is widely used in data center for server consolidation, which can support different operating systems or different isolated applications running on a single server. Besides this usage scenario on server systems, there are other scenarios that require more performance, isolation and security than consolidation. Such scenarios include HPC and Cluster for scientific computing. Because of the particularity of system architectures and usage requirements, existing virtual machine techniques cannot be used in HPC directly. Aiming to provide the features of architecture and requirements for HPC, we present a virtual machine technique for HPC system named High Performance Virtual Zone(HPVZ). HPVZ technique is the first complete solution for virtualization of HPC systems, and can provide users an isolated and secure running environment based on the structure of the HPC system. The evaluation shows that the HPVZ technique is the most cost-effective for HPC, compared to other virtual machine techniques.

Keywords: Virtualization HPC Isolation Security.

1 Introduction

In recent years, virtual execution environments (VEEs), such as Xen [14] and VMware Workstation[4], have grown in popularity. A key advantage of the Virtual Machine is that several different OS images can simultaneously exist on the same machine with strong isolation from each other. This allows easy management and configuration, the virtual machine technique is widely used in Data-Centers or Enterprises to implement the service consolidation. For server consolidation, each VM can run an independent operating system. Different services, which used to run on individual machines in order to avoid interference, are instead running in separate VMs on the same physical machine.

---

* This research is supported by National 973 Plan (2005CB321801) and Funder of Huoyingdong (111072).

Y. Dou, R. Gruber, and J. Joller (Eds.): APPT 2009, LNCS 5737, pp. 205–219, 2009.
© Springer-Verlag Berlin Heidelberg 2009

The desire to run multiple operating systems was the original motivation for virtual machines, as it allowed time-sharing a single computer between several single-tasking OSes. According to the layer where the system virtualization is implemented, the virtual machine can be classed into two major categories. If the VM is running on bare hardware, this kind of VM is called Type-I or native VM. Xen and ESX Server are running on hardware directly and support booting multiple OSes. These OSes are often called guest OSes. The resources of the real machine are controlled by the VM, and then shared by different guest OSes on top of the VM. In order to avoid interference with resource usage, the VM can support quality-of-service (QoS) isolation to prevent a guest operating system from occupying too many resources and preventing access to resources from being obtained by other guest OSes. The Type-II or hosted VM is the kind of VM running on the top of an operating system. The typical system of Type-II VM is VMware. Each VMware process can boot an independent new operating system. The performance of a virtual machine is a big problem you have to consider when you want to use VM technology, especially for I/O performance [12,19].

An alternate technique for isolation is the Container technique of operating system, such as Solaris Zones [15], VServer [2] and Linux Virtuozzo [1]. The Container technique is not a virtual machine, but an example of "operating-system virtualization". The Container technique can provide some form of encapsulation of processes within an operating system. One of the Container technique's advantages is that it is much more performance-efficient than Type-I and Type-II virtual machines, and has better observability into multiple guests simultaneously [1,2,15]. The disadvantage of the Container is that the Container can only support one kind of operating system running environment for applications, which means the Container technique cannot provide two kinds of ABI at the same time, such as Windows and UNIX.

The system architecture and the application requirements will play an important role when designing the system. In this paper, we describe the usage scenarios of super computer and analyze the requirements of Parallel applications. Based on our analysis, we present the first complete virtualization solution for HPC, named High Performance Virtual Zone(HPVZ). The contributions of this paper are as follows.

1. First, this is the first complete solution for High Performance Computer virtualization. Before this work, people would like to use the VMware or Xen technique on small cluster systems directly to construct virtual nodes, but ignoring the characteristics of HPC. This will be analyzed in the later part.

2. Second, based on the distributed computing environment of HPC, we create new optimization techniques to diminish the overheads caused by virtualization.

3. Third, we compare the performance of HPVZ to the machine without virtualization, and also compare the support for isolation and security of HPVZ with other VM techniques.

The rest of the paper is organized as follows. In the next section, we briefly describe the motivation for our HPVZ design. Section 3 describes the structure of HPVZ and its optimizing techniques. In section 4, we compare the performance of HPVZ with the machine without virtualization. We then analyze the isolation and security of HPZV. Section 5 describes the related works of VMs for HPC. In the final section, we summarize the major points of the paper and present our conclusions.

2 Motivation

In this section, we will discuss the background of our work and analyze the HPC's requirements of virtualization.

Rather than a single address space system, modern HPC systems consist of multiple computing nodes with different function. Normally, the HPC system can be divided into three parts: front-end or server nodes, computing nodes and storage nodes. All these three parts are integrated into a tight coupling system by the high-speed inter-connecting network to provide high performance computing capability and massive storage capacity. HPC system is a shared computing environment, and provides service based on the scheduling of resources managing system.

The DARPA High Productivity Computing Systems project [3] is focused on providing a new generation of economically viable high productivity computing systems for national security and for the industrial user community. HPCS program researchers have initiated a fundamental reassessment of how to define and measure performance, programmability, portability, robustness and ultimately, productivity in the HPC domain.

High performance: The performance is the primary evaluation criteria of HPC. According to test, the parallel application can only gain a small part of peak performance of whole HPC system. In order to improve the real performance of applications can gain, the project FAST-OS [6] hopes to use simplified kernel technique to reduce the noise of the operating system and runtime service. FAST-OS project includes SSI research for Petascale Computer, configurable OS and Right-Weight Kernels. These researches hope to use simpler OS to diminish the running noise of the HPC system. But unfortunately, current research of using virtual machine techniques to improve reliability of HPC or save power will bring in more performance overhead to HPC. According to the [7], The performance loss of compiling on ESX server and Xen are 10% and 30% each, and the loss of message passing on ESX server and Xen are 10% and more than 50% each . This is not acceptable for HPC.

Easy use and management: Traditional HPC provides a shared environment to all users. But different users will need different running environments. And sometimes these environments even conflict. For example, different applications need different versions of compilers and libraries. But on shared server nodes, this requirement causes difficulty of management and easy leading to misuse. The demands of easy use and management require the HPC can provide independent running environments for different users.

High security: The system security is often omitted during designing HPC. According to statistics, more than 70% attacks or security threats are induced by interior-users or misuse. To be a public information infrastructure, the capability of protect user's information security is very important to HPC. The leaking of important running information or data files is intolerable. Traditional UNIX OS on HPC uses ACL to prevent un-authority users from accessing others' information, whose isolation capacity is rather weak. Besides the danger caused by un-authority accessing, the misuse can also damage the system. The memory leaking of application will cause the system daemon can't work properly, or even result in this node's crashing. The security isolation and resource usage control are very important to system security.

High availability: The failure of nodes of HPC is inevitable in such a huge system. Normally, people use Checkpoint/Restart technique to diminish the loss when computing nodes crash. Checkpoint/Restart can help application to recover from last checkpoint and can reduce the loss of computing time for batched jobs on computing nodes. But for server nodes, Checkpoint/Restart technique is not enough. The failure of server node will cause the pause of users' operation. Users hope the system can provide a continual service no matter any server node fails. Checkpoint/Restart can't support this function.

According to the former analysis, the factor of performance should always be put on the first position in the design of the virtualized HPC. But using Xen or VMware to construct virtual nodes is not suitable for HPC, the performance loss is unaffordable and the isolation is over powerful for HPC system. Aiming at upper requirements of HPC and the shortcomings of current design, we bring out a complete solution of HPC virtualization in this paper, named High Performance Virtual Zone (HPVZ).

3   HPVZ

3.1   Overview

Current VMM technologies, including Type-I/Type-II and container based virtual technique, provide different isolated running environments based on a shared machine. But for a super computer with multiple independent nodes, these VMM techniques can't provide multiple independent virtual running environments directly. This section introduces the HPVZ, the system of virtual executing environment of High Performance Computer, and describes the techniques used to achieve a secure virtual running environment on a multi-nodes supercomputer with high performance.

3.2   System Structure of HPVZ

HPVZ consists of three parts, Virtual Zone of Server Node (VZSN), High Performance Zone of Computing Node (HZCN) and Zone Based Resource Management (ZBRM). The structure is showed in Fig.1.

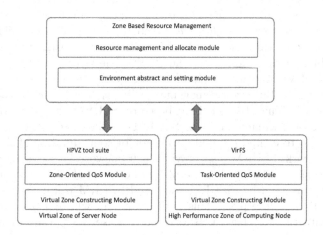

Fig. 1. Structure of HPVZ

The virtual zone of server node is constituted based on the OpenVZ technique [5]. The OpenVZ provides multiple running environments independently in a single OS, including a unique root and system runtime service. The system resource is assigned to each VM whenever it is created. In OpenVZ, the boot and shutdown of each VM just like a regular independent operating system. Because booting a VM in OpenVZ need not the initialization done by the BIOS and operating system kernel, the reboot time may only takes several seconds when necessary. To applications and the users, the management and usage of this zone appears just like a separated host. From this point, there is little difference between a container and hypervisor based VM. However, they differ fundamentally in the techniques they use to implement isolation. Rather than construct multiple virtualized machine, OpenVZ only construct multiple isolated user executing environments, which means only objects needed by application running, such as user's file directory, UID, PID, pty and network address, are virtualized. The advantage of using OpenVZ technique in HPC over Type-I or Type-II VMM is OpenVZ's performance is much higher than Xen or VMware.

The High Performance Zone of Computing Node provides an isolated computing runtime service with high performance on computing nodes compactable with the virtual zone of server node. As mentioned in Section 2, computing nodes have a closed running environment, which means users can't log in the computing nodes directly. They can only submit their jobs from Server nodes to computing nodes. Computing nodes will treat these jobs in batched way. Compared with server nodes, the problems of security and requirements of isolation on computing node are much less. On the contrary, the performance should be more considered about. Based on the situation analyzed before, the HZCN uses *chroot* technique to construct an isolated running environment corresponding to the server nodes. In order to make an isolated file system for different users, we add a VirFS layer between the VFS and the GPFS. When constructing the HZCN, the system will *chroot* to user's working directory. A VirFS will be booted. VirFS will treat the *chrooted* directory as its root, and build the proc file system based on this new root. Based on VirFS, we construct an entirely file system, include process file system and PGFS. The layer of VirFS is very thin, the overhead of VirFS can be omitted when accessing files.

The Zone Based Resource Management (ZBRM) is the central controller of the whole HPVZ. The ZBRM is built based on SLURM [20]. The SLURM is a wildly used resources manage system. SLURM can allocate exclusive and/or non-exclusive access to computing nodes to users for some duration of time so they can perform work. SLURM also provides a framework for starting, executing, and monitoring work (typically a parallel job) on a set of allocated nodes. When user submit jobs by using SLURM commands, ZBRM will extract the virtual zone's actually absolute path. This path parameter will be passed to computing nodes with the job. The SLURM-stepd will use this parameter to create a corresponding isolated running environment on computing nodes. The SLURM system can support batched and interactive jobs. The processing batched job consists of two procedures of interactive jobs. Instead of treating the script of batched jobs as an interactive job, the ZBRM uses different ways to cope with batched jobs and interactive jobs.

There are two kinds of HPVZ in a HPC system. One kind is Common HPVZ (CVZ), and the other is called Special HPVZ (SVZ). The CVZ is established by the system manager by default. The CVZ provides the running environment for most users, just like the environment of traditional HPC before. In CVZ, users can edit, compile and debug their programs, and submit jobs, just like they used to. The SVZ is established for special users. The template of SVZ is provided by the system manager. But the template of SVZ only includes a minimal running requirement. Once the SVZ is established, the management is left to SVZ users. Users in SVZ can install and configure the software of SVZ independently.

3.3   File System Structure

When designing the file system structure of HPVZ image, what should be taken into account includes the contents and the location of the images. There are two kinds of virtual zones in HPVZ, Common VZ and Special VZ. The image contents and location of these two kinds of virtual zone are different.

The images of SVZ are stored on GPFS shared by every server node. Whichever server node the user will log on, the SVZ image will be loaded to that node. When SVZ started, all users belong to this SVZ will log in this SVZ. The CVZ is a common running environment for all users. In order to balance the workload in the whole server nodes array, there are several CVZ instances running concurrently on each server node. The tool suite, including configuration and user management, provides a consistent view of files and users. That means users can log in any server node and has the same operating environment. If the image of CVZ and SVZ are all stored on GPFS, the performance will be a problem. The read latency of files on GPFS is much larger than that of local disks. Because there is only one instance in the whole system and the SVZ user will log in any server node randomly, the SVZ image has to be stored on the shared file system. But for CVZ, there is a CVZ instance running at every server node, and the system runtime services of the CVZs are the same in each instance. Only the files of users in CVZ need be shared by all server nodes from the consistent viewpoint. According to this usage scenario, and in order to improve the performance, we divide the file image of CVZ into system part and global part. The system part of CVZ image includes system directories and files. This part is managed by the system manger, and won't change often. The global user part is the users' working home. In HPVZ, we put the system part on the local file system of each server node, and store the global user part on the GPFS. The performance of CVZ will be improved for running commands in system part of CVZ locally.

Because system part and user part of CVZ image are stored on different partitions, which will result a link from "/HPVZ/root/CVZ/home/" directory to "/PGFS/root/CVZ/home/", as showed in Fig.2. The penetration link of the virtual root set by OpenVZ will cause secure problems, whcih is forbidden by OpenVZ technique. In order to generate a safe penetration, we invent a nail-link technique. The penetrating node will be tagged in the inode structure and linked with real directory when creating the CVZ. When you access the nail-link directory, the system will check the tag and translate the path from local partition to the path of global part. The tag of nail-link can only be set by special tool suite of HPVZ, and only linked to the corresponding directory, this nail-link technique won't add any danger to system.

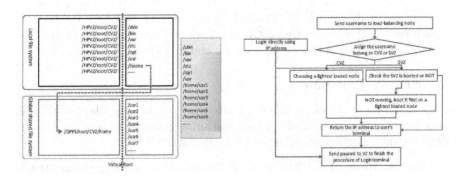

Fig. 2. Nail-link technique   **Fig. 3.** Login procedure in HPVZ

3.4   Resource Isolation

For high available requirement, the multi-level Quality of Service functions are provided by HPVZ. In OpenVZ, the amount of using resource can only be controlled at Zone level. That means you can only configure the maximum and minimum resources limits for a zone, but not for a separated process in a Zone. In HPVZ, we provide different levels of resource limits: process level, job level and VZ level.

On computing node, HPVZ provides a task-oriented resource control. HPVZ divides the tasks running on computing node into two classes. One class is system daemon tasks, like resource manage tasks and communicating tasks, the other is user applications, like users' job. In our design, the system tasks have higher priority than users' applications. So, the resource limit of system tasks is infinite. The maximum of resource of user applications is the total amount of system resource minus the lower limit of system tasks'. This configuration of resources can protect the system daemons from out of resource. The HPVZ can support the resource control at the job and process level. Sometimes in a job, the amount of resource used by each process is imbalance. For example, the first process, who responses for the file operation, will need more resources than other process in the same job. It is unfair to give them the same limit. The job level control can treat the resource usage of each process in the job as a whole. If the total amount of resource doesn't exceed the limit, the applications won't be disturbed. There are two kinds of limits of resource control: soft limit and hard limit. When you exceed the soft limit, the HPVZ will give you a warning. If you overrun the hard limit, the HPVZ will kill the job. In our system, the soft limit is set as 80% of hard limit by default. Based on soft and hard limits, the HPZV provides a QoS negotiable flow.

After the SLURM-stepd spawns a user process, the function *setjobid(jobID)* is called to set the job ID to the process. The processes sharing the same jobID will have the same resource control structure. If the jobID equals to -1, that means the process will have a process level QoS control.

The resource control also can provide the information of the maximum resource usage at different level. This information is very useful to optimize the application's performance. Currently, the majority of resource limits include physical memory, virtual memory, open file and disk spaces.

3.5   HPVZ's Tool Suite

HPVZ management tools include the manage and configure tools of CVZ, user manage tool and login tool, etc. These tool suites provide the functions of creating, deleting, starting, stopping and configuring of HPVZ.

1. **Manage tools of CVZ:** The CVZ has two parts of image as mentioned in Section 3.2. There is a copy of system image on each server node's local disk, and the only copy of global user image stored on the GPFS. When creating the CVZ, the creating tools will copy the system image to each server node and put the user image on the GPFS. Besides these copying

works, the creating tool will set the nail-link in system image pointing to the directory of users' working environment.

2. **Configure tools of CVZ:** Because the system images of CVZ are distributed on every server node. The configurations of CVZ are stored in the system directory in each system image. We provide a configure tool which can keep all configure files in all system images the same. The configuration of CVZ is a trick. Most of configure parameters of system images are the same, but some are not, such as the network address. Each CVZ instance has its own network address. The configuration tool of HPVZ provides an easy way to manage these configure parameters.

3. **User manage tools:** The username is unique in the whole HPVZ, that means each username can only belong to a CVZ or SVZ. The management of username is like NIS. When you add the a new user on a VZ, the *vz_adduser()* command will call a remote server to add this name in a central database first. When successed, the *vz_adduser()* will call local adduser command to add username and passwd in local passwd and shadow files. The *vz_deluser()* command will operate in a reversed way.

4. **Login tool:** When users log in the VZ from remote terminal, the load-balancing node of server array will check the VZ's status which this name belongs to. If VZ is CVZ, the load balancing node will relay the login request to a lightest load node in server array. If the user belongs to a SVZ and this SVZ is alive already, the load balancing node will relay the login request to the node where the SVZ is running. If the SVZ is not active, load balancing node will choose a lightest node to start the SVZ first. The login procedure is shown in Fig.3.

4 Evaluation

4.1 Experimental Environment

We evaluated the performance of the HPVZ on a cluster composed of 8 computing nodes and 2 server nodes. One of server nodes also acts as a load-balancing node. Each node is equipped with dual core Intel Xeon 2.66G CPUs, 8G memory and Mellanox MT25204 PCI-E InfiniBand HCA, which can provide a 20Gb connecting bandwidth. Besides the Infiniband, all nodes in this cluster are also connected by Gigabit Ethernet as controlling network. All nodes in cluster share a global file system supported by Lustre file system.

4.2 Server Node Performance Evaluation

The interacting operations and compiling are main part of Server nodes' workload. In this subsection, we use the micro-benchmark and the way of compiling kernel to evaluate the overhead of using HPVZ technique. The evaluation is compared with the performance of raw machine and HPVZ. The micro-benchmarks we used include Lmbench benchmark(version 3.0-a3) and iozone benchmark. The compiling performance testing is the method of parallel compiling (make -j).

Fig.4 shows the main results for Lmbench benchmark. We can find out that the discrepancy for all testing items of Lmbench's is less than 3%, and only the performance loss of create process (sh proc item) reaches about 10%. The majority works of virtualization is done about management of process. When a process is created, the additional structures, including virtual relation structure and managing structures should be allocated. If we create and destroy processes repeatedly, the additional spending will be cumulated and be obvious in such a specialized test. But in normal usage scenario, this overhead is so small that can be omitted, such like in Fig.8.

Fig.5 shows the bandwidth of read and write for iozone benchmark. From the figure, we can know that the bandwidth of HPVZ is lower than the raw machine by no more than 3%. The main cost is caused by the VirFS between the VFS and real File system. Every I/O operation will be checked first, and then passed from VFS to real file system by the VirFS. The overhead of VirFS is the main overhead of this I/O benchmark. In VirFS, because only the checking and transferring overhead of file operations is involved in, without any file data copy, the performance loss of I/O is quite small.

The compiling performance of server node is always cared by HPC users. The parallel compiling test is a test for overall performance for server nodes. From the Fig.6, we find that the difference for user time of these application compiling tests between HPVZ system and original system is quite small. Only system time is larger in HPVZ than raw machine. The reason is that the image of HPVZ is stored on GPFS. The accessing performance of PGFS is worse than local file system.

But for CVZ, we divide the whole CVZ image into system image and global user image, and store them at local disk and global file system separately. And we also adopt the nail-link technique to diminish the executing time of system applications. In order to figure out the improvement of CVS, we construct a SCZ with the same configuration with CVS, but with only one whole image located on the shared file system. From the Fig.7, we can know that because of a shorter accessing latency of system command and dynamic library, the system time of executing system application is shorten by 19%, and the total compiling time is shorten by 7%.

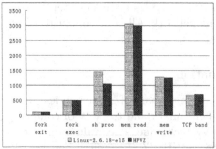

Fig. 4. Lmbenchmark

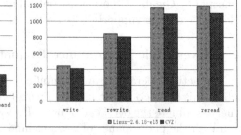

Fig. 5. I/O zone

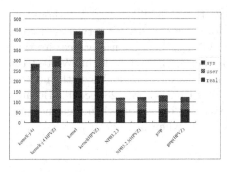 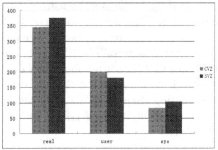

Fig. 6. Compling performance   **Fig. 7.** Optimization of Nail-link technique

4.3 Parallel Application Performance Evaluation

In this subsection we examine the performance of HPC benchmarks on HPVZ. We use the NAS Parallel Benchmarks (NPB) for evaluation. NPB is a representative benchmark for evaluating HPC systems. It can almost utilize the system's CPU and memory fully. We select some typical programs to test HPVZ. The test is made on eight computing nodes. Fig.8 shows the execution time of some NPB programs under these two systems. The comparative results vary little even though the HPVZ technology is adopted. Most of programs have the equivalent results, lu.A even has a better performance than on raw machine. This may be caused by system's noise during the testing. According to our former micro-benchmark test, the observable performance loss on HPVZ only occurs when forking testing item and I/O testing. The NPB benchmarks are mainly computing intensive programs, HPVZ only using *chroot* technique to construct an isolated environment. If the application won't open files too much, the HPVZ's overhead of parallel applications on computing node could be omitted at all.

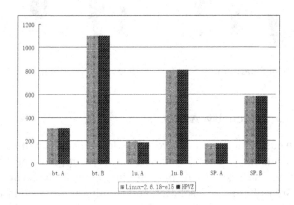

Fig. 8. NPB benchmark

According to the mechanism of HPVZ, the scalability of HPVZ should be quite good. We examine the boot time for HPVZ (both for service and computation) at different scale. Because the CVZ is booted in advance, its time consumption is zero. The SVZ is booted when user want to login. We test the boot time of different number of SVZs on a single server node. When the number of SVZs is no more than 256, the average boot time is about 28 seconds. Because constructing time of HPVZ only involves *chroot* operation when creating jobs, the constructing time of HPVZ remains stable when number of processes in a job changes.

4.4   QoS Performance Evaluation

Qos function is used to control the resource usage and ensuring high quality service on computing nodes. The implementation of Qos function involves creating QoS structure with process and recording the resource usage during each resource consumption. Fig.9 and Fig.10 show the comparative test for Lmbench and programs between the kernels of having Qos functions and without. As shown in figures, except for the test items of fork and exec (20% performance loss because of allocation for management data structure of Qos repeatedly), the other items and programs' performance nearly have no obvious performance loss. These testing results show that the allocation of QoS structure is the main overhead of QoS functions. The recording resource usage in each memory allocating and file opening can be omitted.

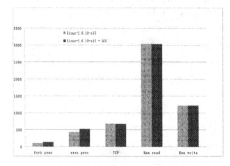   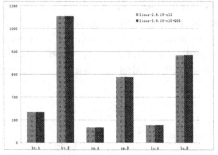

Fig. 9. Lmbenchmark on QoS   **Fig. 10.** NPB benchmark on QoS

4.5   Isolation and Security Analysis

Efficiency can be easily measured by overall performance, including throughput, latency and the scalability. But to isolation and security, it is hard to quantify. The fuller isolation the system can provide, including fault isolation, resource isolation, configure isolation, file isolation and running information isolation, etc, the better the security of the system will be. But on the other side, the better isolation means the more performance overhead. The choice of sufficiency of

Table 1. Comparison of Isolation and Performance

Technique	Fault iso.		File iso.		Resource iso.		Run Iso.	Perf. Rank
	kernel	application	kernel	application	domain	process		
Type-II	X	X	X	X	X	-	X	4
Type-I	X	X	X	X	X	-	X	3
OpenVZ	-	X	-	X	X	-	X	2
HPVZ	-	X	-	X	X	X	X	1

isolation is the key point of a successful design of HPC. The Table 1 lists the capacity of different virtual machine techniques and the rank of the performance. In the columns of fault and file isolation, the "X" stands for this virtual machine technique can support isolation at kernel or application level. From the Table 1, we can know that the isolating functions for fault and files of HPVZ are less than other virtual machine techniques, but sufficient for users. On resource isolation, the HPVZ provides a fine-grained support at the process and job level, while other virtual machine techniques can only provide QoS control at the domain level.

The last column of Table 1 is the performance. According to the testing of [7] and [13], the performance of Type-I virtual machine technique (Xen) is better than Type-II virtual machine (VMware). The performance of resource container technique is even better because it only virtualizes the user running environment. HPVZ is developed based on OpenVZ technique, one kind of resource container technique. And the HPVZ adopts techniques of nail-link optimization and *chroot* as mentioned in Fig.7 and in section 3.2 to gain higher performance. That is the reason why HPVZ occupies the first position in the performance rank column.

Based on the analysis in the Section 2, the performance is the most important to HPC, and other supports, such as easy use, security and high availability follows. From the Table 1, we can find that the HPVZ can provide sufficient isolating support to HPC and with least performance lost.

5   Related Works

The virtual machine technique is mainly used for the consolidation on network servers. In recent years, because of the requirements of high productivity of HPC, the research of how to utilize the virtual machine technique on HPC is becoming hotter and hotter. People hope to use the virtual machine technique to achieve the goals of high available, easy use, high security of HPC designing.

The reliability is a big problem to HPC. The function of dynamic migration of virtual machine can be helpful to improve the reliability of the super computer system. Laura and Santhanam researched the techniques to take the advantage of the VMM to manage and allocate the resource in the super computer [8,9,21].

The efficiency of virtual machine is very important to HPC system. A lot of research are the fields of improving the performance of performance of Xen [14]. The overhead of managing the memory allocations and deletion in Xen is very high. According to the test of malloc/free, and performance of *fork()* and *exec()* will decrease to 40% at most. Even though the shadow page table technique is used in Xen, the memory management performance is still lower to 20% [13,19]. J. Liu researched the technology of bypass I/O to improve the IO performance of Xen for HPC[12]. With the way of bypass I/O, the advantage migration of VMM is absent. Wei Huang did the further research on providing efficient Infiniband-based communication and support dynamic migration as well [11].

The Stephen brought out a container based OS virtualization: Vserver [13], and compared the isolation and efficiency of Vserver and Xen techniques. But about how to construct a virtual environment on HPC, the paper did not mentioned much.

The power consumption becomes a big problem with the scale of the HPC getting larger and larger. Akshat pointed out the principle of how to place the application in the HPC to construct a power-aware system [10]. Currently, taking the advantage of migration of VMM, Tyler [17] and Fabien [18] hope to decrease the total power consumption of the system, and also to avoid the hot spot in the system. This research can save the running expenses of HPC and also can expand the computing node's life-span of HPC.

6   Conclusion

Virtualization technology benefits a wide variety of usage scenarios. It promises such features as configuration independence, software interoperability, better overall system utilization, and resource guarantees. Aiming at the usage scenarios of HPC, we analyze the requirements of the virtualization on HPC. Based on our analysis, this paper has presented a new approach HPVZ to virtualized HPC system. The HPVZ utilizes the container technique of operating system to construct different virtual zones for users. The analysis and evaluation of Section 4 show the HPVZ can fully meet the requirements of resource guarantee and configuration isolation of HPC. And the test results also show the overhead of HPVZ is very small, and can almost get the raw performance of the machine.

Unfortunately, in order to prevent additional overhead of bandwidth and latency, HPVZ does not support dynamic migration on computing nodes. This problem will be conquered in the future.

References

1. SWsoft. Virtuozzo Linux Virtualization, http://www.ncbi.nlm.nih.gov
2. Linux-VServer Project, http://linux-vserver.org
3. HPCS Project, http://www.highproductivity.org
4. VMware, http://www.vmware.com/
5. OpenVZ Project, http://wiki.openvz.org/Main_Page
6. FAST-OS Project, http://www.cs.unm.edu/~fastos/
7. A Performance Comparison of Hypervisors,
   http://www.vmware.com/pdf/hypervisor_performance.pdf

8. Grit, L., Irwin, D., Marupadi, V., Shivam, P.: Harnessing Virtual machine resource control for job management. In: First Workshop on System-level Virtualization for High Performance Computing (March 2007)
9. Santhanam, S., Elango, P., Arpaci-Dusseau, A., Livny, M.: Deploying Virtual Machines as Sandboxes for the Grid. In: Proceedings of the Second Workshop on Real, Large Distributed Systems (WORLDS) (December 2005)
10. Verma, A., Ahuja, P.: Power-aware Dynamic Placement of HPC Applications. In: ICS 2008, Greece (2008)
11. Huang, W., Liu, J., Abail, B.: A case for high performance computing with virtual machines. In: ICS (June 2006)
12. Liu, J., Huang, W., Abali, B., Panda, D.K.: High Performance VMM-Bypass I/O in Virtual Machines. In: Proceedings of USENIX 2006, Boston, MA (2006)
13. Soltesz, S., Potzl, H.: Container-based Operating System Virtualization: A Scalable, High-performance Alternative to Hypervisors. In: EuroSys 2007, Lisboa, Portugal (March 2007)
14. Barham, P., Dragovic, B.: Xen and the Art of Virtualization. In: SOSP 2003, Bolton Landing, New York, USA (October 2003)
15. Solaris Cntainers: Server Virtualization and Manageability, White Paper, http://www.sun.com/software/whitepapers/solaris10/grid_containers.pdf
16. Kamp, P.-H., Watson, R.N.M.: Jails: Confining the omnipotent root, http://www.watson.org/~robert/freebsd/sane2000-jail.pdf
17. Bletsch, T., Lim, M.Y.: Power Aware Domain Migration in a Virtualized Cluster, http://domino.watson.ibm.com/acas/w3www_acas.nsf/images/conf08/$FILE/caspaper-tkbletsc.pdf
18. Hermenier, F., Loriant, N.: Power Management in Grid Computing with Xen. In: Min, G., Di Martino, B., Yang, L.T., Guo, M., Rünger, G. (eds.) ISPA Workshops 2006. LNCS, vol. 4331, pp. 407–416. Springer, Heidelberg (2006)
19. Menon, A.: Diagnosing Performance Overheads in the Xen Virtual Machine Environment. In: VEE 2005, Chicago, Illinois, USA, June 11-12 (2005)
20. Jette, M.: Resource Management using SLURM. In: 7th International Conference on Linux Clusters, University of Oklahoma, May 1 (2006)
21. Nagarajan, A.B.: Proactive Fault Tolerance for HPC with Xen Virtualization. In: ICS 2007, Seattle, WA, USA, June 18-20 (2007)

High Performance Support of Lustre over Customized HSNI for HPC

Yufeng Guo, Xuejun Yang, Li Luo, Qiong Li, and Lu Liu

School of Computer,
National University of Defense Technology, Changsha 410073, China
yfguo21@yahoo.com.cn

Abstract. Parallel I/O needs keep pace with the demand of high performance computing applications. I/O bottleneck still is one of the key problems which restrict the development of high performance computer. Object-based storage combines the advantages of SAN and NAS, adopts an object-based interface, and has been a new orientation of massive storage. The trend as such makes it very promising to build a scalable I/O system for highperformance computing through implementation of object-based storage system based on high-performance interconnects. Lustre is a high performance distributed object parallel file system, is being widely studied and applied. Exploiting performance of Lustre depends on supports of high performance interconnects. In this paper, firstly we designed and implemented a customized high performance interconnect chip, HSNI (High performance Storage Network Interface), and introduced the characteristics of HSNI. Then we analyzed the communication features which support high performance of Lustre. Experimental results show that HSNI can greatly exert the performance of Lustre and has a very good scalability, so its very suitable for building the high performance object-based storage systems for high performance computing.

1 Introduction

With the population of information technology, digital data increased at exponential rates over the past decade, the data gross of whole world increased at rate of 30 percent per year [1]. Storage has entered the age of PB level. The new Moore theorem [2] proposed by Turing award winner Jim Gray told us that the new data arise in the next 18 months would equal to the sum of all the old data arise before under network environment. Information technology has entered into a new developing stage which should center on storage.

Driven by the requirements for extremely high bandwidth and large capacity for high performance computing, storage subsystem architectures are undergoing fundamental changes. Object-based storage combines the advantages of high-speed, direct-access of SAN, and the data sharing and security capabilities of NAS, adopts interface based on objects, store data as objects in a group of self-contained object-based intelligent storage devices (OSD), provides

Y. Dou, R. Gruber, and J. Joller (Eds.): APPT 2009, LNCS 5737, pp. 220–229, 2009.
© Springer-Verlag Berlin Heidelberg 2009

high capacity, throughput, reliability, availability cross-platform data sharing and good scalability. Object-based storage is on the verge of becoming the next generation standard storage interface. The American national standards institute (ANSI) ratified the object-based storage interface standard (OSD T10) [3] in 2005. Object-based storage system separates the storage management from the file hierarchy management. The storage management functionalities, such as data allocation, block mapping, and request scheduling, are all offloaded to storage devices.

At present, object-based storage studies are mainly on distributed parallel file systems over OSD. For example, Lustre [4,6] of Cluster Inc, panFs [5] of Panasas Inc, zFS [7] of IBM, etc. Lustre is a high performance object-based parallel file systems, it comes from Coda project [8] of Carnegie Mellon University, and developed by Cluster File System Inc. Lustre is a POSIX-compliant, object-based parallel file system. It provides fine-grained parallel file services with its distributed lock management, and can serve up to 10,000s of nodes, move 100s of GB/s with state of the art security and management infrastructure. Lustre has been deployed on many supercomputers, such as Jaguar at Oak Ridge National Lab, Thunderbird at Sandia National Lab, Tera-10 at CEA in Europe, and TSUBAME at Tokyo Tech in Japan.

To meet the demand of high performance computing, parallel I/O clusters always adopt to enhance I/O performance, most machines of top500 use this way, through a large number of I/O nodes and concurrent I/O operations to achieve a very high aggregate I/O bandwidth. While this architecture depends on high performance storage interconnects. The trend as such makes it very promising to build a scalable I/O system for high performance computing through implementation of object-based storage system based on high performance interconnects. High performance interconnects such as Myrinet [9], InfiniBand [10], and Quadrics [11] not only have been deployed into large commodity component-based clusters to provide higher computing power, but also have been utilized in commodity storage systems to achieve scalable parallel I/O support [12,13]. So it would have very important practical significance to study on high performance interconnects and communication interface, and provide efficient support for parallel file systems.

The basic contributions of this paper include: firstly we designed and implemented a customized high performance interconnect chip, HSNI. And developed efficient communication features to support high performance of parallel file systems. Finally, we evaluated the performance and scalability of Lustre over HSNI, results show the communication interface designed by us can greatly exert the performance of Lustre, and has a very good scalability.

The organization of this paper is as below: Section1 introduces the challenge of development of storage and I/O system, and analyzes the tread of I/O system. Section2 introduces object based parallel file system, Lustre. Section3 introduces the architecture and communication mechanism of our customized high performance interconnect chip, HSNI. Section4 introduces the communication features which support high performance of Lustre. Section5 evaluates the performance of Lustre over HSNI, and analyzes the results. Section6 is the summary of the paper and future work.

2   Overview of Lustre

Lustre is a POSIX-compliant object-based parallel file system that presents high aggregated I/O bandwidth by striping file extents across many storage devices. It can serve more than 10,000 nodes, and achieve more than 100GB/s aggregated I/O bandwidth. Lustre clusters contain three kinds of components: File system client, which can be used to access the file system. Object storage servers (OSS), which provide file I/O service. Metadata servers(MDS), which manage the names and directories in the file system. All these components connect with storage interconnect.

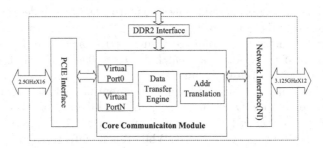

Fig. 1. Architecture of Lustre System

Fig.1 shows the architecture of Lustre system. Clients exchange metadata with MDS, and carry out I/O operation with OSS directly. The role of the client file systems is to provide a directory tree, which provides Unix file sharing semantics. The namespace is managed by metadata services which manage the Lustre inodes. The MDS stores the file inodes for all Lustre files. The information about the file striping pattern, objects of the file, location of the objects are all kept as a part of the extended attributes on the file inode. OSSs are responsible for objects store in the storage devices. Lustre provide numerous ways of handling storage management functions, storage management is achieved through stacks of object modules interacting with each other and dynamically changing the driver stacks. Luster employs a distributed lock manager to handle access to files and directories and synchronize updates, improving on the metadata journaling approach used by most modern file systems. Lustre also provides other features such as read-ahead and write-back caching for performance improvements. Lustre has below key features:

1) **Scalability:** object-based storage architecture that scales to tens of thousands of clients and hundreds of TB of data-a file system without limits.

2) **High Performance:** dramatic increase in throughput and I/O bandwidth by intelligent serialization and separation of metadata operations from data manipulation.

3) Innovative distributed lock manager: intent-based optimizations prevent bottlenecks and increase overall data throughout.

4) Cost effective: support for industry standard platforms and heterogeneous network environments significantly reduce deployment and support costs.

5) High availability: designed to support failover in all server components.

3   Customized High Performance Interconnect-HSNI

3.1   Architecture of HSNI

HSNI is a high performance network interface control chip based on independent light weight communication protocol, and can be applied to high bandwidth, low latency interconnect. HSNI provides a common solution framework for communication within computing nodes and I/O systems. Host interface adopts PCI Express link, and uses customized high performance serial link connect to the system network. HSNI supports virtual address to physical address translation and non-align RDMA to realize user-level communication efficiently.

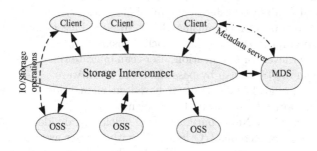

Fig. 2. Architecture of HSNI

As shown by Fig.2, HSNI includes below components:

1) PCI Express Interface: Used as the host interface. HSNI is an endpoint device of PCI Express system. It is compliant with PCI Express1.0a specification, support 16 lanes, 2.5Gbps per lane, up to 4 virtual channels. Max Payload Size is 512B, bidirectional bandwidth is 80Gbps.

2) Network Interface(NI): Used to connect with networks. It's a high speed serial link, implemented optical transmission by photoelectric conversion, supports 12 lanes, 3.125Gbps per lane, and two virtual channels, bidirectional bandwidth is 75Gbps. So the bandwidth can match with PCI Express link, and the performance is balance.

3) DRAM Interface: Adopted DDR2 interface, used to connect out-of-chip DRAM, frequency is 266MHz, data width is 64bit, max DRAM capacity is 4GB. DRAM used to store address translation table for virtual address to physical address, the translation table can be big enough for translation unlimited.

4) Core Communication Module: It's the key module of HSNI, and is designed for high performance communication mechanism. Includes several sub-components: Virtual Ports, Data Transfer Engine, Address Translation Module, e.g. Virtual Ports virtualized the hardware resource, all the operation registers are mapped to VP space, supported users access hardware directly, and provided a communication interface based on descriptors. Data Transfer Engine supports both short messages pass and RDMA, short messages pass used to transfer short package for management and notification, RDMA used for large data block transmission, and supports non-align RDMA transmission. Address Translation Module translates virtual address to physical address, and supports user level communication based on virtual address by search address translation table.

3.2   Characteristics of HSNI

HSNI chip is designed in for a CU-11 process, die size is about 20mmx20mm. Core frequency is 250MHz. The internal data path width is 128b. Power is about 14W.

The major characteristics of HSNI are below:

1. Provide a flexible programming interface based on descriptors mechanism, users can start data transfer by submission of descriptions.
2. Support two transfer mechanisms: Short Message Pass for management and notification, and RDMA for data block transmission.
3. Support user level communication, users can operate HSNI directly, without intervention of OS, so can by pass the costs of software.
4. Support non-align RDMA transfer based on virtual address, data transfer can start at any address needn't alignment.
5. Support Zero-Copy Non-Contiguous I/O efficiently, divided non-contiguous I/O into multi contiguous I/O by driver without user awareness.
6. Short Message Pass supports broadcast and multicast, which can accelerate the scientific applications.
7. Support 32 virtual ports, the descriptors processing of these virtual ports used round-robin arbitrator. Up to 32 processes can operate synchronously.
8. Results of transfer can be reported by interruption or message.
9. Support blocking with ACK validation and non-blocking without ACK validation data transfer.
10. Use key and protected bit to enhance security of communication, prevent misoperations which would destroy the system.

4   High Performance Communication Features

4.1   User Level Communication

User level communication allows user applications access communication interface directly, reduce the cost of software operations. OS kernel maps registers and DRAM space to user address space, so user processes can access them bypass OS kernel, and data can be send from user buffer without copy, so needn't system call, data copy and context switch between kernel and user process, user level communication also reduces the utilization of host CPU. Following we will use RDMA write as an example to show how user level communication process. Firstly, user processes use virtual address to prepare the descriptor and start data transferring. HSNI uses physical address read data from source memory by virtual address to physical address translation, then send data to target HSNI through NI. Target HSNI write data to user data buffer directly by virtual address to physical address translation, too. After all data transmission done, target user process can read from user data buffer without data copy. HSNI adopts virtual address to physical address translation based on address translation table (ATT) to support user level communication. The function of ATT is similar to TLB of memory, ATT can build the virtual address space of communication interface, and the index of table is similar to virtual page address. Contiguous virtual address of communication interface can be mapped to non-contiguous physical memory address by configuration of ATT.

Address translation module is the key component which supports user level communication. Address translation based on ATT is adopted by HSNI. The translation is done by hardware, and doesn't need software intervention. HSNI uses out-of-chip DRAM to build ATT. OS kernel manages ATT, every unit of table is 8B, can keep 64b page physical base address, ATT can be accessed by index. Driver registers the first unit index of a group of continuous ATT and the first page offset of user process space in the identifier of memory, and returns it to user process, so all user address have been translated into index and offset. HSNI only lookup ATT, and shouldn't modify it. To reduce access latency of ATT, we designed cache to store units of ATT, only cache miss would read DRAM. HSNI gets virtual address from descriptors, then uses the index to match ATT and get physical base address, physical base address add to offset will get physical address which used for data transfer. The process of address translation just needs one search operation and one add operation, and can be parallelization and pipeline with data translation, so it's very efficient.

HSNI adopts following methods efficiently realize virtual address to physical address translation:

1. Virtual address to physical address translation is completed by hardware, so it can bypass cost of software, reduce utilization of host CPU.
2. Out-of-chip DRAM can store enough ATT units, address translation invalidation will never happen, so there is no cost of invalid operation.
3. Use cache to reduce the search cost of ATT, and improve the performance of address translation.
4. By parallelization and pipeline with data transfer to reduce the latency and the cost of address translation.

4.2 Zero-Copy Non-contiguous I/O

Non-contiguous I/O access is the main access pattern in scientific applications. Thakur et. al. [14] also noted that it is important to achieve high performance

MPI-IO by providing native support of noncontiguous access in file systems. HSNI can support zero-copy non-contiguous I/O efficiently, user just need start one transfer operation, driver will divide this non-contiguous I/O into multi contiguous I/O, and write multi descriptors in descriptor queue, all these are unaware by user. After all data transfer completion, HSNI can notify host by interruption or short message. Fig.3 shows how zero-copy non-contiguous I/O is carried out: Firstly, the source and destination memory address/length pairs of the IO fragments are collected by the process which would initiate the RDMA operations. Then, user process call RDMA function provided by driver, and passes the non-contiguous address and length link to driver. Drivers separate non-contiguous I/O into multi contiguous I/O, construct descriptors and write in descriptor queue. HSNI start RDMA data transfer. After all data transfers have been done, notify the completion of this non-contiguous I/O to user process.

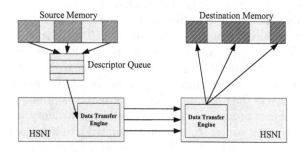

Fig. 3. Zero-Copy Non-contiguous RDMA

4.3   Non-align RDMA

HSNI supports any byte address non-align RDMA transfer, and offset of source and destination can be different. So data needn't copy to buffer which address is align, this can reduce software cost. Data transfer shouldn't cross page boundary, because the start data address offset of source and destination may be different, so source address maybe cross page boundary at destination, so we must align address according to destination address. The align module of HSNI supports non-align RDMA, to reduce the latency of align operations, we pipeline address align process, and pay little impact on communication performance.

5   Performance Evaluations

We construct an object-based storage system based on HSNI. File system adopts object parallel file system Lustre. Then we evaluate the performance of the object-based storage system. Section5.1 will introduce experimental environment and evaluation method. Section5.2 will show the results of test, and we will analyze these results.

5.1 Experimental Setup

Our object storage servers use Intel servers with three PCI Express slots, one used to plug HSNI card, and the other two used to plug RAID card. The disk interface of RAID card uses 3Gb/s SATA II interface, each RAID connects seven 400GB SATA II disks, the disk capacity of single OSS is about 6TB. An Intel server works as MDS, MDS connects to system network by HSNI, too. All clients use HSNI to connect to system network, and run Lustre Client program.

Benchmark uses IOR. IOR [15] (Interleaved or Random) is a parallel file system test code developed by the Scalable I/O Project at Lawrence Livermore National Laboratory. This parallel program performs parallel writes and reads to/from a file using MPI-IO (or optionally POSIX or HDF5) and reports the throughput rates. We used IOR not only to test aggregate bandwidth, but also to test the scalability of our system.

5.2 Experimental Results

In the single client experiments, the client would read from or write to multi OSD concurrently. The total size of I/O file is 64GB, strips across multi OSD uniformly. Fig. 4. shows the changes of I/O read and write bandwidth with an increasing number of OSD. The measurement results show that the read and write performance both improve with an increasing number of OSD. When OSD number is 4, read reaches its peak performance, 590MB/s. When OSD number is 8, write reaches its peak performance, 698MB/s. Also shown in the figure, the read and write performance would decrease appreciably with increase OSD number continuously, that's because just one client, the client communication would be the bottleneck of system. From the measurement results, we find HSNI can provide greatly support of read and write bandwidth for I/O operations of parallel file system.

Fig.5 shows the results of the I/O aggregate bandwidth measurements. The total size of I/O file is 64GB, strips across multi OSD uniformly. The OSD number is 16. The measurement results show the I/O aggregate read and write bandwidth changes with an increasing number of clients, the results would also

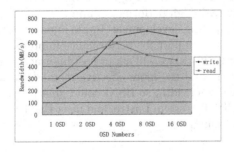

Fig. 4. Single Client I/O Bandwidth

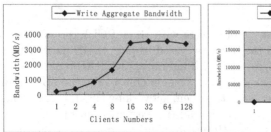 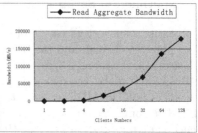

Fig. 5. Aggregate I/O Bandwidth

reflect the scalability of system. The left figure is the result of the write measurement, when the client number is less than 16, that's say every OSD would server no more than one client, the write bandwidth would increase linearly. But the write bandwidth would decrease appreciably if increase client number continuously after that, that's because the competition of OSD and MDS. The right figure shows the read bandwidth changes with an increasing number of clients, the read bandwidth would increase linearly with increase of the client number. Compare the left figure with right figure, we can find the read performance is better than write, and access competition would pay little effect to read performance. That's because the clients used cache. If cache hit, clients can get data directly without access OSD. All the results show that the scalability of the object-based storage system based on HSNI designed by us is very good, so it's very suit for building high performance computing system for scientific applications.

6   Conclusions

With the PB level computing power and storage capacity coming of age, how to construct an I/O system catches the demand of more and more complex applications becomes very important. Object model enhances the intelligent of I/O systems, reduces costs of file systems, cluster enhances parallelism of I/O, so they have been the effective ways to improve I/O performance. Building object-based storage system with high performance interconnects has been the tread of high-performance computing development. Rapid improvement of serial interface bandwidth provides well support for performance improvement of communication interface. In Future work, we will adopt host interface and network interface with higher bandwidth, and use more effective methods to reduce latency and improve data transfer bandwidth, so HSNI could greatly exert the performance of object based parallel file system Lustre, and meet the demand of development of high performance computing.

References

1. Lyman, P., Varian, H.R., et al.: How much information (2003)
2. Gray, J.: What Next? A Few Remaining Problems in Information Technology (1988)
3. Wber, R.O.: SCSI Object-Based Storage Device Commands(OSD), Document Number: ANSI/INCITS 400-2004. International Committee for Information Standards (December 2004)
4. Lustre, http://www.lustre.org
5. David Nagle, A.M., Serenyi, D.: The Panasas ActiveScale Storage Cluster-Dellivering Scalable High Bandwidth Storage. In: Proceedings of Supercomputing 2004 (2004)
6. Braam, P.J.: The Lustre storage architecture. Technical report, Cluster File Systems, Inc. (2002)
7. Rodeh, O., Teperman, A.: zFS- a scalable distributed file system using object disks. In: Proceedings of the 20th IEEE/11th NASA Goddard Conference on Mass Storage Systems and Technologies, pp. 207–218 (2003)
8. Coda Project, http://www.codaproject.org/
9. Myrinet, http://www.myri.com/
10. InfiniBand Architecture Specification, Release1.1. InfiniBand Trade Association (2002)
11. Petrini, F., Feng, W.C., Hoisie, A., Coll., S., Frachtenberg, E.: The Quadrics network: High-Performance Clustering Technology. IEEE Micro. 22(1) (2002)
12. Yu, W., Noronha, R., Liang, S., Panda, D.K.: Benefits of High Speed Interconnects to Cluster File Systems: A Case Study with Lustre. In: IPDPS 2006 (2006)
13. Yu, W., Panda, D.K.: Benefits of Quadrics Scatter/Gather to PVFS2 Noncontiguous IO. In: PACT 2005 (2005)
14. Thakur, R., Gropp, W., Lusk, E.: On Implementing MPI-IO Portably and with High Performance. In: Proceedings of the 6th Workshop on I/O in Parallel and Distributed Systems, pp. 23–32 (1999)
15. IOR Benchmark, http://www.llnl.gov/asic/purple/benchmarks/limited/ior

ViroLab Security and Virtual Organization Infrastructure

Jan Meizner[2], Maciej Malawski[1], Eryk Ciepiela[2], Marek Kasztelnik[2],
Daniel Harezlak[2], Piotr Nowakowski[2], Dariusz Król[2], Tomasz Gubała[2],
Włodzimierz Funika[1], Marian Bubak[1,2], Tomasz Mikołajczyk[3], Paweł Płaszczak[3],
Krzysztof Wilk[3], and Matthias Assel[4]

[1] Institute of Computer Science AGH, al. Mickiewicza 30, 30-059 Kraków, Poland
[2] ACC CYFRONET AGH, ul. Nawojki 11, 30-950 Kraków, Poland
[3] GridwiseTech, ul. Chrobrego 28/4, 31-428 Kraków, Poland
[4] High Performance Computing Center Stuttgart, Nobelstrasse 19 70569 Stuttgart, Germany
jm@jjpm.pl, {malawski,funika,bubak}@agh.edu.pl,
{e.ciepiela,m.kasztelnik,p.nowakowski,
d.harezlak,t.gubala}@cyfronet.pl,
dkrol@student.agh.edu.pl, {tomasz.mikolajczyk,
pawel.plaszczak,chris.wilk}@gridwisetech.com, assel@hlrs.de

Abstract. This paper introduces security requirements and solutions present in the ViroLab Virtual Laboratory. Our approach is to use a federated Single Sign-On mechanism based on the Shibboleth framework that enables multiple partners to authenticate against their local identity systems and use resources provided by all other partners. Since the basic Shibboleth capabilities do not meet our specific requirements related to supporting non-web-based services, we created a set of custom tools that allow us to develop a homogeneous, Shibboleth-based security solution for both Web and non-web-based software components. This paper describes these tools in detail, together with other services of the virtual laboratory which have been integrated with the security infrastructure. A decentralized, attribute-based approach facilitating the creation and management of virtual organizations is the key achievement of our work.

Keywords: virtual laboratory, security, virtual organization, single sign-on, federations, decentralized security, attribute-based authorization, Shibboleth.

1 Introduction

The ViroLab Virtual Laboratory (VL) is a distributed collaborative computing environment, which allows researchers to conduct *in-silico* experiments involving access to multiple data resources and processing of data using complex compositions of computational services [1,2]. The main application field of ViroLab is study of the Human Immunodeficiency Virus (HIV) where experiments combine simulations and analysis of data ranging from molecular dynamics to epidemiological effects [3]. The research results can improve clinical treatment of HIV patients.

The users of the virtual laboratory come from multiple disciplines and include clinicians, virology researchers and computer scientists. Clinicians interact with the system

Y. Dou, R. Gruber, and J. Joller (Eds.): APPT 2009, LNCS 5737, pp. 230–245, 2009.
© Springer-Verlag Berlin Heidelberg 2009

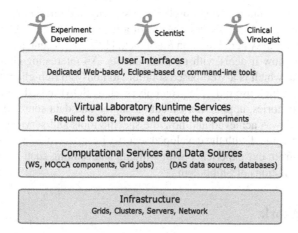

Fig. 1. High-level architecture of the ViroLab Virtual Laboratory

as experiment users, by routinely executing prepared experiments to obtain support in the treatment of their patients. Clinical researchers, virologists and epidemiologists are both designers and users of more advanced experiments needed to analyze the federated datasets of patients from ViroLab databases and acquire new knowledge, suitable for clinical decision support. Finally, the computer scientists' role is to act as experiment developers, supporting the researchers in implementing their experiment plans in an executable format, developing and integrating heterogeneous computing and data resources with the overall environment, and creating novel tools and services facilitating the usage of the entire infrastructure.

A simplified architecture of the Virtual Laboratory is presented in Fig. 1. The users may have multiple roles, such as experiment developers, scientists and clinical virologists, accessing the system via a set of dedicated user interfaces [4]. The user tools provide access to a generic set of virtual laboratory services, which allow execution of the available experiments and management of their results. The experiments are specified using a high-level notation based on Ruby *scripts* [5] and executed by the runtime system (GSEngine) [6]. They can perform computations using a multitude of middleware technologies [7] (such as Web services, MOCCA components [8] and Grid jobs e.g. on EGEE). They can also access multiple data sources, including federated databases, using the Data Access Services [9].

The users come from multiple institutions and can play various roles, which imply different access rights within the system. These aspects are particularly important since in the eHealth domain medical datasets (even those available for research purposes) need to be carefully protected from unauthorized access. For these reasons, there is a need to create a flexible *virtual organization* [10] management mechanism, which allows defining users, resources and policies in order to regulate their trust relationships and secure interactions accordingly.

In this paper we explain how the problem of security and virtual organization management was solved in ViroLab with the use of a federated attribute-based authentication and authorization system based on Shibboleth [11]. We present an overall security model and show how it deals with possible threats. An interesting challenge was to adapt Shibboleth, which is a Web-based solution, to non-web rich-client tools and distributed services which use multiple protocols (such as SOAP-based services, Subversion (SVN) repositories, application execution engine and data sources). We describe in detail how this was achieved and how the specific tools and services of the virtual laboratory are integrated with the developed security infrastructure. We also discuss the lessons learned from our experience with building and running such an infrastructure, including the limitations of Shibboleth.

2   Related Work

Well-established security solutions for Grid systems include authentication, authorization and credential delegation methods based on X.509 certificates. The most notable example of support for authentication and credentials delegation is the Grid Security Infrastructure (GSI) [12]. It enables users to authenticate themselves using so-called proxy certificates (short-lived certificates). Proxies might also be easily delegated to obtain indirect access to services. Following generation the proxy might be used for some time (until it expires); hence this solution is an example of a Single Sign-On (SSO) mechanism. Authorization could be implemented with the help of mechanisms such as VOMS [13] that manages VO membership of Grid users, enabling service providers to grant or deny access based on the user's VO. The main drawback of certificate-based solutions is that their usage that may be too complicated for regular users.

Web-based software is certainly friendlier to the user, as proven by high popularity of web solutions in science (e.g. web interfaces for drug or genetics databases), business as well as in blogs and social networks. This popularity prompted the need for solutions providing the security in those systems. As a result, many web-based security solutions have been created, providing support for SSO mechanisms. Shibboleth [14] is a federated SSO framework based on SAML [15] (a detailed description can be found in Section 4). Another example is the Java Open Single Sign-On (JOSSO) project [16]. Web applications are referred to as SPs (Service Provider) and the part providing user identities is called IdP (Identity Provider). IdP requires a J2EE container (such as plain Tomcat, JBoss or WebLogic), while SP might be developed using either Java or other popular Web technologies, e.g. PHP or ASP.NET. OpenID [17] is currently gaining popularity, although applying it to non-web scenarios is not straightforward.

One of the Shibboleth-based solutions, called GridShib [18], was created specifically for the Globus Toolkit. It integrates Shibboleth with standard Grid certificate solutions by issuing special Grid certificates (with the embedded Shibboleth attributes as an extension) for the users who only have a Shibboleth account. Another similar solution is called ShibGrid [19]. It enables users with and without Grid certificates to access GSI-protected services by either using their certificates for proxy generation or generating short-lived certificates based on the Shibboleth credentials.

3   Basic Threat Model for the ViroLab Infrastructure

The most common security requirements are **authentication** and **authorization**. Our system requires a federated Single Sign-On mechanism which enables different centres to manage their users on their own. Once authenticated, users are able to become authorized to use the services provided by various partners on the basis of the attributes released by their organizations. Other important requirements include **confidentiality** and **integrity** of data both stored in the system, as well as transmitted via the network. We must protect databases, experiments, experiment results and all types of transmitted credentials supplied by the user from being stolen or tampered with. Finally, we must ensure high **availability** of all parts of the architecture, especially security components. Any unavailability of security components might disable or seriously limit access to certain services and resources.

The Virtual laboratory infrastructure contains different types of potentially valuable assets that have to be protected. We present them in Tab. 1. In addition, the table describes possible threats against these assets.

The Virtual Laboratory might be a target of various types of attacks. It is well protected against simple **plain-text transmission eavesdropping** as all communication is encrypted with TLS, but there are other possible techniques, including: **dictionary or brute-force attack against user credentials** guessing user passwords; **phishing** and other **social engineering techniques** to lure potential victims (or **pharming** to redirect them) to a fake portal to intercept their credentials. In addition, the attacker might try to **directly exploit** security services used in the infrastructure (e.g. the LDAP or the Apache web server). To prevent these attacks we have to: enforce reasonably strong passwords, educate users not to give credentials to anyone/anything suspicious and keep our services up-to-date and well-patched.

Table 1. Protected assets and threats against them

Assets				
Medical databases	Users databases	Experiments	Results	Computer and network resources
Description				
HIV virus mutations, drugs; Data is anonymized but still very valueable Must be well protected from theft.	User credentials and attributes; Must be well protected from tampering and theft.	Source code of the experiments; Containing IP, may compromise system if tampered with.	Experiment results;Also intelectual property; Must be protected from being tampered with and stolen.	Computational power and network connectivity; Possible abuse for password cracking or to perform DDoS attacks.
Threats				
DBMS exploited	LDAP exploited	Apache/SVN exploited	Apache/WebDAV exploited	Any service exploited
Plain text eavesdropping, man in the middle attack, theft of credentials, social engineering, compromising node hosting the service (e.g. kernel bugs)				

4   Used Technology

Following in-depth analysis of various possible technologies, Shibboleth was selected as the best solution from the point of view of our requirements.

Shibboleth is a well-established federated Single Sign-On solution, proposed by the Internet2 consortium. It features a group of so-called Home Organizations (HO) in different centers. Each of them hosts an Identity Provider (IdP) composed of the SSO and Attribute Authority (AA) components. SSO supports user authentication against local user databases (in our case – LDAP servers) and produces authentication tokens trusted by other federated HOs. The Attribute Authority (AA) supplies attributes describing and characterizing HO users. AAs also protect the attributes from being released to anyone outside the federation. The exchange of authentication tokens (so-called handles) as well as the attributes is conducted with the help of SAML – a standard for exchanging security assertions.

Shibboleth is a complete solution that suits our security requirements described in this paper. SSO provides a solution for authentication while AA is used for authorization. All communication between the SP and IdP is secured with the TLS protocol and exchange of security assertions features the use of SAML, which guarantees confidentiality and integrity of the transmitted security information. The ability to create many HOs (including backup HO) ensures optimal availability and consistency of the infrastructure.

Despite the fact that Shibboleth seems to be a perfect fit for our needs there is one problem we have had to deal with. Originally, Shibboleth was strictly web-based, designed to protect web applications only. However, we also need to protect our non-web services such as GSEngine, SVN repositories, MOCCA components or the Data Access Services. Because of that we have created a set of tools (described later in this paper) that enable us to acquire and then use the Shibboleth handles in a non-web-based environment.

5   Security Architecture of ViroLab

In this section we describe how we understand the concept of a Virtual Organization (VO) in the context of ViroLab and, subsequently, present an overview of the security architecture. A *ViroLab VO* forms a group of entities (typically users) that share a legitimate need to access similar resources (typically – applications, services, or data). VO membership can be further restricted by other characteristics (*attributes*) common to this group of entities. Membership in a VO is not static – it can be enabled and disabled at any time. For example, two entities (e.g. doctor A and hospital B) within the same VO can dynamically establish each other's identity and initiate secure communication, even if they have no prior knowledge of each other's existence. The novelty of ViroLab VOs comes from the decentralized approach based on attributes. Here we should stress that the security implementation in ViroLab enables easy setup of an unlimited number of VOs in various configurations. The three VOs (developers, users, clinicians) that we are referring to serve as examples for our system validation.

The overall architecture of the ViroLab virtual laboratory, as seen from the security perspective, is shown in Fig. 2. A user can belong to any of the four home organizations.

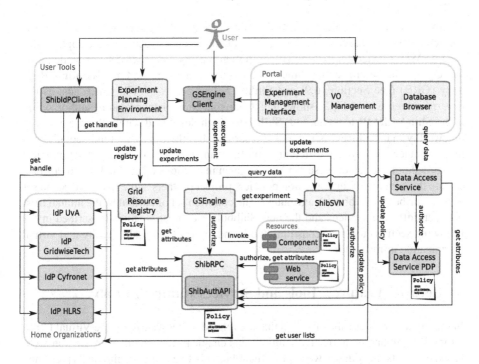

Fig. 2. Overall security architecture in the ViroLab virtual laboratory

Each home organization hosts an Identity Provider (IdP) which enables authentication using a web browser, and which returns user attributes to trusted service providers, like the ViroLab portal, which redirects users to the corresponding authentication capability of the chosen Identity Provider. Once the user is authenticated, the portal server obtains a Shibboleth **handle** that enables it to request user attributes. A *handle*, together with the IdP URL, can be further used as a security credential within the system to obtain access to other resources and services.

A typical Shibboleth handle and IdP URL pair appears as follows:

```
_133e6bb9458bcb1cf0313a#https://idp.gridwisetech.pl/shibboleth-idp
```

The portal offers several tools (available as portlets) for authenticated users, including: the **Experiment Management Interface** (EMI) (see Section 6.6), the **VO Management** (see Section 6.13) and the **Database Browser** – a Web interface to the ViroLab Data Access Services (DAS) (see Section 6.10). In addition to the portal, a user can access the system with a set of specialized tools, both graphical and command-line, such as **ShibIdPClient** (see Section 6.1). The handle can be used directly by the command-line **GSEngine client** tool, which is responsible for the execution of experiments through GSEngine (see Section 6.8). Alternatively, the experiment developer can use the **Experiment Planning Environment** (EPE) (see Section 6.5). The user tools (web-based, GUI-based or command-line) provide access to generic virtual laboratory services, all of which are remotely accessible and protected using the Shibboleth security mechanisms. The main runtime service is called **GSEngine** (see

Section 6.8). It communicates with the client using a dedicated protocol over a secure channel (SSL-based) and, during experiment execution, accesses the application-specific **Web services** or distributed **components** using a *delegated* set of credentials; namely the Shibboleth handle. Other generic services include the **Grid Resource Registry** (GRR) (see Section 6.9) and **ShibSVN** (see Section 6.7), which acts as the *experiment repository*. Fig. 2 shows that the crucial component providing authorization is the **ShibAuthAPI** together with **ShibRPC**, both developed within the project. It is noteworthy that ShibRPC is not a single service, but there may be (and actually are) more instances deployed at different institutions and configured using distinct policies. A detailed description of these modules is given in Sections 6.2 and 6.3. In order to facilitate the creation of authorization policies, project partners agree to use the same set of user attributes (Shibboleth attributes). The common set of attributes, the mutual trust between IdPs, the services and the new Shibboleth-compatible tools (described in the following section) together constitute the foundations of ViroLab security and virtual organization infrastructure.

6 Security Features, Tools and Services within ViroLab

In this section we describe our tools that are related to the security of the Virtual Laboratory. We emphasize innovative solutions that enable us to integrate web and non-web-based elements. In addition we explain the relation between the requirements presented in the threat model and the functionality supplied by these tools.

6.1 ShibIdPClient

ShibIdpClient is a software library designed to enable users to acquire Shibboleth handles by authentication against the SSO, without the need for any web browser. Once supplied with proper configuration and a list of trusted IdP certificates, this component is able to perform automatic authentication of the users based on their credentials. The library fulfills the authentication requirements mentioned in the threat model. It also supports the HTTPS protocol and thus can be used to connect to SSL/TLS secured endpoints, providing confidentiality and integrity of the transmitted data. It might be incorporated in any non-web software to enable it to authenticate users against any Shibboleth IdP protected via basic HTTP authentication and secured with SSL/TLS. In effect, this library constitutes a basic solution to the aforementioned problems with authentication in non-web environments.

ShibIdpCliClient is a command-line tool which uses ShibIdpClient to acquire Shibboleth handles without the need to run any web browser, or even any graphical environment. It is a perfect solution for Unix or Unix-like OS users who prefer to work remotely (e.g. via SSH).

6.2 ShibAuthAPI

The goal of the Shibboleth Attribute Authority API, or ShibAuthAPI for short, is to provide a generic interface that can be used by other developers to shibbolize

(*Shibboleth-enable*) their modules. Users of these modules can be authorized via Shibboleth. ShibRPC (see section 6.3) is an example of a shibbolized module. In other words, ShibAuthAPI is a low-level authentication and authorization Java library that matches non-web use cases, built upon Shibboleth 1.3 and GridShib [18]. ShibAuthAPI contains two elements which are necessary to perform user authentication: (1) AttributeRequestor (responsible for authentication) and (2) PolicyResolver (responsible for authorization).

AttributeRequestor performs authentication of a given user based on the provided Shibboleth handle, which can be obtained either from the portal or from ShibIdPClient. The handle is used for querying a Shibboleth IdP for user attributes. If correct attributes are returned by Shibboleth, we can assume that the given user is known and has been authenticated. PolicyResolver is then asked to make an authorization decision. The AttributeRequestor configuration includes information on all available Shibboleth IdP certificates, Shibboleth SP certificates, a Service Provider certificate (along with a private key) and the access policy file name.

PolicyResolver loads access policies from its configuration file in order to authorize users, or denies authorization, basing on the corresponding policies. If all policy attributes match user attributes, the user is authorized. Each policy has a name (*policy_name*), a publication date (*publication_date*) and a set of attributes (rules).

6.3 ShibRPC

ShibRPC is an XML-RPC service that is implemented as a Java servlet running inside Apache Tomcat. It provides a bridge between Shibboleth and client applications. Using ShibRPC it is possible to shibbolize applications without tight integration with any of the Shibboleth libraries (e.g. ShibAuthAPI). This matches the needs of various applications, including web applications. In order to access the ShibRPC service, a XML-RPC client is necessary. This client complies with the XML-RPC standard specification. Due to the fact that this protocol is popular there are many ready-to-use libraries that are available for C/C++, Java, Ruby, Python, PHP and other programming languages that support TCP/IP sockets. The added value of this library is that it is based on ShibAuthAPI (see section 6.2) and it exposes its key functions. By using ShibRPC, an application can easily access user attributes by passing a Shibboleth handle and the IdP URL to the XML-RPC method. Based on these attributes the application can decide whether the user is allowed to access a dedicated service or not. As ShibRPC is based on ShibAuthAPI, user authorization can also be performed using access policy files on the ShibRPC server side.

6.4 Portal

The goal of the ViroLab Portal, commonly referred to as Portal, is to provide a single entry point to the Virtual Laboratory for experiment users (*scientists* and *physicians*) and Home Organization administrators (see section 6.13). The Portal is especially suited for non-technical users, such as experiment users. The main features of the Portal include distributed security using Shibboleth, support for multiple user institutions, Single Sign-on (SSO) and support for Adobe Flash and AJAX portlets. The Portal uses distributed security mechanisms (federated identity-based security approach), which in turn apply Shibboleth in a standard way: the user is redirected to the Home Organization to perform authentication using a local username and password.

The Portal was designed to offer its services to users from multiple institutions. In order to support authentication and authorization of users from diverse and dispersed groups it uses the Home Organization concept. The user is only requested to select the institution s/he belongs to. The remaining actions are performed automatically behind the scenes.

The Portal provides a means for hosting multiple applications (portlets); hence, it plays the role of a scientific gateway. In other words, once users log on to the Portal, they obtain access to all applications that are installed inside. These applications can then invoke remote services, which perform user authorization using the same credentials. The Portal is powered by the GridSphere portal framework so Java portlets are fully supported, including JSR-168 compliant portlets (plain JSP), AJAX-powered portlets (mixture of JSP, JavaScript, and XML), and Flash-enhanced portlets (JSP files with embedded Flash content).

6.5   Experiment Planning Environment

The Experiment Planning Environment [4] is an Eclipse-based Integrated Development Environment (IDE), which supports developing ViroLab-related experiments in an easy and user-friendly way. This is achieved by gathering different facilities that support each part of the experiment development process: creation, development, execution with GSEngine and sharing via the Experiment Repository. At each of these steps the developer has to take care of obtaining secure access to data and computational resources. Thus, the `ShibIdPClient` library is integrated with the environment. Before experiments can be executed using the GSEngine runtime system, or accessed in the Experiment Repository, the developer must verify his/her identity by obtaining a handle from the Shibboleth system. To do so, the developer can use a dedicated dialog window within the IDE. Upon choosing one of the available Identity Providers and entering the login and password, EPE obtains the security handle and can store it on the local machine. The handle is then *refreshed* automatically in any subsequent EPE session; therefore, the developer can focus on developing new experiments.

All of the security-related information about existing Identity Providers is kept both on the server (where the default GSEngine instance is running) and the client (where the EPE instance is located). On the *server* side a configuration file – `properties.xml` – is maintained. It contains information about various URIs, which describe IdP access points. On the *client* side, public certificates of the IdPs are stored. By distributing the security information to different sites we reduce the likelihood of a successful *men-in-the-middle* attack.

6.6   Experiment Management Interface

The Experiment Management Interface (EMI) [4] allows users to securely execute and monitor experiments by integrating with the Portal in the hosted mode and with a dedicated ShibIdpClient library in the standalone mode. In the former case a web session is used to pass the user's Shibboleth handle from the Portal to the EMI web widget. The handle is then forwarded to GSEngine and the experiment repository to perform corresponding tasks on behalf of the user. The latter, standalone mode requires the user to log in through a dedicated login widget. During this process the user handle is obtained through the ShibIdpClient library and can then be forwarded to underlying components in a similar fashion as in the former case.

6.7 ShibSVN

The goal of the ShibSVN (*Shibboleth-enabled Subversion*) module is to provide access to Subversion repositories with Shibboleth authorization by means of a generic, unmodified Subversion client. The solution depends on ShibRPC (see section 6.3) to which it delegates user credentials so that authorization decisions can be made. The core of ShibSVN is an authorization module for the Apache HTTP Server (bundled with the ShibRPC client), which uses ShibRPC to authorize users.

Authorization for accessing Subversion repositories is based on *Basic Authentication*, i.e. an authentication method included in the HTTP standard since its 1.0 release. By default, the Apache HTTP Server uses user names and passwords stored in text files, LDAP or a database. The developed Apache module provides authorization to any web resource inside an Apache server by invoking XML-RPC methods on a remote server (see section 6.3). In place of a password, the user must provide his or her Shibboleth handle and the IdP URL.

Summing up, due to the fact that Subversion repositories are exposed to the external world as web resources, accessible via URLs using the standard HTTPS (HTTP over SSL) protocol and end users are authorized on the basis of usernames and passwords (namely, their *Shibboleth handles*), each end user is free to use a Subversion client of his/her choice, including any web browser sufficient for read-only access to data in Subversion repositories. In this way both EPE and EMI user tools are integrated with the ViroLab experiment repository based on ShibSVN.

6.8 GSEngine

GSEngine [6] constitutes the central point inside the ViroLab virtual laboratory and therefore it is the first module that requires authorized access in the course of experiment execution. GSEngine is secured in order to restrict access to computational resources for external parties. On the other hand, it is expected to run experiments that access resources (services, components) which are also secured. Therefore, GSEngine maintains a kind of security context for experiments during their execution and delegates security credentials to secured resources in the form of Shibboleth handles.

The GSEngine client communicates with the GSEngine server using an application specific protocol employing the Secure Socket Layer (SSL), thus securing the passing of handles against eavesdropping. GSEngine is integrated with the newest ShibRPC – Shibboleth Authorization Point module, maintained as an external standalone service. Authorization is performed according to a given configurable policy of access to GSEngine within the ViroLab Virtual Organization. The default policy allows access to GSEngine for any identified member of any Home Organization federated in the ViroLab Virtual Organization, or, more accurately, to any user who is assigned a proper value of the homeOrganization attribute and a valid mail attribute. Going beyond default policy definitions, GSEngine providers are technically capable of specifying custom policies. From the architectural point of view, GSEngine encapsulates security integration in a pluggable module that exposes a well-defined interface, thus separating GSEngine business logic and security aspects.

6.9   Grid Resource Registry

The aim of the Grid Resource Registry (GRR) is to store information about all computational resources (Web services, WSRF, MOCCA components, EGEE jobs, etc.) available in the ViroLab Virtual Laboratory. As our laboratory is open for external users, we allow everyone to browse the registry content. A different case should be considered when modifying information stored in the registry. This requires defining a policy that describes who can perform modifications and in what manner. The registry content can be changed by invoking a special web service, secured using WS-Security. By applying the `Username Token Profile` [20] the Shibboleth handle is transmitted to the registry. Subsequently, the registry contacts the ShibRPC component, receives user attributes and checks if the user has the attributes required by the defined GRR security policy. Basing on this information, the registry either allows or denies the possibility to make modifications.

6.10   Data Access Services

For protecting the integrated biomedical data resources appropriately, access to certain underlying resources follows a two-step approach. Firstly, users who want to browse and query particular data sets (using the Database Browser Portlet) need to authenticate themselves with the above described security infrastructure. Afterwards, a properly identified user can take advantage of the Data Access Services (DAS) [9] in order to perform actions on integrated resources. These services accept the user's identity token in order to decide whether the given user is permitted to interact with a particular resource or not.

The final decision on whether a resource is accessible or not is based on the current user attributes (released from the user's home organization) and, of course, on the decision of the local data resource manager [22]. These attributes are requested via a so-called attribute request by sending the user handle (identity token) to the corresponding IdP (using ShibAuthAPI).

For authorization purposes, the user's attributes and the list of all currently available resources are passed to a specific component, the so-called Policy Decision Point (PDP). PDP stores several access control policies that each contain a set of rules specifying the conditions (usually a number of attributes a user has to have) necessary to become authorized for a dedicated resource. The policies are written in a well-established policy description language named XACML [23]. It is a powerful language with many extension mechanisms for defining dedicated policies for custom use cases. In ViroLab, the initial policy structure is kept simple but leaves a lot of freedom for creation of fine-grained rules. In order to easily manage corresponding resources and access rules, a simple application has been developed that enables administrators of particular data resources to dynamically define and (de-)activate certain access rules. This tool directly connects to the PDP, downloads the existing policies, allows manipulation of certain rules, and sends back the policy to the PDP. Once an updated policy is pushed back to the PDP, DAS is automatically notified and can enforce transparent re-authorization of the current user.

6.11 Data Source Registry

The Data Source Registry is a component of the ViroLab architecture, which is responsible for maintaining information about the required data sources and enabling experiment developers to interface with databases and other types of data structures. In order to facilitate this functionality, the Data Source Registry enables developers to register sources and allows them to store credentials necessary for accessing such sources. DSR contains a wallet mechanism, which is based on the Shibboleth user credentials. It uses the Shibboleth client library to request information regarding the user who is actually performing a registry operation and stores the submitted credentials accordingly.

When an experiment user wishes to interface a data source registered in DSR, s/he does not have to supply a separate set of credentials, provided the DSR actually stores valid credentials for a given data source. In order to determine who is running an experiment, the Data Access Client (DAC) [9] queries Shibboleth for user attributes and constructs a handle which uniquely identifies users. This handle is subsequently employed when contacting DSR. If appropriate credentials are found, the given data source can be instantiated with no need for further input on the part of the user.

6.12 MOCCA Component Framework

The reason for the creation of the MOCCA Shibboleth authenticator was to secure access to MOCCA [8] resources with the technology used in the project. We have implemented a new authenticator, which fits into the pluggable authenticator modules of the H2O [24] kernel (a container for MOCCA components). This software enables users to authenticate and become authorized for access based on their handle, previously acquired with the help of the Portal or the ShibIdpCliClient. Once the user supplies his/her Shibboleth credentials the authenticator requests the attributes from the AA via the ShibRPC mechanism. ShibRPC also acts as the primary PDP supplying authorization decisions (based e.g. on the user's HO). In addition, the authenticator contains additional policies that are used for final user authorization and assignment to a specific group. This group defines the privileges that are granted to the users who possess the specified Shibboleth attributes. Each user is also identified by his or her unique username (the combination of the Shibboleth username and the HO).

6.13 VO Management GUI

The objective of the VO Management GUI is to provide HO administrative users with a graphical tool for managing and controlling multiple Virtual Organizations. A crucial requirement suggested by future GUI users was to provide HO administrators with a single tool that would allow them to control the entire ViroLab infrastructure in a secure manner. The most important feature of this tool is the ability to create, modify, store and remove VOs. A new VO can be created by linking users from different institutions (Home Organizations) and granting them access to multiple, geographically-dispersed resources.

In order to meet the aforementioned goals and requirements, the GUI was designed and built as a portlet and then deployed to the ViroLab Portal. Thus, the GUI is always accessible and available everywhere and from any access device (i.e. PC, PDA or smartphone) running a modern graphical Web browser. Moreover, due to the fact that this application is based on the Adobe Flex technology it is both visually pleasing and it has an intuitive user interface.

The GUI is integrated with the ShibRPC, LDAP, ShibSVN and DAS components. ShibRPC is used internally by the GUI to authorise itself when connecting to Apache Tomcat servlets that allow reading and writing ShibSVN and DAS access policies. In other words, these two servlets (one for ShibSVN and one for DAS) are Shibboleth-enabled, which means that they delegate their authorization decisions to ShibRPC. Other ViroLab resources can also be integrated with the GUI in the same manner. An alternative approach to integration between the GUI and other ViroLab resources is to create an Apache Tomcat servlet that implements the public user API. Currently the ShibSVN and DAS services are integrated using this API.

7   Usage Examples

The software components described in this paper were created by the following project partners: GridwiseTech (Shibboleth configuration, ShibAuthAPI, ShibRPC, Portal, ShibSVN, VO Management), Cyfronet (ShibIdpClient, ShibIdPCliClient, EPE, EMI, GSEngine, GRR, DSR, MOCCA), and HLRS (Data Access Services). The developed solutions have been validated in a production infrastructure which enables the virtual laboratory users to run their experiments.

In the ViroLab project, this virtual laboratory is used to plan and execute important virological experiments, focusing on analysis of the HIV virus genotype [25]. This includes calculation of drug resistance, querying historical and provenance [26] information about experiments, and developing a drug resistance measurement system based on multiple rulesets. It has also been applied to other application domains, such as protein folding and structural comparison [27], data mining using the Weka library, and computational chemistry (developing and running a series of Gaussian application on the EGEE infrastructure and as an education tool in computer science classes).

8   Conclusions and Future Work

In this paper we presented our approach to building a security infrastructure in the ViroLab Virtual Laboratory. Instead of using traditional Grid solutions, which are usually based on GSI and its extensions, we have followed a novel approach based on a federated attribute-based security framework.

Our work has yielded considerable results on several fronts. Firstly, we demonstrated that Shibboleth can be used to create a complete decentralized security environment, which can integrate multiple organizations, resources and services, including non-web-based ones. This was achieved by the development of the ShibIdPClient tool, which can obtain a security token (Shibboleth handle) without the need to use a web browser. This security token can be subsequently used to access multiple services, such as GSEngine, Grid Resources Registry, ShibSVN and Data Access Services, as well as application-specific web services and distributed MOCCA components. The authorization decisions on the resource side are fully decentralized and can either be configured by custom local policies or delegated to external entities such as the ShibRPC service or other Policy Decision Points.

It should be noted that we have implemented a user-friendly drag-and-drop interface for dynamic Virtual Organization management. From the users' perspective it is a considerable improvement over traditional command-line tools. This work will be continued and expanded by GridwiseTech (see [28] for more information).

One of the limitation of Shibboleth, which we have encountered, is the problem of the lifetime of the security handle used as a credential that can be delegated to invoke computational services. As computations may take a long time (on the order of hours and possibly days) we had to extend the default lifetime of the handle, which in typical web scenarios is set to 5 minutes. Extending this lifetime may lead to potential security risks, however we assume that the combination of secure communications and mutual trust between identity providers and service providers minimizes the threat of unauthorized handle acquisition and usage. A possible solution could involve migration to Shibboleth 2.0 or applying a combination of Shibboleth and GSI-based proxy certificates, such as in GridShib [18] or ShibGrid [19] projects.

Another limitation of our infrastructure stems from the fact that all client tools (Portal, ShibIdPClient) need to know and trust all the identity providers. This is not a problem if the participating institutions do not change frequently, but in more dynamic scenarios the management of server certificates may become an issue. In such cases a common set of trusted certificates (or CA) should be managed and published. A possible solution would be to use a dedicated institution (such as EUGridPMA [29]), which coordinates authentication in large-scale infrastructures such as EGEE.

It should be noted that XACML is a very extensible language offering substantial flexibility for developers. However, this flexibility and expressiveness can result in complexity and verbosity when creating richly structured policies. Another limitation of the language is the lack of policy versioning and management in the XACML framework. The administrators themselves must solve this issue.

Future work will focus on the enhancement of current policy specifications in order to achieve more fine-grained access control e.g. for individual data sets. Furthermore, we are planning to extend the PDPs and the management tools with further capabilities that provide an improved level of trust among participating entities. We will also investigate advanced sandboxing techniques (e.g. based on virtualization) to provide better isolation between experiments running concurrently in GSEngine on behalf of multiple users. The presented solution can be augmented to support other security mechanisms similar to Shibboleth can be applied in upcoming projects, such as PL-Grid.

Acknowledgments. This work was partly supported by the European Commission ViroLab Project [30] Grant 027446, the corresponding Polish SPUB-M grant, AGH grant 11.11.120.777, and ACC CYFRONET-AGH grant 500-08.

References

1. Bubak, M., Gubala, T., Malawski, M., Balis, B., Funika, W., Bartynski, T., Ciepiela, E., Harezlak, D., Kasztelnik, M., Kocot, J., Krol, D., Nowakowski, P., Pelczar, M., Wach, J., Assel, M., Tirado-Ramos, A.: Virtual laboratory for development and execution of biomedical collaborative applications. In: Proceedings of the Twenty-First IEEE International Symposium on Computer-Based Medical Systems, Jyväskylä, Finland, June 17-19, pp. 373–378. IEEE Computer Society, Los Alamitos (2008)
2. ViroLab team at CYFRONET: The ViroLab Virtual Laboratory Website (2009), http://virolab.cyfronet.pl
3. Sloot, P.M.A., Tirado-Ramos, A., Altintas, I., Bubak, M., Boucher, C.: From molecule to man: Decision support in individualized e-health. Computer 39(11), 40–46 (2006)
4. Funika, W., Harezlak, D., Krol, D., Bubak, M.: Environment for collaborative development and execution of virtual laboratory applications. In: Bubak, M., van Albada, G.D., Dongarra, J., Sloot, P.M.A. (eds.) ICCS 2008, Part III. LNCS, vol. 5103, pp. 446–458. Springer, Heidelberg (2008)
5. Malawski, M., Gubala, T., Kasztelnik, M., Bartynski, T., Bubak, M., Baude, F., Henrio, L.: High-level scripting approach for building component-based applications on the grid. In: Danelutto, M., Fragopoulou, P., Getov, V. (eds.) Making Grids Work: CoreGRID Workshop on Grid Programming Model Grid and P2P Systems Architecture Grid Systems, Tools and Environments, Heraklion, Crete, pp. 307–320. Springer, Heidelberg (2008)
6. Ciepiela, E., Kocot, J., Gubala, T., Malawski, M., Kasztelnik, M., Bubak, M.: Gridspace engine of the virolab virtual laboratory. In: Proceedings of Cracow Grid Workshop 2007, ACC CYFRONET AGH, pp. 53–58 (2008)
7. Bartynski, T., Malawski, M., Gubala, T., Bubak, M.: Universal grid client: Grid operation invoker. In: Wyrzykowski, R., Dongarra, J., Karczewski, K., Wasniewski, J. (eds.) PPAM 2007. LNCS, vol. 4967, pp. 1068–1077. Springer, Heidelberg (2008)
8. Malawski, M., Bubak, M., Placek, M., Kurzyniec, D., Sunderam, V.: Experiments with distributed component computing across grid boundaries. In: Proceedings of HPC-GECO/COMPFRAME Workshop in Conjunction with HPDC 2006, pp. 109–116 (2006)
9. Assel, M., Nowakowski, P., Bubak, M.: Integrating and accessing medical data resources within the ViroLab virtual laboratory. In: Bubak, M., van Albada, G.D., Dongarra, J., Sloot, P.M.A. (eds.) ICCS 2008, Part III. LNCS, vol. 5103, pp. 90–99. Springer, Heidelberg (2008)
10. Foster, I., Kesselman, C., Tuecke, S.: The anatomy of the grid: Enabling scalable virtual organizations. Int. J. High Perform. Comput. Appl. 15(3), 200–222 (2001)
11. Internet 2 Project: Shibboleth (2008), http://shibboleth.internet2.edu/
12. Foster, I.T., Kesselman, C., Tsudik, G., Tuecke, S.: A security architecture for computational grids. In: ACM Conference on Computer and Communications Security, pp. 83–92 (1998)
13. Alfieri, R., Cecchini, R., Ciaschini, V., dell'Agnello, L., Frohner, Á., Lörentey, K., Spataro, F.: From gridmap-file to voms: managing authorization in a grid environment. Future Generation Comp. Syst. 21(4), 549–558 (2005)
14. Internet 2 Consortium: Shibboleth system, http://shibboleth.internet2.edu/
15. OASIS: Security assertion markup language, http://saml.xml.org/saml-specifications
16. Alticore, Inc.: Josso: Java open single sign-on (2009), http://www.josso.org/

17. OpenID Foundation: OpenID specifications, `http://openid.net/specs/`
18. Scavo, T., Welch, V.: A grid authorization model for science gateways. Concurrency and Computation: Practice and Experience (2008) (to appear)
19. Spence, D., et al.: Shibgrid: Shibboleth access for the uk national grid service. In: E-SCIENCE 2006: Proceedings of the Second IEEE International Conference on e-Science and Grid Computing, p. 75. IEEE Computer Society, Washington (2006)
20. OASIS: Web services security: Username token profile v1.0
    `http://docs.oasis-open.org/wss/2004/01/oasis-200401-wss-username-token-profile-1.0.pdf`
21. Globus Alliance: The WS-resource framework toolkit/ (2007),
    `http://www.globus.org/`
22. Assel, M., Kalyoncu, O.: Dynamic access control management for distributed biomedical data resources. In: Cunningham, P., Cunningham, M. (eds.) eChallenges e-2008 Conference, Collaboration and the Knowledge Economy: Issues, Applications, Case Studies, pp. 1593–1599. IOS Press, Amsterdam (2008)
23. Moses, T.: eXtensible Access Control Markup Language TC v2.0 (XACML) (February 2005), `http://docs.oasis-open.org/xacml/2.0/access_control-xacml-2.0-core-spec-os.pdf`
24. Kurzyniec, D., et al.: Towards Self-Organizing Distributed Computing Frameworks: The H2O Approach. Parallel Processing Lett. 13(2), 273–290 (2003)
25. de Oliveira, T., Deforche, K., Cassol, S., Salminen, M., Paraskevis, D., Seebregts, C., Snoeck, J., van Rensburg, E.J.J., Wensing, A.M.J., van de Vijver, D.A., Boucher, C.A., Camacho, R., Vandamme, A.M.: An automated genotyping system for analysis of hiv-1 and other microbial sequences. Bioinformatics 21(19), 3797–3800 (2005)
26. Balis, B., Bubak, M., Pelczar, M., Wach, J.: Provenance tracking and querying in the virolab virtual laboratory. In: 8th IEEE International Symposium on Cluster Computing and the Grid (CCGrid 2008), Lyon, France, May 19-22, pp. 675–680. IEEE Computer Society Press, Los Alamitos (2008)
27. Brylinski, M., Jurkowski, W., Konieczny, L., Roterman, I.: Limited conformational space for early-stage protein folding simulation. Bioinformatics 20(2), 199–205 (2004)
28. ViroLab team at GridwiseTech: GridwiseTech in the ViroLab Project (2009),
    `http://www.gridwisetech.com/virolab`
29. The EUGridPMA: Coordinating grid authentication in e-science,
    `http://www.eugridpma.org/`
30. ViroLab Project Consortium: ViroLab (2009), `http://virolab.org`

E2EDSM: An Edge-to-Edge Data Service Model for Mass Streaming Media Transmission

Junfeng He*, Hui Wang, Ningwu He,
Zhigang Sun, and Zhenghu Gong

School of computer science, National University of Defense Technology,
Changsha 410073, China
{He3.2001,wanghuinudt,Ningwu.He}@gmail.com
{sunzhigang,gzh}@nudt.edu.cn

Abstract. Existing distributed content delivery systems like P2P applications may provide significant benefits for content providers and end users. However, they just shifted the considerable cost and burden to Internet Service Providers (ISPs) and well-behaved end users. In P2P applications, the amount of data served by each ISP and payment of many costly transit links are increasing, but the corresponding service revenue from the peer-hosted data services provided doesnt return. In this paper, we present a novel Edge-to-Edge Data Service Model (E2EDSM) which aims to avoid transferring redundant data over the costly core transit links as well as improving the transmission efficiency of mass streaming media. E2EDSM describes a new way for ISP to take part in the processing of content distribution and makes an effort to achieve a winwin goal. Experimental results based on simulation show that E2EDSM achieves better network performance.

Keywords: Edge-to-Edge network, peer-to-peer network, ISP infrastructure, network architecture.

1 Introduction

Current Internet is very different from its origin. The great majority of Internet's users are normal residential users rather than researchers, and the amount of end users has been increasing greatly. At the same time, information exchanged over Internet changes from small files to mass information like various streaming media. Unlike the traditional C/S service model, end users now prefer to exchange information between each other for their own willingness by the way of peering. Main proportions of Internet traffic are P2P traffic (file sharing and streaming media transmission) in all regions[1][2]. But most existing P2P applications which are based on the End-to-End network architecture[3] have incurred a lot of

---

* This work is supported by a grant from the Major State Basic Research Development Programs of China (973 Programs) (No.2009CB320503), and Chinese National Programs for High Technology Research and Development (863 Programs) (No. 2008AA01A325 and No. 2008AA01A323).

Y. Dou, R. Gruber, and J. Joller (Eds.): APPT 2009, LNCS 5737, pp. 246–258, 2009.
© Springer-Verlag Berlin Heidelberg 2009

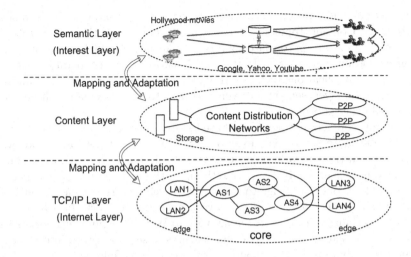

Fig. 1. Network Layers

problems such as network congestion, performance degradation of other applications and so on[4][5]. Lacking of close cooporation between application layer and network layer, a great amount of replicated information is being transferred over Internet and this results in ineffective usage rate of network bandwidth. Those end users who are consumers of P2P applications are trying to utilize their full link speed at all times, which make ISPs bearing heavy load of anxiety.

Most existing solutions are either for the sake of users, or from ISPs view. Few attentions have been paid to the root cause of these problems. We believe that rethinking of the network architecture which most solutions are based on is required indeed.

To understand the complicated relations amongst users, content providers and ISPs, we describe three network layers: Semantic Layer (or Interest Layer), Content Layer and TCP/IP Layer (or Internet Layer), which are depicted in Fig. 1. Semantic layer network with focus on users logic behavior is trying to find out characters of requirements. Content layer is the content distribution layer where most solutions belong to. TCP/IP layer (or Internet Layer) is the actual network layer where data will be transferred.

Some observations can be made, as follows:

End users are both the content producers and consumers, and have diverse interests. Users with the same interest form social networks which are labeled with their interests. As a result of users social property in real world, interests of different regional users show strong geographic features. For example, most Chinese users will visit the famous websites in China such as SOHU, 163, and Youku which may not be known by people of other countries. Contents are distributed over networks of interests and can be classified by users interests.

There are two couplings (semantic layer and content layer, content layer and Internet layer) needed to be considered before figuring out appropriate solutions.

Mapping and adaptation: between Semantic Topology and Content Topology, and between Content Topology and Internet Topology, we think it will be the best way to find out appropriate solutions. Take the content layer as an example, optimization over lower TCP/IP layer: Network-aware, cooperation between ISPs and P2P applications such as P4P[6]. On the other hand, optimization from upper semantic layer: semantic-driven network storage or semantic-driven content distribution networks[7][8].

Moreover, conflicts between distributed system design and network architecture become more severe. For example, excessive use of network middleware technologies in the network makes the concept of end-to-end network architecture existing in name only[9]. After rethinking the architecture of Internet, we introduce the thought of Edge-to-Edge (E2E) architecture, which explicitly divides the whole network into core network and edge network. In a high level, Internet has changed from Research network to Worldwide pubic network- social network, so we can introduce some key features of social network into Internet.

Main contributions of the paper are summarized as follows: (1) we find out that two couplings must be considered before proposing appropriate solutions. (2) We classify the steaming media data transmission into three types by users usage behavior, which are IPTV like type traffic, click and watch type traffic and download and watch type traffic. (3) we present a novel Edge-to-Edge Data Service Model (E2EDSM) in which we explicitly divide the whole network space into core network space and edge network space. E2EDSM aims to avoid redundant data being transferred over the costly core transit links as well as improving the transmission efficiency of mass streaming media. E2EDSM presents a new way for ISP to take part in the processing of content distribution and makes an effort to achieve a win-win goal. (4) we have developed a simulator namely Phoenix and preliminary experiment results show that solutions under Edge-to-Edge architecture have better performances for the large scale streaming media delivery.

This paper proceeds as follows. After a discussion of previous work in Section 2, Section 3 presents our solution under Edge-to-Edge network architecture design. Section 4 presents simulation and preliminary result analysis, and Section 5 makes some discussions. Finally, Section 6 ends this paper with conclusions and future work.

2   Related Work

Our work relates to several aspects of research, such as streaming media applications, mass data transmission, network architecture and distributed system design. Though file sharing and media streaming applications over P2P have been the mainstream of the whole Internet traffic in all regions[1][2], these P2P applications also incur lots of problems such as network congestion, performance degradation of other applications[4][5]. So, many solutions have been presented to solve these issues.

In order to reducing redundant data transferred, researchers came to multicast technology firstly. Li Lao[10] classified multicast technology into three types: IP multicast, overlay multicast and application multicast, and made a comparison among them. Then, solutions of deploying caches in network were proposed. Bing Wang[11] presented an effective proxy cache allocation mechanism for streaming media distribution. Ashok[12] considered deploying cache on router to reduce universal redundant traffic. Mukaddim Pathan[7] introduced the state of the art of content distribution networks, and pointed out the possible research directions of CDN. More and more attentions have been paid to localization of content and service. Frederic[13] suggested that streaming media distribution should combine CDN and P2P. Thomas[4] showed that simple locality-aware P2P delivery solutions can significantly alleviate the induced cost of ISPs, while providing an overall performance approximated to a perfect world-wide caching infrastructure.

Most recently, some researches try to find out the possibility of cooperation between applications and service providers. Arkko[5] analyzed incentives for P2PI (Peer-to-Peer Infrastructure) solutions and presented some deployment considerations. Haiyong Xie[6] presented P4P, a kind of provider portal for applications. Nikolaos[14][15] also shown that ISP storage enable is a feasible way to deal with delay-tolerant data transmission, and presented a new design idea named IPO (Internet Post Office). David D. Clark[16] pointed out that there were many tussles among different stakeholders which were parts of the Internet milieu. Different parties may have interests that may be adverse to each other, so it is very import to understand their requirements clearly before proposing a viable solution.

Applications such as Videos-On-demand or IPTV, which are becoming more and more prevalent, exert a subtle influence on network architecture. How to design the next generation Internet architecture to support these new applications is a question which needs to be paid considerable attention in the research community recently. We believe that study on the requirements of the prevalent applications is the first step to answer the above question. And we notice that the 23rd statistical survey report on the Internet Development in China[17] state that the number of users of video online, music online and network games is increasing continuously and dramatically. Meanwhile, traffic from the P2P applications and streaming media such as PPlive[18] and[19] occupies **50~90%** of the core link bandwidth of Chinas backbone network during night time and 30~50% during daytime which is about four times of American[2].

Saltzer[3] defined the network architecture design principles. However, with the development of Internet, many middle box techniques are widely used, and the heterogeneous network connected to the Internet offend against the End-To-End architecture.

Now it is time for network designers to rethink the network architecture. We argue that the distributed system without well understanding of the network level information will lead to network performance declining and core link bandwidth abusing. Recent studies[11][13] suggest adding cache or storage repositories near users to improve the streaming media transmission quality. But we believe this problem could be solved from the network architecture in which the network itself can satisfy the application requirements of high performance. Inspired by the recent studies, we rethink the network architecture and present an Edge-to-Edge Data Service Model.

3   Edge-to-Edge Data Service Model

3.1   Definitions

The key ideal of our design is to separate the diversity of users network from core transit network. As a result, the core transit network will be simpler and the members of core transit network are the large top transit ISPs all over the world, which are rather stable and responsible. Other ISPs, especially the access ISPs, take part in the network content distribution process by adding some storage nodes at the edge of access network near end users. Therefore, the edge network is more controllable, because all requests form internal end users should first go to an edge network infrastructure (ENI) which is designed to locate at the point of presence of access ISP. See Fig. 2.

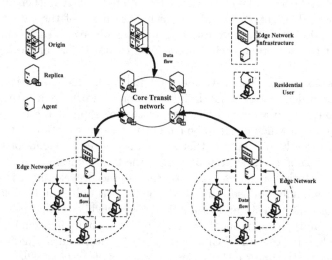

Fig. 2. The sketch map of edge-to-edge network design

Some important notions discussed thorough the paper are explained as follows:

Core Network: A network consists of the large top Transit ISP all over the world. It dedicates to make high speed transmission between its members which are usually big transit ISPs distributed over the whole world.

Edge Network: A network consists of a certain number of users in the same ISP and the ISP constructed Edge Network Infrastructure. It dedicates to meet users various demands of various services.

Edge Network Infrastructure (ENI): An infrastructure which is deployed at the access ISP, i.e., close to end-users. ENI is the only access point to the outside network for all internal end users. It works with responsibility for packets forwarding both in and out of the edge network. Whether the special request is forwarded to the destination depends on ENIs corresponding policies. It can works as Internet Post Office[14]. In order to partaking ENIs burdens, ISP can deploy caches, servers attached to it. It can host a website to offering streaming media service locally. In order to support P2P applications, ISP can also deploy iTracker in the Edge Network Infrastructure according to P4P[6] design principle. The difference is that this particular iTracker will not return peers which are outside of ISPs network (or even edge network), and ENI itself can act as a super peer.

According to our design, Network Space (NS) can be explicitly divided into Core Network Space (CNS) and Edge Network Space (ENS). Different network technologies can be developed and deployed for each space separately.

3.2   Architecture

We expand the concept of End-to-End network architecture[3] to Edge-to-Edge network architecture. A suitable number of end users who belong to the same access ISP make up an edge network that acts as a super end user. ISP constructs Edge Network Infrastructure (ENI) for each edge network to make a management. ENI understands the network topology well, especially the network topology in the same ISP. It can get data from peer edge networks ENI, local ISPs storage nodes if it has, and other networks. See it from Fig. 3. We divide the access ISPs network into a set of edge networks according to some factors such as users location, users access model and so on. End users who are social people in reality have the property of society, so those users who live in a certain area may also have a certain degree of similarity in the special contents that they may be interested in, the periods of using time, and the access model. Based on these observations, we arrange end users into a set of edge networks by making use of the Principle of locality. The scale of edge network can be decided by ISPs according to some rules that may make them benefit from those rules. For example, end users who link to the same Point of Presence (POP) can form an edge network. For the large scale ISP which have thousands POPs, more hierarchies can be constructed by forming a larger edge network over the origin POP level edge network. ISPs can make this decision depending on which level of domination that they want to achieve.

There are advantages from the whole network, ISPs and end users.

The whole network: Benefits by explicitly dividing Network Space into Core Network Space and Edge Network Space, simplicity and effectivity of Core Network Space (CNS) and controllability of Edge Network Space (ENS). According to our design, the traffic load of core transit network can be considerably alleviated. New technologies can be applied and evolved easier both in CNS and ENS.

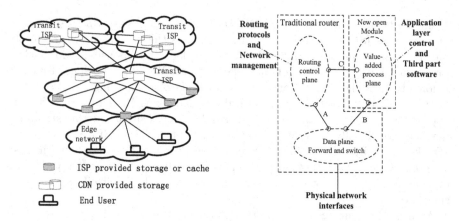

Fig. 3. The data plane of edge-to-edge network design

Fig. 4. New type router based implementation of ENI

ISPs: Benefits by taking full control of the data transmission from end users. First, the traffic load of ISPs backbone network can be reduced remarkably. With ENI deployment, ISP can effectively reduce traffic that out ISPs network and can control the outward traffic to select the economic links. Second, ISP can provide a platform for the application providers to deploy their own programs in ENI to improve application performance, and then charge certain fees from those application providers. Last but not the least, due to the edge network infrastructures of the ISPs, the impact of users activities on the core network is not explicit. The streaming media data can be distributed in the way of CDN, and the contents used frequently are cached by ISPs in the place near users. By this way, ISP can avoid content transmission across over different ISPs and cut down the cost of bandwidth.

Users: Benefits by gaining better services, higher transit speed and lower delay time. For example, in transmission of the streaming media, edge network infrastructures can pre-cache the popular movie data in the local network, and then users can get the videos from the edge network infrastructures directly[12]. The download rates are accelerated and the watch experiences are better.

3.3   Content Distribution under the E2E Network Architecture

We have been considering the implementation of ENI based on new type router. See Fig. 4.

According to our design, the processing of packet transmission will be split into multi-phase, in order to avoiding long-time holding of core transit links. Under the Edge-to-Edge network architecture design, the basic packet processing is described as followed:

Downstream traffic: All requests from internal end users of an edge network should first go to the ENI. If the content that user requesting is already in the storage repositories of ENI, then the request will be accomplished at local. Otherwise, ENI differentiates the flow type of request. If it is the interactive traffic type[5]which is short-lived and delay sensitive, it will be forwarded to the destination of the packets directly. If it is the always-on traffic type such as online streaming traffic or delay-tolerant high-volume file transmission, ENI records this request, and then sends a new request to outside networks to get the content which is requested. After having received the object data, ENI stores the content in its storage repositories and sends the object data to the end user who needs it.

Upstream traffic: All packets from outside should first go to the ENI. If the requested content is already in ENIs storage repositories, then the request will be accomplished immediately without forwarding the packet to destination which belongs to the internal edge network. Other steps are almost the same as downstream traffic, besides the content of interactive type traffic will not be replicated at ENI. Because outside requests may be from various different networks, requested content of interactive type traffic which is short-lived and delay sensitive may not be valuable enough to be stored. Of course, ENI can select to store it or not. Moreover, ENI may have a corresponding algorithm to decide whether to store it or not. See Fig. 5.

As ISPs network (especially, the access ISPs network) has been divided into a set of edge networks, some internet technologies which may be not practice

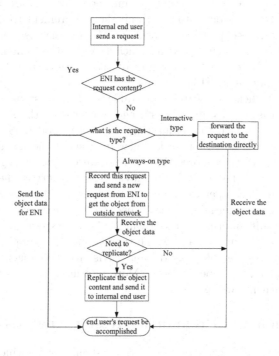

Fig. 5. The Flow chart of request processing

feasible to be widely used in the hole Internet space can be rather suitable for an edge network, like IP multicast and Qos mechanisms. According to Edge-to-Edge network architecture, the whole packet transmission process has been split into several steps. Each small step of packet transmission is completed quicker, so the valuable core transit links and resources can be released in time.

Firstly, bulk data from content providers original server will be transferred to ISPs storage nodes of ISPs network. And then it will be transferred to ENIs storage repositories of edge network. At last, the data will be delivered to its internal end users. If ISP has not deployed storage nodes, the first transfer stage that data from content providers to ISP can make use of CDNs service[8]. In practice, the second step may be not needed. ISP can offer conditions such as equipments and space for Application Provider (AP) or Content Provider (CP) to deploy their own software in the platform of ENI to improve service performance. For example, they can deploy overlay multicast software to develop their own special service. For ISPs, they just provide value-added-cast (VDC).

Streaming media transmission
Based on users usage behavior of streaming media, we classify streaming traffic into three types: IPTV like type traffic, Download_ and_watch type traffic and Click_ and_watch type traffic.

✓In the case of IPTV like type traffic such as live program or video conference, the particular server sends out the same data to a great deal of users at the same time. And users receive data passively, cant replay or forward it. Download_ and_watch type traffic is delay-tolerant and the requirement to delay is not so sensitive to affect users experience, in other words, it is file download type traffic. When it is Click_ and_watch type traffic such as Video-On-Demand, users select the streaming media contents according to their interests and can replay or forward the program at will[13].

✓In the case of Click_ and_watch type traffic, if the request video or other kind streaming media is already in ENIs storage repositories, the streaming media server in ENI can service this request quickly with good QoS guarantee and lower startup delay. If not, ENI sends a new request for the specified data from outside network, and then stores the received data to its storage repositories. After having received the prefix of the movie, ENI can service the users request locally. Obviously, it can get the request data with a higher transfer speed and more stable than its internal end users, because of the location of ENI in the network. As a result, internal end user can get better experience.

✓In the case of Download_ and_watch type traffic, it is simply like file transfer.Due to its delay-tolerant property and ENIs storage capacity, internal end user can also get better experience[14]. More internal end users need the same content, more benefits ISP will gain.

4   Simulation and Preliminary Result Analysis

We implement a customized python version simulator in which the interaction among users, ENIs and servers are described in a precise manner. The simulator captures users actions of requesting multimedia data which are consistent with Poisson distribution just like what happened in real world. Our evaluation shows that E2E network architecture can gain significant network performance improvement in terms of shortening the startup delay and reducing traffic of core links.

Our simulator is event driven. Each interaction among each user, ENI or the server will be taken as an event. We ran the simulator in windows XP on a 2.0 GHz Intel Pentium Dual CPU with 2.0 GB memory.

In this section, we mainly evaluate two important metrics: startup delay and traffic saved in core links. We use a user-ENI-server setup, where the user simulate multiple media players by generating requests for media objects according to a Poisson process which is exponentially distributed with a mean of $1/\lambda$, where λ is the request rate. The selection of the videos is modeled using a Zipf distribution. We sort the videos by access frequency, and then the access frequency for i^{th} the video is given by $f_i = c/i^{1-\theta}$, where θ is the parameter for the distribution and $c = \left[1 \middle/ \sum_{i=1}^{N} \left(1/i^{1-\theta}\right)\right]$ is the normalization constant.

Each movie is divided into 10 segments. The basic unit transferred in our system is a segment. In simulation, we set the delay between user and ENI as 0.001ms and set the delay between ENI and server as 0.001ms, 0.05ms and 0.1 ms respectively.

One benefit brought by deployment of the ENI is effectively reducing redundancy traffic. At the ENI, we setup a buffer whose replacing strategy is LRU. During the period of simulation, we set the buffer with infinite size and leave experiments with finite size as future work. We can use a simple expression to calculate the traffic transmission reducing. r = (TENI - Tserver)/TENI where TENI denotes the total amount of the data transferred from the ENI to the user and Tserver is the total amount of data transferred from the server to the ENI. r shows reduced proportion of core transit link traffic. In the Fig. 6 and Fig. 7, delay ratio means the ratio of the link delay between server and ENI to the link

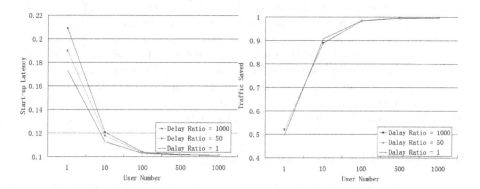

Fig. 6. Start-up delay under different user numbers and different Delay Ratio

Fig. 7. The amount of traffic reduced under different user numbers and different Delay Ratio

delay between ENI and user. Different delay ratio means the different distances between server and ENI. We see that as the user number increases, the reduced traffic in the core link becomes more. When the user number reaches more than 500, we can reduce more than 90% of the traffic which is a big win brought by enabling ENI with a big buffer.

Because the user can fetch the data from ENI, the user start-up latency is shortened dramatically which is shown in Fig. 6.

5   Discussion

In view of the large potential for large amount of streaming media transmission, an important question is "Whether ENI will be the bottleneck of the whole architecture?". This is a complicated question to answer. We make some initial discussions on this issue.

There is a tradeoff between storage and bandwidth. We intend to save the cost of bandwidth and costly transit-links by adding some storage nodes (cache or replica servers) attached to POPs of ISP to construct a new kind of POP-may be called as POPX which is referred to ENI (Edge Network Infrastructure) in this paper.

Whether the storage size needed by ENI will be too large to implement? We do not think so. Because ENI is located at the point of presence of access ISP, the number of end users who link to one ENI will not be too large. And according to the Zipfs law[20], 80 percents users will request the same 20 percentile content at most time. Nikolas[15] also has shown that it is feasible to set up some storage nodes at proper points make ISP storage-enable. Many cache and replica mechanisms can be implemented, which is out of this papers scope,and interested readers can refer to[11].

Whether the computational capacities and link bandwidth of ENI will become the bottleneck? Due to the existence of large amounts redundancy data request, ISPs can implement multicast mechanisms to deliver content to multiple end users at the same time. In addition, we classified users requirement of streaming media into three types to schedule users requests at different time. Also, ENI can do the download and upload work for end users at a higher speed, so the outside links and computational resource will be released earlier. E2EDSM also support existing content distribution solutions such as CDN and P2P.

There may be many edge networks under the authority of one ISP, which can be united to form clusters. A perfect perspective we believe is that the whole edge network is a Cloud[21] where ENI is the portal.

6   Conclusions and Future work

To address the problems brought by large scale data transmission like P2P traffic and streaming media traffic, we should understand the involved parties and their requirements. Take those into account, methodology presented in this paper is an evolutional way. Starting from the understanding two couplings among different network layers, we proposed a solution in the form of Edge-to-Edge network architecture. Moreover, we classify the steaming media data transmission into three types by users usage behavior, which are IPTV like type traffic, Click_ and_watch type traffic and Download_ and_watch type traffic. Then, we presented E2EDSM which aims to avoid redundant data being transferred over the costly core transit links as well as improving the transmission efficiency of mass streaming media. E2EDSM describes a new way for ISP to take part in the processing of content distribution and makes an effort to achieve a win-win goal; we have developed a simulator namely Phoenix and preliminary experiment results show that solutions under Edge-to-Edge architecture have better performances for the large scale streaming media delivery.

There are still much related work need to be studied, such as the relationship between the number of internal end users and the computational capacity and bandwidth requirements of ENI and so on. We have been considering the possibility of deploying agents on new type routers to implement functions of ENI. In addition, we have made a detailed plan to enhance our simulator named Phoenix, which is planned to be putted on our research webpage.

Acknowledgments

This work is supported by a grant from the Major State Basic Research Development Programs of China (973 Programs) (No.2009CB320503), and Chinese National Programs for High Technology Research and Development (863 Programs) (No. 2008AA01A325 and No. 2008AA01A323). The authors would like to acknowledge the help of Wei Peng, Gaowei Cheng, and Bin Dai as well as the anonymous reviewers in improving the paper.

References

1. Schulze, H., Mochalski, K.: Internet Study 2008/2009 (2009),
   http://www.ipoque.com
2. Wu, H.: BroadBand World Forum Asia (2007),
   http://www.iec.org/events/2007/bbwf_asia/
3. Salter, J.H., Reed, D.P., Clark, D.D.: End-to-End Arguments In System Design. In: Second International Conference on Distributed Computing Systems, pp. 509–512 (1981); ACM Transactions on Computer Systems 2(4), 277–288 (November 1984)
4. Karagiannis, T., Rodriguez, P., Papagiannaki, K.: Should Internet Service Providers Fear Peer-Assisted Content Distribution? In: IMC 2005 (2005)
5. Arkko, J.: Ncentives and Deployment Considerations for P2PI Solutions. draftarkko-p2pi-inventives-00, Internet-Draft (2008)
6. Xie, H., Yang, Y.R., Krishnamurthy, A., Liu, Y., Silberschatz, A.: P4P: Provider Portal for Applications. In: ACM SIGCOMM 2008 (2008)
7. Pathan, M., Buyya, R., Vakali, A.: Content Delivery Networks: State of the Art, Insights, and Imperatives. In: Content Delivery Networks. Springer, Heidelberg (2008)
8. http://www.akamai.com

9. Huston, G.: The End of End to End? In: The ISP Columm, ISOC (2008)
10. Lao, L., Cui, J.-H., Gerla, M., Maggiorini, D.: A Comparative Study of Multicast Protocols Top, Bottom, or In the middle. Technical Report TR040054 (2005)
11. Wang, B., Sen, S., Adler, M., Towsley, D.: Optimal Proxy Cache Allocation for Efficient Streaming Media Distribution. In: IEEE INFOCOM (2002)
12. Anand, A., Gupta, A., Akella, A., Seshan, S., Shenker, S.: Packet Caches on Routers: The Implications of Universal Redundant Traffic Elimination. In: ACM SIGCOMM 2008 (2008)
13. Thouin, F., Coates, M.: Video-on-Demand Networks: Design Approaches and Future Challenges. IEEE Nework 21(2), 42–48 (2007)
14. Laoutaris, N., Rodriguez, P.: Good things come to Those Who (Can) Wait or how to handle Delay Tolerant traffic and make peace on the Internet. hotnets2008 (2008)
15. Laoutaris, N., Smaragdakis, G., Rodriguez, P., Sundaram, R.: Delay Tolerant Bulk Data Transfers on the Internet. sigmetric2009 (2009)
16. Clark, D.D., Wroclawski, J., Sollins, K.R., Braden, R.: Tussle in Cyberspace: Defing Tomorrows Internet. In: ACM SIGCOMM 2002 (2002)
17. Statistical Survey Report on the Internet Development (in China), http://www.cnnic.net.cn/uploadfilees/pdf/2009/3/23/131303.pdf
18. http://www.pplive.com
19. http://www.bittorrent.com
20. Zipf, G.K.: Human Behavior and the Principle of Least-Effort. Addison- Wesley, London (1949)
21. Armbrust, M., Fox, A., Griffith, R., Joseph, A.D., Katz, R.H., Konwinski, A., Lee, G., Patterson, D.A., Rabkin, A., Stoica, I., Zaharia, M.: Above the Clouds: A Berkeley View of Cloud Computing. Technical report No. UCB/EECS-2009-28 (2009), http://www.eecs.berkeley.edu/Pubs/TechRpts/2009/EECS-2009-28.html

Iso-Level CAFT: How to Tackle the Combination of Communication Overhead Reduction and Fault Tolerance Scheduling

Mourad Hakem

LIFC Laboratory, Université de Franche-Comté, Belfort, France
Mourad.Hakem@lifc.univ-fcomte.fr

Abstract. To schedule precedence task graphs in a more realistic framework, we introduce an efficient fault tolerant scheduling algorithm that is both contention-aware and capable of supporting ε arbitrary fail-silent (fail-stop) processor failures. The design of the proposed algorithm which we call Iso-Level CAFT, is motivated by (i) the search for a better load-balance and (ii) the generation of fewer communications. These goals are achieved by scheduling a chunk of ready tasks simultaneously, which enables for a global view of the potential communications. Our goal is to minimize the total execution time, or latency, while tolerating an arbitrary number of processor failures. Our approach is based on an active replication scheme to mask failures, so that there is no need for detecting and handling such failures. Major achievements include a low complexity, and a drastic reduction of the number of additional communications induced by the replication mechanism. The experimental results fully demonstrate the usefulness of Iso-Level CAFT.

1 Introduction

With the advent of large-scale heterogeneous platforms such as clusters and grids, resource failures (processors/links) are more likely to occur and have an adverse effect on the applications. Consequently, there is an increasing need for developing techniques to achieve fault tolerance, *i.e.*, to tolerate an arbitrary number of failures during execution. Scheduling for heterogeneous platforms and fault tolerance are difficult problems in their own, and aiming at solving them together makes the problem even harder. For instance, the latency of the application will increase if we want to tolerate several failures, even if no actual failure happens during execution.

In this paper, we introduce the Iso-Level Contention-Aware Fault Tolerant (Iso-Level CAFT) scheduling algorithm (a new version of CAFT [4] that were initially designed to address both problems of network contention and fault-tolerance scheduling) that aims at tolerating multiple processor failures without sacrificing the latency. Iso-Level CAFT is based on an active replication scheme to mask failures, so that there is no need for detecting and handling such failures. Our choice for the active replication scheme is motivated by two important

Y. Dou, R. Gruber, and J. Joller (Eds.): APPT 2009, LNCS 5737, pp. 259–272, 2009.
© Springer-Verlag Berlin Heidelberg 2009

advantages. On the one hand, the schedules obtained are static, thus it is easy to have a guarantee on the latency of the schedule. On the other hand, the deployment of the system does not require complicated mechanisms for failure detection. Major achievements include a low complexity, and a drastic reduction of the number of additional communications induced by the replication mechanism.

We suggest to use the bi-directional one-port architectural model, where each processor can communicate (send and/or receive) with at most one other processor at a given time-step. In other words, a given processor can simultaneously send a message, receive another message, and perform some computation. The bi-directional one-port model seems closer to the actual capabilities of modern networks (see the discussion of related work in [4,5,6]). Indeed, it seems to fit the performance of some current MPI implementations, which serialize asynchronous MPI sends as soon as message sizes exceed a few megabytes [4].

The rest of the paper is organized as follows: Section 2 presents basic definitions and assumptions. Then we describe the principle of the new Iso-Level CAFT algorithm in Section 3. We experimentally compare Iso-Lvel CAFT with its initial version CAFT in Section 4; the results assess the very good behavior of the new algorithm. Finally, we conclude in Section 5.

The review of related work on fault tolerance scheduling is provided in [4].

2   Framework

The execution model for a task graph is represented as a weighted Directed Acyclic Graph (DAG) $G = (V, E)$, where V is the set of nodes corresponding to the tasks, and E is the set of edges corresponding to the precedence relations between the tasks. In the following we use the term node or task indifferently; $v = |V|$ is the number of nodes, and $e = |E|$ is the number of edges. In a DAG, a node without any predecessor is called an *entry* node, while a node without any successor is an *exit* node. For a task t in G, $\Gamma^-(t)$ is the set of immediate predecessors and $\Gamma^+(t)$ denotes its immediate successors. A task is called *ready* if it is unscheduled and all of its predecessors are scheduled. We target a heterogeneous platform with m processors $\mathcal{P} = \{P_1, P_2, \ldots, P_m\}$, fully interconnected. The link between processors P_k and P_h is denoted by l_{kh}. Note that we do not need to have a physical link between any processor pair. Instead, we may have a switch, or even a path composed of several physical links, to interconnect P_k and P_h; in the latter case we would retain the bandwidth of the slowest link in the path for the bandwidth of l_{kh}. For a given graph G and processor set $\mathcal{P}$, $g(G, \mathcal{P})$ is the *granularity*, i.e., the ratio of the sum of slowest computation times of each task, to the sum of slowest communication times along each edge. $\mathcal{H}(\alpha)$ is the head function which returns the first task from a sorted list α, where the list is sorted according to tasks priorities (ties are broken randomly). The number of tasks that can be simultaneously ready at each step in the scheduling process is bounded by the width ω of the task graph (the maximum number of tasks that are independent in G). This, implies that $|\alpha| \leq \omega$.

Our goal is to find a task mapping of the DAG G on the platform $\mathcal{P}$ obeying the one-port model. The objective is to minimize the latency $\mathcal{L}(G)$, while tolerating an arbitrary number ε of processor failures. Our approach is based on an active replication scheme, capable of supporting ε arbitrary fail-silent (a faulty processor does not produce any output) and fail-stop (no processor recovery) processor failures.

3   The Iso-Level CAFT Scheduling Algorithm

In the previous version of CAFT algorithm [4], we consider only one ready task (the one with highest priority) at each step, and we assign all its replicas to the currently best available resources. Instead of considering a single task, we may deal with a chunk of several ready tasks, and assign all their replicas in the same decision making procedure. The intuition is that such a "global" assignment would lead to better load balance processor and link usage.

We introduce a parameter B for the chunk size: B is the maximal number of ready tasks that will be considered at each step. We select the B tasks with the higher bottom levels $b\ell(t)$ (the length of the longest path starting at t to an exit node in the graph) and we allocate them in the same step. Then, we update the set of ready tasks (indeed some new tasks may have become ready), and we sort them again, according to bottom levels. Thus, we expect that the tasks on a critical path will be processed as soon as possible.

The difference between CAFT and the new version, which we call Iso-Level CAFT (or ILC), is sketched in Algorithm 3.1. With CAFT we take the ready task with highest priority all allocate all its replicas before proceeding to the next ready task. In contrast, with Iso-Level CAFT, the second replicas of tasks in the same chunk are allocated only after all first replicas have been placed. Intuitively, this more global strategy will balance best resources across all tasks in the chunk, while CAFT may assign the $\varepsilon + 1$ best resources to the current task, at the risk of sacrificing the next one, even though it may have the same bottom level.

We point out that we face a difficult tradeoff for choosing an appropriate value for B. On the one hand, if B is large, it will be possible to better balance the load and minimize communication costs. On the other hand, a small value of B will enable us to process the tasks on the critical path faster. In the experiments (see Section 4) we observe that choosing $B = m$, the number of processors, leads to good results.

Theorem 1. *The time complexity of Iso-Level CAFT is*

$$O\left(em(\varepsilon + 1)^2 \log(\varepsilon + 1) + v \log \omega\right)$$

Proof. The proof is similar to that given in [4]. Note that since $\varepsilon < m$, we can derive the upper bound $O\left(em^3 \log m + v \log \omega\right)$.

Algorithm 3.1 CAFT vs Iso-Level CAFT (ILC)

1: initialization; $U \leftarrow V$;
2: **while** $U \neq \emptyset$ **do**
3:     $\mathcal{T} \leftarrow \mathcal{H}(\alpha)$; **ILC:** *repeat B times (*CAFT:* $|\mathcal{T}| = 1$ | *ILC:* $|\mathcal{T}| = B$ *)*
4:     **for** $1 \leq i \leq \varepsilon + 1$ **do**
5:         **for** $t \in \mathcal{T}$ **do**
6:             allocate task-replica $t^{(i)}$ to processor with shortest finish time
7:         **end for**
8:     **end for**
9: **end while**

Notice that, allocating many copies of each task will severely increase the total number of communications required by the algorithm: we move from e communications (one per edge) in a mapping with no replication (fault free schedule), to $e(\varepsilon + 1)^2$ with replication (fault tolerant schedule), a quadratic increase. In fact, duplicating each task $\varepsilon + 1$ times is an absolute requirement to resist to ε failures, but duplicating each precedence edge $e(\varepsilon + 1)^2$ times is not mandatory. We can decrease the total number of communications from $e(\varepsilon + 1)^2$ down to $e(\varepsilon + 1)$ as it was proved in [4]. Unfortunatly, this reduction does not work all the time. The linear number of communications $e(\varepsilon + 1)$ holds only in special cases, typically for tasks having a unique predecessor, or when every replica of all predecessors are mapped onto distinct processors or when all the replicas belonging to the same processor communicate with only the same successor-replica.

The problem becomes more complex when tasks have more than one predecessor and several replicas of predecessors mapped on the same processor communicate with different successor-replicas. In the following, we show how to reduce this overhead in the design of Iso-Level CAFT.

3.1   Reducing Communication Overhead

When dealing with realistic model platforms, contention should be considered in order to obtain improved schedules. We account for communication overhead during the mapping process by removing some of the communications. To do so, we propose the following mapping scheme.

Let t be the current task to be scheduled. Consider a predecessor t_j of t, $j \in \Gamma^-(t)$, that has been replicated on $\varepsilon + 1$ distinct processors. We denote by $\mathcal{D}_u$ the set of replicas assigned to processor $\mathcal{P}_u$, and $\eta_u = |\mathcal{D}_u|$ its cardinality. The maximum cardinality is $\eta = \max_{1 \leq u \leq m} \eta_u$. Also we denote by $\mathcal{N}$ the number of processors involved/used by all replicas of tasks in $\Gamma^-(t)$.

We would like to reduce the number of communications from all predecessors t_j to t when possible. The idea is to attempt to place each replica on the non-locked (locked processors are already either involved in a communication with a replica of t, or processing it) processor which currently contains the most predecessor replicas. To this purpose, we sort processors by non increasing order of number of replicas $\eta_u, 1 \leq u \leq m$, assigned to them. At each step in

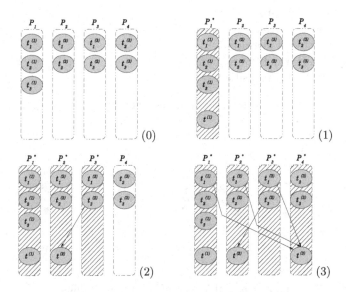

Fig. 1. Iso-Level CAFT Scheduling Steps

the mapping process, we try to take communications from replicas belonging to the non-locked processors, whenever possible. If not, we insert ε additional communications.

Fig. 1 illustrates this procedure. We set $\varepsilon = 2$ in this example. At step (0), no processor is blocked. The three predecessors of the current task t, namely t_1, t_2 and t_3, are assigned. At step (1), we place the first replica $t^{(1)}$ on P_1, which becomes locked. This is represented in the figure with a superscript $*$, and the processor is also hatched in the figure. No communication is added in this case. At step (2), we need to add a communication from P_3 to P_2, and thus we have three locked processors. At step (3), we place replica $t^{(3)}$ on the only non-locked processor which is P_3, and we need to add extra communication since all processors are locked.

Theorem 2. *The schedule generated by Iso-Level CAFT algorithm is valid and resists to ε failures.*

Proof. The proof is similar to that of CAFT (see [4])

In the following, we give an analytical expression of the actual number of communications induced by the *Iso-Level CAFT* algorithm. First we give an interesting upper bound for special graphs, and then we derive an upper bound for the general case.

Special graphs

First, we bound the number of communications induced by Iso-Level CAFT for special graphs like classical kernels representing various types of parallel algorithms [1]. The selected task graphs are:

(a) LU: LU decomposition
(b) LAPLACE: Laplace equation solver
(c) STENCIL: stencil algorithm
(d) DOOLITTLE: Doolittle reduction
(e) LDM^t: LDM^t decomposition

Miniature versions of each task graph are given in Fig. 2.

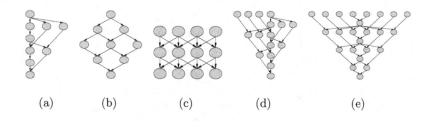

(a)   (b)   (c)   (d)   (e)

Fig. 2. Classical kernels of parallel algorithms

Theorem 3. *The number of messages generated by Iso-Level CAFT for the above special graphs is at most*

$$V_2(\varepsilon + 1) + V_3 \left(\varepsilon \left\lceil \frac{(\varepsilon+2)}{2} \right\rceil + 2 \right),$$

where $V_2 \leq \lfloor \frac{\varepsilon}{2} \rfloor$ is the number of nodes of in-degree 2 and $V_3 \leq \lfloor \frac{\varepsilon}{3} \rfloor$ is the number of nodes of in-degree 3 in the graph.

Proof. One feature of the special graphs is that the in-degree of every task is at most 3. At each step when scheduling current task t, we have three cases to consider, depending upon its in-degree (the cardinal of $\Gamma^-(t)$). Recall that processors are ordered by non increasing η_u values, where η_u is the number of replicas already assigned to P_u, hence which do not need to be communicated again.

(1) $|\Gamma^-(t)| = 1$. In this case, in order to pay no communication, we just need to place each replica of t with a replica of its predecessor.

(2) $|\Gamma^-(t)| = 2$. The two redecessor tasks of t are denoted t_1 and t_2. If replicas of t_1 and t_2 are mapped on the same processor ($\mathcal{P}(t_1^{(z)}) = \mathcal{P}(t_2^{(z')}) = \mathcal{P}$ for some $1 \leq z, z' \leq \varepsilon + 1$), then there is no need for any additional communication. Other replicas of t_1 and t_2 which does not satisfy the previous property are thus mapped onto singleton processors. We perform the *one-to-one mapping* algorithm to allocate the corresponding other replicas of t. For each replica, at most one communication is added.

(3) $|\Gamma^-(t)| = 3$. Here we consider the number of replicas allocated to processor $\mathcal{P}_u$, denoted as η_u.

- We place a replica on each processor with $\eta_u = 3$, thus no communication need to be paid for
- Consider a processor with $\eta_u = 2$. When allocating a replica of t on such a processor $\mathcal{P}_u$, we need to receive data from the third predecessor allocated to $\mathcal{P}_v \neq \mathcal{P}_u$. $\mathcal{P}_v$ may be either a singleton processor ($\eta_v = 1$) or it may handle two predecessors ($\eta_v = 2$).
  - if $\eta_v = 1$, then we need only one communication for mapping the replica of t. In this case $\mathcal{P}_v$ communicates only to $\mathcal{P}_u$.
  - if $\eta_v = 2$, then we may need to add extra communications. For the first $\left\lceil \frac{\varepsilon+1}{2} \right\rceil$ replicas of t, we add only one communication per replica, and lock processors accordingly. But for the remaining set $\left\lfloor \frac{\varepsilon+1}{2} \right\rfloor$ of replicas, we will have to generate $\varepsilon + 1$ communications for each of these replicas. Overall, the number of communications is at most $\left\lceil \frac{\varepsilon+1}{2} \right\rceil + (\varepsilon + 1) \left\lfloor \frac{\varepsilon+1}{2} \right\rfloor$

  Let $X = \left\lceil \frac{\varepsilon+1}{2} \right\rceil + (\varepsilon + 1) \left\lfloor \frac{\varepsilon+1}{2} \right\rfloor$. Let $Y = \varepsilon \left\lceil \frac{(\varepsilon+2)}{2} \right\rceil + 1$. If $\varepsilon = 2k$ is even, then $X = 2k^2 + k + 1 \leq 2k^2 + 2k + 1 = Y$. If $\varepsilon = 2k + 1$ is odd, then $X = 2k^2 + 2k + 1 \leq 2k^2 + 3k + 1 = Y$. In all cases $X \leq Y$, hence the number of communications is at most Y.
- Now, all remaining processors have at most one replica ($\eta = 1$). Thus task t needs its data from two other replicas. So we have to take at most two communications for each replicas mapped. Thus for the mapping of $\varepsilon + 1$ replicas, we will have at most a number of communications equal to $2(\varepsilon+1)$. Note that $2(\varepsilon + 1) \leq Y + 1 = \varepsilon \left\lceil \frac{(\varepsilon+2)}{2} \right\rceil + 2$ for all ε, hence the result.

General graphs

Theorem 4. *For general graphs, the number of messages generated by Iso-Level CAFT is at most*

$$e \left(\varepsilon \left\lceil \frac{(\varepsilon+2)}{2} \right\rceil + 1 \right)$$

Proof. At each step when scheduling current task t:

(i) For the first $\left\lceil \frac{\varepsilon+1}{2} \right\rceil$ replicas, we generate at most $\sum_{u=1}^{\left\lceil \frac{(\varepsilon+1)}{2} \right\rceil} (|\Gamma^-(t)| - \eta_u)$ communications (recall that η_u is the number of replicas already assigned to $\mathcal{P}_u$, hence which do not need to be communicated again). Altogether, we have at most $\left\lceil \frac{(\varepsilon+1)}{2} \right\rceil |\Gamma^-(t)|$ communications for these replicas.

(ii) We still have to map the remaining $\left\lfloor \frac{\varepsilon+1}{2} \right\rfloor$ of t replicas. In the worst case, each replica placed will generate $\varepsilon+1$ communications (this is because processors may be locked in this case).

Thus for this remaining set of replicas, the number of communications is at most $(\varepsilon + 1) \sum_{u=\left\lceil \frac{(\varepsilon+1)}{2} \right\rceil+1}^{\varepsilon+1} (|\Gamma^-(t)| - \eta_u) \leq (\varepsilon + 1) \left\lfloor \frac{\varepsilon+1}{2} \right\rfloor |\Gamma^-(t)|$

From *(i)* and *(ii)*, we have a total number of communications of $|\Gamma^-(t)|X$, where $X = \left\lceil \frac{\varepsilon+1}{2} \right\rceil + (\varepsilon + 1) \left\lfloor \frac{\varepsilon+1}{2} \right\rfloor$. As in the proof of Theorem 3, we knwo that $X \leq Y$, where $Y = \varepsilon \left\lceil \frac{(\varepsilon+2)}{2} \right\rceil + 1$. Hence the number of communications is at most Y.

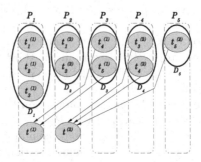

Fig. 3. Complementary/disjoint sets of replicas

Thus, summing up for all the v tasks in G, the total number of messages is at most $\sum_{u=1}^{v} |\Gamma^-(t)| \left(\varepsilon \left\lceil \frac{(\varepsilon+2)}{2} \right\rceil + 1 \right) = e \left(\varepsilon \left\lceil \frac{(\varepsilon+2)}{2} \right\rceil + 1 \right)$.

The following last Theorem deals with disjoint and complementary replica sets. In fact, the number of communications can be drastically reduced in such a case:

Theorem 5. *For general graphs, if at each step when scheduling a task t, we can determine replica sets $\mathcal{D}_u$ that are both disjoint ($\mathcal{D}_u \cap \mathcal{D}_{u'} = \emptyset$ if $u \neq u'$) and complementary ($\sigma_{u=1}^{m} |\mathcal{D}_u| = |\Gamma^-(t)|$, or in other words $\cup_{1 \leq u \leq m} \mathcal{D}_u$ contains a replica of each predecessor of t), then the number of messages is at most $e(\varepsilon+1)$.*

Proof. We map a replica on $\mathcal{D}_u$ and add communications from all complementary sets, which generates at most $|\Gamma^-(t)| - |\mathcal{D}_u| = |\cup_{1 \leq u' \leq m, u' \neq u} \mathcal{D}_{u'}| \leq |\Gamma^-(t)|$.

Thus, for the mapping of $\varepsilon + 1$ replicas, and summing up for the set V of tasks in G, the total number of messages is at most $\sum_{t \in V} |\Gamma^-(t)|(\varepsilon + 1) = e(\varepsilon + 1)$.

Fig. 3 illustrates, for the mapping of the first replica $t^{(1)}$ we have $|\Gamma^-(t)| - |\mathcal{D}_1| = 5 - 3 = 2 = |\mathcal{D}_3|$. In addition, both $\mathcal{D}_1$ and $\mathcal{D}_3$ are mutually complementary/disjoints and they form a complete instance of all predecessors. Also, for the mapping of the second replica $t^{(2)}$, we have $|\Gamma^-(t)| - |\mathcal{D}_2| = 5 - 2 = 3 = |\mathcal{D}_4 \cup \mathcal{D}_5|$. Similarly, the condition of complementarity/disjunction of the sets $\mathcal{D}_2$, $\mathcal{D}_4$ and $\mathcal{D}_5$ holds.

4   Experimental Results

We assess the practical significance and usefulness of the Iso-Level CAFT algorithm through simulation studies. We compare the performance of Iso-Level CAFT with its initial version CAFT algorithm. We use randomly generated graphs, whose parameters are consistent with those used in the literature [4]. We characterize these random graphs with three parameters: (i) the number of tasks, chosen uniformly from the range [80, 120]; (ii) the number of incoming/outgoing edges per task, which is set in [1, 3]; and (iii) the granularity of the task graph $g(G)$. We consider two types of graphs, with a granularity (a) in $[0.2, 2.0]$ and increments of 0.2, and (b) in $[1, 10]$ and increments of 1. Two types of platforms are considered, first with 10 processors and $\varepsilon = 1$ or $\varepsilon = 3$, and then with 20 processors and $\varepsilon = 5$ (a full set of results is available in the dedicated research report [3]). To account for communication heterogeneity in the system, the unit message delay of the links and the message volume between two tasks are chosen uniformly from the ranges $[0.5, 1]$ and $[50, 150]$ respectively. Each point in the figures represents the mean of executions on 60 random graphs. The fault free schedule is defined as the schedule generated without replication, assuming that the system is completely safe. Recall that the upper bounds of the schedules are computed as explained in [2].

Each algorithm is evaluated in terms of achieved latency and fault toler-ance overhead $\dfrac{\text{CAFT}^0|\text{Iso-Level CAFT}^0|\text{CAFT}^c|\text{Iso-Level CAFT}^c - \text{CAFT}^*}{\text{CAFT}^*}$, where the superscripts $*$, c and 0 respectively denote the latency achieved by the fault free schedule, the latency achieved by the schedule when processors effectively fail (crash) and the latency achieved with 0 crash. We have also compared the behavior of each algorithm when processors crash down by computing the real execution time for a given schedule rather than just bounds (upper bound and latency with 0 crash).

Comparing the results of Iso-Level CAFT to the results of CAFT, we ob-serve in Fig. 4 and 5 that Iso-Level CAFT gives the best performance. It always improves the latency significantly in all figures. This is because the Iso-Level CAFT algorithm tries incrementally to ensure a certain degree of load balanc-ing for processors by scheduling a chunk of ready tasks before considering their corresponding replicas. This better load balancing also decreases communica-tions between tasks. Consequently, this leads to minimize the final latency of the schedule.

We also find in Fig. 6 and 7 that the performance difference between CAFT and Iso-Level CAFT increases when the granularity increases. This interesting result comes from the fact that larger granularity indicates that we are deal-ing with intensive computations applications in heterogeneous platforms. Thus, in order to reduce the latency for such applications, it is important to better parallelize the application. That is why we changed the backbone of CAFT to perfectly balance the load of processors at each step of the scheduling process.

Finally, we readily observe from all figures that we deal with two conflict-ing objectives. Indeed, the fault tolerance overhead increases together with the number of supported failures. We also see that latency increases together with granularity, as expected. In addition, it is interesting to note that when the number of failures increases, there is not really much difference in the increase of the latency achieved by CAFT and Iso-Level CAFT, compared to the schedule length generated with 0 crash. This is explained by the fact that the increase in the schedule length is already absorbed by the replication done previously, in order to resist to eventual failures.

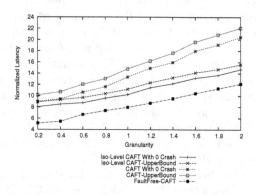

(a) Latency bounds

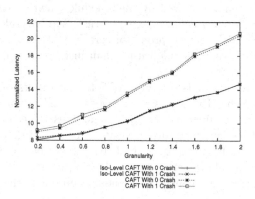

(b) Latency achieved with crash

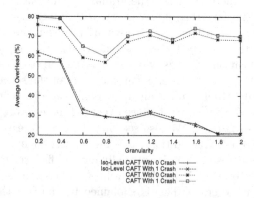

(c) Fault tolerance overhead

Fig. 4. Average normalized latency and overhead comparison between Iso-Level-CAFT and CAFT (Bound and Crash cases, $m = 10, \varepsilon = 1$)

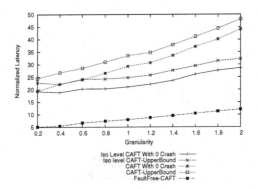

(a) Latency bounds

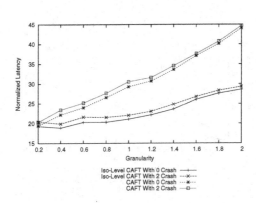

(b) Latency achieved with crash

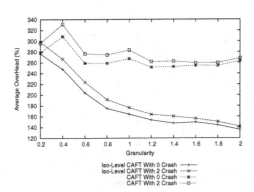

(c) Fault tolerance overhead

Fig. 5. Average normalized latency and overhead comparison between Iso-Level-CAFT and CAFT (Bound and Crash cases, $m = 10, \varepsilon = 3$)

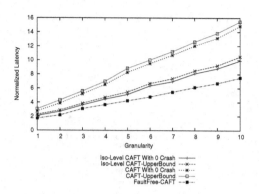

(a) Latency bounds

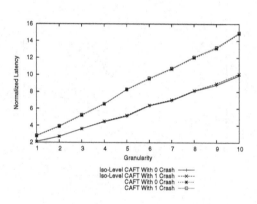

(b) Latency achieved with crash

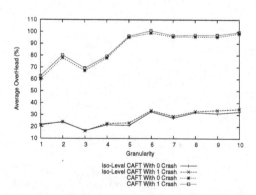

(c) Fault tolerance overhead

Fig. 6. Average normalized latency and overhead comparison between Iso-Level-CAFT and CAFT for coarse grain graphs $g(G) \geq 1$ (Bound and Crash cases, $m = 10, \varepsilon = 1$)

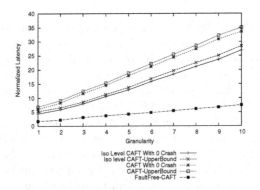

(a) Latency bounds

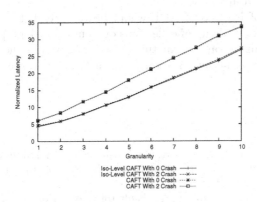

(b) Latency achieved with crash

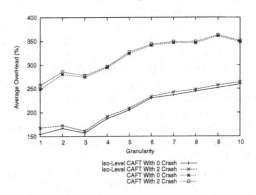

(c) Fault tolerance overhead

Fig. 7. Average normalized latency and overhead comparison between Iso-Level-CAFT and CAFT for coarse grain graphs $g(G) \geq 1$ (Bound and Crash cases, $m = 10, \varepsilon = 3$)

5   Conclusion

In this paper, an efficient fault-tolerant scheduling algorithm (Iso-Level CAFT) for heteorgeneous systems is studied and analysed. Iso-Level CAFT is based on an active replication scheme, and is able to drastically reduce the communication overhead induced by task replication, which turns out a key factor in improving performance when dealing with realistic, communication contention aware, platform models. The design of Iso-Level CAFT is motivated by (i) the search for a better load-balance and (ii) the generation of fewer communications. These goals are achieved by scheduling a chunk of ready tasks simultaneously, which enables for a global view of the potential communications. To assess the performance of Iso-Level CAFT, simulation studies were conducted to compare it with CAFT, which seems to be its main direct competitor from the literature. We have shown that Iso-Level CAFT is very efficient both in terms of computational complexity and quality of the resulting schedule.

An extension of Iso-Level CAFT would be to extend it to the context of pipelined workflows made up of collections of identical task graphs (rather than dealing with a single graph as in this paper). We would then need to solve a challenging tri-criteria optimization problem (latency, throughput and fault-tolerance).

References

1. Beaumont, O., Boudet, V., Robert, Y.: A realistic model and an efficient heuristic for scheduling with heterogeneous processors. In: Proc. of the 11th Heterogeneous Computing Workshop HCW 2002 (2002)
2. Benoit, A., Hakem, M., Robert, Y.: Fault tolerant scheduling of precedence task graphs on heterogeneous platforms. In: Proc. of the 10th Int. Workshop in Advances Parallel and Distributed Computational Models APDCM 2008, pp. 1–8 (2008), http://graal.ens-lyon.fr/~abenoit/
3. Benoit, A., Hakem, M., Robert, Y.: Iso-Level CAFT: How to Tackle the Combination of Communication Overhead Reduction and Fault Tolerance Scheduling. In: RR 2008-25, LIP, ENS Lyon, France (July 2008), http://graal.ens-lyon.fr/~mhakem/
4. Benoit, A., Hakem, M., Robert, Y.: Realistic models and efficient algorithms for fault tolerance scheduling on heterogeneous platforms. In: Proc. of the 37th IEEE Int. Conference on Parallel Processing ICPP 2008, pp. 246–253 (2008), http://graal.ens-lyon.fr/~abenoit/
5. Sinnen, O., Sousa, L.: Experimental evaluation of task scheduling accuracy: Implications for the scheduling model. IEICE Transactions on Information and Systems E86-D(9), 1620–1627 (2003)
6. Sinnen, O., Sousa, L.: Communication contention in task scheduling. IEEE Trans. on Parallel and Distributed Systems 16(6), 503–515 (2005)

MaGate Simulator: A Simulation Environment for a Decentralized Grid Scheduler

Ye Huang, Amos Brocco, Michele Courant,
Beat Hirsbrunner, and Pierre Kuonen

Department of Informatics, University of Fribourg, Switzerland
Department of Information and Communication Technologies, University of Applied
Sciences Western Switzerland (Fribourg)
{ye.huang,amos.brocco,michele.courant,beat.hirsbrunner}@unifr.ch,
pierre.kuonen@hefr.ch

Abstract. This paper presents a simulator for of a decentralized modular grid scheduler named MaGate. MaGate's design emphasizes scheduler interoperability by providing intelligent scheduling serving the grid community as a whole. Each MaGate scheduler instance is able to deal with dynamic scheduling conditions, with continuously arriving grid jobs. Received jobs are either allocated on local resources, or delegated to other MaGates for remote execution. The proposed MaGate simulator is based on GridSim toolkit and Alea simulator, and abstracts the features and behaviors of complex fundamental grid elements, such as grid jobs, grid resources, and grid users. Simulation of scheduling tasks is supported by a grid network overlay simulator executing distributed ant-based swarm intelligence algorithms to provide services such as group communication and resource discovery. For evaluation, a comparison of behaviors of different collaborative policies among a community of MaGates is provided. Results support the use of the proposed approach as a functional ready grid scheduler simulator.

Keywords: Grid Scheduling, SmartGRID, MaGate Simulator, Simulation.

1 Introduction

Distributed heterogeneous systems under decentralized control are conventionally understood as grid computing [1], pervasive computing [2] or peer-to-peer (P2P) computing [3] systems. Grid nodes are organized as decentralized virtual organizations (VO) with each member sharing its resources with the community. The goal of a grid is thus to construct and manage a powerful shared pool of resource that enables large scale usage and better resource throughput.

Grid scheduling services, also known as 'high level' scheduling [4], are considered as a crucial component for grid computing because they determine the effectiveness and efficiency of the grid. Scheduling services are in charge of identifying, characterizing, discovering, selecting, and allocating the resources best suited for a particular job.

Y. Dou, R. Gruber, and J. Joller (Eds.): APPT 2009, LNCS 5737, pp. 273–287, 2009.
© Springer-Verlag Berlin Heidelberg 2009

The contribution of this paper is a simulation based implementation of a decentralized modular grid scheduler named MaGate. As a grid scheduler, the MaGate enables the scheduling of a job across a variety of grid resources such as computational clusters, parallel supercomputers, desktop machines that belong to different VOs. More precisely, submitted job may not be executed only on nodes within same VO, but also on appropriate remote resource from other VO with independent scheduling systems and polices. By allocating user's jobs to a proper resource, selected from the entire grid community, improvement of the rate of successfully job execution can be expected. In other words, the MaGate schedulers are designed to cooperated with each other, in order to provide intelligent scheduling for the scope of serving the grid community as a whole, not just for a individual grid nodes.

The MaGate simulator is implemented on GridSim [5] and Alea [6], which together provide the modeling of different kinds of essential grid components, such as grid jobs with various parameters, heterogeneous grid resources, and grid users. Based on this simulated grid ecosystem, each MaGate scheduler receives locally submitted jobs throughout its lifecycle, and matches job requirements with local resource characteristic using the adopted scheduling policies. Jobs suited for local execution are kept, whereas for each unsuited job, a resource search query is propagated to other grid nodes in order to discover remote Ma-Gates accepting remote execution of the job.

This work is implemented within the SmartGRID[7] project, which aims at developing a flexible grid middleware supported by fully decentralized bio-inspired algorithms. Accordingly, in order to support scheduling activities, the MaGate simulator relies on a grid overlay simulator that provides services such as group communication and resource discovery. Due to the requirements of the SmartGRID project, actual implementation only considers fully decentralized peer-to-peer systems where nodes are connected over an unstructured topologies. Communication between the MaGate and overlay simulators is achieved by means of asynchronous message passing: the scheduler simulator can control the grid overlay one by requesting connection of new nodes, disconnection or crash of existing nodes, as well as by starting resource discovery queries. Currently the overlay simulator supports static overlays, as well as dynamic unstructured overlays managed by different algorithms such as BlatAnt [8], Gnutella[9], and Newscast [10].

Both the MaGate and the overlay simulator are designed and developed within the SmartGRID project, which aims at bringing a decisive increase in efficiency, robustness, and reliability regarding the volatile, dynamics, and heterogeneous grid computing infrastructure. The SmartGRID is comprised of two layers and one internal interface: the *Smart Resource Management Layer (SRML)* to support grid scheduling; the *Smart Signaling Layer (SSL)* to provide reactive resource discovery, and the *Datawarehouse Interface (DWI)* to facilitate data exchanging between SRML and SSL. Detailed description of SmartGRID can be found at [7] [11].

The remainder of the paper is organized as follows: in section 2, an overview of related work is introduced. Section 3 and Section 4 details the framework of MaGate simulator and Overlay simulator respectively, followed by a discussion on the experimental results as an illustration of its usage in Section 5. Conclusions and future work are presented in section 6.

2   Related Work

This section provides an overview of related work concerning both the scheduling simulator, as well as the grid overlay simulator.

2.1   Grid Simulator

The management of a real grid system has shown its complexity, which limits researchers' capability to test and explore ideas at the investigating stage. In order to remedy the unnecessary pain at an early phase, a simulation system is quite necessary.

GridSim. GridSim [5] is a toolkit implemented in Java, which allows parallel modeling and simulation of different grid entities, such as distributed grid users, applications, resources, schedulers, and resource brokers. It provides the facility for creating different classes of heterogeneous resources that can be aggregated by resource brokers, and mapped to job requirements.

GridSim supports modeling of uni-processor and/or multi-processors machines with time-shared and/or space-shared scheduling policies. Furthermore GridSim lets users define their own application behaviors, and supports various types of jobs, which are known as *gridlets* and are parameterized by information like MIPS, I/O, etc. A range of protocols enable the *gridlets* to be mapped on different kinds of resources.

Other salient features of GridSim toolkit include: resource time zone, special time slots for resources (weekend, holidays, etc), advance reservation, market-driven economic models, network speed specification, statistic and analyzing of GridSim actions, etc.

Alea. Alea [6] is a simulator based on GridSim, developed for the purpose of dealing with common scheduling problems in grid environment, such as heterogeneous resources and jobs, dynamic job arriving flow, etc.

Alea is a strong addition to GridSim because it brings many important and useful features including an experimental centralized grid scheduler with advanced scheduling techniques for schedule generation, support of jobs requesting single-processor and/or multi-processor, a set of separated profiles for describing job requirement and resource capability, various implemented queue based algorithms (FCS, EDF, Easy Backfilling, EDF-Backfilling), improved simulation determinism, and support of Grid Workload Format (GWF) [12].

GSSIM. GSSIM [13] is another simulation framework based on GridSim, which provides an easy-to-use grid scheduling framework for enabling simulations of a wide range of scheduling algorithms in multi-level heterogeneous grid infrastructures. GSSIM is structured with a set of flexible and replaceable plugin components, such as grid scheduling plugins, local scheduling plugins, and runtime calculation plugins. Moreover by means of a specific developed network manager, GSSIM improves the speed of grid simulations by avoiding the need to packetize large network transfers, and by providing a network-aware scheduling simulation in distributed environment.

2.2   Overlay Simulator

To simulate the underlying network connecting grid nodes, a variety of networks simulators are available [14] [15]. Although these tools provide precise discrete simulation and evaluation of network protocols, they are too low-level for the purpose of evaluating the SmartGRID approach. Accordingly, a more high-level network simulator geared toward peer-to-peer protocols was considered. In this respect, there exist different simulators that allow rapid prototyping and evaluation of peer-to-peer algorithms, both for simple membership management as well as for resource discovery.

PeerSim. PeerSim [16] is a Java simulator that provides a set of classes to ease the implementation of peer-to-peer algorithms. In order to keep the simulation process simple, PeerSim is not concerned with the transport layer. Two simulation models are provided: an event-based and a cycle-based model. As concurrency is not supported, nodes operate in a sequential order.

PlanetSim. PlanetSim [17] provides a simulation environment for overlay networks and services. The platform enables the implementation and evaluation of network services on top of different overlay algorithms, as well as the implementation of new network management protocols. Furthermore, PlanetSim allows seamless deployment on the PlanetLab[1] network for real world experiments.

AntHill. In contrast to the previously described simulators, AntHill focuses on multi-agent systems and distributed bio-inspired ant colony algorithms: software agents can migrate between peers and collaborate to solve complex tasks.

The simulator implemented within SmartGRID borrows ideas from these projects and provides an environment for the evaluation of fully distributed algorithms based both on swarm intelligence, as well as on traditional peer-to-peer protocols.

3   MaGate Simulator

In this section we introduce the MaGate simulator framework. First the design goals are presented, followed by an overview of the framework, and an in-depth discussion of its components.

---

[1] http://www.planet-lab.org/

3.1   Design Goals

The MaGate simulator is developed with goal of providing a set of easy-to-use simulated decentralized grid schedulers, which are able to interact with each other for job exchanging, collaborate with external grid services and/or simulations, and help researchers to evaluate different scheduling relevant algorithms/models under various using scenarios.

3.2   MaGate Simulator Modules

As the adopted grid scheduler by SmartGRID, the MaGate scheduler is dedicated to tackle different grid scheduling relevant events within an uniform and loosely coupled architecture, including delegating jobs with appropriate remote nodes, using dynamic resource discovery service, open structured for cooperating with external grid components, etc. The MaGate simulator addresses such goals with a modular architecture that corresponds to the real world, as illustrated in Figure 1.

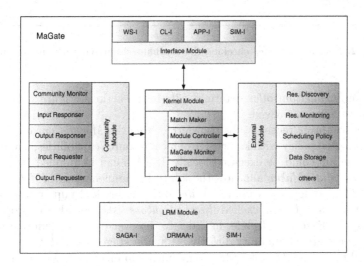

Fig. 1. MaGate Modular Architecture

Kernel Module. The Kernel Module is responsible for MaGate's self-management, which addresses various MaGate internal events, provides local scheduling decisions, and interacts with other modules to make the MaGate work as a whole. Meanwhile, the Kernel Module is also in charge of system logging and analysis.

The *ModuleController* plays an important role because it is in charge of processing the continuously incoming internal simulation events during the scheduler lifecycle, including: job submission/scheduled/completion events, community knowledge updates, system self-inspection requests. In response to these

```
...
Sim_event ev = new Sim_event();
while (Sim_system.running()) {
  super.sim_get_next(ev);
  <routine code for system/community checking>
  if (ev.get_tag() == Message.JobToMatchMaker) {
    <code to process job submission>
    continue;
  } if (ev.get_tag() == Message.ScheduleMadeByMatchMaker) {
    <code to process schedules made due to local scheduling policy>
    continue;
  } ...
  if (ev.get_tag() == GridSimTags.END_OF_SIMULATION) {
    <code to process signal of end of simulation>
    break;
  }
}
<code to finalize the simulation>
```

Fig. 2. *ModuleController* checking the continuously arriving internal events

events, the *ModuleController* determines its future actions. Figure 2 shows how self-management is achieved.

The *MatchMaker* receives jobs transferred from the *ModuleController*, evaluates the adopted policy with knowledge of local resource capabilities, and decides whether the job could be executed locally. If a job can be fulfilled by local resources, the *MatchMaker* allocates the job to the implemented *SIM-I* interface of the LRM Module; otherwise, the *MatchMaker* either looks up appropriate remote nodes from the local cached *direct neighbors list*, or sends the propagated queries to the External Module, in order to discover potential suitable remote nodes from the grid community directly. At a later stage, the *MatchMaker* filters discovered results, and invokes the Community Module to delegate corresponding jobs to the selected remote resources. The *MaGateMonitor* is used to record MaGate behavior and scheduling history for statistical purposes.

Interface Module. The Interface Module manages the interfaces for accepting job submission from multi-type local invokers, such as grid users, high level grid applications, and simulation based instances, and for giving the responses back.

The *CL-I* provides a command line based interface to receive parametrized job submission. Similarly, both the *APP-I* and the *WS-I* offer alternative approaches for receiving job submission from specific grid applications and web service based invokers respectively.

Furthermore, for the purpose of MaGate simulator validation, the *SIM-I* also accepts submission of simulated grid jobs.

Community Module. The Community Module is a vital component of the MaGate scheduler, because it mediates the interaction between different schedulers, and facilitates the work (job) exchange among the interconnected grid community. With help from the Community Module, jobs that cannot be satisfied by local resources are allowed to be delegated for remote execution. In other words, connected schedulers collaborate to construct a dynamic and interoperable grid scheduler community, namely a *Smart Resource Management Layer*. The design of the Community Module follows the suggestion of the Scheduling Instance [18].

As illustrated in Figure 3, the *OutputRequester* firstly checks whether jobs need to be delegated to remote nodes. In that case, the *OutputRequester* is responsible for searching appropriate remote MaGate schedulers based on adopted resource searching policy, and tries job delegation to each discovered remote nodes, until the delegation request is accepted. Inversely, the *InputRequester* is responsible for incoming job delegation requests, has to determine job delegation acceptance depending on the utilized community collaborative policy, and manages transfer of accepted delegated jobs to the Kernel Module for local execution.

After delegated jobs are processed, the *OutputResponser* is used to construct corresponding responses, and deliver them back to the delegation initiators. Similarly, the *InputResponser* monitors the incoming delegation response information from other grid schedulers.

The *CommunityMonitor* keeps a cached *direct neighbors list*, which is established and maintained by the interconnected resource discovery service through

```
... JobInfo fetchedJobInfo = null;
while(!this.maGate.getStorage().isEmpty_localUnsuitedJob()) {
  <code to fetch well presented jobs for delegation>
  boolean status = false;
  if(RDProtocol.equals(Message.RDFromDirectNeighbors)) {
    remoteNodes = this.maGate.getStorage().getNeighborList();
  } else if (RDProtocol.equals(Message.RDFromCommunitySearch)) {
    remoteNodes = searchRemoteMaGate(fetchedJobInfo.getJobProfile());
  } else {
    <code of other resource discovery approaches>
  }
  for(Node rNode : remoteNodes) {
    status = inputRequestToRemoteMaGate(rNode, fetchedJobInfo);
    if(status) { break; }
  }
  <code to process job delegation success/failure result>
}
```

Fig. 3. *OutputRequester* delegate local unsuited jobs

the External Module. Each member of such list mainly contains the information of remote scheduler's published profile, as well as the recent node status. In this case, each MaGate has a partial knowledge of its grid community, enabling fast resource discovery, work exchanging, load balancing and failure recovery of the entire grid.

LRM Module. The LRM Module bridges the interaction between the MaGate and existing grid infrastructure, e.g., local resource management systems. Accepted local suited jobs, from both local users and the grid community, are allocated to the interconnected local resources, and retrieved back once the process is completed. Instead of supporting all of the existing facilities, the LRM Module prefers to make use of emerging standardized API-based specifications, such as *SAGA-I* (Simple API For Grid Application) [19] and *DRMAA-I* (Distributed Resource Management Application API) [20], to support various heterogenous resources.

At current stage, in order to validate the MaGate simulator, implementation of the *SIM-I* is focused on processing simulated jobs on simulated resources.

External Module. The External Module offers a plug-in mechanism, which strengthen each MaGate scheduler instance by integrating available external grid components/services/algorithms, and makes the grid scheduler fit various usage scenarios.

The *ResourceDiscovery* is a critical component because it connects the MaGate scheduler to an existing grid community, which makes the job delegation

```
HashMap<String,Object> maGateProfile = new HashMap<String,Object>();
maGateProfile.put("os", this.maGate.getLRM().getOsType());
<code to put other resource characteristic>
this.maGate.setMaGateProfile(maGateProfile);
this.maGate.getMaGateInfra().updateProfile(maGateId, maGateProfile);
```

Fig. 4. Resource community profile publish

```
getMaGateInfrastructure().startQuery(this.maGateId, queryId, queryProfile);
this.results.put(queryId, queryProfile);
Thread.sleep(MaGateParam.timeAllowedForCommunitySearch);
SearchResult result = this.results.get(queryId);
this.results.remove(queryId);
```

Fig. 5. Resource discovery from grid community

on remote nodes to be possible. As shown in Figure 4, once a MaGate scheduler applies to join an existing grid community, its community available capability information has to be published in the meantime. Afterward, once the *ResourceDiscovery* is invoked to discover remote resources with expected characteristic, the published community profile of each arrived remote scheduler will be used for mapping and resource selection (shown in Figure 5). The *ResourceMonitoring* component works in a similar way as the *ResourceDiscovery* component, by monitoring changes in the published community profile of already contacted remote MaGate schedulers.

Besides that, the *SchedulingPolicy* offers a parameter based approach for adopting external scheduling algorithms, which follow the uniform I/O parameter schema and may be developed by other organizations. Finally, the *DataStorage* component enables the storage of MaGate's data into external storage facilities.

4 Overlay Simulator

The overlay simulator provides both membership management for grid nodes, as well as resource discovery and group communication services. The topology maintained within the simulator is fully controllable by the MaGate simulator: nodes can be connected to the network, disconnected, or forced to crash (i.e. disconnect abruptly from the network).

Although the implementation focuses on BlatAnt [8] as the main overlay management algorithm, several other are also available (for example, Gnutella[9] and Newscast [10]). BlatAnt constructs and maintains a self-structured overlay using a collaborative approach inspired by the behavior of ant colonies. The overlay is resilient to node failures, and exhibits low path distances between nodes, as well as a small number of connections between nodes.

Communication between the overlay simulator and MaGates is based on an asynchronous message passing protocol: this ensures independence between the simulators, and permits them to be executed on different computers. Each MaGate interact with a corresponding overlay node to publish its resource profile (used to match resource discovery queries), request new connections to other nodes or disconnect from a node. The interface with the MaGate simulator only exposes these high-level services, and is not tied to the actual algorithm used to manage the overlay.

Resource discovery is currently achieved using a restricted flooding algorithm. When a MaGate issues a resource discovery query the overlay node propagates the query to all of its neighbors. Each receiving node will forward the query up to a determined distance. Forwarding is stopped when a node with a profile matching the query is found: in this case a notification is sent to the requesting MaGate for each matching node found. As queries are tagged with a unique identifier, nodes will not forward queries that have already been received in the past.

5 Case Study

As an example of usage of the MaGate simulator, this section presents a reference experiment made by using the simulator, and the adopted community collaborative policies. In Subsection 5.1, the internal interaction workflow of the MaGate simulator is given. In Subsection 5.2 and 5.3, the adopted community collaborative policies are discussed as reference for future work. The configuration of the experiment is illustrated in Subsection 5.4, followed by the results discussion in Subsection 5.5.

5.1 Interaction Scenarios

Once a new MaGate scheduler instance is established within the simulation, an external resource discovery service must be interconnected for future community collaboration; meanwhile, a profile with regards to the MaGate's community capability contribution has to be published.

Afterward, the newly established MaGate receives job submission from its local users, and decides whether the job requirement could be satisfied by the local resources. If yes, the job is accepted and allocated to the local resource management system for local execution; if not, the MaGate tries to discover an appropriate remote node which matches the job requirement, and delegates the local unsuited job for remote execution.

Once a MaGate scheduler instance receives a job delegation request from the grid community, acceptance decision is made according to the adopted community policies. If such a request is acceptable, the delegated job will be preserved locally until the process is completed; if not, the reject response is delivered back to the request initiator, with optional reject reasons. Then it is the responsibility of the request initiator to decide whether another re-negoation process should be issued later, depending its the adopted community policy again.

Noteworthy that once a delegated remote job is accepted by the local MaGate instance, there is no difference between jobs submitted locally, and jobs delegated from the grid community.

5.2 Resource Discovery Policies

To delegate local unsuited jobs to appropriate remote resources, such resources have to be discovered firstly. Concerning the ecosystem of MaGate simulator, we address the problem of decentralized resource discovery by using flooding based protocols on a self-structured overlay topology maintained with the help of a bioinspired algorithm that borrows ideas from the swarm intelligence and ant colony optimization.

Two alternative approaches are evaluated in the reference experiment, and illustrated as follows:

Neighbors look-up policy. The *Neighbors* means that each MaGate scheduler instance is supposed to discover remote MaGates from a local cached *direct* *neighbors list*, which is maintained and kept up-to-date by the adopted overlay resource discovery service, regarding to the network connection status with the local MaGate.

Community search policy. The *Search* stands for each MaGate scheduler instance is responsible for propagating resource discovery queries according to the job requirement, submitting such queries to the grid community, and obtaining the return results after a certain period of waiting time. For example, the *Search100* presents the waiting time between query submission and result obtaining is 100 milliseconds.

5.3   Job Delegation (Re)Negotiation and Acceptance Rules

Many rules can be applied to determine whether a job delegation request should be accepted, as well as the subsequent behaviors. During experiments two simple rules to be the reference benchmark for the future work has been used.

Job delegation (re)negotiation rule. The *Nego* defines the maximal allowed number of times of negotiation for each individual job delegation. For example, the *Nego1* stands implies that if a job delegation is rejected by a remote MaGate, the same request should not be resent to the same remote MaGate anymore; inversely, the *Nego10* implies that a rejected delegation request is allowed to be retried with the same remote MaGate for ten times, with same or different parameters.

Job delegation acceptance rule. The *Queue* stands for the length limit of the *Community Input Queue*. Each time the host MaGate approves a job delegation request, the accepted but unprocessed remote job will be preserved in the *Community Input Queue* until the job is processed and sent back to the delegation initiator. In our experiment, for example, the *Queue5* presents that the host MaGate is able to manage at most five accepted but unprocessed remote jobs, as long as the length limit is reached, the subsequent delegation requests to the host MaGate will be rejected.

5.4   Simulation Configuration

The experiment were performed on an Intel Core Duo 2.2GHz physical machine, with 2GB RAM. In order to obtain stable values, the results were averaged from 10 repeated iterations. The experiment is done on a grid with 100 MaGates, each MaGate manages a Massive Parallel Processor System (MPP) with 64 or 128 processors. Each MaGate is supposed to receive 100 jobs submitted from the local user during 12 hours, each job may require 1 to 5 processors. the choices of operating system owned by all MPPs fall into the same distribution as the job requirement: [Linux, Windows, Mac]; similarly, the processors MIPS owned by all MPPs is configured as same as the job requirement.

Additionally, size of the *direct neighbors list* of each MaGate is 6, the number of times allowed for (re)negotiation is either 1 or 3, and length of the *Community Input Queue* is either 5 or 10.

5.5   Results and Discussion

The benefit of large scale grid computing has been verified by many researchers
[21] [22]. In our work, a new criterion titled *RJC (Rate of successfully executed
Jobs from the entire grid Community)* is proposed to demonstrate the functionalities of the MaGate simulator. The reference experiment aim at increasing the
value of *RJC*, as it represents the effectiveness of allowing local unsuited jobs
to be shared amongst different grid schedulers, from the grid's point of view.
Other criterions such as resource throughput and network workload are not yet
considered.

The behaviors of different scenarios in a 100-MaGate community illustrated
in Figure 6.

The *Local* represents a reference scenario where no jobs sharing between Ma-
Gate scheduler instances is allowed. If a locally submitted job cannot be fulfilled
by the local resource, it is considered as a *local unsuited job* and marked as failure. Considering that each MaGate manages one MPP machine with a single
operating system, and the submitted jobs vary their operating system requirements from an uniform three-option distribution, in average each MaGate could
only process 1/3 locally submitted jobs on its local resource. Conversely, considering that the choices of operating system owned by all MPPs within the grid
community fall into the same distribution as job requirements, it is expected
that for each individual local unsuited job an average of 1/3 of the MaGates of
the entire grid community has the expected capabilities to accept them.

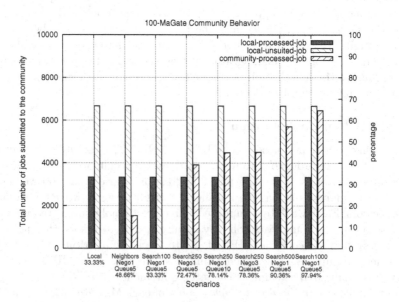

Fig. 6. Grid community of 100 MaGates

Next, as presented by scenario *Neighbor-Nego1-Queue5*, if the *Neighbors Look-up Policy* is adopted as the resource discovery approach, it is evident that useful remote MaGates can be discovered sometimes when needed by job delegation requests. In this case, the *RJC* has been improved by approximate 15%.

An alternative way of seeking remote MaGates for job delegation is the *Community Search Policy*. It is to be expected that if appropriate remote MaGates exist, are connected within the same community, are represented properly, and are pproved to be publicly available by their community policies, the corresponding resource discovery queries will be matched within a reasonable time delay. However, as shown in scenario *Search100-Nego1-Queue5*, if the waiting time is too limited, for example 100 milliseconds, no remote MaGates can be discovered, which makes no difference in the obtained *RJC*.

If the waiting time allowed for *Community Search Policy* is increased a little, such as 250 mili-seconds by scenario *Search250-Nego1-Queue5*, and 500 milliseconds by scenario *Search500-Nego1-Queue5*, discovery becomes more successful, and the *RJC* is improved by 39.14% and 57.03% respectively.

Additionally, results illustrated in scenario *Search250-Nego1-Queue10* and *Search250-Nego3-Queue5* demonstrate that even within the same waiting time for the *Community Search Policy*, the *RJC* can be still improved by utilizing various job delegation related rules, such as increased times for (re)negotiation and expanded length limit of the *Community Input Queue*.

Finally, it is noteworthy that allowing enough waiting time for resource discovery using the *Community Search Policy*, as shown by scenario *Search1000-Nego1-Queue5*, is a necessary condition to achieve an *RJC* of 100%. Nonetheless, failure to obtain results might still be possible either because of limits of the restricted flooding algorithm used by the Overlay simulator, or because candidate remote MaGates that may already reached their length limit of the *Community Input Queue* and have not been released during the delegation waiting period.

6   Conclusion and Future Work

In this paper, we presented the MaGate simulator as a grid simulation environment. The MaGate simulator is composed of different modules, and aims at providing a simulation based implementation for the MaGate scheduler, an interoperable decentralized grid scheduler used within the SmartGRID project [7], and dedicates to cooperate with each other to provide intelligent scheduling for the scope of serving the grid community as a whole, not just for a single grid node. Moreover the simulator itself can be easily extended, and adopted for evaluating newly developed decentralized scheduling algorithms, models, or workflows. An overlay simulator is employed by the MaGate simulator, to provide services such as group communication and resource discovery on fully decentralized peer-to-peer network.

As an example, two resource discovery polices, along with another two job delegation (re)negotiation and acceptance rules have been used as reference scenarios, and the validated results have shown the use of a functionally ready grid scheduler simulator.

Future work will focus on the the extension of the simulator with an advanced Community Module supporting web services technology (especially the WS-Agreement specification [23]), as well as better support to other existing local scheduling algorithms. Furthermore, a study of an automatic mechanism to dynamically generate user customized community collaborative policies will be carried out, in order to evaluate all the different parameters that can be used to generate various community collaborative policies. This work our may bring increased flexibility and adaptability in grid scheduling.

Acknowledgements

MaGate simulator is developed within SmartGRID project, a collaborative work led by PAI group[2] from University of Fribourg, and GridGroup[3] fromUniversity of Applied Sciences Western Switzerland (Fribourg). This work is supported by the Swiss Hasler Foundation[4], in the framework of the ManCom Initiative (ManCom for Managing Complexity of Information and Communication Systems), project Nr. 2122.

References

1. Foster, I., Kesselman, C., Tuecke, S.: The Anatomy of the Grid: Enabling Scalable Virtual Organizations. International Journal of High Performance Computing Applications 15(3), 200 (2001)
2. Satyanarayanan, M.: Pervasive computing: vision and challenges. IEEE Personal Communications, [see also IEEE Wireless Communications] 8(4), 10–17 (2001)
3. Milojicic, D., Kalogeraki, V., Lukose, R., Nagaraja, K., Pruyne, J., Richard, B., Rollins, S., Xu, Z.: Peer-to-Peer Computing. HP Laboratories Palo Alto (March 2002)
4. Schwiegelshohn, U., Yahyapour, R.: Attributes for communication between scheduling instances. Global Grid Forum, GGF (December 2001)
5. Buyya, R., Murshed, M.: GridSim: a toolkit for the modeling and simulation of distributed resource management and scheduling for Grid computing. Concurrency and Computation: Practice and Experience 14(13-15), 1175–1220 (2002)
6. Klusacek, D., Matyska, L., Rudova, H.: Alea-Grid Scheduling Simulation Environment. In: Wyrzykowski, R., Dongarra, J., Karczewski, K., Wasniewski, J. (eds.) PPAM 2007. LNCS, vol. 4967, pp. 1029–1038. Springer, Heidelberg (2008)
7. Huang, Y., Brocco, A., Kuonen, P., Courant, M., Hirsbrunner, B.: SmartGRID: A Fully Decentralized Grid Scheduling Framework Supported by Swarm Intelligence. In: Seventh International Conference on Grid and Cooperative Computing, 2008. GCC 2008, China, pp. 160–168. IEEE Computer Society, Los Alamitos (2008)

---

[2] http://diuf.unifr.ch/pai/
[3] http://gridgroup.tic.hefr.ch/
[4] http://www.haslerstiftung.ch/

8. Brocco, A., Frapolli, F., Hirsbrunner, B.: Bounded diameter overlay construction: A self organized approach. In: IEEE Swarm Intelligence Symposium, SIS 2009. IEEE, Los Alamitos (2009)
9. Ripeanu, M., Foster, I.: Peer-to-peer architecture case study: Gnutella network. In: First Conference on Peer-to-peer Computing, Sweden, pp. 99–100. IEEE Computer Press, Los Alamitos (2001)
10. Jelasity, M., van Steen, M.: Large-scale newscast computing on the internet. Technical Report IR-503, Vrije Universiteit Amsterdam, Department of Computer Science, Amsterdam, The Netherlands (October 2002)
11. Brocco, A., Hirsbrunner, B., Courant, M.: A modular middleware for high-level dynamic network management. In: Proceedings of the 1st workshop on Middleware-application interaction: in conjunction with Euro-Sys 2007, pp. 21–24. ACM Press, New York (2007)
12. GridWorkloadsArchive: http://gwa.ewi.tudelft.nl/pmwiki/
13. Kurowski, K., Nabrzyski, J., Oleksiak, A., Weglarz, J.: Grid scheduling simulations with GSSIM. In: 3rd Workshop on Scheduling and Resource Management for Parallel and Distributed Systems, Proceedings of the 13th International Conference on Parallel and Distributed Systems, Hsinchu, Taiwan (2007)
14. Henderson, T., Lacage, M., Riley, G.: Network simulations with the ns-3 simulator. Demo paper at ACM SIGCOMM 2008 (2008)
15. Mathieu Lacage, T.R.H.: Yet another network simulator. In: WNS2 2006: Proceeding from the 2006 workshop on ns-2: the IP network simulator, p. 12. ACM, New York (2006)
16. Jelasity, M., Montresor, A., Jesi, G.P., Voulgaris, S.: The Peersim simulator, http://peersim.sf.net
17. García, P., Pairot, C., Mondéjar, R., Pujol, J., Tejedor, H., Rallo, R.: Planetsim: A new overlay network simulation framework. Software Engineering and Middleware, 123–136 (2005)
18. Tonellotto, N., Wieder, P., Yahyapour, R.: A proposal for a generic grid scheduling architecture. In: Integrated Research in Grid Computing Workshop, Greece, pp. 337–346. Springer, Heidelberg (2005)
19. Goodale, T., Jha, S., Kaiser, H., Kielmann, T., Kleijer, P., von Laszewski, G., Lee, C., Merzky, A., Rajic, H., Shalf, J.: SAGA: A Simple API for Grid Applications. High-level application programming on the Grid. Computational Methods in Science and Technology 12(1), 7–20 (2006)
20. Troger, P., Rajic, H., Haas, A., Domagalski, P.: Standardization of an API for Distributed Resource Management Systems. In: CCGRID 2007: Proceedings of the Seventh IEEE International Symposium on Cluster Computing and the Grid, pp. 619–626. IEEE Computer Society, Washington (2007)
21. Ernemann, C., Hamscher, V., Yahyapour, R.: Benefits of global grid computing for job scheduling. In: Fifth IEEE/ACM International Workshop on Grid Computing, Pittsburgh, USA, pp. 374–379. IEEE Press, Los Alamitos (2004)
22. Ernemann, C., Hamscher, V., Schwiegelshohn, U., Yahyapour, R., Streit, A.: On Advantages of Grid Computing for Parallel Job Scheduling. In: 2nd IEEE International Symposium on Cluster Computing and the Grid (CC-GRID 2002), Berlin, Germany, pp. 39–46. IEEE Press, Los Alamitos (2002)
23. Andrieux, A., Czajkowski, K., Dan, A., Keahey, K., Ludwig, H., Pruyne, J., Rofrano, J., Tuecke, S., Xu, M.: Web Services Agreement Specification (WS-Agreement). Technical report, Open Grid Forum, USA (2004)

A Distributed Shared Memory Architecture for Occasionally Connected Mobile Environments*

Christophe Schneble[1], Thomas Seidmann[2], and Hansjörg Huser[1]

[1] Institute for Networked Systems,
University of Applied Science Rapperswil, Switzerland
{christophe.schneble,hhuser}@hsr.ch
[2] Cdot AG, Altishofen (LU), Switzerland
thomas.seidmann@cdot.ch

Abstract. In this paper we present a distributed cache architecture for occasionally connected systems. The system is realised using an underlying P2P-infrastructure. The gridNet Framework provides a transparent interface for working with distributed cache-objects. The paper also contains a description of an envisioned example application running on top of the GridNet framework.

Keywords: Distributed Shared Memory, object cache, peer to peer, P2P, healthcare, occasionally connected systems, mobile environments, mobile grids.

1 Introduction

Peer-to-peer (P2P) networks are very popular nowadays. The peer-to-peer model has been widely used on file-sharing applications such as *Bittorent* [2] or *Gnutella* [1]. Those systems have proved the usage of peer-to-peer in an highly dynamic and large-scale setting. However, they share immutable files, thus dealing only with read-only data. *Distributed Shared Memory Systems (DSM-Systems)* have been well studied over the past years, and the problem of sharing mutable data in distributed environments has thereby been addressed. A large number of consistency models and their protocols have been presented [6,7,10,11,14,19]. However, most of those systems use either a well-defined static topology in which reconfiguration events occur infrequently or they need at least one coordinator to handle change and transaction management.

In this paper we present gridNet, a distributed shared memory architecture that combines the advantages of the P2P-Model with the notion of a shared memory. The gridNet Framework is intended for occasionally connected systems. Thus dealing in an environment of mobile clients where a highly dynamic topology is of main concern. The Framework provides programmers with a simple and easy-to-use programming interface, thus letting developers work like on

---

* This work was partially founded by the Swiss Innovation Promotion Agency CTI (KTI) within the project Cdot.gridNET: Grid-Computing Framework for distributed and mobile Applications KTI P-Nr:9540.1.

Y. Dou, R. Gruber, and J. Joller (Eds.): APPT 2009, LNCS 5737, pp. 288–301, 2009.
© Springer-Verlag Berlin Heidelberg 2009

local objects. The Framework is being developed using Microsoft's .Net Framework. The *Peer Channel* and its underlying *Peer Name Resolution Protocol*[4], which is provided by the *Windows Communication Foundation (WCF)*, is used for P2P communication. Querying for objects can be achieved by sending a *LINQ* Query [3] out to the wire.

The rest of this paper is organised as follows: Related work in this area is presented in section 2; the novel DSM approach is presented in section 3; some typical use cases will be discussed in section 4; the architectural implementation is outlined in section 5; the API is presented in section 6; and finally conclusions and future work are discussed in section 7.

2   Related Work

2.1   General Considerations

The grid computing infrastructure was already implemented in an earlier project state [9]. This infrastructure consists at each node of a job queue, a resource chooser, and a communication framework. The whole grid infrastructure works as a fully distributed peer-to-peer application, thus allowing a highly flexible topology.

There are various approaches to the architecture and design of cache systems for computing grids both in academia and industry. Juxmem [5] applies distributed shared memory (DSM) principles to object cache systems, yet it is more focused on cluster-like systems and precludes permanent accessibility of the participating nodes. Globe [17] (pp 472), an object-based distributed system, uses the entry consistency model for replication, which by its nature also requires the participating nodes to be connected.

Numerous database system vendors try to position their products as cache components for grid systems, namely Oracle. The common characteristic in this case is the relational (n-tuple)-based nature of these systems, which poses a well known impedance mismatch between classes (of objects) and relational tables. On the other hand, such systems usually cope well with occasionally connected scenarios.

None of cache systems studied actually fulfils the requirements we have postulated, namely:

- Replaceable consistency model and coherence protocol,
- Support for occasionally connected systems,
- Object-based nature,
- Full distribution (without any centralised components).

2.2   P2P-Systems

Three major characteristics of a peer-to-peer Network can be identified as follows:

- Each node provides both client and server functionality and in that way can act as either provider or consumer of services or data.
- *Decentralisation* : there is no central coordinating authority for the organisation of the network or the use of resources and communication between the peers in the network.
- *Autonomy* : Each node can autonomously determine when and to what extent it makes its resources available.

A great variety of P2P frameworks have been developed such as Pastry and Chord [13]. Common to all those frameworks is the DHT approach for name resolution and the use of a seed server for getting an initial set of neighbour nodes. This is also true in the PeerChannel architecture of the .Net Framework, which will be outlined in the following paragraph.

WCF Peer Channel. Our P2P-Infrastructure uses the WCF Peer Channel provided by the Microsoft .Net Framework 3.5. The Peer Channel enables scalable message delivery. Before sending messages to the mesh, a node needs to discover its peer neighbours. This is achieved either by using a self-implemented resolver or the provided Peer Name Resolution Protocol *(PNRP)* [4]. Based on IPv6, the PNR Protocol enables joining the mesh over the whole Internet. A *PNRP node* can participate in one or more clouds. A cloud is a group of nodes that can communicate with one another to resolve names into addresses. Each node maintains a cache of *PNRP* ID-to-endpoint mappings. A node is required

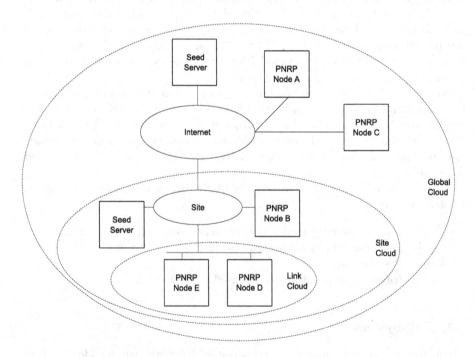

Fig. 1. PNRP-Cloud Hierarchy

to cache its leaf set, plus any other it knows of. A cloud has a scope property that may be *Global, Site Local* or *Link Local* as illustrated in Figure 1. Communication between nodes never crosses from one cloud to another. Cloud discovery (the process by which a node outside the cloud finds existing nodes within the cloud) is different at different scope levels. To discover nodes on the same link (*Link local*) a node uses the *Simple Service Discovery Protocol* (*SSDP*, as specified by the *UPnP Architecture*) [4]. If there are no other nodes in the cloud that exist on the node's link then the discovery mechanism uses a seed server. To discover nodes in the global cloud (*Global*) a node contacts one of the well-known seed servers. Discovery at the site level (*Site local*) is achieved by contacting a seed server whose address can be supplied either manually, by configuration, or by an application.

2.3   DSM Systems

Over the last decades numerous research activities have been carried out in the area of Distributed Shared Memory (DSM) [15]. However, this architectural element of distributed computing systems has not thus far become mainstream. The only applications of DSM that have surfaced until now are those of (distributed) caches of distributed object systems and distributed file systems, mainly when replication comes into play [16] [8]. On the other hand, such cache systems are very often designed and built using simplified semantics compared to what is involved int the design of DSM systems. For example, some of them do not include a coherence protocol at all: Neither write-invalidate nor write-update messages are sent upon performing write operation to shared objects. Instead they simply rely on lifetimes expressed as (global) time spans after whose expiry the object state somehow gets refreshed upon the next access. Such an approach is clearly insufficient in situations where full replication (multiple readers and multiple writers, MRMW) is needed. In our research we have committed ourselves to cache systems with real DSM semantics. A large number of consistency models and their protocols have been developed over the last decade [6,7,10,11,14,19] and play an important role in designing a DSM-System.

2.4   The Basic Gossip Protocol

One particularly interesting species of coherence protocols, used mainly in distributed file systems for keeping replicas up-to-date, is the *gossip* protocol [17] (pp 170). These algorithms belong to a broader family of *epidemic* protocols very well suited for fast and reliable spreading of information within very large-scale distributed systems. The primary purpose of gossip protocols is to support high availability in an environment where failures of nodes are likely and reliable multicast of updates is impractical or impossible. The simplest form of a gossip protocol is the basic gossip protocol [8], which uses Lamport's logical clock timestamps for versioning update messages while maintaining an open group of participants and *overwrite* semantics for updates (although it is desirable to control the granularity of these overwrite updates, as depicted in section 5.3).

We decided to apply a modified basic gossip protocol and to use the underlying peer-to-peer network in order to deliver write-update messages.

3   A Novel DSM-Approach for Occasionally Connected Systems

A DSM system's most important building blocks are the *consistency model* and *coherence protocol*. The coherence protocol can be understood to implement the consistency model. We do not wish to hard-wire one particular consistency model into the cache implementation but rather to define clear interfaces and keep the consistency model pluggable (see section 5.3).

All employed algorithms and protocols must be fully distributed. This precludes the use of some consistency models based on synchronisation variables constituting a kind of critical section that must be respected by all participants. In occasionally connected systems (OCS) such a requirement would be impossible to achieve.

Another important design concept of our cache system is the desired lack of any central component or element, which could otherwise become a single point of failure, as well as the occasionally connected nature of participating nodes. However when the PNR Protocol is used in global mode at least one seed Server must be specified which may be clustered, thus reducing the chance of a single point of failure. Using PNRP on a local network eliminates a single point of failure as cloud discovery is achieved using the SSDP protocol [4].

Security plays an important role in our system. Standard claim-based authentication mechanism such as SAML tokens will be used for authentication.

The proposed DSM-System consists of an unlimited number of Nodes interconnected with the already mentioned peer-channel provided by the Microsoft .NET Framework. As we are dealing with an occasionally connected system each node may join or leave the mesh at will. During an offline phase, a node may modify its local dataset or a synchronised one. Those changes will be propagated upon reconnect, based on a modified basic gossip protocol, to be described later.

4   Application Example

Healthcare's data sovereignty is still dedicated to the healthcare-provider (hospital, home for the aged, doctor). Thus this is a case of highly distributed data. For example getting all data about a patient involves querying all participants data stores. Even inside an organisation, data may be distributed over various nodes or data stores. This implies the need for a distributed grid infrastructure. Our application example will prove the usage of our grid.Net Framework in such a complex environment. An excerpt of some of the following scenarios will be used in our application example.

4.1 Activity Recording

Doctors or nurses record their activities involving medical treatments to the electronic patient record which is synchronised to the local node before the users goes offline. We assume that the client will be disconnected during activity recording. Upon reconnect, the recorded activities are propagated to the mesh. Working on the same patient record is allowed and supported.

4.2 Benchmarking

Getting statistics about treatments involves all participating nodes. Thus a query is formulated and sent to the mesh. The nodes evaluate the query and send back an aggregated result.

4.3 GetPatientData

A doctor treating a patient's disease wants to access all data available on the mesh. Thus, he sends a request for a specified patient. It may be necessary for a third party to grant access to the data. However, it may be necessary to access all data in case of an emergency. For such a case access rules will be provided.(see [18]).

5 Architectural Implementation

This section is organised as follows: In section 5.1 the main building-blocks of our cache architecture shall be presented and described. In section 5.2 our implementation of a *cacheable object* shall be outlined. Section 5.3 describes the consistency and coherence protocol. The change tracking and notification is described in section 5.4. In section 5.5 different message-types as well as their triggering based on cache operations shall be discussed. In section 5.6 we reason about our *conflict handling mechanism*. Section 5.7 finally presents the *finite state machine* of cacheable objects.

5.1 System Overview

Every node consists of the same components. However, based on the different roles (replier or requester) a node is currently assigned to, different components will be used to fulfil the operation. As depicted in Figure 2 the main components are the following

- Local Object Cache
- Query Processor
- Coordinator
- Persistence Layer (Log- and Application-Store)
- Log
- Job Engine

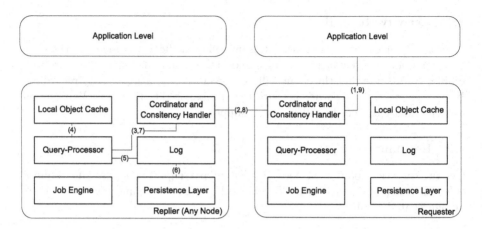

Fig. 2. Main-Cache-Entities (Connecting lines depecit the chronology of the usage of components when querying for an Object)

Query Processor. The *Query-Processor* handles any incoming *query-message*. It is responsible for getting an object out of the *Persistence Layer*, or the *Local Object Cache*, as well as returning all log entries of the queried object.

Persistence Layer. The *Persistence Layer* stores all application data.

Local Object Cache. Currently active objects are stored in a *local memory object cache*, thus allowing efficient access.

Coordinator and Consitency Handler. The Coordinator is responsible for handling requests from the application layer as well as handling incoming messages from other nodes. It takes the appropriate actions based on the role the node is in for handling an operation. The Coordinator also consists of a queue that stores all write update messages that cannot be sent when the node is offline (see also Section 5.5). Another part of the coordinator is the pluggable (and thus replaceable) module of the consistency handler. This module's task is to implement the consistency model and coherence protocol, as will be explained in section 5.3.

Log. The Log stores every write update message. It is a central component as the consistency of all object states relies on the persitent log entries. Whenever a node crashes the object states have to be reconstructed by querying the log, using a *bootstrapping mechanism*.

Job Engine. The job engine executes jobs sent by another node and returns the result to the initiator.

5.2   Cacheable Objects

A cacheable object is a serialisable plain-old CLR object. Every cacheable object is identified by a system-wide unique identifier. Furthermore, each object contains a version number (scalar logical clock) identifying its current version. Operation on variables that may alter any value within an object are conducted over Properties. This allows a lightweight change tracking mechanism as described in section 5.4. The level of granularity can be set at different levels as described below.

5.3   Consistency and Coherence Protocol

The goal of our system is to allow grid applications to access data in a distributed environment. In such a system data is mutable and can be read and updated by multiple peer nodes in a sequential manner or at the same time. When a node modifies data, the consistency protocol is in charge of updating or invalidating the modified object to avoid returning invalid data. We provide an extensible and exchangeable consistency protocol allowing one to choose between different consistency models. Currently the sequential and causal consistency models are supported. Other advanced consistency models may be supported in the future.

Sequential consitency. Sequential consitency guarantees that changes to any object are seen by all nodes in the same order. Sequential consitency is weaker then strict consitency, which assumes ordering by (global) physical time (which actually doesn't exist in distributed systems).

Causal consitency. Weakens the notion of sequential consitency in that it makes distinction between events that are potentially causally related and those that are not. Only causally related operations must be seen by all nodes in the same order, whereas causally unrelated can be observed by differemt nodes in any order.

The cache system architecture includes the concept of a pluggable consistency model and its corresponding coherence protocol, called consistency handler. This is achieved by submitting the object version of a newly received write-update message and the current object version to the consistency handler. The consistency handler keeps a list of pending updates and decides in which order these get applied based on comparison of object versions.

5.4   Change Tracking and Notification

With the use of an event notification mechanism a lightweight change-tracking mechanism can be implemented without the use of complex interception. The level of granularity (whole object/ fields, members) can be configured for each cacheable object type. Setting the granularity level influences how the consistency model will handle updates on objects. Setting the level to *object granularity* will replace one object state with the newer one. This can be a problem if two nodes propagate updates on the same object resulting in an equal version number. Here is where *tie breaking* criteria come into operation. On the other hand, setting the level to *field granularity* allows merging the field and members of two objects with the same version if no conflicts are detected in the comparison of the change-vector.

Change Vector. The change vector is the Boolean representation of changes of the data on an object's properties and members. Modification of a property triggers changing the Boolean value of at specified dimension of the vector. This allows a performant conflict checking of two write update messages (with the same object ID and version number).

5.5   Message Handling

Modifying, adding, and querying for an object triggers a message. The following subsections present a brief explanation of each message type. These messages are the main component of our modified basic gossip protocol. Messages are sent through a flooding mechanism. This in fact does not ensure reliable message delivery to all nodes in the mesh. Ladin et al. [12] ensure reliable message delivery by sending an acknowledgment message upon arrival of the *write update message* so that the sender can keep track of whether or not all nodes received the *write update message*. This architecture assumes that the node knows the entire mesh topology even if some nodes are disconnected. Let us consider the sending of a *write update message*. We cannot guarantee that the Message arrives at all nodes: a node may be broken or in an offline state. Thus, the task of receiving changes is transferred to the node by having it get all changes which occurred during its offline phase, upon reconnecting to the mesh.

Write Update Message. The message consists of the following set <NodeID, ObjectID, ObjectVersion, ObjectState, Change Vectors>. Whenever a cacheable object is modified, or added, a *write update message* is sent onto the wire to notify the resulting nodes about changes. Modification occurring during an offline phase on the same object would result in as many messages as alternations in the object's values. Consider that the node is an in offline state and the object to be modified has field granularity then multiple changes would result in multiple write update messages. If comparison of the change vectors does not detect a conflict , then the messages can be compacted into one *write update message*.

Query Message. Querying the grid for an object triggers the sending of a *query message*. The result of a *query message* returns a cacheable object and the corresponding object log. The requester (here sender of the query-message) only accepts responses within a well-defined time span since the *query message* was sent. The enquiring node may obtain multiple responses or it may not receive any response. Possible reasons for this include following:

- The object is not present or the node holding the object is in an offline state.
- The node is working on an offline copy,
- The node is working on a completely new object.

Adding an Object to the Cache. Adding an object to the cache is done by calling the update method. Each cacheable object is assigned a unique identifier. Adding the object triggers the sending of a *write update message*.

5.6   Conflict-Handling Mechanism

Conflicts are the result of the sending of at least two *write update messages* with the same version number and object ID. If the granularity-level is set to field granularity, conflicts may be resolved by merging the two objects together. A failing match would result in a conflict. Resolving conflicts requires an overall agreement of all nodes on a tie-breaking criterion. The message to be applied when a conflict is detected is computed by the tie-breaking algorithm.

Tie-Breaking Criteria and -Algorithm. The tie-breaking criteria used by the tie-breaking-algorithm should be configurable. Currently the messages with the highest node ID will be applied in case of conflicting write update messages. Future implementations could for example implement a quorum-consensus or a home-based approach[19].

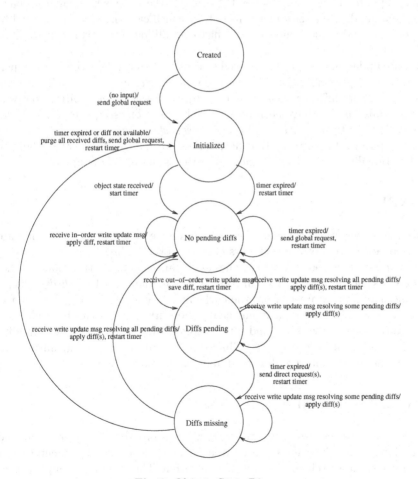

Fig. 3. Objects State Diagram

5.7   Finite State Machine of Cached Objects

Figure 3 represents the Mealy state machine of an object. As illustrated, an object can be in five states during its life cycle, which are *created, initialised, no pending diffs, diffs pending, diffs missing*. When an object is created a *global request message* is sent, requesting other nodes for the state of the newly created object (in case any other node has it) and a timer is started. The object state is then changed to *initialised*.

After either this timer has expired or a write update message answering the object state query has been received, the state is changed to *no pending diffs*. This state is maintained if any write update messages are received in correct order (updates can be applied then) or the timer expires again, in which case it is restarted and a global request message is sent to query changes.

If however the received message is out of order, the state of the object is changed to *pending diffs* and another timer is started. This state is maintained until an update arrives that resolves the conflict (the state is then changed back to no pending diffs) or the timer runs out, in which case the state is changed to *diffs missing* and a query message is sent to get all log entries corresponding to the object.

If write update messages are received that resolve all conflicts the state is then changed to *no pending diffs*; otherwise, the object state stays in *diffs missing*. In any case, the diffs are applied to the object. If the timer expires, however, before all missing diffs have been received, all received messages are purged, the state is changed to *initialised*, and a *global request message* is sent.

It is important to point out that during all state changes the local availability and functionality of the shared (cached) object is not at all disrupted.

6   API

Table 1 provides an overview of the cache interface. We agree on the semantic as proposed by most of the cache systems. However dealing with OCS-systems (occasionally connected systems) implies an enhancement over traditional cache-systems. As shown in Table 1 we introduced the method *GetAndScheduleQuery*. This method gets an object from the cache and a timer is started to query the mesh (at a specified interval) about changes occurring. This can be useful if a node goes temporarily offline and after reconnecting wants to get new modification which occurred during the offline-Phase. Implications of our finite state machine for the design were discussed above in section 5.7.

7   Conclusion and Future Work

The described cache system constitutes a work in progress: We have completed the design and architecture and are presently at work on the implementation of the base system as well as a reference application. The design and implementation of the job scheduling system as a separate part of the whole project gives

Table 1. API-Interfaces

Interface	Description
Add(Object,GUID)	Adds the object with the specified unique identifier to the cache.
Get(CacheableObject, Timeout)	Gets an object that matches the fields of the assigned prototype-object. [a]
Get(GUID,Timeout)	Retrieves the object with the specified GUID.
Get(LinqQuery,Timeout)	Retrieves an IEnumerable of objects as specified in by the LINQ-query.
GetAndScheduleQuery(CacheableObject, Timeout,Interval)	Gets an object that matches the fields of the assigned prototype-object. Object is added to a queue and updated periodically.
GetAndScheduleQuery(GUID,Timeout, Interval)	Retrieves the object with the specified GUID. Object is added to a queue and updated periodically.
Put(CachableObject)	Adds the modified object to the cache. This method triggers sending a write-update-message.
GetUpdateLog(CachableObject)	Retrieves the change-log of the specified object.
GetUpdateLog(CachableObject, Revision)	Retrieves the change-log of the specified object since the specified version.

[a] A prototype-object is an instance of an object that should be retrieved from the cache. Along with the specified fields filled out that must match.

us confidence that the choice of the underlying technology was sound and that the peer network infrastructure we are using fulfils our needs. In addition, we can conclude that the job scheduling, control, and monitoring we designed and implemented works as desired.

The next logical step is proof-of-concept of our grid cache design by implementing the base system along with a reference application. Part of this is also design of the security subsystem used both within the grid as well as for interfacing with it. Although outside the scope of this paper, the security subsystem will be claims-based; that is, all messages within the grid system will carry tokens containing appropriate claim sets that will be evaluated for authentication and authorisation purposes.

One major issue we will have to tackle in the near future is system testing of a large-scale distributed system using the technology we develop. Even though we are applying a test-drive approach by means of unit testing during development, this is not sufficient for a system test. For this reason we are considering and evaluating simulation techniques prior to and as a first step in system-testing real distributed systems.

References

1. The annotated gnutella protocol specification v0.4.,
   `http://rfc-gnutella.sourceforge.net/developer/stable/index.html`
2. Bittorent protocol specification (2009),
   `http://www.bittorrent.org/beps/bep0003.html`
3. The linq project (2009),
   `http://msdn.microsoft.com/en-us/vbasic/aa904594.aspx`
4. Peer name resolution protocol (pnrp) version 4.0 specification (2009),
   `http://download.microsoft.com/download/a/e/6/`
   `ae6e4142-aa58-45c6-8dcf-a657e5900cd3/MS-PNRP.pdf`
5. Antoniu, G., Bougé, L., Jan, M.: Juxmem: An adaptive supportive platform for data sharing on the grid. Scalable Computing: Practice and Experience 6(33), 43–45 (2005)
6. Bershad, B.N., Zekauskas, M.J., Sawdon, W.A.: The midway distributed shared memory system, February 1993, pp. 528–537 (1993)
7. Carter, J.B., Bennett, J.K., Zwaenepoel, W.: Implementation and performance of munin. In: SOSP 1991: Proceedings of the thirteenth ACM symposium on Operating systems principles, pp. 152–164. ACM, New York (1991)
8. Chow, R., Johnson, T.: Distributed Operating Systems & Algorithms. Addison Wesley Longman, Inc., Amsterdam (1997)
9. Thomas Corbat and Lukas Felber. Cdot.gridnet: Internal working paper (2009)
10. Gharachorloo, K., Lenoski, D., Laudon, J., Gibbons, P., Gupta, A., Hennessy, J.: Memory consistency and event ordering in scalable shared-memory multiprocessors, May 1990, pp. 15–26 (1990)
11. Iftode, L., Singh, J.P., Li, K.: Scope consistency: A bridge between release consistency and entry consistency. In: Proceedings of the 8th Annual ACM Symposium on Parallel Algorithms and Architectures, pp. 277–287 (1996)
12. Ladin, R., Liskov, B., Shrira, L., Ghemawat, S.: Lazy replication: Exploiting the semantics of distributed services. In: IEEE Computer Society Technical Committee on Operating Systems and Application Environments, pp. 43–57. IEEE Computer Society, Los Alamitos (1990)
13. Liben-Nowell, D., Balakrishnan, H., Karger, D.: Analysis of the evolution of peer-to-peer systems. In: PODC 2002: Proceedings of the twenty-first annual symposium on Principles of distributed computing, pp. 233–242. ACM, New York (2002)
14. Protic, J., Tomasevic, M., Milutinovic, V.: Distributed shared memory: concepts and systems. IEEE Parallel & Distributed Technology: Systems & Applications 4(2), 63–71 (summer 1996)
15. Seidmann, T.: Distributed Shared Memory in Modern Operating Systems. PhD thesis, Slovak University of Technology in Bratislava (2004)

16. Tanenbaum, A.S.: Distributed Operating Systems. Prentice Hall, Inc., Englewood Cliffs (1995)
17. Tanenbaum, A.S., van Steen, M.: Distributed System, Principles and Paradigms, 2nd edn. Pearson Education, Inc., Upper Saddle River (2007)
18. Moses, E.T.: Xacml 2.0 rsa 2008 interop scenarios walk through - version 0.7 (2009), http://xml.coverpages.org/RSA-UseCasesGuideV7-20081020.pdf
19. Zhou, Y., Iftode, L., Li, K.: Performance evaluation of two home-based lazy release consistency protocols for shared virtual memory systems. SIGOPS Oper. Syst. Rev. 30(SI), 75–88 (1996)

Time-Adaptive Vertical Handoff Triggering Methods for Heterogeneous Systems*

Qingyang Song, Zhongfeng Wen, Xingwei Wang, Lei Guo, and Ruiyun Yu

Department of Information Science and Engineering, Northeastern University,
Shenyang, China

Abstract. Vertical handoff decision is an important process in heterogeneous systems. In order to find an appropriate time to trigger a handoff, deciding a stability period before performing the handoff has been studied formerly. In this paper, we introduce the definition of the residence time of a handoff zone (HZ) into the stability period decision method. Then two algorithms, Stability Period Decision Scheme with HZ Residence Time (SPDRT) and Stability Period Decision Scheme Based on Fuzzy Logic (SPDFL), are proposed to adjust the stability period dynamically. Moreover, we apply the two schemes to solve the handoff call queuing problem. Simulation results show that the proposed methods can decrease handoff call dropping rate effectively and adjust the stability period intelligently and sensibly.

1 Introduction

With the prevalent development of the current third-generation (3G) networks, the heterogeneous wireless networks, called next-generation networks (NGN) or fourth-generation (4G) networks [1] coordinating many different types of networks such as Wireless Local Area Networks (WLAN), Wireless Metropolitan Area Networks (WMAN) and 3G Cellular Networks (WWAN) are going to appear. Nowadays, there is an obvious trend to integrate the 3G Cellular Networks and WLANs. The 3G Cellular Networks will provide the limited bandwidth and expensive service price but universal coverage as an upper layer. At the same time, the WLAN will offer high-speed and low-cost data services within limited coverage areas as a lower layer. The integration of all kinds of networks enables users to obtain always-best-connected (ABC) services [2] at any time and in any location.

In all radio technologies of heterogeneous networks, vertical handoff is a challenging problem and has been studied widely. The vertical handoff is the process of maintaining the communication connections between the mobile terminal (MT)

---

* This work is supported by the National Natural Science Foundation of China under Grant No. 60673159, No. 70671020 and No. 60802023; the Key Project of Chinese Ministry of Education under Grant No. 108040; the National High-Tech Research and Development Plan of China under Grant No. 2007AA041201; Specialized Research Fund for the Doctoral Program of Higher Education under Grant No. 20060145012, No. 20070145017 and No. 20070145096.

Y. Dou, R. Gruber, and J. Joller (Eds.): APPT 2009, LNCS 5737, pp. 302–312, 2009.
© Springer-Verlag Berlin Heidelberg 2009

and systems when a user is roaming in different types of networks [3], which includes three steps: system discovery, handoff decision, and handoff execution [4]. The second step is especially important. For vertical handoff decision algorithms, there are three directions mainly referred in the field [5]. The first direction is the traditional received signal strength (RSS) -based method combined with other parameters such as hysteresis margin and dwell time [6]. The second approach is the multiple-attribute decision making scheme of vertical handoff, which quotes several metrics such as available bandwidth, signal to noise ratio (SNR), cost, and speed in a utility function [7]. The third way uses artificial intelligence techniques such as fuzzy logic and neural networks with a few parameters about the quality of service (QoS). For example, the fuzzy logic theory has been referred to dealing with the vertical handoff decision problem in [8] and [9].

In [10], a handoff decision scheme has been presented to deal with handoff decision problem. The users should use cost function to measure the QoS of all the candidate networks and select the best as the target network. Then the stability period T_S is set as follows:

$$T_S = l_{handoff} + \frac{l_{handoff}}{(r-1)}, \tag{1}$$

where $r = f_{current} / f_{better}$, $l_{handoff}$ presents the handoff latency, $f_{current}$ and f_{better} are the cost function value of current and target network, respectively. Stability period is expressed as a waiting period from finding a network to switch to triggering handoff. Only if the target network is consistently the best of all networks within a stability period does the MT execute handoff. Equation (1) is based on making up handoff latency and the lost time due to it. In real world, the handoff latency of every network varies all the time but the latency in [10] is assumed to be fixed. Afterward, a few improvements have been done in [4] and [11]. In [4], the authors presented two methods to adjust stability period based on network utility ratio. Reference [11] emphasized on obtaining handoff metrics by using the MAC layer sensing technique to adjust stability period dynamically. However, all the optimization methods are based on (1). The setup of handoff latency is unavoidable. In fact, handoff latency is hard to measure in wireless network.

In this paper, we apply the utility function to measure the QoS provided by all networks and find a right one as the target network to perform handoff. Two time-adaptive vertical handoff triggering methods, which both focus on adjusting the stability period dynamically, are proposed. The remainder of this paper is organized as follows. Section 2 describes the proposed methods. In Sect.3, simulations are done through two scenarios. Finally, conclusions are drawn in Sect.4.

2   Time-Adaptive Vertical Handoff Triggering Methods

This section describes the time-adaptive vertical handoff triggering methods: Stability Period Decision Scheme with HZ Residence Time (SPDRT) and Stability Period Decision Scheme Based on Fuzzy Logic (SPDFL). We will present the definition of so called Handoff Zone (HZ) residence time and focus on the setup of the stability period.

2.1 HZ

The boundary between cells is determined by average RSS from adjacent cells in wireless communication networks. However, due to shadowing and fading effects, the RSS varies from time to time although the transmitting signal strength is constant and distance from a base station or an access point is fixed. Figure 1 presents an example of our proposed system model, the 3G network is used to cover universal area and the WLAN can provide local coverage. Here, we regard the area lying in the common boundary between WLANs as HZ. Generally, the cell shape is defined as a hexagon in the cellular environment. We assume that the HZ shape is ellipse because that will be close to real condition.

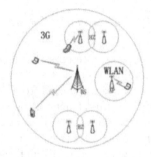

Fig. 1. Handoff zone in wireless overlay networks

2.2 HZ Residence Time

The residence time presents the time that an MT resides in the current cell before it enters the adjacent cell. Because of that, we define the HZ residence time as the time between the moment an MT begins to accept service in HZ and the moment it leaves HZ or the time an MT spent when crossing the HZ. The calculation of residence time has been studied extensively in the past. In [12], the negative exponential distribution model is presented and the Gamma distribution model is shown in [13]. Those methods are quite complex and time-consuming. Here, we adopt the geometrical analysis method which can calculate the HZ residence time simply and fast. Equation (2) is the trajectory function of the HZ boundary.

$$\frac{x^2}{a^2} + \frac{y^2}{b^2} = 1, \tag{2}$$

where a and b are the major axis and minor axis of the ellipse, respectively.

The trajectory function of the MT's movement can be determined by

$$(x - x_0) * tan\theta = y - y_0, \tag{3}$$

where θ is the angle of user's current moving direction and (x_0, y_0) is the user's coordinate point of his initial position in the HZ. From (2) and (3), the intersection point of the trajectory of the MT's movement and the trajectory of the HZ boundary can be found. Then the MT's moving distance d in the HZ before it leaves the HZ may be achieved. Finally, the HZ residence time T_H is given as:

$$T_H = \frac{d}{v}, \tag{4}$$

where v is the user's current moving velocity which is obtained randomly by the initialization process.

2.3 SPDRT

As discussed in Sect.1, after selecting a target network, the MT should perform the process of stability period decision. The stability period is deduced based on the idea of making up. In (1), the handoff latencies of different wireless networks are derived from a large amount of experiments [10]. In order to simplify the simulation process, (5) is applied to define stability period T_{S-P} in our SPDRT scheme.

$$T_{S-P} = T_{min} + (T_{max} - T_{min})(1 - r), \tag{5}$$

where $r = U_{tar}/U_{cur}$, T_{min} and T_{max} are the lower bound and the higher bound of the initialization time value. U_{cur} is the utility function value of the network that the user resides in currently. U_{tar}, which is larger than U_{cur}, is the utility function value of the network that the user will perform handoff into. Likewise, r is also used to adjust the stability period. The utility function value of any network varies from time to time with the continuing changes of the network conditions. Then the stability period changes simultaneously. Therefore, the stability period can be dynamically adjusted according to the actual network conditions. Moreover, T_{S-P} is a linear function of r. The stability period will vary more sharply with the slight change of r than the condition in (1).

When the MT enters the HZ, it needs a better network to switch because of the QoS's getting worse in the current network. After choosing a network as the target, it starts the measure process of QoS within a stability period. As there are several better networks to be selected and any of the candidate networks may be the optimal option, the measure process of QoS will be performed frequently. If the MT doesn't perform handoff successfully before it moves out of the HZ boundary, the handoff call is dropped. So we use the HZ residence time to be the final time for triggering the handoff, the MT will be forced to perform handoff once the final time exceeds the HZ residence time. As a result, the dropped handoff calls caused by frequent QoS measurements in corresponding stability period are effectively avoided.

2.4 SPDFL

The fuzzy multiple-attribute decision making algorithm has been used to deal
with the vertical handoff decision problem. Through measuring network's QoS
parameters and selecting a suitable network, it can provide adaptive and accurate
handoff decision because of its intelligent character. The method based on fuzzy
logic is especially sensitive to QoS parameters' change, so in this section, we use
it for realizing stability period's dynamic adjustment and call it SPDFL scheme.
As shown in Fig.2, a fuzzy logic controller is applied in the SPDFL scheme. The
fuzzifier receives the considered context parameters and transforms them to the
fuzzy sets which have a varying degree of membership. Therefore, the real-time
measurements will change to a series of values like low, medium or high if the
bandwidth alone is considered. Then every value is mapped onto a membership
value and all the values become a membership function together.

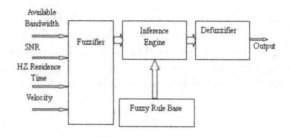

Fig. 2. Fuzzy logic controller

   In our scheme, we consider four parameters: available bandwidth, SNR, velocity, HZ residence time as the input variables of the fuzzifier as shown in Fig.2.
We transform them to the linguistic variables as: Available Bandwidth = {High
(H), Medium (M), Low (L)}; SNR = {High (H), Medium (M), Low (L)}; Velocity = {Fast (F), Medium (M), Slow (S)}; HZ residence time = {Long (L),
Medium (M), Short (S)}. Figure 3 illustrates the membership functions of the
parameters.
   Unlike conventional application of fuzzy logic that the output parameter is a
precise quantity which is mapped to the membership value, the output variable
in our scheme is a degree which presents a time value. We set the time value as
the stability period here. According to fuzzy rule base shown in Table 1[1], there
are 81 rules. Also, the 81 rules stand for 81 different stability period time at
the corresponding degree. The degrees are determined by the QoS parameters of
the target network such as available bandwidth, SNR, velocity and HZ residence
time. The suitable stability period varies with the network's real-time QoS.

---

[1] It is a breviary of the entire table due to space.

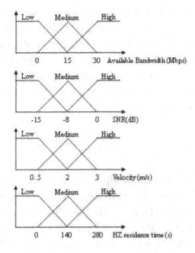

Fig. 3. Membership functions

Table 1. Fuzzy rule base

Rules	HZ residence time	Available bandwidth	SNR	Velocity	Degrees
1	S	H	H	F	1
2	S	H	H	M	2
3	S	H	H	S	3
4	S	H	M	F	4
5	S	H	M	M	5
6	S	H	M	S	6
7	S	H	L	F	7
8	S	H	L	M	8
9	S	H	L	S	9
10	S	M	H	F	10
...	...	...	...	...	...
79	L	L	L	F	79
80	L	L	L	M	80
81	L	L	L	S	81

2.5   Delaying Handoff Scheme in HZ

Here we discuss a particular phenomenon: several users enter the HZ at the same moment, which is called the handoff call queuing problem. In the utility function-based method, the MT will switch to the most appropriate one once the target network can provide the best QoS. But the problem appears when all the users need to perform handoff: the users will execute the handoff into the same network and the limited resource can't fulfill so many service requests for a network. Subsequently, some of the users will be out of service. A general idea, which delays some handoff calls, is presented to deal with this problem. Although this method can reduce the occurrence of handoff call dropping, the handoff delay process will last too long and the handoff will not be triggered in time. In order to achieve the purpose of adjusting delay time dynamically, we apply the theory of (5) to decide the delay time T_{D-T} and rewrite it as (6). We call this dynamic delay scheme here.

$$T_{D-T} = T_{min} + (T_{max} - T_{min})(1 - r), \tag{6}$$

where $r = U_{tar}/U_{cur}$.

Also, the SPDFL scheme can be adopted to deal with this problem. We call it fuzzy logic-based delay scheme. In addition, it is important to differentiate real-time and non-real-time applications in the handoff decision process because the real-time applications such as voice service need to perform handoff as soon as possible. So we add the service level of the application as an input parameter of the fuzzifier. This proposal makes the delay time more sensible to the real-time applications.

3   Performance Evaluation

The performance of the proposal is evaluated by simulations. We set a heterogeneous structure where a 3G system and two WLANs overlay, as shown in Fig.4. In Table 2, we list the simulation parameters of network environment. An MT is randomly generated within the whole simulation area. In the simulation model, the arrival of the MT follows a Poisson distribution and the total number of users is set to be 1000. The initial velocity of an MT is set to be a random number between 0.5 m/s and 3 m/s. In order to simplify the simulation process, the MT is assumed to do the rectilinear motion. The range of movement direction is uniformly distributed from 0 to 2π. Three applications, voice conversation,

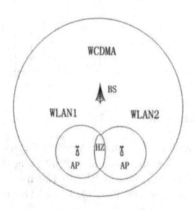

Fig. 4. Simulation environment

Table 2. Simulation parameters of the networks

Wireless environment	WCDMA	WLAN
Cell radius (m)	800	100
Shadowing deviation (dB)	6	6
Tx power (dBm)	37	24
Frequency (Hz)	2.1e9	2.4e9
Transmitter antenna height (m)	50	1
Receiver antenna height (m)	2	1
Transmitter antenna gain (dB)	1	1
Receiver antenna gain (dB)	1	1
Rx sensitivity (dBm)	-98	-94

Table 3. Service characteristics

Service class	Bandwidth	Real-time or not
Voice conversation	0.384M	Real-time
Video streaming	1M	Real-time
Data download	2M	Non-real-time

video streaming and data download, are chosen by the users. The bandwidths occupied by these services are shown in Table 3.

In Fig.5, we compare the handoff call dropping rates of using the following methods: utility function-based scheme, stability period decision (SPD) scheme [10], SPDRT and SPDFL. In SPDRT, T_{min} and $T_{máx}$ are set to be 2s and 5s, respectively. The simulation results show that the utility function-based scheme has the higher handoff call dropping rate compared to all other schemes since the target network conditions changed so fast that there could be no enough resource to provide for the user after he performed handoff to the network without measuring the network's QoS within a stability period. The SPDRT is slightly better than SPD as it introduces the HZ residence time, which avoids handoff call dropping by the time-consuming stability period decision process. In SPDFL, more parameters of the target network are collected in order to obtain an appropriate stability period and choose a suitable time point to trigger handoff. However, it achieves the highest sensitivity in stability period's adjustment.

Figure 6 and 7 are the simulation results about dealing with the handoff call queuing problem. The comparisons among the four algorithms are shown in Fig.6. They are non-delay, fixed delay, dynamic delay and fuzzy logic-based delay schemes. When multiple users enter the HZ at the same time, some calls could be blocked due to the limited resource. So, the non-delay scheme has very high handoff call dropping rate. Though the Fixed delay scheme can solve the blocking problem, the handoff time point can't be decided flexibly because the delay time is fixed, and the MT may lose the best opportunity of triggering the handoff. The dynamic delay scheme resolves this delay problem. Moreover, the dropping would happen frequently if the handoff request of an MT with real-time application can't be satisfied. In fuzzy logic-based delay scheme, we consider the service level of the application as an input parameter. In this way, the handoff request of the real-time service will be dealt with timely. So this

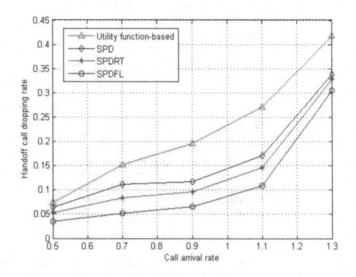

Fig. 5. Handoff call dropping rate versus call arrival rate

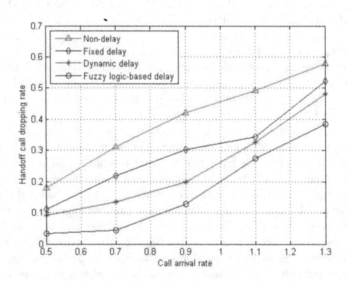

Fig. 6. Handoff call dropping rate versus call arrival rate

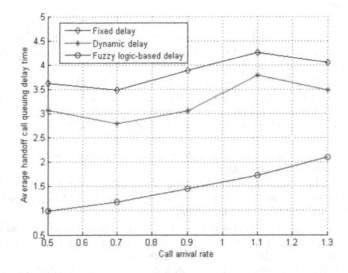

Fig. 7. Average handoff call queuing delay time versus call arrival rate

scheme obtains the lowest rate and shows about 6% decrease for handoff call dropping rate over the dynamic delay scheme averagely.

As shown in Fig.7, the average handoff call queuing delay time of all users entering the HZ is compared. We can see that the average handoff call queuing delay time in the fixed delay scheme is longer than that in the dynamic delay scheme due to inappropriate delay time setting. The fuzzy logic-based delay scheme has the shortest average handoff call queuing delay time. This indicates that the fuzzy logic-based scheme is more intelligent and sensible in deciding delay time. Though the average handoff call queuing delay time is longer than conventional handoff latency and may lead to handoff call dropping to some extent, but the delaying handoff method prevents a lot of handoff calls being blocked and makes a tradeoff between them.

4   Conclusion

In this paper, we proposed two time-adaptive vertical handoff triggering schemes that find an appropriate time point to trigger handoff based on the residence time in the HZ. The two schemes, SPDRT and SPDFL, both focus on deciding the stability period dynamically. Furthermore, we apply them to solve the handoff call queuing problem. The simulations show that the proposed schemes outperform previous schemes in decreasing handoff call dropping rate. Moreover, the schemes are intelligent and sensible in adjusting the stability period.

References

1. Bria, A., Gessler, F., Queseth, O., Stridh, R., Unbehaun, M., Jiang, W., Zander, J.: 4th-generation wireless infrastructures: scenarios and research challenges. IEEE Wireless Communications 8(6), 25–31 (2001)
2. Chen, Y.P., Yang, Y.H.: A new 4G architecture providing multimode terminals always best connected services. IEEE Wireless Communications 14(2), 36–41 (2007)
3. Zhu, F., Mcnair, J.: Optimizations for vertical handoff decision algorithms. In: Wireless Communications and Networking Conference, vol. 2, pp. 867–872 (2004)
4. Chen, W.T., Liu, J.C., Huang, H.K.: An adaptive scheme for vertical handoff in wireless overlay networks. In: IEEE International Conference on Parallel and Distributed Systems, pp. 541–548 (2004)
5. Zahran, A.H., Liang, B., Saleh, A.: Signal Threshold Adaptation for Vertical Handoff in Heterogeneous Wireless Networks. Mobile Networks and Applications (MONET) journal 11(4), 625–640 (2006)
6. Liu, M., Li, Z.C., Guo, X.B., Lach, H.Y.: Design and Evaluation of Vertical Handoff Decision Algorithm in Heterogeneous Wireless Networks. In: IEEE International Conference on Networks, vol. 2, pp. 1–6 (2006)
7. Lee, D.Y., Han, Y.N., Hwang, J.Y.: QOS-based Vertical handoff decision algorithm in heterogeneous networks. In: Personal. IEEE International Symposium on Indoor and Mobile Radio Communications, pp. 1–5 (2006)
8. Guo, Q., Zhu, J., Xu, X.H.: An adaptive multi-criteria vertical handoff decision algorithm for radio heterogeneous network. In: IEEE International Conference on Communications, vol. 4, pp. 2769–2773 (2005)
9. Barolli, L., Xhafa, F., Durresi, A., Koyama, A., Takizawa, M.: An intelligent handoff system for eireless cellular networks using fuzzy logic and random walk model. In: International Conference on Complex, Intelligent and Software Intensive Systems, pp. 5–11 (2008)
10. Wang, H.J., Katz, R.H., Giese, J.: Policy-enabled handoffs across heterogeneous wireless networks. In: Proc. of the Second IEEE Workshop on Mobile Computing Systems and Applications, New Orleans, Louisiana, pp. 51–61 (1999)
11. Jia, H.L., Cheng, P., Zhang, Z.Y., Li, S.J.: An improved adaptive decision scheme for vertical handoff in heterogeneous wireless networks. In: IEEE International Conference on Communications, Circuits and Systems, vol. 3, pp. 1816–1820 (2006)
12. Zonoozi, M., Dassanayake, P.: User mobility modeling and characterization of mobility patterns. IEEE Journal on Selected Areas in Communication 15(7), 1239–1252 (1997)
13. Fang, Y.G., Chlamtac, I., Lin, Y.B.: Call performance for a PCS network. IEEE Journal on Selected Areas in Communication 15(8), 1568–1581 (1997)

Energy-Saving Topology Control for Heterogeneous Ad Hoc Networks

Lei Zhang and Xuehui Wang

School of Computer,
National University of Defense Technology, Changsha 410073, China
findzhanglei@hotmail.com

Abstract. Topology control with per-node transmission power adjustment in wireless ad hoc networks has been shown to be effective with respect to prolonging network lifetime and increasing network capacity. In this paper, we propose a fully distributed, asynchronous and localized energy-saving topology control algorithm for heterogeneous ad hoc networks with non-uniform transmission ranges. We prove the topology derived from the algorithm preserves the network connectivity and bi-directionality. It need not the position system support and dramatically reduces the communication overhead compared to other topology control algorithms. Simulation results show the effectiveness of our proposed algorithm.

1 Introduction

Wireless ad hoc networks have been the focus of many recent research and development efforts for its applications in military, commercial, and educational environments. Since wireless nodes are usually powered by batteries, energy-saving is a prime consideration in these networks. Topology control via per-node transmission power adjustment has been shown to be effective in extending network lifetime and increasing network capacity (due to better spatial reuse of spectrum), but reducing transmission power arbitrarily on each node may result in a disconnected network. Energy-saving topology control aims at reducing the transmission power as much as possible while maintaining the network connectivity.

Most of the literature in this area has focused on the topology control problem in homogeneous ad hoc networks with uniform transmission ranges. Ramanathan et al. [1] proposed a centralized algorithm CONNECT that requires global information, thus cannot be applied to large ad hoc networks. He also presented two distributed algorithms LINT and LILT, but both are heuristic and cannot preserve the network connectivity. Roger Wattenhofer al. [2] introduced a cone-based distributed topology control algorithm (CBTC) with the support of directional antenna. The basic idea is that a node i transmits with the minimum power p such that there is at least one neighbor in every cone of angle centered at i. The obtained communication graph is made symmetric by adding the reverse edge to every asymmetric link. The authors show that setting $\beta \leq \pi2/3$ is a sufficient condition to ensure connectivity. Ning Li [3] proposed a distributed

Y. Dou, R. Gruber, and J. Joller (Eds.): APPT 2009, LNCS 5737, pp. 313–322, 2009.
© Springer-Verlag Berlin Heidelberg 2009

topology control algorithm LMST basing on the local minimum spanning tree theory, each node builds its local minimum spanning tree and only keeps on-tree nodes that are one-hop away as its neighbors in the final topology.

The assumption of homogeneous nodes does not always hold in practice, because the devices in the network may have dramatically different capabilities, for instance, the communication network in the battle field involves different wireless devices on soldiers, vehicles and UAVs. Ning Li and Jennifer C. Hou [4] showed that most existing topology control algorithms cannot be directly applied to heterogeneous wireless multi-hop networks in which the transmission range of each node may be different. They proposed two localized topology control algorithms for heterogeneous wireless ad hoc networks with non-uniform transmission ranges: Directed Relative Neighborhood Graph (DRNG) and Directed Local Minimum Spanning Tree (DLMST). The authors prove that if the original network is bi-directional and strongly connected, both DRNG and DLMST are localized algorithms to preserve the network connectivity, but if the original network is not bi-directional (this is not uncommon in heterogeneous ad hoc networks), the neighborhood topology information needed by DRNG and DLMST cannot be obtained locally, which will result in extensive global broadcasts in the network. Jilei Liu and Baochun Li [5] proposed a solution that is based on the minimum-power vicinity tree (MPVT), each node gets its vicinity topology and build a minimum-power vicinity tree using the single source shortest-paths algorithm, such as the Bellman-Ford or Dijkstra's algorithms, but the vicinity topology also cannot be obtained locally if there exist unidirectional links. Moreover, all the mentioned topology control algorithms for heterogeneous ad hoc networks need GPS or other position system to obtain the location information of each node, which maybe inapplicable in practice.

In this paper, we propose a distributed energy-saving topology control algorithm MINS (minimum-power ingress neighbor sub-network) for heterogeneous ad hoc networks with non-uniform transmission ranges. Each node builds a minimum-power ingress neighbor sub-network based on the locally collected ingress neighbor (defined in section 2) topology information and adjusts its transmission power according to the received transmission power control messages from its ingress neighbors. Compared with other topology control algorithms for heterogeneous ad hoc networks, MINS need not position system support and dramatically reduces the communication overhead, the topology generated by MINS preserves the network connectivity and has less average node degree.

The rest of the paper is organized as follows. The network model is described in Section 2. Then we present the MINS topology control algorithm in Section 3, and discuss its scalability, preservation of network connectivity and bi-directionality in Section 4. Finally, we present a simulation-based performance study in Section 5, and conclude the paper in Section 6.

2   Network Model

Consider n heterogeneous nodes are randomly deployed in a two-dimensional plane. Each node is assigned a unique id (such as an IP/MAC address) and equipped with an omni-directional antenna with adjustable transmission power. Since nodes are heterogeneous, they have different maximum transmission powers and radio ranges, which will result in unidirectional links in the network.

Let V denote the node set in the network, we assume the wireless channel is symmetric and obstacle-free, each node has the ability to gather its location information via position system, such as GPS. $\forall u \in V$, suppose d_u^{max} is its maximum transmission range, we define ingress neighbor and ingress neighbor set as follows.

Definition 1. *Ingress Neighbor and Ingress Neighbor Set.* $\forall u, v \in V$, $d(u,v)$ is *the distance between node u and v, if $d_u^{max} > d(u,v)$, u is an ingress neighbor of v, denoted as $u \rightarrow v$, all these ingress neighbors of node v constitute its ingress neighbor set V_{IG}^v (including node v itself).*

Since the maximum transmission range of each node may be different, ingress neighbor is asymmetric, i.e., $u \rightarrow v$ does not imply $v \rightarrow u$. If u is an ingress neighbor of v, there exists a directed link (u,v) from u to v, its weight is $d(u,v)$. The network topology generated by having each node transmit with its maximum power is a directed graph, denoted as $G = (V, E)$, where $E = \{(u, v) : u \rightarrow v, u \in V, v \in V\}$.

The objective of the energy-saving topology control algorithm is to minimize the transmission power of each node while preserving the network connectivity.

3   The MINS Topology Control Algorithm

In this section, we propose a distributed energy-saving topology control algorithm MINS (Minimum-power Ingress Neighbor Sub-network) for heterogeneous wireless ad hoc networks with non-uniform transmission ranges, which is composed of four phases: topology information collection, local topology construction, transmission power adjustment and mobility manipulation.

3.1   Topology Information Collection

In this phase each node collects its ingress neighbor information locally and constructs a ingress neighbor topology $G_{IG}^v = (V_{IG}^v, E_{IG}^v)$, where V_{IG}^v is the ingress neighbor set, $E_{IG}^v = \{(x,y) : x \rightarrow y, x \in V_{IG}^v, y \in V_{IG}^v\}$ is the directed edge set among all the nodes in V_{IG}^v, $G_{IG}^v = (V_{IG}^v, E_{IG}^v)$ is a subgraph of $G = (V, E)$, which can be obtained as follows.

Each node in the network periodically broadcasts a HELLO message using its maximum transmission power (in this paper, broadcast means 1-hop broadcast, global broadcast means broadcast in the entire network). The information contained in a HELLO message should at least include the node *id*, the node position and its maximum transmission power P_u^{smax}. If $u \rightarrow v$, v will receive u's HELLO message, assume the received signal power level is $P_{(u,v)}^r$, according to the path loss model commonly adopted by previous work [6], it satisfies

$$P_{(u,v)}^r = c * \frac{P_u^{smax}}{d(u,v)^r} \tag{1}$$

where $d(u, v)$ is the mutual distance between node u and v, c is a constant, r is the propagation loss coefficient, its value ranges from 2 to 5 depending on the environment.

Let $P_{(u,v)}^{smin}$ represents the receiving threshold of the node vs radio interface (e.g. it is 3.652E-10w for 914MHz Lucent WaveLAN DSSS radio interface). According to equation (1),

$$P_v^{rmin} = c * \frac{P_{u,v}^{smin}}{d(u,v)^r} \tag{2}$$

where $P_{(u,v)}^{smin}$ is the minimum transmission power for node u to reach node v, combine equation (1) and (2), we get

$$P_{(u,v)}^{smin} = P_u^{smax} * \frac{P_v^{rmin}}{P_{(u,v)}^r} \tag{3}$$

where P_v^{rmin} and P_u^{smax} are known, $P_{(u,v)}^r$ is the signal power of the received HELLO message, so by equation (3) node v can calculate the minimum transmission power of each ingress neighbor, it records these information in a ingress neighbor link list (INLL) as Table 1.

The information in the ingress neighbor link list will be broadcasted by each node in a INLL message using its maximum transmission power. After receiving the INLL messages from all the ingress neighbors, node v can build its ingress neighbor topology $G_{IG}^v = (V_{IG}^v, E_{IG}^v)$, which is the basis of our energy-saving topology control algorithm.

Table 1. Ingress neighbor link list

Link	Minimum transmitting power for this link
(a, v)	$P_{(a,v)}^{smin}$
(b, v)	$P_{(b,v)}^{smin}$
...	...

3.2   Local Topology Construction

With the knowledge of ingress neighbor topology $G_{IG}^v = (V_{IG}^v, E_{IG}^v)$, node v constructs a minimum-power ingress neighbor sub-network $G_{IG}^{v}{}' = (V_{IG}^v, E_{IG}^v{}')$ using the following algorithm.

Step 1. Construct a subgraph $G_{IG}^{v}{}' = (V_{IG}^v, E_{IG}^v{}')$ without any edges and initialize the minimum transmission range d_v^{min} of each node in V_{IG}^v to 0.

$$E_{IG}^v{}' = \phi \qquad d_v^{min} = 0 \qquad V_t = V_{IG}^v - v$$

Step 2. Sort the edges in E_{IG}^v according to its weight $d(u, v)$ in a non-decreasing order, the sort result is denoted as S.

Step 3. Retrieve the first directed edge (x,y) from S.

Step 4. If $x \in V_t$ and node x is not connected to node y, add edge (x,y) to $E_{IG}^{v}{}'$ and update d_x^{min}:

$$if \;\; d_x^{min} < d(x,y), \;\; set \;\; d_x^{min} = d(x,y)$$

Step 5. If node x is connected to node v, delete node x from V_t.

Step 6. If V_t is empty, terminate the algorithm, else go to step 3.

The algorithm is greedy, it iteratively adds edge to $E_{IG}^{v}{}'$ until each neighbor node can reach node v, the maximum power of all edges in the sub-network is minimized.

3.3   Transmission Power Adjustment

On termination of the local topology construction algorithm, node v obtains the minimum transmission range for each ingress neighbor. It will send these information to its ingress neighbors within a transmission power control (TPC) message.

Since ingress neighbor is not symmetric, node v may be unable to reach some of its ingress neighbors directly using its maximum transmission power. In this case, if v broadcasts the TPC message globally, it will result in excessive communication overhead. Instead of globally broadcasting the TPC message to all the ingress neighbors, node v only broadcasts the TPC message to those ingress neighbors that are directed connected to it in $G_{IG}^{v}{}' = (V_{IG}^{v}, E_{IG}^{v}{}')$, which is sufficient to guarantee the network connectivity (proved in Theorem 1).Figure 1 gives an illustration, Fig 1(a) is the ingress neighbor topology of node v, in which $u \rightarrow v$ but 4 cannot reach u directly, Fig 1(b) is the minimum-power ingress neighbor sub-network $G_{IG}^{v}{}' = (V_{IG}^{v}, E_{IG}^{v}{}')$ constructed by v. To guarantee both ingress neighbor w and u can reach node v in the final topology, v need only send the TPC message to node w, because u is also w's ingress neighbor, edge (u,w) will be added to the minimum-power ingress neighbor sub-network of node w, which will eventually broadcasting the TPC message to node u.

The only case that node v must globally broadcast the TPC message is that there is not a ingress neighbor in the green area of figure 2(b), which will result u is directly connected to v in $G_{IG}^{v}{}' = (V_{IG}^{v}, E_{IG}^{v}{}')$, but this rarely happens in the strongly connected ad hoc networks. Extensive simulations show this method dramatically reduces the communication overhead caused by global broadcast (see section 5).

Upon receiving a TPC message, node v compares the transmission power requirement from the TPC message with its current power setting, and adjusts its transmission power to the larger value. The final network topology is denoted as $G_0 = (V, E_0)$ after the transmission power adjustment.

3.4   Mobility Manipulation

To manipulate the mobility of wireless nodes, each node should broadcast HELLO message periodically, the interval between two broadcasts is determined by the

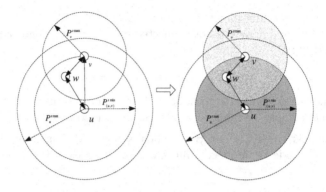

Fig. 1. Illustration of TPC message sending policy

mobility speed. When any node finds the ingress neighbor topology is changed, it will rebroadcast the INLL message to notify its neighbors to update the ingress neighbor topology information and readjust the transmission power from scratch.

4   Properties of MINS Algorithm

In this section, we discuss the scalability, connectivity and bi-directionality of the MINS algorithm.

4.1   Scalability

The MINS algorithm is a fully distributed and localized algorithm to be executed on each node in the network. Since every node in the network can run the algorithm independently based on its local ingress neighbor topology information, it is scalable to large heterogeneous ad hoc networks. Moreover, in MINS algorithm each node need only the ingress neighbor topology instead of the egress neighbor (the neighbors it can reach) topology as in MPVT[4], DRNG or DLMST[3]. Ingress neighbor topology can be obtained by exchanging the HELLO and INLL messages locally, and the number of global broadcasts during transmission power adjustment can be dramatically reduced using the minimum-power ingress neighbor sub-network. While obtaining the egress neighbor information need extensive global broadcasts [3] [4], which will result in too much communication overhead.

Furthermore, MINS algorithm is asynchronous. Each node executes the algorithm periodically and independently, it can start running the algorithm at any time, transmission power adjustment is activated by the received TPC message, synchronization mechanism is not needed among the wireless nodes.

Finally, when the node density increases in the network, each node's transmission power becomes less to maintain the network connectivity, the average node degree and consequently the network contention level are consistent despite of the node density in the network. The percentage of nodes that globally broadcast TPC messages is also decreased (see section 5).

4.2 Connectivity

Theorem 1. *If the original topology $G = (V, E)$ is strongly connected, then $G_0 = (V, E_0)$ obtained by MINS algorithm is also strongly connected.*

Proof. Since $G = (V, E)$ is strongly connected, $\forall u, v \in V$, there exists a directed path form u to v in $G = (V, E)$, without loss of generality, we denote it as $p(u, x_1, x_2...x_{k-1}, x_k, v)$, where $x_1, x_2...x_{k-1}, x_k$ are the k intermediate nodes from u to v.

Since $x_k \rightarrow v$, by the MINS algorithm , there must exist a directed path in $G_0 = (V, E_0)$ through which node x_k can reach node v. Similarly, $x_{k-1} \rightarrow x_k$ implies x_{k-1} can reach x_k, $x_{k-2} \rightarrow x_{k-1}$ implies x_{k-2} can reach x_{k-1}, which continues until node u can reach node x_1. As a result, node u can reach node v in $G_0 = (V, E_0)$, therefore $G_0 = (V, E_0)$ is strongly connected.

4.3 Bi-directionality

It is very important to guarantee the network bi-directionality, because MAC protocols usually require bidirectional links for proper operation, such as the RTS-CTS-DATA-ACK handshake protocol in IEEE 802.11 standard. MINS algorithm does not always preserve the bi-directionality even if the initial topology is bi-directionally connected, as illustrated in figure 2. But MINS algorithm can be easily extended as follows to guarantee the bi-directionality of the network.

In the first phase of MINS algorithm, after obtaining the ingress neighbor topology $G_{IG}^v = (V_{IG}^v, E_{IG}^v)$, delete all the unidirectional links in $G_{IG}^v = (V_{IG}^v, E_{IG}^v)$ and continue the algorithm.

In the second phase of MINS algorithm, once we add an edge (x, y) to $E_{IG}^{v\prime}$, the corresponding reverse edge (y, x) is also added to $E_{IG}^{v\prime}$ simultaneously:

$$if \ P_x < P_{(x,y)}^{smin}, set \ P_x = P_{(x,y)}^{smin}$$

$$if \ P_y < P_{(y,x)}^{smin}, set \ P_y = P_{(y,x)}^{smin}$$

so the minimum-power ingress neighbor topology obtained in this phase is bi-directional.

We denote the modified algorithm as EMINS algorithm.

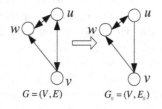

Fig. 2. Illustration of TPC message sending policy

Theorem 2. *If the original topology $G = (V, E)$ is strongly connected and bi-directional, then $G_0 = (V, E_0)$ obtained by MINS algorithm is also strongly and bi-directionally connected .*

Proof. Since $G = (V, E)$ is strongly connected and bi-directional, $\forall u, v \in V$, there exists a bi-directional path $p(u, x_1, x_2 ... x_{k-1}$ between u and v in $G = (V, E)$, where $x_1, x_2 ... x_{k-1}, x_k$ are the k intermediate nodes.

Since x_k is node v's ingress neighbor and the minimum-power ingress neighbor sub-network obtained by EMINS algorithm is bi-directional, there exists a bi-directional path between node x_k and v, thus node x_k is bi-directionally connected with node v in $G_0 = (V, E_0)$. Similarly, node x_{k-1} is bi-directionally connected with s_k, node x_{k-2} is bi-directionally connected with s_{k-1}, which continues until node u is bi-directionally connected with x_1. As a result node u is bi-directionally connected with node v in $G_0 = (V, E_0)$. Therefore $G_0 = (V, E_0)$ is strongly and bi-directionally connected.

5   Performance Simulation

In this section, we evaluate the performance of the MINS algorithm through simulations. Assume n nodes are uniformly distributed in a ll square area, two-ray ground propagation model is used for the wireless channel. The transmission ranges are uniformly distributed in $[200m, 250m]$ (the corresponding maximum transmission power is in the range of 0.1154w and 0.2818w), the receiving threshold is 3.652E-10w.

We use the following metrics to evaluate the performance of the topology control algorithm.

(1) Average Out Degree: A smaller average out degree usually implies less contention/interference and better spatial reuse.

(2) Communication Overhead: Less communication overhead implies better scalability and less bandwidth consumption. We use the percentage of the nodes that make global broadcast during the execution of topology control algorithms to quantify the communication overhead.

(3) Average Transmission Power: Lower transmission power implies higher energy efficiency and better network spatial reuse.

In the first simulation, we fix the distribution area $l=1000m$ and vary the number of nodes from 50 to 300 (node density increases). We compare the average out degree, communication overhead and average transmission power for the topologies generated using maximum transmission power, MPVT, DRNG and MINS algorithm. In Fig. 3(a) the topology under MINS has less average out degree than those under maximum transmission power, MPVT and DRNG. Fig. 3(b) shows communication overhead of different algorithms, in MINS algorithm only a few nodes globally broadcast the TPC messages, and the percentage of nodes decreases rapidly with the increase of node density, while in MPVT and DRNG, plenty of nodes need global broadcast to construct the egress neighbor topology. The average transmission power under different algorithms is shown

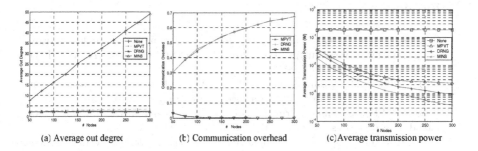

(a) Average out degree   (b) Communication overhead   (c) Average transmission power

Fig. 3. Performance under fixed network size

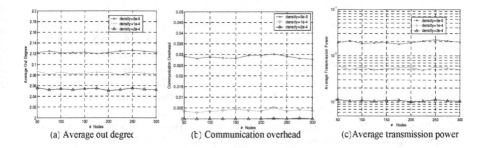

(a) Average out degree   (b) Communication overhead   (c) Average transmission power

Fig. 4. Performance under fixed node density

in Fig. 3(c), the MINS algorithm outperforms others, which implies it provides higher energy efficiency and better spatial reuse.

To observe the influence of network size on the performance of the MINS algorithm, we fix the node density and vary the number of nodes in the network from 50 to 300 (the network size increases accordingly), the average node degrees, communication overhead and average transmission power for the topologies generated using the MINS algorithm when density=$2e$-4 , $1e$-4 and $5e$-5 are shown in Fig. 4 (a) (b) (c). Under a fixed node density, the average out degree, communication overhead and average transmission power are almost invariable despite of the network size, which implies MINS algorithm is scalable to large wireless ad hoc networks without performance degradation.

6 Conclusion

In this paper, we propose a distributed topology control algorithm for heterogeneous ad hoc networks with non-uniform transmission ranges. Each node constructs a minimum-power ingress neighbor sub-network based on the locally collected topology information to save energy and preserve the network connectivity, the transmission power adjustment process is optimized to reduce the communication overhead. Performance simulation shows the effectiveness of our proposed algorithm.

References

1. Ramanathan, R., Rosales-Hain, R.: Topology control of multihop wireless networks using transmit power adjustment. In: Proc. IEEE INFOCOM 2000, Tel Aviv, Israel, March 2000, pp. 404–413 (2000)
2. Li, L., Halpern, J.Y., Bahl, P., Wang, Y.-M., Wattenhofer, R.: Analysis of a cone-based distributed topology control algorithm for wireless multi-hop networks. In: Proc. ACM Symposium on Principles of Distributed Computing, Newport, Rhode Island, United States, August 2001, pp. 264–273 (2001)
3. Li, N., Hou, J.C.: Topology Control in Heterogeneous Wireless Networks: Problems and Solutions. In: Proc. IEEE INFOCOM 2004, Hong Kong, China (March 2004)
4. Liu, J., Li, B.: Distributed Topology Control in Wireless Sensor Networks with Asymmetric Links. In: Proc. GLOBECOM 2003, San Francisco, USA (December 2003)
5. Li, N., Hou, J.C., Sha, L.: Design and analysis of an MSTbased topology control algorithm. In: Proc. IEEE INFOCOM 2003, San Francisco, CA, USA (April 2003)
6. Rodoplu, V., Meng, T.H.: Minimum energy mobile wirelessnetworks. IEEE Journal on Selected Areas in Communications 17(8), 1333–1344 (1999)
7. Tseng, Y.-C., Chang, Y.-N., Tzeng, B.-H.: Energy-efficient topology control for wireless ad hoc sensor networks. In: Proc. Int. Conf. Parallel and Distributed Systems, ICPADS 2002 (2002)
8. Calinescu, A., Mandoui, I., Zelikovsky, A.: Symmetric connectivity with minimum power consumption inradio networks. In: Proc. of IFIP TCS (2002)
9. Hu, L.: Topology control for multihop packet radio networks. IEEE Trans. on Communications 41(10) (October 1993)
10. Blough, D.M., Leoncini, M., Resta, G., Santi, P.: The k-Neighbors Approach to Symmetric Topology Control in Ad Hoc Networks. IEEE J. on Selected Areas in Communications (submitted)
11. Narayanaswamy, S., Kawadia, V., Sreenivas, R.S., Kumar, P.R.: Power control in ad-hoc networks: Theory, architecture, algorithm and implementation of the compow protocol. In: Proc. of European Wireless 2002, Next Generation Wireless Networks: Technologies, Protocols, Services and Applications, Florence, Italy, February 2002, pp. 156–162 (2002)
12. Wattenhofer, R., Bahl, P., Li, L., Wang, Y.M.: Distributed Topology Control for Power Efficient Operation in Multihop Wireless Ad Hoc Networks. In: Proceedings of INFOCOM (April 2001)
13. Manber, U.: Introduction to Algorithms. Addison-Wesly, London (1989)

Computational Performance of a Parallelized Three-Dimensional High-Order Spectral Element Toolbox

Christoph Bosshard[1], Roland Bouffanais[2], Christian Clémençon[3],
Michel O. Deville[1], Nicolas Fiétier[1], Ralf Gruber[1], Sohrab Kehtari[4],
Vincent Keller[1], and Jonas Latt[1]

[1] Laboratory of Computational Engineering,
École Polytechnique Fédérale de Lausanne,
STI – ISE – LIN, Station 9,
CH–1015 Lausanne, Switzerland
[2] Massachusetts Institute of Technology,
77 Massachusetts Avenue, Room 5-326,
Cambridge MA 02139, USA
[3] DIT,
École Polytechnique Fédérale de Lausanne,
CH–1015 Lausanne, Switzerland
[4] Swiss Federal Institute of Technology Zurich,
HG J 47, Rämistrasse 101,
8092 Zurich, Switzerland

Abstract. In this paper, a comprehensive performance review of an MPI-based high-order three-dimensional spectral element method C++ toolbox is presented. The focus is put on the performance evaluation of several aspects with a particular emphasis on the parallel efficiency. The performance evaluation is analyzed with help of a time prediction model based on a parameterization of the application and the hardware resources. A tailor-made CFD computation benchmark case is introduced and used to carry out this review, stressing the particular interest for clusters with up to 8192 cores. Some problems in the parallel implementation have been detected and corrected. The theoretical complexities with respect to the number of elements, to the polynomial degree, and to communication needs are correctly reproduced. It is concluded that this type of code has a nearly perfect speed up on machines with thousands of cores, and is ready to make the step to next-generation petaflop machines.

1 Introduction

The **S**pectral **u**nstructured **E**lements **O**bject-**O**riented **S**ystem (SpecuLOOS) is a toolbox written in C++ [1]. SpecuLOOS is a spectral and mortar element analysis toolbox for the numerical solution of partial differential equations and more particularly for solving incompressible unsteady fluid flow problems [2]. The main

Y. Dou, R. Gruber, and J. Joller (Eds.): APPT 2009, LNCS 5737, pp. 323–329, 2009.
© Springer-Verlag Berlin Heidelberg 2009

architecture choices and the parallel implementation were elaborated and implemented by Van Kemenade and Dubois-Pèlerin [3]. Subsequently, SpecuLOOS' C++ code has been further developed, see [4].

It is well known that spectral element methods [5] are easily amenable to parallelization, as the domain decomposition into spectral elements can be made to correspond in a natural way to an attribution to parallel nodes [6].

The numerous references previously given and the ongoing simulations based on SpecuLOOS highlight the achieved versatility and flexibility of this C++ toolbox. Nevertheless, ten years have passed between the first version of SpecuLOOS' code and the present time and tremendous changes have occurred at both hardware and software levels. Fast dual DDR memory, RISC architectures, 64-bit memory addressing, compilers improvement, libraries optimization, libraries parallelization, and increase in inter-connecting switch performance are all among the SpecuLOOS improvements.

Here we discuss adaptation of SpecuLOOS to thousands of multi-core nodes. Performance measurements on a one-core node, on a cluster with hundreds of nodes, and on a 4096 dual-core BlueGene/L are presented. The obtained complexities are compared with theoretical predictions. First results show that small cases gave good complexities, but huge cases gave poor efficiencies. These results led to the detection of a poor parallel implementation. Once corrected, the complexity of SpecuLOOS corresponds to the theoretical one up to the 8192 cores used.

Test case description

The test case belongs to the field of CFD and consists in solving the 3D Navier–Stokes equations for a viscous Newtonian incompressible fluid. Based on the problem at hand, it is always physically rewarding to non-dimensionalize the governing Navier–Stokes equations which take the following general form

$$\frac{\partial \mathbf{u}}{\partial t} + \mathbf{u} \cdot \nabla \mathbf{u} = -\nabla p + \frac{1}{\mathrm{Re}} \Delta \mathbf{u} + \mathbf{f}, \qquad \forall (\mathbf{x}, t) \in \Omega \times I, \qquad (1)$$

$$\nabla \cdot \mathbf{u} = 0, \qquad \forall (\mathbf{x}, t) \in \Omega \times I, \qquad (2)$$

where $\mathbf{u}$ is the velocity field, p the reduced pressure (normalized by the constant fluid density), $\mathbf{f}$ the body force per unit mass and Re the Reynolds number

$$\mathrm{Re} = \frac{UL}{\nu}, \qquad (3)$$

expressed in terms of the characteristic length L, the characteristic velocity U, and the constant kinematic viscosity ν. The system evolution is studied in the time interval $I = [t_0, T]$. Considering particular flows, the governing Navier–Stokes equations (1)–(2) are supplemented with appropriate boundary conditions for the fluid velocity $\mathbf{u}$ and/or for the local stress at the boundary. For time-dependent problems, a given divergence-free velocity field is required as initial condition in the internal fluid domain.

The test case corresponds to the fully three-dimensional simulation of the flow enclosed in a lid-driven cubical cavity at the Reynolds number of $12\,000$ placing us in the locally-turbulent regime. It corresponds to the case denoted under-resolved DNS (UDNS) in Bouffanais *e.a.* [7]. The reader is referred to Bouffanais *e.a.* [7] for full details on the numerical method and on the parameters used.

The complexity is proportional to the total number of elements E in the three dimensional space. Each element is transformed to a cube. Since the Gauss–Lobatto–Legendre basis functions of degrees $N = N_x = N_y = N_z$

$$h_j(r) = -\frac{1}{N(N+1)}\frac{1}{L_N(\xi_j)}\frac{(1-r^2)\,L'_N(r)}{(r-\xi_j)}, \qquad -1 \leq r \leq +1, \quad 0 \leq j \leq N,$$
(4)

are orthonormal, the complexity for the pressure is $(N-1)^3$, while the complexity for the velocity is $(N+1)^3$. During the computations, the variables are frequently re-interpolated between the collocation, and operation which has a leading complexity of N^4, due to the tensorization of the implied linear operations. At large values of N, these re-interpolations therefore dominate the total computation time. It should be remarked that from a complexity standpoint, a term like $(N-1)^3$ is equivalent to a term like $(N+1)^3$. In the following, a term $N-1$ has been applied systematically to read the complexity from experimental performance curves, while the notation of the equations is simplified by use of the term N.

The CPU time T of the SpecuLOOS spectral code can then be estimated to

$$T(N_1, N_{CG}, E, N) = a_1 N_1 N_{CG} E N^{a_3},$$
(5)

where N_{CG} is the number of conjugate gradient steps, N_1 is the number of time steps, a_1 is found through simulation, and $3 < a_3 < 4$.

2   Complexity on One Node

First, we run SpecuLOOS on one node without any communication using the Couzy preconditioner [8]. One time iteration step of SpecuLOOS is divided into three main parts: (1) computes the tentative velocity (through a Helmholtz equation solved by preconditioned conjugate gradient method), (2) computes the pressure (through a sophisticated conjugate gradient), and (3) corrects the tentative velocity. The relative importance of each of these three components depends on the parameters in a given simulation. With a fine discretization of the time axis, the second part becomes dominant, and takes as much as 90 % of the total CPU time in the example described below.

Table 1 presents the results of SpecuLOOS on one node of an Intel Xeon cluster. The CPU time measurements, $T_{CG,(1\ iter)}$, for one time step and one CG iteration step ($N_1 = N_{CG} = 1$) are used to minimize $\sum (T - T_{CG,(1\ iter)})^2$, where

$$T(1, 1, E, N) = a_1 E^{a_2} N^{a_3},$$
(6)

Table 1. SpecuLOOS on one node of an Intel Xeon cluster. The number of conjugate gradient iterations N_{CG} is an average value over all time steps for the pressure.

N_1	E	N	T_{exec} [s]	N_{CG} # iter	T_{CG} [s]	$\frac{T_{CG}}{T_{exec}}$	$T_{CG,(1\ iter)}$ [s]
1	256	8	40.1	198	32.8	0.818	0.17
1	256	10	119.3	247	103.8	0.870	0.42
1	512	6	43.2	205	33.9	0.785	0.17
1	512	8	116.4	268	106.7	0.917	0.40
1	512	10	394.3	344	342.3	0.868	1.00
1	1024	6	105.2	259	83.4	0.793	0.32
1	1024	8	311.0	339	265.4	0.853	0.78

This minimization procedure gives the scaling law.

$$T(1,1,E,N) = 2.01 \cdot 10^{-6} E^{0.97} \cdot N^{3.3} \, . \tag{7}$$

One realises that this complexity law corresponds well to the theoretical one, (Eq. 5).

Generally, the number of iteration steps is not known. If in the optimization procedure one includes N_{CG} in the parameters E and N,

$$T(N_1, \cdot, E, N) = 1.15 \cdot 10^{-5} \cdot N_1 \cdot E^{1.30} \cdot N^{4.19} \, . \tag{8}$$

As a consequence, the estimated number of $N_{CG,est}$ is

$$N_{CG,est} = 5.72 \cdot E^{0.33} \cdot N^{0.89} \, . \tag{9}$$

This prediction is also close to the expected theoretical complexity $N_{CG,theo}$:

$$N_{CG,theo} \approx E^{\frac{1}{3}} \cdot N \, . \tag{10}$$

The same type of studies have been made for a diagonal precoditioner varying the polynomial degree. The complexity found is $N_{CG,est} \approx N^{1.47}$. Thus, for $N \geq 12$ the diagonal preconditioner is faster, while for $N < 12$ the Couzy preconditioner is faster. Since we treat cases with $N = 12$ or smaller, we concentrate on the Couzy preconditioner.

3   Wrong Complexity on the BlueGene/L

The SpecuLOOS code has been ported to the IBM BlueGene/L machine at EPFL with 4096 dual core nodes. Since interelement communication is not that important, all the cores can be used for computation. Table 2 presents the results obtained with the original version of the SpecuLOOS code, before important adaptations described below where performed. One element is running in a core. The polynomial degree is fixed to N=12 for the velocity components, and

Table 2. SpecuLOOS on the BlueGene/L machine up to $P = 8192$ cores. The number of elements per core have been fixed to one. The polynomial degree for the pressure is equal to $N - 2 = 10$.

N_1	$E = E_x E_y E_z$	N	P	$\frac{\# \; elem}{node}$	T_{exec}
1	8x8x16	12	1024	1	17.22
1	8x16x16	12	2048	1	29.91
1	16x16x16	12	4096	1	57.05
1	16x16x32	12	8192	1	140.50

to $N - 2 = 10$ for the pressure. The resulting complexity given by the pressure computation is illustrated on Table 2, and is identified as

$$T \approx E^2. \tag{11}$$

This result shows that the complexity of the original parallel code is far away from the $E^{1.3}$ law, which is expected for theoretical reasons and verified numerically in a serial program execution, eq. 8. The reasons for this bad result could be identified as follows. An IF instruction over all elements had been introduced in the code, in order to identify the attribution of elements to computational nodes dynamically, at each iteration of the conjugate gradient method. Such an instruction is typical for rapid corrections in a code, which are made to parallelize a program rapidly without realising its impact on future program executions. This did not affect the CPU time for less than $P = 100$ nodes, but became dominant for $P > 1000$. This IF instruction has now been replaced by the use of a precomputed list, pointing to the elements which are active on a core.

4   Fine Results on the BlueGene/L

The corrected SpecuLOOS code has been rerun again on the BlueGene/L machine. The effect of the communication has been studied, and results are presented in Fig. 1. The ideal speedup is presented in the upper straight line. The measurements for the case of one element per core are presented through the circular markers. Inter-element communication takes a very small amount of time in the case of 1024 elements, and about 12% of the total time for 8192 cores. If the number of elements per core is increased, the communication/computation decreases, and the computation is closer to ideal scalability.

The measurements in Table 3 show that the symmetric cases with E=16x16x16 take less iteration steps than non-symmetric cases. The complexity laws $T \approx E^a$ for the unsymmetric cases give exponents of a_2=(1.35, 1.28, 1.36, 1.34) for $P =$ (1024, 2048, 4096, 8192). These exponents correspond very well to the expected one, i.e. to a_2=1.3, eqs. 6 and 8. This tells us that the present version of the SpecuLOOS code is well scalable on the BlueGene/L up to 8192, and will for bigger cases, scale to petaflop machines.

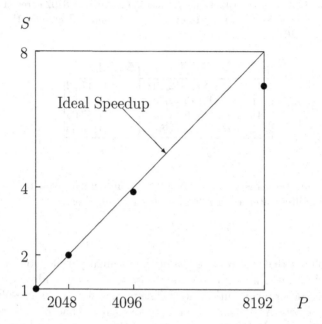

Fig. 1. Speedup S on BlueGene/L as a function of P for the case E=16x16x32, Table 3. The 12% loss in speedup for P=8192 is due to communication between the cores.

Table 3. SpecuLOOS on the BlueGene/L machine up to $P = 8192$ cores. The polynomial degree for the pressure is equal to $N - 2 = 10$. The number of elements per core vary from 1 to 8. The number of iteration steps is an average value, with a clear drop for $E_x = E_y = E_z$.

P	$E = E_x E_y E_z$	$\frac{E^3}{P}$	N_{it}	$T[sec]$
1024	8x8x16	1	689	29.9
1024	8x16x16	2	966	82.8
1024	16x16x16	4	912	155.3
1024	16x16x32	8	1463	494.2
2048	8x16x16	1	950	42.1
2048	16x16x16	2	912	79.1
2048	16x16x32	4	1461	249.9
4096	16x16x16	1	912	41.9
4096	16x16x32	2	1463	128.4
4096	16x32x32	4	1925	331.2
8192	16x16x32	1	1463	70.7
8192	16x32x32	2	1958	179.1

5   Conclusions

The performance review presented in this paper for the high-order spectral and mortar element method C++ toolbox, Speculoos, has shown that good performances can be achieved with relatively common internode network communication systems, available software and hardware resources—small commodity clusters with non-proprietary compilers installed on it.

The parallel implementation of Speculoos based on MPI has shown to be efficient. Reasonable scalability and efficiency can be achieved on commodity clusters. The results support the original choices made in Speculoos parallel implementation by keeping it at a very low-level.

One of the goal of this study was to estimate if Speculoos could run on a massively parallel computer architecture comprising thousands of computational units, specifically on the IBM Blue Gene machine at EPFL with 4'096 dual core units. After detection and correction of a poor implementation choice in the parallel version, perfect scalabilities on up to 8192 cores have been detected.

The present version of the SpecuLOOS code is well scalable on the Blue-Gene/L up to 8192, and will for bigger cases, even scale to petaflop machines.

Acknowledgments

This research is being partially funded by a Swiss National Science Foundation Grant (No. 200020–101707) and by the Swiss National Supercomputing Center CSCS, whose supports are gratefully acknowledged.

References

1. The OpenSPECULOOS project,
   http://sourceforge.net/projects/openspeculoos/
2. Van Kemenade, V.: Incompressible fluid flow simulation by the spectral element method, Tech. rep., "Annexe technique projet FN 21-40'512.94", IMHEF–DGM, Swiss Federal Institute of Technology, Lausanne (1996)
3. Dubois-Pèlerin, Y., Van Kemenade, V., Deville, M.: An object-oriented toolbox for spectral element analysis. J. Sci. Comput. 14, 1–29 (1999)
4. Bouffanais, R.: Simulation of shear-driven flows: Transition with a free surface and confined turbulence, EPFL, Thèse no. 3837 (2007)
5. Deville, M.O., Fischer, P.F., Mund, E.H.: High-order methods for incompressible fluid flow. Cambridge University Press, Cambridge (2002)
6. Fischer, P.F., Patera, A.T.: Parallel spectral element solution of the Stokes problem. J. Comput. Phys. 92, 380–421 (1991)
7. Bouffanais, R., Deville, M.O., Leriche, E.: Large-eddy simulation of the flow in a lid-driven cubical cavity. Phys. Fluids 19, Art. 055108 (2007)
8. Couzy, W., Deville, M.O.: Spectral-element preconditioners for the Uzawa pressure operator applied to incompressible flows. J. Sci. Comput. 9, 107–112 (1994)

Research on Evaluation of Parallelization on an Embedded Multicore Platform

Tao Liu, Zhenzhou Ji, Qing Wang, Dali Xiao, and Shuyan Zhang

School of Computer Science and Technology, Harbin Institute of Technology,
Harbin, Heilongjiang, 150001, China
{liutao07,jizhenzhou}@hit.edu.cn

Abstract. In order to solve the problem of serious performance bottleneck in traditional embedded platform, the parallelization of evaluation algorithms based on an embedded multicore platform is implemented. By analyzing the process of the parallel algorithms on the embedded chip multicore platform, and effectively using the limited memory and cache resource, the evaluation algorithms are implemented in an embedded multicore processor FPGA full function simulation platform. After comparing the parallelization effects of the two multithread models, a conclusion can be made that the shared memory model of parallel multithread fits the embedded multicore platform well. The parallel model generates substantial overall performance increase. An average relative speedup of 3.28 is achieved and meets the low memory resource in embedded architecture. And with the increase in core number the parallelization based on OpenMP model has shown good scalability.

Keywords: embedded, multicore processor, parallelization, FPGA.

1 Introduction

With the increasing performance requirements of digital signal processing applications, the design of embedded processor is changing from the single-core to the chip multicore architecture[1]. A multicore system will face the performance bottleneck of traditional single-core algorithms and a good relative speedup cann't be got by simply using the multicore platform directly. It's required to take reasonable multithread scheduling means of implementation on an embedded multicore platform[2,10]. However, embedded systems have their own unfavorable factors in less storage resource and cache with simple architecture, it has important theoretical and applicational significance in how to make algorithm research and parallelization evaluation on the characteristics of embedded multicore platform. By analyzing the algorithms base on the embedded SMP multicore platforms and reasonably allocating the limited storage resource for the efficient realization of multithread mode, making evaluation of parallelization for the common parallel algorithms in embedded computing area, we research on the suitable parallelization model for embedded parallel platform in order to significantly improve the algorithm performance.

Y. Dou, R. Gruber, and J. Joller (Eds.): APPT 2009, LNCS 5737, pp. 330–340, 2009.
© Springer-Verlag Berlin Heidelberg 2009

The main contents of this paper is based on the embedded multicore architecture platform to complete the evaluation tasks, including Cannon matrix multiplication algorithm, Fast Fourier Transform(FFT), discrete wavelet transform(DWT), image processing algorithm of SUSAN and 2-D non-steady-state heat conduction equation (HCE), then evaluate the performance in two parallelization model as OpenMP[3] and Pthread, the execution time of the evaluation can be obtained through the embedded system timer and by analyzing the parallelization efficiency of the embedded multicore platform we make research on the parallelization design under limited storage resource condition.

2   The Embedded Multicore Processor Platform

Therefore, an embedded platform with four 32-bit RISC cores working in seven-stage pipeline and with 64bit FPU has been simulated by FPGA. The structure of LEON3 processor core[4] is shown in Figure 1.

The platform is setup with XILINX XC4VLX160 chip FPGA, the FPGA main chip has 67,584 slice or 152064 logical units, the equivalent scale of 10 million gates can be designed. In order to make an on-chip quad-core simulation design, the structure code of the IP core has been written into the PROM with the detailed parameters shown in table 1. With built-in cache snooping for data coherency the processor provides hardware support for cache coherency, processor enumeration and interrupts steering. An AMBA round-robin arbiter provides fair bus utilization for the cores, and the layout and interconnection of the functional components are implemented in SMP configuration[5]. Due to the power limit of embedded platform, L2 cache isn't taken into account in this simulation. In order to evaluate the parallelization a linux host with GRMON debug tool is connected to the evaluation platform. Here the onchip enabled core number can be changed from 1 to 4 by debug commands, then load the parallel algorithms to evaluate the performce of parallelization models. OpenMP on the embedded platform is quite different from desktop applications, which compiled with the limited storage resource to optimize the integration[6]. In order to build OpenMP compiler for embedded cross-compiler environment[7,8], and there are two keys to setup the embedded OpenMP cross-compiling environment:

Firstly the compiler should support the precompilation of the OpenMP source code, secondly there should be standard POSIX[9] thread library supporting the compiler to deal with the compiled multithread programs[10]. Then the schedule of multithread needs to configure the embedded operating system to establish real-time operating system for high-performance embedded applications with the support for multi-task priority mechanisms, and all the necessary synchronization primitives for the embedded platform, additionally with multi-level queue scheduler for multithread approach. In order to meet the demands of performance monitoring and extensional functions of embedded applications, the components of embedded configurable operating system (eCos) kernel functions are enabled with the cross-compiling procedure[11]. The Embedded multicore platform need to modify the initialization method of precompiling as $cyg\_start()$, the main function takes into charge after the initialization and the implementation of parallel

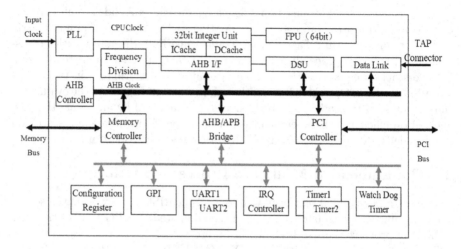

Fig. 1. The core architecture

Table 1. The Simulation Parameters

Simulation Items	Value Description
FPGA chip	VIRTEX4 XC4VLX160
configuration PROM	$6 \times 18V04 - VQ44$
SRAM	4Mbyte ($4 \times 512 \times 16bit$)
FLASH	64Mbyte
processing Cores	$1 - 4$ (Configurable)
L1 Instruction Cache	8Kbyte per core, direct mapped, 32byte per line
L1 Data Cache	8Kbyte per core, 2-way associated, 32byte line
core feather	SMP mode
instruction set	SPARC V8

programs start. Additionally the script of the linker named target.ld should be reconfigured and be enabled to setup the interrupts and the vectors[12] when the eCos kernel starts the initial execution.

3   The Implementation of Evaluation Algorithms for Embedded Multicore Platform

3.1   The Parallelization of Cannon Algorithm on Embedded Platform

The Cannon algorithm has good scalability with the increase in processor number. In our tests, the number of processor cores is four, the detail algorithm is like the following:

1. Generate $N \times N$ integer matrix A and B randomly and define two 2D integer arrays in size $N \times N$ with name A and B and four matrix C_{11}, C_{12}, C_{21}, C_{22} in size $N/2 \times N/2$ to store the result.
2. Divide A into four equal size blocks and do the same to B, so there are eight blocks. If we go on defining eight 2D-arrays in size $N/2 \times N/2$ requires too much memory here, additionally there would be too much critical resource that may cause some trouble to the synchronization among the threads. Actually during the execution the processor cores all get their data by accessing the public data bus in turn, so the execution is parallel but the data fetching is still serial. Here we define two 2D-arrays in size $N/2 \times N/2$ named tmp_A and tmp_B as template buffer to deal with blocks from A and B. Define a global variable named t as a state sign for tmp_A and tmp_B, the value of t shows which thread is fit for the content in tmp_A and tmp_B. For example, when there are A_{11} in tmp_A and B_{11} in tmp_B, t will be 1 to show that $thread\_1$ needs the data.
3. Assign the eight blocks to four processor cores, then OpenMP code would generate four threads automatically and each thread runs on an individual processor core. When assigning the blocks to each thread, the threads should wait for the t value until the required blocks have been written into tmp_A and tmp_B, then the threads can get data from blocks and begin to do multiply and add operations. After the result has got ready the threads would halt.

3.2   The Parallelization of FFT Algorithm on Embedded Platform

Transform N-length FFT into two $N/2$-length FFTs and then induce an iterative procedure, this method accelerated FFT greatly. Next each odd and even sequence Fourier Transform can be divided into a combo of two subsequence and go on repeating these operations. The time complexity of FFT would be decreased from N^2 to $N \cdot \log N$. The FFT process is composed by two steps: the bit-reverse step and the butterfly computing step, The OpenMP can complete each step in parallel to shrink the execution time and increase the acceleration ratio.

1. Bit-reverse: The following codes are the step of bit-reverse. There's no data or control dependencies, so directives can be added to make parallel execution.
2. Butterfly computing: There would be $\log N$ times computing operations in the process of butterfly computing, if the number of processor cores is M, then cut the dataset N into M parts, each core takes charge of one part, when all parts are calculated out they would be merged together to finish the computing, the serial merging step would be $\log M$ in time complexity. This method can greatly shrink the running time of FFT.

3.3   The Parallelization of DWT Algorithm on Embedded Platform

Set p as the number of processing cores, then allocate $C_n^k(n = 0, 1, ..., N/2^j - 1)$ as the input data to these processing cores, the core i would get data: $C_n^k(n = i\frac{N}{p2^j}, ..., (i+1)\frac{N}{p2^j} - 1)$.

First of all randomly generated the L length low-pass coefficient H and the high-pass coefficient G, N length of the input sequence for C, apply two L-size integer arrays H and G, and a N-size array C, call *srand()* function to generate random contents for G, H and C. The DWT task will be divided into four parts; the four parts of the task are assigned to the four processor cores. Algorithm begins from the main thread and initialize the timer, in the main thread call *fork()* to create four subthreads, every subthreads have the same priority, according to the kernel of the multi-level queue scheduling mechanism, each subthread will be assigned to a different processor core. After the first calculation round the cores make synchronization and exchange data to update the array C. When the round counter reaches $\log(n)$, the DWT results would be in array C.

3.4   The Parallelization of SUSAN Algorithm by Blocks

From the image point of view, the method makes a big image divided into a few parts of the same size and then allocates each part to an individual processing thread, lastly combine each of the small images into one large image[13]. The key procedure of the algorithm is like the following:

1. The number of sub-images with equally partitioning. The actual number of image sub-blocks is associated with the number of system threads, and according to the characteristics of the SUSAN algorithm the complexity of the calculation depends on the image resolution, and has nothing to do with the gray value of the image pixels, so the image is divided into blocks in same size to ensure inter-thread load balancing. The image segmentation processing is a common problem. In some image formats it's very difficult to find sub-points. SUSAN algorithm processes pgm format images which have the resolution data in file header, so segmentation can be done according to the resolution data.
2. Image sub-blocks processing. Each edge of the image pixels will take some overlaps to ensure that the special points of the correct image extraction, to prevent missing the edges of small parts in the overlap area. If the block does not overlap the small image, then it usually causes loss of two-phase image pixels department information. In the algorithm parallelization the overlapping area uses the edges of 5-pixel length region, the overlap area is processed twice during the segmentation procedure.

Commonly used methods of sub-images are shown in Figure 2, (a) for an average of the image is divided into four parts horizontally, the shadow part of the edge of the block is the part that need to be processed twice, set up w as the width of the image, h as the height of the image , d for the distance over shadow part in pixels, then in (a) the shadow part has pixels number of $3wd$, in (b) the images are divided into four parts, each part needs to be processed twice, then in (b) the shadow part has pixels number of $(w + h)d$, in (c) the image are divided into four parts vertically, then in (c) the shadow part has pixels number of $3hd$.

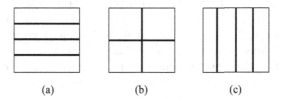

Fig. 2. Image segmentation methods for SUSAN

Therefore, in accordance with the specific image pixel value, we can select the optimal sub-block approach to allow double-handling of the smallest number of pixels. In this paper, Figure (a) is the selected method.

3.5   The Parallelization of 2-D Non-steady-state HCE

Given two-dimensional non-steady-state heat conduction equation:

$$Pc \times dT/dt = d(K \times dT/dx)/dx + d(K \times dT/dy)/dy + S \qquad (1)$$

T, K, p, c, S are x, y, t function, p: dielectric coefficient, c: specific heat, K: thermal conductivity medium, S: The heat generated per unit volume rate (with heat), T to be a function of demand, and its significance is the temperature of a point in a plane at a certain time.

Here using the first boundary condition: $T = b(x, y, t)$. To solve the differential equation, use two-dimensional Crank-Nicolson difference scheme [14], make Integral on both sides of the equation was:

$$\int_S^N \int_W^E \int^{t+\Delta t} pc\frac{\partial T}{\partial t} dt dx dy = \int^{t+\Delta t} \int_S^N \int_W^E \frac{\partial}{\partial x}(K\frac{\partial T}{\partial x}) dx dy dt + \qquad (2)$$

$$\int^{t+\Delta t} \int_W^E \int_S^N \frac{\partial}{\partial y}(K\frac{\partial T}{\partial y}) dy dx dt + \int^{t+\Delta t} \int_S^N \int_W^E S dx dy dt$$

Assuming that the region is divided into $n \times n$ blocks, that is, the total grid has $(n+1) \times (n+1)$ nodes, except the nodes around the boundary, and the remaining $(n-1) \times (n-1)$ nodes are waiting to be processed. Then a large-scale sparse matrix equation is got:

$$AX = b \qquad (3)$$

$$A = \begin{pmatrix} g_1 \ h_1 & & & & \\ f_2 \ g_2 \ h_2 & & & & \\ & f_3 \ g_3 \ h_3 & & & \\ & & \cdot \ \cdot \ \cdot & & \\ & & \cdot \ \cdot \ \cdot & & \\ & & & \cdot \ \cdot \ \cdot & \\ & & & f_{n-2} \ g_{n-2} \ h_{n-2} \\ & & & & f_{n-1} \ g_{n-1} \end{pmatrix}, X = \begin{pmatrix} x_1 \\ x_2 \\ \cdot \\ \cdot \\ \cdot \\ x_{n-2} \\ x_{n-1} \end{pmatrix}, b = \begin{pmatrix} b_1 \\ b_2 \\ \cdot \\ \cdot \\ \cdot \\ b_{n-2} \\ b_{n-1} \end{pmatrix}$$

Here, $g_i(i = 1, 2, ..., n - 1)$ is a $(n - 1) \times (n - 1)$ size triple diagonal matrix, $f_i(i = 1, 2, ..., n-1)$ and $h_i(i = 1, 2, ..., n-1)$ are $(n-1) \times (n-1)$ size diagonal matrices. X_i and $b_i(i = 1, 2, ..., n - 1)$ for n-1 column vector. The HCE is transformed into linear equations. The actual matrix in the implementation is sparse matrix (3) and the parallelization can be put here to solve it.

4   Embedded Multicore Parallel Model Evaluation

4.1   Evaluation Algorithm Parameters

The OpenMP multithread programming model and the Linux system Pthread model are used to make evaluation to the effectiveness and performance of the parallelization in all five parallel algorithms on an embedded multicore platform. The evaluation is performed in the way that each algorithm is executed with a small and a large input sets to assess the efficiency:

1. Cannon matrix multiplication with the matrices of 100 dimensions and 400 dimensions,
2. FFT computation with operating parameters 2^{11} and 2^{15},
3. Parallel algorithm for DWT Input $N = 512$ and 2048 with the parameters $L = 500$,
4. Image size for SUSAN algorithm to process 8.9Kbyte and 61.2Kbyte,
5. The numbers of HCE equations respectively are 50 and 140.

In the embedded quad-core platform the evaluation generates OpenMP model and Pthread model parallelized task running time and the corresponding single-core serial computing time. Calculate the relative speedup according to the Amdahl's law[15] and use eCos system timer to provide execution times. Firstly define the system clock $cyg\_tick\_count\_t$ handle and then the exact time is got by calling $cyg\_currunt\_time()$ function. The time unit is 10ms.

4.2   Test Data Analysis

The five parallelized tasks for embedded multicore platform run in accordance with the small and large-scale input sets, every task executes with 10 groups of input data. The total run time and relative speedup between single-core and quad-core computing for each task are shown in table 2. The overall behavior from the evalutaion tasks can be found: With the size of the input data increased, both OpenMP and Pthread model have a higher speedup ratio, which shows the performance improvement is well worth the overhead from initialization and synchronization. The specific performance of each algorithm, such as Cannon algorithm demonstrates the highest performance relative speedup of more than 3.80 because of the little impact from data correlation. But by the algorithm structure and some data correlation, the speedup of SUSAN algorithm and HCE equations task are relatively lower, however they have still shown significant performance increase.

Table 2. The Execution Time of the Two Models

Algorithm	Model	OpenMP		Pthread	
		Single-Core	4 Cores	Single-Core	4 Cores
Cannon	Small	5.861	1.548	5.833	1.566
	Large	381.077	98.784	380.952	99.892
FFT	Small	6.936	2.393	6.902	2.426
	Large	235.417	68.298	234.989	69.732
DWT	Small	2.161	0.668	2.100	0.654
	Large	7.435	2.210	7.383	2.215
SUSAN	Small	4.362	1.621	4.304	1.598
	Large	31.730	11.413	31.123	11.505
HCE	Small	14.143	4.928	14.085	4.776
	Large	52.997	17.878	52.913	17.896

A run time difference comparative analysis is shown in Figure 3 for the two parallelization models. Y-axis is on behalf of the time difference between the two models as OpenMP task run time minus Pthread task run time. A positive value means the run time of OpenMP task is longer than that of Pthread task. On the contrary, a negative value means OpenMP task run time is shorter than that of Pthread task. X-axis for the five kinds of algorithms corresponding to the different core numbers, such as the "Small input single (4)" is on behalf of with the smaller input set running on single (or 4) core(s), "Large input single (4)" is on behalf of with the larger input set running on single (or 4) core(s). As can be seen in the single-core conditions, the Pthread model overhead is relatively low; the corresponding algorithms run at a slightly faster speed, but only a very small gap here. In the quad-core with large input set conditions OpenMP run time are all shorter than Pthread model with all algorithms except HCE.

It can be seen that with the increase in the number of threads, OpenMP model has a better effect. In particular, Cannon matrix multiplication and FFT algorithms have more obvious changes in run time difference of the two models. The OpenMP model changes from being slower than the Pthread model tasks in single-core execution to taking over in the quad-core tasks. So it's clear that the OpenMP model in embedded multicore environment has significantly more effective for calculating the greater data input set with few data correlation tasks.

A speedup comparison between two multithread parallelization models with large and small input sets on an embedded quad-core platform is shown in Figure 4. The relative speedup is calculated according to the Amdahl's law. "OpenMP(Pthread) small" is on behalf of the OpenMP(Pthread) model task speedup with small input set, "OpenMP(Pthread) large" is on behalf of the OpenMP(Pthread) model task speedup with large input set.

After the comparison two parallel models of multithread both have obvious effects on raising performance. In OpenMP model four out of all the five tasks have shown better relative speedup with comparison to Pthread model and can produce greater performance embedded computing. However, in the HCE

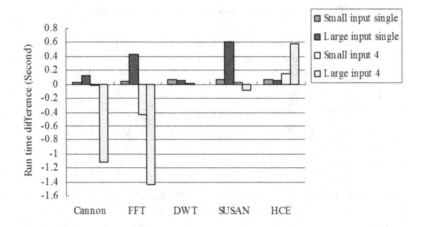

Fig. 3. The Run time difference between two parallelization models

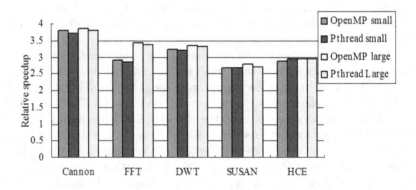

Fig. 4. The Relative Speedup of Two Parallelization Models on an Embedded Quad-core Platform

parallelization because of the need to wait for the sync signal, Pthread model shows better flexibility, but the design process is relatively complex. It can also been seen that OpenMP model reduces the speedup gap and gets more speedup in performance when the input set scale gets larger. Because OpenMP model has simple features in tasks development, it can be expected on the high-performance embedded platform in more parallel threads condition with better scalability. An average relative speedup of 3.28 can be achieved by OpenMP model.

5   Conclusions and Future Work

By analyzing the realization of the parallel process based on embedded multicore platform, configurations for embedded system scheduling and multi-threaded runtime library are made in the limited memory resource and cache. The parallelization of five evaluation tasks are implemented on an embedded multicore architecture FPGA fully functional simulation platform, including Cannon matrix multiplication, FFT, discrete wavelet transform, image processing algorithm of SUSAN and 2-D non-steady-state heat conduction equation. After comparing the effect of OpenMP and Pthread multi-thread model, the OpenMP multithread model is a little better for the current embedded multicore platform. An average relative speedup of 3.28 can be achieved in the evaluation of five OpenMP parallelized embedded tasks. It's a very attractive overall performance improvement on embedded multicore platform, and can meet the low memory overhead requirement. With the increasing trend of core number, OpenMP model is relatively a more efficient way than Pthread in performance and has good scalability. At the same time OpenMP model significantly reduces the difficulty of parallel development. The parallelization of both OpenMP and Pthread based on embedded multicore in the near future can have a significant performance increase on the new embedded architecture platform.

The future work will be based on the embedded multicore architecture for performance and energy efficiency for further evaluation and optimization, the parallelization can be further improved by reducing the synchronization overhead with different means of communication, in order to look forward to getting better performance and efficiency in new embedded multicore or manycore architectures.

Acknowledgments. This work is supported by the Science and Technology Development Project fund of Shandong Province(No.2007GG10001020).

References

1. Burger, D., Goodman, J.R.: Billion-Transistor Architectures: There and Back Again. Computer 37(3), 22–28 (2004)
2. Hwu, W.M., Ryoo, S., Ueng, S.Z., et al.: Implicitly Parallel Programming Models for Thousand-Core Microprocessors. In: Proceeding of the 44th annual conference on Design automation, San Diego, California, USA (2007)
3. Dagum, L., Menon, R.: OpenMP: An Industry-Standard API for Shared-Memory Programming. Computational Science & Engineering 5(1), 46–55 (1998)
4. Gaisler, J., Catovic, E., Isomaki, M., et al.: GRLIB IP Core User's Manual. Gaisler Reserch (2009), http://www.gaisler.com
5. Leon3 Processor Datasheet of Gaisler Reserch,
   http://www.gaisler.com/doc/leon3_product_sheet.pdf
6. Berrendorf, R., Nieken, G.: Performance characteristics for OpenMP constructs on different parallel computer architectures. Concurrency-Practice and Experience 12(12), 1261–1273 (2000)
7. Cuvillo, J.D., Zhu, W., Gao, G.R.: Landing OpenMP on Cyclops-64: An Efficient Mapping of OpenMP to a Many-Core System-on-a-Chip. In: Proceding of the 3rd conference on computing frontiers, Ischia, Italy, pp. 41–50 (2006)

8. Bull, J.M.: Measuring synchronization and scheduling overheads in OpenMP. In: Proceedings of the First European Workshop on OpenMP, Lund, Sweden, pp. 99–105 (1999)
9. IEEE Std 1003.1-2001. Standard for Information Technology - Portable Operating System Interface (POSIX) Base Definitions. IEEE, New York (2001)
10. Cuvillo, J.D., Zhu, W.R., Hu, Z., et al.: FAST: A functionally accurate simulation toolset for the Cyclops64 cellular architecture. In: Proceedings of the Workshop on Modeling, Benchmarking and Simulation, Wisconsin, USA, pp. 11–20 (2005)
11. Massa, A.J.: Embedded Software Development with eCos. Prentice Hall, Indianapolis (2002)
12. Bryant, R.E., O'Hallaron, D.: Computer System: A Programmer's Perspective, pp. 461–501. China Electric Power Press, Beijing (2007)
13. Jie, W., Zhang, S., Tao, L., et al.: Multi-core Embeded Processor Based on FPGA and Parallelization of SUSAN Algorithm. Chinese Journal of Computers 31(11), 1995–2004 (2008)
14. Wenqia, W.: The alternating segment crank-nicolson method for solving convection-diffusion equation with variable coefficient. Applied Mathematics and Mechanics 24(1) (2003)
15. John, L.H., David, A.P.: Computer Architecture: A Quantitative Approach, 4th edn. Elsevier, Singapore (2007)

MapReduce-Based Pattern Finding Algorithm Applied in Motif Detection for Prescription Compatibility Network

Yang Liu, Xiaohong Jiang*, Huajun Chen, Jun Ma, and Xiangyu Zhang

College of Computer Science, Zhejiang University,
Zheda Road. 38, Hangzhou, China, 310027
{darkwarrior,jiangxh,huajunsir,majun,xiangyu}@zju.edu.cn

Abstract. Network motifs are basic building blocks in complex networks. Motif detection has recently attracted much attention as a topic to uncover structural design principles of complex networks. Pattern finding is the most computationally expensive step in the process of motif detection. In this paper, we design a pattern finding algorithm based on Google MapReduce to improve the efficiency. Performance evaluation shows our algorithm can facilitates the detection of larger motifs in large size networks and has good scalability. We apply it in the prescription network and find some commonly used prescription network motifs that provide the possibility to further discover the law of prescription compatibility.

Keywords: complex network, motif detection, pattern finding, MapReduce, prescription compatibility.

1 Introduction

Network motifs are specific pattern of local interconnections with potential functional properties and can be seen as the basic building blocks of complex network [1]. Pattern finding in a complex network is the first and most important step to analyze motifs. Some pattern finding methods are already used to analyze the network motifs in real world such as biochemistry network, ecology network, neurobiology network, and engineering network [1]. And these applications obtain many valuable research results. However, in the pattern finding area, there are many NP-complete problems, such as determining graph isomorphism and maximum independent set [2]. For this reason, the pattern finding algorithms always have high time-space complexity. Moreover, when the size of the pattern is big (usually bigger than 4), the number of the intermediate becomes very large (above millions of items), which makes pattern finding time consuming and memory exhausted.

Google's MapReduce framework is known as the framework of Clouding Computing. MapReduce built on top of the distributed Google File System provides a parallelization framework that has garnered considerable acclaim for its ease-of-use,

---

* Corresponding Author.

Y. Dou, R. Gruber, and J. Joller (Eds.): APPT 2009, LNCS 5737, pp. 341–355, 2009.
© Springer-Verlag Berlin Heidelberg 2009

scalability, and fault-tolerance [3]. Therefore, we try to use the Google's Mapreduce framework to speed up pattern finding and avoid running-out-of memory in a PC-cluster environment. We design a MapReduce-based Pattern Finding algorithm (MRPF) that provides good efficiency and scalability. We also apply it in prescription network and successfully find some commonly used prescription structures that propose the possibility to discover law of prescription compatibility.

In our MRPF algorithm, we reorganize the traditional pattern finding process into four steps: distributed storage, neighbor vertices finding and pattern initialization, pattern extension, and frequency computing. Each step is implemented by a MapReduce pass. In each MapReduce pass, the task is divided into a number of sub-tasks of the same size and each sub-task is distributed to a node of the cluster. MRPF uses an extended mode to find the target size pattern. That is trying to add one more vertex to the matches of i-size patterns to create patterns of size i+1. The extension doesn't stop until patterns reach the target size.

To test the computational efficiency of MRPF, we apply it to the prescription compatibility structure detection. The knowledge discovery of prescription compatibility is an important part of Traditional Chinese Medicine (TCM) research. Prescription compatibility investigates the composite structure of herbal medicines. One prescription contains five or six herbal medicines. However prescriptions are commonly given based on experiences without theoretical instruction on prescription structures. So we construct the prescription compatibility network and use our algorithm to detect the prescription compatibility structure.

The rest of the paper is organized as follows. Section 2 introduces some related works on pattern finding methods, applications of MapReduce and some data mining method used in TCM. Section 3 describes our MRPF algorithm in detail. Section 4 gives the case study on prescription compatibility using our algorithm. Section 5 provides some concluding remarks and discussion for future work.

2   Relate Works

The main step in motif detection is pattern finding in the complex network. There are two distinct problem formulations for pattern finding in graph datasets. One is the graph-transaction setting that use a set of relatively small graphs as input data, the other is the single-graph setting using a single large graph instead[4]. Pattern finding in graph-transaction attracts more attention, so that a number of efficient algorithms [5-10] have been developed. However, few investigations have been made in pattern finding from the single-graph setting. Moreover, some algorithms, such as GBI [11] and SUBDUE [12], will lose a large number of patterns, and at the same time not scale well for large datasets due to computational complexity. In recent years, with the application of pattern finding increasingly used in many fields, researchers start to pay more attention in designing algorithms for single-graph setting. In 2005, Michihiro Kuramoch and George Karrypis developed an algorithm to find patterns in a large sparse graph [4]. Falk Schreiber and Henning Schwobbermeyer designed a FPF multiple-thread algorithm [13] to improve the performance of Michihiro's algorithm. Jin Chen et al. designed a NeMoFinder algorithm that can mine meso-scale network motifs in large protein-protein interaction networks [14]. In 2007, Chen Chen et al. invented a gApprox algorithm that does consider approximate matching in its search space [15]. However all these algorithms mentioned above ignored to consider the limitation of the main memory of one computer. So for further improving the performance of pattern finding and breaking through single computer resource constraints, we design a parallel pattern finding algorithm based on MapReduce Framework. It's a complete algorithm without losing any target-size pattern in the network.

MapReduce Framework, as a parallel model, is often used in data mining, such as machine learning [16], svm [17]. These experiments demonstrate that MapReduce Framework is effective for problems with high complexity and large dataset. It is also proved that MapReduce can be adapted to manipulating graphs. Implementation of pattern finding in the context of MapReduce Framework is able to address the issues of insufficient memory, computational complexity and fault tolerance. Many of data mining methods have been used in the Modernization of Traditional Chinese Medicine. Text mining method is used for finding functional community of TCM Knowledge [18]. Mining compatibility rules are used for TCM databases [19]. Clustering method is applied to analyzing Chinese Text Categorization [20]. Prescription compatibility is investigated in [21-23], but very little work has been done on motif detection in prescription network, which is very important for law discovery of prescription compatibility. We analyze the prescription compatibility using the complex network and find some commonly used prescription structures.

3   MRPF: MapReduce-Based Pattern Finding

MapReduce-based pattern finding (MRPF) framework aims to implement frequent pattern finding on complex graphs based on Hadoop. Although it also works well on undirected graphs, here we still focus on introducing its application on directed graphs. It's more interesting and representative to apply this framework on directed graphs. For clearly depicting MRPF, we show the serial pattern finding algorithm in Algorithm 1.

3.1   MRPF Framework

Here we define the size of a pattern by its vertices number. We use the generation of a canonical label described in [24] to check graphs for isomorphism. After loading a dataset of a network, MRPF uses one MapReduce pass to parse the dataset and form three information tables. Another MapReduce pass is used to extend *matches* that are subgraphs of the network from size i to i+1. The frequency of new patterns will be calculated after all matches of patterns of size i+1 have been obtained. Fig. 1 depicts the outline of MRPF.

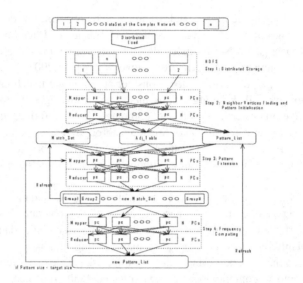

Fig. 1. The MRPF framework

Algorithm 1. Normal Pattern Finding

Data: Dataset of Graph G, target pattern size s, minimum support (f_min)

Result: Set P of pattern of target size

begin

    P ← {all pattern of size 2};

    size ← 2; /* initial size */

    MATCH$_{p2}$ ← all matches of p2;

    TPS ← Φ; /* TPS: target pattern size */

    while size < target size do

      foreach pattern p ∈ P do

        foreach match m ∈ MATCH$_p$ do

          foreach incident vertex v of m do

            m′ ← m ∪{v };

            p′ ← pattern of {m′};

            TPS ← TPS∪{p};

            MATCH$_{p'}$ ← MATCH$_p$∪{ m′};

```
        end

    end

end

P ← Φ;

foreach  p ∈ TPS do

    frequency ← sizeof ( MATCH_p);

    if frequency > f_min then P  ← PU{p};

    end

    size++;

end.
```

Step 1: Distributed storage. MRPF is based on Hadoop, a Google's GFS implementation, hosted as a project of the Apache Software Foundation [16]. In Step 1, the target network is stored as textual files in a specific format. Using Hadoop, the file can be easily divided into a set of blocks with the same size and distributed on nodes of the cluster to keep load balance in the cluster. Hadoop can process the blocks concurrently on nodes where the data is located.

Step 2: Neighbor vertices finding and pattern initialization. In this step we use a MapReduce pass to do two tasks, one is to find adjacent neighbor of each vertex to form an adjacent vertices table *(Adj_Table)*, the other is to find patterns of size two (one edge and two vertices) and their matches. Each mapper inputs one block of the dataset. The results are respectively stored in *Adj_Table, Match_Set* and *Pattern_List*. Please note that Adj_Table is distributed to every node in the cluster and it will be used in pattern extension (Step 3). It is used to detect the patters on the borders of blocks and to guarantee our algorithm to be complete (against losing patterns). Match_Set and Pattern_List are updated by Step 3 and Step 4 respectively. We will introduce the details in Section 3.2.

Step 3: Pattern extension. It is the key step of the MRPF. This step also takes one MapReduce pass. The map stage working with reduce stage extends patterns of size i to i+1. The details will be explained in Section3.3.

Mapper – extend the matches of size i to i+1, calculate their patterns and produce a group key with the patterns and matches. Each mapper outputs one or more key-value pairs, and the pairs with the same key will automatically be grouped into the same reducer.

Reducer - remove the duplicated matches. Since different matches may get the same subgraph of size i+1 when the matches i are extended. During the grouping process mentioned above, we compare the canonical label of each match and keep just one of the same matches. The outputs of reducers are grouped into different files according to the pattern label.

Step 4: Frequency computing. After pruning the identical subgraphs, a MapReduce pass is used to count the support value of all patterns that appear in the big simple graph. We prune the patterns lower than the minimum required frequency. Then we store new patterns in Pattern_List. Go back to Step 3 to process iteratively till the target pattern size is reached. The details are given in Section 3.4.

3.2 Neighbor Vertices Finding and Pattern Initialization

Just like a classical application of MapReduce, each mapper of the first MapReduce pass is fed with one block of dataset. The input key-value pairs would be like <key, value = edge (V_i, V_j) > (V_i and V_j are adjacent vertex to each other), where edges belong to dataset. Mappers produce two kinds of keys: the vertex key according to vertex label and the pattern key according to the pattern *canonical label*. Mappers travel through all edges of the graph, each Mapper outputs three key-value pairs <$key_1 = V_i$, $value_1 = V_j$>, <$key_2 = V_j$, $value_2 = V_i$> and <key_3 = pattern2, $value_3$ = edge (V_i, V_j) >.

After all mapper instances have finished, the MapReduce infrastructure automatically collects and groups the key-value pairs according to the keys. The values with the same key are put into the same group, called G (key), and reducers receive the key value pairs <key, G (key)> where G (key) is adjacent vertices of a vertex or the match of a pattern whose size is two. Reducers compose the G (key) into an adjacent vertices list or match list and outputs <key, list> into Adj_Table or Match_Set according to the class of each key, where the list is vertices list or match list. Algorithm 2 presents the pseudo code of this step. Through this process, it registers each vertex's adjacent vertices. Meanwhile, it finds the smallest patterns (of size 2) and their matches.

Algorithm 2. Neighbor Vertices Finding and Pattern Initialization

```
Procedure: Mapper(key, value = Edge(V_i :V_j))
   /*  p is the canonical label of Edge(V_i:V_j)  */
      p getPattern(Edge(V_i:V_j))
      EmitIntermediate (<key = V_i, value = V_j>)
      EmitIntermediate (<key = V_j, value = V_i>)
      EmitIntermediate (<key = p, value = Edge(V_i:V_j)>)

Procedure: Reduce(key, value = G(key))
   /* Adj_List : adjacent vertices list;
      Match_List: matches of the same pattren */
   Adj_List
   Match_List
   if key is vertex label then
```

```
foreach item v_i  in G(key) do
   Adj_List Adj_List {v_i}
end
Emit(<key, Adj_List >)
else
   foreach item match_i in G(key) do
     Match_List Match_List { match_i}
   end
   Emit(<key, Match_List>)
end
```

3.3 Pattern Extension

This step is the key part of the MRPF algorithm. This step, together with the step 4 frequency computing, will be repeated until the target size pattern is obtained. In the pseudo code of the Algorithm 3 below we will see the procedure of how we use the MapReduce Framework clearly.

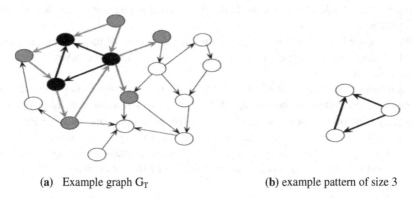

(a) Example graph G_T (b) example pattern of size 3

Fig. 2. (a) G_T is a graph. The subgraph (highlighted with bold lines) in G_T is a match of the pattern in (b). Gray vertices in G_T are *incident* vertices of the match and gray edges are *detected* edges. (b) A pattern of size 3.

First, we load the adjacent vertices table (Adj_Table) which can be stored in memory to find incident vertices of matches. Then load the Pattern_List where keeps all the patterns of size i. The initial state of the Pattern_List is defined as "Starting". The input of mapper is from Match_Set. As shown in Fig. 2, if a match (highlighted in bold black line) is found in the graph, we call the vertices (in gray) adjacent to the matched vertices (in black) incident vertex of a match. And the edge between an incident vertex and the match is called detected edge.

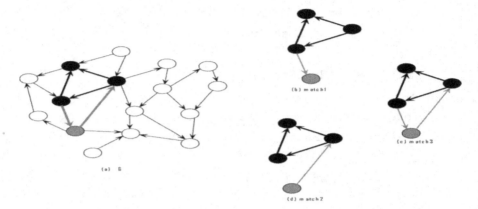

Fig. 3. (a) A graph with a randomly selected subgraph (highlighted with bold lines). The subgraph is a match (M_3) of some pattern. (b), (c), (d) are the extension matches from M_3.

In mappers, the input pair would be like <key, value=Pattern$_i$ & match$_i$> from the Match_Set, where Pattern$_i$ means the pattern has i vertices and match$_i$ means the match has i vertices. If the Pattern$_i$ is contained in Pattern_List or Pattern_list is in initial state, it extends match$_i$ to matchi+1 through adding each incident vertex into match$_i$ as shown in Fig.3. Then it adds various combinations of detected edges into match$_i$ and forms new matches.

We compute Pattern$_{i+1}$ of match$_{i+1}$ and the canonical label of the Pattern$_{i+1}$ as part of output value. Each mapper outputs one or more pairs like <key'= match$_{i+1}$, value'=pattern $_{i+1}$>.

Each reducer receives a <key'= match$_{i+1}$, S (key'))> where the S (key') has only one element------the pattern of the match$_{i+1}$ that is the key of key-value pair. In this way we can easily wipe off the identical matches. Each reducer outputs one <key'' = Pattern$_{i+1}$, key'>, the MapReduce infrastructure sorts and groups the key-value pairs according the key'' value, then produces the successive block based on grouping. Blocks are stored in N different computers, which is convenient to deal with the data in the next MapReduce process.

Algorithm 3. Pattern Extension

```
Procedure: Mapper(key, value = Pattern_i & match_i)
  Load  Adj_Table
  Load  Pattern_List
  if Pattern_i in Pattern_List
    or Pattern_list is in the Starting state then
    foreach incident vertex of match_i  do
      foreach combination C_i of detected edges
        between the incident vertex and match_i do
```

```
        match_{i+1}   match_i  { C_i }
        Pattern_{i+1}   corresponding pattern of match_{i+1}
        EmitIntermediate(<key = match_{i+1}, Pattern_{i+1}>)
    end
end

Procedure: Reduce(key= match_{i+1}, S (key))
    Pattern_{i+1}   one of S (key)
    Emit(<key = Pattern_{i+1}, match_{i,j}>)
```

3.4 Frequency Computing

Frequency computing is a simple counting process, a classical application of MapReduce. Its input is the output of the step3. Algorithm 4 presents the pseudo code of the two steps: grouping and parallel counting. The mapper's input is <key, value = T>, where T is composed of pattern canonical label and matches. It picks up the pattern canonical (P) from T. The mapper outputs a key-value pair <key' = P, value'=1>.

After completing all of the Mapper instances, for each key transmitted by Mapper, a value set (S (key')) is automatically formed. And each reduce is fed with <key', S (key')>. The reducer outputs <key''= key' value'' = sum(S (key'))>.

Then the pattern frequency is calculated based on the occurrence quantity of each pattern. In this paper, to show the full potential of the prescription network we use the frequency concept which counts every match of the pattern. It gives a complete overview of all possible occurrences of a pattern even if elements of the target graph are used several times. So it does not satisfy the Downward Closure Property [4]. And we do not prune the infrequent patterns that lower than the target pattern size. Note that the occurrence quantity of some patterns is too small to affect the pattern finding results. We call these patterns *dust patterns*. A minimum required frequency variable (f_min) is defined to prune the dust patterns. The value of f_min is given by experts according to their experience.

Algorithm 4. Frequency Computing

```
Procedure: Mapper(key, value = Pattern_i & match_i)
    /* PL: pattern label*/
    PL   the canonical label of Pattern_i
    EmitIntermediate(<key = PL, '1'>)

Procedure: Reduce(key , S (key))
    Sum 0
    foreach item '1' in S(key) do
        Sum Sum + 1
```

```
end
/* total is the quantity of all patterns, f_min is a minimum
required frequency variable */
if   Sum total * f_min
    Emit(<key = Pattern_{i+1},   Sum>)
end
```

4 Application to Prescription Compatibility Structure Detection

4.1 Motifs Detection Results

A key subject of prescription research is theoretical study on prescription compatibility regularity. The structure of Monarch, Minister, Assistant and Guide is the compatibility principle for prescriptions and the base for the overall efficacy of prescriptions. However, people as yet know nothing about the commonly used compatibility structure. In other words, people still have no acquaintance with most appropriate ratio of these four kinds (e.g. Monarchs, Ministers, Assistants and Guides) of Chinese herbal medicines respectively participating in the compatibility of a prescription, which is very important to exert the overall efficacy.

In the prescription compatibility network, node represents Chinese herbal medicine, while edge describes the compatibility relation that might exist between the two herb nodes, and edge direction indicates the relative position between the two connected herb nodes from the higher one to the lower one. According to the multi-types of the relative positions between any two herb nodes, the compatibility relations of them vary greatly. Table1 shows in detail all types of possible compatibility relations in terms of criteria for the classification of herbs.

Table 1. All types of possible compatibility relations

Herbal	compatibility relation	Herbal	compatibility relation
Monarch, Minister	Monarch → Minister	Monarch, Assistant	Monarch → Assistant
Monarch, Guide	Monarch → Guide	Minister, Assistant	Minister → Assistant
Minister, Guide	Minister → Guide	Assistant, Guide	Assistant → Guide

We select 201 prescriptions that are explicit in the compatibility structure from [25] to construct the prescription compatibility network. The network contains about 300 vertices and 2, 000 edges, as shown in Fig.4.

We apply our algorithm in the prescription network, and after comparing with random networks, we find a number of motifs of prescription network (see Fig.5) and their occurrence quantity shown in table 2.

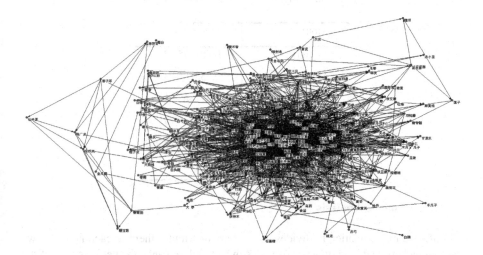

Fig. 4. The topological structure of the prescription compatibility network

These motifs are the basic structure of the prescription compatibility. For example, Motif1 consists of one Monarch, one Minister, one Assistant and one Guide; Motif3 contains one Monarch, one Minister, one Assistant and one Guide; Motif5 contains one Monarch, two Ministers and two Assistants. They are of great value to further discover the law of prescription compatibility.

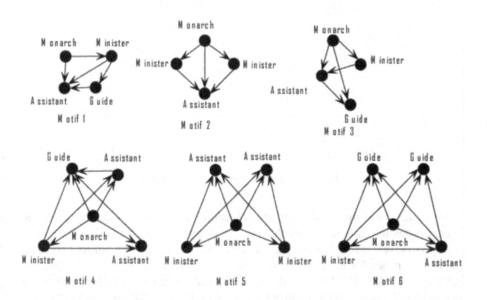

Fig. 5. Six motifs of size 4 and size 5 separately

Table 2. Frequency for each motif in Fig.4

Motif	Frequency
Motif1	0.4093750%
Motif2	0.3534964%
Motif3	0.3728833%
Motif4	0.0038188%
Motif5	0.0026400%
Motif6	0.0018862%

4.2 Performance Analysis

Our algorithm automatically divides the job and distributes them to each node. So we can dynamically add the quantity of nodes, which will enhance the performance of the algorithm. We run the program on a blade-cluster with 48 nodes. Each node is equipped with Intel (R) Xeon (TM) CPU 2.80 GHZ and 1 GB memory. In the experiment, we run the algorithm to do the same task on cluster of varying nodes. And the experiment results of finding size 4 and size 5 motifs are shown in Fig.6.

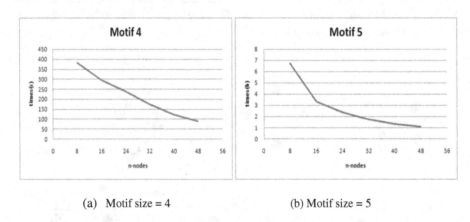

(a) Motif size = 4   (b) Motif size = 5

Fig. 6. Algorithm performance on the cluster

From the above figure, it's clear that execution time decreases quickly while the cluster nodes increase. It implies that our algorithm scales well with the computing nodes. However, the performance acceleration decreases when the cluster exceeds a number of nodes for a fixed size task. In this experimentation, we just prove the scalability of MRPF. Here we theoretically analyze reasons of the acceleration decreasing. We define the formula of the execution time of MRPF as followed:

$$T_{total}(N) = \frac{C_{fix}}{N} + T_{overhead} = \frac{C_{fix}}{N} + T_{map}(N) + T_{reduce}(N) + T_{M/s}(N). \qquad (1)$$

In the formula (1), N is the number of data nodes; C_{fix} is a constant that represents the computation complexity of the fixed size task and it is distributed to each node evenly; $T_{map}(N)$, $T_{reduce}(N)$ and $T_{M/s}(N)$ respectively denote Map Task initialization time, the time for each reducer receiving the intermediate, and the time for the communication between the master node and slave nodes. The Map Task initialization time $T_{map}(N)$ includes assigning tasks, preparing data and task issuing. According to our experience, the total number of map tasks is better to be set about 3 or 4 times of the number of nodes, which can make full use of the resource of the cluster. So we divide the task dynamically according to N. While the number of the data blocks increasing with N, the number of the Map Task increases and the total time of map initialization and intermediate distribution increase too. It is obvious that $T_{map}(N)$ and $T_{reduce}(N)$ are increasing with N. And the cluster is organized in master/slaves mode, with only one master node responsible for data retrieval, task assignment and task snooping on the slave nodes. So while the node number N increase, the communication overhead between master and slaves will also increase. So the value of $T_{M/s}(N)$ is increasing with N. The speedup of MRPF can be calculated using the following formula:

$$Speedup = \frac{T_{total}(N)}{T_{total}(N+1)} = \frac{\frac{C_{fix}}{N} + T_{map}(N) + T_{reduce}(N) + T_{M/s}(N)}{\frac{C_{fix}}{N+1} + T_{map}(N+1) + T_{reduce}(N+1) + T_{M/s}(N+1)}. \qquad (2)$$

From the formula (2), it can be deduced that the speedup might degrade due to the increasing overhead even if C_{fix} is allocated by the cluster nodes. It can be clearly observed that there is an inflection point in exertion time curve in figure 6(b) when the number of the data nodes equals 16. It may be caused by the topology of the cluster or architecture of MapReduce Framework. We need to do further experiments to investigate into it.

5 Conclusion

In summary, the contributions of this paper are as follows:

1. We designed a MapReduce-based pattern finding algorithm (MRPF) for analyzing the complex network. We reorganized the pattern finding process and implemented each step using the MapReduce framework, which makes MRPF parallelizable and extensible. The experiment evaluation on the expending of nodes in Section 4.2 indicated that increasing the number of the nodes would enhance the performance of MRPF.

2. We applied the complex network analysis method to the prescription compatibility network and used MRPF to find the commonly used compatibility structure. And we found some prescription structures which reflect characters of the law of compatibility of medicines in prescriptions in some way.

More experiments need to be done to evaluate the algorithm performance considering the factors of data block size, node number, and network bandwidth, etc. In fact, developing MapReduce based pattern finding algorithm is actually the first step to our target, to develop a parallel data mining library based on MapReduce that can be applied in many fields. And we will also testify these parallel algorithms in data mining in TCM.

Acknowledgements

Supported by Program for Changjiang Scholars and innovative Research Team in University (IRT0652, PCSIRT), China 863 project under grant 2006AA01A123, the National 973 Basic Research Program of China under grant No.2007CB310900, National Science Fund for Distinguished Young Scholars under grant No.60525202, J20060103, J20050710, the Defense Advanced Research Foundation of the General Armaments Department of the PLA under Grant No.9140A06060307JW0403.

References

1. Milo, R., Shen-Orr, S., Itzkovitz, S., Kashtan, N., Chklovskii, D., Alon, U.: Network Motifs: Simple Building Block of Complex Networks. Science 5594, 824–827 (2002)
2. Garey, M.R., Johnson, D.S.: Computers and Intractability: A Guide to the Theory of NP-Completeness. W. H. Freeman and Company, New York (1979)
3. Dean, J., Ghemawat, S.: MapReduce: Simplified data processing on large clusters. In: ACM OSDI (2004)
4. Kuramochi, M., Karypis, G.: Finding Frequent Patterns in a Large Sparse Graph. In: Data Mining and Knowledge Discovery, vol. 5810, pp. 243–271. Springer, Heidelberg (2005)
5. Yan, X., Han, J.: gSpan: Graph-based substructure pattern mining. In: 2002 IEEE International Conference on Data Mining, 2002. ICDM 2002. Proceedings, pp. 721–724. IEEE Press, Maebashi City (2002)
6. Inokucbi, A., Wasbio, T., Motoda, H.: Complete mining of frequent patterns from graphs: Mining graph data. Machine Learning 50(3), 321–354 (2003)
7. Hong, M., Zhou, H., Wang, W., Shi, B.: An efficient algorithm of frequent connected subgraph extraction. In: Whang, K.-Y., Jeon, J., Shim, K., Srivastava, J. (eds.) PAKDD 2003. LNCS, vol. 2637, pp. 40–51. Springer, Heidelberg (2003)
8. Yan, X., Hart, J.: CloseGraph: Mining closed frequent patterns. In: The 9th ACM SIGKDD International Conference on Knowledge Discovery and Data Mining (KDD 2003), pp. 286–295. ACM, Washington (2003)
9. Huan, J., Wang, W., Prins, J.: Efficient mining of frequent subgraph in the presence of isomorphism. In: 2003 International Conference on Data Mining (ICDM), Melbourne, pp. 549–552. IEEE, Florida (2003)
10. Gudes, E., Shimony, S.E., Vanetik, N.: Discovering frequent graph patterns using disjoint paths. IEEE Transactions on Knowledge and Data Engineering 18(11), 1441–1456 (2006)
11. Yoshida, K., Motoda, H., Indurkhya, N.: Graph-based induction as a unified learning framework. Journal of Applied Intelligence 4, 297–328 (1994)

12. Cook, J., Holder, L.: Substructure discovery using minimum description length and background knowledge. J. Artificial Intelligence Research, 231–255 (1994)
13. Schreiber, F., Schwöbbermeyer, H.: Frequent Concepts and Pattern Detection for the Analysis of Motifs in Networks. In: Priami, C., Merelli, E., Gonzalez, P., Omicini, A. (eds.) Transactions on Computational Systems Biology III. LNCS (LNBI), vol. 3737, pp. 89–104. Springer, Heidelberg (2005)
14. Chen, J., Hsu, W., Lee, M.-L., Ng, S.-K.: Nemofinder: dissecting genome-wide protein-protein interactions with meso-scale network motifs. In: KDD, pp. 106–115 (2006)
15. Chen, C., Yan, X., Zhu, F., Han, J.: gApprox: Mining frequent approximate patterns from a massive network. In: Perner, P. (ed.) ICDM 2007. LNCS (LNAI), vol. 4597, pp. 445–450. Springer, Heidelberg (2007)
16. Chu, C., Kim, S.K., Lin, Y., Yu, Y.Y., Bradski, G.: Map-Reduce for Machine Learning on Multicore. NIPS (2006)
17. Chang, E., Zhu, K., Wang, H., Bai, H., Li, J., Qiu, Z., Cui, H.: PSVM: Parallelizing Support Vector Machines on Distributed Computers. NIPS (2007)
18. Wu, Z., Zhou, X., Liu, B., Chen, J.: Text Mining for Finding Functional Community of Related Genes using TCM Knowledge. In: Boulicaut, J.-F., Esposito, F., Giannotti, F., Pedreschi, D. (eds.) PKDD 2004. LNCS (LNAI), vol. 3202, pp. 459–470. Springer, Heidelberg (2004)
19. Ying, T., Guo-fu, Y., Gui-bing, L., Jian-ying, C.: Mining Compatibility Rules from Irregular Chinese Traditional Medicine Database by Apriori Agorithm. Journal of Southwest Jiaotong University (English Edition) 15, 288–292 (2007)
20. Xuezhong, Z., Zhaohui, W.: Distributional Character Clustering for Chinese Text Categorization. In: Zhang, C., Guesgen, H.W., Yeap, W.-K. (eds.) PRICAI 2004. LNCS (LNAI), vol. 3157, pp. 575–584. Springer, Heidelberg (2004)
21. Xiao, H., Liang, X., Lu, P., Chan, C.: New method for analysis of Chinese herbal complex prescription and its application. Chinese Science Bulletin 44, 1164–1172 (1999)
22. Feng, Y., Wu, Z., Zhou, X., Zhou, Z., Fan, W.: Knowledge discovery in traditional Chinese medicine: State of the art and perspectives. Artificial Intelligence in Medicine. 38(3), 219–236 (2006)
23. Chang, Y.-H., Lin, H.-J., Li, W.-C.: Clinical evaluation of the traditional Chinese prescription Chi-Ju-Di-Huang-Wan for Dry Eye. Phytotherapy Research 19(4), 349–354 (2005)
24. Kuramochi, M., Karypis, G.: An efficient algorithm for discovering frequent subgraphs. Technical Report 02-026, Department of Computer Science, University of Minnesota (2002)
25. Fujing, D.: Prescription: for the Specialty of Chinese Traditional Medicine. Shanghai Publishing House of Science and Technology Press, Shanghai (2006)

Parallelization of the LEMan Code with MPI and OpenMP

N. Mellet and W.A. Cooper

Ecole Polytechnique Fédérale de Lausanne (EPFL)
Centre de Recherches en Physique des Plasmas
Association Euratom-Confédération Suisse
CH-1015 Lausanne, Switzerland
nicolas.mellet@epfl.ch
http://crppwww.epfl.ch

Abstract. The low-frequency wave propagation code LEMan has been parallelized. Due to large memory requirement but fast computation with the cold model, the parallelization is limited to a low number of processors. The specific block-tridiagonal structure of the matrix to be solved has been taken into account for the MPI implementation. It has then been compared with the performance of OpenMP in order to determine the optimal method depending on the case studied.

Keywords: Plasma physics, Alfvén, ICRF, Parallelization, MPI, OpenMP.

1 Introduction

Thermonuclear fusion is a very promising source of energy. The reaction that is based on fusion of light nuclei needs specific conditions to happen. These can be reached for example by confining plasma in a magnetic field with sufficient density and temperature. A great variety of waves can then propagate in this case. The low-frequency domain studied by the LEMan code [1] is especially interesting. Waves can be sources of instabilities or be used for heating purpose to obtain parameters required for a self-sustained reaction.

The concept of the LEMan code is to provide a fast computation of the wave field in fully three-dimensional geometries. As plasma is a charged fluid, it consists then essentially in the direct solution of the Maxwell's equations. These are solved using a Galerkin weak form with a discretization that is characteristic of a toroidal topology: radial finite elements, toroidal and poloidal Fourier harmonics. Such a scheme leads to a full block tridiagonal matrix for the linear system.

2 Parallelization

The parallelisation of the LEMan code can mainly be separated in three parts: the matrix construction, the solver and the diagnostics. The third point corresponds essentially to the computation of the plasma quantities relative to the

Y. Dou, R. Gruber, and J. Joller (Eds.): APPT 2009, LNCS 5737, pp. 356–362, 2009.
© Springer-Verlag Berlin Heidelberg 2009

solution (electric and magnetic fields, power deposition, etc). The tasks are however easy to share between processors in this case. This paper will then concentrate on the two first steps of the computation.

A first point has to be mentioned about the solver. Due to the huge size of the matrix, it is impossible to use a parallel library like SCALAPACK. As the matrix width is large, the temporary arrays reach quickly the memory limit of the machine. The method that will involve parallelization with MPI has to be implemented directly on the matrix blocks. It uses Gauss elimination which is expressed for one processor as:

$$
\begin{pmatrix}
B_1 & C_1 & 0 & \cdots & 0 \\
A_1 & B_2 & C_2 & \ddots & \vdots \\
0 & A_2 & B_3 & \ddots & 0 \\
\vdots & \ddots & \ddots & \ddots & C_{n-1} \\
0 & \cdots & 0 & A_{n-1} & B_n
\end{pmatrix}
\begin{pmatrix}
f_1 \\ f_2 \\ f_3 \\ \vdots \\ f_n
\end{pmatrix}
=
\begin{pmatrix}
d_1 \\ d_2 \\ d_3 \\ \vdots \\ d_n
\end{pmatrix}
\qquad
\begin{aligned}
\mathcal{B}_1 &= B_1, \\
\mathcal{B}_i &= B_i - A_{i-1}\mathcal{D}_{i-1}, \\
\mathcal{D}_i &= d_i - A_{i-1}\mathcal{e}_{i-1},
\end{aligned}
\qquad (1)
$$

where $\mathcal{e}_i = \mathcal{B}_i^{-1}\mathcal{D}_i$ and $\mathcal{D}_i = \mathcal{B}_i^{-1}C_i$. Once the matrix has been factorized, the second step is to perform the backsolve:

$$ f_i = \mathcal{e}_i - \mathcal{D}_i f_{i+1}, \qquad (2) $$

We note that with this method, only one block ($\mathcal{D}_i$) has to be stored for each radial node. Compared to the usual band matrix storage in LAPACK, this represents a gain of 82%. The main memory concern does not, however, come from the total matrix storage as hard drives can be used for this purpose but from the memory required for the blocks that correspond to a single radial position. As a huge number of Fourier modes is needed for the more complex geometries and cases, their memory can represent altogether more than 10 GB. In such cases, the optimal machines are SMP whose memory is shared over processors. As OpenMP can be used on those computers, the number of MPI tasks can be kept very low. A method that provides a good scaling is Cyclic Reduction. It has however the disadvantage to require 31 times more operation that a simple Gauss decomposition in the present case where the matrix blocks are full. This technique becomes then faster than a serial run only with more than 32 MPI tasks. With the possibility to take advantage of OpenMP and other parallelization methods, the use of Cyclic Reduction can be avoided. In what follows, we will concentrate on the optimization of the solver with a much lower number of processors.

The first technique that is used is a two-processor method. The method called BABE (Burn At Both Ends) [2] consists in applying a Gauss decomposition with one processor from the top and with the other from the bottom of the matrix:

$$
\begin{aligned}
\text{Processor 1:} \quad & \mathcal{B}_i = B_i - A_{i-1}\mathcal{D}_{i-1}, & \text{Processor 2:} \quad & \mathcal{B}_i = B_i - C_i\mathcal{D}_{i+1}, \\
& \text{where } \mathcal{D}_i = \mathcal{B}_i^{-1}C_i, & & \text{where } \mathcal{D}_i = \mathcal{B}_i^{-1}A_{i-1}, \\
& \mathcal{D}_i = d_i - A_{i-1}\mathcal{e}_{i-1}. & & \mathcal{D}_i = d_i - C_i\mathcal{e}_{i+1}.
\end{aligned}
$$

$$ (3) $$

The elimination process is performed until a central system that contains 4 blocks is obtained:

$$\begin{pmatrix} \mathcal{B}_1 & C_1 & 0 & & \cdots & & 0 \\ 0 & \mathcal{B}_2 & \ddots & & & & \\ 0 & \ddots & \ddots & C_{\frac{n}{2}-1} & \ddots & & \\ & 0 & \mathcal{B}_{\frac{n}{2}} & C_{\frac{n}{2}} & & & \\ \vdots & & \ddots & A_{\frac{n}{2}} & \mathcal{B}_{\frac{n}{2}+1} & 0 & \\ & & & A_{\frac{n}{2}+1} & \ddots & \ddots & 0 \\ & & & & \ddots & \mathcal{B}_{n-1} & 0 \\ 0 & & \cdots & & & 0 & A_{n-1} & \mathcal{B}_n \end{pmatrix} \begin{pmatrix} f_1 \\ f_2 \\ \vdots \\ f_{\frac{n}{2}} \\ f_{\frac{n}{2}+1} \\ \vdots \\ f_{n-1} \\ f_n \end{pmatrix} = \begin{pmatrix} \partial_1 \\ \partial_2 \\ \vdots \\ \partial_{\frac{n}{2}} \\ \partial_{\frac{n}{2}+1} \\ \vdots \\ \partial_{n-1} \\ \partial_n \end{pmatrix}. \tag{4}$$

Its solution is given by the following expression:

$$f_{\frac{n}{2}} = \left(\mathcal{B}_{\frac{n}{2}} - C_{\frac{n}{2}} \mathcal{B}_{\frac{n}{2}+1}^{-1} A_{\frac{n}{2}} \right)^{-1} \left(\partial_{\frac{n}{2}} - C_{\frac{n}{2}} \mathcal{B}_{\frac{n}{2}+1}^{-1} \partial_{\frac{n}{2}+1} \right) \tag{5}$$

Once this element has been computed, the backsolve can be undertaken simultaneously until the top and bottom of the matrix:

Processor 1: $f_i = \mathfrak{e}_i - \mathcal{D}_i f_{i+1}$.   Processor 2: $f_i = \mathfrak{e}_i - \mathcal{D}_i f_{i-1}$. $\quad$ (6)

Such a method has the advantage to divide the time by two in separating totally the tasks between processors. As for the simple Gauss decomposition, only the $\mathcal{D}_i$ block is stored involving a reduced memory usage. It must be mentioned that this element has a different definition for each processor.

In order to reduce the computation time further, other possibilities exist but do not give the same scalability as the BABE algorithm. For example, the computation of the matrix elements and the solver can be alternated. This method gives very different results depending on the resolution used for the problem. It is obvious that the biggest gain is obtained if those two tasks last the same amount of time.

Finally $\mathcal{D}_{i-1}$ in Eq. (1) is computed by factorizing $\mathcal{B}_{i-1}$ and solving with C_{i-1} as right-hand side. It is possible to take advantage of the fact that in this case the solution needs three times more time than the factorization. All processors perform then the decomposition as the columns of the right-hand side matrix are shared among them. Possible gain with this technique is limited by the time required to undertake the factorization.

3   CPU Time Results

In this section, we will concentrate on three types of case that appear when performing computations with LEMan. It must be mentioned that the requirements depend mostly on the model under consideration and on the geometry.

As we want to compute the wave propagation in a plasma, Maxwells equations are used and can be written as:

$$\nabla \times \nabla \times \mathbf{E} - k_0^2 \hat{\epsilon} \cdot \mathbf{E} = ik_0 \frac{4\pi}{c} \mathbf{j}_{ant}. \tag{7}$$

where $\mathbf{E}$ is the electric field and j_{ant} is the antenna excitation that appears in the right-hand side of the linear system. The ϵ term is the dielectric tensor. As it relates together the electric current density and the electric field, the physical model is crucial to determine its value. In the cold formulation it is calculated with the help of Newton's equation by considering a charged element of fluid submitted to an electromagnetic field. In this case its value is obtained in the real space and can be inserted directly inside the equation to be solved. As the same number of operations is required to compute each term of the matrix, it is proportional to N_{mn}^2 where N_{mn} is the number of Fourier Harmonics. The solver in itself involves inversions and multiplications of square matrices with N_{mn} rows and columns and scales then as N_{mn}^3. With a great number of Fourier harmonics, the solver dominates over the matrix computation.

In the warm model where the effects of the distribution function of the particles in the velocity space have to be taken into account, the requirements for the matrix computation changes drastically. The dielectric tensor is then calculated by using the Vlasov equation which describes the distribution function (f) evolution:

$$\frac{\partial f}{\partial t} + \mathbf{v} \cdot \frac{\partial f}{\partial \mathbf{x}} + \frac{q}{m} \left[\mathbf{E} + \mathbf{v} \times \mathbf{B} \right] \cdot \frac{\partial f}{\partial \mathbf{v}} = 0. \tag{8}$$

Several simplifications are then performed on (8) postulating that the radius of the particle trajectories around the magnetic field lines is negligible compared to the wavelength of the perturbation and to the characteristic length of variation of the plasma parameters. In order to solve the relation obtained after simplification and to conserve the exact expression for all the terms in general three-dimensional geometry, the dielectric tensor is determined as the convolution connecting together the electric current density and the electric field. The inversion of a polynomial linear system of degree 1 in $v_{\parallel}$ is in this case needed:

$$\begin{pmatrix} a_{1,1} + b_{1,1}v_{\parallel} & a_{1,2} + b_{1,2}v_{\parallel} & \cdots & a_{1,p} + b_{1,p}v_{\parallel} \\ a_{2,1} + b_{2,1}v_{\parallel} & a_{2,2} + b_{2,2}v_{\parallel} & & a_{2,p} + b_{2,p}v_{\parallel} \\ \vdots & & \ddots & \\ a_{p,1} + b_{p,1}v_{\parallel} & a_{p,2} + b_{p,2}v_{\parallel} & & a_{p,p} + b_{p,p}v_{\parallel} \end{pmatrix} \begin{pmatrix} f_{l,1} \\ f_{l,2} \\ \vdots \\ f_{l,p} \end{pmatrix} = g(\mathbf{v}, \mathbf{E}, l). \tag{9}$$

The number of operations required for this inversion scales as N_{mn}^5. It becomes then obvious that the matrix construction is much longer than the solver as the latter has a N_{mn}^3 dependence.

3.1 Warm Model

The first situation is relative to the warm model. The speed-up plotted against the number of processor is displayed in Fig 1. As the computation time is much

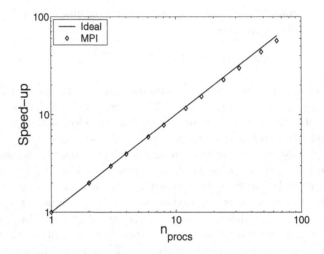

Fig. 1. Speed vs number of processors for the warm model with 96 Fourier harmonics

higher for the matrix construction than for the solver, the parallelization consists simply in sharing equally the number of radial nodes on every processor. The CPU time behaviour is then theoretically $1/n_{procs}$. Fig 1 shows that it is effectively close to it. In the warm case, the parallelization seems not to be then a major problem.

3.2   Cold Model

Now that the warm case, where simple parallelization can be performed, has been investigated, we will concentrate on the cold model where it is subtler. Two different situations are presented. The first one contains a reduced number of Fourier harmonics ($N_m = 319$). The idea is that the matrix construction and the solver take almost the same time. As we work on a SMP machine, it is also interesting to compare parallelization between MPI and OpenMP. The results are presented in Figure 2 against the ideal behaviour. OpenMP has a better scaling than MPI but is far away from perfect when it reaches 16 processors. It must be pointed out than this technique has been implemented in order to compute cases with a high number of Fourier harmonics. This is obviously not the case here. Concerning the behaviour of the MPI curve, some explanations must be given. The first scheme used for 2 processors is BABE. The speed-up is very close to what has been obtained with OpenMP but is not as perfect as expected. The step to 4 processors is performed by alternating the matrix construction and the solver. This is quite efficient as those two computations take roughly the same order of computational time. For a higher number of tasks, the separation of the right-hand side matrices in the solver between processors has been used. The gain of time is quite interesting from $n_{procs} = 4$ to $n_{procs} = 8$ but it is practically

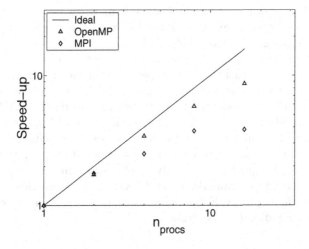

Fig. 2. Comparison of the speed-up with a parallelization using OpenMP and MPI for the cold model with an intermediate number of Fourier harmonics ($N_m = 319$)

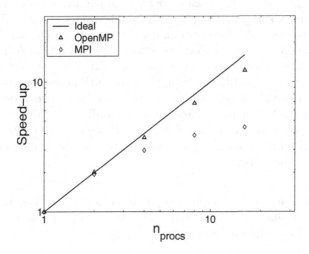

Fig. 3. Comparison of the speed-up with a parallelization using OpenMP and MPI for the cold model with a high number of Fourier harmonics ($N_m = 841$)

negligible for the last step. MPI seems then to give satisfactory results when limited to less than 8 tasks.

The final simulation is made with a higher number of Fourier modes ($N_m = 841$). Results are expected to be better as the code is mainly optimised for this kind of situation. They are effectively those which require the most resources. The speed-up is shown in Fig. 3. Again OpenMP exhibits a better dependence than MPI. In this case, this method uses BABE for two processors. For a higher number of tasks, sharing of the right-hand side matrices has been used for the solver. Going from 2 to 4 processors is efficient with this method. For a higher number of tasks the gain progressively diminishes.

The highest number of Fourier harmonics that has been used with the LEMan code is around 2000. In this case, the dependence in increasing the number of processors is better than for the cases shown here. Taking account of them, we can deduce that the best results would be obtained using the BABE method and OpenMP inside the nodes. In that situation, a speed-up of about 24 is reached. A possible gain with cyclic reduction would be achieved with more than 744 processors as this method requires more than 31 times more operations. This is a very large requirement for solving of a single linear system. With 32 processors, the largest case can take about 2 days. Furthermore, this computation applies for a single frequency. For a frequency scan, it is possible to separate the computation by dividing the spectrum.

4   Conclusions

The warm model for plasma wave propagation, destabilisation and absorption has been shown to give a good scaling with a simple decomposition of the task along the magnetic surfaces. The size of the problem can be increased directly by incrementing the number of processors. For the cold model, the problem is more complex as it depends on the characteristics of the resolution. A high number of Fourier harmonics gives a better scaling. A balance has to be found for the parallelization between MPI and OpenMP. If the SMP nodes contain a sufficient number of processors, the best method is obviously to use two nodes related by the BABE algorithm when the computation is parallelized with OpenMP inside them for the processors with shared memory. If the cyclic reduction would be implemented, a huge number of processors would then be required for a single linear system to be solved.

Acknowledgments. The computations have been performed on the Pleiades2 cluster of EPFL and Blanc at CSCS. This work was partly supported by the Swiss National Foundation and Euratom.

References

1. Popovich, P., Cooper, W.A., Villard, L.: A full-wave solver of the Maxwell's equations in 3D cold plasmas. Comput. Phys. Comm. 175, 250 (2006)
2. Gruber, R., Cooper, W.A., Beniston, M., Gengler, M., Merazzi, S.: Software development strategies for parallel computer architectures. Physics Reports 207, 167 (1991)

The Recursive Dual-Net and Its Applications

Yamin Li[1], Shietung Peng[1], and Wanming Chu[2]

[1] Department of Computer Science
Hosei University
Tokyo 184-8584 Japan
{yamin,speng}@k.hosei.ac.jp
[2] Department of Computer Hardware
University of Aizu
Aizu-Wakamatsu 965-8580 Japan
w-chu@u-aizu.ac.jp

Abstract. In this paper, we propose a universal network, called recursive dual-net (RDN). It can be used as a candidate of effective interconnection networks for massively parallel computers. The RDN is generated by recursively applying dual-construction on a base-network. Given a regular and symmetric graph of size n and node-degree d, the dual-construction generates a regular and symmetric graph of size $2n^2$ and node-degree $d+1$. The RDN has many interesting properties including low node-degree and small diameter. For example, we can construct an RDN connecting more than 3-million nodes with only 6 links per node and a diameter of 22. We investigate the topological properties of the RDN and compare it to other networks including 3D torus, WK-recursive network, hypercube, cube-connected-cycle, and dual-cube. We also describe an efficient routing algorithm for RDN.

Keywords: Interconnection networks and routing algorithm.

1 Introduction

In massively parallel processor (MPP), the interconnection network plays a crucial role on the issues such as communication performance, hardware cost, computational complexity, fault-tolerance, etc. Much research has been reported in the literatures for interconnection networks that can be used to connect parallel computers of large scale (see [2,6,12] for the review of the early work). The following two categories have attracted a great research attention. One is the hypercube-like family that has the advantage of short diameters for high-performance computing and efficient communication [5,7,8,9,10]. The other is 2D/3D mesh or torus that has the advantage of small and fixed node-degrees and easy implementations. Traditionally, most MPPs in the history including those built by NASA, CRAY, FGPS, IBM, etc., use 2D/3D mesh or torus or their variations with extra diagonal links. The recursive networks also have been proposed as effective interconnection networks for parallel computers of large

Y. Dou, R. Gruber, and J. Joller (Eds.): APPT 2009, LNCS 5737, pp. 363–374, 2009.
© Springer-Verlag Berlin Heidelberg 2009

scale. For example, the WK-recursive network [4,13] is a class of recursive scalable networks. It offers a high-degree of regularity, scalability, and symmetry and has a compact VLSI implementation.

Recently, due to the advance in computer technologies, the community of supercomputers rises competition to construct supercomputers of very-large scale that might contain millions of nodes [11]. For example, the IBM new Blue Gene system was proposed that will contain more than a million processors. It was predicted that the MPPs of the next decade will contain 10 to 100 millions of nodes [3]. For such a parallel computer of very-large scale, the traditional interconnection networks may no longer satisfy the requirements for the high-performance computing or efficient communication. For the future generation of MPPs with millions of nodes, the node-degree and the diameter will be the critical measures for the effectiveness of the interconnection networks. The node-degree is limited by the hardware technologies and the diameter affects directly all kind of communication schemes. Other important measures include bisection bandwidth, scalability, and efficient routing algorithms.

In this paper, we propose a set of networks, called *Recursive Dual-Net* (RDN). A recursive dual-net is based on the recursive dual-constructions of a regular base-network. The dual-construction extends a regular network with n nodes and node-degree d to a network with $2n^2$ nodes and node-degree $d+1$. The recursive dual-net is especially suitable for the interconnection network of the parallel computers with millions of nodes. It has the merits of regularity, scalability and symmetry and can connect a huge number of nodes with just a small number of links per node and very short diameters. For example, a 2-level RDN with $n = 25$ can connect more than 3-million nodes that has only 6 links per node and its diameter equals to 22. For parallel computers with millions of nodes, most of the known topologies will either require a large number of links per node (hypercube-like family) that is difficult to implement or have a large diameter (3D torus or WK-recursive network) that affects tremendously its performance.

We investigate the topological properties of the recursive dual-net and show some examples of recursive dual-net with rather simple base-networks. Then we compare them with other networks such as 3D torus [1], WK-recursive network [13], hypercube [10], CCC (cube-connected-cycle) [9], and dual-cube [7,8]. We also propose efficient basic routing algorithms for the recursive dual-net.

The rest of this paper is organized as follows. Section 2 describes the recursive dual-net in details. Section 3 discusses the topological properties of the recursive dual-net. Sections 4 compares recursive dual-net with other networks. Section 5 gives a few examples of recursive dual-net for parallel computers of large-scale or very large-scale. Section 6 describes an efficient routing algorithm. Section 7 concludes the paper and presents some future research directions.

2   Recursive Dual-Net

Let G be an undirected graph. The size of G, denoted as $|G|$, is the number of vertices. A path from node s to node t in G is denoted by $s \to t$. The length of the path is the number of edges in the path. For any two nodes s and t in G, we denote $D(s, t)$ as the length of a shortest path connecting s and t. The diameter of G is defined as $D(G) = \max\{D(s,t) | s, t \in G\}$. For any two nodes s and t in G, if there is a path connecting s and t, we say G is a connected graph.

Suppose we have a symmetric connected graph B and there are n_0 nodes in B and the node degree is d_0. A k-level Recursive Dual-Net $RDN^k(B)$, also denoted as $RDN^k(B(n_0))$, can be recursively defined as follows:

1. $RDN^0(B) = B$ is a symmetric connected graph with n_0 nodes, called *base network*;
2. For $k > 0$, an $RDN^k(B)$ is constructed from $RDN^{k-1}(B)$ by a dual-construction as explained below (also see Figure 1).

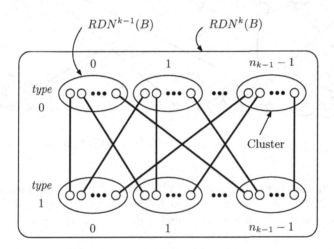

Fig. 1. Build an $RDN^k(B)$ from $RDN^{k-1}(B)$

Dual-construction. Let $RDN^{k-1}(B)$ be referred to as a *cluster* of level k and $n_{k-1} = |RDN^{k-1}(B)|$ for $k > 0$. An $RDN^k(B)$ is a graph that contains $2n_{k-1}$ clusters of level k as subgraphs. These clusters are divided into two sets with each set containing n_{k-1} clusters. Each cluster in one set is said to be of *type* 0, denoted as C_i^0, where $0 \le i \le n_{k-1} - 1$ is the cluster ID. Each cluster in the other set is of *type* 1, denoted as C_j^1, where $0 \le j \le n_{k-1} - 1$ is the cluster ID. At level k, each node in a cluster has a new link to a node in a distinct cluster of the other type. We call this link *cross-edge* of level k. By following this rule, for each pair of clusters C_i^0 and C_j^1, there is a unique edge connecting a node in C_i^0 and a node in C_j^1, $0 \le i, j \le n_{k-1} - 1$. In Figure 1, there are n_{k-1} nodes within each cluster $RDN^{k-1}(B)$.

We give two simple examples of recursive dual-nets with $k = 1$ and 2, in which the base network is a ring with 3 nodes, in Figure 2 and Figure 3, respectively. Figure 2 depicts an $RDN^1(B(3))$ network. There are 3 nodes in the base network.

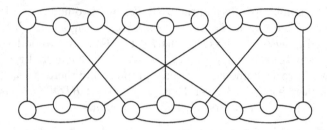

Fig. 2. A Recursive Dual-Net $RDN^1(B(3))$

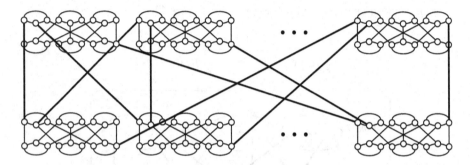

Fig. 3. A Recursive Dual-Net $RDN^2(B(3))$

Therefore, the number of nodes in $RDN^1(B(3))$ is 2×3^2, or 18. Figure 3 shows the $RDN^2(B(3))$ constructed from the $RDN^1(B(3))$ in Figure 2. We did not show all the nodes in the figure. The number of nodes in $RDN^2(B(3))$ is 2×18^2, or 648.

Similarly, we can construct an $RDN^3(B(3))$ containing 2×648^2, or 839,808 nodes with node-degree of 5 and diameter of 22. In contrast, the 839,808-node 3D torus machine (adopt by IBM Blue Gene/L [1]) configured as $108 \times 108 \times 72$ nodes, the diameter is equal to $54 + 54 + 36 = 144$ with a node degree of 6.

3   Topological Properties of RDN

We can see from the recursive dual-construction described above that an $RDN^k(B)$ is a symmetric connected network with node-degree $d_0 + k$, where d_0 is the node-degree of the base network B. The number of nodes n_k in $RDN^k(B)$ satisfies the recurrence $n_k = 2n_{k-1}^2$ for $k > 0$. Solving the recurrence, we get $n_k = (2n_0)^{2^k}/2$.

Concerning the diameter D_k of $RDN^k(B)$, we know that the worst-case (the longest one) for the shortest path $P(u, v)$ connecting any two nodes u and v in $RDN^k(B)$ is as follow: u and v are of the same type and path $P = u \rightarrow u' \rightarrow w \rightarrow w' \rightarrow v$, where $u \rightarrow u'$ and $w \rightarrow w'$ are cross-edges of level k, and $|u' \rightarrow w| = |w' \rightarrow v| = D_{k-1}$, as shown as in Figure 4. Therefore, the diameter

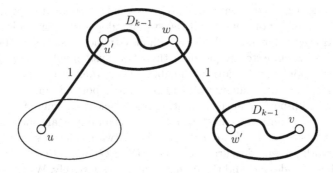

Fig. 4. The diameter of the Recursive Dual-Net

of $RDN^k(B)$ satisfies the recurrence $D_k = 2D_{k-1} + 2$ for $k > 0$. Solving the recurrence, we get $D_k = 2^k D_0 + 2^{k+1} - 2$, where D_0 is the diameter of the base network.

The bisection bandwidth is important for fault-tolerance. Next, we investigate the bisection bandwidth of the $RDN^k(B)$ for $k \geq 1$. From the dual-construction, we know that there is no link between the clusters of level k that are of the same type. Therefore, the minimum number of links those removal will disconnect two halves occurs when both halves contain equal numbers of clusters of type 0 or 1. That is, the minimum number of links those removal will disconnect two halves equals to half of the total number of cross-edges of level k which is $\lceil (2n_0)^{2^k}/8 \rceil$.

Notice that if n_0 is odd and $k = 1$ we should divide the RDN into two halves such that one half contains $\lfloor n_0/2 \rfloor$ (or $\lceil n_0/2 \rceil$) type 0 clusters and $\lceil n_0/2 \rceil$ (or $\lfloor n_0/2 \rfloor$) type 1 clusters. For example, the bisection bandwidth of $RDN^1(B(3))$ is $\lceil 6^2/8 \rceil = \lceil 9/2 \rceil = 5$.

We summarize the discussion above about the fundamental properties of the Recursive Dual-Net in the following theorem.

Theorem 1. *Assume that the base network B is a symmetric graph with size n_0, node-degree d_0, and the diameter D_0. Then, the size, the node-degree, the diameter and the bisection bandwidth of $RDN^k(B)$ are $(2n_0)^{2^k}/2$, d_0+k, $2^k D_0 + 2^{k+1} - 2$, and $\lceil (2n_0)^{2^k}/8 \rceil$, respectively.*

4   Comparison to Other Interconnection Networks

An interconnection network is evaluated in terms of a number of parameters such as node-degree, diameter, bisection width, average distance, regularity, symmetry, etc. Let G be a regular, symmetric graph. There are trade-offs among the node-degree, the diameter, and the size of a graph G. It is not easy and maybe unfair to use a single parameter to compare the effectiveness of networks that have different topologies and sizes. However, it should be worth to have such a parameter that shows the combined effects of the topology on three important measures: node-degree, diameter and size. There might be an argument that the diameter is not an important issue if the system adopts the wormhole switching technique. However, for the MPPs with millions of nodes, it seems not possible to use wormhole switching technique since the whole system will occupy a big hall and the connection must be done with cables. Therefore, for the interconnection networks of MPPs, the diameter should play an important role for measuring the ability of high-performance computing and efficient communication.

In this paper, we introduce *cost ratio* $CR(G)$ as an important measure for the combined effects of the hardware cost and the software efficiency of an interconnection network presented as graph G. Let $|(G)|$, $d(G)$, and $D(G)$ be the number of nodes, the node-degree, and the diameter of G, respectively. We define $CR(G)$ as

$$CR(G) = (d(G) + D(G))/\lg|(G)|$$

The motivation here is that the node-degree and diameter should not increase faster than the logarithm of the size of of the graph. It should be considered as a basic rule for high-performance MPPs. The design of interconnection network should make effort to reduce the cost ratio, especially for an MPP with very large scale. The cost ratio of hypercube is a constant 2 for any size. One of the reasons that hypercube has been and will be still popular as an interconnection network of MPPs is that its node-degree and diameter grow logarithmically with its size. However, for an MPP with more than a million of nodes, the logarithmic growth rate of the node-degree is still too big for the current hardware technologies (each node requires more than 20 ports and channels).

Other important measures for the performance of networks include the existence of simple and efficient routing and communication algorithms for certain communication patterns such as multicast or total exchange. We present a simple and efficient routing algorithm on RDN. The design of efficient algorithms for collective communication is beyond the scope of this paper. It should be an interesting subjects for the further research.

Table 1 summarizes the number of nodes, the node-degree, the diameter, and the cost ratio for 3D torus, hypercube, CCC, dual-cube, WK-recursive network and recursive dual-net. The *torus*, also called *wrap-around mesh* or a *toroidal mesh*, was adopt by IBM Blue Gene/L. This topology includes the p-ary, q-cube which is a q-dimensional torus with the restriction that each dimension is of the same size p. In a $CCC(n)$, each node in an n-cube is replaced with an n-node ring [9]. A dual-cube $DC(n)$ contains 2^n $(n-1)$-cubes called *clusters* [7]. Half of the clusters are of type 0 and the other half are of type 1. There is a unique link (cross-edge) connecting each pair of clusters of distinct types. $DC(n)$ is equal to $RDN(2^{n-1}, 1)$, where the base network is an $(n-1)$-cube.

A WK-recursive network of level t denoted as $WK(n,t)$ can be constructed recursively as follows [13]. $WK(n,1)$ is an n-node complete graph augmented with n open links each at a node. Each node of $WK(n,t)$ is incident with $n-1$ substituting links and one flipping link (or open link). The substituting links are those within basic building blocks, and the j-flipping links are those connecting two embedded $WK(n,j)$. Figure 5 shows a WK-recursive network with $n = 4$ and $t = 2$.

Table 1. CR of recursive dual-net and the other networks

Network	Number of nodes	Node-degree	Diameter
p-ary, 3-cube	p^3	6	$3p/2$
n-cube	2^n	n	n
$CCC(n)$	$n * 2^n$	3	$2n + \lfloor n/2 \rfloor - 2$
$DC(n)$	2^{2n-1}	n	$2n$
$WK(n,t)$	n^t	n	$2^t - 1$
$RDN^k(B)$	$n_k = (2n_0)^{2^k}/2$	$d_0 + k$	$2^k * D_0 + 2^{k+1} - 2$

Network	CR
p-ary, 3-cube	$(6 + 3p/2)/3 \lg p$
n-cube	2
$CCC(n)$	$(2n + \lfloor n/2 \rfloor + 1)/(n + \lg n)$
$DC(n)$	$3n/(2n - 1)$
$WK(n,t)$	$(n + 2^t - 1)/\lg n^t$
$RDN^k(B)$	$(d_0 + k + D_k)/\lg n_k$

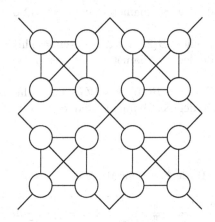

Fig. 5. A WK-recursive network $WK(4, 2)$

5   Samples of RDN for Massively Parallel Computers

In this section, we describe some selections of base-networks such that the corresponding recursive dual-net will be the candidate as an effective interconnection network for MPPs of different sizes. A good choice for the base-network is p-ary, q-cube. The p-ary, q-cube has many nice properties and is suitable as an interconnection network for parallel computers of small sizes. For example, a 5-ary, 2-cube or a 3-ary, 3-cube can be easily built into a 2D or 3D chip. The second choice for the base-network is a WK-recursive network with $n = 4$ and $t = 2$ or 3. The nature of WK-recursive network makes it easily to be implemented on a 2D chip. The selection of value k for recursive dual-net depends on the sizes of the MPPs. For the MPPs of large-scale (thousands of nodes), $k = 1$ is a good choice, while for the MPPs of very large-scale (millions of nodes), we can set $k = 2$ that applies dual-construction twice. We list below a few examples of the RDN as candidates of interconnection networks for MPPs based on the discussion above.

1. MPPs of large-scale:
   - $RDN^1(B(25))$, where $B(25)$ is a 5-ary, 2-cube: Since $n_0 = 25, d_0 = 4$, and $D_0 = 4$, this network has 1250 nodes. its node-degree, diameter and cost ratio are 5, 10, and 1.46, respectively.
   - $RDN^1(B(27))$, where $B(27)$ is a 3-ary, 3-cube: Since $n_0 = 27, d_0 = 6$, and $D_0 = 3$, this network has 1458 nodes. its node-degree, diameter and cost ratio are 7, 8 and 1.43, respectively.
   - $RDN^1(B(16))$, where $B(16)$ is a $WK(4, 2)$: Since $n_0 = 16, d_0 = 4$, and $D_0 = 3$, this network has 512 nodes. its node-degree, diameter and cost ratio are 5, 8 and 1.44, respectively.
2. MPPs of very large-scale:
   - $RDN^2(B(25))$, where $B(25)$ is a 5-ary, 2-cube: This network has 3,125,000 nodes. its node-degree, diameter and cost ratio are 6, 22 and 1.30, respectively.
   - $RDN^2(B(27))$, where $B(27)$ is a 3-ary, 3-cube: This network has 4,251,528 nodes. its node-degree, diameter and cost ratio are 8, 18 and 1.18, respectively.
   - $RDN^2(B(16))$, where $B(16)$ is a $WK(4, 2)$: This network has 524,288 nodes. its node-degree, diameter and cost ratio are 6, 18 and 1.26, respectively.

Table 2. CR for MPPs of large-scale

Network	n	d	D	CR
10-ary 3-cube	1,000	6	15	2.11
10-cube	1,024	10	10	2.00
CCC(8)	2,048	3	18	1.91
$WK(8, 3)$	512	8	7	1.67
$DC(6)$	2,048	6	12	1.64
$RDN^1(B(25))$	1,250	5	10	1.46
$RDN^1(B(27))$	1,458	7	8	1.43
$RDN^1(B(16))$	512	5	8	1.44

We show the comparisons of the RDN and other networks for MPPs of large-scale and very large-scale in Table 2 and Table 3, respectively. It can be seen from the tables that the RDN with properly selected base-networks are superior to other networks.

Table 3. CR for MPPs of very large-scale

Network	n	d	D	CR
100-ary 3-cube	1,000,000	6	150	7.83
20-cube	1,048,576	20	20	2.00
CCC(16)	1,048,576	3	38	2.05
$WK(8,7)$	2,097,152	8	127	6.43
$DC(11)$	2,097,152	11	22	1.57
$RDN^2(B(25))$	3,125,000	6	22	1.30
$RDN^2(B(27))$	4,251,528	8	18	1.18
$RDN^2(B(16))$	524,288	6	18	1.26

Finally, concerning the physical layout of an MPP with recursive dual-net, it can be described briefly as follows. The base-network that is a 5-ary, 2-cube, or a 3-ary, 3-cube, or an $WK(4,2)$ can be built on a 2D or 3D chip. The MPP of large-scale that contains clusters of level 1 can be packed into a dual-rack that connects to sets of clusters face-to-face. The MPP of very large-scale can be built and displayed in a big hall with dual-racks connected through cables. With the advance of technologies, the above configuration of an MPP with the recursive dual-net might become a reality.

6 An Efficient Routing Algorithm in RDN

The problem of finding a path from a source s to a destination t and forwarding a message along the path is known as the basic routing problem. In this section, we present efficient algorithms for the basic routing in RDN.

In order to describe the routing algorithm, we first give a presentation for $RDN^k(B)$ that provides an unique ID to each node in $RDN^k(B)$. Let the IDs of nodes in B, denoted as ID_0, be i, $0 \le i \le n_0 - 1$. The ID_k of node u in $RDN^k(B)$ for $k > 0$ is a triple (u_0, u_1, u_2), where u_0 is a 0 or 1, u_1 and u_2 belong to ID_{k-1}. We call u_0, u_1, and u_2 typeID, clusterID, and nodeID of u, respectively.

More specifically, ID_i, $1 \le i \le k$, can be defined recursively as follows: $ID_i = (b, ID_{i-1}, ID_{i-1})$, where $b = 0$ or 1. The ID of a node u in $RDN^k(B)$ can also be presented by an unique integer i, $0 \le i \le (2n_0)^{2^k}/2 - 1$, where i is the lexicographical order of the triple (u_0, u_1, u_2). For example, the ID of node $(1, 1, 2)$ in $RDN^1(B)$ is $1 * 3^2 + 1 * 3 + 2 = 14$. It can be verified easily that the definition is consistent with the definition of the recursive dual-net in Section 2.

With this ID presentation, (u, v) is a cross-edge of level k in $RDN^k(B)$ iff $u_0 \ne v_0$, $u_1 = v_2$, and $u_2 = v_1$.

Assume that a routing algorithm for the base network B is available. The proposed routing algorithm that routes node u to node v in $RDN^k(B)$ for $k > 0$ is a recursive one. If u and v are in the same cluster of level k then just call itself for $k - 1$. Otherwise, we assume that u and v has distinct typeID (for the case $u_0 = v_0$, we simply route u to w via a cross-edge of level k then we treat w as u). We route u to u' with $u_2' = v_1$ and v to v' with $v_2' = u_1$ inside the clusters of level k where u and v belong to. This can be done by recursive calls for $k - 1$. Then we can route u' to v' in 1 hop since there is a cross-edge of level k from u' to v'. The proposed routing algorithm is described formally as Algorithm 1.

Algorithm 1: RDN_routing($RDN^k(B), u, v$)
begin
  if $k = 0$ **then** RDN_routing($RDN(m, 0), u, v$)
  else
    Case 1:$u_0 = v_0$ and $u_1 = v_1$
      RDN_routing($RDN_{u_0,u_1}^{k-1}(B), u_2, v_2$);
      /* $RDN_{u_0,u_1}^{k-1}(B)$ is the cluster with typeID $= u_0$
        and clusterID $= u_1$. */
    Case 2: $u_0 \neq v_0$
      RDN_routing($RDN_{u_0,u_1}^{k-1}(B), u_2, v_1$);
      $u' = (u_0, u_1, v_1)$;
      RDN_routing($RDN_{v_0,v_1}^{k-1}(B), v_2, u_1$);
      $v' = (v_0, v_1, u_1)$;
      connect u' and v' via a cross-edge of level k;
    Case 3: $u_0 = v_0$ and $u_1 \neq v_1$
      route u to w via the cross-edge of level k;
      route node w to node v as in Case 2;
  endif
end

Example (also see Fig. 6):
$k = 2$:
  $u = (u_0, u_1, u_2) = (0, (0, 0, 0), (0, 0, 0))$
  $v = (v_0, v_1, v_2) = (1, (1, 2, 2), (0, 2, 2))$
  $u_0 = 0, u_1 = (0, 0, 0), u_2 = (0, 0, 0)$
  $v_0 = 1, v_1 = (1, 2, 2), v_2 = (0, 2, 2)$
  $u_0 \neq v_0$ (Case 2, cross-edge):
  $u' = (u_0, u_1, v_1) = (0, (0, 0, 0), (1, 2, 2))$
  $v' = (v_0, v_1, u_1) = (1, (1, 2, 2), (0, 0, 0))$
  $u_2 = (0, 0, 0) \rightarrow v_1 = (1, 2, 2)$, see $k = 1$ (1)
  $v_2 = (0, 2, 2) \rightarrow u_1 = (0, 0, 0)$, see $k = 1$ (2)
$k = 1$ (1): in cluster $(0, (0, 0, 0), *)$
  $u = (u_0, u_1, u_2) = (0, 0, 0)$
  $v = (v_0, v_1, v_2) = (1, 2, 2)$
  $u_0 = 0, u_1 = 0, u_2 = 0$
  $v_0 = 1, v_1 = 2, v_2 = 2$
  $u_0 \neq v_0$ (Case 2, cross-edge):

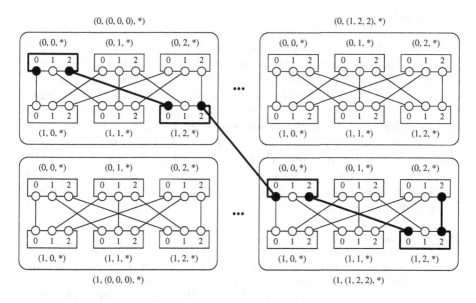

Fig. 6. Routing in $RDN^2(B)$

$$u' = (u_0, u_1, v_1) = (0, 0, 2)$$
$$v' = (v_0, v_1, u_1) = (1, 2, 0)$$
$$u_2 = 0 \rightarrow v_1 = 2, \text{ (Case 1, } k = 0)$$
$$v_2 = 2 \rightarrow u_1 = 0, \text{ (Case 1, } k = 0)$$
$$k = 1 \text{ (2): in cluster } (1, (1, 2, 2), *)$$
$$u = (u_0, u_1, u_2) = (0, 2, 2)$$
$$v = (v_0, v_1, v_2) = (0, 0, 0)$$
$$u_0 = 0, u_1 = 2, u_2 = 2$$
$$v_0 = 0, v_1 = 0, v_2 = 0$$
$$u_0 = v_0 \text{ and } u_1 \neq v_1 \text{ (Case 3)}$$
$$w = (w_0, w_1, w_2) = (1, 2, 2)$$
Let $u = w$, then do similarly in $k = 1$ (1).

Theorem 2. *In $RDN^k(B)$, routing from source s to destination t can be done in at most $2^k * D_0 + 2^{k+1} - 2$ steps, where D_0 is the diameter of the base network.*

Proof. The correctness of the algorithm 1 can be proved easily by induction on k. The worst-case for the length of the routing path is Case 3. In Case 3, the length of routing path $d(u, v)$ satisfies the inequality $d(u, v) \leq d(w, w') + d(v, v') + 2$ for $k > 0$, where $d(w, w') \leq D_{k-1}$ and $d(v, v') \leq D_{k-1}$. Therefore, we have $d(u, v) \leq 2^k * D_0 + 2^{k+1} - 2$, where D_0 is the diameter for the base network. □

7   Conclusion

In this paper, we described a universal network, recursive dual-net, that can be used as an effective interconnection network of an MPP with very large scale (having millions of nodes). If the base-network is properly selected, the recursive dual-net has many attractive properties including small and flexible node-degree, short diameter, recursive structure, and efficient routing algorithms. We studied the topological properties of the recursive dual-net. We also described an efficient routing algorithm in $RDN^k(B)$ for $k > 0$. To design efficient algorithms for collective communications, parallel prefix computation, sorting, and numerical computations in recursive dual-net are certainly worth of the further research. The other direction of the future work includes the study of architectural aspects of the proposed network.

References

1. Adiga, N.R., Blumrich, M.A., Chen, D., Coteus, P., Gara, A., Giampapa, M.E., Heidelberger, P., Singh, S., Steinmacher-Burow, B.D., Takken, T., Tsao, M., Vranas, P.: Blue gene/l torus interconnection network. IBM Journal of Research and Development 49(2/3), 265–276 (2005),
   http://www.research.ibm.com/journal/rd/492/tocpdf.html
2. Aki, S.G.: Parallel Computation: Models and Methods. Prentice-Hall, Englewood Cliffs (1997)
3. Beckman, P.: Looking toward exascale computing, keynote speaker. In: International Conference on Parallel and Distributed Computing, Applications and Technologies (PDCAT 2008), University of Otago, Dunedin, New Zealand, December 2 (2008)
4. Chen, G.H., Duh, D.R.: Topological properties, communication, and computation on wk-recursive networks. Networks 24(6), 303–317 (1994)
5. Ghose, K., Desai, K.R.: Hierarchical cubic networks. IEEE Transactions on Parallel and Distributed Systems 6(4), 427–435 (1995)
6. Leighton, F.T.: Introduction to Parallel Algorithms and Architectures: Arrays, Trees, Hypercubes. Morgan Kaufmann, San Francisco (1992)
7. Li, Y., Peng, S.: Dual-cubes: a new interconnection network for high-performance computer clusters. In: Proceedings of the 2000 International Computer Symposium, Workshop on Computer Architecture, ChiaYi, Taiwan, December 2000, pp. 51–57 (2000)
8. Li, Y., Peng, S., Chu, W.: Efficient collective communications in dual-cube. The Journal of Supercomputing 28(1), 71–90 (2004)
9. Preparata, F.P., Vuillemin, J.: The cube-connected cycles: a versatile network for parallel computation. Commun. ACM 24, 300–309 (1981)
10. Saad, Y., Schultz, M.H.: Topological properties of hypercubes. IEEE Transactions on Computers 37(7), 867–872 (1988)
11. TOP500. Supercomputer Sites (June 2008), http://top500.org/
12. Varma, A., Raghavendra, C.S.: Interconnection Networks for Multiprocessors and Multicomputers: Theory and Practice. IEEE Computer Society Press, Los Alamitos (1994)
13. Vicchia, G., Sanges, C.: A recursively scalable network vlsi implementation. Future Generation Computer Systems 4(3), 235–243 (1988)

Parallelization Strategies for Mixed Regular-Irregular Applications on Multicore-Systems

Gudula Rünger and Michael Schwind

Department of Computer Science,
Chemnitz University of Technology, Germany
{ruenger,schwi}@informatik.tu-chemnitz.de

Abstract. Scientific simulation codes often exhibit a mixed structure of regular and irregular data accesses. Since the organization of data accesses has a large influence on the overall performance of parallel code, a careful planning of parallelism is required. In this article, we consider a mixed regular-irregular particle simulation code and investigate several parallelization strategies for multicore architectures consisting of several multicore processors in a shared memory system. The interaction of irregular and regular data accesses are the specific challenge for a cache optimized parallel multicore-code. We present performance experiments on three different multicore systems and show that a mixture of parallelization techniques for irregular and regular applications leads to the best performance.

1 Introduction

Many codes from scientific computing combine irregular and regular features. Examples are particle simulation codes which have a natural irregular behavior caused by a non-predictive movements of particles. Due to the computational demands these simulation codes require parallelism to deliver simulation results in a reasonable timescale. For pure irregular as well as pure regular computation pattern there are well-known parallelization strategies for a good data distribution and cache utilization leading to a good performance. However, these strategies are complementary and for a specific mixed irregular-regular algorithm a specific parallel implementation has to be determined. In this article, we consider a parallel simulation algorithm with an internal loop nest with irregular and regular access pattern in the different loops. Specifically, we investigate parallelization strategies leading to a good cache utilization on parallel multicore platforms.

Recent multicore systems offer a cost effective way to execute parallel simulation algorithms. These systems consist of several multicore processors which can access a shared memory. Each multicore processor consists of several cores and a common memory with several cache levels. Altogether a shared memory parallel system with a hierarchical memory results. To achieve a good performance for a parallel application, the parallel program has to be designed such that the memory hierarchy is exploited. Program parts accessing the same or neighboring

Y. Dou, R. Gruber, and J. Joller (Eds.): APPT 2009, LNCS 5737, pp. 375–388, 2009.
© Springer-Verlag Berlin Heidelberg 2009

data elements should be performed on cores accessing the same cache. However, spatial or temporal locality of data accesses are difficult to achieve for mixed irregular-regular algorithms.

The scientific algorithm we consider in this paper is a particle simulation for a Lennard-Jones fluid [6]. This application code executes a sequence of time steps. Within each time step the algorithm computes the reference trajectory, the tangent space and an orthogonalization step. The execution of the tangent space consists of a nested loop with mixed irregular-regular data accesses. In an earlier article [7], we have investigated transformations on this nested loop for the sequential and parallel implementation on distributed memory high performance computers. In this article, we consider shared memory multicore machines and use OpenMP for the implementation. Our focus in this paper is a cache optimized implementation exploiting the memory hierarchy. The starting point for the parallelization is the best sequential algorithm from [7]. The contribution of this article is the design of different parallelization strategies for shared memory machines, the mapping of data and computation to cores of the multicore system, and the investigation of the performance on recent multicore systems. Performance tests have been performed on three multi-core systems, an AMD Opteron System without shared cache, an AMD Opteron System, where 4 cores share a level 3 cache, and an Intel XEON System, where 2 cores share a second level cache.

The rest of the article is organized as follows. Sections 2 describes the simulation algorithm. Section 3 introduces different parallelization strategies. Section 4 presents performance experiments. Section 5 discusses related work and Section 6 concludes.

2   Mixed Regular-Irregular Simulation Program

Mixed regular-irregular computation structures occur in many advanced simulation algorithms from scientific computing. One class of simulation algorithms are many-particle system, for which a large variety of different algorithms and implementations exists. The many-particle codes differ in the physical model, the numerical method used for the computer program and the data, which reflect the different aspects to be simulated. The mixed regular-irregular simulation pattern usually stems from the movement of particles and the varying interactions of particles on the one hand and the accesses to data stored in a fixed order on the other hand. In both, a sequential or parallel implementation, the data storage and the calculation of varying interactions has to be organized carefully to avoid a large overhead when calculation interaction in consecutive time steps on fixed data layouts. The memory hierarchy of a specific machine and the cache utilization is the challenging task. The data information of the many-particle simulation and the amount of data plays a crucial role to achieve efficiency.

In this article, we consider a many-particle simulation with N particles based on a Lennard-Jones system in d dimensions [11]. This physical model belongs to the short range particle simulations so that in the numerical simulation the interaction of particles with a distance larger than a predefined cut-off radius is treated as zero. Thus, interactions do not occur between all particles but only between particles within a certain area. An interaction between particles corresponds to a calculation on the data stored for the two interacting particles. Due to the movement of particles, the interaction partner of a particle may change in each time step since particles leave the area within the cutoff radius of this particle. The interaction partners are stored in a specific data structure, called the interaction list, which is updated after each time step. The specific simulation code is a statistical molecular dynamic method which determines the reference trajectory of particles in the phase space. This leads to a very large set of data of size $2dN \times 2d$ to be stored for each particle. The data of all particles are stored in two two-dimensional arrays a and p of size $2dN \times d$. The array p holds positions and the array a holds accelerations later used to update the positions. Typical numbers for d and N are $d = 3$ and N between $100 - 1000$. We concentrate on the main loop of the computation of tangent space dynamics which suffers most from the the mixed regular-irregular computation pattern. This code has the form

---

Algorithm 1. Basic sequential code

```
begin
  for i = 1 to N do
    for each j ∈ interaction_list(i) do
      calculation of data of size 2dN in a loop k = 1, ..., 2dN

end
```

Algorithm 2. Sequential code with block data accesses

```
  begin
1   for w = 1 to 2dN/s do
2     for i = 1 to N do
3       for each j ∈ interaction_list(i) do
4         -computation of constant values
5         for k = (w − 1) · s + 1 to w · s do
6           computation of interaction

  end
```

In a previous investigation, we have shown that a transformed computation pattern and a reorganized data storage leads to much higher performance. The code structure is given in Algorithm 2 and is the starting point for an implementation on multicore systems. The code structure results from the original code by a loop exchange of the loop over the particles and the loop over the data for each partner as well as a blocking of data. The data are stored in blocks of size s so that each block contains $2dN \cdot s$ data. Each data block contains $d \cdot s$ data for each of the N particles, see Figure 1 for an illustration.

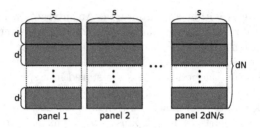

Fig. 1. Data layout for the $2dN \times 2d$ arrays a and p

The loop in line 1 visits the blocks of data, the loop in line 2 visits each particle and its interactions in line 3, and the loop in line 5 visits the data in each block. For a sequential implementation, the blocked version leads to a good cache utilization since entire blocks fit into cache and calculation for interactions occur only within the same column block. This code structure also leads to good performance for a parallel implementation on distributed memory machines by distributing blocks of data. In this article, we investigate parallel implementations with OpenMP on shared memory systems and especially on multicore architectures, see Section 3.

3   Parallel Implementation on Multicore Systems

In this section, we present several parallel implementation strategies for the mixed regular-irregular code on multicore systems. The multicore systems have a hierarchical structure consisting of multicore processors accessing a shared memory, where each multicore processor has several cores and a cache hierarchy consisting of L1, L2, and L3 caches. Figure 2 depicts three different multicore architectures used in this article. The systems are also described in Table 2.

The parallel programs use OpenMP for a threaded shared memory implementation but differ in the decomposition into tasks which are assigned to threads. The number of threads corresponds to the number of cores in the multicore system. Furthermore, a thread is mapped to a specific core in the system so that the different implementation strategies can be investigated. This is done by mapping a thread name `t=omp_get_thread_num()` to a specific operating system thread.

3.1   Parallelization with Respect to Data Blocks

In the first parallel program, the parallel tasks are formed according to a decomposition into data blocks. The starting point is the sequential code shown in Algorithm 2, which already exhibits an outer loop over panels of data, see also Figure 1. Each of the panels of data consists of $2dN \cdot s$ elements of the array a and p where s is the number of columns of the panel. The parallel program version uses the OpenMP `#pragma omp for` for the parallelization of the loop over loop parameter w; the pseudocode is given in Algorithm 3. The loop bodies of the w-loop are mapped to the cores for execution in a round-robin way to achieve load balance.

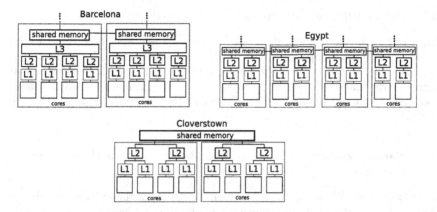

Fig. 2. Different Multicore Architectures: AMD Opteron (Barcelona and Egypt), Intel XEON (Cloverstown)

Algorithm 3. Parallel code with regular parallelization

Procedure   begin
| #pragma omp for schedule(static,1)
1 | **for** $w = 1$ **to** $6N/s$ **do**
2 | | **for** $i = 1$ **to** N **do**
3 | | | **for** each $j \in interaction\_list(i)$ **do**
4 | | | | -compute of constant values
5 | | | | **for** $k = (w - 1) \cdot s + 1$ **to** $w \cdot s$ **do**
6 | | | | | -computation of interaction

  end

The data for this program are stored in the so-called numa allocation which means that the data are stored in the parts of the memory directly connected to the processors. The data are accessible by all processors, but the data accesses of a processor to the local parts of the shared memory connected to processors are faster, which is exploited here. To make sure that the data accesses of the cores of a processor access the data stored at this processor, blocks of data panels are mapped to processors in a round robin way. For a number of cores nc of a processor, blocks of nc data panels are mapped to processors. The static scheduling with blocksize 1 assigns exactly those computations on panels to a core for which the processor owns the data in its parts of shared memory. For static scheduling with a larger blocksize b, the mapping of data panels to memory parts uses $b \cdot nc$ data panels in a round robin way.

The parallel implementation parallelizing the w-loop can be considered as a parallelization of the regular part of the application. The entire irregular computation on data within the same panel are executed on the same core so that irregular data accesses cause no conflict between different cores.

3.2   Parallelization with Respect to Data Blocks Variation

The order of interactions in line 3 of Algorithm 3 is unspecified. In [7] we have presented how this loop can be modified to use a different order of interactions and have shown that this reordering of interaction transformation results in a higher performance of the computations. here, we consider this transformation too, and replace the loops of line 2 and 3 with a the version described as algorithm 5 of [7].

3.3   Parallelization with Respect to Particle Interactions Using Barriers

In the next parallelization strategy, the interactions of the w-loop over the data panels are executed one after another and the internal irregular calculation are performed in parallel by all cores of the system. The data are distributed over all memories on per page (4KByte) basis in a round robin way.

For each iteration of the w-loop, the interactions between the particles are calculated in a recursive way on boxes which are subvolumes of the entire volume of the simulation. The subvolumes of the entire d-dimensional volume are divided into d-dimensional subvolumes according to the dimensions so that $n_1 \times n_2 \times \ldots \times n_d$ smaller boxes result. The computation of particle interactions in the same box are combined and form one task which is mapped to a single thread. Also, the computation of particle interactions between particles in two different boxes form one task to be computed by a single thread. These tasks can be described by an interaction matrix S of size $n \times n$, where $(i, j), i, j = 0, \ldots, n-1$, denotes the interactions of particles p_i in subvolume i with particles p_j in subvolume j. Since interactions are computed only once, the upper triangular part of S describes all interactions. The diagonal of S contains the interactions $(i, i), i = 0, \ldots, n - 1$, of the particles within the same subvolume.

The mapping of tasks (i, j) to cores, denoted by numbers $c \in \{0, \ldots, p - 1\}$, is done in a recursive way, as described in the pseudocode in Algorithm 4. The interaction matrix is subdivided recursively into 4 submatrices of equal quadratic size. The number of subdivisions depends on the number of cores p (where we assume $p < n$); for a number $p = 2^k$ there are k subdivisions. The tasks are mapped to cores such that no conflict of data accesses results and, thus, no locking is needed. The mapping of tasks (i, j) to cores $c \in T = \{0, \ldots, p - 1\}$ is done within the recursive subdivision.

Algorithm 4 shows the mapping of the tasks to cores in an example. Different colors indicate the different cores. The number of subvolumes 128 comes from a decomposition of a 3-dimensional volume into $4 \times 4 \times 8$ boxes in the $x-$, $y-$ and $z-$ direction. The linear numbering of the subvolumes is done according to these dimensions.

3.4   Parallelization with Respect to Particle Interactions Using Locks

The next parallel program is a modification of Algorithm 4. It is possible to replace the barrier synchronization from the previous algorithm by using lock synchronization. Lock synchronization uses for each subvolume u a lock-variable $lock_u$ of type `omp_lock_t`. This lock-variable protects the data of all particles residing in the subvolume u. To use lock synchronization in Algorithm 4, all barrier synchronizations have been removed; lock-statements have been inserted before and unlock-statements after line 2 in Alg. 4. The lock-statements lock both lock-variables $lock_i$ and $lock_j$, if i and j are different. If i and j are identical only one lock-variable is used. The unlock-statements release both $lock_i$ and $lock_j$ or only one lock-variable, if i and j are identical.

3.5   Combined Parallelization with Barriers

A third parallelization strategy considered is a combination of Algorithm 3 and Algorithm 4. Each iteration from the outer $w - loop$ is assigned in a round robin way to a multicore-CPU and not to cores as it was done in Alg. 3. The irregular computations are parallelized according to Algorithm 4. On machines with memories directly connected to the processor (numa), we allocate each panel on that multicore-CPU which computes the panel.

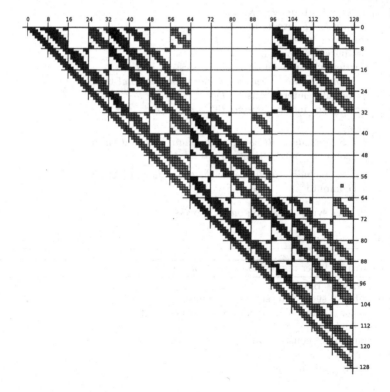

Fig. 3. Interaction matrix S of size 128×128. A 3-dimensional volume is subdivided into $4 \times 4 \times 8$ boxes. The different shaded boxes denote different cores executing the interactions between boxes.

Algorithm 4. Parallel code with irregular parallelization

Procedure begin

	input : S 2-dimensional interaction matrix
	input : w block to compute
	input : T 1-dimensional index set of core numbers
1	**if** *size of S is* 1×1 **then**
	/* subspace has 1 block with $(i,j) \in S$ */
2	compute interactions in S_{ij} on block w by Processor T_s using Alg. 5 ;
3	**else**
4	decompose S into four quadratic submatrices S_1, S_2, S_3, S_4
5	**if** $\#T = 1$ **then**
	/* size of thread space is one sequential computation */
6	compute_interactions(S_1, T)
7	**if** S_2 *includes entries below the main diagonal* **then**
8	compute_interactions(S_2, T)
9	compute_interactions(S_3, T)
10	**if** S_4 *is* **then**
11	compute_interactions(S_4,T)
12	**else**
	/* Parallel decomposition */
13	decompose T into T_1 and T_2
14	compute_interactions(S_1, T_1)
15	compute_interactions(S_3,T_2)
16	Barrier synchronization on all processors in T
17	**if** S *includes no entries below the main diagonal* **then**
18	compute_interactions(S_2,T_1)
19	compute_interactions(S_4,T_2)
20	**else**
21	**if** S_2 *includes entries below the main diagonal* **then**
22	compute_interactions(S_2, T)
23	**if** S_4 *includes entries below the main diagonal* **then**
24	compute_interactions(S_4,T)
25	Barrier synchronization on all processors in T

end

Algorithm 5. Inner regular loop of Algorithm 4

Procedure begin

	input : S set of interactions to compute
	input : w block of matrix on which to compute
1	**for** *each* $(i,j) \in S$ **do**
2	-compute of constant values
3	**for** $k = (w - 1) \cdot s + 1$ **to** $w \cdot s$ **do**
4	-computation of interaction

end

3.6 Combined Parallelization with Locks

The parallelization from the previous section uses Algorithm 4 for the parallelization of the irregular loop. As in Section 3.4 the barrier synchronization can be removed using lock-synchronization. In contrast to Section 3.3, where every subvolume is protected by one lock-variable, in this parallelization there exist $L = p \times n$ lock-variables, where p is the number of multicore-CPUs and n the number of subvolumes, resulting in a two-dimensional array of lock-variables. Each row of lock-variables is assigned to a multicore-CPU. Each column of lock-variables protects the same subvolume but for different panels (different iteration of the w-loop). The cores of each multicore-CPU calculate the same panel w and synchronize the updates to different parts of the panel associated to different subvolumes using the lock-variables of the multicore-CPU they belong to.

3.7 Array Privatization

This parallelization technique uses a buffer of size $2dN \cdot s$ for each core of the system. In this parallelization the outer w-loop of Alg. 2 remains a sequential loop. The irregular computations in Line 2 and Line 3 are parallelized. For the parallelization, both loops in line 2 and line 3 are merged to get one loop iterating on a list of tuples. Each tuple stores the interaction between two particles. Each core computes an equal amount of interactions. For each interaction computed on a core the core updates only its private buffer after all interactions are calculated for one panel. The cores accumulate their private results and store it in panel w.

4 Experiments

The efficiency of the different parallel algorithms has been tested on three different multi-core systems with the characteristics described in Table 2; the names are given according to the codenames of the manufacture. Figures 4, 5 and 6 present performance results in GFlop/s for $N = 1000$ particles on the test systems with a varying number of cores used. The size of the data read and written in all Figures is $2 \times 2dN \times dN = 2 \times 6000 \times 3000$. This data is stored into panels with a blocksize $s = 40$ (Fig. 4), $s = 80$ (Fig. 5), and $s = 120$ (Fig. 6). A description of the curves is given in Table 1. The algorithms from Sections 3.3, 3.4, 3.5 and 3.6 use a decomposition of the simulation volume into $4 \times 4 \times 4$ boxes along the x-, y-, z-axis; the total number of boxes is 64. In Figure 7 the

Table 1. Description of curves in Figures 4, 5 and 6

diagram label	Section	diagram label	Section
data-blocks	3.1	mixed-barrier	3.5
data-blocks-irr	3.2	mixed-locks	3.6
irr-barrier	3.3	repl-bufs	3.7
irr-locks	3.4		

Table 2. Multicore systems used for the experiments

Codename	Egypt	Barcelona	Clovertown
Processor	AMD Opteron 870	AMD Opteron 8347	Intel XEON E5345
Frequency	2.0 GHz	1.9GHz	2.33 GHz
GFlop/s per Core (Total)	4 (64)	7.6 (121.6)	9.32 (74.56)
Number of CPU	8	4	2
Cores per CPU (Total)	2 (16)	4 (16)	4 (8)
Architecture	Numa	Numa	Bus
Shared-Cache	-	Level 3 (2MB) shared by 4 Cores	Level2 (2MB) shared by 2 Cores

Table 3. Maximum performance in GFlop/s

Algorithm	Egypt			Barcelona			Clovertown		
	s=40	s=80	s=120	s=40	s=80	s=120	s=40	s=80	s=120
data-blocks	1.2	1.3	1.0	2.5	2	1.5	2.8	2.9	3.1
data-blocks-irr	13.7	11.4	13.9	18	16.9	20.4	17.46	15.74	18.5
irr-barrier	9.4	10.4	12.44	15.38	13.7	18	11.7	13.6	14.65
irr-locks	7.0	8.6	9.6	11.2	11	14.7	10.1	10.8	12.1
mixed-barrier	10.5	13.6	17.6	19.54	18.98	22.2	13.8	16.79	18.88
mixed-locks	10.5	13.9	14.6	17.33	18.02	21.1	13.3	15.1	16.9
repl-bufs	3.5	3.5	4.0	5.56	5.6	6.3	6	5.6	6.06

number of misses for the case $s = 120$ on the system Cloverstown is shown, the other systems show a similar behavior.

The diagrams show that on all platforms the Algorithm from Section 3.1 (data-blocks) has the lowest performance. The performance does not increase when more cores are used. The highest performance for the Algorithm from Section 3.1 was measured on the system Cloverstown with $3.1 GFlop/s$. The algorithm from Section 3.2 (data-blocks-irr) scales well with an increasing number of processors. The highest performance of $20.4 GFlop/s$ is achieved on the system Barcelona with an block size of $s = 120$. This shows that the parallelization is not responsible for the low performance of the algorithm from Section 3.1 since both algorithms use a parallelization of the outer w-loop. The difference of both algorithms is that the algorithm from Section 3.2 uses a different order of computing interactions, which tries to increase locality of memory accesses. The number of L1-, L2- and TLB-misses in Figure 7 substantiate this, because the Algorithm from Section 3.1 has the most misses in all three cases.

The performance of the algorithm from Section 3.3 (irr-barrier) increases with an increasing number of cores. The best performance was measured on the system Barcelona with $18 GFlop/s$. The corresponding version without barrier synchronization using locks from Section 3.4 (irr-locks) has a lower performance. It reaches at its maximum $14.7 GFlop/s$ on the system Barcelona. We think that the algorithm using locks has a lot more synchronization points. This is the case because the algorithm use a lock for every access to a subvolume; the algorithm using barrier synchronization calculates the interaction of subvolumes without synchronization, when the number of processors in the processor sets T is one.

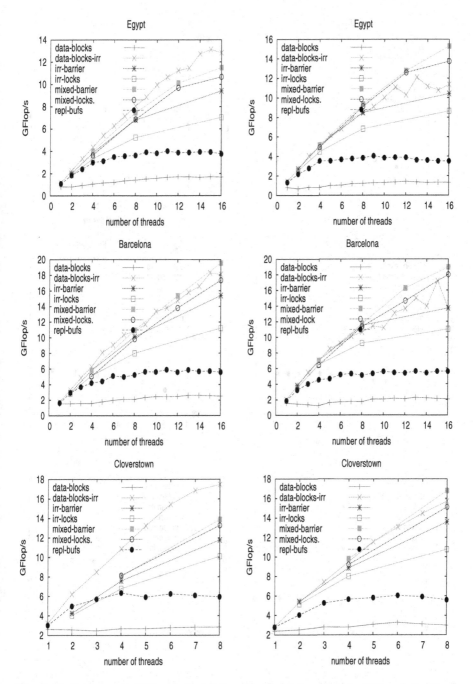

Fig. 4. Performance in GFlops/s for block size $s = 40$ on the systems Egypt, Barcelona and Cloverstown

Fig. 5. Performance in GFlops/s for block size $s = 80$ on the systems Egypt, Barcelona and Cloverstown

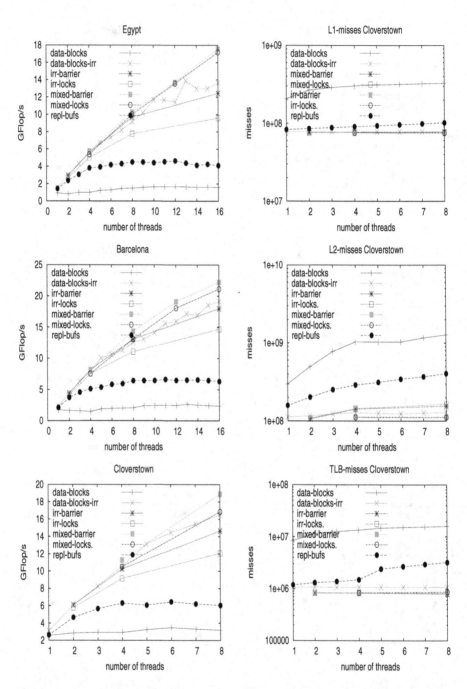

Fig. 6. Performance in GFlops/s for block size $s = 120$ on the systems Egypt, Barcelona and Cloverstown

Fig. 7. L1-,L2-Cache and TLB-Cache misses on system Cloverstown for block size $s = 120$ on the system Cloverstown

The algorithm using a combination of parallelizing the regular loop and the irregular loop from Section 3.5 has the best performance of $22.2GFlop/s$ on the system Barcelona. This algorithm has the lowest L1-, L2- and TLB-cache misses for $s = 120$, which shows that this strategy is most appropriate to reduce cache misses on our multicore-systems. Mainly the L2-misses are reduced compared to the Algorithm from Section 3.1, since the L2-Cache is a shared cache on the system Cloverstown, the reduced number of misses might come from the sharing of the common L2-cache on this system. The corresponding Algorithm using locks from Section 3.6 has lower performance.

The algorithm from Section 3.7 (repl-bufs) has a little better performance than the algorithm from Section 3.1. The number of misses are higher than the number of misses of the Algorithms from Sections 3.2 to 3.3. The use of the extra buffer introduce extra memory accesses which might introduce the cache-misses.

A comparison of all three block-sizes shows that the algorithm from Section 3.5 has its highest performance with a blocksize of $s = 120$. The two smaller blocksizes give a smaller performance. The reason is that the regular computation in the inner loop of Algorithm 5 have a higher performance when the blocksize is higher.

5 Related Work

Due to the importance of many-body simulations as a tool for scientists there are numerous articles about sequential and parallel algorithms and implementations. Many articles consider distributed memory machines like [10] and [5] to mention only two.

Another class of research which is related to this article are parallel algorithms for irregular reduction. An irregular reduction is the accumulation of updates to objects, where the order of the updates is not known at compile time. The update to data elements in the irregular loop of Alg. 2 can be considered as an irregular reduction. A good survey on parallelizing techniques algorithms for irregular reductions is given in [4]. They present a scheme named Local Write for parallel irregular reductions targeting distributed shared memory (DSM) systems. We do not consider this scheme for parallelizing the irregular loop, since it would considerable increase the amount of floating point computations. A technique called array privatization [1] is used in Section 3.7; we have adapted it for our problem of mixed irregular-regular problems. However, none of the mentioned work addresses the problem of a tightly coupled regular-irregular computations on modern multicore architectures with caches.

Locality optimization techniques are closely related to this article, they increase the efficiency of memory access using caches efficiently. [3] presents a technique to increase locality for n-body simulations. It sorts particles into boxes similar to Algorithm 3.3. In [4], a hierarchical graph partitioning algorithm is presented and applied to the reordering of particles in arrays to increase spatial locality. They compare their algorithm with different locality transformations. The article [8] presents different algorithms for reordering irregular loops based on hypergraphs. They present metrics to select different reordering techniques.

In [2] and [9] mixed regular and irregular computations are considered. In both articles a problem is addressed for which first a regular computation and afterwards an irregular computation is performed. Thus, the problems differ from our application algorithm with tightly coupled irregular and regular computations.

6 Conclusion

In this article, we have presented different parallelization strategies for a many-body simulation program. The algorithm has the special property of tightly coupled regular and irregular computations. The experiments on recent multi-core platforms from AMD and Intel have been shown that an algorithm which parallelizes regular and irregular computations gives the best performance.

Acknowledgement

We are very grateful to Günter Radons from the Department of Physics, Chemnitz University of Technology for providing the code for calculating many-body interactions.

References

1. Blume, B., Eigenmann, R., Faigin, K., Grout, J., Hoeflinger, J., Padua, D., Petersen, P., Pottenger, B., Rauchwerger, L., Tu, P., Weatherford, S.: Polaris: The next generation in parallelizing compilers. In: Proc. of the Workshop on Languages and Compilers for Parallel Computing, pp. 10–1. Springer, Heidelberg (1994)
2. Chakrabarti, D.R., Shenoy, N., Choudhary, A.N., Banerjee, P.: An Efficient Uniform Run-time Scheme for Mixed Regular-irregular Applications. In: Proc. of the Int. Conf. on Supercomputing, Melbourne, Australia, July 1998, pp. 61–68 (1998)
3. Crummey, J.M., Whalley, D., Kennedy, K.: Improving Memory Hierarchy Performance for Irregular Applications Using Data and Computation Reorderings. Int. J. Parallel Program. 29(3), 217–247 (2001)
4. Han, H., Tseng, C.-W.: Improving Locality for Adaptive Irregular Scientific Codes. In: Midkiff, S.P., Moreira, J.E., Gupta, M., Chatterjee, S., Ferrante, J., Prins, J.F., Pugh, B., Tseng, C.-W. (eds.) LCPC 2000. LNCS, vol. 2017, pp. 173–188. Springer, Heidelberg (2001)
5. Plimpton, S.: Fast parallel algorithms for short-range molecular dynamics. J. Comp. Phys. 117, 1–19 (1995)
6. Radons, G., Yang, H.L.: Static and Dynamic Correlations in Many-Particle Lyapunov Vectors, nlin.cd/0404028, and references therein
7. Rünger, G., Schwind, M.: Cache optimization for mixed regular and irregular computations. In: Proc. of the POHLL 2008 Workshop on Performance Optimization for High-Level Languages and Libraries (POHLL 2008). IEEE, Los Alamitos (2008)
8. Strout, M.M., Hovland, P.D.: Metrics and models for reordering transformations. In: Proc. of the The Second ACM SIGPLAN Workshop on Memory System Performance (MSP), June 8, pp. 23–34 (2004)
9. Ujaldon, M., Zapata, E.L.: Efficient Resolution of Sparse Indirections in Data-Parallel Compilers. In: Proc. of the Int. Conf. on Supercomputing, Barcelona, Spain, July 1995, pp. 117–126 (1995)
10. Warren, M.S., Salmon, J.K.: A parallel hashed Oct-Tree N-body algorithm. In: Supercomputing 1993: Proceedings of the 1993 ACM/IEEE conference on Supercomputing, pp. 12–21. ACM, New York (1993)
11. Yang, H., Radons, G.: Lyapunov instabilities of Lennard-Jones fluids. Phys. Rev. E 71(3), 036211 (2005)

Performance Improvement of Multimedia Kernels by Alleviating Overhead Instructions on SIMD Devices

Asadollah Shahbahrami[1,2] and Ben Juurlink[1]

[1] Computer Engineering Laboratory,
Delft University of Technology, 2628 CD Delft, The Netherlands
{a.shahbahrami,b.h.h.juurlink}@tudelft.nl
[2] Department of Computer Engineering, Faculty of Engineering,
University of Guilan, Rasht, Iran

Abstract. SIMD extension is one of the most common and effective technique to exploit data-level parallelism in today's processor designs. However, the performance of SIMD architectures is limited by some constraints such as mismatch between the storage and the computational formats and using data permutation instructions during vectorization. In our previous work we have proposed two architectural modifications, the extended subwords and the Matrix Register File (MRF) to alleviate the limitations. The extended subwords, uses four extra bits for every byte in a media register and it provides additional parallelism. The MRF allows flexible row-wise as well as column-wise access to the register file and it eliminates data permutation instructions. We have validated the combination of the proposed techniques by studying the performance of some multimedia kernels. In this paper, we analysis each proposed technique separately. In other words, we answer the following questions in this paper. How much of the performance gain is a result of the additional parallelism? and how much is due to the elimination of data permutation instructions? The results show that employing the MRF and extended subwords separately obtains the speedup less than 1 and 1.15, respectively. In other words, our results indicate that using either extended subwords or the MRF techniques is insufficient to eliminate most pack/unpack and rearrangement overhead instructions on SIMD processors. The combination of both techniques, on the other hand, yields much more performance benefits than each technique.

1 Introduction

Multimedia extensions are one of the most common approach to exploit Data-Level Parallelism (DLP) in multimedia applications on General-Purpose Processors (GPPs). With this approach, multiple data items are packed into a wider

This research was supported in part by the Netherlands Organization for Scientific Research (NWO).

Y. Dou, R. Gruber, and J. Joller (Eds.): APPT 2009, LNCS 5737, pp. 389–407, 2009.
© Springer-Verlag Berlin Heidelberg 2009

media register which can be processed using a Single Instruction and Multiple Data (SIMD) instruction. These extensions can improve the performance of several multimedia applications. Nevertheless, they have some limitations. First, there is a mismatch between the computational format and the storage format of multimedia data. Because of this many data type conversion instructions are used in SIMD implementations. Second, existing SIMD computational instructions cannot efficiently exploit DLP of the 2D and interleaved multimedia data. In order to vectorize 2D and interleaved multimedia data, many rearrangement instructions are needed.

In our previous work, two architectural enhancements, the Matrix Register File (MRF) and extended subwords techniques have been proposed to overcome the above limitations [16]. Extended subwords use registers that are wider than the packed format used to store the data. Extended subwords avoid data type conversion instructions. The MRF allows to load data stored consecutively in memory to a column of the register file, where a column corresponds to corresponding subwords of different registers. This technique avoids the need of data rearrangement instructions. The MMX multimedia extension [12] has been modified by the proposed techniques that was called the Modified MMX (MMMX) architecture. The MMMX architecture have been validated by studying the performance of several important multimedia kernels. Our results show that the performance benefits by employing both proposed techniques is higher than just using the extended subwords technique. In other words, those multimedia kernels which employ the MRF and extended subwrods techniques obtain more speedups than just using the extended subwords technique. However, we did not determine how much of the performance gain is a result of employing the extended subwords technique and how much is due to the employing the MRF. Our goal in this paper is to analysis each technique separately.

We make the following contributions compared to other works.

- We have applied the proposed techniques on a wide range of multimedia kernels.
- In order to determine the performance benefits of each proposed technique, we analysis each technique separately. In other words, we have enhanced the MMX architecture with extended subwords (MMX + ES) and with an MRF (MMX + MRF) separately.
- Our results indicate that using either extended subwords or the MRF techniques is insufficient to eliminate most pack/unpack and rearrangement overhead instructions. In addition, using the MRF is both unuseful and causes performance loss. The MMMX architecture that employs both proposed techniques, on the other hand, yields much more performance benefits.

This paper is organized as follows. In Section 2, we present background information related to the multimedia extensions and their performance bottlenecks. In Section 3, we describes the MMMX architecture that features the extended subwords and the MRF techniques. We discuss several multimedia kernels selected for performance evaluation in Section 4 followed by performance evaluation in Section 5. We analysis each proposed technique separately in Section 6. Finally, conclusions are given in Section 7.

2 Background

We present a short explanation of the multimedia extensions in this section.

2.1 GPPs Enhanced with Multimedia Extension

In order to increase the performance of multimedia applications, GPPs vendors have extended their ISAs. These ISA extensions use the Subword Level Parallelism (SLP) concept [10]. A subword is a smaller precision unit of data contained within a word. In SLP, multiple subwords are packed into a word and then whole word is processed. SLP is used in order to exploit DLP with existing hardware without sacrificing the general-purpose nature of the processor. In SLP, a register is viewed as a small vector with elements that are smaller than the register size. This requires small data types and wide registers.

The first multimedia extensions are Intel's MMX [12], Sun's Visual Instruction Set (VIS) [17], Compaq's Motion Video Instructions (MVI) [3], MIPS Digital Media eXtension (MDMX) [8], and HP's Multimedia Acceleration eXtension (MAX) [10]. These extensions supported only integer data types and were introduced in the mid-1990's. 3DNow [1] was the first to support floating-point media instructions. It was followed by Streaming SIMD Extension (SSE) and SSE2 from Intel [13]. Motorola's AltiVec [4] supports integer as well as floating-point media instructions. In addition, high-performance processors also use SIMD processing. An excellent example of this is the Cell processor [7] developed by a partnership of IBM, Sony, and Toshiba. Cell is a heterogeneous chip multiprocessor consisting of a PowerPC core that controls eight high-performance Synergistic Processing Elements (SPEs). Each SPE has one SIMD computation unit that is referred to as Synergistic Processor Unit (SPU). Each SPU has 128 128-bit registers. SPUs support both integer and floating-point SIMD instructions. Table 1 summarizes the common and distinguishing features of existing multimedia instruction set extensions [15].

2.2 Performance Bottlenecks

SIMD architectures generally provide two kinds of SIMD instructions. The first are the SIMD computational instructions such as arithmetic instructions. The second are the SIMD overhead instructions that are necessary for data movement, data type conversions, and data reorganization. The latter instructions are needed to bring data in a form amenable to SIMD processing. These instructions constitute a large part of the SIMD codes. For example, Ranghanathan et al. [14] indicated that the SIMD implementations of the MPEG/JPEG codecs using the VIS ISA require on average 41% overhead instructions such as packing/unpacking and data re-shuffling. In addition, the dynamic instructions count

Table 1. Summary of available multimedia extensions. Sn and Un indicate n-bit signed and unsigned integer packed elements, respectively. Values n without a prefix U or S in the last row, indicate operations work for both signed and unsigned values. [1] Note that 68 instructions of the 144 SSE2 instructions operate on 128-bit packed integer in XMM registers, wide versions of 64-bit MMX/SSE integer instructions.

GPP with Multimedia Extension ISA Name	AltiVec/VMX	MAX-1/2	MDMX	MMX/ 3DNow	VIS	MMX/ SIMD	SSE	SSE2	SPU ISA
Company	Motorola/IBM	HP	MIPS	AMD	Sun	Intel	Intel	Intel	IBM/Sony/Toshiba
Instruction set	Power PC	PARISC2	MIPS-V	IA32	P. V.9	IA32	IA64	IA64	-
Processor	MPC7400	PA RISC	R1000 PA8000	K6-2	Ultra Sparc	P2	P3	P4	Cell
Year	1999/2002	1995	1997	1999	1995	1997	1999	2000	2005
Datapath width	128-bit	64-bit	64-bit	64-bit	64-bit	64-bit	128-bit	128-bit	128-bit
Size of register file	32x128b	(31) /32x64b	32x64b	8x64b	32x64b	8x64b	8x128b	8x128b	128x128b
Dedicated or shared with	Dedicated	Int. Reg.	FP Reg.	Dedicated	FP Reg.	FP Reg.	Dedicated	Dedicated	Dedicated
Integer data types:									
8-bit	16	-	8	8	8	8	8	16	16
16-bit	8	4	4	4	4	4	4	8	8
32-bit	4	-	-	2	2	2	2	4	4
64-bit	-	-	-	-	-	-	-	2	2
Shift right/left	Yes	Yes	Yes	Yes	Yes	Yes	Yes	Yes	Yes
Multiply-add	Yes	No	No	Yes	Yes	Yes	Yes	Yes	Yes
Shift-add	No	Yes	No	No	No	No	No	No	No
Floating-point	Yes	No	Yes	Yes	No	No	Yes	Yes	Yes
Single-precision	4x32	-	2x32	4x16 2x32	-	-	4x32	4x32	4x32
Double-precision	-	-	-	1x64	-	-	-	2x64	2x64
Accumulator	No	No	1x192b	No	No	No	No	No	
# of instructions	162	(9) 8	74	24	121	57	70	144[1]	213
# of operands	3	3	3-4	2	3	2	2	2	2/3/4
Sum of absolute-differences	No	No	No	Yes	Yes	No	Yes	Yes	Yes
Modulo addition/ subtraction	8, 16, 32	16	8, 16	8, 16 32	16, 32	8, 16 64	8, 16 32, 64	8, 16 32,64	8, 16 32,64
Saturation addition/ subtraction	U8, U16, U32 S8, S16, S32	U16, S16	S16	U8, U16 S8, S16	No	U8, U16 S8, S16	U8, U16 S8, S16	U8, U16 S8, S16	-

of the EEMBC consumer benchmarks running on the Philips TriMedia TM32 shows that over 23% of instructions are data alignment instructions such as pack/merge bytes (16.8%) and pack/merge half words (6.5%) [5]. The execution of this large number of the SIMD overhead instructions decreases the performance and increases pressure on the fetch and decode steps.

To illustrate where overhead instructions are needed in the SIMD implementations of multimedia kernels, we explain it in more detail. Data reordering and data type conversion instructions are used after loading the input data and before storing the outputs. For example, in case of the RGB-to-YCbCr color space conversion, 35 and 6 instructions are needed in each loop iteration to convert 8 pixels from the band interleaved format to the band separated format and unpack the packed byte data types to packed 16-bit word data types, respectively. In addition, 12 instructions are needed to pack the unpacked results and store in memory. On the other hand, the number of SIMD computational instructions is 78. This means that the number of overhead instructions is significant compared to the number of SIMD computational instructions. As another example, matrix transposition is a very common operation in multimedia applications. 2D multimedia algorithms such as the 2D Discrete Cosine Transform (DCT) consists of two 1D transforms called horizontal and vertical transforms. The horizontal transform processes the rows while vertical transform processes the columns. SIMD vectorization of the vertical transform is straightforward, since the corresponding data of each column are adjacent in memory. Therefore, several columns can be processed without any rearranging of the subwords. For horizontal transform on the other hand, corresponding elements of adjacent rows are not continuous in memory (in a row-major storage format). In order to employ SIMD instructions, data rearrangement instructions are needed to transpose the matrix. This step takes a significant amount of time. For example, transposing an 8 × 8 block of bytes, requires 56 MMX/SSE instructions, if the elements are two bytes wide, then 88 instructions are required. Consequently, it is important either to eliminate, to alleviate, or to overlap these instructions with other SIMD computational instructions.

3   MMMX Architecture

The MMMX architecture is MMX enhanced with extended subwords, the MRF, and a few general-purpose SIMD instructions that are not present in the MMX and SSE extensions. The employed techniques in the MMMX architecture are discussed briefly in the following section. More detail about this architecture can be found in [15].

3.1   Extended Subwords

Image and video data is typically stored as packed 8-bit elements, but intermediate results usually require more than 8-bit precision. As a consequence, most 8-bit SIMD ALU instructions are wasted. In the SIMD extensions, the choice is either to be imprecise by using saturation operations at every stage, or to loose parallelism by unpacking to a larger format. Using saturation instructions produces inaccurate results. This is because saturation is usually used at the end of computation. It is more precise to saturate once at the end of the computation rather than at every step of the algorithm. For instance, adding three signed 8-bit values $120 + 48 - 10$, using signed saturation at every step produces 117 and using signed saturation at the last step produces 127.

SIMD architectures support different packing, unpacking, and extending instructions to convert the different data types to each other. For example, the MMX/SSE architectures provide packss{wb,dw,wb} and punpck {hbw,hwd,hdq, lbw,lwd,ldq} instructions for data type conversions.

To avoid the data type conversion overhead and to increase parallelism, extended subwords are employed. This means that the registers are wider than the data loaded into them. Specifically, for every byte of data, there are four extra bits. This implies that MMMX registers are 96 bits wide, while MMX has 64-bit registers. Based on that, the MMMX registers can hold 2×48-bit, 4×24-bit, or 8×12-bit elements.

3.2   The Matrix Register File

The ability to efficiently rearrange subwords within and between registers is crucial to performance. To overcome this problem, a matrix register file is employed, which allows data loaded from memory to be written to a column of the register file as well as to a row register. In the MMMX architecture, the MRF provides parallel access to 12-, 24-, and 48-bit subwords of the row registers that are horizontally located. This is similar to conventional SIMD architectures, which provide parallel access to 8-, 16-, and 32-bit data elements of media registers. In addition, the MRF provides parallel access to 12-bit subwords of the column registers that are vertically arranged.

Figure 1(a) depicts a block diagram of a register file with one write port (Port C) and two read ports (Port A and Port B). The input and output of this block diagram is based on eight 96-bit registers. Figure 1(b) illustrates the combination

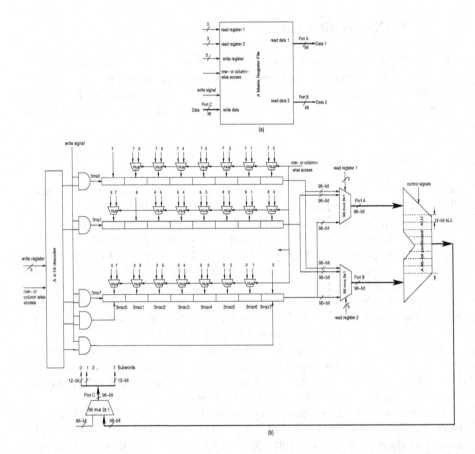

Fig. 1. (a) A register file with eight 96-bit registers, 2 read ports, and 1 write port, (b) the implementation of two read ports and one write port for a matrix register file with 8 96-bit registers as well as a partitioned ALU for subword parallel processing

of the MRF with a 96-bit partitioned ALU for the MMMX architecture. The partitioned ALUs have been designed based on the subword adder. Multiplexers have been used in subword boundaries to propagate or prevent the subword carries in the carry chain [6]. There are eight 12-bit adders. These adders operate independently for 12-bit data. They can also be coupled to behave an four pairs of two adders to perform four 24-bit operations, or combined into two groups of four adders for two 48-bit format.

3.3   MMMX Instruction Set Architecture

The MMMX architecture has different load/store, ALU, and multiplication instructions, which some of them are discussed in the remainder of this section.

The `fld8u12` instruction loads eight unsigned bytes from memory and zero-extends them to a 12-bit format in a 96-bit MMMX register. The `fld8s12` instruction, on the other hand, loads eight signed bytes and sign-extends them to a 12-bit format. These instructions are illustrated in Figure 2 for little endian. The `fld16s12` instruction loads eight signed 16-bit, packs them to signed 12-bit

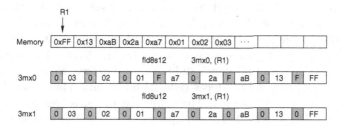

Fig. 2. The `fld8s12` instruction loads eight signed bytes and sign-extends them to 12-bit values, while the `fld8u12` instruction loads eight unsigned bytes and zero-extends them to 12-bit values

format, and writes in a row register. This instruction is useful for those kernels that their input data can be represented by the signed 12-bit, while they use the signed 16-bit storage format. For example, in the DCT kernel, the input data is the signed 9-bit format. It uses the signed 16-bit storage format, while it uses the signed 12-bit for computational format. The instruction `fldc8u12` ("load-column 8-bit to 12-bit unsigned") is used to load a column of the MRF.

Load instructions automatically unpack and store instructions automatically pack and saturate, as illustrated for the load instructions in Figure 2. Store instructions automatically saturate (clip) and pack the subwords. For example, the instruction `fst12s8` saturates the 12-bit signed subwords to 8-bit unsigned subwords before storing them to memory.

Most MMMX ALU instructions are direct counterparts of MMX/SSE instructions. For example, the MMMX instructions `fadd{12,24,48}` (packed addition of 12-, 24-, 48-bit subwords) and `fsub{12,24,48}` (packed subtraction of 12-, 24-, 48-bit subwords) correspond to the MMX instructions `padd{b,w,d}` mm,mm/mem64 and psub{b,w,d} mm,mm/mem64, respectively. MMMX, however, does not support variants of these instructions that automatically saturate the results of the additions to the maximum value representable by the subword data type. They are not needed because as was mentioned the load instructions automatically unpack the subwords and the store instructions automatically pack and saturate. In other words, the MMMX architecture does not support saturation arithmetic.

In several media kernels all elements packed in a register need to be summed, while in other kernels adjacent elements need to be added. Rather than providing different instructions for summing all elements and adding adjacent elements, it has been decided to support adding adjacent elements only but for every packed data type. Whereas summing all elements would probably translate to a multicycle operation, adding adjacent elements is a very simple operation that can most likely be implemented in a single cycle.

Another operation that has been found useful in implementing of several multimedia kernels such as the (I)DCT kernels is the possibility to negate some or all elements in a packed register. The instructions fneg{12,24,48} 3mx0, 3mx1, imm8 negate the 12-, 24-, or 48-bit subwords of the source operand if the corresponding bit in the 8-bit immediate imm8 is set. If subwords are 24- or 48-bit, the four or six higher order bits in the 8-bit immediate are ignored.

The MMMX architecture supports three kinds of multiplication instructions. The first are full multiplication instructions fmulf{12,24}. For example, the fmulf12 instruction multiplies each 12-bit subword in 3mx0 with the corresponding subwords in 3mx1 and produces eight 24-bit results. This means that each result is larger than a subword. Therefore, the produced results are kept in both registers. The second kind of multiplication instructions are the partitioned multiply-accumulate instructions fmadd{12,24}. These instructions perform the operation on subwords that are either 12- or 24-bit, while the MMX instruction pmaddwd performs the MAC operation on subwords that are 16-bit. The MAC operation is an important operation in digital signal processing. This instruction multiplies the eight signed 12-bit values of the destination operand by the eight 12-bit values of the source operand. The corresponding odd-numbered and even-numbered subwords are summed and stored in the 24-bit subwords of the destination operand.

The third type of multiplication is truncation. Truncation is performed by the fmul{12l,12h,24l,24h} instructions. It means that the high or low bits of the results are discarded. When n-bit fixed point values are multiplied with fractional components, the result should be n-bit of precision. Specifically, the instructions fmul12{l,h} multiply the eight corresponding subwords of the source and destination operands and write the low-order (fmul12l) or high-order (fmul12h) 12 bits of the 24-bit product to the destination operand.

4   Multimedia Kernels

Most of the execution time of multimedia applications is spent in multimedia kernels. Therefore, in order to evaluate the proposed techniques, some time

Table 2. Summary of multimedia kernels

Multimedia Kernels	Description
Matrix transpose	Matrix transposition is an important kernel for many 2D media kernels.
Vector/Matrix Multiply	Vector/matrix multiply kernel is used in some multimedia standards.
Repetitive Padding	In this kernel, the pixel values at the boundary of the video object is replicated horizontally as well as vertically.
RGB-to-YCbCr	Color space conversion, which is usually used in the encoder stage.
Horizontal DCT	Horizontal DCT in used in most media standards to process the rows of images in order to remove spatial redundancy.
Horizontal IDCT	Horizontal Inverse DCT is used in the multimedia standards in order to reconstruct the rows of the transformed images.
Vertical DCT	Vertical DCT in used in most media standards to process the columns of images in order to remove spatial redundancy.
Vertical IDCT	Vertical IDCT is used in the multimedia standards in order to reconstruct the columns of the transformed images.
Add block	The add block is used in the decoder, during the block reconstruction stage of motion compensation.
2 × 2 Haar transform	The 2 × 2 haar transform is used to decompose an image into four different bands.
Inverse 2 × 2 Haar transform	The inverse 2 × 2 haar transform is used to reconstruct the original image from different bands.
Paeth prediction	Paeth prediction is used in the PNG standard.
YCbCr-to-RGB	Color space conversion, which is usually used in the decoder stage.
SAD function	The SAD function, which is used in motion estimation kernel to remove temporal redundancies between video frames.
SAD function with interpolation	The SAD function with horizontal and vertical interpolation is used in motion estimation algorithm.
SAD function for image histograms	The SAD function is used for similarity measurements of image histograms.
SSD function	The SSD function, which is used in motion estimation kernel to remove temporal redundancies between video frames.
SSD function with interpolation	The SSD function with horizontal and vertical interpolation is used in motion estimation algorithm.

consuming kernels of multimedia standards have been considered. Table 2 lists the media kernels along with a small description. In order to clarify which proposed techniques have been used in SIMD implementations of media kernels, the presented kernels are divided into two groups. First, kernels that use both extended subwords and the MRF techniques, for instance, the first six kernels. Second, kernels that just use extended subwords technique, for example, the rest of the kernels (twelve kernels).

As was mentioned, the 2D transforms such as (I)DCT are decomposed into two 1D transforms called horizontal and vertical transforms. In order to increase DLP in SIMD implementation of vertical transform, the extended subwords technique is used, while in SIMD implementation of horizontal transform both proposed techniques are needed in order to increase DLP and also to avoid data rearrangement instructions.

5   Performance Evaluation

In this section we evaluate the proposed techniques by comparing the performance of the SIMD implementations that employ the SIMD architectural enhancements to the performance of the MMX and SSE implementations on a single issue processor.

5.1   Evaluation Environment

In order to evaluate the SIMD architectural enhancements, we have used the sim-outorder simulator of the SimpleScalar toolset [2]. We have synthesized MMX/SSE and MMMX instructions using the 16-bit annotate field, which is available in the instruction format of the PISA ISA. More detail about our extension to the SimpleScalar toolset can be found in [9].

The main objective is to compare the performance of the MMX and SSE extensions without the proposed techniques to the those extensions with the SIMD architectural enhancements. The main parameters of the modeled processors are depicted in Table 3. The latency and throughput of SIMD instructions are set equal to the latency and throughput of the corresponding scalar instructions. This is a conservative assumption given that the SIMD instructions perform the same operation but on narrower data types. The latency and throughput of SIMD multiplier units are set to 3 and 1 respectively, the same as in the Pentium 3 processor. The latency of SIMD multiplier units in the Pentium 4 processor is 8 cycles.

Three programs have been implemented by C and assembly languages and simulated using the SimpleScalar simulator for each kernel. Each program consists of three parts. One part is for reading the image, the second part is the computational kernel, and the last part is for storing the transformed image. One program was completely written in C. It was compiled using the gcc compiler targeted to the SimpleScalar PISA with optimization level -O2. The reading and storing parts of the other two programs were also written in C, but the second part was implemented by hand using MMX/SSE and MMMX. These programs will be referred to as C, MMX, and MMMX for each kernel. All C, MMX, and MMMX codes use the same algorithms. In addition, the correctness of the MMX and MMMX codes were validated by comparing their output to the output of C programs.

The speedup was measured by the ratio of the total number of cycles for the computational part of each kernel for the MMX implementation to the MMMX implementation. In order to explain the speedup, the ratio of dynamic number of instructions has also been obtained. These metrics formed the basis of the comparative study. Ratio of dynamic number of instructions means the ratio of the number of committed instructions for the MMX implementation to the number of committed instructions for the MMMX implementation.

5.2   Performance Evaluation Results

Figure 3 and Figure 4 depict the speedup of MMMX over MMX for media kernels that either use extended subwords technique or use both proposed techniques, respectively. The results have been obtained for one execution of media kernels on a single block on the single issue processor. In addition, these figures show

Table 3. Processor configuration

Parameter	Value
Issue width	1
Integer ALU, SIMD ALU	1
Integer MULT, SIMD MULT	1
L1 Instruction cache	512 set, direct-mapped 64-byte line LRU, 1-cycle hit, total of 32 KB
L1 Data cache	128 set, 4-way, 64-byte line, 1-cycle hit, total of 32 KB
L2 Unified cache	1024 set, 4-way, 64-byte line, 6-cycle hit, total of 256 KB
Main memory latency	18 cycles for first chunk, 2 thereafter
Memory bus width	16 bytes
RUU (register update unit) entries	64
Load-store queue size	8
Execution	out-of-order

the ratio of committed instructions (MMX implementation over MMMX). Both figures show that MMMX performs better than MMX for all kernels except SAD. The speedup in Figure 3 ranges from 0.74 for the SAD kernel to 2.66 for Paeth kernel. MMMX yields a speedup ranging from 1.10 for the 2D IDCT kernel to 4.47 for the Transp.(12) kernel in Figure 4. The most important reason why MMMX improves performance is that it needs to execute fewer instructions than MMX. In the SAD kernel, on the other hand, MMMX needs to execute more instructions than MMX. As Figure 3 shows, the ratio of committed instructions for the SAD kernel is 0.72.

An Special-Purpose `psadbw` Instruction (SPI) [13] has been used in the MMX implementation of the SAD function and the SAD function with interpolation, while in the MMMX implementation this SPI has been synthesized by a few general-purpose SIMD instructions. Both MMX and MMMX employ 8-way parallelism in the SAD function, while MMMX uses more instructions than MMX. MMX employs both 4- and 8-way parallelism in the SAD function with interpolation, which means that it uses many data type conversion instructions. On the contrary, MMMX always employs 8-way parallelism in the SAD function with interpolation kernel. This is the reason that the speedup is almost two for this kernel.

The speedup obtained for the Paeth kernel in Figure 3 is 2.66. The reason is that intermediate data is at most 10 bits wide and MMMX can, therefore, calculate the prediction for eight pixels in each loop iteration while MMX computes the prediction for four pixels. The speedups of MMMX over MMX for the vertical IDCT and 2D IDCT kernels in those figures is less than the speedups for other kernels. This is because the input data of these kernels is 12-bit and some intermediate results are larger than 12-bit. Therefore, the MMMX implementation cannot employ 12-bit functionality (8-way parallel SIMD instructions) all

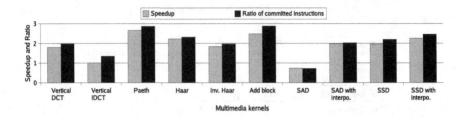

Fig. 3. Speedup of MMMX over MMX as well as the ratio of committed instructions (MMX over MMMX) for multimedia kernels, which use extended subwords technique on a single block on the single issue processor

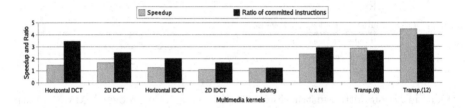

Fig. 4. Speedup of MMMX over MMX as well as the ratio of committed instructions (MMX over MMMX) for multimedia kernels, which use both proposed techniques on a single block on the single issue processor

the time but sometimes has to convert to 4×24-bit packed data types. The MMX implementation, on the other hand, is able to use 16-bit functionality all the time.

The reason why MMMX improves performance by just 20% for the Padding kernel in Figure 4 is that the MMX implementation employs the special-purpose `pavgb` instruction which computes the arithmetic average of eight pairs of bytes. More precisely, the `pavgb` instruction is supported in the SSE integer extension to MMX. MMMX does not support this instruction because with extended subwords it offers little extra functionality since it can be synthesized using the more general-purpose instructions `fadd12` and `fsar12` (shift arithmetic right on extended subwords). Nevertheless, because the matrix needs to be transposed between horizontal and vertical padding MMMX provides a speedup.

The two kernels for which the highest speedups are obtained are the 8×8 matrix transpose on 8-bit (Transp.(8)) and 12-bit data (Transp.(12)). If the matrix elements are 8-bit, MMMX can use the MRF to transpose the matrix, while MMX requires many pack and unpack instructions to realize a matrix transposition. Furthermore, if the elements are 12-bit (but stored as 16-bit data types), MMMX is able to employ 8-way parallel SIMD instructions, while MMX can only employ 4-way parallel instructions. As a result, MMMX improves performance by more than a factor of 4.47.

The average speedup and ratio of committed instructions for kernels that only use the extended subwords technique are 1.90 and 2.08, respectively, while for the kernels that use both proposed techniques are 2.05 and 2.56. The reduction of the dynamic instruction count in Figure 3 is due to extended subwords and in Figure 4 it is due to extended subwords and the MRF techniques. As a result, the performance benefits obtained by employing both techniques is higher than just using the extended subwords technique. Consequently, a part of the performance benefits is due to extended subwords, which increases DLP and the other part of the performance improvement is due to the MRF that eliminates the data rearrangement instructions. In order to clarify how much of the performance gain is a result of the additional parallelism provided by extended subwords and how much of it is due to the MRF, we disccuss some examples, horizontal transform of DCT and 2D DCTin the following section.

6   Analysis of Each Proposed Technique Separately

As already indicated in Table 2, in the SIMD implementations of some kernels such as the horizontal DCT both proposed techniques have been employed. Consequently, a part of the performance benefits is due to extended subwords, which increases DLP and the other part of the performance improvement is due to the MRF that eliminates the data rearrangement instructions. This section discusses an example, horizontal DCT in order to clarify how much of the performance gain is a result of the additional parallelism provided by extended subwords and how much of it is due to the MRF.

6.1   LLM Algorithm to Implement Discrete Cosine Transform

The discrete cosine transform and its inverse are widely used in several image and video compression applications. JPEG and MPEG partition the input image into 8×8 blocks and perform a 2D DCT on each block. The input elements are often either 8- or 9-bit, and the output is an 8×8 block of 12-bit 2's complement data. In this section, we discuss the LLM [11] technique to implement the DCT.

One of the fastest algorithm to compute the 2D DCT is LLM [11] technique. This algorithm performs a 1D DCT on each row of the 8×8 block followed by a 1D DCT on each column of the transformed 8×8 block. The algorithm has four stages, the output of each stage is the input of next stage. Figure 5 depicts the data flow graph of this algorithm for 8 pixels using fixed-point arithmetic.

Four SIMD implementations of the DCT namely, MMX, MMMX, MMX enhanced with extended subwords, and MMX enhanced with the MRF using LLM algorithm are explained and then their performance evaluation are presented.

6.2   Four Different SIMD Implementations for Horizontal DCT

In this section different SIMD implementations are discussed.

MMX Implementation: In the MMX implementation of this algorithm, however, 16-bit functionality (4-way parallelism) has been used because the input
data is either 8- or 9-bit. This means that this kernel needs 16-bit storage format,
while the intermediate results are smaller than 16-bit. Data type conversion instructions are not needed because four 16-bit can be loaded from memory to the
four subwords of a media register. Although many rearrangement instructions
are used in this implementation, this implementation exploits 4-way parallelism
in all stages. Figure 6 depicts the MMX/SSE implementation of the first stage of
the LLM algorithm for horizontal DCT. As this figure shows some rearrangement
instructions are required in this implementation.

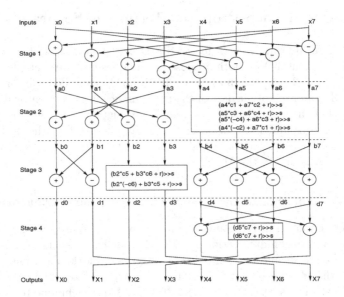

Fig. 5. Data flow graph of 8 pixels DCT using LLM [11] algorithm. The constant
coefficients of c, r, and s are provided for fixed-point implementation.

`movq   mm0, (dct)` ;mm0 =	x03	x02	x01	x00
`movq   mm3, 8(dct)` ;mm3 =	x07	x06	x05	x04
`pshufw mm1, mm0,27` ;mm1 =	x00	x01	x02	x03
`pshufw mm2, mm3,27` ;mm2 =	x04	x05	x06	x07
`paddsw mm0, mm2` ;mm0 =	x03+x04	x02+x05	x01+x06	x00+x07
`psubsw mm1, mm3` ;mm1 =	x00-x07	x01-x06	x02-x05	x03-x04

Fig. 6. The MMX/SSE code of the first stage of the LLM algorithm for horizontal
DCT

```
fldc16s12 3mxc0, (dct)     ; 3mxc0 =
fldc16s12 3mxc1, 16(dct)  ; 3mxc1 =
fldc16s12 3mxc2, 32(dct)  ; 3mxc2 =
fldc16s12 3mxc3, 48(dct)  ; 3mxc3 =
fldc16s12 3mxc4, 64(dct)  ; 3mxc4 =
fldc16s12 3mxc5, 80(dct)  ; 3mxc5 =
fldc16s12 3mxc6, 96(dct)  ; 3mxc6 =
fldc16s12 3mxc7, 112(dct) ; 3mxc7 =
fst12s16s 112(dct), 3mx7  ; (mem) =
fmov      3mx7 ,  3mx0    ; 3mx7 =
fadd12    3mx0 ,  112(dct) ; 3mx0 =
fsub12    3mx7 ,  112(dct) ; 3mx7 =
```

x07	x06	x05	x04	x03	x02	x01	x00
x17	x16	x15	x14	x13	x12	x11	x10
x27	x26	x25	x24	x23	x22	x21	x20
x37	x36	x35	x34	x33	x32	x31	x30
x47	x46	x45	x44	x43	x42	x41	x40
x57	x56	x55	x54	x53	x52	x51	x50
x67	x66	x65	x64	x63	x62	x61	x60
x77	x76	x75	x74	x73	x72	x71	x70
x77	x67	x57	x47	x37	x27	x17	x07
x70	x60	x50	x40	x30	x20	x10	x00
X	X	X	X	X	X	X	x00+x07
X	X	X	X	X	X	X	x00-x07

Fig. 7. A part of the MMMX implementation for the horizontal DCT algorithm. "X" denotes to $xi0 \pm xi7$, where $0 \leq i \leq 7$.

MMMX Implementation: MMMX processes eight rows in one iteration. A complete 8×8 block is loaded into eight column registers. After that row registers which have eight subwords are processed. Figure 7 depicts a part of the MMMX implementation of the LLM algorithm. In this figure, "X" refers to $xi0 \pm xi7$, where $0 \leq i \leq 7$. First, eight load column instructions are used to load a complete 8×8 block into column registers. After that two fadd12 and fsub12 instructions are needed to process 16 pixels simultaneously. In MMX, on the other hand, four instructions (two pshufw instructions, a paddsw, and a psubsw instructions) are required to process eight pixels.

MMX Enhanced with Extended Subwords: In MMX enhanced with extended subwords (MMX + ES), there are eight 12-bit subwords in each media register. In order to bring these subwords in a form amenable to SIMD processing, new data permutation instructions such as fshuflh12, fshufhl12, fshufhh12, fshufll12, and frever12 are needed. This is because of the following reasons. First, there is no shuffle instructions in MMX. MMX performs data permutation using pack and unpack instructions, while these instructions are not useful for MMX + ES. Second, there is a pshufw (packed shuffle word) instruction in SSE that is used for rearrangement of four subwords within a media register, while MMX + ES has eight subwords.

Figure 8 depicts a part of the horizontal DCT code that has been implemented by the MMX + ES. In each loop iteration of this implementation eight pixels are processed, the same as the MMX implementation that was already discussed.

MMX Enhanced with an MRF: In MMX enhanced with an MRF, there are four 128-bit column registers and eight 64-bit registers the same as MMX. Each

`fld16s12 mm0, (dct) ;mm0=`	x7	x6	x5	x4	x3	x2	x1	x0
`frever12 mm2, mm0   ;mm2=`	x0	x1	x2	x3	x4	x5	x6	x7
`fneg12   mm2, mm2,15;mm2=`	x0	x1	x2	x3	-x4	-x5	-x6	-x7
`fadd12   mm0, mm2   ;mm0=`	x0+x7	x1+x6	x2+x5	x3+x4	x3-x4	x2-x5	x1-x6	x0-x7

Fig. 8. A part of the code for horizontal DCT that has been implemented by MMX enhanced by extended subwords

`fldc16s16  cmm0 ,  (dct)   ; cmm0 =`	x07	x06	x05	x04	x03	x02	x01	x00
`fldc16s16  cmm1 ,  16(dct); cmm1 =`	x17	x16	x15	x14	x13	x12	x11	x10
`fldc16s16  cmm2 ,  32(dct); cmm2 =`	x27	x26	x25	x24	x23	x22	x21	x20
`fldc16s16  cmm3 ,  48(dct); cmm3 =`	x37	x36	x35	x34	x33	x32	x31	x30
`movq       (dct),  mm7    ; (mem) =`	x37		x27		x17		x07	
`movq       mm7  ,  mm0    ; mm7  =`	x30		x20		x10		x00	
`paddsw     mm0  ,  (dct)  ; mm0  =`	x30+x37		x20+x27		x10+x17		x00+x07	
`psubsw     mm7  ,  (dct)  ; mm7  =`	x30-x37		x20-x27		x10-x17		x00-x07	

Fig. 9. A part of the MMX + MRF implementation of the horizontal DCT algorithm

column register has eight 16-bit subword. Each subword in a column register corresponds to a subword in a row register. Each load column instruction can load eight 16-bit pixels into a column register. In addition, Figure 9 depicts a part of the MMX + MRF implementation of the horizontal DCT algorithm. There are two loop iterations to process an 8×8 block. This means that in each loop iteration, four rows (32 pixels) are processed.

6.3   Experimental Results

Figure 6.3 depicts the speedup of MMX + ES, MMX + MRF, and MMMX over MMX for one execution of an 8×8 horizontal DCT on a single issue processor. In addition, this figure shows the ratio of committed instructions (MMX over the other architectures). The speedup of MMX + ES is 1.15, while the speedup of MMX + MRF is less than 1. These results indicate that using either extended subwords or the MRF techniques is insufficient to eliminate most pack/unpack and rearrangement overhead instructions. In addition, using the MRF is both unuseful and causes performance loss. The MMMX architecture that employs both proposed techniques, on the other hand, yields much more performance benefits. Its speedup is 1.52.

In order to explain the behavior of Figure 6.3, Figure 6.3 shows the number of SIMD computation, SIMD overhead, SIMD ld/st, and scalar instructions for the four different architectures: MMX, MMX + MRF, MMX + ES, and MMMX

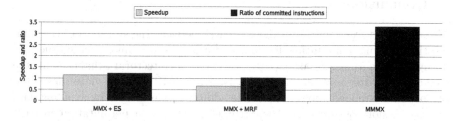

Fig. 10. Speedup of the MMX + ES, MMX + MRF, and MMMX over MMX as well as ratio of committed instructions for an 8 × 8 horizontal DCT on a single issue processor

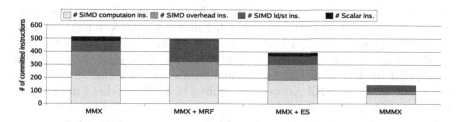

Fig. 11. The number of SIMD computation, SIMD overhead, SIMD ld/st, and scalar instructions in four different architectures, MMX, MMX + MRF, MMX + ES, and MMMX for an 8 × 8 horizontal DCT kernel

for an 8 × 8 horizontal DCT kernel. As this figure shows, the total number of instructions in the MMX + MRF is almost the same as MMX. This means that the former architecture cannot reduce the total number of instructions. The MMX + MRF reduces the number of SIMD overhead instructions, but it increases the number of SIMD ld/st instructions. This is because the MMX + MRF transposes four rows in each iteration and this causes that all eight 64-bit registers are filled. In order to use some of the filled registers for intermediate computations, they are stored and loaded in memory hierarchy and this increases the number of SIMD ld/st instructions. The latency of SIMD ld/st instructions is almost more than the latency of the SIMD overhead instructions. This is the main reason why the MMX + MRF has a performance penalty. MMX + ES, on the other hand, reduces the total number of instructions. The ratio of committed instructions is 1.23 as shown in Figure 6.3.

The extended subwords technique reduces the number of SIMD computation and SIMD ld/st instructions more than the MRF technique, while the latter technique reduces the number of SIMD overhead and scalar instructions more than the former technique. Consequently, these experimental results indicate that using either of these techniques is insufficient to mitigate SIMD computation, SIMD overhead, SIMD ld/st, and scalar instructions. The MMMX architecture that employs both proposed techniques reduces the total number of instructions much more than MMX + MRF and MMX + ES.

7 Conclusions

SIMD architectures suffer from the mismatch between the storage and the computational formats of multimedia data and using data permutation instructions during vectorization. We already proposed two architectural enhancement, the extended subwords and the Matrix Register File (MRF) to alleviate these limitations. The extended subwords provide additional parallelism by avoiding data tyep conversion instructions. The MRF eliminates data permutation instructions. The MMX architecture has been modified by the proposed techniques that was called the Modified MMX (MMMX) architecture. In this paper, we validated the MMMX architecture on a wide range of multimedia kernels. In addition, in order to determine the performance benefits of each proposed technique, we analysised each technique separately. The results showed that employing the MRF (MMX + MRF) and extended subwords (MMX + ES) separately obtain the speedup less than 1 and 1.15, respectively. This is because the total number of instructions in the MMX + MRF is almost the same as MMX. This means that the former architecture cannot reduce the total number of instructions. The MMX + MRF reduces the number of SIMD overhead instructions, but it increases the number of SIMD ld/st instructions. MMX + ES, on the other hand, reduces the total number of instructions. The results indicate that using either extended subwords or the MRF techniques is insufficient to eliminate most pack/unpack and rearrangement overhead instructions. The combination of both techniques should be employed in SIMD implementation.

References

1. Advanced Micro Devices Inc. 3DNow Technology Manual (2000)
2. Austin, T., Larson, E., Ernst, D.: SimpleScalar: An Infrastructure for Computer System Modeling. IEEE Computer 35(2), 59–67 (2002)
3. Bannon, P., Saito, Y.: The Alpha 21164PC Microprocessor. In: IEEE Proc. Compcon 1997, February 1997, pp. 20–27 (1997)
4. Diefendorff, K., Dubey, P.K., Hochsprung, R., Scales, H.: AltiVec Extension to PowerPC Accelerates Media Processing. IEEE Micro 20(2), 85–95 (2000)
5. Hennessy, J.L., Patterson, D.A.: Computer Architecture: A Quantitative Approach, 3rd edn. Morgan Kaufmann, San Francisco (2002)
6. Huang, L., Lai, M., Dai, K., Yue, H., Shen, L.: Hardware Support for Arithmetic Units of Processor with Multimedia Extension. In: Proc. IEEE Int. Conf. on Multimedia and Ubiquitous Engineering, April 2007, pp. 633–637 (2007)
7. IBM. Synergistic Processor Unit Instruction Set Architecture (January 2007)
8. Jennings, M.D., Conte, T.M.: Subword Extensions for Video Processing on Mobile Systems. IEEE Concurrency 6(3), 13–16 (1998)
9. Juurlink, B., Borodin, D., Meeuws, R.J., Aalbers, G.T., Leisink, H.: The SimpleScalar Instruction Tool (SSIT) and the SimpleScalar Architecture Tool (SSAT), http://ce.et.tudelft.nl/~shabahrami/
10. Lee, R.B.: Subword Parallelism with MAX-2. IEEE Micro 16(4), 51–59 (1996)
11. Loeffler, C., Ligtenberg, A., Moschytz, G.S.: Practical Fast 1-D DCT Algorithms With 11 Multiplications. In: Proc. Int. Conf. on Acoustical and Speech and Signal Processing, May 1989, pp. 988–991 (1989)

12. Peleg, A., Weiser, U.: MMX Technology Extension to the Intel Architecture. IEEE Micro 16(4), 42–50 (1996)
13. Raman, S.K., Pentkovski, V., Keshava, J.: Implementing Streaming SIMD Extensions on the Pentium 3 Processor. IEEE Micro 20(4), 47–57 (2000)
14. Ranganathan, P., Adve, S., Jouppi, N.P.: Performance of Image and Video Processing with General Purpose Processors and Media ISA Extensions. In: Proc. Int. Symp. on Computer Architecture, pp. 124–135 (1999)
15. Shahbahrami, A.: Avoiding Conversion and Rearrangement Overhead in SIMD Architectures. PhD thesis, Delft University of Technology (September 2008)
16. Shahbahrami, A., Juurlink, B., Vassiliadis, S.: Versatility of Extended Subwords and the Matrix Register File. ACM Transactions on Architecture and Code Optimization (TACO) 5(1) (May 2008)
17. Tremblay, M., Michael 0'Connor, J., Narayanan, V., He, L.: VIS Speeds New Media Processing. IEEE Micro 16(4), 10–20 (1996)

Large Matrix Multiplication on a Novel Heterogeneous Parallel DSP Architecture

Joar Sohl, Jian Wang, and Dake Liu

Department of Electrical Engineering, Linköping University, 581 83 Linköping, Sweden
{joar,dake,jianw}@isy.liu.se

Abstract. This paper introduces a novel master-multi-SIMD on-chip multi-core architecture for embedded signal processing. The parallel architecture and its memory subsystem are described in this paper. We evaluate the large size matrix multiplication performance on this parallel architecture and compare it with a SIMD-extended data parallel architecture. We also examine how well the new architecture scales for different numbers of SIMD co-processors. The experimental results show that the ePUMA[1] architecture's memory subsystem can effectively hide the data access overhead. With its 8-way SIMD data path and multi-SIMD parallel execution, the ePUMA architecture improves the performance of matrix multiplication with a speedup of 45x from the conventional SIMD extension.

Keywords: ePUMA, matrix multiplication, parallel DSP, SIMD, vector memory, permutation.

1 Introduction

Parallel computing has been used in embedded signal processing for several decades to meet the increasing demand of computing power. Particularly, massive parallelism is of much importance for streaming DSP processors to achieve real-time processing on large volume streaming data[1].

One kind of data parallel architecture is the SIMD extension which is used in ARM's Media Extensions[2] and PowerPC's AltiVec[3]. It improves processing capability for streaming media applications while still offering low power consumption. The SIMD extensions also simplify software development by providing a single tool-chain and processing core. Another parallel architecture known as VLIW[4] has also been proved to be an industrial success by TI's DaVinci and ADI's TigerShark. The VLIW processors take advantages of Instruction Level Parallelism (ILP) and efficiently use the hardware resources to improve the application performance. However, both the SIMD based and the VLIW based architectures have shown their bottlenecks in today's embedded systems. These systems are characterized by high performance and real-time requirements as well as power and cost constraints. The SIMD extensions' drawback is due to its data access overhead for instructions such as vector load, shuffle, pack, and unpack, which becomes an obstacle to the performance enhancement [5]. The VLIW architecture has disadvantages at providing power-efficient and cost-effective embedded processing[6]. Moreover, both of these two parallel architectures fail to scale to

---

[1] ePUMA: embedded Parallel DSP processor architecture with Unique Memory Access.

Y. Dou, R. Gruber, and J. Joller (Eds.): APPT 2009, LNCS 5737, pp. 408–419, 2009.
© Springer-Verlag Berlin Heidelberg 2009

even higher performance demanding applications such as high definition video codec, baseband signal processing in communication base-stations, and radar signal processing. Recently, a new trend of master-multi-SIMD on-chip multi-core architectures has emerged in high performance parallel DSP design, for example the CELL processor from STI. The Cell architecture provides high performance processing for a wide range of applications. It has one master processor extended by eight SIMD co-processors aimed at data-intensive processing. Each co-processor is assigned a local memory and a DMA controller. The interconnection of these processors is through the Cell Element Interconnect Bus (EIB), which consists of four ring buses to provide high throughput at low cost[7].

The ePUMA project is carried out at the Computer Engineering Division of the Department of Electrical Engineering at Linköping University. This project aims to develop a novel master-multi-SIMD parallel embedded DSP processor for real-time high performance computing with low power consumption and low silicon cost. The goal will be achieved by maximally hiding the data access and control overhead of the parallel architecture. This project has design challenges that include a power efficient memory subsystem with the highest possible throughput, and a local multi-bank vector memory and address permutation design for low latency parallel vector data access. A parallel programming model and a program-friendly tool chain is another key design challenge.

In this paper, we evaluate the performance of the ePUMA parallel architecture using an example of large-size matrix-matrix multiplication. Large matrix operations can be found in many data intensive computing applications. It is also a good candidate for parallel processing. The performance is evaluated on two different parallel architectures; a single 8-way SIMD extension, and ePUMA with different numbers of SIMD co-processors.

The rest of this paper is organized as follows. An overview of the ePUMA master-multi-SIMD architecture is provided in Section II. The memory subsystem is described in Section III. Section IV presents the implementations of matrix multiplication. The evaluation results are in Section V and Section VI concludes the paper.

2   Overview of the ePUMA Architecture

The ePUMA parallel DSP architecture is a master-multi-SIMD on-chip multi-core architecture. It consists of one master processing core, eight SIMD cores, and a memory subsystem. Each SIMD core has a local data memory and program memory. The memory subsystem includes two main memories, two ring buses, and two DMA controllers. The master core and all of the SIMD cores have access to both two buses for data and command communications. The overall architecture is illustrated in Figure 1.

The master core performs scalar operations and program control, while the eight SIMD cores are assigned by the master with parallel tasks of vector processing. This parallel DSP architecture has two interfaces to two off-chip main memories. One main memory attached to Ring Bus 1 is used for streaming data storage. The second main memory on Ring Bus 2 is used for software programs and coefficient data. The data

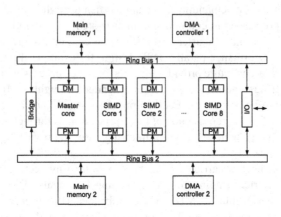

Fig. 1. ePUMA master-multi-SIMD architecture

communications are handled by the DMA controller on each bus. Data exchange between two main memories is performed by going through the bridge module.

3   Memory Subsystem

In the design of multi-core embedded processors, the memory subsystem keeps being an important component to achieve high computing performance. The memory access latency is one of the major factors that affect performance. Moreover, the memory subsystem is the key component to reduce power consumption and silicon cost. The design of the memory subsystem determines the implementation complexity. For example, Cell EIB chooses the ring bus architecture instead of the crossbar interconnection for the purpose of getting the highest possible throughput from the wire-efficient ring-bus implementation with the limits on area, power and complexity costs[7].

The memory subsystem of ePUMA architecture consists of two main memories, local store unit in each SIMD core, the interconnection buses, and the DMA controller, as illustrated by the region in the dash line in Figure 1.

3.1   Interconnection Buses

All the processing cores and memory modules are connected through this interconnection bus architecture, which contains two ring buses. A bridge module connects these two buses to enable data communication between them.

Ring bus 1. Ring bus 1 connects the master and all SIMD cores to main memory 1 which is for streaming data storage. A DMA controller is attached to this bus for direct memory access. A DMA transaction task can be configured and triggered by either the master processor or any of the SIMD cores. Ring bus 1 uses a cross-bar bus protocol which supports multi-connections simultaneously.

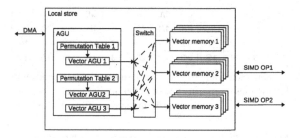

Fig. 2. Local store unit with three vector memories and two permutation tables

Ring bus 2. Ring bus 2 connects all the master and SIMD cores to main memory 2 which is prepared for software programs and coefficient data. Here the data communication load is not as high as in ring bus 1. To simplify implementation complexity, ring bus 2 applies a shared bus protocol, meaning that at one time only one bus master is granted the bus to perform its data transfer.

3.2 Vector Memory and Data Permutation

ePUMA's local store unit in each SIMD core consists of three vector memories and two permutation tables, as shown in Figure 2. The use of a multi-bank vector memory and data permutation can provide parallel vector data access with various addressing patterns at very short latency, usually within one cycle[8][9]. At execution time the local store unit connects two of the three vector memories to the SIMD data path for vector operands fetch. The remaining vector memory is connected to the DMA controller for data communication to the global memory. The SIMD unit works under two modes; a SIMD mode and a SIMT[1] mode[1]. In SIMD mode, data are loaded to register file first and then used by the data path. While in SIMT mode, the data path can access vector memory directly. The purpose of using three vector memories is to provide a "ping-pong" buffer for simultaneously loading data and executing SIMD tasks. A switch logic is used to swap the ping-pong buffers.

Data permutation is used with the vector memories to provide conflict-free parallel access[8]. The permutation process decides each vector element's storage position in the vector memory. This position information includes a bank number and a local address of the selected memory bank. A simple way to use a vector memory without permutation is to use a number of LSB bits from its address for bank selection, and use the rest bits as the local address. This common solution performs well for consecutive data access. For more complex SIMD or vector based high performance computing, many different access patterns are involved. Take matrix multiplication as an example. One matrix is accessed in row-wise order, and the other one is accessed in column-wise order. If permutation is available to provide such a column-wise vector access, the time for matrix transpose can be eliminated. This will improve the performance for matrix multiplication and other algorithms which access data that is not in row-major order. Here we give an example of using permutation to achieve conflict-free column-wise

---

[1] SIMT stands for Single Instruction-flow Multiple Tasks [1].

0	1	2	3	0/0	1/0	2/0	3/0	0/0	1/0	2/0	3/0
4	5	6	7	0/1	1/1	2/1	3/1	1/1	2/1	3/1	0/1
8	9	10	11	0/2	1/2	2/2	3/2	2/2	3/2	0/2	1/2
12	13	14	15	0/3	1/3	2/3	3/3	3/3	0/3	1/3	2/3

(a) Input matrix and (b) Storage position (c) Storage position
its addresses   in vector memory in vector memory
                       without permutation with permutation

Fig. 3. Conflict-free vector memory access with permutation

data access, shown in Figure3. Figure 3(a) shows the source 4×4 matrix with its sequential addresses. Figure 3(b) and Figure 3(c) use a representation of {S/r} in each block to present each matrix element's storage position in the vector memory, where S represents the bank assignment, r is the local address within the memory bank. Now we consider the access of vector {0,4,8,12}, that is, access the first column of the input matrix. Using the approach in Figure 3(b), it can be seen that all the elements are stored in memory bank 0, and a bank conflict occurs in this case. This means that four cycles are required to load this column data. When permutation is used as illustrated in Figure 3(c), the elements of the column vector reside in different memory banks, and no bank-conflict occurs and the access latency is reduced to one cycle. The calculation of storage position {S/r} is discussed in [8] and formulated in [9]. The permutation function used in this example is shown in Equations 1 and 2.

$$S(i) = \lfloor i + i/4 \rfloor \bmod 4 \tag{1}$$

$$r(i) = \lfloor i/4 \rfloor \tag{2}$$

In the ePUMA local store unit, data permutation is applied on both sides of the vector memory in the form of lookup tables; the DMA controller uses one permutation table during a DMA transaction, the SIMD unit uses the other permutation table to generate data addresses for vector memory. A permutation table takes a single address either from DMA input or from SIMD load/store unit as an entry to the table, and gets an output of vector addresses for the vector memory. Each element in the address vector contains two parts, the bank number and the sub-address within that bank. These addresses are calculated by the master and the table is configured by the master processor.

3.3 Multi-task DMA Controller

Each bus is allocated a DMA controller for direct memory access. A DMA transaction task can be configured either by the master core or by any of the SIMD cores. The DMA controller enables a task queue which supports multiple tasks in the queue. Thus as soon as one DMA transfer is finished, the next task can start immediately. Another useful feature of the DMA controller is the priority policy in the task queue. A task with a higher priority will be issued earlier. Simple data manipulations such as endian reordering and data width adjustment are also performed in the DMA transactions.

4   Matrix Multiplication Implementations

The main application domain for ePUMA is streaming DSP. I.e., the important algorithms that must be considered let us load a chunk of data to the vector memories, compute using a regular data access pattern, write back the results, and repeat.

Algorithms that cannot be decomposed into smaller parts which have this property, i.e. those who requires irregular data access patterns and/or frequent access to main memory during the compute phases are not a priority. We do not expect the performance achieved when running these algorithms on ePUMA to deviate from the performance on other architectures in any significant way.

In this section, we compare the performance of matrix multiplication of matrices with dimension 64 * 64. We chose this as our initial algorithm to be evaluated as it has very regular data access patterns and is typical for the application domain.

The performance will be evaluated on two different architectures using three different software implementations. Both architectures are assumed to have an identical 8-way SIMD datapaths. The difference between them is the complexity in memory subsystem. The first implementation is on a conventional SIMD extension data parallel architecture. The second and third implementation is on our ePUMA multi-SIMD architecture.

First of all, a mathematical definition of matrix multiplication is provided in Equation 3:

For $A \in \mathbb{R}^{m \times n}$, $B \in \mathbb{R}^{n \times p}$, then $C = AB \in \mathbb{R}^{m \times p}$, where

$$C_{i,j} = \sum_{r=1}^{n} A_{i,r} B_{r,j} \tag{3}$$

4.1   Architecture 1 - 8-Way SIMD Extension

First we consider the case when an 8-way SIMD extension is used with a cache. For simplicity we assume that the matrices A and B are already present in the cache. We also ignore the time it takes for the output matrix C to be written back after when it is moved from the cache. However, compared to the cycles necessary for this architecture to complete the matrix multiplication it can be considered negligable.

Since matrix B is in row-major order and it needs to be accessed in column-major order, we need to transpose B. Using a standard SIMDized version on 8*8 blocks this take 4810 cycles. The kernel for the matrix multiplication after B is transposed can be implementad as shown in Listing 1. While most of of the code code is quite self-explanatory some details are worth mentioning. Using a NISO SIMD datapath[1] the computation for *conv8wdw* is given in Equation 4:

$$\text{rDest.slot} = \sum_{i=0}^{7} \text{Src1.i} * \text{Src2.i}. \tag{4}$$

Similiarly, *sum4dwdw* is given by Equation 5:

$$rDest.slot = \sum_{i=0}^{3} Src1.i + Src2.i. \tag{5}$$

To avoid lengthy code but not add overhead from jumps and managing a counter in the would be innermost loops *generate* is run at compile time. Similarly we use *macro* to avoid unneccessary repetition.

Listing 1. Matrix multiplication for the 8-way SIMD extension

```
macro  CONV(REG)
    generate for  j  in  0 .. 3
        ld          r0 ,( rA , rI .0 )
        ld          r1 ,( rB , rI .1 )
        stall       2
        conv8wdw  REG.%j , r0 , r1
        addvs       rI ,8 -- Increment  address  offsets
        nop
    endgenerate
endmacro

set  rA ,A              -- rA = address  for  matrix  A
set  rB ,B              -- rB = address  for  matrix  B
set  rC ,C              -- rC = address  for  matrix  C
for  i  in  0 .. 63
    mul  rI .0 , i ,64*WORDSIZE -- set  offset  for  A
    set  rI .1 ,0                -- reset  B  offset
    repeat  64
        CONV( r0 )
        CONV( r1 )
        mul         rI .0 , i ,64*WORDSIZE -- reset  A  offset
        stall       2
        sum4dwdw  r2 .0 , r0 , r1
        stall       4
        st          m1 ( rC ) , r4 .0
        add         rC ,2*WORDSIZE
    endrepeat
endfor
```

4.2   Architecture 2 - SIMD Co-processor with Vector Memory

Using a vector memory with permutation we can implement the multiplication as shown in Figure 4. A naive implementation can be seen in Listing 2. However, since so much of the addressing overhead is removed we get a significant number of nops in the inner loop. A simple optimization by overlapping the iterations results in the code shown in Listing 3.

The *conv8wdw* and some others instructions now use the notation $< memory > (op)$ for operands, where *op* is the operation to be performed to get the address for the next

Fig. 4. Implementation on the system with a co-processor and vector memory

operand. When we are in SIMT mode the address generator calculates these in parallel with the other instructions.

The total cost of the DMA transfer is 2057 cycles.

Listing 2. Matrix multiplication for ePUMA

```
macro  CONV(REG)
      generate for  j in 0 .. 3
            conv8wdw  REG.%j , M1r(+8) ,
                              M2c(+64*WORDSIZE*8)
      endgenerate
endmacro

set  rM1B , C
for  i in 0 .. 63
      set  rM1 , A                -- set  offset  for  A
      mac  rM1 , i , 64*WORDSIZE
      set  rM2 , B                -- reset  B  offset
      add  r3 , B , WORDSIZE
      repeat  64
            CONV( r0 )
            CONV( r1 )
            set  rM1 , A          -- reset  A  offset
            mac  rM1 , i , 64*WORDSIZE
            set  rM2 , r3++
            stall      3
            sum4dwdw  r2 . 0 , r0 , r1
            stall      4
            st          M1B(+2*WORDSIZE) , r2 . 0
      endrepeat
endfor
```

Listing 3. Overlapping implementation for ePUMA

```
macro  8CONV(REG1 , REG2)
      generate for  j in 0 .. 3
            conv8wdw  REG1.%j , M1r(+8*WORDSIZE) ,
                              M2c(+64*WORDSIZE*8)
      endgenerate
      generate for  j in 0 .. 2
            conv8wdw  REG2.%j , M1r(+8*WORDSIZE) ,
                              M2c(+64*WORDSIZE*8)
      endgenerate
      conv8wdw  REG2.3 , M1r(r6) ,
                        M2c(r7++)
```

```
endmacro

set  rM2C,C
for  i  in  0 .. 63
     set        rM1,A
     mac        rM1,i,64*WORDSIZE
     set        r6,rM1
     set        rM2,B
     add        r7,B,WORDSIZE
     8CONV(r4,r5)
     8CONV(r0,r1)
     sum4dwdw  r2.0,r4,r5
     repeat 62
          8CONV(r0,r1)
          st          M2C(+2*WORDSIZE),r2.0
          sum4dwdw  r2.0,r0,r1
     endrepeat
     stall      6
     st         M2C(+2*WORDSIZE),r2.0
     sum4dwdw  r2.0,r0,r1
     stall      4
     st         M2C(+2*WORDSIZE),r2.0
endfor
```

4.3   Architecture 2 - Overlapping DMA

We can improve the performance by overlapping some DMA transactions with computation. We do not want to split matrix B into sections because the overhead per iteration
for the inner loop will increase significantly. Instead we transfer matrix B in full, and
then transfer each row in matrix A and the destination matrix C by themselves. This
strategy lends itself well to a parallel solution by using a cyclic distribution of the rows
of A and C among the SIMD processors. This is demonstrated in Figure 5 and Figure 6.

In Figure 5 $p = 3$. We broadcast B and then send each processor one row in A. We
then transfer any finished rows in C to global memory.

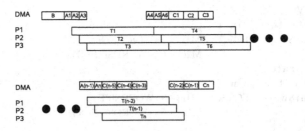

Fig. 5. Overlapping DMA

In Figure 6 we see the vector memory usage. We store B in vector memory 1. Since we need to access B column-wise we use a permutation table for AGU1. Since we access A and C row-wise we do not need any permutation table for these, and we can use AGU2 and AGU3 for address generation for these memories. We do however swap vector memories 2 and 3 in the local store unit between each processed row, so that when we use one memory for calculations while the other one is used for DMA transfers.

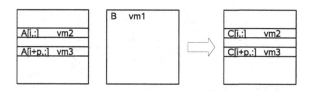

Fig. 6. Usage of vector memories

5   Experimental Results

We define the ratio R as in Equation 6:

$$R = \frac{\text{Total cycles}}{\text{Arithmetic instructions}}. \tag{6}$$

The number of arithmetic instructions is defined as the number of *conv8wdw* and *sum4dwdw* instructions. For the considered implementations this value is 36864. We can then use R as a measurement for the amount of overhead for the different implementations.

In Table 1 we find the results for when we use one core for processing for all the implementations.

The ePUMA system is not that far from the ideal R value of one. We get an overhead of 19.5% with the naive DMA transactions. Being a bit more clever we get down to 15.4% by overlapping DMA transactions with computation. Using only SIMD extensions impose quite a significant overhead of 647%.

The speedup of the implementations on ePUMA are quite significant, almost 6.5 when using overlapping DMA. We should also remember that we did not account for memory transfers for architecture 1, so the improvements by ePUMA should be slightly larger.

Table 1. Results

Architecture	Arch. 1	Arch. 2	Arch. 2 - Overlapping DMA
Total cycles	275342	44043	42531
R	7.469	1.195	1.154
Speedup	1.00	6.25	6.47

5.1   ePUMA Scalability

In Table 2 we observe the relative speedup of the overlapping DMA implementation when using more than one SIMD processor. It is not quite linear; however, considering how much overhead that has already been removed it is not all that surprising that we cannot entirely hide the DMA transfers.

Table 2. ePUMA scalability

Processors	1	2	4	8
Speedup	1.000	1.973	3.832	7.176

5.2   Permutation Tables vs Parallel Transpose

In Table 3 we compare the relative execution times of using permutation tables vs performing a parallel transpose of matrix B for different numbers of processors. We use the values for ePUMA with permutation tables as the baseline. We can see that the added cost when not using permutation tables is 11-12%. As the transpose is $\Theta(n^2)$ and the matrix multiplication is $\Theta(n^3)$ we expect this value to be larger for algorithms with less computation compared to the input size. Still, avoiding an added cost of 11-12% of the total execution time is quite significant.

Table 3. Using permutation tables vs parallel transpose

Processors	1	2	4	8
Permutation tables	1.0000	1.0000	1.0000	1.0000
Parallel transpose	1.1147	1.1148	1.1152	1.1164

6   Conclusion

Reviewing the performance increase offered by ePUMA compared to SIMD extensions we believe that ePUMA holds great promise. Using the same number of processors as the SIMD extended architecture we increase the performance with a factor of 6.47, and by using the full 8 SIMD processor version with a factor of 45.64.

While the problem at hand fits ePUMA very well it is quite reasonable to expect similar results for other algorithms with regular addressing patterns. However, we require that the data access patterns are predictable and that we will be able to load data from main memory in advance. As ePUMA is geared towards streaming DSP this is an acceptable constraint.

Acknowledgements

The authors would like to thank SSF, Swedish Foundation for Strategic Research, for the support of this project.

References

1. Liu, D.: Embedded DSP Processor Design, ch. 20. Morgen-Kaufmann, Linköping (2008)
2. ARM Media Extensions, http://www.arm.com/products/CPUs/arch-simd.html
3. Tyler, J., Lent, J., Mather, A., Nauyen, H.: AltiVec^{TM}: Bringing Vector Technology to the PowerPC^{TM} Processor Family. In: IEEE International IPCCC 1999, February 10-12, pp. 437–444 (1999)
4. Kumura, T., Ikekawa, M., Yosbida, M., Kuroda, I.: VLIW DSP for mobile applications. IEEE Signal Processing Magazine 19(4), 10–21 (2002)
5. Chang, H., Cho, J., Sung, W.: Performance Evaluation of an SIMD Architecture with a Multi-bank Vector Memory Unit. IEEE SIPS, Banff, 71–76 (2006)
6. Weiss, M., Fettweis, G.: Dynamic Codewidth Reduction for VLIW Instruction Set Architectures in Digital Signal Processors. In: 3rd International Workshop on Image ana' Signal Processing, pp. 517–520 (1996)
7. Ainsworth, T.W., Pinkston, T.M.: Characterizing The Cell Eib On-Chip Network. IEEE Micro 27(5), 6–14 (2007)
8. Gössel, M., Rebel, B., Creutzburg, R.: Memory Architecture and Parallel Access. Elsevier Science, Amsterdam (1994)
9. Lundgren, B., Ödlund, A.: Expose of patterns in parallel memory access. Master thesis, Linköping university, LiTH-ISY-EX–07/4005-SE

Implementing Fast Packet Filters
by Software Pipelining on x86 Processors[*]

Yoshiyuki Yamashita[1] and Masato Tsuru[2]

[1] Saga University, Honjyo 1, Saga, 840-8502 Japan
yaman@is.saga-u.ac.jp
[2] Kyushu Institute of Technology, Kawazu 680-4, Iizuka, 820-8502 Japan
tsuru@ndrc.kyutech.ac.jp

Abstract. Packet filters are essential for network traffic/security management on the Internet. Filters implemented by software on general-purpose CPUs are very flexible but occasionally suffer from poor performance. In order to address this problem, we have investigated software pipelining techniques for loops with a number of conditional branches for use in software-based fast packet filters. Based on our previous researches, we herein apply the software pipelining approach in an attempt to increase the filter performance for large filter rules. We validate the effectiveness of the proposed approach on Intel x86-32/64 series, as well as Intel Itanium 2 processors, which speaks to the generality and practicality of the proposed approach. The software pipelined program codes on x86-64 processors are 2.2 times faster than C-compiler-based codes and 1.8 times faster than carefully optimized hand-compiled codes. In addition, the performance of the pipelined codes we obtained on x86-64 processors is comparable to that on Itanium 2 processors with predicate registers.

1 Introduction

Packet filters basically inspect the header and/or payload of each incoming packet and, accordingly, perform appropriate actions (pass, discard, logging, modification, etc.) on the packet based on a given filter rule (a set of filter patterns). Packet filters are essential for network traffic management and security management, and so are implemented in a variety of systems and devices, including not only IP routers and firewalls, but also various types of network equipment. Software-based packet filters on general-purpose CPUs are cost-effective and flexible, but are generally relatively slow, whereas hardware-based packet filters (e.g., packet filters using ASIC or FPGA [9,14]) are fast, but expensive and less flexible. Recently, the rapid growth of network bandwidth has led to the requirement for high-speed packet filters. On the other hand, emerging applications of packet filters require much more scalability and flexibility in handling filter

---

[*] This work was supported in part by Hitachi, Ltd, National Institute of Information and Communications Technology, and JSPS.KAKENHI (S 18100001).

Y. Dou, R. Gruber, and J. Joller (Eds.): APPT 2009, LNCS 5737, pp. 420–435, 2009.
© Springer-Verlag Berlin Heidelberg 2009

rules, which should be easily modifiable in response to changes in circumstances or requirements. In order to realize packet filters that enable both flexibility and high-speed operation in a cost-effective manner, it is of practical importance to make software-based packet filters fast enough that the filters would be effective even for a large filter rule consisting of a number of filter patterns or under intensive traffic load. This requires an effective combination of both the higher-level optimization related to algorithmic structures that are adaptable for the input packet sequence and the lower-level (machine code) optimization related to acceleration techniques in a compiler study.

To address this problem, the authors have focused on the lower-level optimization and have investigated software pipelining techniques for loops with a number of conditional branches as key techniques for accelerating software-based packet filters. Several studies have attempted to produce native machine code from a packet filter rule and to make the filter faster compared with the conventional interpreter-based packet filter [2,4,8]. However, to the best of our knowledge, none of these studies applied state-of-the-art optimization techniques based on software pipelining and fully exploited the performance of modern general-purpose processors. Although software pipelining is a common technique in compiler construction, it is technically difficult to apply software pipelining to a packet filter because the filter consists of a few tens of (more than 20 in some cases) conditional branches. We solve this problem with predicated execution [5] and enhanced modulo scheduling [10]. We investigated optimization on the packet-based loop (see Section 2) [11,12], and also reported experimental results on rule pattern-based loop optimization using the Itanium 2 processor [13]. Based on these studies, in the present paper, we try to validate the effectiveness of our approach to accelerating large filter rules (consisting of a number of filter patters) through extensive experiments using not only the Itanium 2 processor but also x86-32/64 series processors, which are the most widely deployed general-purpose processors.

We discuss and compare the results for both types of processors, thereby demonstrating the generality of the proposed approach. The software pipelined codes developed herein are 2.9 times and 2.2 times faster than C-compiler-based codes run on the Itanium 2 and x86 processors, respectively, and 1.5 times and 1.8 times faster than carefully optimized hand-compiled codes run on the Itanium 2 and x86 processors, respectively.

2   Framework

In the present study, we consider the following two types of optimizations:

Type A optimization applies software pipelining to a packet-based loop to process intensive input traffic (i.e., for *a huge number of* input packets).

Type B optimization applies software pipelining to a pattern-based loop to handle *a lot of* filter patterns.

```
for(i = 0; i < n_packets; i++){
    result = filter1(packet[i]);
    action(packet[i],result);
}
```

(a) Type A program

```
for(i = 0; i < n_packets; i++){
    result[i] = filter1(packet[i]);
}
for(i = 0; i < n_packets; i++){
    action(packet[i],result[i]);
}
```

(b) Type A program revised

```
result = REJECT;
for(i = 0; i < n_patterns; i++){
    r = filter2(packet,pattern[i]);
    if(r != NULL){
        result = r;
        break;
    }
}
action(packet,result);
```

(c) Type B program

Fig. 1. Packet filter programs of types A and B

2.1   Type A Optimization

Suppose that a one-line packet filter (e.g., tcpdump) suffers from highly intensive input traffic such as a Denial Of Service (DOS) attack or an unexpected
traffic load by misconfiguration. In this case, the filter program, which iterates the loop body in terms of input packets, can be regarded as in Figure 1
(a), where the function call filter1(packet[i]) decides the action for the i-
th input packet packet[i], and the function call action(packet[i],result)
processes the packet according to the decision.

   In recent years, we have been investigating the case in which a filter pattern is
represented in the syntax of the tcpdump based on the Berkeley Packet Filter [7].
In our approach, the above-described loop is divided into the two loops given
in Figure 1 (b). The first loop is optimized because the function filter1()
contains only logical and arithmetic operations, while the function action()
contains system-calls, which are difficult to optimize. The body of the function
filter1() varies in terms of the contents of the given filter pattern so that a
compiler that translates each filter pattern into an optimized loop code is needed.

   We have shown previously that, on an Itanium 2 processor, software pipelining
a program can speedup the program by approximately three to four times compared to the naive C-based program and by approximately two times compared
to the non-pipelined optimized program [11,12].

2.2   Type B Optimization

Type B optimization is the main subject of the present paper. Suppose that a
large packet filter (i.e., a packet filter that consists of a number of filter patterns)
suffers from low throughput due to the long processing time of each input packet.
Figure 2 shows an example of the filter patterns considered herein. Like the
Cisco IOS access list, the example is based on a typical static IP filter rule

```
ip filter 1 reject X.X.X.0/24 * * * *
ip filter 2 pass * X.X.X.0/24 established * *
ip filter 3 pass X.X.X.X/29 X.X.X.X tcp * smtp
ip filter 4 pass X.X.X.0/24 X.X.X.X tcp * 5000-6000
ip filter 5 pass * * udp * domain
ip filter 6 pass X.X.X.X/29 X.X.X.X tcp * pop3
...
```

Fig. 2. Example of a filter rule (each X.X.X.X is replaced with a concrete IP address)

representation [3]. This filter rule consists of one or more lines of filter patterns, and a filter pattern represents various conditions of IP addresses, protocols, and port numbers of an input packet. The details are described in Section 3.

In this case, the filter program, which iterates the loop body in terms of rule patterns, can be regarded as in Figure 1 (c), where the function call filter2(packet,pattern[i]) returns PASS or REJECT if the input packet matches the *i*-th pattern and the program exits the loop. Otherwise, the program proceeds to the next pattern. In contrast to filter1() in type A, the body of filter2() is invariant in terms of the contents of filter patterns because the syntax of filter patterns are restricted so that we can easily translate and store an arbitrary filter pattern into a memory array of fixed format. Thus, it is sufficient to construct a program to access to the memory array and check whether the input packet matches pattern by pattern. We construct such a program using a code optimizer that performs software pipelining. Note that it is very hard to perform software pipelining by hand because the loop body includes a few tens of conditional branches and the optimized code is too complex to write by hand. We obtained a preliminary result on an Itanium 2 processor, indicating the potential applicability of the proposed approach [13].

Hereinafter, if there is no confusion, we refer to a packet filter based on type A (or type B) optimization as a *type A packet filter* (or *type B packet filter*).

3 Filter Rule and Execution Model

The syntax and semantics of the proposed filter rule are based on the syntax and semantics of the common popular static IP filter rules, such as the Cisco IOS access list [3]. In this section, we summarize the proposed filter rule and then discuss how to analyze the execution time of type B packet filters.

3.1 Filter Rule

We assume that a filter rule consists of one or more *filter patterns*, which are stored in a text formatted file. Figure 2 is such an example; in which each line represents one filter pattern to check the IP addresses, protocol, and port numbers of every input packet.

After being invoked, a packet filter program reads the rule file and translates the contents of the filter patterns into an inner binary representation stored in a memory array. The program then checks whether an input packet matches the conditions that each filter pattern represents. The program proceeds from the first filter pattern at the top line to the bottom line in descending order. If the packet matches a filter pattern, the program performs the corresponding action of the pattern. Otherwise, the program drops the packet[1] if the packet matches no filter pattern in the rule.

Hereinafter, we generally refer to the entire set of rule patterns simply as a *rule* and each filter pattern simply as a *pattern*.

The following is the syntax of every filter pattern in this paper:

$$\texttt{ip filter } n \ action \ sip \ dip \ proto \ spt \ dpt$$

The parameters n, *action*, *sip*, *dip*, *proto*, *spt*, and *dpt* are defined below.

n is a pattern identification number (unsigned 16-bit integer). We assume that the numbers of patterns are arranged in ascending order.

action is an action when the pattern is chosen. Usually, the action is `pass`, `reject`, or another special action.

sip (or *dip*) is the source (destination) IP address of the input packet, which is one of the following three patterns. "`*`" is a wild card, which indicates an arbitrary address. "$x_1.x_2.x_3.x_4$" is a concrete address, where each x_i is an unsigned 8-bit integer value. "$x_1.x_2.x_3.x_4/m$" is a concrete address with a mask bit-width m, where m is a non-negative integer such as $0 \le m \le 32$.

proto is a protocol identifier, which is one of the following four patters. "`*`" is a wild card, which indicates an arbitrary protocol. "`tcp`" indicates the tcp protocol. "`udp`" indicates the udp protocol. "`established`" indicates the tcp packet after the tcp connection is established[2].

spt (or *dpt*) is the source (destination) port number of the input packet, which is one of the following four patterns. "`*`" is a wild card, which indicates an arbitrary port number. We specify an arbitrary port number if the protocol of the pattern is not `tcp`/`udp`. "p" is a concrete port number (unsigned 16-bit integer). "p_1-p_2" is a range of port numbers specified by two port numbers $p_1 \le p_2$. "*name*" is a specific port name such as `smtp`, `www`, or `domain`.

3.2   Model of Execution Time

Before proceeding to the experiments and the evaluation thereof, we consider a simple theoretical model for the execution times of type B packet filters.

We assume that a rule consists of N filter patterns, and that the execution time t of a packet filter is represented by the linear equation $t = T_O + kT_P$ when the input packet matches the k-th pattern (at the k-th line from the top of the rule), where the constant T_0 is the pre-/post-processing time (overhead time) of the filter program, and the constant T_P is the unit processing time for each

---

[1] This is referred to as a default rule. In some cases, the default rule may be to accept the packet if there is no pattern to match.

[2] The packet filter must check the `ack` and `rst` bits in the flag field of the tcp packet.

pattern. If the input packet matches no pattern, we assume $t = T_O + NT_P$. Let p_k be the probability for the case in which the packet matches the k-th pattern, and let $p_0 = 1 - \sum_{k=1}^{N} p_k$ be the probability for the case in which the input packet matches no pattern. We can define the average (expected) execution time to check an arbitrary input packet as follows:

$$\bar{t} = \sum_{k=1}^{N} p_k(T_O + kT_P) + p_0(T_O + NT_P) = T_O + \alpha T_P \quad (1)$$

where $\alpha = \sum_{k=1}^{N} kp_k + Np_0$. This is the relation between the filter rule and its expected execution time for an arbitrary input packet. Suppose that a set P of sample input packets and several types of sample rules R_1, R_2, ..., R_n are given. Then, for each pair (P, R_i), we can calculate α_i, i.e., the coefficient of the second term of equation (1), by analyzing which filter pattern in R_i matches a packet in P. Moreover, given a concrete implementation (an executable code) F of our type B optimization, we can experimentally obtain the average execution time $\bar{t}_i$, as the left-hand side of equation (1), for the pair (P, R_i). Thus, there are n equations with unknown constant values T_O and T_P, as follows:

$$\bar{t}_1 = T_O + \alpha_1 T_P, \quad \bar{t}_2 = T_O + \alpha_2 T_P, \quad ..., \quad \bar{t}_n = T_O + \alpha_n T_P$$

Using the method of least squares, we can obtain the values T_O and T_P. We will later see that the above approximation works well, although it is quite simple.

Suppose that, for two given implementations F and F' of our packet filter program, we can obtain pairs of constant values (T_O, T_P) and (T_O', T_P'), respectively. Then, the ratio of the expected execution times $\bar{t}$ and $\bar{t}'$ of the implementations is given as follows:

$$\bar{t}/\bar{t}' = (T_O + \alpha T_P)/(T_O' + \alpha T_P')$$

Note that α is invariant, independent from program implementations, and is likely to increase when the number N of filter patterns increases. Hence, $\bar{t}/\bar{t}' \approx T_P/T_P'$ holds when α is sufficiently large, which shows that the constants T_P and T_P' are fundamentally important when comparing two different implementations. The value T_P/T_P' is regarded as the acceleration ratio of F' to F.

4   Code Optimization Techniques

Before explaining code optimization, we restrict our focus on filter patterns for TCP packets. An input packet for which the IP protocol is p never matches a filter pattern for which the *proto* field is neither p nor a wild card *. Therefore, the filter patterns should be sorted by the IP protocol type. Figure 3 shows the concrete but straightforward form of the loop in Figure 1 (c) specialized for TCP packets. Here, the input packet is stored in the variable packet, and the filter patterns are stored in the array tcp_pattern. Their data entities are structured with the data members such as sip, dip, and proto. Hereinafter, we concentrate on optimizing this loop.

```
result = REJECT;
for(int i = 0; i < n_tcp_patterns; i++){
  SIP = packet.sip & tcp_pattern[i].sip_bit_mask;
  if(SIP == tcp_pattern[i].sip){                                    //(1)
    DIP = packet.dip & tcp_pattern[i].dip_bit_mask;
    if(DIP == tcp_pattern[i].dip){                                  //(2)
      if(tcp_pattern[i].proto == tcp){                              //(3)
        if(packet.spt >= tcp_pattern[i].spt_minimum_value){         //(4)
          if(packet.spt <= tcp_pattern[i].spt_maximum_value){       //(5)
            if(packet.dpt >= tcp_pattern[i].dpt_minimum_value){     //(6)
              if(packet.dpt <= tcp_pattern[i].dpt_maximum_value){   //(7)
                FLAGS =  packet.tcp_flag_field
                       & tcp_pattern[i].tcp_flag_field_bit_mask;
                if(FLAGS == tcp_pattern[i].tcp_flag_field){         //(8)
                  result = tcp_pattern[i].action;
                  break;
                }
                ...
      } else if(tcp_pattern[i].proto == *){                         //(9)
        result = tcp_pattern[i].action;
        break;
      }
  ...
}
```

Fig. 3. C program for filtering tcp packets

Four types of code optimization techniques have been applied for type A optimization in our previous studies [11,12], and these types except predicated execution will also be applied on x86 processors for type B optimization in the present paper. These are explained briefly in the following.

4.1 Compiling a Naive C Program

The most primitive code optimization technique considered herein is to compile this program in a straightforward manner with the optimizing option -O3 of the compiler. We herein refer to this program (and its compiled binary code) as *naive code*, because compiling a common C program by a common C compiler is the simplest solution among the optimization methods considered herein.

4.2 Compiling by Hand

One reason a hand-compiled code is faster than a compiler-generated code is that the assembly programmer deliberately selects a set of CPU instructions suitable for a given computation, which cannot be done by the compiler. In the present case, multimedia instructions that are usually contained in recent commercial processors are effective for the parallel comparison of IP addresses and port numbers. In preliminary experiments, gcc and even icc, Intel's C compiler, did not generate such a code.

Thus, the second code optimization technique considered herein is to compile the program in Figure 3 by hand. We refer to the code as a *hand compiled code*.

4.3 Software Pipelining

Software pipelining [1] can rearrange the instructions and execute successive iterations in parallel if the iterations have no dependence on each other[3]. For loops in which the body has no conditional branch, this technique is common now because most compilers, including gcc, can apply the technique. However, the target loop in Figure 3 has conditional branches and can be software pipelined by existing compilers. For loops with conditional branches, we apply software pipelining using the two techniques introduced below.

Predicated Execution. Predicated execution (PE) with predicate registers [5] eliminates branch instructions, which may seriously slow program execution due to branch penalties, and transforms a loop body into a straight line code without branches. If a loop body is a straight-line code, we can optimize the loop by applying a standard software pipelining technique [1].

The third optimization technique considered in the present paper is to construct such a software pipelined predicated code from the hand compiled code in Section 4.2. Let us refer to the code obtained in this manner as a *PE code*. Since Itanium 2 processor is the only existing commercial processor having the predication facility, this technique is not applicable to any x86 processor.

Enhanced Modulo Scheduling. It is difficult to precisely explain enhanced modulo scheduling (EMS) [10] in the limited space available in the present paper. Put simply, EMS transforms a software pipelined PE code into a code that does not use predicate registers. Enhanced modulo scheduling simulates predication by generating a combination of all possible sequences of unpredicated instructions. Since EMS uses no predicate register, any processor (including, of course, x86 processors) can execute the code generated by EMS. One drawback of EMS is that the combination causes an exponential increase in code size, which may cause the I-cache overflow. Strictly speaking, the EMS algorithm originally proposed in [10] treats a loop having a few unnested conditional branches and is not sufficient for the optimization of the target loop shown in Figure 3. Thus, we have extended the algorithm so as to be applicable to loops with *a few tens of deeply nested* conditional branches[4].

The fourth optimization technique considered herein is to apply EMS to the hand compiled code presented in Section 4.2. Let us refer to the code generated in this manner as a *EMS code*.

Readers who are interested in software pipelining techniques by PE and EMS can refer to [12] for an easy-to-understand introduction.

---

[3] It is natural to assume that there is no dependence between filter patterns in a static IP packet filter rule.

[4] The authors are currently preparing another paper that explains how to extend the original EMS.

4.4   Two Approaches to Fast Type B Packet Filters

In order to obtain a fast code in type B optimization, we consider the following two approaches.

The first approach is to develop a code optimizer which automatically exploits characteristics of the targeted processor. By this approach, we have obtained the PE and EMS codes on an Itanium 2 with the same software pipelining techniques for type A described in the previous paper [12]. In Section 6, we refer to the experimental results obtained in our paper [13], in which we use the code optimizer developed in the previous study [12], with only small modifications, depending on the differences between type A and type B optimizations.

The second approach is to look for a fast code in *generate-and-test* manner. By this approach, we have obtained an optimized EMS code on x86 processors by performing a *generate-and-test* method described in the next section. For any C loop, theoretically, there are an enormous (or an infinite) number of EMS codes. Some of which are faster or slower, but we do not know which the code is the fastest. Thus, we first select one EMS code from among the EMS codes. Then, with sample input packets and a sample rule of filter patterns, we examine the code in terms of its execution time. Next, we select the second EMS code and examine this code. In this way, we examine numerous EMS codes, so that we are expected to eventually obtain the optimal one.

At this moment, a code optimizer (in the first approach) is not developed for x86 processors because we have little experience in applying EMS to x86 processors and we do not obtain a detail algorithm how to generate faster EMS codes yet. Of course, the code optimizer for the Itanium 2 cannot be used for x86 processors because their architectures are quite different. The behaviors of x86 processors are described in Intel's IA-32 manuals [6]. However, the behaviors of out-of-order completion type processors are generally vague, whereas the behaviors of in-order completion type processors like the Itanium 2 are strictly defined in the manuals [5]. Hence, in the future, after validating the effectiveness of the EMS technique, we intend to establish a concrete optimization algorithm for x86 processors.

5   Optimizations on x86 Processors

5.1   Generate-and-Test Procedure

The following illustrates the overall procedure for performing generate-and-test experiments on x86 processors.

1. First, we translate the C program in Figure 3 into a hand compiled code on an x86 processor. ¿From this code, we select *primary* instructions that essentially determine the total order of all instructions executed (explained in Section 5.2 below).
2. Next, we rearrange the primary instructions according to a certain rule (explained in Section 5.2). In general, such a rearranged sequence of primary

instructions does not preserve the semantics of the original hand compiled code. However, by carefully restricting the sequence as a skeleton (or a kernel) of the software pipelined code, we can derive an executable software pipelined code equivalent to the original code. Then, we examine the execution time of the code using a lot of pairs of a sample data (a set of input packets) and a sample rule.

3. Iterating step 2 above, we generate and test a large number of software pipelined codes to search for the fastest code.

We apply the procedure to extended 64-bit mode in x86 processors (hereinafter x86-64) and to common 32-bit mode in x86 processors (hereinafter x86-32).

5.2   Codes for x86-64 Processors

We wrote the hand compiled code for x86-64 processors, as given in Figure 4 (a), where LOOPBACK(*label*) is a macro to update a loop counter register and jump back to the entry point *label* of the loop.

The 64-bit operation instructions and multimedia (MMX) instructions are aggressively used in this code in order to decrease the number of conditional branches. As a result, the nine conditions shown in Figure 3 are reduced to the five conditional branches shown in Figure 4 (a). Moreover, we prevent any two basic blocks in the code from sharing local registers because a software pipelined code derived from this code may execute those blocks in parallel.

The primary instructions are numbered 0 through 15 (see the ends of lines in Figure 4 (a)). Note that no conditional branch is a primary instruction because, in x86 architecture, a branch instruction always works with the preceding compare instruction. Thus, we select a compare instruction as a primary instruction, but not a branch instruction. A loop back jump (or the macro LOOPBACK(*label*)) is not a primary instruction because it plays an idiomatic role in the loop execution, i.e., it is not directly associated with the computational contents.

Now, we assume that the sequence of the sixteen numbers 0, 1, ..., 15 denotes the execution order of the primary instructions in the corresponding software pipelined code. For example, the sequence

$$0,1,2,3,4,5,6,7,8,9,10,11,12,13,14,15$$

is assumed to denote the hand compiled code in Figure 4 (a), because the primary instructions are executed in the same order as in Figure 4 (a). As another example, the sequence

$$11,12,13,14,15,0,1,2,3,4,5,6,7,8,9,10$$

is assumed to denote the software pipelined code, in which the primary instructions numbered 0 through 10 are executed in the last half of an iteration and instructions numbered 11 through 15 are executed in the first half of the next iteration. Thus, a code generator can automatically derive the actual code, as in Figure 4 (b). In the same way of the software pipelined codes without conditional branches, this software pipelined code consists of the prologue, kernel, and

```
Lxxx:
        movq    %rsi,%r8          // 0
        andq    8(%rbp),%r8       // 1
        cmpq    0(%rbp),%r8       // 2
        je      Ltxx
        LOOPBACK(Lxxx)
Ltxx:
        cmpb    $6,36(%rbp)       // 3
        jne     Ltfx
Lttx:
        movq    16(%rbp),%mm1     // 4
        movq    %mm7,%mm0         // 5
        pcmpgtd %mm0,%mm1         // 6
        pcmpgtd 24(%rbp),%mm0     // 7
        por     %mm1,%mm0         // 8
        movd    %mm0,%r9          // 9
        testq   %r9,%r9           // 10
        je      Lttt
        LOOPBACK(Lxxx)
Lttt:
        movzbl  38(%rbp),%r10d    // 11
        movl    %r14d,%r11d       // 12
        andl    %r10d,%r11d       // 13
        cmpl    %r11d,%r10d       // 14
        je      Laccept
        LOOPBACK(Lxxx)
Ltfx:
        cmpb    $0,36(%rbp)       // 15
        je      Laccept
        LOOPBACK(Lxxx)
```

(a) Hand compiled code

```
Lxxx_zzz:   // PROLOGUE PART
        movq    %rsi,%r8          // 0
        andq    8(%rbp),%r8       // 1
        cmpq    0(%rbp),%r8       // 2
        je Ltxx_zzz_8

        ... (29 lines are omitted)

Lxxx_ttt:   // KERNEL PART
        movzbl  -2(%rbp),%r10d    // 11
        movl    %r14d,%r11d       // 12
        andl    %r10d,%r11d       // 13
        cmpl    %r11d,%r10d       // 14
        je      Laccept
        movq    %rsi,%r8          // 0
        andq    8(%rbp),%r8       // 1
        cmpq    0(%rbp),%r8       // 2
        je      Ltxx_ttt
        LOOPBACK(Lxxx_fxx)
Ltxx_ttt:
        cmpb    $6,36(%rbp)       // 3
        jne     Ltfx_ttt
Lttx_ttf:
        movq    16(%rbp),%mm1     // 4
        movq    %mm7,%mm0         // 5
        pcmpgtd %mm0,%mm1         // 6
        pcmpgtd 24(%rbp),%mm0     // 7
        por     %mm1,%mm0         // 8
        movd    %mm0,%r9          // 9
        testq   %r9,%r9           // 10
        je      Lttt_ttf
Lttf_ttf:
        LOOPBACK(Lxxx_ttf)
Lttt_ttf:
        LOOPBACK(Lxxx_ttt)

        ... (112 lines are omitted)

Lzzz_ttt:   // EPILOGUE PART
        movzbl  -2(%rbp),%r10d    // 11
        movl    %r14d,%r11d       // 12
        andl    %r10d,%r11d       // 13
        cmpl    %r11d,%r10d       // 14

        ... (14 lines are omitted)
```

(b) An example of EMS code

Fig. 4. Codes on an x86-64 processor

epilogue parts. The total code size is 193 lines in this case and and the sizes of EMS codes are likely to be over 500 lines when the number of software pipeline stages are bigger.

In this manner, there is a (partial) mapping from a set of number sequences to a set of software pipelined codes. Note that not every number sequence can generate a software pipelined code, but a sequence that satisfies certain conditions can generate a code due to several restrictions of software pipelined codes (details are not discussed herein due to space limitations). Thus, generating such a number sequence iteratively, we can generate a code that corresponds to the number sequence and examine its execution time.

5.3   Codes for x86-32 Processors

The above-described method is also applicable to x86-32 processors. One exception is that x86-32 processors cannot use 64-bit operation instructions, so that such instructions are decomposed into two or more 32-bit operation instructions, and the number of primary instructions in the hand compiled code increases to 18 (the actual code is omitted here).

5.4   Experiments

The sample input packets used in the present experiments were captured from the network of our lab using tcpdump -w. The total number of packets is 10, 000. In these experiments, 10, 000 packets are loaded onto a large buffer in main memory (virtual network). Then, each packet is copied from the virtual network buffer to a receiving buffer and processed repeatedly (10, 000 times). The total execution time is then divided by 10, 000 to obtain the number of executions per packet. The execution time of the function call action(packet,result) is excluded. Five sample rules, which have 2, 9, 18, 35, and 71 filter patterns, are prepared. Therefore, five pairs, consisting of a set of input packets and a rule, are examined in the present experiments. The α coefficients in the right-hand side of equation (1) are 2.00, 8.99, 17.68, 34.36, and 69.73 for the five pairs.

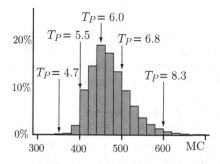

Fig. 5. Probability histogram of the execution times of the massively generated codes on an X86-64 Xeon (2.66 GHz, OSX 10.5.5) for $\alpha = 69.73$

Table 1. Execution times on various x86 processors

# machine	optimized code	execution time t (MC) $\alpha = ...$					$t = T_O + \alpha T_P$	
		2.00	8.99	17.68	34.36	69.73	T_O	T_P
1 Xeon	naive C code	47.4	124.5	168.0	411.8	699.2	30.0	9.8
(2.66 GHz,	hand compiled...	33.8	73.2	176.0	303.4	577.8	17.5	8.1
OSX 10.5.5)	EMS code	32.6	68.5	108.6	180.9	354.8	23.7	4.7
2 Core 2 Duo	naive C code	28.4	81.4	115.8	339.8	771.4	−31.4	11.3
(1.83 GHz,	hand compiled...	29.9	71.2	176.3	304.6	543.7	22.0	7.7
FedoraCore 9)	EMS code	30.0	65.7	106.3	181.8	358.2	20.4	4.8
3 Core 2 Duo	naive C code	48.1	123.9	167.2	409.5	696.1	30.2	9.8
(2.00 GHz,	hand compiled...	31.5	68.6	178.5	317.6	605.9	12.0	8.6
OSX 10.5.5)	EMS code	32.2	67.9	108.0	180.8	355.0	23.1	4.7
1 Xeon,	naive C code	63.2	190.1	289.5	681.4	1203.0	31.8	17.1
same as above	hand compiled...	42.0	92.7	206.1	321.4	685.3	18.0	9.5
machine #1	EMS code	45.1	97.8	158.3	267.0	542.3	28.4	7.3
2 Core 2 Duo,	naive C code	38.0	113.1	228.7	598.0	1033.2	−1.6	15.2
same as above	hand compiled...	39.2	96.7	212.3	356.5	645.8	32.2	9.0
machine #2	EMS code	39.2	90.4	149.1	262.2	527.5	22.9	7.2
3 Xeon	naive C code	53.0	195.7	347.0	647.2	1502.3	−20.1	21.3
(2.13 GHZ,	hand compiled...	38.8	89.5	201.0	334.6	629.8	26.5	8.8
Linux v.2.6)	EMS code	40.4	90.0	150.2	263.7	523.3	24.5	7.1

(64 — machines #1–3; 32 — machines #1–3)

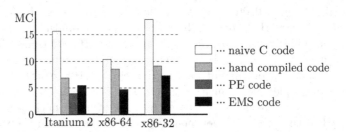

Fig. 6. Comparisons of the average values of T_P on three types of processors

The experimental results are summarized in Table 1. Several machines in the our lab were used in the experiments. These machines are listed in Table 1 along with the CPU clock cycles and type of operating system. The execution time listed in each line of the "EMS code" is that of the fastest code among all of the generated and tested codes.

The code generator tool developed by the authors can generate more than a billion lines of software pipelined codes and requires more than several months to examine all of them. Thus, a subset of codes sampled was examined so that the experiments could be completed in one day or so.

Figure 5 is the probability histogram of the execution times of the codes massively generated on x86-64 machine #1 (Xeon, 2.66 GHz) when the coefficient α in equation (1) is 69.73. The shortest time is 354.8 MC, as listed in Table 1, whereas the longest time is 756.8 MC. The probability of obtaining a code for which the execution time is less than 400.0, 445.0, 500.0, and 600.0 (or for which T_P is less than 5.5, 6.0, 6.8, and 8.3) is 2.4%, 50.0%, 75.8%, and 99.1%, respectively. Thus approximately 75% of EMS codes are faster than the hand compiled code, and $1 \sim 2\%$ of EMS codes are semi-optimal.

6   Evaluation of the Experiments

The values of T_P, a unit rule-pattern execution time in MC, on the x86-64 (or x86-32) machines are approximately 10.0, 8.0, and 4.7 (or 18.0, 9.1, and 7.2) for the naive, hand compiled, and EMS codes, respectively, despite the differences in CPU type, clock cycles, and type of operating system. This is considered to be because the processors have a common or very similar architecture on the lineups of Intel CPU generations.

Next, we compare the Itanium 2, the x86-64, and the x86-32 processors with respect to factors other than the differences of the individual machines. Table 2 shows the values of T_P for the three types of processors, where the values for the Itanium 2 are referred from our paper [13], and the values on the x86-64/32 are the averages of the results for three machines as calculated from Table 1. The values of T_P are also illustrated in Figure 6. Table 3 lists the acceleration ratios of all of the codes to the execution times of the naive codes and the hand compiled codes. These tables and graph reveal the followings.

The acceleration ratios of 2.2 and 1.8 of the EMS codes on the x86-64 and x86-32 processors show that the EMS code is approximately two times faster than the naive code and the hand compiled code, respectively. This means that software pipelining techniques are generally effective for x86 processors.

Table 2. Average values of T_P on three types of processors

optimized code	Itanium 2[†]	x86-64	x86-32
naive C code	15.7	10.3	17.9
hand compiled code	7.9	8.3	9.1
PE code	3.9	—	—
EMS code	5.4	4.7	7.2

† The values are referred from [13].

Table 3. Acceleration ratios compared to naive codes and hand compiled codes

optimized code	ratios to naive codes			ratios to hand compiled...		
	Itanium 2	x86-64	x86-32	Itanium 2	x86-64	x86-32
naive C code	1.0	1.0	1.0	0.5	0.8	0.5
hand compiled...	2.0	1.2	2.0	1.0	1.0	1.0
PE code	4.0	—	—	2.0	—	—
EMS code	2.9	2.2	2.5	1.5	1.8	1.3

Table 2 indicates that the execution times of 8.3 and 9.1 of the hand compiled codes on both the x86-64 and x86-32 processors are similar, whereas the execution time of 4.7 of the EMS code on the x86-64 processor is considerably smaller than the execution time of 7.2 of the EMS code on the x86-32 processor. Simply speaking, this is considered to be because the 64-bit mode, but not the 32-bit mode, can use a special hardware facility that is effective for software pipelined codes. The authors, however, are unclear as to why the 64-bit mode is so much faster than the 32-bit mode.

7   Future Research

Table 4 summarizes the authors' past and present researches and future plans to develop the code optimization techniques for fast packet filters.

The authors started the research [11,12] at the category I in the table, and further applied the same code optimization techniques to the research at the category II [13]. The present research state in this paper is at the category III. Here we have shown that the proposed software pipelining technique is effective for improving the execution speed of type B packet filters on x86 processors. Since the x86 series of processors are the most widely deployed general-purpose processors, we are ready to embed this technique in existing packet filters. Surprisingly, the obtained x86-64's EMS code can achieve a considerably short execution time close to the optimal Itanium 2's PE code, which exploits the special function of Itanium 2. Thus, one of our future researches is to verify the implementation of high-speed packet filters based on the proposed technique in actual equipment. The other future research is at the category IV, where we need to establish a concrete code optimization algorithm to obtain an optimal x86 code, although the generate-and-test method is useful to try unclear things. We have already gained significant insight into such an algorithm, including the enormous number of relations of number sequences, actually generated codes, and their execution times. For example, the following number sequence generates the fastest code on the x86-64 machine #1.

   0,1,2,14,15,9,10,3,11,12,13,4,5,6,7,8

Analyzing this information, we expect to determine the common properties of the faster software pipelined codes (EMS codes) on the x86 processor. Finally

Table 4. Research categories on fast packet filters and code optimization techniques

	Type A fast packet filter	Type B fast packet filter	generalized fast packet filter
Itanium 2	I	II	V
x86	IV	III	V

the studies at the categories I to IV will give us various code-level optimization techniques to construct generalized fast packet filters categorized in V.

References

1. Appel, A.W.: Modern Compiler Implementation in C. Cambridge University Press, Cambridge (1997)
2. Begel, A., McCanne, S., Graham, S.: BPF+: Exploiting Global Data-Flow Optimization in a Generalized Packet Filter Architecture. In: ACM SIGCOMM 1999 (1999)
3. Cisco: Configuring IP Access Lists, Document ID: 23602, http://www.cisco.com/warp/public/707/confaccesslists.html
4. Cristea, M.L., Bos, H.: A Compiler for Packet Filters. In: Proceedings of ASCI 2004 (2004)
5. Intel: Intel Itanium Architecture Software Developer's Manual (2005), http://www.intel.com/
6. Intel: Intel64 and IA-32 Architectures Optimization Reference Manual (2007), http://www.intel.com/
7. Jacobson, V., et al.: tcpdump(1), bpf...., Unix Manual Page (1990)
8. Okumura, T., Mossé, D., et al.: Network QoS Management Framework for Server Clusters An End-Host Retrofitting Event-Handler Approach using Netnice. In: 3rd Int. Symp. on Cluster Computing and the Grid (2003)
9. Singh, S., Baboescu, F., Varghese, G., Wang, J.: Packet Classification Using Multidimensional Cutting. In: ACM SIGCOMM 2003 (2003)
10. Warter, N.J., Haab, G.E., Bockhaus, J.W.: Enhanced Modulo Scheduling for Loops with Conditional Branches. In: IEEE MICRO-25 (1992)
11. Yamashita, Y., Tsuru, M.: Code Optimization for Packet Filters. In: SAINT 2007 Workshops CD-ROM (2007)
12. Yamashita, Y., Tsuru, M.: Software Pipelining for Packet Filters. In: Perrott, R., Chapman, B.M., Subhlok, J., de Mello, R.F., Yang, L.T. (eds.) HPCC 2007. LNCS, vol. 4782, pp. 446–459. Springer, Heidelberg (2007)
13. Yamashita, Y., Tsuru, M.: Implementations of Fast packet Filters and their Evaluations. IPSJ Transactions on Advanced Computing System (TACS) 1(1), 1–11 (2008) (in Japanese)
14. Yusuf, S., Luk, W.: Bitwise Optimised CAM for Network Intrusion Detection Systems. In: Int. Conf. Field Programmable Logic Appl. (2005)

OSL: Optimized Bulk Synchronous Parallel Skeletons on Distributed Arrays

Noman Javed and Frédéric Loulergue

Université d'Orléans – LIFO, France
{noman.javed,frederic.loulergue}@univ-orleans.fr

Abstract. The existing solutions to program parallel architectures range from parallelizing compilers to distributed concurrent programming. Intermediate approaches propose a more structured parallelism: Algorithmic skeletons are higher-order functions that capture the patterns of parallel algorithms. The user of the library has just to compose some of the skeletons to write her parallel application. When one is designing a parallel program, the parallel performance is important. It is thus very interesting for the programmer to rely on a simple yet realistic parallel performance model such as the Bulk Synchronous Parallel (BSP) model. We present OSL, the Orléans Skeleton Library: it is a library of BSP algorithmic skeletons in C++. It offers data-parallel skeletons on arrays as well as communication oriented skeletons. The performance of OSL is demonstrated with two applications: heat equation and FFT.

1 Introduction

The existing solutions to program parallel architectures range from parallelizing compilers to distributed concurrent programming offered by libraries such as MPI [46]. For shared-memory machines or multi-core machines, libraries based on threads are widely in use [40,11,1]. Intermediate approaches propose a more structured parallelism. The parallelism is exposed to the programmer to a less extend, but still allows her to specify parallel aspects of the algorithm to be implemented. These intermediate approaches thus give more control over parallelism than automatic parallelization but are less complex than message passing or thread-based libraries.

Algorithmic skeletons [13,18,41] are one of these approaches. An algorithmic skeleton is a higher-order function that captures the pattern of a parallel algorithm such as a pipeline, a parallel reduction, *etc*. Often the sequential semantics of the skeleton is quite simple and corresponds to the usual semantics of similar higher-order functions in functional programming languages. The user of a skeleton library has just to compose some the skeletons to write her parallel application. In skeletal parallelism, data-structures are mostly considered globally for the whole parallel machine, even in the case of distributed memory machine. That eases the writing and reading of parallel programs compared to the Single Program Multiple Data (SPMD) paradigm in which data structures can only be described locally to a process. The development of SPMD or threaded programs

Y. Dou, R. Gruber, and J. Joller (Eds.): APPT 2009, LNCS 5737, pp. 436–451, 2009.
© Springer-Verlag Berlin Heidelberg 2009

for shared memory machines is also difficult because they may contain indeterminism and deadlocks. This is confirmed by the high complexity of related
verification problems [3,45,42].

When one is designing a parallel program, the parallel performance is of course
important. It is thus very interesting for the programmer to rely on a simple yet realistic parallel cost model such as BSP [48,38,15] (Bulk Synchronous Parallelism)
or CGM [19] (Coarse Grained Model). The BSP model targets all general purpose
parallel architectures even if the abstract BSP computer is a distributed memory
machine. Its execution model separates synchronization and communication and
obliges both to be collective operations. It proposes a simple and accurate cost
model (in this context, cost means the estimate of parallel execution time) making it possible to predict performances in a realistic and portable way. The theory
of the proof of BSP programs [31,24] is also close in complexity to the sequential
case. The BSP model was used successfully for a broad variety of problems: scientific computation [7], genetic algorithms [9], genetic programming [20], neural
networks [44], parallel databases [4], constraints solvers [26], *etc.*

In this paper we present OSL the Orléans Skeleton Library. OSL provides a set
of data parallel skeletons which follow the BSP model of parallel computation.
OSL is a library for C++ currently implemented on top of MPI and it uses meta-
programming techniques to offer a good efficiency. Our goal is thus to provide
an easy to use library for a widely used programming language and that allows
simple reasoning about parallel performances based on a simple and portable
cost model. We first begin by giving some elements on the Bulk Synchronous
Parallel model (section 2). In section 3, we then give an overview of OSL. The
use of OSL is illustrated through two small applications (section 4): the Fast
Fourier Transform computation and a one dimension simulation of heat diffusion.
Experiments and comparisons of the programming and running times of these
applications with respect to SkeTo [37,21] and Muesli [33,35,12] are presented
in section 5. Sections 6 and 7 are devoted to related work, conclusion and
future work.

2   The Bulk Synchronous Parallel Model

The Bulk Synchronous Parallel (BSP) model [48,38,15,7] describes: an abstract
parallel computer, a model of execution and a cost model.

The BSP architecture. A BSP computer has three components: (a) a set of
homogeneous processor-memory pairs, (b) a network allowing point-to-point in-
ter processor communications, (c) a global synchronization unit that performs
synchronization barriers.

Any general purpose parallel architecture can be seen as a BSP computer.
For example a shared memory machine could be used in such a way that each
processor only accesses a subpart of the shared memory (which is then "private")
and communications could be performed using a dedicated part of the shared
memory. Furthermore in most cases the synchronization unit is not a hardware

unit but is rather emulated by software ([29] presents global synchronization barrier algorithms).

The performance of the BSP computer is characterized by four parameters (including the local processor speed) or three parameters (expressed as multiples of the local processing speed): **p** the number of processor-memory pairs ; **L** the time required for a global synchronization ; **g** the time required for collectively delivering a 1-relation (communication phase where every processor receives/sends at most one word), the network can deliver an h-relation (communication phase where every processor receives/sends at most h words) in time $g \times h$. These parameters can easily be obtained using benchmarks [28].

The execution model

A BSP program is a sequence of *super-steps*. The execution of a super-step is divided into (at most) three successive and logically disjoint phases:

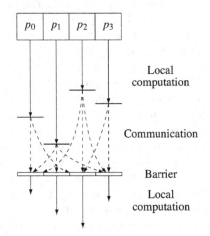

1. Each processor uses its local data (only) to perform sequential computations and to request data transfers to/from other nodes ;
2. The network delivers the requested data transfers ;
3. A global synchronization barrier occurs, making the transferred data available for the next super-step.

The cost model. The execution time of a super-step s is thus the sum of the maximal local processing time, the data delivery time, and the global synchronization time. It is expressed by the following formula:

$$\text{Time}(s) = \max_{0 \le i < p} w_i^{(s)} + \max_{0 \le i < p} h_i^{(s)} \times g + L$$

$w_i^{(s)}$ = local processing time on processor i during super-step s
$h_i^{(s)} = \max\{h_{i+}^{(s)}, h_{i-}^{(s)}\}$ where $h_{i+}^{(s)}$ (resp. $h_{i-}^{(s)}$) is the number of words transmitted (resp. received) by processor i during super-step s.

The execution time $\sum_s \text{Time}(s)$ of a BSP program composed of S super-steps is, therefore, a sum of 3 terms:

$$W + H \times g + S \times L \text{ where } W = \sum_{s=1}^{S} \max_{0 \le i < p} w_i^{(s)} \text{ and } H = \sum_{s=1}^{S} \max_{0 \le i < p} h_i^{(s)}.$$

In general, W, H and S depends on the number of processor-memory pairs, on the size of data n, or on more complex parameters like data skew. The design of BSP algorithms is therefore a tradeoff in order to minimize execution time by jointly minimizing the number S of super-steps, the total volume H and imbalance of communication, the total volume W and imbalance of local computation.

3   OSL: An Overview

OSL is a library for BSP algorithmic skeletons. The library is implemented in the C++ language using an MPI library for communications. At the moment the library offers a distributed array data structure. Data parallel and communication skeletons are offered for computing with distributed arrays. OSL supports both standard and oblivious [8] BSP synchronization. The library provides a set of utility functions to help the programmer to write parallel applications.

3.1   Distributed Arrays

The idea behind using the distributed arrays is to avoid programmer being indulged into the details of scattering and then gathering back the data. A distributed array is implemented in the form of a generic class. A handful set of constructors are provided. Programmer can fix the global size, initialize the data by some value or by applying some function, copy data from already existing distributed array.

The Dist_Array class acts as a front end wrapper and controller for the original data storage SArray class. As a wrapper class Dist_Array is used in the engineering of the composition of data parallel skeletons. Programmer needs not to worry about the SArray class. The signatures of basic public functionality of the Dist_Array class are given below:

```
inline size_t size() const;
inline size_t get_local_size() const;
inline size_t get_local_start() const;
inline T operator[] (size_t idx) const;
inline T& operator[] (size_t idx);
inline T& get(int idx);
inline T& get(int idx) const;
inline Rep const& rep() const;
inline Rep& rep();
```

3.2   Operators

Algorithmic skeletons can be seen as higher-order functions. However thus functions cannot be handled directly in most object oriented languages. To pass a function as argument to another function, the common practice is to encapsulate it in an object.

OSL provides operators that are used to save the input and output types of the function object. Any function object should be inherited from one of the two OSL operator classes in order to pass it as an argument to some skeleton or distributed array. For the moment only two operator classes are provided in compliance with the requirements of the available skeleton set: unary and binary operators. Operator classes along with a simple function object are presented below:

```
template<class I, class O>
struct unary_operator{
    typedef I input_type;
    typedef O output_type;
};
template<class I1, class I2, class O>
struct binary_operator{
    typedef I1 input_type_1;
    typedef I2 input_type_2;
    typedef O output_type;
};

struct index: public unary_operator < int, int > {
  double operator()( int idx ) const {
    return idx;
  }
} index; // index function object inherited from unary_operator class
```

3.3   Data Parallel Skeletons

Classic data parallel skeletons map, map_index, zip, zip_index are implemented in the library.

map takes a function object as the first argument and applies it to every element of its second argument, a distributed array. Note that the input function object should be inherited from one of the two operator classes as mentioned in the previous section. The semantics of a map can be viewed as:

$$\texttt{map}(f, [x_0; \ldots; x_{n-1}]) = [f(x_0); \ldots; f(x_{n-1})]$$

map_index applies the function object to the global index of every element of the distributed array. The semantics of map_index can be represented as

$$\texttt{map\_index}(f, [x_0; \ldots; x_{n-1}]) = [f(0, x_0); f(1, x_1); \ldots; f(n-1, x_{n-1})]$$

zip applies the function object on every element of the two input distributed array. Its semantics can be represented as:

$$\texttt{zip}(f, [x_0; \ldots; x_{n-1}], [y_0; \ldots; y_{n-1}]) = [f(x_0, y_0); \ldots; f(x_{n-1}, y_{n-1})]$$

zip_index applies the function object to the global indexes of the two input distributed arrays. The semantics of zip_index can be viewed as:

$$\texttt{zip\_index}(f, [x_0; \ldots; x_{n-1}], [y_0; \ldots; y_{n-1}]) = [f(0, x_0, y_0); \ldots; f(n-1, x_{n-1}, y_{n-1})]$$

The BSP cost associated with all the above mentioned data parallel skeletons is $\mathcal{O}(\frac{n}{p})$ where n is the global size of the distributed array and p is the number of processes.

These data parallel skeletons are implemented in the form of function objects. A corresponding calling function is provided to create the data parallel skeleton's function object with the arguments function object and distributed array. This function object is then wrapped into the `Dist_Array` class wrapper to be used as a resultant distributed array. This mechanism optimizes the composition of these skeletons. The implementation of the `map` class along with its calling function is presented below:

```
template <typename F, typename OP1>
class MAP {
private:
  F& f;
  typename A_Traits<OP1>::ExprRef op1;
public:
  typename F::output_type inline operator[] (size_t idx) const {
    return f(op1[idx]);
  }
  inline size_t get_local_size() const {
    return op1.get_local_size();
  }
};
template <typename T, typename F, typename R1>
Dist_Array<T,MAP<F,R1> >
inline map (F& f, Dist_Array<T,R1> const& a) {
  return Dist_Array<T,MAP<F,R1> >
    (MAP<F,R1>(f,a.rep()));
}
```

3.4   Communication Skeletons

OSL implements three communication skeletons `shift_right`, `shift_left` and `permute_partition`. These communication skeletons request a BSP synchronization barrier at the end of their call.

`shift_right` shifts the entire distributed array to one position on the right and puts the given value as the first element of the first process. During the process of shifting it communicates the last element of every process i to the process $i+1$. `shift_right` can be represented as:

$$\texttt{shift\_right}(v, [x_0; \ldots; x_{n-1}]) = [v; x_0; \ldots; x_{n-2}]$$

`shift_left` does the same thing on the left.

The BSP cost of `shift` skeletons is $\mathcal{O}(\frac{n}{p}) + s \times g + L$ where s is the size of a single element.

`permute_partition` permutes the sub-arrays of a distributed array. It takes as argument a bijection f from processor identifiers to processor identifiers. For all processor i, the sub-array it contains after the call to `permute_partition` is the sub-array that was contained by processor $f^{-1}(i)$. The function object f thus determines the receivers of the sub-arrays. It is the most heavy skeleton in terms of communication. The BSP cost of permute partition is $\mathcal{O}(p) + \frac{n}{p} \times s \times g + L$.

These communication skeletons are also implemented as function objects. However their composition is currently not optimized as is the composition of communication-free data parallel skeletons.

3.5   Synchronization

In BSP model every communication step should be followed by synchronization. As OSL is developed over MPI, `MPI_Barrier` is used as synchronization primitive. However the oblivious synchronization introduced in the PUB library [8] could be used: when the processors know in advance the number of messages they should exchange during a super-step, they can proceed to a new super-step as soon as they have exchanged all the expected messages. This saves a call to the global synchronization unit. OSL supports BOTH standard synchronization and oblivious synchronization. The selection of any of the two is done by setting the appropriate flag during compilation.

3.6   Optimization Using Expression Templates

All the above mentioned data parallel skeletons can be simply composed in an optimized fashion. This is based on the principle of expression template [49]. The principle of expression templates is to encode abstract syntax trees using C++ template mechanism. By overloading the appropriate operator it is then possible to produce actual code from an expression template. In this way by composing the data parallel skeletons we can get rid of temporaries and the intermediate loops.

The difference between non-optimized and optimized OSL code is show below:

```
// bar1 and bar2 are already created
Dist_Array bar_map = map(increment,bar1);
Dist_Array bar_zip = zip(add,bar2,bar_map);
Dist_Array result = zip(add,bar_map,bar_zip);
// Note: Above version is valid but not optimized
// Below is the optimized one
Dist_Array result = zip( add, map(increment,bar1),
        zip(add, bar2,
            map(increment, bar1) ) );
// Instead of three separate loops and two temporary Dist_Arrays the
//optimized version is doing the same thing within a single loop and
//without any temporary.
```

4   Applications in OSL

Programming with OSL is presented by developing the following two applications.

4.1   Heat Equation

The simulation of one dimensional heat diffusion could be performed by solving the heat equation using a discretization approach:

$$u(x, t+1) \doteq \text{diffuse} \times \frac{\Delta_t}{\Delta_x^2} \times \left(u(x+1, t) + u(x-1, t) - 2 \times u(x, t) \right) + u(x, t)$$

Here we represent the line of metal by a distributed array and we iterate over time. We present the algorithm using skeletons from this formula:

1. $u(x+1, t)$: Left shifting the original array,
2. $u(x-1, t)$: Right shifting the original array,
3. $u(x+1, t) + u(x-1, t)$: Zipping the above two arrays by adding them,
4. $-2 \times u(x, t)$: Mapping original array by multiplying by -2 (given as an object function instance of the Mult_by class),
5. $u(x+1, t) + u(x-1, t) - 2 \times u(x, t)$: Zipping resultant arrays of 3 and 4 using the add object function,
6. diffuse $\times \frac{\Delta_t}{\Delta_x^2}$: Initializing function object,
7. diffuse $\times \frac{\Delta_t}{\Delta_x^2} \times \left(u(x+1, t) + u(x-1, t) - 2 \times u(x, t) \right)$: Mapping function object of step 6 on resultant array of step 5,
8. diffuse $\times \frac{\Delta_t}{\Delta_x^2} \times \left(u(x+1, t) + u(x-1, t) - 2 \times u(x, t) \right) + u(x, t)$: Zipping the original array with result of step 7 by adding them.

We have used our skeleton functions to implement the above algorithm. This implementation is presented in the following listing

```
int main (int argc, char *argv[])
{
  osl::init(&argc,&argv);
  Mult_by by_minus2( - 2 );
  Add add;
  int count = 0;
  for(double t = delta_t; count < time/delta_t; t += delta_t, count++){
    Dist_Array< double > right = shift_left(boundary, bar);
    Dist_Array< double > left = shift_right(boundary, bar);
    Mult_by by_gamma((diffuse*delta_t)/(delta_x*delta_x));
    bar = zip(add_fun, bar,
            osl::map(by_gamma, zip(add, zip(add, left, right),
                                osl::map(by_minus2, bar))));
  }
  // Printing the result
  osl::finalize();
}
```

The BSP cost of the heat equation program can be calculated from the costs of the individual skeletons:

$$8 \times \left(\frac{n}{p}\right) + 2 \times s \times g + L$$

4.2   Fast Fourier Transform

Fast Fourier Transform is implemented in OSL and compared with Muesli. We borrow the implementation of FFT algorithm in terms of skeletons from Muesli. First step in FFT is to decompose the original n size data in n discrete signals in an interlaced fashion. In case of sequential algorithm it takes $\log_2 n$ stages. But in parallel as the original n is already distributed among p processors, it takes $\log_2 p$ stages. Next step is to find the frequency spectra of 1 dimensional time domain signals. Frequency spectra of 1 point signal is equal to itself. Last step is to combine n frequency spectra in exact reverse order that time decomposition takes place. This process requires $\log_2 n - \log_2 p$ iterations in parallel.

First step of this algorithm can be implemented by creating a copy of the original array and then calling `map_index`, `permute_partition`, `map_index`. Second step can be implemented by `map_index` and third step can be implemented by `zip_index`. In our implementation we use the optimized OSL composition of second and third step:

```
int main (int argc, char *argv[])
{
  osl::init(&argc,&argv);
  Dist_Array< double > bar( problemsize, 1.0 );
  init_complex initc(bar);
  Dist_Array<complex > bar_comp(initc,problemsize);
  Dist_Array<complex > bar_t(problemsize);
  log2p = (int)log2(mysize);
  log2size = (int)log2(problemsize);
  for(int j = 0; j < log2p; j++){
      bar_t = bar_comp;
      bitcomplement bitcomp(log2p - 1 - j);
      permute_partition(bitcomp,bar_t);
      combine comb(j);
      bar_comp = zip_index(comb,bar_comp,bar_t);
    }
  for(int j = log2p; j < log2size; j++){
      fetch fch(bar_comp,j);
      combine cmbin(j);
      bar_comp = zip_index(cmbin,bar_comp,map_index(fch,bar_t));
    }
  // Outputting the result
  osl::finalize();
}
```

`cmbin` and `fch` are function objects. In OSL we have not implemented currying (which is implemented in Muesli). Thus in order to pass a curried function in OSL, the programmer should create a function object encapsulating certain parameters via the constructor. Then function object could act as a curried function.

The BSP cost of FFT is

$$\log_2 p \times (2n + \mathcal{O}(p) \times s \times g + L)) + (\log_2 n - \log_2 p) \times 2n$$

5   Experiments and Comparisons

All the experiments were conducted on a cluster of PC built in two parts of 8 nodes each. Each of the first 8 nodes contains two Quad-Core AMD Opteron 2376 processors with a 2.3 GHz frequency. Each node has 16 Gb of memory. The other 8 nodes contain each two Dual-Core AMD Opteron 2216 with a 2.4 GHz frequency. Each node has 4Gb of memory. These 16 nodes are linked by a Gigabit-Ethernet network, each node having one network card. The operating system is Ubuntu 8.04. The MPI library used was Open MPI 1.3. The compiler was GCC 4.2.3. All the examples were compiled using the second level of optimization.

In the experiments we used each core as a BSP processor. However the number of processes by multi-core processor is balanced (separately on each part of the cluster: for less than 64 BSP processors only the first half is used with a balanced number of BSP processors on each physical processor. For more than 64 BSP processors the second part of the cluster is also used. The BSP parameters are thus worsened when p is increased since only one network card is used by several processors.

We also ran the examples written with two other libraries: SkeTo [37,21] and Muesli [35,12]. For data-parallel operations on distributed arrays, OSL, SkeTo and Muesli are very similar.

SkeTo offers data-parallel operations on other data structures: matrices and trees. We used the latest public release[1]: 0.21. The SkeTo release contains the heat equation example. It is not possible to program efficiently the FFT example since there is no communication skeleton in SkeTo similar to `permute_partition` (the only available communication skeletons are `shift` and `gather` skeletons).

Muesli offers data-parallel and task-parallel skeletons [34]. The set of skeletons operate on distributed arrays, distributed matrices and distributed sparse matrices [12]. In Muesli the size of distributed arrays should be a multiple of the number of processors. This constraint does not exist for OSL and SkeTo. There is no `shift` skeleton in Muesli. The `shift` skeleton could be obtained by a composition of `map` and `permute`. However the `permute` and `fold` skeletons and all their variants could not be used if the number of processors is not a power of two. Thus heat equation example could be executed with Muesli only for particular cases. The experiments were only performed for the FFT example, included in the latest Muesli release[2]: 1.79.

We have compared the performances of our heat equation programs with SkeTo for heat diffusion in copper. The program takes as input the length of the metal, Δ_x, the duration of the simulation, and Δ_t the time step. We experimented on a 100mm bar of copper and fix the time of simulation to 1 second. We have experimented with both the oblivious and non oblivious versions of our program. The timings (average of 5 runs) are presented in figure 1 for some input values. The oblivious version of OSL always attain better performances than SkeTo. The non-oblivious version is closer to SkeTo in term of performances. For

---

[1] http://www.ipl.t.u-tokyo.ac.jp/sketo
[2] http://www.wi.uni-muenster.de/pi/forschung/Skeletons/index.html

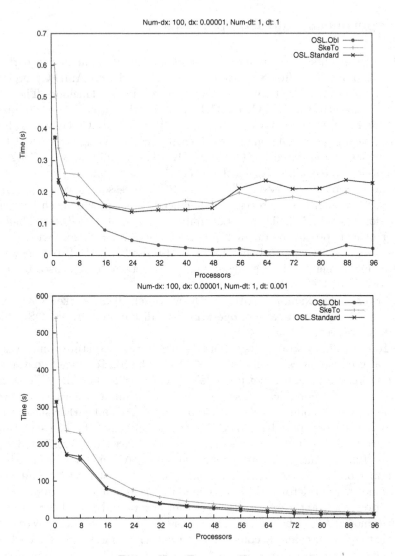

Fig. 1. Heat Equation Timings

only one iteration, the non-oblivious OSL version is about 10 times faster than SkeTo for a large number of processors: it is due to our optimized composition of skeletons. For 1000 iterations, OSL is still more than 40% faster than SkeTo.

If for a given number of processors we examine the timings by varying the sizes of distributed arrays, we could see that the performances follow the BSP cost given in the previous section.

The FFT program takes as argument the size of the array. It should be a multiple of the number of processors. The number of processors should be a power of 2. We measured the performances of OSL FFT with both type of synchronizations and also of the Muesli version of FFT. For small sizes, depending on the

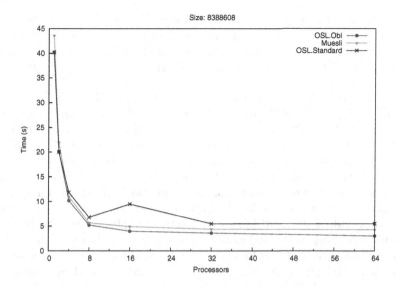

Fig. 2. FFT Timings

number of processors, Muesli and oblivious OSL have similar performances but one may be slightly better than the other. For large sizes, oblivious OSL have better performances than Muesli. In figure 2, for 64 processors, OSL is more than 20% faster than Muesli.

6   Related Work

Skeletons and Object-Oriented Languages. There are many algorithmic skeleton libraries or linguistic extensions for C and C++. We already discussed Muesli and SkeTo. Quaff [23] does not have a distributed data structure: the scattering and gathering of data is done by the framework (but of course for specific data-structure the user has to specify the scatter/gather methods). Quaff relies heavily on meta-programming techniques for optimization, but no implementation is currently publicly available which explains why we did not perform a comparison with it. Most of its proposed skeletons are task parallel skeletons. eSkel [14,5] is an attempt to bridge the gap between skeletons libraries and MPI. The programming style of eSkel is thus very close to MPI style but with skeleton capabilities. The integration within MPI code is easy but the signatures of the propose skeletons are much more complicated. OSL provides skeletons easier to use but integration with MPI programs is not considered currently.

DatTel [6] is a partial parallel implementation of the STL library, which is also partly the case for STAPL. Intel Threading Building Blocks [43] could be seen as a skeleton library: it offers a kind of map, and also reduce and scan parallel algorithms. BSFC++ [16] uses C++ templates in order to obtain a functional bulk synchronous parallel language. However the code was difficult to write for a C++ programmer and not very efficient. There are also several skeleton libraries for the Java programming language. They are more dynamic by nature and targets more heterogeneous and changing architectures such as grids than the C/C++ libraries: Lithium [2], Muskel [17], Calcium [10].

Libraries for Bulk Synchronous Parallel Programming. BSPlib [28], PUB [8] and BSPonMPI [47] are three libraries for C that support bulk synchronous parallel programming. The proposed set of functions is quite small compared to MPI, yet efficient. However the programming style of these libraries is not as high level than skeleton libraries and OSL. JBSP [27] is a Java version of the BSP libraries. BSML [36] is a functional language that support BSP programming. It has a very small core of functions, nice semantical properties. The provided operations are not so easy to handle for a beginner but its higher-order nature allows to provide a standard library of functions implemented with the primitives only but easier to use and close to more classical skeletons. However being based on the Objective Caml functional language hinders its use by a large audience. ScientificPython [30] contains a BSP module inspired by BSML. Both NestStep [32] and Ct [25] provide a parallel programming model based on nested data structures and a BSP-like execution model.

7   Conclusions and Future Work

OSL is a library for manipulating distributed arrays through bulk synchronous parallel algorithmic skeletons in C++. Preliminary performance comparisons show that our library is very efficient. OSL is currently limited to distributed arrays. In the future, we plan to address other data structures, in particular matrices and multidimensional arrays. We also plan to use OSL for implementing various scientific computing applications.

The optimization technique used to improve the performance of composed calls to data-parallel skeletons is in the current version limited to non-communicating skeletons. The next version of OSL will address the composition of arbitrary skeletons. For this our expression templates will target a kind of BSP algebra (such as [39] whose terms will be translated into C++ code with MPI calls, in a similar way the QUAFF library uses expression templates to translate skeleton compositions into a process algebra [22]. We also plan to have an optimized implementation of OSL dedicated to multi-core architectures not relying on MPI.

The verification of the correctness of the implementation of OSL with respect to the functional semantics of skeletons is also a long term goal of our research.

References

1. OpenMP Application Program Interface version 3.0 (May 2008)
2. Aldinucci, M., Danelutto, M., Teti, P.: An Advanced Environment Supporting Structured Parallel Programming in Java. Future Generation Computer Systems 19, 611–626 (2002)

3. Apt, K.R., Olderog, E.-R.: Verification of sequential and concurrent programs, 2nd edn. Springer, Heidelberg (1997)
4. Bamha, M., Exbrayat, M.: Pipelining a Skew-Insensitive Parallel Join Algorithm. Parallel Processing Letters 13(3), 317–328 (2003)
5. Benoit, A., Murray, C., Gilmore, S., Hillston, J.: Flexible Skeletal Programming with eSkel. In: Cunha, J.C., Medeiros, P.D. (eds.) Euro-Par 2005. LNCS, vol. 3648, pp. 761–770. Springer, Heidelberg (2005)
6. Bischof, H., Gorlatch, S., Leschinskiy, R.: DatTeL: A Data-Parallel C++ Template Library. Parallel Processing Letters 13(3), 461–472 (2003)
7. Bisseling, R.: Parallel Scientific Computation. A structured approach using BSP and MPI. Oxford University Press, Oxford (2004)
8. Bonorden, O., Juurlink, B., von Otte, I., Rieping, I.: The Paderborn University BSP (PUB) Library. Parallel Computing 29(2), 187–207 (2003)
9. Braud, A., Vrain, C.: A parallel genetic algorithm based on the BSP model. In: Evolutionary Computation and Parallel Processing GECCO & AAAI Workshop, Orlando (Florida), USA (1999)
10. Caromel, D., Leyton, M.: Fine tuning algorithmic skeletons. In: Kermarrec, A.-M., Bougé, L., Priol, T. (eds.) Euro-Par 2007. LNCS, vol. 4641, pp. 72–81. Springer, Heidelberg (2007)
11. Chapman, B., Jost, G., van Der Pas, R.: Using OpenMP. MIT Press, Cambridge (2008); about OpenMP 2.5
12. Ciechanowicz, P., Poldner, M., Kuchen, H.: The Münster Skeleton Library Muesli – A Comprenhensive Overview. Technical Report Working Paper No. 7, European Research Center for Information Systems, University of Münster, Germany (2009)
13. Cole, M.: Algorithmic Skeletons: Structured Management of Parallel Computation. MIT Press, Cambridge (1989)
14. Cole, M.: Bringing Skeletons out of the Closet: A Pragmatic Manifesto for Skeletal Parallel Programming. Parallel Computing 30(3), 389–406 (2004)
15. Skillicorn, D.B., Hill, J.M.D., McColl, W.F.: Questions and Answers about BSP. Scientific Programming 6(3), 249–274 (1997)
16. Dabrowski, F., Loulergue, F.: Functional Bulk Synchronous Programming in C++. In: 21st IASTED International Multi-conference, Applied Informatics (AI 2003), Symposium on Parallel and Distributed Computing and Networks, February 2003, pp. 462–467. ACTA Press (2003)
17. Danelutto, M., Dazzi, P.: Joint Structured/Unstructured Parallelism Exploitation in Muskel. In: Alexandrov, V.N., van Albada, G.D., Sloot, P.M.A., Dongarra, J. (eds.) ICCS 2006. LNCS, vol. 3992, pp. 937–944. Springer, Heidelberg (2006)
18. Darlington, J., Field, A.J., Harrison, P.G., Kelly, P., Sharp, D., Wu, Q., While, R.: Parallel Programming Using Skeleton Functions. In: Reeve, M., Bode, A., Wolf, G. (eds.) PARLE 1993. LNCS, vol. 694, pp. 146–160. Springer, Heidelberg (1993)
19. Dehne, F., Fabri, A., Rau-Chaplin, A.: Scalable parallel ceometric algorithms for coarse grained multicomputer. In: 9th Symposium on Computational Geometry, pp. 298–307 (1993)
20. Dracopoulos, D.C., Kent, S.: Speeding up genetic programming: A parallel BSP implementation. In: First Annual Conference on Genetic Programming. MIT Press, Cambridge (1996)
21. Emoto, K., Matsuzaki, K., Hu, Z., Takeichi, M.: Domain-Specific Optimization Strategy for Skeleton Programs. In: Kermarrec, A.-M., Bougé, L., Priol, T. (eds.) Euro-Par 2007. LNCS, vol. 4641, pp. 705–714. Springer, Heidelberg (2007)

22. Falcou, J., Sérot, J.: Formal Semantics Applied to the Implementation of a Skeleton-Based Parallel Programming Library. In: Bischof, C.H., Bücker, H.M., Gibbon, P., Joubert, G.R., Lippert, T., Mohr, B., Peters, F.J. (eds.) Parallel Computing: Architectures, Algorithms and Applications, ParCo 2007. Advances in Parallel Computing, vol. 15, pp. 243–252. IOS Press, Amsterdam (2007)
23. Falcou, J., Sérot, J., Chateau, T., Lapresté, J.-T.: Quaff: Efficient C++ Design for Parallel Skeletons. Parallel Computing 32, 604–615 (2006)
24. Gava, F.: Formal Proofs of Functional BSP Programs. Parallel Processing Letters 13(3), 365–376 (2003)
25. Ghuloum, A., Smith, T., Gansha, W., Zhou, X., Fang, J., Guo, P., So, B., Rajagopalan, M., Chen, Y., Chen, B.: Future-Proof Data Parallel Algorithms and Software on Intel Multi-Core Architecture. Intel Technology Journal 11(4) (2007)
26. Granvilliers, L., Hains, G., Miller, Q., Romero, N.: A system for the high-level parallelization and cooperation of constraint solvers. In: Pan, Y., Akl, S.G., Li, K. (eds.) Proceedings of International Conference on Parallel and Distributed Computing and Systems (PDCS), Las Vegas, USA, pp. 596–601. IASTED/ACTA Press (1998)
27. Gu, Y., Lee, B.-S., Cai, W.: JBSP: A BSP Programming Library in Java. Journal of Parallel and Distributed Computing 61(17), 1126–1142 (2001)
28. Hill, J.M.D., McColl, B., Stefanescu, D., Goudreau, M., et al.: BSPlib: The BSP Programming Library. Parallel Computing 24, 1947–1980 (1998)
29. Hill, J.M.D., Skillicorn, D.B.: Practical Barrier Synchronisation. In: 6th EuroMicro Workshop on Parallel and Distributed Processing (PDP 1998). IEEE Computer Society Press, Los Alamitos (1998)
30. Hinsen, K., Langtangen, H.P., Skavhaug, O., Odegård, Å.: Using BSP and Python to simplify parallel programming. Future Generation Computur Systems 22(1), 123–157 (2006)
31. Jifeng, H., Miller, Q., Chen, L.: Algebraic laws for BSP programming. In: Fraigniaud, P., Mignotte, A., Robert, Y., Bougé, L. (eds.) Euro-Par 1996. LNCS, vol. 1124, pp. 1123–1124. Springer, Heidelberg (1996)
32. Kessler, C.W.: Managing Distributed Shared Arrays in a Bulk-Synchronous Parallel Environment. Concurrency and Computation: Practice and Experience 16, 133–153 (2004)
33. Kuchen, H.: A Skeleton Library. In: Monien, B., Feldmann, R.L. (eds.) Euro-Par 2002. LNCS, vol. 2400, pp. 620–629. Springer, Heidelberg (2002)
34. Kuchen, H., Cole, M.: The Integration of Task and Data Parallel Skeletons. Parallel Processing Letters 12(2), 141–155 (2002)
35. Kuchen, H., Poldner, M.: On Implementing the Farm Skeleton. Parallel Processing Letters 18(1), 204–219 (2008)
36. Loulergue, F., Gava, F., Billiet, D.: Bulk Synchronous Parallel ML: Modular Implementation and Performance Prediction. In: Sunderam, V.S., van Albada, G.D., Sloot, P.M.A., Dongarra, J. (eds.) ICCS 2005. LNCS, vol. 3515, pp. 1046–1054. Springer, Heidelberg (2005)
37. Matsuzaki, K., Iwasaki, H., Emoto, K., Hu, Z.: A Library of Constructive Skeletons for Sequential Style of Parallel Programming. In: InfoScale 2006: Proceedings of the 1st international conference on Scalable information systems. ACM Press, New York (2006)
38. McColl, W.F.: Scalability, portability and predictability: The BSP approach to parallel programming. Future Generation Computer Systems 12, 265–272 (1996)
39. Merlin, A., Hains, G.: A bulk synchronous process algebra. Computer Languages, Systems and Structures 33(3-4), 111–133 (2007)

40. Nichols, B., Buttlar, D., Proulx Farrell, J.: Pthreads Programming: A POSIX Standard for Better Multiprocessing. O'Reilly, Sebastopol (1996)
41. Pelagatti, S.: Structured Development of Parallel Programs. Taylor & Francis, Abington (1998)
42. Pervez, S., Gopalakrishnan, G., Kirby, R.M., Palmer, R., Thakur, R., Gropp, W.: Practical Model-Checking Method for Verifying Correctness of MPI Programs. In: Cappello, F., Herault, T., Dongarra, J. (eds.) PVM/MPI 2007. LNCS, vol. 4757, pp. 344–353. Springer, Heidelberg (2007)
43. Reinders, J.: Intel Threading Building Blocks: Outfitting C++ for Multi-core Processor Parallelism. O'Reilly, Sebastopol (2007)
44. Rogers, R.O., Skillicorn, D.B.: Using the BSP cost model to optimise parallel neural network training. Future Generation Computer Systems 14(5-6), 409–424 (1998)
45. Siegel, S.F.: Model Checking Nonblocking MPI Programs. In: Cook, B., Podelski, A. (eds.) VMCAI 2007. LNCS, vol. 4349, pp. 44–58. Springer, Heidelberg (2007)
46. Snir, M., Gropp, W.: MPI the Complete Reference. MIT Press, Cambridge (1998)
47. Suijlen, W.J.: BSPonMPI, http://bsponmpi.sourceforge.net
48. Valiant, L.G.: A bridging model for parallel computation. Comm. of the ACM 33(8), 103 (1990)
49. Veldhuizen, T.: Techniques for Scientific C++. Computer science technical report 542, Indiana University (2000)

Evaluating SPLASH-2 Applications Using MapReduce

Shengkai Zhu, Zhiwei Xiao, Haibo Chen, Rong Chen, Weihua Zhang, and Binyu Zang

Parallel Processing Institute, Fudan University

Abstract. MapReduce has been prevalent for running data-parallel applications. By hiding other non-functionality parts such as parallelism, fault tolerance and load balance from programmers, MapReduce significantly simplifies the programming of large clusters. Due to the mentioned features of MapReduce above, researchers have also explored the use of MapReduce on other application domains, such as machine learning, textual retrieval and statistical translation, among others.

In this paper, we study the feasibility of running typical supercomputing applications using the MapReduce framework. We port two applications (Water Spatial and Radix Sort) from the Stanford SPLASH-2 suite to MapReduce. By completely evaluating them in Hadoop, an open-source MapReduce framework for clusters, we analyze the major performance bottleneck of them in the MapReduce framework. Based on this, we also provide several suggestions in enhancing the MapReduce framework to suite these applications.

1 Introduction

MapReduce [1], advocated and popularized by Google, has been prevalent for data-parallel applications due to its simplicity yet still powerful processing capability. It has been widely deployed in Google's own clusters and used for various applications such as web-search, indexing and log analysis.

Though Google's implementation detail is fairly secretive for the public domain, Apache has provided Hadoop [2], an open-source implementation of the MapReduce framework. It has gained significant popularity recently due to its practicality, cost-effectiveness and openness. Thus, it has been widely adopted in various application domains such as statistical machine translation [3], textual retrieval [4] and machine learning [5].

The elegance of MapReduce, the readily availability of the cost-effective Hadoop implementation would also open opportunities to run many parallel or supercomputing applications on commodity clusters. Running parallel or supercomputing applications on MapReduce, if applicable, would make the power of solving many difficult scientific problems ubiquitously accessible at a very low cost. Bryant [6] has recently discussed the possibility of running some data-intensive supercomputing applications such as genomic sequences and earthquake modeling on commodity clusters. Unfortunately, there are currently few studies on the performance characteristics of parallel applications on commodity clusters with multi-core.

In this paper, we port and evaluate two parallel applications from the SPLASH-2 [7] benchmark suite which originally run in large shared-memory multiprocessors to a

Y. Dou, R. Gruber, and J. Joller (Eds.): APPT 2009, LNCS 5737, pp. 452–464, 2009.
© Springer-Verlag Berlin Heidelberg 2009

small-scale commodity clusters with multi-core, aiming at studying the performance characteristics of these applications on commodity clusters.

We have conducted a detailed evaluation on the performance characteristics of these applications. Our evaluation results in a 17 dual-core cluster (1 master node, 16 slave nodes) show there are some performance bottlenecks and we further summarize the key causes of the slowdown. With a detailed and complete analysis, we also present several potential optimization opportunities.

The rest of the paper is organized as follows. The next section presents the necessary background knowledge on MapReduce and Hadoop. In section 3, we port two typical scientific applications from SPLASH-2 suite to run on Hadoop and illustrate the major issues associated with the porting. Section 4 presents a detailed performance evaluation of Hadoop on a commodity cluster. Section 5 discusses several optimization opportunities to improve the performance of MapReduce for supercomputing applications on commodity clusters. Section 6 discusses the related work and section 7 concludes this paper.

2   Background

This section presents the necessary background information on the general MapReduce programming model and the design and implementation of Hadoop.

2.1   MapReduce Programming Model

The programming model of MapReduce is inspired by the functional programming primitives such as *Map* and *Reduce*. MapReduce processes the input and intermediate data in a Single Program Multiple Data (SPMD) fashion. The *Map* processes the input data and generated a set of $\langle key, value \rangle$ pairs, while the *Reduce* aggregates all $\langle key, value \rangle$ pairs according to the key.

The following pseudo-code in Figure 1 shows the *Word Count* application written using the MapReduce programming model, which counts the number of occurrences of each word in a document. The *Mapper* function emits a $\langle word, 1 \rangle$ pair for each *word* in document, and the *Reducer* function counts all occurrences of a *word* as the output.

```
//input = a document            //key = word
//pairs: key = word, value = 1   //values = a set of value
Mapper (input){                  Reducer (key, values){
   for each word in input:          int sum = 0;
      emit_inter( word, 1 );         for each value in values:
}                                        sum += value;
                                     emit( key, sum );
                                 }
```

Fig. 1. *Mapper* and *Reducer* of *Word Count* in MapReduce

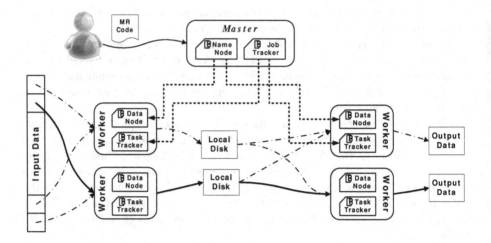

Fig. 2. MapReduce Execution Flow

2.2 The Hadoop Design and Implementation

Hadoop is an open-source implementation of the MapReduce framework. Hadoop uses a distributed file system, namely Hadoop Distributed File System (HDFS) to store the input and the final results. HDFS manages a number of local disks owned by the nodes in a cluster and maps them to a single file system. The HDFS resembles the Google File System in the fashion of handling storage failures using several replicas of the same data. One of the key principles in Hadoop is that "moving computation is much cheaper than moving data". Thus, Hadoop schedules the MapReduce tasks to the node near the data storage to minimize the data transfers.

An overview of the architecture and the execution flow of Hadoop are shown in Figure 2, which uses a master-slave mode. There is a master node that runs the *Job Tracker* for task allocation and scheduling, and *Name Node* for HDFS metadata management. To run a MapReduce task, the *Job Tracker* allocates the *Task Trackers* on the slave nodes to run the *map* or *reduce* tasks. Each slave node may also be the data node, which stores the data blocks of file in HDFS. The task tracker consults the *Name Node* to get the specific *Data Node* to get the data for a file.

3 Implementing SPLASH-2 Applications with Hadoop MapReduce

This section introduces the SPLASH-2 benchmark suite and how two of them are ported to the MapReduce framework.

3.1 SPLASH-2 Suite

The SPLASH-2 suite consists of a set of complete applications and computational kernels. The programs represent a variety of computation workloads in scientific, graphics computing and engineering. The suite is designed to facilitate the study of centralized and distributed shared address-space multiprocessors. We choose *Water Spatial*, a water molecule simulation system and *Radix Sort*, an integer radix sort kernel for porting and evaluation. We believe that these two typical scientific and engineering programs cover the major characteristics of supercomputing with MapReduce.

Water Spatial is an N-body molecules dynamics application that evaluates the forces and potentials which occur over time in a cluster of water molecules in a liquid state. It is improved from the program water in SPLASH [8]. In an initial state, configurable number of water molecules are scattered in a cubical space. They are generated globally with random coordinate and velocity. Also many other physical and system parameters are carried by each molecule. Most of them will be updated several times during the whole life time of the application. Further documentation and details of the Water Spatial models can be found in [9, 10, 11].

Radix Sort is a small computational kernel performing sorting on integers using an iterative algorithm. Its implementation is based on [12].

3.2 Implementing Water Spatial(WS) and Radix Sort(RS) in MapReduce

Data Structures. In typical supercomputing applications, lots of mathematical, physical and system parameters are involved during the whole computation. Arrays and matrices are the most commonly adopted data structures. And in a system with large amounts of elements, the items are also kept in a list-based structure.

Due to well-defined partition methods and synchronization mechanisms, access to shared data is not difficult in a shared address-space environment. However, in a cluster environment, data structures need to be serialized into the distributed storage system for remote access. In Hadoop, the HDFS (Hadoop Distributed File System) is deployed to hold the data.

As a result of heavy network communications, access to shared data turns to be a significant source of overhead. Hence, the data partition policy in MapReduce determines the efficiency of the parallel algorithm implemented. A well-designed data structure and partition method could avoid a lot of unnecessary network communications, which could be the bottleneck in many cases.

Data updates in MapReduce can be done in different approaches. For fields owned by each basic element, its information can be refreshed through a direct update in the map/reduce phase. A global aggregative variable is usually updated in a synchronization point, accomplished by a MapReduce job with single reduce task. Data movements are the most complicated and common cases in typical supercomputing applications, resulting from changes of inter-data relation, which in turn forces a reconstruction of data partitions.

Computation Steps. Many supercomputing applications can be divided into several computation steps, often with a number of iterations doing a series of calculation. Between two consecutive steps, global data synchronization is performed to ensure the correctness of succeeding computing.

In MapReduce, unlike the shared-memory environment, data synchronization can only be performed after completion of a job and is costly. Usually, the number of global barriers defines a lower bound of the number of MapReduce jobs.

According to different behaviors of MapReduce jobs, jobs composing a typical supercomputing can be classified into three categories: element-update jobs, global-variable aggregation jobs and mixed jobs. The mixed job performs the element-update and does aggregation for a global variable in the same phase.

During a MapReduce computation, each map/reduce task works on their local copy of data. Data updates on global storage have to be performed after each MapReduce job. The distributed file system significantly affects the efficiency of the data-sharing. There is also consistency problem associated with it. The computation in each phase is thus required to dump the updated data into distributed storage with a specific format, which can be recognized and read effectively by the next worker. Usually the formats are designed specifically for each situation.

A Walkthrough for Water Spatial. At the beginning of a Water Spatial instance, random input data is generated and stored in HDFS, with only append operation allowed. Thus, the data file has to be reconstructed after each update.

The storage format of the basic element, water molecule, is shown in Figure 3. It consists of coordinates and other parameters holding the force and energy information. However, these two parts of parameters are rarely modified simultaneously in the same phase. This makes it unnecessary to hold these two parts in the same chunk of storage. During the data reconstruction, accesses to the part not involved in computation would unnecessarily increase the network load. Taking this into consideration, we store the coordinates of molecule and other physical information in two separated chunks. Each molecule will be assigned a unique identifier used as an index to refer to the both parts.

Water Spatial consists of a series of complex computations, with all three kinds of MapReduce jobs involved. The detail computation flow is shown in the Figure 4. Three phases can be transformed as mixed jobs, while the rest perform only element update.

Input data in Water Spatial is partitioned on the molecules according to their coordinates. In the shared-memory version of SPLASH-2, molecules with the same

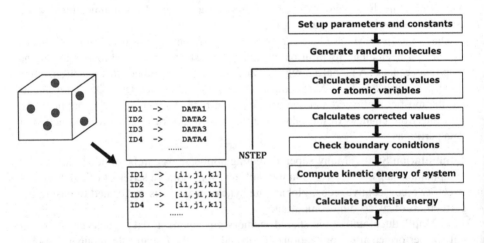

Fig. 3. Data Format of Molecules   **Fig. 4.** Execution Flow of Water Spatial

```
Mapper (input){                      Reducer (key, values){
    for each molecule in input:          global_sum = 0;
    local_sum = Collect(molecule );      for each value in values:
    emit_inter( id, local_sum );             global_sum += value;
                                             emit( key, global_sum );
}                                    }
```

Fig. 5. Mapper and Reducer for Aggregation Job

```
                                     Mapper (input){
                                         for each molecule in input:
                                         if ( isFake(molecule) )
Mapper (input){                              molecule.value = local_val;
    for each molecule in input:          else
    Update( molecule );                      local_val += Update( molecule );
    emit_inter( NULL, molecule );        emit_inter( NULL, molecule );
}                                    }
```

Fig. 6. Mapper for Update-Only Job   **Fig. 7.** Mapper for Mix Job

coordinates are processed in a single thread together. We keep such a design here but hold their coordinates and other parameters in different chunks.

An aggregation-only job can be performed intuitively by MapReduce. The *Mapper* in Figure 5 collects information from all molecules. The *Mapper* calculates concerned value from some fields and emits it to the intermediate key-value pair. Each key in these pairs represents the different global variables aggregated.

Most update-only jobs can also be processed easily in MapReduce. The fields of each element are modified through the computation. The *Mapper* described in Figure 6 needs only to update the molecule passed in and then bounces it to the *Reducer*.

Since the output key-value pair should always be the same type during a computation phase, the *Mapper* designed for a mixed job in Figure 7 is much more complicated. In our implementation, the *Molecule* is taken as our output key-value pair type. Besides, we use fake molecules to carry the aggregation values.

The *Reducer* for all kinds of job can be easily set to the *IdentityReducer*, which is built in the Hadoop framework, simply doing sorting on the map outputs. In some aggregation jobs, the number of reduce workers has to be set to one. Otherwise, a routine out of the framework should do the aggregation for *Reducer*.

There are two special phases in Water Spatial which compute inter-water forces and their potential energy. The computation needs to calculate the molecules with all their neighbors within effective radius. While the radius is larger than a single data partition block, this *Mapper* would process much more molecules than regular cases. Further, the inter-neighbor communication in a 3D space significantly increases the network load for these redundant transmissions.

A Walkthrough for Radix Sort. Data involved in Radix Sort is a list of integers to be sorted. The input set can be partitioned intuitively and will not be modified during the computation. This makes its storage format much simpler than that of Water Spatial.

Radix Sort consists of iterative histogram computing. The computation involved in the program is a simple histogram performing for each radix r digits. The number of the MapReduce jobs is determined by the iteration number, which is in turn determined by the max integer provided by users. The *Mapper* for Radix Sort simply ranks the entire integer passed in on the specific r digits for each iteration, forming a histogram with 2^r buckets, whose indices range from 0 to 2^r-1. Each integer is processed from the least significant r digits to the most significant r digits through the loop.

All the local histograms constructed in the map tasks will be merged into a single global histogram. Thus, the number of reduce tasks is required to be set to one. According to the global histogram, a partial sorting on those r digits can be performed correctly. After the last iteration, these integers come to an ordered state.

Instead of only ranking the 2^r buckets of each iteration, our implementation of Radix Sort takes the whole integer as the element for histogram in computation and collects those integers with the same r digits value in the corresponding bucket. This implementation ensures that an ordered sequence can be reached just in the time of processing each reduce phase. No more efforts for permutation are needed in the client end that starts the job, which is necessary if *Reducer* only ranks the buckets. In that case, a large amount of data transmission would occur on this single node to copy all integers required at each permutation computing.

Table 1. Line of Code in MapReduce version

Application	Components	Line of Code
Water Spatial	Original code	1984
	Append code	2002
	Interface and Framework	1226
	Data storage and communication	776
Radix Sort	Original code	705
	Append code	318
	Interface and Framework	301
	Data storage and communication	17

Porting Effort. Table 1 shows the porting effort to translate these two programs onto the Hadoop framework. The original amount of code in MapReduce is 1984 lines. By reusing most of the computation code, we still need to append other 2002 lines of code. The major part of the extra code for Water Spatial is for the interface and framework supports required by Hadoop-0.19.1. Data partition and distributed file system operations code also result in some extra code. The large number of code for framework is caused by many similar routines to setup MapReduce jobs with different configurations.

Data sharing in memory are replaced with network communication on the MapReduce cluster, which is also a source of extra code. As much more inevitable data dumping and loading occur in this condition, the code for defining formats to store the data structure is also needed in this non-sharing address-space environment. However, the data format code for Water Spatial can be well reused by other scientific applications. In contrast, Radix Sort needs almost no data communication between the consecutive permutation steps. Most of its code is for *Mapper* and *Reducer*, making its porting quite easy. By using a same algorithm design but different coding in Java, Radix Sort does not reuse many original code, which are programmed mostly on dealing with memory in C.

4   Evaluation

In this section, we present and analyze the experimental results of Water Spatial and Radix Sort.

4.1   Experiment Setup

We conduct our experiments on a cluster consisting of 1 master node and 16 slave nodes. We have single master node running *Job Tracker* and *Name Node*. All slavers run as both *Task Trackers* and *Data Nodes*. Each slave machine has a dual-processor, 2GB main memory and a SATA disk. Network connectivity is by 100M/sec Ethernet links connecting into the campus local network.

In our experiments for Water Spatial and Radix Sort, we evaluate the performance characteristics of our MapReduce implementation. Its core computation algorithms are the same as the original ones in SPLASH-2. We use Hadoop-0.19.1, the most recent version of Hadoop and Java SE Runtime Environment 1.6 as our experiment platform. The input size of Water Spatial experiments varies from 18^3 to 57^3, indicating the number of molecules. The size of input data file for Radix Sort varies from 12.5MB to 100MB.

4.2   Overall Performance

Figure 8 and Figure 9 show the overall performance of these two applications. In both applications, the scalability with input size demonstrated on cluster is poor.

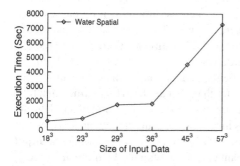

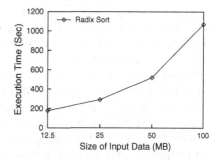

Fig. 8. The overall execution time of WS on a commodity cluster

Fig. 9. The overall execution time of RS on a commodity cluster

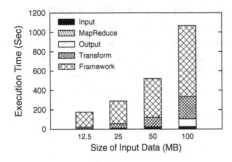   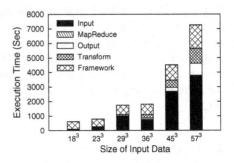

Fig. 10. The execution time breakdown of RS on a commodity cluster

Fig. 11. The execution time breakdown of WS on a commodity cluster

4.3 Performance Breakdown

The time breakdown of Water Spatial in Figure 11 presents the execution time spent in different components of Hadoop. The overall time is divided into five parts. The **Input** and **Output** parts count for the time spent for data reading/writing from/to HDFS for *Mapper/Reducer*. The **MapReduce** part here stands for the time spent in the computation inside *Mapper* and *Reducer*, which execute as the core computation algorithms. The **Transform** part denotes the data transformation time from the output of a MapReduce job to the required format in the next step. The last part, **Framework** time, is the time spent in MapReduce job creation, Hadoop scheduling and the map/reduce task initialization. The intermediate data transmissions are also accounted for the **Framework** part.

From the time breakdown, we notice that time for computation in *Mapper* and *Reducer* is negligible. This part does the major computation for the Water Spatial simulation. And compared with the overall execution time in shared-memory environment, time in this part has a speedup more than 2x. And this speedup shows the advantage of parallel-computing in MapReduce for the general application without heavy loads of data communication. On the other hand, the MapReduce framework causes much more negative side-effects for the scientific application. From the figure, we notice the time in **Input** part increases rapidly with the data input size. This is because our implementation has to scan through some data files more than one time in certain phases, such as the inter-molecule phase and potential energy phase. Thus the network loads for this part can increase much more quickly than that of the **Output** and **Transform** parts. The molecule layout at the input size 29^3 is a little irregular. It can not be scanned sequentially well and thus suffers a significant amount of HDFS cache miss. We can see that the execution time at 29^3 is only sightly shorter than that at 36^3. The **Framework** time grows with input size because of the increased transmission of intermediate data. As Figure 10 illustrates, Radix Sort also spends most of its execution time on data communication. Because of its less data synchronization and simpler storage format, the **Input** and **Output** time of Radix Sort is insignificant compared with the **Framework** time.

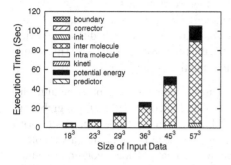

Fig. 12. The execution time breakdown of WS on a single machine

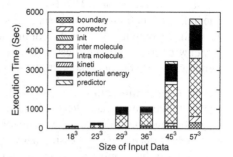

Fig. 13. The execution time breakdown of WS on a commodity cluster

4.4   Affects with Application Characteristics

With the breakdown time in Figure 12 and Figure 13, we further investigate the distribution of time spent in different computation phase of Water Spatial. The computation phases here are divided according to the program flow described in Figure 4. The time of Water Spatial is mainly spent in inter-water force computing and potential energy calculating. These are the only two phases involving the neighbor partitions of data. Thus they are dominant in a whole run since their greater computation loads. The inter-water force computing time is longer since it works as a mixed job in MapReduce while potential energy calculating is an update-only job. And in the MapReduce version with a large input size, time of other phases start to become obvious. This happens because a large number of data communications is raised.

5   Optimization Opportunities

Storage System. The HDFS used in Hadoop framework is designed to work with regular data-intensive applications. Files in the HDFS can only be appended at the tail. The in-place data updating cannot be supported or worked out with a simple alternative using existing approaches. By studying Water Spatial and Radix Sort, we found the matrices and multi- or many-dimension arrays are the most common structure used to hold data. Frequent update operations on these kinds of structures result in quiet a lot of overhead in reconstruction. The dumping and loading from arrays or matrices force other extra efforts to be done. The large proportion of HDFS time showed in our experimental results of Water Spatial just verifies that. Considering the native characteristics of supercomputing applications, a specific lower-level storage system is necessary. And good support to distributed arrays and matrices access will lead to a great improvement on data communication. The general-purpose distributed storage system or sequential file system cannot work well with those structures.

Output Directing. In supercomputing applications, work completion by multiple MapReduce jobs causes another performance problem. The output from previous job needs to be dumped onto HDFS. Such data is then read by tasks from the next job. The indirect data transmission costs a large fraction of execution time. Actually, before dumping the output, tasks for the coming jobs have already been scheduled. Allowing output written directly to its destination can save the time writing to HDFS. This avoids a great waste of network resource and also saves the time significantly.

Simple Aggregation Function. Simple aggregation operation in a supercomputing application, like sum of variables, is also a common kind of computation. For a global aggregation function computed, the number of reduce worker has to be one, which forms a bottleneck during the processing. However, the overhead from passing a variable to sum is negligible compared to the creation time of a heavy reduce worker. Note that, a functional enhancement should be augmented. It should allow pass the variables for simple aggregation directly to the application submission end and skip the unnecessary reduce phase. Thus quite a lot of time caused by framework during the reduce phase and its corresponding HDFS operations could be saved.

Multi-Phase in Single Pass. The mixed job we introduced often leads to a difficult situation for programming. Thinking of the element update and variable sum in the same pass in Water Spatial, fake elements are created for carrying aggregated variable. In most cases, several operations on the same partition of data are independent during the same pass. Due to lack of support from the MapReduce framework, the operations have to be separated apart or programmed with a bad understandability. A multi-functional *mapper* for MapReduce can improve the working efficiency greatly. Furthermore, since MapReduce cannot ensure the tasks processing the same partition to be assigned to the same nodes, which causes many avoidable data communication.

6   Related Work

The evolvement of the MapReduce programming model, MapReduce, invented and popularized by Google, has been widely deployed into the production systems inside Google. Outside Google, Apache has designed and implemented Hadoop, an open-source alternative of Google's MapReduce, which is implemented using Java and built upon the Hadoop Distributed File System (HDFS). Due to the simplicity of MapReduce, the database community also extends the MapReduce programming model by adding an additional stage, called Merge, to support the joint of two tables [13].

There have been a lot of efforts in trying MapReduce to other domains other than the web-search domain. Chu et al. [14] proposed using MapReduce to run machine learning algorithms on multi-core. Dyer et al. [3] also built the statistical machine translation using MapReduce. Besides, Ekanayake et al. [15] applied MapReduce for scientific data analysis. Specifically, they evaluated MapReduce with High Energy Physics data analysis and K-Means clustering. Our work differs from the above ones in that we studied in another domain of applications , supercomputing, on commodity clusters and provided a more detailed study on their performance characteristics.

The prevalent of heterogeneous multi-core systems open opportunities to run MapReduce originally for clusters in a signal machine. Ranger et al. [16] recently provide a MapReduce implementation, namely Phoenix, which runs on multi-core platforms. Their implementation indicates that applications written using MapReduce, are comparable in performance and scalability to their pthread counterparts. The popularity of MapReduce is also embodied in running MapReduce on other heterogeneous environments, such as on GPUs [17] and Cell [18].

7 Conclusion

MapReduce has been prevalent for running data-parallel applications without effort for non-functionality parts. The features mentioned make the programming model popular in various domains like textual retrieval and machine learning. In this paper, we ported and evaluated two typical scientific applications from the SPLASH-2 suite using MapReduce. Based on a detailed study and analysis, we identified that the requirement of frequent data communication in the kind of application results in a huge overhead on network. Based on our experience, we also proposed several potential enhancements on the MapReduce framework to make the model much more suitable for supercomputing applications.

References

1. Dean, J., Ghemawat, S.: MapReduce: simplified data processing on large clusters. Communications of the ACM 51(1), 107–113 (2008)
2. Bialecki, A., Cafarella, M., Cutting, D., O'Malley, O.: Hadoop: a framework for running applications on large clusters built of commodity hardware (2005),
   http://lucene.apache.org/hadoop
3. Dyer, C., Cordova, A., Mont, A., Lin, J.: Fast, easy, and cheap: Construction of statistical machine translation models with MapReduce. In: Proceedings of the Third Workshop on Statistical Machine Translation at ACL, pp. 199–207 (2008)
4. Elsayed, T., Lin, J., Oard, D.W.: Pairwise document similarity in large collections with mapreduce. In: Proceedings of the 46th Annual Meeting of the Association for Computational Linguistics, pp. 265–268 (2008)
5. Wolfe, J., Haghighi, A., Klein, D.: Fully distributed EM for very large datasets. In: Proceedings of the 25th international conference on Machine learning, pp. 1184–1191. ACM, New York (2008)
6. Bryant, R.: Data-intensive supercomputing: The case for DISC (2007)
7. Woo, S.C., Ohara, M., Torrie, E., Singh, J.P., Gupta, A.: The SPLASH-2 Programs: Characterization and Methodological Considerations. In: Proc. ISCA (1995)
8. Singh, J.P., Gupta, A., Levoy, M.: SPLASH: Stanford parallel applications for shared memory. Computer Architecture News 20(1), 5–44 (1994)
9. Lie, G., Clementi, E.: Molecuelar-dynamics simulation of liquid water with an ab initio flexible water-water interaction potential. Physical Review A33, 2679–2693 (1986)
10. Matsuoka, O., Clementi, E., Yoshimine, M.: CI study of the water dimer potential suface. Journal of Chemical Physics 64(4), 1351–1361 (1976)
11. Barlett, R., Shavitt, I., Purvis, G.: The quartic force field of H_2O determined by many-body methods that include quadruple excitation effects. Journal of Chemical Physics 71(1), 281–291 (1979)
12. Blelloch, G.E., Leiserson, C.E., Maggs, B.M., Plaxton, C.G., Smith, S.J., Zagha, M.: A comparison of sorting algorithm for the connection machine CM-2. In: Proc. SPAA (1991)
13. Yang, H., Dasdan, A., Hsiao, R., Parker, D.: Map-reduce-merge: simplified relational data processing on large clusters. In: Proc. SIGMOD (2007)

14. Chu, C., Kim, S., Lin, Y., Yu, Y., Bradski, G., Ng, A., Olukotun, K.: Map-reduce for machine learning on multicore. In: Advances in Neural Information Processing Systems: Proceedings of the 2006 Conference, p. 281. MIT Press, Cambridge (2007)
15. Ekanayake, J., Pallickara, S., Fox, G.: MapReduce for Data Intensive Scientific Analyses. In: IEEE Fourth International Conference on eScience, 2008. eScience 2008, pp. 277–284 (2008)
16. Ranger, C., Raghuraman, R., Penmetsa, A., Bradski, G., Kozyrakis, C.: Evaluating mapreduce for multi-core and multiprocessor systems. In: Proc. HPCA (2007)
17. He, B., Fang, W., Luo, Q., Govindaraju, N., Wang, T.: Mars: a MapReduce framework on graphics processors. In: Proc. PACT (2008)
18. de Kruijf, M., Sankaralingam, K.: MapReduce for the Cell BE Architecture. University of Wisconsin Computer Sciences Technical Report CS-TR-2007

MPTD: A Scalable and Flexible Performance Prediction Framework for Parallel Systems

Chuanfu Xu, Yonggang Che, and Zhenghua Wang

National Laboratory for Parallel and Distributed Processing,
School of Computer, National University of Defense Technology,
Changsha 410073, China
xuchuanfu@nudt.edu.cn

Abstract. The increasing complexities of today's parallel systems pose new challenges for performance prediction. Effective performance prediction can provide insight, deepen understanding and further identify potential performance bottlenecks of system/application combinations. In this paper, we present and evaluate a multi-phase trace-driven (MPTD) performance prediction framework for parallel systems. In the trace generation phase, based on a relatively simple performance model, MPTD performs parallel performance simulation to generate primary prediction results and traces rapidly. In the trace adjustment phase, traces are transformed or re-simulated based on performance models of new component architecture or more detailed performance models. This phase is self-repeatable (it can be performed more than once and need not go back to the former phase) to enable more flexible reuse of traces. We implemented an instantiation of MPTD to predict the performance of popular multi-core cluster systems. Analysis and tests show that MPTD is scalable, flexible, and can help researchers for better balancing accuracy and efficiency of performance prediction.

1   Introduction

Performance prediction of applications on parallel systems is very important and can be used throughout the life-cycle of systems including design, implementation, optimization, procurement, installation, upgrade, etc [1]. Performance of parallel systems is often determined by many interacting factors and involves architecture of node and processor, interconnection, algorithm, implementation, compiler, operating system, etc. Consequently, efficient and accurate performance prediction is very difficult. With the development of technology, current parallel systems are becoming increasingly complex and huge. For example, IBM Roadrunner, the No.1 machine of TOP500 [2] supercomputer list issued in November 2008, consists of 122400 computation cores. It is undoubtedly a challenging problem to predict the performance of parallel applications on such a complex and huge high performance computer system.

Performance simulation and analytical model are two well-known performance prediction approaches. Accuracy and efficiency are the main tradeoffs for both

Y. Dou, R. Gruber, and J. Joller (Eds.): APPT 2009, LNCS 5737, pp. 465–476, 2009.
© Springer-Verlag Berlin Heidelberg 2009

techniques. The main disadvantage of simulation is its high costs and low efficiency. Cycle-accurate simulation of applications is often more than 3 magnitude's slower than realistic execution [3]. Therefore, it is infeasible to carry out cycle-accurate simulation of large-scale parallel systems as far as cost is concerned. Although researchers have recently proposed some techniques such as sampling simulation and parallel simulation [3] to speed up simulation, most simulators still have limited scalability of capability. For example, it is hard to extend a simulator to support new component architecture such as new acceleration processing units. An analytical model is generally tailored to particular kind of applications. To construct it, researches often need to analyze the application's control workflows and data structures; therefore, the analytical model is usually limited in scope and fails to capture subtle interactions between architecture and software. Moreover, researches usually select one performance tool and apply it continually; it is hardly possible for them to combine different prediction results from various performance tools or models to efficiently balance the speed and accuracy of performance prediction.

We think performance prediction should mirror the development of the application and/or system dynamically. As details are refined through implementations, the performance model adopted by performance prediction should also be refined. Based on this idea, we present a multi-phase trace-driven (MPTD) performance prediction framework for parallel systems. In the trace generation phase, prediction results and traces are obtained via parallel performance simulation implementing relatively simple performance model. This phase only needs to carry out once for a combination of system and application under given execution configuration. It can be used as a rapid, primary performance evaluation at early stage of system design. In the trace adjustment phase, traces are transformed or re-simulated based on performance models of new component architecture or more detailed performance models. This phase is self-repeatable (it can be performed more than once and need not go back to the former phase) to enable more flexible reuse of traces. MPTD efficiently combines various prediction results from performance tools in different phases via trace transformation. We design a trace model for parallel performance simulation of message passing parallel applications in MPTD. We implement an instantiation of MPTD to predict performance of popular multi-core cluster systems. Analysis and tests show that MPTD is scalable, flexible and can help researchers for better balancing accuracy and efficiency of performance prediction.

The paper is organized as follows. In Section 2, we describe MPTD framework in details, including its components, workflows, and trace transformation model. Then we demonstrate an instantiation of MPTD and present the results in Section 3. Section 4 gives a review of related work. Finally, in Section 5, we conclude and discuss some future works of this paper.

2   MPTD Framework

MPTD aims to predict an application's performance on parallel systems under a given execution configuration. In consideration of clear expression, we assume that target applications are standard message passing interface (MPI) applications; furthermore, we have a simplifying hypothesis similar to [4] that a message passing parallel application's performance is often dominated by two major factors: 1) local computation component performance and 2) interconnection network performance. Accordingly, performance prediction needs to take local execution code block (LECB) and MPI message communication statements into account. A LECB is the sequence of local statements executed between two message passing statements. As we will see in section 2.4, our approach and idea are easy to expand beyond the above assumptions.

2.1 Components of MPTD

In MPTD, there are generally 3 kinds of performance tools which can be used in different phases of performance prediction.

- Parallel simulator. Compared to sequential cycle-accurate simulation, parallel simulator [5,6,7] can improve its efficiency by parallelizing simulation task. A parallel simulator used in MPTD must support tracing to generate trace files along with prediction results.
- Trace transformation tool. Taking trace files as input, trace transformation tool can adjust timing information in traces by simply modifying parameters about CPU or interconnection network. Further, trace transformation can combine new predictions results from third-party performance tools reflecting new component architecture or performance models.
- Third-party performance tools. These tools implement a certain degree of details of performance models for architecture components of parallel systems (cycle-accurate processor simulator, detailed contention-based interconnection network simulator, for example). They are often very slow and hard to integrate with fast performance tools such as parallel simulator directly.

2.2 A Typical Workflow for MPTD

Fig. 1 illustrates a typical workflow for MPTD framework. It involves all three kinds of tools mentioned above. In the trace generation phase (denoted by rectangle with red dashed line), target application is executed on the parallel performance simulator and primary prediction results and trace files are produced. In the trace adjustment phase (denoted by rectangle with blue dashed line), cycle-accurate predictions of some key LECBs are obtained by performing cycle-accurate simulating of these LECBs. New predictions along with original traces are taken as inputs to the trace transformation tool which will output adjusted traces. The new traces are again simulated by a detailed network simulator for message passing among target processes to generate final prediction result based on more detailed network performance model. The workflow only includes two phases, but the trace adjustment phase is slef-repeatable: Users may reuse the same original traces to perform prediction without need to go back to the former phase.

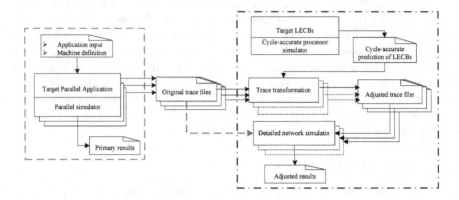

Fig. 1. A typical performance prediction workflow for MPTD. Grey rectangles denote programs, and white rectangles with the upper right corner turned down denote files. Stacked symbols indicate multiple instances of programs or files running or being processed in parallel, while stacked symbols with dashed lines indicate programs may be optionally implemented as a parallel one.

In MPTD, workflows, particularly in the trace adjustment phase, will be slightly different due to specific implementations of performance tools. For example, traces can be fed to detailed network simulator directly without transformation (denoted by blue dashed line in Fig. 1). Users usually need to take following issues into account while implementing prediction workflows in MPTD framework:

- Combination with third-party performance tools. For example, to combine with cycle-accurate prediction results of some key LECBs, users may insert a pair of functions at the start and the end of these LECBs to mark them. Firstly, a parameter file containing primary predictions of the marked LECBs' durations will be generated by parallel simulation. Then, the cycle-accurate processor simulator can update durations of the LECBs in the parameter file according to new estimations. At last, the trace tools will adjust affected parts of the original traces according to the rewritten parameter file. Besides, users may implement a trace-driven detailed network simulator to re-simulate message communication behavior in the original traces.
- Implementation of trace tool. Trace tool can be implemented independently and provides standard interfaces for other performance tools. Moreover, it can also be parallelized like in [8] to improve efficiency.

2.3   Design of Trace Model

In MPTD, trace files produced in the trace generation phase contains an abstract representation   of   execution   behaviors   and   corresponding   timing information about parallel performance simulation of target application on target machine. Therefore, our trace model is directly relevant to the principle of parallel simulation.

Firstly, each simulating process will be allocated a number of target processes in parallel simulation. Traces generated by a simulating process must contain information about all traversed code regions (CR) of the target processes running on it. According to assumptions in Section 2, two kinds of CR must be included: LECB and MPI statement.

Secondly, every target process maintains a virtual clock T in parallel simulation. T will be advanced according to the simulation of application code and synchronized via message communication among the target processes. For example, suppose current timestamps of target process A and B are $T^A_{current}$ and $T^B_{current}$ respectively; A sends a message msg to B and predicts that it will take ΔT seconds for msg to arrive its destination, then the predicted receive timestamp of msg is set to $T^A_{current} + \Delta T$ (i.e. $T^{msg}_{predicted} = T^A_{current} + \Delta T$); B will set its timestamp to be the maximum of $T^{msg}_{predicted}$ and $T^B_{current}$ (i.e. $T^B_{current} = max\{T^B_{current}, T^{msg}_{predicted}\}$) while scheduling msg according to synchronization strategy. Consequently, Traces in MPTD also need to include information about message communications across target processes.

Thus, our trace model consists of two types of traces as described below:

- Summary trace. Summary trace contains information about target system, target application and execution configuration of parallel simulation. Given the summary trace, Trace transformation tools can determine which performance trace a target process is belonged to.
- Performance trace. Each simulating process will generate a performance trace containing all CRs and related timing information (start time, end time, etc.) of target processes. More importantly, following timestamps are needed to preserve timestamp dependency in trace transformation: for sending a message, send timestamp and predicted receive timestamp are needed; for receiving a message, received timestamp (timestamp after update while receiving a message) and receive timestamp (timestamp before synchronization) are both needed. Besides, messages sent by a target process and attributes such as message communicator, destination tag, size will also being included to support re-simulation of message transferring by a detailed network simulator.

Timing information in performance trace records each target process's progress of virtual clock in parallel simulation and we use timeline to denote it. In trace transformation, the earliest timestamp in a timeline is firstly adjusted, and then all subsequent timestamps in the same timeline will be adjusted accordingly. At last, other affected timelines which may be in different performance traces will be checked to maintain timestamp dependency across target processes.

Fig. 2 shows a simple example about trace transformation. In Fig. 2(a), there are two target processes A and B in the original trace. Firstly, A executed a LECB and then called a MPI_Send to send a message to B (denoted as e_1 in

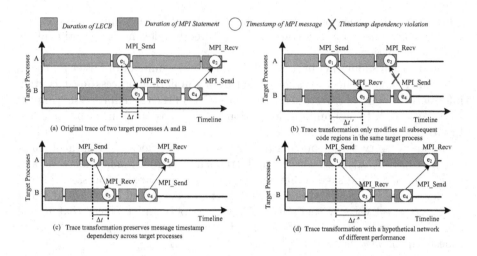

Fig. 2. Trace transformation process

A's timeline). B called MPI_Recv to receive the message from A (denoted as e_3 in B's timeline) and then executed a LECB before calling another MPI_Send (denoted as e_4 in B's timeline) to send a message back to A (denoted as e_2 in A's timeline). In this example, e_3 depends on e_1 and e_2 depends on e_4; we use directed lines with arrow to represent this kind of dependency. We show an illegal trace transformation in Fig. 2(b) while only subsequent timestamps in the same timeline are adjusted. Although the timestamp of e_3 is still late than e1, one of its attributes (predicted receive time) is actually changed from $\triangle t$ to $\triangle t'$; Even more serious is the fact that now the timestamp of e2 is earlier than the timestamp of e_4. Such kind of situations is known as timestamp dependency violation (TDV) in MPTD. In Fig. 2(b), we use a red cross to represent TDV. Trace transformation must assure that no TDVs exist in the modified trace. Fig. 2(c) shows the timelines for A and B after final trace transformation. Compared to Fig. 2(a), durations of LECBs are altered and TDVs in Fig. 2(b) are eliminated. We also show a hypothetical adjustment of network performance in Fig. 2(d): predicted receive time of e_1 has changed from $\triangle t$ to $\triangle t''$.

2.4   Advantage Analysis

Here we discuss and analyze some underlying advantages of MPTD. As compared to traditional performance prediction approaches, we think MPTD is much more scalable, efficient and flexible.

- Scalability. In MPTD, users can choose available tools in different phases to improve prediction speed. For example, although performance models adopted by parallel simulator in the trace generation phase are relatively simple, it can produce prediction results in a timely manner. This is especially useful in early stage of system design. In the trace adjustment phase, performance measurement is much faster than cycle-accurate simulation if target processor is available. By extending trace model appropriately, MPTD also provides feasible approach to support performance prediction of systems with up-to-date architecture. This is very important for performance prediction of current supercomputers with popular acceleration computation components and multi-tier parallelism.

- Efficiency and flexibility. MPTD offers users more flexible options of tools and phases to better balance between efficiency and accuracy. Usually prediction results of trace generation phase are enough in the case of relative accuracy is considered when users often compare enhanced systems with baseline system. Efficiency and flexibility of MPTD is helpful for researchers to identify potential performance bottleneck and investigate scalability of applications or systems: Users may change their system sizes, try new-type processors or network in MPTD to yield insight into achievable performance.

3   An Instantiation of MPTD

We have implemented an instantiation of MPTD framework and it includes the following prototype systems:

- MCPSim. It is a parallel simulator for multi-core SMP cluster systems. Message transfer time was estimated by simple Latency/Bandwidth [9] network performance model. LECB execution time was predicted by host machine's wall-clock time multiplying a scalefactor.
- EPSim. It is a detailed contention-based Gigabit Ethernet parallel simulator implemented based on [10]. Message transferring was simulated among entities such as network interface cards, switches and etc. EPSim contains a built-in trace transformation module to adjust message transfer latency according to realistic simulation.
- Trace tool. It provides trace generation and parsing interfaces for MCP-Sim and EPSim. Besides, it implemented our trace transformation model described in Section 2.3.

3.1   Experiment Setup

We use 2 typical MPI programs to validate prediction accuracy of MPTD: GAUSS and Jacobi3D. GAUSS is a program that solves the matrix system of linear equations (i.e. $Ax = b$) using Gaussian Elimination. Jacobi3D is a 7-point stencil program with 3-D decomposition [5]. Further, we have written a MPI synthetic application (MPISA) to support precisely changing computation to communication ratio. MPISA includes a computation loop and a communication loop: duration of the computation loop can be varied by adjusting the number of floating point operations executed, while the communication loop implemented multiple communication patterns and message distribution patterns. We use MPISA to demonstrate MPTD's capability of performance bottleneck analysis. Parallel system used in our tests is a 64 nodes multi-core SMP cluster system connected by Gigabit Ethernet. Each node consists of two 2.33 GHz quad-core Xeon with 8GB DDRII ECC memory. We use the parallel system as our host machine and target machine while running MCPSim in the trace generation phase.

Accuracy validation of MPTD was shown in Fig. 3 and Fig. 4 for GAUSS and Jacobi3D respectively. In each figure, the program's observed runtime by actual execution, predicted runtime by MCPSim in the trace generation phase and

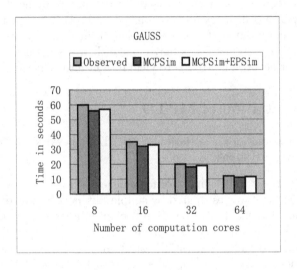

Fig. 3. Validation of MPTD for GAUSS

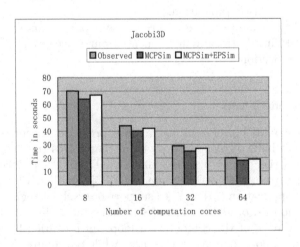

Fig. 4. Validation of MPTD for Jacobi3D

predicted runtime by EPSim using MCPSim-generated traces in the trace adjustment phase were presented. Error% is defined as (observed runtime - predicted runtime) / (observed runtime*100). For the two programs, average errors% are both decreased from EPSim to MCPSim+EPSim: from about 7.2% to about 2.1% for GAUSS and from about 9.0% to 2.2% for Jacobi3D. We can see that a detailed contention-based network simulation in trace adjustment phase has effectively decreased error% resulted from relatively simple performance model in the trace generation phase. This is especially true for programs like Jacobi3D whose message passing performance is critical.

Users can also use MPTD to identify performance bottlenecks of an application. Fig. 5 shows a case study of this kind of analysis for MPISA. MPISA_1 and MPISA_2 represent computation-intensive and communication-intensive versions of MPISA respectively. The target machine size is fixed to 32 computation cores. The results are obtained by separately modify the network parameters (e.g., bandwidth) and CPU speed (e.g., cpuscalefactor) in trace transformation tool. If significantly improving network or CPU has little or no effect on the performance of the application, then it is clear that the limiting factor or bottleneck for the application is not the corresponding hardware, but something inherent in the application or some other aspects. For MPISA_1, when we improved the network without improving the CPU, almost no performance gains resulted. But when we improved the CPU without improving the network, we can obtain about 40% speedup, confirming that the bottleneck of this application is not interconnection network but CPU. Likewise, we can see that network upgrade

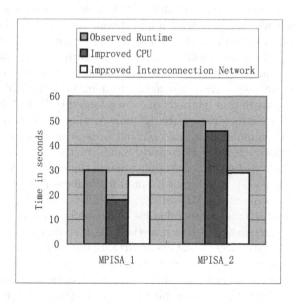

Fig. 5. A case study of performance bottleneck analysis in MPTD using MPISA

will benefit MPISA_2 the most (about 42%). In MPTD, this kind of analysis can be performed efficiently by reuse of traces.

4   Related Work

The principle of performance prediction for parallel systems has already been intensively studied and various performance tools existed. Here we only present a review of some trace-based performance prediction approaches that are most relevant to this paper.

Two early trace performance prediction tools are introduced in [9] and [11]. Both of them use traces previously generated to perform transformation according to a prediction model. The prediction model describes relative process speed, optionally differentiated by code section, and message transfer times as a function of message size. AIMS [12] is another performance-analysis toolkit offering trace-based simulation capabilities. It can estimate the scalability of parallel applications by extrapolating previously generated execution traces to higher numbers of processors and larger problem sizes. SCALASCA [8] is a trace analysis toolset for large-scale message passing applications. One of its distinctive features is the ability to identify wait states in MPI message communication by searching characteristic patterns in traces. Although the focuses of the above tools are different, they all collected traces by application instrumentation and execution which limit their scopes to the existed systems. MPTD focuses on the integration of different predictions tools, especially performance simulation tools, through multi-phase and traces from parallel simulation.

PERC (Performance Evaluation Research Center) presented a performance prediction framework [4,13] for HPC applications. To carry out the framework, firstly users need to obtain system profiles (e.g., memory performance and communication performance) and application signatures (e.g., memory access pattern, communication pattern), then convolution method is adopted to map signatures to profiles to get the predicted performance results. Different application tracers and convolution methods may be adopted in PERC, but it did not take some complex characteristics like dynamic overlap (for example, overlap of computation and communication) into account because of its separate prediction of CPU and network related performance. Similarly, the application signatures are also determined by executing the application in the framework, which require that the application scale is sufficiently small for framework user's system.

Most of parallel simulators (MPI-SIM [7], LAPSE[6], etc.) don't support tracing and are difficult to extend capability for new models or architectures. BigSim [5] also adopts a trace-driven two step method. At first step, it uses an emulator to run application with larger numbers of virtual processes on a smaller number of physical processors to generate trace logs, then at second step, a postmortem simulator uses generated traces accounts for network contention and topological characteristics to predict network performance. In BigSim, users must finish the two steps to reach a prediction result. However, in MPTD, prediction workflow is more flexible: trace adjustment phase is optional and trace transformation tool may be independent. Moreover, tracing in BigSim is designed for its implementation language Charm++, our trace model is designed for standard message passing application which makes it much more general for tracing in parallel performance simulator.

5   Conclusion and Future Works

In this paper, we present a multi-phase trace-driven framework MPTD for performance prediction of parallel computer systems. MPTD enables users to choose performance tools of various complexities in different phases and combine prediction results from them via trace transformation. Analysis and tests show that MPTD can obtain better tradeoff between accuracy and efficiency of performance prediction; it is also scalable, efficient and flexible. As for future works, we will further validate MPTD using more MPI programs and optimize implementation of performance tools used in MPTD.

Acknowledgement

This paper was supported by the National Science Foundation of China (NSFC) under Grant No.60603055, and the National High-Tech Research and Development Plan of China under Grant No.2007AA01Z116.

References

1. Nudd, G., Kerbyson, D., Papaefstathiou, E., Perry, S., Harper, J.S., Wilcox, D.: Pace: A toolset for the performance prediction of parallel and distributed systems. Int. J. of High Performance Computing Applications 14, 228–251 (2000)
2. Top500supercomputersite (2008), http://www.top500.org/
3. Yi, J.J., Lilja, D.J.: Simulation of computer architectures: Simulators, benchmarks, methodologies, and recommendations. IEEE Transactions on computers 55(3), 268–280 (2006)
4. Carrington, L., Snavely, A., Wolter, N., Gao, X.: A performance prediction framework for scientific applications. In: Sloot, P.M.A., Abramson, D., Bogdanov, A.V., Gorbachev, Y.E., Dongarra, J., Zomaya, A.Y. (eds.) ICCS 2003. LNCS, vol. 2659. Springer, Heidelberg (2003)
5. Zheng, G., Wilmarth, T., Jagadishprasad, P., Kaĺe, L.V.: Simulation-based performance prediction for large parallel machines. International Journal of Parallel Programming 33, 183–207 (2005)
6. Dickens, P.M., Heidelberger, P., Nicol, D.M.: A distributed memory lapse: parallel simulation of message-passing programs. SIGSIM Simul. Dig. 24(1), 32–38 (1994)
7. Bagrodia, R., Deelman, E., Docy, S., Phan, T.: Performance prediction of large parallel applications using parallel simulations. In: ACM SIGPLAN Symposium on Principles and Practice of Parallel Programming (PPoPP) (May 1999)
8. Geimer, M., Wolf, F., Wylie, B., Mohr., B.: Scalable parallel trace-based performance analysis. In: Mohr, B., Träff, J.L., Worringen, J., Dongarra, J. (eds.) PVM/MPI 2006. LNCS, vol. 4192, pp. 303–312. Springer, Heidelberg (2006)

9. Mendes, C.: Performance prediction by trace transformation. In: Proc. of the 5th Brazilian Symposium on Computer Architecture, Florianopolis (September 1993)
10. Jagadishprasad, P.K.: Parallel simulation of large scale interconnection networks used in high performance computing. Master's thesis, University of Illinois at Urbana-Champaign (2004)
11. Labarta, J., Girona, S., Pillet, V., Cortes, T., Gregoris, L.: Dip: A parallel program development environment. In: Fraigniaud, P., Mignotte, A., Robert, Y., Bougé, L. (eds.) Euro-Par 1996. LNCS, vol. 1124, pp. 665–674. Springer, Heidelberg (1996)
12. Yan, J., Sarukkai, S., Mehra, P.: Performance measurement, visualization and modeling of parallel and distributed programs using the aims toolkit. Software Practice and Experience 25(4), 429–461 (1995)
13. Snavely, A., Carrington, L., Wolter, N., Labarta, J., Badia, R., Purkayastha, A.: A framework for application performance modeling and prediction. In: Proceedings of SC 2002, Baltimore (November 2002)

Author Index